BREVARD S. CHILDS
THE BOOK OF EXODUS

THE OLD TESTAMENT LIBRARY

General Editors

BREVARD S. CHILDS

THE BOOK
OF
EXODUS

A Critical, Theological Commentary

THE WESTMINSTER PRESS
Philadelphia

Copyright © 1974 Brevard S. Childs

Published in Great Britain
under the title *Exodus, A Commentary*
Third printing, 1976
Published by The Westminster Press®
Philadelphia, Pennsylvania

2 2 2 . 1 4
C 5 3 7 6

Library of Congress Cataloging in Publication Data

Childs, Brevard S.
  The book of Exodus.

  (The Old Testament library)
  Bibliography: p.
  1. Bible. O. T. Exodus—Commentaries.
I. Bible. O. T. Exodus. English. 1974.
II. Title. III. Series.
BS1245.3.C45   222'.12'07   73–23120
ISBN 0–664–20985–8

*This book is gratefully dedicated
to my mother
and to the memory of
my father*

CONTENTS

PREFACE

THE PURPOSE of this commentary is unabashedly theological. Its concern is to understand Exodus as scripture of the church. The exegesis arises as a theological discipline within the context of the canon and is directed toward the community of faith which lives by its confession of Jesus Christ.

Yet the author is also aware that serious theological understanding of the text is dependent on a rigorous and careful study of the whole range of problems within the Bible which includes text and source criticism, syntax and grammar, history and geography. Nor can the hearing of the text by the Christian church be divorced from that other community of faith which lives from the same Bible, and from the countless other stances outside of any commitment to faith or tradition.

It will be immediately clear from this perspective that a different understanding of the role of biblical interpretation is being offered from that currently held by the majority of scholars within the field. Even the format of the exegesis offers an implicit criticism of the usual concept of a commentary. The issue at stake does not lie in the degree of technicality of the exegesis – whether or not a knowledge of Hebrew and Greek is assumed – but in the concept of the task. The rash of recent popularizations offers nothing qualitatively different from the technical volumes.

I am fully aware of the risks involved when one cuts oneself away from the safe and well-charted boundaries which the canons of historical critical scholarship have come to regard as self-evident, and perhaps even sacrosanct. Nevertheless, it seems to me imperative for the health of the discipline and certainly of the church that the generally accepted areas in which the exegete works be greatly broadened. I have tried to show why an adequate interpretation of the Bible for the church must involve a continuous wrestling with the history of interpretation and theology. Yet who can control equally well the fields of Semitic philology, ancient Near Eastern history, text and form criticism, rabbinics, New Testament, patristics, medieval and Reformation studies, philosophy and dogmatics? Still the effort has to be made to sketch the true parameters of the discipline of biblical interpretation, even if there are gaps and deficiencies in one man's attempt.

Since any commentary must be selective in its choice of material, I have at least tried to shift the scale of priorities. I have not followed the usual pattern of the English-language commentary in offering a long introduction in which one rehearses the traditional problems of literary criticism and history of Israel. Because the field is well-supplied in good text-books covering these areas, a repetition seems unnecessary. Moreover, in my judgment, a false impression of their importance is created. There are other areas in which I have imposed restrictions. The philological notes are offered only in those places where an understanding of the biblical text of Exodus is directly affected. The area of textual criticism has also been curtailed and no attempt has been made to pursue all the problems of the text's recensional history. Obviously no effort has been made to be exhaustive in the history of exegesis, but hopefully the selection is representative enough not to distort the complete picture seriously.

My academic interest in the book of Exodus goes back some twenty years to an unforgettable seminar on Moses which was conducted by Professor Walter Baumgartner of Basel in the summer semester of 1952. Well-worn copies of Dillmann, Gressmann, Driver, and Noth indicate their constant use over two decades. Active work on this commentary extends over ten years. During that period I have gone through many different stages in my own thinking. Somewhere *en route* I discovered that Calvin and Drusius, Rashi and Ibn Ezra, belong among the giants. I have tried to show why these great expositors – the term 'pre-critical' is both naïve and arrogant – need to be heard in concert with Wellhausen and Gunkel. When I began my work, there were few commentaries on Exodus available. Since that time some commentaries, mostly of a popular form, have appeared, but, in my judgment, the need is still a pressing one.

I would like to express my appreciation for financial support in preparing this commentary. In 1963 I received a grant for study at the Hebrew University in Jerusalem from the Simon M. Guggenheim Foundation. In 1970 I was granted a fellowship to study at Cambridge University from the American Council of Learned Societies. To both of these foundations I am deeply grateful.

Finally, I am indebted to my colleague, R. Lansing Hicks, for innumerable suggestions for improving the manuscript. My sincere thanks also goes to the SCM Press staff, particularly to Miss Jean Cunningham, for the careful editing of the book.

INTRODUCTION

1. *The Goal of the Exegesis*

THE AIM OF this commentary is to seek to interpret the book of Exodus as canonical scripture within the theological discipline of the Christian church. As scripture its authoritative role within the life of the community is assumed, but how this authority functions must be continually explored. Therefore, although the book in its canonical form belongs to the sacred inheritance of the church, it is incumbent upon each new generation to study its meaning afresh, to have the contemporary situation of the church addressed by its word, and to anticipate a fresh appropriation of its message through the work of God's Spirit.

The author does not share the hermeneutical position of those who suggest that biblical exegesis is an objective, descriptive enterprise, controlled solely by scientific criticism, to which the Christian theologian can at best add a few homiletical reflections for piety's sake. In my judgment, the rigid separation between the descriptive and constructive elements of exegesis strikes at the roots of the theological task of understanding the Bible. Nevertheless, it does belong to the task of the scholar in the church to deal seriously with the Old Testament text in its original setting within the history of Israel and to make use of research done by many whose understanding of the exegetical task differs widely from the one being suggested. Conversely, it is to be hoped that the actual exegesis of this commentary can prove useful and illuminating to those who do not share the author's general concept of the discipline.

It seems inappropriate in a commentary to launch into an essay on hermeneutics. Whether or not the exegesis is successful cannot be judged on its theory of interpretation, but on the actual interpretation itself. However, perhaps it is in order to explain briefly the rationale for the format of the commentary and to offer suggestions as to how the various sections within a chapter can be used by the reader.

2. The Format of the Commentary

1. Each section begins with a new translation of the Hebrew text. The ancient versions have been constantly checked, with the goal not only of restoring the best text, but of seeking to understand how the text was heard and interpreted by later communities. Although the most significant textual variants are discussed in detail, the emphasis of the section falls on syntactical problems which most often affect the actual exegesis. Alternative renderings by modern translators have frequently been noted and evaluated as an aid to the non-specialist.

2. The historical development which lay behind the final form of the biblical text is treated in considerable detail with regard to both the oral and literary levels. In this section a form-critical, traditio-historical analysis is offered which seeks to explore the early forces at work in the shaping of the oral tradition. Again, a fresh source analysis has been attempted which treats the various literary strands which comprise the present narrative. Finally, observations on the history of redaction discuss the final ordering of the passage. At times the results of the prehistory of the text have direct bearing on the interpretation of the canonical text; at other times the prehistory is quite irrelevant to understanding the synchronistic dimension of the biblical text. In the exegetical section which follows the pre-history, an evaluation of the role of the various earlier stages of the text is usually attempted, but by design no general theory of a relation-ship which obtains in every case within Exodus is proposed. The section is printed in smaller type to indicate its subsidiary role within the commentary.

3. The first major section, entitled Old Testament context, forms the heart of the commentary. This section attempts to deal seriously with the text in its final form, which is its canonical shape, while at the same time recognizing and profiting by the variety of historical forces which were at work in producing it. In my judgment, the failure of most critical commentaries to deal with the final shape of the text without falling into modern midrash is a major deficiency. From a literary point of view there is a great need to understand the present composition as a piece of literature with its own integrity. The concentration of critical scholars on form-critical and source analysis has tended to fragment the text and leave the reader with only bits

and pieces. But an even more important reason for interpreting the final text is a theological one. It is the final text, the composite narrative, in its present shape which the church, following the lead of the synagogue, accepted as canonical and thus the vehicle of revelation and instruction. Much of the frustration which the preacher experiences in using commentaries stems from the failure of the interpreter to deal with the text in its canonical shape. Rather, the interest of the commentator centers on various problems of its prehistory. In my judgment, the study of the prehistory has its proper function within exegesis only in illuminating the final text.

4. The section on the New Testament's treatment of the Old Testament is a conscious attempt to take seriously the church's confession that her sacred scripture consists of an Old and a New Testament. The New Testament's reading of the Old is therefore not just included within the section on history of interpretation, but functions as the voice of the apostles which the church hears along with that of the prophets. The New Testament uses the Old Testament in a variety of ways. Its exegesis shares a Hellenistic environment both in form and content, and often reflects the ongoing exegetical traditions of Judaism which had developed beyond the Old Testament. This section attempts to describe how the early church understood the Old Testament scripture in the light of the new confession of Jesus Christ.

5. The section on history of exegesis offers an analogy to the section on the prehistory of the text. The one deals with the period before the text's complete formation, the other with its interpretation after its formation. Both have a significant, albeit indirect, relationship to the major exegetical task of interpreting the canonical text. The history of exegesis is of special interest in illuminating the text by showing how the questions which are brought to bear by subsequent generations of interpreters influenced the answers which they received. No one comes to the text *de novo*, but consciously or unconsciously shares a tradition with his predecessors. This section therefore tries to bring some historical controls to the issue of how the present generation is influenced by the exegetical traditions in which we now stand.

The concern of this commentary with the history of exegesis is also an attempt to broaden the increasingly narrow focus of the field on a few names within recent Old Testament scholarship. This tendency has not only ignored the impressive scholarship of many earlier generations, but finds itself unable to comprehend many of the major issues which the biblical text has evoked. Because this section must be highly selective, I have tried to deal with the major Jewish and Christian expositors throughout the commentary, and in addition bring in those special studies which were influential for each particular passage at crucial periods.

6. The last section offers a theological reflection on the text within the context of the Christian canon. It seeks to relate the various Old Testament and New Testament witnesses in the light of the history of exegesis to the theological issues which evoked the witness. It is an attempt to move from witness to substance. This reflection is not intended to be timeless or offer biblical truths for all ages, but to present a model of how the Christian seeks to understand the testimony of the prophets and apostles in his own time and situation. The section is not simply random homiletical ruminations; it attempts to build on the previous exegetical and historical work of the commentary, and to develop a more rigorous method of actualizing the text for the church's present task. The commentary aims to bring more precision into its concluding section, which in most recent series is either missing or attached as an unrelated appendix to critical exegesis. (Cf. my evaluation of various Old Testament commentary series in *Interpretation* 18, 1964, pp. 432–49.) It is my deep concern that the task of relating biblical exegesis and theology can be thus aided, and the systematic and moral theologian will recognize issues which directly affect his discipline and which will evoke his joint participation in a common enterprise.

This particular format attempts to make easier the use of the commentary by a variety of different readers. The first two sections are directed primarily to the technical scholar and seek to push along the research of the discipline in the areas of form and traditio-historical criticism. These sections can be omitted by the student, pastor, and Sunday school teacher without seriously jeopardizing the comprehension of the exegetical section. The exegesis attempts to incorporate that material in the prehistory of the text which is directly relevant to the exposition of the canonical text. The history of exegesis is also subsidiary to the exegesis and can be studied on its own as part of intellectual history or passed over on a first reading. The sections on Old Testament context, New Testament context, and theological reflection form the heart of the commentary and are directed to both the technical and non-professional reader.

ABBREVIATIONS

AASOR	*Annual of the American Schools of Oriental Research*, New Haven
AfO	*Archiv für Orientforschung*, Berlin
AJSL	*American Journal of Semitic Languages*, Chicago
AmTr	An American Translation of the Bible, Chicago 1931
ANEP	*The Ancient Near East in Pictures relating to the Old Testament*, Princeton and London 1954
ANET²	*Ancient Near Eastern Texts relating to the Old Testament²*, Princeton and London 1955
ARN	*Abot de Rabbi Nathan*
ARW	*Archiv für Religionswissenschaft*, Leipzig
ASTI	*Annual of the Swedish Theological Institute in Jerusalem*, Leiden
AV	Authorized Version of the Bible, 1611
BA	*Biblical Archaeologist*, New Haven
BASOR	*Bulletin of the American Schools of Oriental Research*, New Haven
BBB	*Bonner Biblische Beiträge*, Bonn
BDB	F. Brown, S. R. Driver and C. A. Briggs, eds., *A Hebrew and English Lexicon of the Old Testament*, Oxford 1906, rev. ed. 1957
BH	Biblia Hebraica³, ed. R. Kittel, Stuttgart 1937
BHH	*Biblisch-historisches Handwörterbuch*, ed. B. Reicke and L. Rost, Göttingen 1962ff.
BJRL	*Bulletin of the John Rylands Library*, Manchester
BRL	*Biblisches Reallexikon*, ed. K. Galling, HAT 1.1, 1937
BWAT	Beiträge zur Wissenschaft vom Alten Testament, Leipzig
BZ	*Biblische Zeitschrift*, Freiburg
BZAW	Beihefte zur *Zeitschrift für die Alttestamentliche Wissenschaft*, Giessen, Berlin
BZNW	Beihefte zur *Zeitschrift für die Neutestamentliche Wissenschaft*, Giessen, Berlin
CAD	*Chicago Assyrian Dictionary*

CBQ	*Catholic Biblical Quarterly*, Washington, D.C.
CCL	Corpus Christianorum, Series Latina, Turnhout
CH	The Code of Hammurabi
DBS	*Dictionnaire de la Bible. Supplément*, Paris 1928ff.
ET	English translation
ETL	*Ephemerides Theologicae Lovanienses*, Louvain
EvTh	*Evangelische Theologie*, Munich
EVV	English versions of the Bible
FRLANT	Forschungen zur Religion und Literatur des Alten und Neuen Testaments, Göttingen
G-K	Gesenius-Kautzsch, *Hebrew Grammar*, ET Oxford 1910
HAT	Handbuch zum Alten Testament, Tübingen
HDB	Hastings' *Dictionary of the Bible*, 5 vols, Edinburgh 1898–1904
HNT	Handbuch zum Neuen Testament, Tübingen
HTR	*Harvard Theological Review*, Cambridge, Mass.
HUCA	*Hebrew Union College Annual*, Cincinnati
IB	*The Interpreter's Bible*, New York 1951–57
ICC	The International Critical Commentary, Edinburgh
IDB	*The Interpreter's Dictionary of the Bible*, New York 1962
IEJ	*Israel Exploration Journal*, Jerusalem
JANES	*Journal of Ancient Near Eastern Studies of Columbia University*, New York
JAOS	*Journal of the American Oriental Society*, New Haven
JBL	*Journal of Biblical Literature*, Philadelphia
JCS	*Journal of Cuneiform Studies*, New Haven
JNES	*Journal of Near Eastern Studies*, Chicago
JQR	*Jewish Quarterly Review*, London
JSS	*Journal of Semitic Studies*, Manchester
JTS	*Journal of Theological Studies*, Oxford
KEKNT	Kritisch-exegetischer Kommentar über das Neue Testament, Göttingen
KS	*Kleine Schriften*
LXX	Septuagint
MGWJ	*Monatsschrift für Geschichte und Wissenschaft des Judentums*, Breslau
MPG	Migne, Patrologia, Series Graeca, Paris
MPL	Migne, Patrologia, Series Latina, Paris
MT	Massoretic Text
MUSJ	*Mélanges de l'Université Saint-Joseph*, Beirut

NAB	The New American Bible, New York and London 1970
NEB	New English Bible, Oxford and Cambridge 1970
NF	Neue Folge
NJPS	The Jewish Publication Society's new translation of The Torah, Philadelphia 1962
NTS	*New Testament Studies*, Cambridge
NTT	*Nieuw Theologisch Tijdschrift*, Haarlem
OLZ	*Orientalistische Literaturzeitung*, Berlin
OTS	*Oudtestamentische Studiën*, Leiden
PEQ	*Palestine Exploration Quarterly*, London
PRE	Pirkê de Rabbi Eliezer
RB	*Revue Biblique*, Paris
RE	*Realencyklopädie für protestantische Theologie und Kirche*[3], Leipzig 1896ff.
REJ	*Revue des Études Juives*, Paris
RGG	*Die Religion in Geschichte und Gegenwart*, Tübingen, [2]1927–31; [3]1957–65
RHD	*Revue Historique de Droit Français et Étranger*, Paris
RHPR	*Revue de l'Histoire et de Philosophie Religieuses*, Strasbourg, Paris
RIDA	*Revue International des Droits de l'Antiquité*, Brussels
RSV	Revised Standard Version of the Bible, New York and London 1952
SBT	Studies in Biblical Theology, London and Naperville
SC	Sources Chrétiennes, Paris
ShR	*Exodus Rabbah*
THAT	*Theologisches Handwörterbuch zum AT*, ed. E. Jenni and C. Westermann, 2 vols, Munich and Zürich 1971f.
ThBl	*Theologische Blätter*, Leipzig
ThLZ	*Theologische Literaturzeitung*, Leipzig
TDNT	*Theological Dictionary of the New Testament* (ET of *TWNT*), Grand Rapids, Michigan, 1964ff.
ThR	*Theologische Rundschau*, Tübingen
ThRe	*Theologische Revue*, Münster i. W.
TWAT	*Theologisches Wörterbuch zum AT*, ed. G. J. Botterweck and H. Ringgren, Stuttgart 1970ff.
TWNT	*Theologisches Wörterbuch zum NT*, ed. G. Kittel, Stuttgart 1933ff.
ThZ	*Theologische Zeitschrift*, Basel
VT	*Vetus Testamentum*, Leiden

WA   Martin Luther, *Werke*, Kritische Gesamtausgabe, Weimar 1883ff.

WMANT Wissenschaftliche Monographien zum Alten und Neuen Testament, Neukirchen-Vluyn

WO   *Die Welt des Orients*, Göttingen

WThJ   *Westminster Theological Journal*, Philadelphia

ZA   *Zeitschrift für Assyriologie*, Leipzig, Berlin

ZAW   *Zeitschrift für die Alttestamentliche Wissenschaft*, Giessen, Berlin

ZDMG *Zeitschrift der Deutschen Morgenländischen Gesellschaft*, Leipzig

ZDPV *Zeitschrift des Deutschen Palästina-Vereins*, Wiesbaden

ZNW   *Zeitschrift für die Neutestamentliche Wissenschaft*, Giessen, Berlin

ZThK   *Zeitschrift für Theologie und Kirche*, Tübingen

BIBLIOGRAPHY

1. *Commentaries on Exodus*

Church Fathers and Schoolmen

Augustine, *Quaestiones in Heptateuchum* (MPL 34; CCL 33)
Bede, *In Pentateuchum Commentarii* (MPL 91)
Cyril of Alexandria, *Glaphyrorum in Exodum Liber* (MPG 69)
Nicholas of Lyra, *Postillae perpetuae, seu brevia commentaria in Universa Biblia*
Origen, *In Exodum Homilia* (MPG 12) = *Homélies sur l'Exode* (SC 16, 1947)
Rabanus Maurus, *Commentaria in Exodum* (MPL 108)
Rupert of Deutz (Tuitiensis), *In Exodum* (CCL 22)
Theodoret, *Quaestiones in Exodum* (MPG 80)
Walafrid Strabo, *Glossa Ordinaria. Liber Exodus* (MPL 113)

Medieval Jewish Commentators

David Isaac Abarbanel (1437–1508), *Commentary on the Torah*, Tel-Aviv 1960
Joseph ben Isaac Bechor Shor (12th century), *Commentary on the Torah*, Jerusalem 1956
Levi ben Gershom (Gersonides: 1288–1344), *Commentary on the Torah*, Venice 1514; often reprinted
Abraham Ibn Ezra (1089–1164), *Abraham Ibn Ezra's Commentary to Exodus*, ed. L. Fleischer, Vienna 1926
Moshe ben Nachman (Nachmanides, Ramban; 1194–c.1270), *Commentary on the Torah*, Jerusalem 1962
Saadia Gaon (882–942), *Commentary to the Pentateuch*, Jerusalem 1963
Solomon ben Isaac (Rashi; 1040–1105), *Commentary on the Pentateuch*, ed. Berliner, Jerusalem 1962

Solomon ben Meir (Rashbam; 1085-1174), *Commentary on the Torah*, New York 1949
Menahem ben Solomon (12th century), *Sechel Tob*, ed. Buber, Berlin 1900-1902

Reformation and Post-Reformation Commentators
Henry Ainsworth, *Annotations on the Five Books of Moses*, London 1639
A. Calmet, *Commentaire littéral sur tous les livres de l'Ancien et du Nouveau Testament* I, Paris 1724
John Calvin, *Commentaries on the Four Last Books of Moses Arranged in the Form of a Harmony*, 1564; ET Grand Rapids 1950
Adam Clarke, *The Holy Bible . . . with a Commentary and Critical Notes*, Liverpool 1810-26; often reprinted
J. Clericus, *Pentateuchus Mosis ex eius translatione cum paraphrasi perpetua*, Amsterdam 1735
Critici Sacri sive doctissimorum vivorum in S.S. Biblia Annotationes et Tractatus, ed. J. Pearson et al., Amsterdam 1669; contains the commentaries of Münster, Fagius, Grotius, Drusius, Vatablus, etc.
John Gill, *An Exposition of the Old Testament*, London 1852; often reprinted
H. Grotius, *Annotata in Vetus Testamentum*, Paris 1644
Matthew Henry, *An Exposition of the Old and New Testaments*, London 1708-10; often reprinted
Cornelius Jansen, *Pentateuchus, seu Commentarius in quinque libros Mosis*, Louvain 1639
Cornelius a Lapide, *Commentaria in Scripturam Sacram* I, Antwerp 1616; reprinted Paris 1859
Martin Luther, *Auslegungen über das zweite Buch Mosis*, 1524-26, WA XVI, 1899, pp. 1-654; Concordia Walch ed. III, 1894, pp. 673ff.
Symon Patrick, *Commentary on the Pentateuch*, London 1695-1700
B. Pererius, *Disputationes in Exodum*, Venice 1601
J. Piscator, *Commentaria in omnes Veteris et Novi Testamenti libros* Herborne 1646
M. Poole, *Synopsis Criticorum*, London 1669-76
C. F. K. Rosenmüller, *Scholia in Vetus Testamentum*, Leipzig 1820-34
Thomas Scott, *The Holy Bible with Explanatory Notes*, London 1788-92; often reprinted
Jacobus Tirinus, *Commentarius in Vetus et Novum Testamentum*, Antwerp 1632
Andrew Willet, *Hexapla in Exodum*, London 1608

U. Zwingli, *Farrago Annotationum in Exodum*, 1527; reprinted, *Opera* V, ed. Schuler and Schulthess, Zürich 1835

Modern Commentators

B. Bäntsch, *Exodus-Leviticus-Numeri*, Göttingen 1903
G. Beer, *Exodus*, mit einem Beitrag von K. Galling, HAT 3, 1939
F. M. Th. Böhl, *Exodus*, Groningen 1928
U. Cassuto, *A Commentary on the Book of Exodus*, ET London 1967
A. Clamer, *L'Exode*, Paris 1956
R. E. Clements, *Exodus*, Cambridge 1972
B. Couroyer, *L'Exode*, Paris 1958
G. Henton Davies, *Exodus*, London 1967
A. Dillmann, *Die Bücher Exodus und Leviticus*[3] ed. V. Ryssel, Leipzig 1897
S. R. Driver, *The Book of Exodus*, Cambridge 1911
F. C. Fensham, *Exodus*, Nijkerk 1970
H. Frey, *Die Botschaft des Alten Testaments*, vols. 5–6, Stuttgart 1949–53
S. Goldman, *From Slavery to Freedom*, New York and London 1958
M. Greenberg, *Understanding Exodus*, New York 1969
H. Gressmann, *Die Anfänge Israels*, Schriften des AT I.2[2], Göttingen 1922
P. Heinisch, *Das Buch Exodus*, Bonn 1934
H. Holzinger, *Exodus*, Tübingen 1900
F. de Hummelauer, *Commentarius in Exodum et Leviticum*, Paris 1897
J. P. Hyatt, *Exodus*, London 1971
B. Jacob, *Das Zweite Buch der Torah*, Microfilm, Jerusalem n.d.
M. M. Kalisch, *Historical and Critical Commentary on the Old Testament*: II, *Exodus*, London 1855
C. F. Keil, *Commentary on the Pentateuch*, ET Edinburgh 1864
A. Knobel, *Exodus*, Leipzig 1857
S. D. Luzzatto, *Commentary to the Pentateuch* (Heb.), Padua 1871; reprinted Tel-Aviv 1965
A. H. McNeile, *The Book of Exodus*, London 1908
J. Murphy, *Commentary on Exodus*, Edinburgh 1866
M. Noth, *Exodus*, ET Old Testament Library, London and Philadelphia 1962
J. C. Rylaarsdam, 'Introduction and Exegesis to the Book of Exodus', *IB* I, pp.833–1099
G. Te Stroete, *Exodus*, Roermond 1966

2. Selected Critical Monographs on Exodus

G. Auzou, *De la Servitude au Service*, Paris 1961
B. W. Bacon, *The Triple Tradition of the Exodus*, Hartford 1894
M. Buber, *Moses*, Oxford and London 1946
B. D. Eerdmans, *Alttestamentliche Studien, III: Das Buch Exodus*, Giessen 1910
O. Eissfeldt, *Hexateuch-Synopse*, Leipzig 1922
G. Fohrer, *Überlieferung und Geschichte des Exodus*, Berlin 1964
E. Galbiati, *La Struttura letteraria dell' Esodo*, Milan 1956
H. Gressmann, *Mose und seine Zeit*, FRLANT 18, 1913
M. Noth, *Überlieferungsgeschichte des Pentateuch*, Stuttgart 1948, ET *A History of Pentateuchal Traditions*, Englewood Cliffs N.J. 1971, Hemel Hempstead 1972
K. G. O'Connell, *The Theodotionic Revision of the Book of Exodus*, Cambridge, Mass., 1972
E. Osswald, *Das Bild des Mose*, Berlin 1962
J. Plastaras, *The God of Exodus*, Milwaukee 1966
W. Rudolph, *Der 'Elohist' von Exodus bis Josua*, Berlin 1938
H. Schmid, *Mose. Überlieferung und Geschichte*, Berlin 1968
R. Smend, *Die Erzählung des Hexateuch*, Berlin 1912
J. Wellhausen, *Die Composition des Hexateuchs und der historischen Bücher des Alten Testaments*[3], Berlin 1899
F. V. Winnett, *The Mosaic Tradition*, Toronto and London 1949

3. General

A. Alt, *Kleine Schriften zur Geschichte Volkes Israel* I–III, Munich 1953–59; partly translated in *Essays on Old Testament History and Religion*, Oxford 1966, New York 1967
C. Brockelmann, *Hebräische Syntax*, Neukirchen 1956
B. S. Childs, *Memory and Tradition in Israel*, SBT 37, 1962
S. R. Driver, *A Treatise on the Use of the Tenses in Hebrew*[3], Oxford 1892
A. B. Ehrlich, *Randglossen zur hebräischen Bibel* I, Leipzig 1908
W. Eichrodt, *Theology of the Old Testament* I–II, ET Old Testament Library, London and Philadelphia 1961, 1967
W. Gesenius and F. Buhl, *Hebräisches und aramäisches Handwörterbuch über das AT*[17], Leipzig 1915
E. König, *Historisch-kritisches Lehrgebäude der hebräischen Sprache*, Leipzig 1881–97

H. M. Orlinsky, *Notes on the New Translation of the Torah*, New York 1969

G. von Rad, *Old Testament Theology* I–II, ET Edinburgh and New York 1962, 1965

—, *Gesammelte Studien zum AT*, Munich 1958 (cited as *GSAT*); ET *The Problem of the Hexateuch and Other Essays*, Edinburgh and New York 1966

W. Schottroff, *'Gedenken' im Alten Orient und im AT*, WMANT 15[2], 1967

R. de Vaux, *Ancient Israel: Its Life and Institutions*, ET London and New York 1961

W. Zimmerli, *Gottes Offenbarung*, Munich 1963

I

INTRODUCTORY

1.1–7

A. Besters, '"Israël" et "Fils d'Israël"', *RB* 74, 1964, pp.5–23, 322–55; G. W. Coats, 'A Structural Transition in Exodus', *VT* 22, 1972, pp.129ff.; M. Greenberg, *Understanding Exodus*, 1969, pp.18ff.; A. Lacocque, *Le Devenir de Dieu*, Paris 1967, pp.25ff.; Th. C. Vriezen, 'Exodusstudien, Exodus 1', *VT* 17, 1967, pp.334–53.

1 ¹These are the names of the Israelites who came to Egypt with Jacob, each with his household: ²Reuben, Simeon, Levi, and Judah, ³Issachar, Zebulon, and Benjamin, ⁴Dan and Naphtali, Gad and Asher. ⁵The tribal offspring of Jacob was seventy persons, Joseph being already in Egypt. ⁶Then Joseph died, and all his brothers, and all that generation. ⁷But the Israelites were fruitful and prolific; they multiplied and increased greatly so that the land was filled with them.

1. Textual and Philological Notes

Cf. F. M. Cross, *The Ancient Library of Qumran*, Garden City, N.Y. 1958, pp.137f., for a preliminary treatment of the text 4QExᵃ.

1.1. The MT begins with a conjunction which the LXX omits. Cf. Lev.1.1; Num.1.1; Josh.1.1; *G–K* §49bN.

5b.A nominal clause of circumstantial force. A parallel construction is Gen.1.2. Cf. König, *Lehrgebäude* III, §302a, 362k.

2. Old Testament Context

The book of Exodus begins by recapitulating information which has already been given in Genesis. The list of the sons of Jacob who entered Egypt has appeared in Gen.46.8ff. with the tradition of seventy persons. The death of Joseph has been recounted in Gen.50.26. At the same time new material is introduced within the first few verses which goes beyond the Genesis account, especially the death of the entire generation of Joseph and the multiplication of the people. The introduction, therefore, points both backward to the patriarchs and forward to the exodus story. The initial task is to examine more closely this dual function of the introduction.

There is general agreement among literary critics regarding the source division: P = 1–5, 7; J = 6. However, this initial source division does not in itself solve many problems, but simply focuses the issues at stake more sharply. Why did the Priestly writer recapitulate his earlier material in this form and how did he couple his introduction to the earlier Exodus traditions (J) in 8ff.?

The Priestly writer begins with the phrase 'These are the names . . .' This formula serves the author much in the same way as the phrase 'These are the generations of . . .' (Gen. 2.4, etc.) to provide a structure for the narrative. The formula which connects the names to the entrance into Egypt derives from the tradition in Gen. 46. This chapter had also included the tradition of seventy persons (v. 27). However, in its new role in the Exodus narrative the writer is forced to adjust the older material to the different historical situation. He repeats the tradition of the seventy in v. 5, but adds the comment on Joseph's being already in Egypt to accord with the narrative. (For later interpreters – the LXX records 75 souls – the problem of reconciling the numbers in the genealogies became an issue.) It is of interest to note that, although the Priestly writer of Exodus uses the genealogical framework of Gen. 46.8ff. in v. 1, the actual order of the names follows the older tradition of Gen. 35 which organized the names according to the eponymic wives of Jacob.

Verse 1 begins with the tradition of the patriarchs. The *bᵉnê Israel* are the sons of Jacob, but the transitional function of the introduction emerges in v. 7. Now the *bᵉnê Israel* are the Israelites, the people of Israel. The writer has moved from the tradition of a family to that of the nation. (Cf. A. Besters, *op. cit.*, pp. 5ff.) His fusion of the two traditions makes it clear that he understands the exodus as a direct continuation of the history begun in Genesis. Indeed the nature of the continuity is made explicit in v. 7. In this verse the Priestly writer goes beyond the Genesis narrative of 46.27 and begins the exodus account. The vocabulary of v. 7 reflects the promise of blessing to Adam (Gen. 1.28; 9.1) as well as the promise to Abraham (12.1ff.). God, the creator, has fulfilled his promise to the fathers. Verse 7 now functions as a transitional verse by pointing in both directions. It serves as a fulfillment of the patriarchal promise of the past, but now forms the background for the events which initiate the exodus (cf. 1.9).

Vriezen (*op. cit.*, pp.334ff.) has made a strong case for seeing a traditional formula in v.6. The repetition of Joseph's death in v.6 belongs to the formula of the rise of the new king in v.8. The beginning of the new age is marked by the ending of the old (cf. the close parallel in Judg.2.10). The final Priestly redactor has retained the traditional formula of the earlier source in v.6, but he has skillfully intertwined it with his own transitional material in v.7 which sets the new period of Israel's history within the broad framework of the one great plan of God with his people from creation.

II

ISRAEL'S PERSECUTION AND
THE BIRTH OF MOSES
1.8–2.10

E. Auerbach, *Moses*, Amsterdam 1963; G. Binder, *Die Aussetzung des Königskindes Kyros und Romulus*, Beiträge zur klass. Philologie 10, Meisenheim 1964; B. S. Childs, 'The Birth of Moses', *JBL* 84, 1965, pp.109ff.; M. Cogan, 'A Technical Term for Exposure', *JNES* 27, 1968, pp.133–5; C. Cohen, 'The Legend of Sargon and the Birth of Moses', *JANES* 4, 1972, pp.46–51; G. R. Driver, 'Hebrew Mothers', *ZAW* 67, 1955, pp.246–8; G. Fohrer, *Überlieferung und Geschichte des Exodus*, 1964, pp.9ff.; H. Gressmann, *Mose und seine Zeit*, 1913, pp.1ff.; H. G. Güterbock, 'Die historische Tradition und ihre literarische Gestaltung bei Babyloniern und Hethitern bis 1200', *ZA* 42, 1934, pp.62–4; W. Helck, 'Ṯkw und die Ramsesstadt', *VT* 15, 1965, pp.35ff.; I. Mendelsohn, 'On Corvée Labor in Ancient Canaan and Israel', *BASOR* 167, 1962, pp.31–5; E. Meyer, *Die Israeliten und ihre Nachbarstämme*, Halle 1906, reprinted Darmstadt 1967, pp.41ff.; F. Nims, 'Bricks without Straw', *BA* 13, 1950, pp.22–8; J. Plastaras, *The God of Exodus*, 1966, pp.26ff.; G. von Rad, 'Beobachtungen an der Moseerzählung Exodus 1–14', *EvTh* 31, 1971, pp.579–88; D. B. Redford, 'Ex.1, 11', *VT* 13, 1963, pp.401–18; 'The Literary Motif of the Exposed Child', *Numen* 14, 1967, pp.210ff.; F. V. Winnett, *The Mosaic Tradition*, 1949, pp.16ff.

1 [8]Then there arose a new king over Egypt who did not know Joseph. [9]And he said to his people, 'Look, the Israelite people are too numerous and strong for us. [10]Come on, let's deal shrewdly with them, lest they increase and, in the event of war, should join forces with our enemies in fighting against us and go up out of the land.' [11]Accordingly, they put gang-foremen in charge of them to oppress them with forced labor; and they built storage cities for Pharaoh, Pithom and Raamses. [12]But the more they oppressed them the more they multiplied and spread about so that they (the Egyptians) came to loathe the Israelites. [13]So the Egyptians subjected the Israelites to cruel slavery. [14]They made their lives bitter with heavy work at mortar and brick, and with all kinds of labor in the fields. All the work they exacted of them with ruthlessness.

15 Then the king of Egypt spoke to the Hebrew midwives, one of whom was named Shiphrah and the other Puah. 16'When you deliver the Hebrew women, look at the birthstool; if it is a boy, kill him; if it is a girl, let her live.' 17But the midwives feared God and did not do as the king of Egypt had commanded them, but let the male children live. 18So the king of Egypt summoned the midwives and said to them: 'Why have you done this and let the male children live?' 19The midwives said to Pharaoh, 'Because the Hebrew women are not like the Egyptian women, for they are vigorous; and before the midwife reaches them, they have given birth.' 20And God dealt favorably with the midwives and the people multiplied and increased greatly. 21And because the midwives feared God, he established houses for them. 22Then Pharaoh commanded all his people, 'Every boy that is born you shall throw into the Nile, but let all the girls live.'

2 1Now a man from the house of Levi went and married the daughter of Levi. 2She conceived and bore a son. When she saw how beautiful he was, she hid him for three months. 3When she could no longer hide him, she got a papyrus basket for him, and sealed it with bitumen and pitch. She put the child into it and placed it among the reeds at the bank of the Nile. 4Her sister posted herself at some distance to learn what would happen to him.

5 Now the daughter of Pharaoh came down to bathe at the Nile while her maids walked along the Nile. She caught sight of the basket among the reeds and sent her maid to get it. 6On opening it, she saw the child – a boy – crying. She took pity on him and said, 'This must be a Hebrew child.' 7Then his sister said to Pharaoh's daughter, 'Shall I go and summon for you a nurse from the Hebrew women to nurse the child for you?' 8Pharaoh's daughter answered: 'Yes.' So the girl went and called the child's mother. 9And Pharaoh's daughter said to her: 'Take this child and nurse it for me, and I will pay your wages.' So the woman took the child and nursed it. 10When the child grew up, she brought him to Pharaoh's daughter, and she made him her son. She named him Moses, saying, 'because I drew him out of the water'.

1. Textual and Philological Notes

1.8. The AmTr catches the sense in its paraphrase 'who knew nothing about Joseph'. B. Jacob, *Das zweite Buch Mose, ad loc.*, reads too much into the Hebrew: 'he did not choose to know Joseph'.

10. NJPS translates the final verb $w^{e'}āl\bar{a}h$ as 'gain ascendancy over' which greatly improves the sense of the sentence. However, the philological warrant for this meaning is too weak to justify it. Still cf. Orlinsky, *Notes on the New Translation*, p. 149. The 3 fem.pl. form should be emended to $tiqrā'\bar{e}n\hat{u}$ with BH[3]. Cf. the use in Lev. 10.19.

14. The syntax of the final clause remains an old crux. Cf. the discussion by J. Blau, *VT* 4, 1954, pp. 7ff., and P. Saydon, *VT* 14, 1964, p. 201.

15. The LXX and V do not read 'Hebrew' as an attributive adjective but in construct state: 'the midwives of the Hebrews', which leaves open the question of nationality.

16. The exact meaning of the noun '*obnayim* is still debated. Cf. the parallel in Jer. 18.3 = 'potter's wheel'. The most probable explanation remains a type of delivery stool of two stones on which the woman knelt. However, the translation 'genitals' is adopted by the AmTr and others because of the context. NAB follows the LXX in reading 'giving birth'. Cf. H. A. Brongers, *NTT* 20, 1966, pp. 241ff.

19. *ḥāyôṭ* from *ḥāyeh*, 'lively'. The common emendation to *ḥayyôṭ* 'animals' does not commend itself either philologically or exegetically. The problem is dealt with in detail by G. R. Driver, 'Hebrew Mothers', *ZAW* 67, 1955, pp. 246ff.

21. It is uncertain whether the connotation of *bāttîm* is narrowly construed (house) or broadly (family).

23. The LXX, followed by NAB, adds 'to the Hebrews', which appears to be a clarifying expansion.

2.1. The syntax of the last phrase is difficult. '*eṭ-baṭ-lēwî* does not normally mean 'a daughter of Levi' because of the definite article (König, *Lehrgebäude* III, 304a), nor a Levite woman as in NJPS, NAB which would be rather *baṭ 'îš lēwî*. Cf. Ex. 6.18a, 20a.

2. Cf. W. F. Albright on the idiom *rā'āh kî ṭôb* in *Mélanges bibliques redigés . . . A. Robert*, Paris 1956, pp. 22ff.; also Meek, *JBL* 82, 1963, p. 268; *JBL* 64, 1945, p. 12.

5. The middle clause is circumstantial: 'while the maidens were walking'.

8. An affirmative answer in Biblical Hebrew repeats the verb of the question.

9. *hêlîkî* 'take' is difficult and often emended to *hôlîkî*. It is thought to have been influenced by the nearby *hêniqihû*. Ehrlich, *Randglossen I*, p. 264, argues against this emendation that the hiph. of *hlk* is normally used of that which can move itself. Only in late Hebrew does it become synonymous with *hēbî'*. He follows the Syriac and Rashi in reading *hê' lāk* = 'here, it's yours!' Perhaps a technical term is reflected here. Cogan (*op. cit.*, p. 10) argues for a Hebrew equivalent of the Akkadian *nadu*, 'to throw, or cast'. An Akkadian formula from the act of adoption offers a certain parallel: 'take the child, he is your child'. (*ta-ab-li zu-ḫa-ra-am lu-ú ma-ru-ki*). Cf. M. Schorr, *Urkunden des altbabylonischen Zivil- und Prozessrechts*, Vorderasiatische Bibliothek 5, Leipzig 1907, p. 122 #78, and M. David, *Die Adoption in altbabylonischen Recht*, Leipzig 1927, pp. 79f. However, the semantic problems involved in such a reconstruction are difficult, as J. Barr, *Comparative Philology and the Text of the Old Testament*, London and New York 1968, has rightly argued.

10a. Ehrlich, *Randglossen I*, p. 265, suggests emending *wayyigdal* to *wayyiggāmēl* (when it was weaned); however, the parallel in Gen. 21.8 shows that the verb in the qal can refer specifically to the age of weaning.

10b. The older attempt to understand the expression *wayyehî lebēn* figuratively: 'he was to her like her own son', breaks down in the light of the increasing number of Near Eastern parallels. Cf. *The Brooklyn Museum Aramaic Papyri*, ed. E. G. Kraeling, New York 1953, p. 226.

10c.Cf. Koehler-Baumgartner, *Lexicon in VT libros*, London 1953, *s.v.*, for the innumerable attempts, both ancient and modern, at the derivation of the name. There is now a general consensus that the name is of Egyptian origin from the root *ms(w)* meaning to 'beget'. It is a hypocoristic form of a theophoric name built on the pattern of Tutmose. Cf. J. G. Griffiths, 'The Egyptian Derivation of the Name Moses', *JNES* 12, 1932, pp.225–31; H. Cazelles, *Moïse, l'Homme de l'Alliance*, Tournai 1955, pp. 14ff.

2. *Literary and History of Tradition Problems*

A. *Literary*

The vast majority of critical commentators assign the section 1.8–2.10 to a variety of different literary sources, although recognizing at the same time a unified quality to the narrative in its present form. There is a wide consensus in assigning to P vv. 13 and 14. The characteristic style, vocabulary, and continuity with the introduction to Exodus and with the P source in Genesis confirm this judgment. However, the division of the rest of the chapter between J and E has produced much diversity of opinion. The usual criteria of the divine name or duplicated story occur too infrequently to aid.

The disagreement turns on two major decisions. First, does the first section extend from vv. 8–12 or 8–10? Meyer (also Gressmann, Bäntsch, Beer) defended the view that the plan which began in v. 8 'to deal shrewdly' (v. 10) found its continuation in v. 15 with the story of the midwives, and not in the heavy work of vv. 11f. Conversely, Wellhausen, followed by Bacon, Driver, Noth, saw vv. 8–12 as a unit (usually J) which had its duplicate in vv. 15–20. The second issue turns on the lack of agreement in determining which source is represented in 15–20 and 2.1–10. The majority assign these verses to E, although Noth opts for J.

Regarding the first problem, we accept 8–12 as the unit. The inconsistency of the plan to deal shrewdly in conjunction with the subsequent reference to undisguised slave labor does not rest on a source division, but arises from the fusion of two traditions (cf. below). Again, v. 12 seems to refer to v. 10 which would speak against separating at this point. Regarding the second problem, there are no very sure criteria for deciding. Clearly v. 22 belongs to the same stratum as 8–10, but to which source is not clear. On the thin basis of vocabulary differences we tend to assign to J vv. 8–12 and to E vv. 15–20, 22; 2.1–10. However, the source division is not definite, nor does it seem to be very significant exegetically. Both J and E seem to follow the same major lines of the tradition and therefore show few characteristic peculiarities. The more significant issues lie on the level of oral tradition.

B. *History of Traditions*

The nature of the history of traditions problem first emerged with sharp clarity in the analysis of Gressmann (*Mose und seine Zeit*, pp. 1ff.). Building on the earlier work of E. Meyer (*Die Israeliten und ihre Nachbarstämme*) Gressmann attempted to determine the relation of the birth story tradition to the other traditions of the exodus and to clarify the nature of the story's prehistory. Briefly his conclusions were as follows: the story of Moses' birth is a saga which belongs to the youngest of the exodus traditions and stands in tension with the earlier traditions. The motif of the Egyptians seeking to reduce the number of Hebrew slaves in ch. 1 is dependent on the Moses' birth narrative of ch. 2. The original motif had to do only with the king's attempt to destroy the promised hero-child. This motivation was secondarily expanded to include a threat to the whole people and thus to provide the background for the birth legend of Moses. Gressmann concluded that the parallels, particularly the Babylonian legend of Sargon of Akkad, demonstrated that the common *Märchenmotif* of the promised child who was exposed and rescued, had been applied to Moses. By and large, a majority of critical commentators have accepted Gressmann's analysis (Böhl, Beer, Auerbach, Rylaarsdam, Noth, Fohrer, and Clamer with reservation).

However, in spite of this apparent consensus certain problems arise in connection with his analysis. First of all, the meaning and function of the Sargon legend is not at all clear. In the most recent translation of Speiser (*ANET²*, p. 119), he renders the opening lines as follows:

> Sargon, the mighty king, king of Agade, am I
> My mother was a *changeling* (*enitum*), my father I knew not,
> The brother(s) of my father *loved* the hills
> My city is Azupiranu, which is situated on the banks of the Euphrates.
> My *changeling* mother conceived me, in secret she bore me
> She set me in a basket of rush. . . .

Speiser follows Güterbock (*op cit.*, pp. 62ff.) in arguing that the term *enitum* is uncertain. Driver (in G. R. Driver and J. C. Miles, *The Babylonian Laws*, Oxford and New York 1952, I, pp.361ff.), had also dismissed as false the identification of *enitum* with the common *entu* = priestess. However, in spite of this dissent, the identification is more than probable. Both von Soden, *Akkadisches Handwörterbuch* I, Wiesbaden 1965, p.220, and *CAD*, vol.4, p.173, defend a translation of 'high priestess'. Most recently, C. Cohen (*op. cit.*, pp.47f.) has reviewed the philological evidence used by *CAD* along with the new text recently published by W. G. Lambert (*Atraḥasis*, Oxford 1969, p.102), and he concludes that the identification of *entu* with *enetu* = priestess is incontrovertible.

What is the effect of this clarification on the meaning of the passage as a whole? One could argue that Sargon's claim of an *entu* as a mother automatically implied that his father was a king (cf. the passages cited in *CAD* which would point to some form of *hieros gamos*). The force of this argument is that it offers a consistent interpretation of the whole Sargon legend. It functions to legitimate Sargon by claiming a royal ancestry.

However, Güterbock's alternative interpretation cannot be lightly dismissed. The line 'in secret she bore me . . .' is interpreted as indicating an illegitimate birth which led to the child being concealed. The line 'my father I knew not' could point in this same direction. Moreover, the several texts cited by *CAD* and Lambert all emphasize the requirement of chastity on the part of the high priestess which would further explain the secrecy. Finally, the strongest evidence for Güterbock's interpretation is his ability to explain the text in its function as *naru* literature. In place of a hypothesis that the legend performed the role of legitimating Sargon's kingship, Güterbock has shown conclusively its real function. The *Märchenmotif* of the first ten lines simply introduces the main point of the text which is the report on the deeds of Sargon's reign. 'The black-headed (people) I ruled, I governed, mighty mountains . . . I conquered, the upper ranges I scaled . . .' There then follows an oracle of blessing in the imperative style directed to 'whatever king may come after me' in which the same deeds are repeated seriatim: 'Let him rule, let him govern . . ., let him conquer . . . let him scale the upper ranges . . .' Güterbock concludes that the function of the oracle was to determine the future by binding it to the past, which is closely related to omen literature. To summarize up to this point, the Sargon legend functions as an introduction to a blessing oracle. It is a *Märchenmotif* rather than a mythological fragment and seems to have had no cultic or etiological role.

Gressmann argued at great length that the original form of the birth legend always contained a threat on the child's life which arose from a prophecy regarding the child's destiny. Indeed, the Moses' story is cast into this form in Josephus, Philo, *Exodus Rabbah*, and in Greek mythology. (Cf. G. Binder, *op. cit.*; D. B. Redford, *op. cit.*, *Numen* 14, pp. 210ff.) However, it seems most unlikely that this motif of a threat was present in the Sargon legend which was a motif of the 'rags-to-riches' type and related how a rejected child was exposed, rescued, nurtured into manhood, and finally succeeded to a position of honor. Again, it seems unlikely that if the original story had included this element, it would have been later removed, since the announcement of a coming child by a divine messenger is a feature indigenous to Israel's tradition (Gen. 16.11; 18.9; Judg. 13.7, etc.). Therefore, we argue that the motivation for the exposure is not part of the inherited tradition but belongs to the special feature of the Moses story.

Once the question of the shape of the *Vorlage* has been discussed, the more difficult problem in Gressmann's analysis still remains, namely, what is the relation of the traditions of Israel's persecution in ch. 1 to the birth and rescue of Moses in ch. 2? Is Gressmann correct in claiming that the primary element in the history of tradition was the birth legend which was secondarily expanded to include the broad threat to the people?

At the outset it is important to distinguish between the various traditions which are represented in ch. 1. First, vv. 7 and 12 (P and J) speak of the miraculous increase of the people to form a large nation, a tradition which is elsewhere reflected in Gen. 1.28; Deut. 10.22; Josh. 24.3, etc. Again, vv. 11f. and 13f. refer to this bitter slavery of Israel in Egypt which is the dominant tradition respecting the early period and is reflected throughout the Old Testament (Deut. 6.20ff.; 26.6ff.; I Sam. 12.8, etc.). Finally, vv. 15–22 recount the efforts of Pharaoh actually to destroy the Israelites, at first in a covert fashion, but later openly. For convenience we shall designate this latter theme as the 'genocide' tradition.

In ch. 1 these three traditions have been joined. Moreover, the fusion has preceded the literary level. The source represented in vv. 8–12 (probably J) not only has the tradition of the miraculous increase and bitter slavery, but the vocabulary of v. 10 ('deal shrewdly') would imply a knowledge of the genocide tradition as well (cf. Gressmann). As the chapter is now composed, the genocide tradition provides the structure of the entire chapter, and the two other traditions have been worked into this framework. This means that the genocide tradition cannot be regarded in any sense as a late interpolation into an older slavery-in-Egypt tradition.

Nevertheless, there remain major tensions within the chapter which have long since been pointed out. Ordinarily a ruling nation, particularly in the Ancient Near East, would not think of destroying its labor supply, but would look with favor on its increase. Again, one does not reduce the number of a people by destroying the males, but rather the females. Both of these difficulties seem to argue against joining the slavery-in-Egypt tradition with the genocide tradition. Moreover, how is one to explain the fact that there are no other references in the Old Testament to the genocide tradition (except Ps. 105.25)? Moreover, the later stories in Exodus seem to contradict the picture of Israel's slave conditions as an exercise in genocide. As Gressmann remarks (p. 3), to intensify the oppression in ch. 5.1ff. by removing the straw for making bricks would be a 'Kinderspiel' and an unthinkable continuation from ch. 1.

There have been several efforts to avoid the force of Gressmann's argument. Dillmann and recently Plastaras have argued that the genocide tradition was a short-lived, momentary intensification, but this is a conjecture without any support from the text. Again, it has been argued that the lack of further Old Testament references to genocide in Egypt is not decisive because elsewhere in the Bible we have examples of single, isolated traditions of great antiquity. While this phenomenon can be readily granted in theory, it seems highly unlikely in respect to the exodus. The tradition does not appear as an undigested ancient fragment, but provides exactly those features needed to introduce ch. 2, namely an attempted genocide on the male children.

We conclude, therefore, that in respect to the history of traditions problem Gressmann's reconstruction remains the most probable one. Ch. 2 provided the primary tradition to which ch. 1 was secondarily joined.

C. *The Transformation of the Tradition*

The purpose of studying the traditional material has been to provide a perspective from which to understand more clearly the newer, non-conventional elements of the chapter. Even Gressmann was concerned that the particular Hebrew stamp of the story not be overlooked. Once the outlines of the common Near Eastern material have been sketched, it is possible to see how the story has been altered by means of newer elements.

First, the common motif of the exposed child, who is rescued to become king, has been seriously altered. The simple 'rags-to-riches' motif is no longer applicable to Moses. He is not an unknown child who becomes king; rather the whole weight of the story has been shifted. Moses is first 'exalted' and later returns to a position of humility by identifying with his people. The story now serves to illustrate the special handling of this particular child. The reader is led to feel that the significance of these events is not fully clear. The real action still lies in the future. The rescue is only a preparation.

Secondly, the Egyptian local color has been skillfully used in the story by the writer who represents throughout a Hebrew point of view. The introduction of the princess as the rescuer of the child is certainly not characteristic of Egyptian folk tales where a goddess would be expected to play this role (G. Roeder, *Altägyptische Erzählung und Märchen*, Jena 1927, pp. 12ff., 102ff.). The picture of the Egyptian princess is also that viewed by an outsider and not from within the Egyptian court. Not only does she speak Hebrew, but she is able to recognize the foundling as one belonging to the Hebrews and is willing to seek out a nurse from among them.

Thirdly, the etymology of the name belongs to the newer elements of the story. As Noth has observed, the Hebrew writer was unaware of the Egyptian origin of the name. Otherwise he would have made use of this fact. The naming follows the usual pattern of Old Testament etymological etiologies, and derives from a loose association in sound.

Finally, the motivation for the exposure is one of the boldest alterations of the common tradition. It was unthinkable to speak of Moses as a foundling with unknown parentage. Moreover, Hebrew parents do not willingly expose their children. This practice was repudiated at an early date in Israel. The only alternative open to the narrative was to provide an adequate reason which would force the parents to this action.

D. *The Transmission of the Story*

There is one final set of questions to raise regarding the transmission of this tradition. The above analysis has attempted to show that there was a period of oral tradition in which conventional Near Eastern material received a particular Hebrew stamp. The delineation of Moses in the birth story was made on the oral level. This implies that there were bearers of this tradition, circles within Israel who were active in its preservation. Can one make more precise this process of transmission?

In my earlier article (*JBL* 1965, *op. cit.*) I suggested as a working hypothesis that the unusual features of the birth story might be best explained in reference to wisdom literature. Although it is immediately clear that the story is not wisdom literature in the strict sense of the term, it has some affinity to historicized wisdom tales. The evidence is along the following lines:

1. The characters in the chapter, especially Pharaoh, seem to represent typical figures. Pharaoh thinks to act shrewdly, but is really the wicked fool who is duped by the clever midwives. Cf. the parallel to Haman in the Esther story (Talmon, *VT* XIII, 1963, pp. 419ff.).

2. The piety of the midwives reflects the religious ideal of the wisdom circles. Their refusal to obey Pharaoh stems from a 'fear of God'. This piety evidences itself in cleverness and in the ability to meet the accusation of Pharaoh with rational arguments.

3. Another important feature of the story which might point toward wisdom circles is the completely open and positive description of the Egyptian princess. It is not because of ignorance or deception that she adopts the child. Rather, the narrator emphasizes her spontaneous pity for the child, as well as her awareness that he is a Hebrew. This positive attitude toward the foreigner is characteristic of the international flavor of wisdom circles.

4. Finally, the concept of God's role is unusual for the Exodus traditions and parallels more closely the Joseph stories of Genesis. Direct theological statements concerning God's activity are used sparingly (cf. von Rad, *GSAT*, pp. 272ff.; ET *The Problem of the Hexateuch*, pp. 292ff.). Nowhere does God appear to rescue the child; rather, everything has a 'natural' cause. Yet it is clear that the writer sees the mystery of God's providence through the action of the humans involved.

It is not easy to set a date for the emergence of the birth story tradition. As with most Old Testament birth stories it belongs to one of the youngest layers of tradition. The fact that it was incorporated in the oldest literary strand would set a *terminus ad quem* to its oral formation. It seems probable that Ps. 105.23ff. knew the tradition in a shape which differed little from its present literary form. The Psalmist makes reference to the same major feature of Ex. 1.7–14.

3. Old Testament Context

Although the study of the developments of the tradition of the birth story has confirmed the probability that ch. 1 is secondary to 2.1–10, the present task of the interpreter is to seek to understand the final form of the narrative.

The main thrust of the story is clear. The sons of Jacob increase miraculously in accordance with the divine promise (Gen. 12) to become a mighty people. However a new Egyptian king, who assumed the throne without any knowledge of Israel's past privileged position under Joseph, saw the increase as a threat. He decided on a plan to check Israel's expansion, which began with slavery forced on the people. When this failed in its purpose, he resorted to secret treachery in attempting to murder the male children and finally, in desperation, ordered the open drowning by the Egyptian populace of all male Hebrew babies. Against this background, the child Moses was born. Unable to conceal him for long, his mother set him into the Nile in a basket. From there he was rescued by the daughter of Pharaoh, reared in safety, and adopted as a son by the princess.

One of the major themes which ties the narrative together is the contrast between the plan of God for the good of his people and the evil designs of the Egyptian king. The Egyptian's plan unfolds in three steps, which increase in oppression and the exploitation of crass power. Each time the plan is thwarted, in different and strange ways, and Israel hangs on by a string. God's plan for his people, however, is not clearly stated. Only the writer makes it apparent that it has begun to unfold in accordance with a prior divine commitment and focuses finally on this child, who has been miraculously saved from destruction and prepared for a special mission. Within this broad framework there are a variety of other themes, some of which are simply received from the tradition, others which are skillfully developed in a fresh way.

[1.8–14] This first episode relates in the simple, narrative style of the folk-tale the change in Israel's position which was undoubtedly a complex historical process involving many political factors (cf. Cassuto, p. 10). The tradition marks the transition from being members of a large family to the emergence of a nation in the period of Egyptian slavery. The cause of the change from a position of privilege and prosperity to one of want and oppression is attributed to a new king 'who did not know Joseph'. At this point, it is a mistake for modern commentators to try to bring this vague reference into sharper focus by learned discussions of Egyptian history. This move fails to deal seriously with the biblical style which makes use of stereotyped idioms in order to highlight the beginning of a new epoch in Israel's life. The writer describes the king simply as 'new', and he is immediately seen addressing 'his people'. (Again, to suggest that 'his' people is a technical term for 'advisers' is to misunderstand the style of the narrative.) The Egyptian king is not presented as the incarnate Son of Re, who rules with absolute sovereignty over a nation, but as a clever despot who sets about to convince his supporters of his plan. Identifying himself with them ('us', 'we'), he sketches the nature of the danger and a suitable course of action. Calvin appropriately describes the king's action as a classic example of using an alleged threat as an occasion for one's own wickedness. Up to that moment the Hebrews had done nothing to wrong the Egyptians. Note that they are not even accused of holding the best land. Rather, the accusation turns on a series of hypothetical situations: 'Were they to continue to multiply, and were enemies to come from some other direction, then if the Hebrews were to join with them, they could succeed in escaping from the country.' The translation of the NJPS seeks to bolster the logic of the remark by rendering the final clause 'gain control of the land', but without adequate warrant from the text.

One might argue that the biblical writer was so accustomed to having Pharaoh resist Israel's departure from the land in the subsequent narrative that he attributed the same motivation to this king even before Israel was enslaved. But actually the effect is to dramatize the ill-founded nature of the charge. A king and people who are so foolish now seek 'to deal shrewdly' with the situation. Thus Israel is enslaved. The author makes use of older material within the tradition to describe in detail the nature of the slavery: heavy burdens, construction of store houses with brick and mortar, work in the fields. But the variety of activity produces a single effect. Life was made bitter by the rigor of the oppression.

Just how the Egyptians expected the enforced labor to impede the expansion of the Hebrews is not fully clear. Would the hard labor enervate the people or were the men kept away from their wives? The narrative is not bothered by lack of rigorous logic. Nevertheless the first plan of Pharaoh failed in its purpose. Indeed, it backfired because the multiplication accelerated in proportion to the oppression. What is more, a revulsion fell on the Egyptians which they had not experienced up to then.

[1.15–21] The writer moves abruptly to the second stage of oppression without pausing to assess Pharaoh's reflection over his failure. Nor does he employ any deceptive devices to introduce his conversation with the midwives. Rather in accord with the style of the folk tale he launches immediately into the dialogue, filling in the bare minimum of details. There were two Hebrew midwives named Shiphrah and Puah. Commentators have long puzzled over why only two are mentioned and suggested various explanations. Thus Rashi suggests that the two were the head officials of the guild. However, Cassuto is obviously correct in attributing this factor to the poetic character of the narrative.

A more serious question has to do with the nationality of the midwives. Were they Hebrew or Egyptian? The minor variation in the grammatical forms between the two alternative constructions of the text, namely 'Hebrew midwives' or 'midwives of the Hebrews', has continued to engage the commentators. On the one hand, those who opt for the midwives being Hebrew argue that the names of the women are Hebrew (cf. Rashi's etymologies), and that it is highly unlikely that Egyptians would have been accepted in this delicate task (B. Jacob). On the other hand, those who opt for their Egyptian nationality argue that Pharaoh could never have expected Hebrew women to betray in secret their own people in this way. In addition, the fact that the midwives 'feared God' is presented in the narrative as a great surprise, a miracle with which Pharaoh never reckoned. The force of this description is reduced if the midwives were Hebrew. Finally, the reward proffered the midwives in v. 21 'he gave them families' seems to make the best sense in terms of providing a posterity within the people of Israel. However, the meaning of v. 21 is too obscure to carry much weight in the debate. (The difficulty of this verse was obviously felt very early. Verses 20b and 21c already seem to be an attempt at clarification which does not fully succeed.) Whatever is thought to have been the original reading, it is clear that the Massoretic Text accepted the first alternative and described the midwives as Hebrew.

The story of Pharaoh and the midwives continues the folk-tale style with the Egyptian king himself instructing the women. The writer underplays the circumstances surrounding the command by omitting both the elements of threat or the response of the midwives to a scheme which was to require action diametrically opposed to their office as bearer of life. Rather, the author offers the real reason which was to thwart the plan. It was not because they boldly defied the king, nor because of their loyalty to the Hebrews, but because they 'feared God', that they refused to obey the command. The king is immediately aware of a breakdown in his plan and summons the midwives. Using the fixed form of the accusation (Gen. 20.9ff.) he charges them with a felony. Cassuto remarks perceptively: 'in truth they did not do anything, on the contrary they refrained from taking action; but this is the way the wicked despot puts it: he who refused to obey him acts . . . against him' (p. 14).

The response of the midwives is so clever as to have convinced not only Pharaoh, but a number of modern commentators who accept its veracity on face value. Others see in the answer a sagacious half-truth since, had the Hebrews not used midwives, one wonders why there would have been such an office at all. Actually, the true reason for the failure of Pharaoh's plan has already been given in v. 17, namely, their fear of God. The clever response serves to highlight the stupidity of the king who would 'act wisely'. Once again, the frail resources of two women have succeeded in outdoing the crass power of the tyrant.

The narrative now moves quickly to its conclusion. Pharaoh throws off the cloak of secrecy. He commanded all his people: 'Every male child [Hebrew is surely understood] shall be thrown into the Nile.' The pogrom has reached its height. All Egypt has been recruited to destroy the population explosion of the enemy. Then Moses is born.

In the birth story which follows there is no direct reference to the plan of Pharaoh to destroy Israel, but the pogrom is everywhere assumed to be the background. In fact, the material in ch. 1 serves so perfectly as the setting for ch. 2 that the two chapters could hardly have circulated independently. Still the author does not narrate the birth story as an immediate continuation of the story in ch. 1. He takes a fresh start by introducing a new style of narrative which is quite unrelated at first. Only as he develops his story does its relation to the larger history become all too evident.

[2.1–10] The focus suddenly narrows to fall on one man. A certain Levite – his name is unknown to the tradition at this point – takes to wife a daughter of Levi. (The text may be in some disorder, but the emphasis lies on the ordinary character of the event.) In accordance with the typical idiom, the conception and birth of a son follows immediately. Then suddenly the connection between chs. 1 and 2 is clear. In an effort to save the life of the child, the mother conceals it for three months. The reason given is again not an explicit reference to Pharaoh's command, but intimate and subjective: 'When she saw how healthy he was . . .' To lose a frail child is bad enough, but such a child . . . The writer allows the reader to link the two ideas, and moves immediately to her action: 'she hid him for three months'. Then when she could no longer conceal him – whether his cries were too loud or whether for some other reason we are not told – she prepared a basket in which to set the child out into the river. The writer portrays the intense care with which the basket was prepared to prevent its leaking – it even had a top – and placed at the edge of the river's bank. At this point, we are not told anything respecting the mother's motivation. Had she decided to abandon the child in resignation? Hardly this, because the sister stood at a distance 'to see what would be done to him'. The Hebrew idiom expresses far more than simply a neutral observation of what transpired (cf. Esther 2.11). Rather, the emphasis falls on the child's being an object of an activity, the exact nature of which is still unknown.

Certainly one of the most delightful features in the narrative is the role of the sister. Commentators have long noted a tension in the chapter caused by her appearance in v. 4, whereas v. 1 implies by its use of the stereotyped formula that Moses was the first and only child of the couple. Yet this element is neither to be harmonized (e.g. girls were not counted in Israel), nor relegated to different sources. Rather, it should be seen as a literary device of the author. The sister plays a key role as the agent in the story who joins the introductory theme of the mother and child with that of the princess and child. Moreover, the sister tempers the harshness of the exposure by keeping watch at a distance. From this position she appears instantaneously before Pharaoh's daughter to negotiate a Hebrew wet nurse. Not only is the child saved and returned to his mother with royal protection, but she is even paid for taking care of her own child. Some commentators have wondered whether this is a form of irony being directed toward the Egyptians, but in the light of the favorable portrayal of the Egyptian princess, this is hardly likely. She is touched immediately by the sight of the crying baby. Although she recognizes that he is one of the Hebrew children, which ties the story back to the decree of the king, she does not hesitate to offer it protection. In fact, the child is not only rescued, but adopted into the royal household as her son.

Ordinarily the naming of the child occurs directly after birth. Here it is postponed to fit the story. Still it serves as an appendix to the narrative and is not a major force which called the whole birth story tradition into being (so Noth). The naming reflects the usual pattern of Old Testament etymological etiologies and derives the name from a loose association in sound. It has long been recognized that the name Moses is Egyptian in derivation, meaning 'son', which usually appears in the shortened form of Egyptian names like Thutmose. However, the Hebrew writer was unaware of this Egyptian origin or he would certainly have made use of this information. The author connects the name with the Hebrew root 'to draw out', deriving it from the passive form ('the one drawn out') rather than from the philologically more accurate active form ('the drawer out') in order to match the story.

Once again Pharaoh's plan has been thwarted and in a doubly miraculous way. The child has been rescued from exposure, even by the very daughter of the one who made the decree. God's plan for his people rested on the helpless child, floating down the river. But the child is not lost, and the story points expectantly toward the future. What will become of this child on whom such special care has been lavished?

Detailed Notes

1.8. Frequent attempts have been made to bring the vague references to a dynastic change into sharper historical focus (cf. Driver, ad loc.), but it is uncertain to what extent historical memory lay behind this narrative idiom. The same point can be made respecting the alleged threat of war in v. 10. The assumption of many commentators that the sharper the historical focus, the more accurate the interpretation of a passage, is not warranted, particularly if the biblical author uses the material in a blurred state within his narrative. However, a good survey of the historical evidence for this period in Egyptian history can be found in S. Herrmann, *Israels Aufenthalt in Aegypten*, Stuttgart 1970, pp. 34ff.; ET *Israel in Egypt*, SBT 2.27, 1973, pp. 19ff.

11. The term 'Pharaoh' designated originally the royal palace and was later transferred to the king himself as a royal title. Cf. *BHH* III, col. 1445.

11. Pithom is the Hebrew transcription of the Egyptian *Pr-Tm*, 'house of the god Tem' (Atum). It was a city in the east of the Wadi Tumilat and identified with either Tell el-Maskhutah or Tell er-Ratabah. (Cf. the controversy between Gardiner and Naville summarized by Lambdin, *IDB* III, p.821.) Raamses is the Hebrew transcription of the Egyptian (*pr*)-*r^c-ms-sw*, 'House of Ramses', and was the royal residence of the Pharaohs of the nineteenth and twentieth dynasties. The city was located at either Tanis or Qantiz, which are some 15 miles apart. (Cf. the discussion between D. B. Redford, *VT*, *op. cit.*, and W. Helck, *VT*, *op. cit.*, and again Redford, *Numen*, *op. cit.* Also see B. Couroyer, *op. cit.*)

15. 'Hebrew'. The use of the term Hebrew has been much discussed in recent times. A connection has been long since proposed with the *Ḫabiru* which comprised a larger beduin group of peoples who appear in Ugaritic, Akkadian, and Egyptian texts in the 3rd and 2nd millennia BC and who served as a work force for Egyptian building projects. Cf. the specialized studies of J. Bottéro, 'Le Problème des Ḫabiru', *Rencontre Assyriologique Internationale*, Paris 1954, and M. Greenberg, *The Ḫab/piru*, New Haven 1955. The two midwives have apparently Semitic names. Puah may mean 'splendid one' or perhaps 'girl' related to the Ugaritic cognate *pqt*. Shiphrah appears as *šp-ra* on a list of Egyptian slaves and means 'fair one'. Recent discussion has usually started with W. F. Albright's treatment in *JAOS* 74, 1954, pp.222–32, and sought to make refinements. Cf. J. J. Stamm, *Suppl. VT* 16, 1967, p.327.

16. 'birthstools'. Cf. the pictorial representations in A. Erman, *Die Religion der Ägypter*, Berlin 1934, p.55.

21. 'fear of God', cf. H. W. Wolff, *EvTh* 29, 1969, pp.59ff.

2.1. 'a man of Levi'. Ex.6.20 provides the names of Moses' father and mother.

4. 'his sister'. Cf. le Déaut, 'Miryam, soeur de Moise', *Biblica* 45, 1964, pp.198ff.

5. 'the daughter of Pharaoh'. In later tradition she was known by several names (cf. Driver *ad loc.*).

7. Cf. the discussion of wet nurse contracts in B. S. Childs, *JBL* 84, pp.112ff.

4. New Testament Context

G. H. Box, 'The Gospel Narratives of the Nativity and the Alleged Influence of Heathen Ideas', *The Interpreter*, 1906, pp.195ff.; D. Daube, *The New Testament and Rabbinic Judaism*, London and New York 1956, pp.5–12; M. Dibelius, 'Jungfrauensohn und Krippenkind', *Botschaft und Geschichte* I, Tübingen 1953, pp.1ff.; J. Jeremias, '*Mωυσῆς*', *TWNT* IV, pp.874ff. = *TDNT* IV, pp.848ff.; M. Gaster, *The Asatir. The Samaritan Book of the 'Secrets of Moses'*, London 1927, pp.262ff.; I. Heinemann, 'Moses', *Pauly Wissowa* 16, 1935, pp.359ff.; K. Koch, 'Das Lamm, das Ägypten vernichtet', *ZNW* 57, 1966, pp.79–93; B. Lindars, *New Testament Apologetic*, London and Philadelphia 1961, pp.216ff.; E. Lohmeyer-Schmauch, *Das Evangelium des Matthäus*², Göttingen 1958; H. Strack and P. Billerbeck, *Kommentar zum NT aus Talmud und Midrasch* I, Munich 1922, pp.76ff.; K. Stendahl, 'Quis et unde? An Analysis of Mt 1–2', *Judentum, Urchristentum, Kirche*, BZNW 26², 1964, pp.26ff.; A. Vögtle, *Messias und Gottessohn, Herkunft und Sinn der matthäischen Geburts- und Kindheitsgeschichte* (Düsseldorf 1971).

The most extensive use made of the Moses birth story in the New Testament is in Matthew's account of the visit of the magi and Herod's attempt to destroy the promised Messiah (ch. 2; cf. also Heb. 11.23). Although there are no explicit quotations in Matt. 2 of Ex. 2, the connection between the two accounts has long been recognized. Evidence for the comparison was first seen in the parallel sequence and content of the stories. Both have to do with the birth of a young male child, whose life is threatened by the ruling monarch, at first secretly, but later in open hostility. The child is rescued in the nick of time, but the other children are slaughtered in a vain effort to remove the threat of the one child. A closer study, moreover, reveals other features of Matthew's account which tie the gospel to the Moses story. The quotation from Hos. 11.1, 'Out of Egypt have I called my son', draws a typological parallel between Israel's deliverance from Egypt and Jesus' ascent from the same land. Again, the order to return to the land of Israel in 2.20 is a clear reference to Moses' instructions in Ex. 4.19.

Perhaps the most important observation to be made is that Matthew has not made use of the Moses story in its Old Testament form. Rather, the Matthew account reflects a variety of elements stemming from the Hellenistic reading of the biblical text which the New Testament shares in common with Josephus, Philo, the Targums, and rabbinic and Samaritan midrashim. Thus King Herod is apprised of the threat to his throne through the new-born child by a wise man from the East in an announcement formula which is a feature characteristic of all the above-mentioned texts. Ultimately, this form of the birth narrative goes back to Greek mythology which was imposed on the earlier Near Eastern tradition. (Cf. the detailed discussion of the Perseus tradition in Roscher's *Ausführliches Lexikon der griechischen und römischen Mythologie* III/II, Leipzig 1902ff., cols. 1986ff. and G. Binder, *op. cit.*) In the Samaritan tradition, because Moses had assumed all the features of the eschatological Redeemer figure, his birth was signalled by a host of cosmological wonders: 'the star of Israel ascending in the heights', and 'the star of glory in the heaven' (S. J. Miller, *The Samaritan Molad Mosheh*, New York 1949, p. 12f.). In the rabbinic midrashim the story of Moses' birth also becomes a magnet for attracting a variety of folklore motifs. (Cf. L. Ginzburg, *Legends of the Jews* II, Philadelphia 1910, pp. 262ff.; Daube, *op. cit.*, pp. 5ff.)

Although the Moses story in Matthew bears an unmistakable

Hellenistic stamp, it is significant that these elements of the story have been simply assumed by the New Testament tradition. There is no conscious effort made to establish a close connection between the birth of Jesus and that of Moses by means of proof texts. Indeed, Old Testament passages which seem just below the surface in the Matthew account, such as the 'star arising out of Jacob' (Num. 24.17), never actually play a part in the final shape of the text. For this reason the attempt of scholars such as Box (*op. cit.*, pp. 195ff.) to see the Matthean account as a midrash on the Old Testament cannot be really sustained.

The major characteristic of Matthew's use of the Moses birth story tradition is the manner in which the Exodus material has been read through the eyes of other Old Testament texts in an effort to interpret the life and death of Jesus. The original framework of the birth story has been retained in its Hellenistic form, but the interest of Matthew has certainly shifted. Stendahl (*op. cit.*) and Lindars (*op. cit.*) are probably correct in emphasizing the apologetic element in Matthew's attempt to establish by means of proof texts the messianic claim of Jesus in terms of Bethlehem and Nazareth. Moses' birth serves as a type to foreshadow the birth of the Messiah who according to Micah 5 was to be born in Bethlehem. His descent into Egypt marks his identification with the history of Israel whose deliverance he effected. The slaughter of the innocents is read through the eyes of Jer. 31.15, which in effect reverses the grief in its prophetic form (Lindars, p. 218). The Moses birth story provides a traditional framework in which the messianic claims of Jesus were placed, but the real christological development emerged as these elements of the birth story were refracted through the whole Old Testament and made to focus on Jesus, the Christ.

5. *History of Exegesis*

The classic Jewish commentators continued to use the midrashic form of the earlier period in their handling of the Exodus passage, but added to it a great variety of other elements. Thus the eight major questions which Abarbanel poses to ch. 1 continue, by and large, along many of the same lines as in the past. With Rashi and others, Abarbanel initially focuses on such questions as the repetition of the patriarchal names (cf. Gen. 46.8ff.), the special mention of Joseph in Egypt, the unmodified reference in 1.22 to 'every son shall be cast into the Nile', and the naming of Moses. Jewish commentators consistently address the question of the legality of Amram's marrying his father's sister (6.20), particularly in the light of other biblical legislation (Lev. 18.12). However, Abarbanel goes considerably beyond the usual midrashic question in pursuing the inner logic of the chapter. How did the exposure of Moses by his parents in the river really differ from the king's edict? Why was not Pharaoh suspicious of the Hebrew child raised in his house? The majority of the classic commentaries see the theological significance of ch. 1 to lie in the growth of the nation in fulfillment of the commandment in Gen. 1.28, and the divine promise to Abraham (Rashi, Ramban, Luzzatto).

Early and medieval Christian interpreters pursued the details of the text with much less exegetical rigor. Interest in the allegorical and homiletical interpretation replaced the midrashic questions. Moses in the ark becomes a type of Christ in the cradle, or the Egyptian princess foreshadows the Gentile acceptance of the gospel in contrast to the synagogue's rejection (cf. the selection of the fathers cited by Cornelius a Lapide, *ad loc.*). However, the dominant exegetical question of ch. 1 focused on the response of the midwives. Had the midwives lied and then been rewarded by God for it? Augustine first treated the Exodus passage at some length in his treatise on lying (*De Mendacio* iv.5), concluding that lying is never justified. The midwives were rewarded because of their benevolence toward Israel, not because of their deceit (*De Mendacio* xv.32). Gregory (*Moralia* XVIII. iii.6 *on Job*, MPL 76.41) also argues that the midwives' lying was reprehensible and diverted their true reward of eternal life into a mere earthly recompense. This Exodus passage became the classic passage for all later medieval discussions of lying, and is treated by Aquinas, Peter Martyr and others.

The same interest in the problem of lying continued in Christian exegesis of the Reformation and post-Reformation periods. Calvin argued in his commentary that the lying of the midwives was reprehensible and displeasing to God. Notwithstanding, since no action is free of sin, God rewarded their good works even if mixed with impurity (cf. Lapide's vigorous response). Luther's exegesis on Ex. 1 is much more homiletical and christological than Calvin's, and although rejecting the allegory of the Fathers, he sought to see in the chapter a model for Christian living under the pressures of persecution. He tended to justify the midwives' lying which was directed to aid, rather than injure. In the post-Reformation period several

Protestant commentators, notably John Lightfoot of Cambridge ('The words of the Hebrew midwives not a lie, but a glorious confession of their faith', *A Handful of Gleanings out of the Book of Exodus, Works* II, London 1822, p.357), denied that the midwives had ever lied (so also Patrick, Clarke).

Another feature of the post-Reformation interpretation which had precedence in the earlier periods as well was the strong rationalistic overtones of the exegesis. Detailed mathematical proofs were offered to demonstrate the validity of the increase from seventy persons to a nation of several million within the alloted time (cf. the examples cited by M. Poole, *Synopsis Criticorum, ad loc.*).

The modern period brought a major shift in the assessment of the historical character of chs. 1 and 2, although the implications of the new approach were not immediately felt. Rosenmüller (1822) continued to treat the Exodus chapters as fully historical. Kalisch (1855) argued that the infancy narratives of antiquity which were largely fictitious differed widely from the truths of the Moses narrative (p.24). Dillmann (1880) and Driver (1911) still felt it impossible to determine how much of the narratives were historical. Bäntsch (1903) felt that one could no longer look for a historical kernel in the birth story, but this opinion brought no radical change in his handling of the text in comparison with his predecessors. Rather, it was the consistent *religionsgeschichtliche* approach of Eduard Meyer and, above all, of H. Gressmann which attempted to deal seriously with the Ancient Near Eastern parallels, and as a result raised a whole new battery of questions respecting the growth and appropriation of traditions within Israel. By and large, the period following Gressmann lost interest completely in the earlier questions of the 'pre-critical' period.

6. *Theological Reflection*

The witness of both Testaments has much in common. In both accounts of Ex. 1–2 and Matt. 2, God's plan for his people has a fragile beginning. In both the child serves as the not-yet-revealed instrument of God's intervention, and in both cases the thread on which everything hangs is exceedingly thin. God seems to be taking such an enormous risk to let everything ride on two helpless midwives, a frail ark as protection from the sea, and a last-minute flight to Egypt.

In contrast, the power of the world seems so impressive and

invulnerable. Because God's salvation always appears as a threat, the world can unleash its power against this frail beginning. Pharaoh senses a threat and devises his plan long before the Hebrews are in the least prepared to resist. The magi appear so naïve and powerless before the scheming intrigue of the king. And in both cases, when the secret plans fail, the ungloved fist is ready in an instant to strike.

Again, both stories witness to the wonderfully unexpected rescue from a humanly impossible situation. The Exodus writer delights in the rescue by Pharaoh's daughter and marvels at the mystery of God's work. Matthew allows the magi the full and complete joy of the Christ-child, as they rejoice at the star and worship the child with gifts, before warning them – almost in an afterthought – of the terrible danger from the king.

Finally, both stories testify to the suffering of the people which accompanies the redemption. Rachel, eponymic mother of the people, weeps for her children who have been destroyed. Israel participates in the death of her children, in the slaughter of the infants. The grim reality is that even when redemption finally comes, it is accompanied, not by the heroic martyrdom of the brave partisan, but by the senseless murder of children. The salvation promised by God is not greeted by a waiting world, but opposed with the hysterical fanaticism which borders on madness.

It is also clear that the New Testament wishes to go beyond the Old Testament witness. Moses was only a type of the Messiah and the deliverance from Egypt only a prelude to eschatological redemption. Already the word had been sounded to weeping Rachel: 'Keep back your voice from weeping . . . there is hope for your future and your children shall come back to their own country' (Jer. 31.16f.). The deliverance from Egypt had not brought true freedom, but Israel still awaited her true redemption. The Messiah identifies himself with the history of his people, descending into Egypt, and coming out as the true son.

A polemical note can also be discerned in the New Testament's use of the Moses birth story. The pattern of the threat remained the same. The child of promise is endangered; the Gentiles announce and welcome his coming. But in the New Testament the threat no longer comes from the pagan king of a hostile empire, but from Herod, the king of the Jews. The Messiah of God has forced a wedge into the solidarity of the chosen people. Christ calls forth his most bitter opposition from within his own people. In Rev. 12 both the traditions have been radically transformed with apocalyptic imagery. The struggle for the child has taken on cosmological dimensions with war erupting in heaven itself. Now the whole church, not just the innocents, is enveloped in a struggle for life, and is urged both to rejoice and to endure. The end is already in sight.

In spite of the transformation and radicalization of the tradition in the New Testament, the Old Testament story continues to provide the basic context for the church's hope. Jesus comes to fulfill the promise to Israel. He comes also as a human child, to human parents, in a historical setting. The incarnation demands the historical context. His coming was not a mythological drama. Matthew's birth story, far from being an invasion of pagan fantasy, is a reaffirmation of the witness made to the ancient people of God.

III

MOSES SLAYS AN EGYPTIAN
AND FLEES TO MIDIAN

2.11-25

W. F. ALBRIGHT, 'Jethro, Hobab and Reuel in Early Hebrew Tradition', *CBQ* 25, 1963, pp. 1–11; G. FOHRER, *Überlieferung und Geschichte des Exodus*, 1964, pp. 24ff.; M. GREENBERG, *Understanding Exodus*, 1969, pp. 44ff.; A. H. J. GUNNEWEG, 'Mose in Midian', *ZThK* 61, 1964, pp. 1–9.

2 [11]It happened after some time that Moses grew up and he went out to his kinsmen and looked on their toil. He saw an Egyptian beating a Hebrew, one of his kin. [12]Turning this way and that and seeing no one, he struck down the Egyptian and hid him in the sand. [13]When he went out the next day, there were two Hebrews struggling together. Then he said to the one who was in the wrong: 'Why do you strike your companion?' [14]He replied, 'Who made you a ruler and judge over us? Do you mean to kill me as you killed the Egyptian?' Then Moses was afraid, and thought: Surely the thing is known. [15]When Pharaoh learned of the matter, he sought to kill Moses, but Moses fled from Pharaoh, and settled in the land of Midian, and sat down beside a well.

16 Now the priest of Midian had seven daughters and they came and drew water, and filled the troughs to water their father's flock, [17]but some shepherds came and drove them off. So Moses rose to their defense and watered their flock. [18]When they came to their father Reuel, he said, 'How did you manage to get home so soon today?' [19]They answered: 'An Egyptian rescued us from the shepherds and even drew water for us and watered the flock.' [20]He said to his daughters, 'Then where is he? Why did you leave the man? Invite him to have a meal.' [21]Moses was agreeable to stay with the man, and he gave Moses his daughter Zipporah. [22]She bore a son, and he called his name Gershom; for he said, 'I have been a stranger in a foreign land.'

23 A long time afterward the king of Egypt died. The Israelites groaned under the bondage and cried out for help, and their cry under

bondage came up to God. [24]God heard their groaning and God remembered his covenant with Abraham and Isaac and Jacob. [25]And God saw the Israelites and God took notice.

1. Textual and Philological Notes

2.11. *wayyigdal* cannot be subordinated to *wayyēṣē'* as a circumstantial clause, as in the LXX and most modern translations. Cf. Gen. 34.25 for such a construction and the discussion of E. König, *ZAW* 19 (1899), pp. 260ff.

makkeh. Cf. the section on literary analysis for the different nuances in the story of the verb 'to strike'.

12. *kōh wākōh*, 'this way and that'. Without direct parallel in the OT, but cf. Num. 11.31; 23.15, etc.

13. *bayyôm haššēnî*, a definite sequence, Judg. 20.24, 30.

niṣṣîm, 'struggling', cf. Ex. 21.22; Deut. 25.11.

rāšā', 'the offending party'. Here a legal term to designate the one judged wrong in a particular case. Cf. Deut. 25.1; I Kings 8.32; Prov. 24.24.

rēa' in the weaker sense of 'fellow'. The overtones of kinsman are from the larger context. Compare LXX πλησίον with Acts. 7.26.

14. *'îš šar.* *šar* is in apposition; compare *'îš kōhēn*, Lev. 21.9; *'îš nābî'* Judg. 6.8, etc.

16. The LXX harmonistically supplies the name Jethro. On the question of his identity, cf. W. F. Albright, *CBQ*, *op. cit.*, pp. 1f.

25. The last clause is difficult. The MT 'and God knew' lacks the usual object. The LXX reads καὶ ἐγνώσθη αὐτοῖς 'he was made known to them', which would be equivalent to the Hebrew niphal. Others suggest an emendation such as Dillmann who proposes *wayyērā'*, 'and he appeared to them' (cf. Ex. 6.3). D. Winton Thomas, *JTS* 49 (1948), pp. 142f., suggests the meaning 'cared for, kept in mind', and cites an Arabic cognate. M. Greenberg (*op. cit.*, p. 54) points out a close parallel in Gen. 18.21 with the meaning 'consider, take thought of what to do'. This latter seems to be the best suggestion.

2. Literary and Form-critical Analysis

There is general agreement that vv. 11–22 stem from the same source in spite of a certain unevenness in the text (cf. Noth on vv. 15 and 18). The relation of 11–22 to 1–10 remains a problem since solid criteria on which to make a source judgment are lacking. Wellhausen hesitated when attempting to separate J and E, but suspected different sources in vv. 10 and 11 because of the repetition of *wayyigdal*. I tend to agree with Noth that vv. 11–22 are a continuation of vv. 1–10 with a few secondary glosses and belong to J. The last few verses in the chapter, 23b–25, are clearly from P.

It has long been observed that the story which begins in v. 11 serves as a means of bringing Moses out of Egypt into Midian for the decisive event at the bush (cf. Gressmann). The common motif of the hero's withdrawal into the desert before his return to Egypt in 4.18ff. can be recognized. However, it is also apparent that this connection is not merely a literary, novelistic device, but involves a fusion of early traditions. Gunneweg (*op. cit.*, pp. 1ff.) has suggested that a complex traditional problem emerges once vv. 11ff. are seen in connection with the Midian traditions of ch. 18. These texts seem to reflect early layers of tradition in which the Hebrews share a common cult with the Midianites, and in which cult the name of Yahweh is rooted. From there a whole cluster of problems, often treated under the rubric of the Kenite hypothesis, is raised. (Cf. the treatment of the problem in ch. 18.)

This passage reflects several interesting examples of stylistic features. First of all, there are several examples in which the same verb appears in close proximity, but with a different meaning each time. Note: v. 10 *wayyigdal*, 'reached the stage to be weaned' and v. 11 'grew to manhood'; v. 11 *wayyar' be* 'looked with sympathy' and *wayyar'* 'he saw'; v. 11 *makkeh* 'striking' and v. 12 *wayyak* 'strike dead'; v. 15 *wayyēšeb* 'dwell' and *wayyēšeb* 'he sat down'. In the first example of *wayyigdal*, the relation seems to be quite accidental and not a result of a conscious literary device. Two stories are joined with a slight overlapping. The syntax of v. 11 prevents this from being taken circumstantially as a resumptive clause. However, the remaining examples show the conscious artistic skill of the author who uses a semantic shift to transfer the action from a broad or continuous scene to a narrow, specific event (cf. Gen. 34.1 for a parallel). This device enables the writer to move quickly through large areas of time and space and yet focus briefly with great detail on three particular events within a huge background.

Another similar technique is revealed in the writer's play on various meanings of the verb *nkh* = strike. Moses sees an Egyptian 'striking' a Hebrew. Noth follows an old scholarly tradition in interpreting this as actual killing. However, this translation, while perhaps correct in substance, overlooks the writer's subtlety in leaving its meaning indefinite. Moses then reacts by also striking, but this time clearly striking dead. On the next day one Hebrew is again striking another. He first introduces the ugly word 'kill' (*hrg*) to describe Moses' act. Then Pharaoh hears and seeks in turn to avenge by killing Moses.

Finally, it is remarkable to observe the skill with which the author is able to picture a whole range of strong subjective emotions by means of objective, descriptive language. In each case there is a marked underplay. Moses goes out to his brethren and looks on their toil. The implied sympathy shifts immediately to passionate anger, then instinctive caution. Fear swells up before the saucy impudence of the betrayer. Again, in the retelling of Moses' act of heroism, the daughters' enthusiasm breaks out – why he even drew water for us! – to be quenched by the obvious irritation of the father (*we'ayyô*) at their inhospitality.

3. Old Testament Context

[**2.11–15**] The passage is somewhat loosely connected with the birth story which precedes. The writer moves immediately to his first major theme: Moses goes out to look with sympathy on the toil of his kinsmen. No words in the story are wasted on describing where Moses lived or how he knew that he was a Hebrew. Rather, the concern focuses on Moses' purposeful seeking out his kinsmen and his regard for their oppression. The repetition of the phrase 'from his kin' (v. 11) connects the slaying of the Egyptian in a causal relation with Moses' identification with his Hebrew brother. Then the second major theme of the first story is introduced. Moses is anxious that his act be done in secrecy. The sequence indicates that the slaying was not initiated in a burst of passion or following a vain attempt to dissuade the oppressor (so B. Jacob). Verse 12 emphasizes the note of secrecy and stealth in the piling up of clauses: he looked both ways; he observed no one; he struck him; there was no struggle as in v. 13; he buried him quickly because the ground was sandy.

In v. 13 the narrative returns to the first theme: again he goes out to his brothers, and to his surprise (*wehinnēh*) two Hebrews are fighting. Moses attempts to mediate. The use of the technical legal term for the offending party (*lārāšāʿ*) expresses succinctly that Moses' concern is with the issue of justice. His is not a sentimental identification with the Hebrews. The reference to 'his fellow' is a neutral one and does not explicitly express the incongruity of kinsmen fighting together (cf. Gen. 13.8; Acts 7.26). Now the tension of the story mounts as the two chief themes clash. The offending Hebrew rudely rejects the mediation of Moses, and challenges his authority to play this role. The second question referring to the killing of the Egyptian does not arise out of a genuine self fear but is a cynical means of warding off the reproach and turning it into a threat. The knowledge of the act is no longer a secret but is shared by one who has already started to use it as an insidious weapon. The reaction of Moses confirms the point. Moses is afraid because his secret is out, and with good reason. When Pharaoh hears, he seeks to kill him.

The point of the first story emerges in the conflict between the themes of active sympathy and required secrecy. The latter theme leads to the heart of the issue: Moses must act in secrecy because he has no authority! The impudent Hebrew saw this correctly. The story ends on two related notes. First, Moses does not succeed in his attempted deliverance. He must flee for his life like every other political fugitive. (Cf. the parallel vocabulary in I Sam. 21.11ff.; I Kings 11.17ff.; Jer. 26.20ff.; Story of Sinuhe, *ANET*², p. 19.) Secondly, his failure was initiated by the betrayal of his own kin who rejected not only his authority, but his demand for justice as well.

[2.16–22] The reader is led immediately to the second episode. Some commentators have tried to speculate on how much time elapsed between stories, but the text lends no support whatever to the question. The story is recounted in extremely simple prose – note the recurrence of the verb 'come' – which alternates between description of action and conversation. Moses is seated at the well. In v. 16 the writer brings the bare minimum of background information which is needed for understanding the event which ensues. The setting at the well is paralleled in several patriarchal stories (Gen. 24; 29), and is the traditional setting for human encounter in the semi-desert areas of the Near East. Since water was the source of all life and wealth, it is obvious that strife regarding its proper use was common. In a few strokes the writer pictures the deliberate ruthlessness of the shepherds. They wait until the women have finished the tedious work of drawing water and filling the water troughs before driving them away with force.

Then Moses arises and comes to their aid. The writer is extremely restrained in his description of this intervention. He is obviously not interested in portraying Moses as a folk hero. (Contrast this reservation with the description of Samson or Jonathan in action.) A more elaborate description emerges from conversation which is skilfully evoked by the writer's use of Jethro's questions, and the daughters' answer. The emphasis falls on the unusual circumstances that an Egyptian rescued them and the added surprise that he both drew water and watered their flock. Jethro's three remarks, each of which reflects a slightly different emotion, not only serves to express the reaction of a beduin whose deep-seated sense of responsibility for hospitality has been aroused. It also works as a literary device to enhance the contrast in response between an earlier example of aid which had been rejected and one of true gratitude. Once the main point has been made the story hastens toward completion. The return of the daughters to Moses, the invitation to a meal, and the meeting with Jethro are passed over as unessential. Rather, the bare outlines of the essential history are sketched. Moses agrees to stay with Jethro; he is given a wife; he has a son, and the child is named. Although the formula for the naming is traditional, it serves as an essential conclusion to the episode. The name indicates that Moses still remembers that he is a sojourner in a foreign land. He belongs to another people, in another land.

The two stories which now form one unit have been linked together in an interesting manner. There is the initial continuity of fleeing to the land of Midian (v. 15), and the priest of Midian (v. 16). But significant are the contrasts drawn between the two episodes. In the first (v. 11), the Egyptian is the enemy who oppresses; in the second, Moses is called an Egyptian (v. 18) who offers help against the oppressor. In the first, the strife is between an Egyptian and a Hebrew, in the second between two non-Hebrew people. In the first, Moses flees from his home; in the second he finds a home.

Moreover, these contrasts serve to highlight the many similarities which bind the stories together into a unit. First, the emphasis falls in both on Moses' active concern for justice to the weak which transcends the narrow bounds of nation and people. Secondly, Moses is an exile who is forced to live apart from his people whom he has not succeeded in delivering.

[2.23–25] Finally, it is a question how best to interpret the last few verses. The NEB and NAB begin the next section of the revelation at the bush with these verses, but this seems hardly correct. The verses relate primarily to what has already been recounted and conclude the section by returning to the earlier theme of Israel's misery. However, the verses do mark a decided break, both in time and perspective, with what is past. First, the narrative takes the reader back to Israel in Egypt and records the passing of time. Nothing has improved since Moses' departure. Israel continues to groan under its burden. Secondly, their suffering has not gone unnoticed. God remembers his covenant with the patriarchs. But in both instances there is a glimpse toward the future as well. The old king of Egypt whose reign first marked the beginning of Israel's trouble (1.8) has died. What will the future bring? Moreover, God takes notice of their misery. What will his plan for them be?

Detailed Notes

2.15. 'to the land of Midian'. Cf. G. Landes, 'Midian', *IDB*, s.v., for a discussion of the geographical problems and a survey of the role of the Midianites in the Old Testament.

16. 'Jethro'. Cf. Albright, *op. cit.*, and the fuller discussion of the problem in ch. 18.

22. 'he called his name . . . for he said'. For a study of the etiological formulae, cf. Fichter, *VT* 6 (1956), pp. 372ff.; B. Long, *The Problem of Etiological Narrative in the OT*, BZAW 108, 1968, pp. 4ff.

4. New Testament Context

On *Acts*: Beside the standard commentaries of Knowling (Expositor's Greek, 1900), K. Lake and H. J. Cadbury (*Beginnings of Christianity*, New York and London 1920ff.), Haenchen (KEKNT 3¹⁴, 1965, ET Oxford 1971) and Conzelmann (HNT 7², 1963), cf. B. W. Bacon, 'Stephen's Speech', *Biblical and Semitic Studies*, New Haven 1901, pp. 213ff.; M. Dibelius, *Studies in the Acts of the Apostles*, ET London and New York 1956, pp. 138ff.; A. T. Hanson, *Jesus Christ in the Old Testament*, London 1965, pp. 82ff.; M. Simon, *St Stephen and the Hellenists in the Primitive Church*, London 1958, with additional bibliography.

On *Hebrews*: beside the standard commentaries of Westcott (1889), Riggenbach (KNT 14, 1913), Moffatt (ICC 1924), Windisch (HNT 14², 1931), Michel (1949) and Spicq (1952–53), cf. A. T. Hanson, *op. cit.*, pp. 72ff.; E. Käsemann, *Das wandernde Gottesvolk*, Göttingen 1939, pp. 5ff.; William Manson, *The Epistle to the Hebrews*, London and Toronto 1951, pp. 36ff.; A. Schlatter, *Der Glaube im Neuen Testament*³, Stuttgart 1905, pp. 524ff.; J. Schneider, *'ὄνειδος'* *TWNT* V, pp. 238ff. = *TDNT* V, pp. 238f.

Exodus 2.11ff. receives two extended interpretations within the New Testament.

A. *Acts* 7.23–29, 35

In the Stephen speech the recounting of Israel's history continues with the story of Moses' slaying the Egyptian and his flight to Midian. As one would expect from the earlier analysis of the Moses birth story, the chapter reflects several features of the Hellenistic Jewish midrash. In general, the parallels to Philo's treatment (*De Vita Mosis*) are closer to Acts than the early rabbinic exegetical traditions, although the differences with both remain striking. Along with

Philo, Acts 7 understands the slaying of the Egyptian as an abortive attempt to carry out a deliverance which became the mission of ch. 3. However, the New Testament account connects the passage in terms of prophecy and fulfillment within a redemptive history (cf. v. 17, 'as the time of the promise grew near . . .'), whereas Philo has Moses exhorting the people to patience in the light of the changing fortunes of nature (I.40ff.). The style of the two midrashic interpretations also has common features. Both Acts and Philo offer an interpretation of the slaying by describing a subjective motivation ('Moses considered that his action . . . was a righteous one' *V. Mos.* I.44; 'he supposed that his brethren would understand', Acts 7.25). In both cases the description goes considerably beyond the Old Testament text. It also differs from the style of the rabbinic midrash which is also vitally interested in providing a motivation, but provides it after a different fashion.

There are several elements in Philo's treatment which stem from an inherited midrashic tradition common to the rabbinic traditions as well, such as Moses' initial attempt to assist the Hebrews, the particular cruelty of the overseer, and the concern to justify the killing as an ethical act (cf. Ginzberg, *Legends of the Jews* V, Philadelphia 1925, p.404 for references). Acts shares also some common features such as the chronological datum, and the toning down of the fear element in the flight. However, more characteristic is the restrained use of the midrashic traditions. The strong theological interests of the author force the interpretation to move along quite different lines from either the rabbis or Philo.

The category of prophecy and fulfillment by which the Old Testament traditions are read leads to the New Testament writer's attributing a purpose to Moses' act which is not given in the Old Testament account. He thought that his brothers would understand the true significance of his intervention as the instrument of God's deliverance. The lack of understanding, which is certainly an important Old Testament theme in the passage, is then employed apologetically by the New Testament writer as an example of a larger pattern of disobedience which extends throughout Israel's history, vv.35ff. The pattern of disobedience culminates in the rejection of Jesus, the Righteous One (v.52) which unleashes the implied threat of Deut. 18.

Again, it is significant to note how the New Testament writer from his new perspective has interpreted the theme of deliverance in terms of reconciliation. Naturally the Old Testament text provided the starting point for his understanding. The Exodus account stressed the incongruity of two Hebrews fighting, which called forth Moses' intervention. Acts 7.26 is explicit in describing Moses' act as an attempt at reconciliation (συνήλλασσεν). His retort in v. 26 goes much beyond both the MT and the LXX. The neutral *rēaʿ* becomes 'brother', the interrogative is replaced by the indicative, and both men rather than just the offending party are addressed: 'Men, you are brothers!' (Alford's reading of ἄνδρες ἀδελφοί together without punctuation increases the parallelism with Gen. 13.8, LXX.) The callousness of the rejection is highlighted by the addition of the phrase, 'he thrust him aside'.

The second story in Ex. 2 of Moses in Midian is reduced to a bare minimum in Acts 7 since interest falls immediately on the revelation at the bush which confirms Moses' authority by divine sanction. The mention of the two sons which were born in Midian perhaps reflects the common midrashic harmonization of Ex. 4.20 and 18.4. Of considerably more importance is the interpretation of Moses as an 'exile' in v. 29 (cf. *TWNT* V, pp. 840ff. = *TDNT* V, pp. 841ff.). Note the use of the word in Acts 7.6. In the Old Testament the *gēr* designated originally a social class of the landless sojourner who lived without the protection of a clan. But the term had already been greatly expanded theologically when the people of Israel were described as a 'sojourner' in Egypt (Deut. 23.8f.). A further spiritualization of the term is evident in the Chronicles and Psalms (I Chron. 29.15; Pss. 39.13; 119.19). Philo quotes Ex. 2.22 (*De Confusione Ling*. 82) to prove that man only sojourns in the body, but his real home lies in the realm of the spirit (cf. P. Katz, *Philo's Bible*, Cambridge 1950, pp. 73f.). In Hebrews the term reflects to some degree this Hellenistic polarity of earth and heaven, but within a central eschatological framework (cf. I Peter 1.17; 2.11; Eph. 2.19). In the light of these different alternatives, it is significant to see that Acts 7.29 holds to the original, concrete meaning of the term. The fact that Moses was forced to become an exile serves to emphasize his rejection by his own people. This interpretation of the term illustrates very clearly the strikingly different setting between Acts 7 and Heb. 11. In the former, the Old Testament is used for an apologetic purpose against the synagogue in order to establish the grounds of Israel's history of disobedience, while in the latter the Old Testament message functions as encouragement to a Christian audience.

B. *Hebrews* 11.24–28

Ex. 2.11ff. receives another surprisingly full interpretation in Heb. 11. In the light of the compression of the exodus events into a few verses in this chapter the interest in this one Old Testament story is even more remarkable. The literary form of the chapter is striking, and sets the interpretation immediately into a different context from that of Acts (cf. H. Windisch, *Hebräerbrief*, pp. 98f., on the form). Under the theme of faith a whole series of Old Testament figures are presented which serve as witnesses of faith for the New Testament writer in his attempt to evoke a similar response in his readers (12.1ff.). Even Jesus is placed in the series (12.2), but then set apart as the 'pioneer and perfecter of faith'. The style has a strong rhetorical flavor, and has its closest parallel in the martyr literature of Hellenistic Judaism (cf. IV Macc. 16). The dominant Hellenistic flavor is also immediately evident in the vocabulary and religious perspective. (Cf. the parallels, especially in Josephus, *Antiq*. II. 215ff.)

The writer uses the event in a series to illustrate his understanding of faith. Windisch notes that the element of faith is not an explicit motif; moreover, the one explicit reference to Abraham's faith in Gen. 15 is omitted. It is evident that the writer is coming to the Old Testament with interests which are less dependent on the exact wording of the text and a set of categories which operate in a powerful fashion in transforming the tradition for its theological purposes than was the case in Acts 7. In using the Moses story as an illustration of faith, the writer often goes beyond the sense of the Old Testament text.

First of all, the writer stresses the active choice of faith which is involved. Moses 'refused to be called the son of Pharaoh, choosing rather to share ill-treatment with the people of God'. The element of choice is emphasized by setting up the alternatives: 'ill-treatment with the people of God' instead of the 'fleeting pleasures of sin'; 'abuse suffered for Christ rather than treasures of Egypt'. The fact that Moses did make a choice appears, of course, implicitly in the Old Testament story, but the New Testament expands greatly on it. Especially in the description of Israel as the 'people of God', 'the fleeting pleasures of sin', and 'suffering abuse for Christ', the writer has introduced a vocabulary which is far removed from that of the Old Testament.

The element of a real choice made in faith serves the writer's central concern of illustrating the power of faith which has been unleashed in Israel's history. A certain heroic element of those involved is present, but it is closely tied and subordinated to the great events which faith evoked. The strong selective tendency from among the events is revealed in v. 27 which omits the Midian episode, and fuses Moses' first leaving with the exodus from Egypt. (Cf. the addition in the Western text which describes the killing of the Egyptian as an act of faith.) The explicit reference to Moses' lack of fear of the king in the light of Ex. 2.14 shows the writer's freedom in respect to the actual wording of the text. That this freedom is not completely arbitrary can be defended in the light of the larger narrative context which portrays a consistent picture of Moses' bold confrontation with Pharaoh. In other words, the writer is interpreting the content of the exodus story and does not feel bound to the text of Exodus.

The boldest innovation of the writer, however, turns on his understanding of the event as 'abuse suffered for Christ'. This christological interpretation is important in giving the writer's meaning to his contrast between the 'visible and the invisible', the 'transient' and the 'enduring' which pervades the chapter. In spite of the long history of scholarly debate on the meaning of the phrase several things seem clear. The use of the term 'abuse' stems from the LXX, as is evident from Paul's explicit reference in Rom. 15.3 to Ps. 69.10. Moreover in Ps. 89.50f. the term appears in reference to the despised, Anointed One, who suffers persecution for the sake of God. These verses seem to provide the specific background for the allusion in Hebrews.

What then is meant by Moses 'suffering abuse for Christ'? The attempt to interpret it merely typologically – as the Christ once suffered so must also any who represent him (Westcott) – avoids the difficulty rather than explaining it. Nor can the phrase simply mean 'suffering for Christ's sake' which would call for a different Greek construction (cf. II Cor. 4.5, 11; I Peter 3.14; Phil. 1.29). Rather, the phrase indicates an actual participation by Moses in Christ's shame in the same way as the saints who follow Christ later also share (cf. Heb. 10.33; 13.13). The statement does not appear to be dependent on a theory of pre-existence, but rather the whole emphasis falls on the unmediated identification. The union which binds the faith of Israel to the Christ is not merely a formal pattern of hope in the visible world, but actually shares in the selfsame content: 'he endured as seeing him who is invisible' (v. 27).

The striking feature in the thought of the New Testament writer is his creative use of several separate theological alternatives. He speaks of a 'timeless' identification of almost ontological homogeneity; he uses a polarity between the visible and the invisible with its strong affinities to popular Hellenistic thought; he retains the strong Old Testament flavor of prophetic expectation by placing all the stories within the framework of waiting for the promise (v. 39). Usually, modern interpreters have isolated one element and used it to the detriment of the others. However, this tends to destroy the sensitive balance. The christological reference provides the content of the invisible: Christ was always present among God's people. Nevertheless, the divine reality appears in a real polarity – he does not speak of a 'not-yet-visible' – which is not merely a vehicle for eschatology. Thus all Old Testament history must be read as a witness to God's promise to a wandering people which is yet to be fulfilled.

Finally, the characteristic feature of the New Testament's hearing of the Old can be illuminated when contrasted and compared with the typical tendencies found in the rabbinic midrashim. The aim of such an analysis is not to raise truth claims for one type of interpretation at this point. Rather, the purpose is to sharpen the lines in describing the New Testament's understanding by setting it over against an alternative reading of a common text. The plotting of both the common and divergent elements will be useful for determining the way which the Old Testament functioned in a latter context.

In the first place, the rabbinic midrashim, Philo, and the New Testament all heard v. 11 as a major theme of the Exodus passage: Moses' voluntary participation in the sufferings of his people. All the interpretations went beyond the Old Testament text in attributing to this a positive value judgment. Again, there was a common tendency to play down the explicit Old Testament reference to the secrecy of the act, and to Moses' subsequent fear of his being discovered.

However, more striking are the different directions in which the later exegetical traditions moved. In the rabbinic midrashim Moses' deed is used as the legitimation of his special status in Israel. God now speaks of the 'Torah of Moses' and the 'people of Moses' because of this special concern for Israel: 'he devoted his whole soul to them' (*Mekilta*, Shirata I, 49f.; *Sh.R.*30.4; cf. Philo, *Vita Mos.* I.32ff.). Moreover, Moses' deed now functions analogically in providing a model for God's action toward Israel. 'Thou hast put aside thy work and hast gone to share the sorrow of Israel . . . I will also leave those on high . . .' (*Sh.R.* I 27). This characteristic rabbinic analogy functions under the rubric of 'sufficient reward' or 'measure for measure'. (Cf. *Mekilta*, Beshallah I, 193ff. for the rubric and pattern in respect to Abraham.) The righteous deed of a man – usually a Patriarch – provides the grounds for God's corresponding act of mercy. Here the New Testament's use of analogy is characteristically different from the rabbinical, although the typology functions in distinct ways in Acts and Hebrews. In both, the Old Testament story provides a christological pattern. In Acts the rejection of Moses foreshadows Christ's; in Hebrews the sufferings of Moses are anticipations of his. In the New Testament the analogy functions as an incomplete adumbration or a proleptic identification rather than as the grounds for the divine action. Particularly in Acts the analogy is a negative one, illustrating a pattern of unbelief, a point which would be unthinkable for the midrash. Moses functions as the bearer of the word of promise (Acts 7.37). There are several other characteristic differences in approach to the Old Testament story. The rabbinic midrashim see the major issue in both episodes in Egypt and Midian to be Moses' attempt to execute justice for the oppressed. It is obviously there that the midrashim find clear scriptural warrants for this move within the biblical text itself, but there is an expansion beyond the Old Testament when the 'beating of a Hebrew' is assumed to be an unjust beating with intent to kill (*Sh.R.* I 28; Philo, *Vita Mos.* I. 44; cf. Ginzberg, *Legends* V, p.405 for further parallels). However, the major issue is the question of justice. The midrash focuses its main attention on explaining and justifying Moses' act of slaying the Egyptian. Indeed a variety of reasons are given: he was the cruellest of all Egyptians; there was no one else to help; Moses saw that no proselyte would ever arise; the law demanded his death, etc. (Targum Jonathan, Fragmentary Targum, *ad loc.*; *Midrash Haggadol Exodus*, ed. M. Margulies, Jerusalem 1956, p.29; *Sh.R.*).

In the New Testament the issue of justice is subordinated to that of deliverance. Acts 7 does touch the question of justice, in fact it expands its scope along with the midrash (cf. ἀδικέω in vv.24 and 26), but it understands Moses' intervention as the beginning of the fulfillment of the promised deliverance. For this reason the issue of justifying the killing by Moses does not emerge. In Hebrews the author is even further removed from this issue in his focus on the promise, and omits both the killing and betrayal.

Finally, the issue of Moses' authority is treated by both traditions but in different ways. The midrash interprets the controversy with the Hebrew in vv. 13ff. as referring specifically to the evil Dathan and Abiram. To this extent the tendency of this interpretation leads to a restriction of the problem of authority. It was caused by their characteristic wickedness, or there was a genuine halachic question at stake regarding Moses' age and lineage (Targum Jonathan, *Mekilta*, Amalek 3, 129; *ARN* 20; Ginzberg, *Legends* V, p.405). However, the midrashic interpretation moves in another direction when it designates the sin of slander to be the fundamental cause for Israel's suffering. The New Testament's use in Acts is akin to this second interpretation, but is far more radical in its application. It generalizes the example according to the prophetic model of Jer. 19.13 and Amos 5.25ff. to find a negative pattern which involves ontological dimensions of disobedience.

In summary, the midrash understands Moses' action to be a model of obedience to Torah even though it preceded the giving of the covenant at Sinai. The interpretation seeks to explore and develop the full implications of this central fact to the life of the community, whereas, the fundamental eschatological interest of the New Testament controls the essential function of the text and establishes the new christological setting in which the story now is used.

5. *History of Exegesis*

In the history of interpretation of this Old Testament passage, commentators can initially be divided into two groups: (*a*) those who give Moses' deed of slaying the Egyptian a positive evaluation, and (*b*) those who judge it in an unfavorable light.

The first group includes several of the church Fathers (Gregory Nazianen, *Epist.* 76; Tertullian, *Contra Marc.* IV. 28; Ambrose, *De Officiis* I. 36), Luther, Calvin, and the bulk of orthodox Protestant exegetes of the seventeenth and eighteenth centuries (Ainsworth, Henry, Patrick, Scott). Generally these interpreters take their lead from the New Testament and see it as a divinely inspired act. Calvin's interpretation is typical, especially of the classic Protestant position, when he writes: 'He was armed by God's command, and, conscious of his legitimate vocation, rightly, and judiciously assumed that character which God had assigned to him' (*ad loc.*).

Although these interpreters have attempted to adopt the New

Testament's perspective, the context in which they wrote has tended to alter the function which this interpretation served. The question of justice, the rightness or wrongness of the act, has moved very much to the foreground of the discussion. Luther addressed himself to the specific issue and suggested a positive evaluation by using reasons provided only in part by the New Testament, but also by rational arguments which had been borrowed from the rabbis. Several commentators found themselves in the position of defending the rightness of the act while at the same time arguing that its special divine warrant removed it from the area of moral judgment (Henry). Moreover, the commentators who stressed the revelatory character of Moses' act often felt constrained to explain the absence of an explicit reference to such a revelation in scripture and sought to supply the link through conjecture or deduction. This exegetical move of combining reasons based on revelation and reason to defend the action remained a dominant one in both Catholic and Protestant orthodoxy (cf. summary of opinions in Lapide, *Commentaria in Sacram Scripturam*, and M. Poole, *Synopsis Criticorum*). Aquinas' defence of the action (*Summa*, 2a 2ae, 60) on the grounds that it was not a crime to defend the innocent was generally followed by the Catholic commentators such as Lyra and Pererius. (But cf. the objections of Cornelius Jansen, *Pentateuchus, ad loc.*)

The other major alternative in the history of interpretation finds its authoritative representative in Augustine (*Contra Faustum* XXII.70) who contests Moses' authority to kill the Egyptian in spite of the injustice, and compares him with Peter, who also sinned in his untrained impulsiveness (cf. the later modification in *Quaest. in Hept.* II.2). Frequently the act was judged to be premature because it preceded the call in ch. 3 (so Keil). However, the most characteristic element in the group is the strong psychological interest. Very early the 'turning this way and that' (v. 12) was attributed to his bad conscience. Driver is typical of the late nineteenth-century Liberal Protestant view, which appreciated Moses' sympathy for the oppressed, but in the end could not but condemn it as ill-considered. H. Frey, writing with a different theological interest, spoke of 'his all too human failing' in which Moses moved from a stance of faith to disobedience. Another typical position, which is closely akin, focused to such an extent on the psychological traits of Moses as to subordinate almost entirely the ethical question (cf. already Gregory of Nyssa, *Vita Mosis*). The commentators' interests center on the traits of the hero, his courage, burning patriotism, and feelings for justice (cf. especially Dillmann, Bäntsch, Beer). At times there is a tacit approval of Moses' deed because of its passionate quality.

The classic Jewish medieval commentators fit into the first group of interpretation. Taking their lead from the early midrashim, they naturally evaluate Moses' act in a positive light. Rashi follows faithfully the midrashic tradition with little addition. Maimonides attributes to Moses the first degree of prophecy which spirit moved him to slay the Egyptian (*Guide for the Perplexed* II.45). Abarbanel, after attacking the idiosyncratic interpretation of Ibn Ezra, elaborates on the qualities of Moses which are revealed in this act of courage and which would not tolerate insult to his brothers, even though he had to risk his life to avenge the sons of Israel. All agreed on the justice of Moses' act.

Modern Jewish commentators with few exceptions (B. Jacob) continue the exegetical tradition of the medieval commentators (Kalisch, Cassuto). But even this tradition has not been immune from the influence of new elements from modern psychology and philosophy. André Neher, for example, understands the intervention as 'breaking through the selfishness of his own ego, he discovers his neighbors . . . The estrangement between men has disappeared . . . Now all men are neighbors and friends' (*Moses and the Vocation of the Jewish People*, ET New York and London 1959, p.92).

6. *Theological Reflection*

My purpose is to attempt to reflect on the theological significance of the Exodus passage in the light of its total witness within the canon. How does one hear the message of both testaments in respect to this specific passage? First, if we take our lead from the epistle to the Hebrews in an attempt to understand the Old Testament in the light of the New, we see that Moses' act of identification with his brothers is judged to be a model of Christian faith. Indeed, the specific ingredients of this faith are described in terms of this story. He suffered abuse for Christ, he shared ill-treatment with the people of God, and he looked for his reward. Moses' decision is a pattern of Christian faith because he responded to God in his decision of obedience, and endured by faith in his promise.

However, if we now turn to the Old Testament, the picture of Moses' decision is a wholly different one. Nowhere are Moses' motives discussed. He did make a conscious decision in identifying with the plight of his kinsmen. But although this element appears in the text, the emphasis falls fully on the act, not on the decision itself. Moreover the events which are subsequently described point in no way to a single-hearted commitment to a divine purpose. Rather, an occurrence is described which touches off a series of incidents, most of which are only accidentally connected with each other. He kills an Egyptian, thinking that his act is secret. But he is seen, rebuffed by his fellow Hebrew, and betrayed. In terror for his life he flees as a fugitive from his country to seek shelter in Midian. There he remains shepherding sheep for a living, and raising a family. There is very little here of the hero of faith who decides for God.

Nevertheless, the relationship of these two portrayals is not wholly arbitrary and poses by their very juxtaposition an important theological problem. In both the Old Testament and New Testament passages there are elements of faith as sharing another's suffering, and faith as hope. But the perspective is a totally different one. Hebrews describes Moses' whole behavior as eschatologically oriented. Exodus speaks of the here and now, and only in the naming of the child is there a momentary glimpse into a hope and a future. Hebrews brackets all the story under the rubric of faith; Exodus has no one rubric and describes a complex of actions. In a real sense, the issue at stake is the understanding of the nature of man's decision for God. Seen from one perspective, the issue is black and white, unequivocal in its character, the clear call to discipleship. In another sense, it is a living and deciding among the variety of relations in which we live, seeking in the complexity of mixed sinful emotions and historical accidents to live an obedient life. The selfless act is soon beclouded by violence and nothing of lasting effect is accomplished for Israel's plight. Confessing that only in Jesus Christ do these two perspectives fall together, the witness of both testaments to Moses remains in the tension and points to man's continuing obligation of wrestling with the decision of faith in the context of a multitude of small decisions of living.

To interpret from the context of the canon would seem to mean that the biblical witness to the nature of Moses' faith is viewed from a double perspective: faith as eschatological hope and faith as response in the present. Faith is seen as a clear-cut decision of commitment and trust, and faith as confused action toward obedience in the complexity of several alternatives.

The book of Acts interprets the story in a different way, as we have already seen. The sequence of Moses' identifying with his brothers' suffering, of risking his life for the cause of his people, and being then misunderstood and rebuffed, is understood as a recurring pattern of Israel's disobedience. This history of unbelief finds its parallel in the prophets and its climax in the rejection of the Messiah. But is not this a completely arbitrary and tendentious reading of the facts? The Jews did not ever reject the authority of the Messiah. The issue at stake was that Jesus' claim to be the Messiah was not acknowledged. But is this not exactly the theological issue which emerges when Old and New Testament are seen together? The rejection stemmed from a lack of recognition. The claim to authority was not accepted because the right to the office of God's deliverer was not acknowledged. 'Who made you judge over us?'

However, precisely to this issue both testaments address themselves. Neither Moses nor Jesus were recognized, at least by their own people. But Moses was 'recognized' by the Midianites in spite of looking like an Egyptian! And Jesus found a response among the poor and out-cast. The basic point is that lack of recognition is disobedience because the act itself discloses the bearer to be from God. 'Believe me for my work's sake.' The quality of the deed was self-authenticating. This is the message to John the Baptist (Matt. 11.2ff). It is the same issue with Moses. The fact that God's deliverer is not recognized reflects the condition of blindness on the part of his people. To the objection 'If you are the Christ, tell us plainly' (John 10.24), the whole Bible responds: 'The works that I do in my Father's name, they bear witness to me.'

Finally, there is another theological avenue into the text which begins with a modern problem and seeks to discover the interaction between the Bible and the issue. As a modern Christian I am con-cerned with the much discussed issue of using physical violence as a means for social change. I would like to know if it is ever justified, and if so, under what conditions. What about the so-called 'theology of revolution'? I approach the Exodus text with this problem in mind, seeking some guidance. What can I learn?

We have already noticed that the Old Testament does not moralize on Moses' act of violence. Nowhere is there an explicit evaluation that either praises or condemns it. Rather, a situation is painted with great realism and sensitivity, and the reader is left to ponder on the anomalies of the deed. Moses acts in order to right an injustice, not for his own sake, but for another. He is motivated to react with violence out of love for his people which even jeopardizes his own life. But the ambiguity of the situation is that the act does not carry only one meaning. It is open to misunderstanding and a variety of possible interpretations. Moses supposed that his motivation was obvious, but the Hebrew who was abusing his fellow attributed a totally different intention from that which Moses has envisioned. 'Who made you a ruler over us?' Implied in both of Moses' acts, the killing of the Egyptian and the attempt to reconcile the Hebrew, was a claim to authoritity and a definition of justice. From the perspective of the offending Hebrew this man posed a threat because his behavior was being called into question. He was not willing to accept Moses' help when it was offered under these conditions. Therefore, he rebuffed Moses and sought to destroy him by imputing an interpretation to his deed which impugned his honesty. To his chagrin Moses discovered that his altruism had made for him an enemy, not an ally.

Again, the story points to Moses' attempt to act in secret. He killed the Egyptian thinking that he was not being observed, and even cautiously disposed of the incriminating evidence. Obviously, his being in hostile Egypt dictated this prudence. Yet one wonders whether an act of justice can really be done under these circumstances. Once Moses is discovered, he is unusually vulnerable. In terror he flees for his own life, leaving behind the repercussions of his act. He has become indistinguishable from every other political fugitive. Moreover, what did he really solve? The biblical text, without drawing explicit conclusions regarding the ethics of the matter, does make it fully clear that no deliverance occurred. Moses had to be sent back to Egypt with a different authority and with a new mission.

Lastly, the interpretation in Acts points to another aspect of the problem. The New Testament writer is concerned with the intervention as an attempt at reconciliation. Moses is cast into the role of Abraham and uses the patriarch's words in addressing the fighting Hebrews: 'Men, you are brothers.' But the incongruity of Moses' arguing for genuine reconciliation is pointed out by the impudent Hebrew. His act of killing had put him in a different position from Abraham. He was now unable to act as a reconciler. The prior action has robbed all his later words of significance.

In sum, the text does not provide one clear answer to the complex problem of using violence for the sake of justice. But it does raise a whole set of issues which are inherent in such action. By uncovering the ambiguities in the act of violence, the reader is forced to confront rather than evade those basic factors which constitute the moral decision.

IV

THE CALL OF MOSES

3.1–4.17

M. A. Beek, 'Der Dornbusch als Wohnsitz Gottes (Deut. xxxiii 16)' *OTS* 14, 1965, pp. 155–61; O. Eissfeldt, 'Die Komposition von Exodus 1–12', *KS* II, Tübingen 1963, pp. 16off.; G. Fohrer, *Überlieferung und Geschichte des Exodus*, 1964, pp. 24ff.; D. N. Freedman, 'The Burning Bush', *Biblica* 50, 1969, pp. 245–6; M. Greenberg, *Understanding Exodus*, 1969, pp. 67ff.; H. Gressmann, *Mose und seine Zeit*, 1913, pp. 21ff.; N. Habel, 'The Form and Significance of the Call Narratives', *ZAW* 77, 1965, pp. 297ff.; J. Hempel, 'Berufung und Bekehrung', *Festschrift G. Beer*, Stuttgart 1935, pp. 41–61; B. Jacob, 'Mose am Dornbusch', *MGWJ* 66, 1922, pp. 11–33, 116–38, 180–200; C. A. Keller, 'Über einige alttestamentliche Heiligtums-legenden', *ZAW* 67, 1955, pp. 141–68; 68, 1956, pp. 85–97; R. Kilian, 'Die prophetischen Berufungsberichte', *Theologie im Wandel*, Tübinger Theologische Reihe 1, Munich 1967, pp. 356–76; E. Kutsch, 'Gideons Berufung und Altarbau Jdc. 6, 11–24', *ThLZ* 81, 1956, cols. 75–84; A. Lacocque, *Le Devenir de Dieu*, Paris 1967, pp. 71ff.; H. D. Preuss, 'Ich will mit dir sein', *ZAW* 80, 1968, pp. 139–73; G. von Rad, *Old Testament Theology* II, 1965, pp. 50ff.; W. Richter, *Die sogenannten vorprophetischen Berufungsberichte*, Göttingen 1970; L. Rost, 'Die Gottesverehrung der Patriarchen im Lichte der Pentateuchquellen', *Suppl. VT* 7, 1960, pp. 346–59; H. Schmid, *Mose: Überlieferung und Geschichte*, Berlin 1968, pp. 27ff.; H. Seebass, *Mose und Aaron, Sinai und Gottesberg*, Bonn 1962, pp. 5ff.; J. A. Soggin, 'Kultätiologische Sagen und Katechese im Hexateuch', *VT* 10, 1960, pp. 341ff.; R. Tourney, 'Le nom de "Buisson ardent"', *VT* 7, 1957, pp. 410–13; G. Westphal, 'Aaron und die Aaroniden', *ZAW* 26, 1966, pp. 227ff.; E. J. Young, 'The Call of Moses', *WThJ* 29, 1967, pp. 117–35; 30, 1968, pp. 1–23; W. Zimmerli, 'Zur Form- und Traditionsgeschichte der prophetischen Berufungs-geschichte der prophetischen Berufungserzählungen', *Ezechiel* I, Neukirchen 1955, pp. 16–21.

3 ¹Now Moses was tending the flock of his father-in-law, Jethro, the priest of Midian, and he led the flock behind the wilderness and came to the mountain of God, to Horeb. ²The angel of the Lord appeared to him as a flame of fire from the midst of a bush. And he looked, and to his amazement the bush was burning with fire without being consumed. ³And Moses said, 'I must go across to see this marvellous

sight, why the bush does not burn up.' 4When the LORD saw that he went across to look, God called to him from the midst of the bush, saying, 'Moses, Moses.' He answered, 'Here I am.' 5He said, 'Do not come any closer; take off your sandals from your feet, for the place where you are standing is holy ground.' 6Then he said, 'I am the God of your father, the God of Abraham, the God of Isaac, and the God of Jacob.' And Moses hid his face, for he was afraid to look at God.

7 The LORD said, 'I have certainly seen the misery of my people in Egypt and I have heard their cry because of their overseers. Surely I am aware of their sufferings, 8and I have come down to deliver them from the Egyptians, and to bring them out of that land to a good and spacious land, a land flowing with milk and honey, the home of the Canaanites, the Hittites, the Amorites, the Perizzites, the Hivites, and the Jebusites. 9Now the cry of the Israelites has reached me; moreover I have seen the brutality with which they terrorize them. 10Come now, I will send you to Pharaoh that you may bring forth my people, the Israelites, from Egypt.' 11But Moses said to God, 'Who am I that I should go to Pharaoh and lead out the Israelites from Egypt?' 12He said, 'I will be with you, and this will be the sign for you that I have sent you: when you have brought forth the Israelites out of Egypt, you shall worship God on this mountain.'

13 Then Moses said to God, 'If I went to the Israelites and was saying to them, "The God of your fathers has sent me to you," and they asked me, "What is his name?" what should I say to them?' 14God said to Moses, 'I AM WHO I AM.' And he said, 'So you shall speak to the Israelites, "I AM has sent me to you."' 15And God spoke further to Moses, 'So you shall say to the Israelites, "The LORD (YHWH), the God of your fathers, the God of Abraham, the God of Isaac, and the God of Jacob, has sent me to you." This is my name for ever, this my designation in every generation. 16Go and assemble the elders of Israel together and say to them, "The LORD, the God of your fathers, the God of Abraham, Isaac, and Jacob, has appeared to me saying, 'I have paid close attention to you and all that is being done to you in Egypt, 17and I am resolved to bring you up out of the misery of Egypt to the land of the Canaanites, the Hittites, the Amorites, the Perizzites, the Hivites, and the Jebusites, to a land flowing with milk and honey.' " 18They will listen to you, and you shall go with the elders of Israel to the king of Egypt and say to him, "The LORD, the God of the Hebrews, has met with us. Now let us go a distance of three days into the wilderness, to sacrifice to the Lord our God." 19Yet I well know that the king of Egypt will not let you go except by force. 20So I shall stretch out my hand and smite Egypt with all the marvels which I will perform upon them. After that he will let you go. 21And I will bring this people into such favor with the Egyptians that when you go, you will not depart empty-handed. 22Each

woman shall ask her neighbor, or any woman living in her house, for objects of silver and gold, and clothing, and you shall put them on your sons and daughters. Thus you shall plunder the Egyptians.'

4 ¹Then Moses spoke up and said, 'Look, they will never believe me or listen to me, but they will say, "The LORD has not appeared to you."' ²The LORD said to him, 'What is that in your hand?' He said, 'A rod.' ³He said, 'Throw it on the ground.' So he threw it on the ground and it became a snake and Moses ran from it. ⁴Then the LORD said to Moses, 'Put out your hand and take it by the tail.' So he put out his hand and seized it, and it became a rod in his hand. ⁵'This is in order that they may believe that the LORD, the God of their fathers, the God of Abraham, the God of Isaac, and the God of Jacob, did appear to you.' ⁶The LORD said to him further, 'Put your hand into the upper fold of your cloak.' He put his hand into his cloak, and when he drew it out, his hand was diseased, white as snow. ⁷Then he said, 'Put back your hand into your cloak,' and when he drew it out of his cloak, there it was as healthy as the rest of his body. ⁸'If they will not believe you, or heed the first sign, they may believe the second. ⁹If they will not believe even these two signs or listen to you, you shall take some water from the Nile and pour it on the dry ground; and the water that you have taken from the Nile will turn to blood on the dry ground.'

10 But Moses said to the LORD, 'Please, O Lord, I have never been a man who is good with words, either in the past or now that you have spoken to your servant; rather I am slow and hesitant in speaking.' ¹¹Then the LORD said to him, 'Who is it that gives man speech? Who makes him dumb or deaf, seeing or blind? Is it not I, the LORD? ¹²Now go, and I will help your speech, and teach you what to say.' ¹³But he said, 'Please, O Lord, send anybody else.' ¹⁴Then the LORD became angry with Moses and said, 'Don't you have a brother, Aaron, the Levite? I know that he can speak fluently. He is already on his way to meet you, and he will be happy to see you. ¹⁵You shall speak to him and put words in his mouth; I will help both of you to speak and teach you both what to do. ¹⁶He will do the speaking for you to the people, and he will be your mouthpiece and you will play the role of God for him. ¹⁷And take this rod in your hand with which you will perform the signs.'

1. Textual and Philological Notes

3.1. *hāyāh* with participle denotes continuous action in the past. *G–K* § 116 r.
The LXX omits the *hā'elōhîm* which is an attempt to ease the difficulty.
The primary meaning of *'aḥar* is 'behind'. 'West' is a derivative orientation which assumed that one faced east.

2. 2a functions as a superscription to the story (cf. Ex. 18.1), whereas 2b describes the chronological sequence. The different perspectives account for the tension

rather than sources in this verse (contra Richter, *op. cit.*, p. 74ff.). *BDB* suggests that *labbaṭ* is a contracted form of *lahbaṭ* meaning 'flame'. Ibn Ezra and others opt for the philologically improbable explanation of *leḇ* *'ēš* 'heart of the fire'. The preposition should probably be taken as a *beth essentiae* with G–K § 119i.

sᵉneh, 'bush', is a rare word, appearing otherwise only in Deut. 33.16. Cf. the discussion of cognates by Tourney, *VT* 7, 1957, pp. 410ff.

3. *maddûaᶜ*, 'why'. Cf. A. Jepsen ('Warum? Eine lexikalische und theologische Studie', *Das ferne und nahe Wort. Festschrift Rost*, Berlin 1967, pp. 106f.), who lays emphasis on the element of surprise, which he contrasts with the use of *lāmāh*.

D. N. Freedman (*Biblica, op. cit.*) suggests interpreting the *lō'* as the emphatic rather than negative particle. Cf. also F. Nötscher, 'Zur emphatischen Lamed', *VT* 3, 1953, pp. 374f. The suggestion may be correct, although it is hardly necessary in the light of the wide semantic range of the verb. Cf. LXX.

12. Cf. the extended note below on the syntactical problem of the verse. The issue at stake is the antecedent for the *zeh*.

13. On the use of *hinnēh* in a conditional sentence, cf. König, *Lehrgebäude* III § 390m.

mah-šᵉmô. Buber (*Moses*, p. 48) argued that the Hebrew phrase can only mean 'What lies concealed behind that name?' and never 'What is your name?' (cf. B. Jacob). This explanation is not correct, as is clear from the parallel in Gen. 32.27.

14. *'ehyeh 'ᵃšer 'ehyeh*, 'I am who I am.' In a very learned article E. Schild (*VT* 4, 1954, pp. 296ff.) puts forward the theory that the syntax of the Hebrew relative clause had been misunderstood by the traditional translation. Using as his starting point the rule on congruence in a relative clause – the predicate of the relative clause agrees with the personal pronoun of the governing substantive (G–K § 138d) – he argued for the translation: 'I am He who is.' J. Lindblom (*ASTI* 3, 1964, pp. 4–15) accepted Schild's proposal. Cf. the NAB: 'I am who am.' However, B. Albrektson ('On the Syntax of *'ehyeh 'ᵃšer 'ehyeh* in Exodus 3:14', see p. 60 below) has pointed out major problems with Schild's theory, particularly the fact that the function of the verbal clause in Ex. 3.14 cannot be equated with nominal clauses such as I Chron. 21.17. Schild's denial of the circular *idem per idem* construction is not convincing either. Therefore, the traditional translation must still be preferred.

15. NEB has felt constrained to reintroduce the term 'Jehovah' as the traditional rendering of the Tetragrammaton. Perhaps this choice could be defended in a particular ecclesiastical context. However, its use in the NEB, which is committed wholeheartedly to the comparative philological method, strikes one as curious.

19. The MT *wᵉlō'* is difficult and usually emended to *'im lō'* following the LXX.

22. On the meaning of the verb *šā'al* in the context of the 'despoiling of the Egyptians', cf. the excursus, pp. 175ff.

4.1. 'believe me', vv. 1, 5, 8. For a discussion of the phrase 'believe on Moses', cf. H. Gross, 'Der Glaube an Mose nach Exodus', *Wort-Gebot-Glaube. Eichrodt Festschrift*, Zürich 1970, pp. 57–65.

1. The particle *hēn* is not used here conditionally since there is no apodosis, rather as an introduction to a lively encounter (Gen. 18.27; 27.37).

4. The syntactical sequence in 4ff. and 7ff. is difficult since the narrative description breaks into the divine speech. The translation of the NEB which assumes a complete sentence in v. 5 is probably to be preferred to the punctuation of the RSV and NJPS, although the issue is more one of English style than Hebrew syntax.

6. *ḥêq* means literally 'bosom', but the meaning is clearly that of the folds of the clothing (Ps. 74.11; Prov. 6.27).
The disease is described in Lev. 13.9 and Num. 12.10, and traditionally identified with leprosy.

2. Literary and Form-critical Analysis, 3.1–4.17

A. The Scope of the Section

There is considerable disagreement among commentators on fixing the limits of this section. The issue is contested in respect of both the beginning and the end of the unit. Noth (*Exodus, ad loc.*) argues that the unit extends from 2.11–4.23 because the flight from Egypt and the return to Egypt 4.18ff. frame the section. His division recognizes that 2.11ff. and 2.23ff. belong together, and therefore is to be preferred over the division at 2.23 (Bäntsch, Holzinger, Cassuto, Plastaras). According to Noth (*Überlieferungsgeschichte*, p. 31 = ET, p. 30) 3.1–4.16 is not only secondary in terms of the history of traditions, but is also a literary interpolation. He argues that 2.23aα was originally joined to 4.19. However, there remain some serious objections of Noth's hypothesis: (i) No evidence can be adduced for an original literary connection between 2.23a and 4.19 on the basis of the LXX, which reflects a later attempt to harmonize the difficulty. (ii) The style of the narrative in chs. 2 and 4 is not continuous. In ch. 2 the scene is viewed entirely from the human perspective. Moses did not hear a word from God directing him to flee. The command to return in 4.21 is of a different order. (iii) Noth's literary analysis of this chapter is unduly influenced by his theory of the separate transmission of the Sinai and Exodus traditions. We conclude that the unit begins at 3.1.

How far does the section extend? Again, the opinions diverge. Some scholars find no real break between the commission of Moses in chs. 3 and 4 and his first encounter with Pharaoh in 5.1 (cf. Driver's unit from 3.1–6.1). This decision may be dictated in part by source analysis which recognized the Priestly parallel of the commission in 6.2ff. However, the majority of commentators prefer to divide between the commission of Moses and the first encounter with

Pharaoh. Some begin the new section at 4.18 (Bäntsch), others at
4.24 (Noth), still others at 5.1 (Dillmann, Holzinger, McNeile,
Clamer). This lack of agreement as to where the break comes, would
indicate the lack of clear signs of a division. In my opinion, it is
unlikely that 5.1 can be seen as the beginning of a section because
in none of the other occurrences of the term 'afterward' (*we'aḥar*)
does it mark a break in the narrative, but rather indicates continuity
(Gen. 10.18; 30.21, etc.). Again, there seems to be a catchword
connection between 4.23 and 24 which would argue against a
beginning at v. 24. Therefore, I tend to agree with Bäntsch in ending
the commission section at 4.17 and beginning the new section at 4.18.
Certainly some of the difficulty in determining the end of the section
stems from a secondary expansion in 4.21ff. which blurred the lines
between the sections. The section dealing with Aaron, 4.13–16,
27–31 has long been recognized as secondary in the main narrative.

B. *The Problem of Sources*
    There is general agreement among the commentators who reckon
with three major strands on the division of the chapter into sources
(cf. Meyer, Bacon, Bäntsch, Gressmann, Noth, etc.). Criteria for
distinguishing the strands are found in the interchange of divine
names (5//4b; 7.8//6), and in the divergent place designation (J
speaks of Sinai and the bush; E of Horeb). Moreover, characteristic
tendencies of two sources are felt to be reflected in the appearing of
the angel in J in contrast to God's calling in E. Accordingly, J is
assigned verses 2–4a, 5, 7, 8, 16–22; 4.1–16 whereas E receives 1, 4b,
6, 9–15; 4.17. Nevertheless there remain difficulties which exert
pressure for even further literary refinement. Many commentators
find elements of J in v. 1 and assign the expression 'priest of Midian'
to J as a parallel to E's 'Jethro'. A characteristic of J is the reference
to the burning bush; however, the expression appears in 4b in an
E section. Again, clear source criteria seem to be missing in 16ff.
(Gressmann prefers E).
    Critics of this analysis have offered several alternative solutions.
Rudolph eliminates E, but is forced to remove a good many verses as
secondary glosses and rearrange the order (cf. Eissfeldt, *op. cit.*,
pp. 162f.). In my judgment the recent, very detailed analysis of
W. Richter (*op. cit.*, pp. 59ff.) is too hair-splitting and as a result has
unduly atomized the text. For example, Richter eliminates the
appearance of the angel of Yahweh in v. 2 as being sequentially

out of place and reconstructs a 'smooth text'. But this move has failed to reckon with the literary style of the biblical author, paralleled in Gen. 18.1, in which v. 2 serves as a type of superscription to the narrative.

The other extreme is found in Buber, who seeks to defend the unity of the section, but at the cost of considerable elimination of alleged accretions. Jacob, Cassuto, and Lacocque defend the traditional view that the interchange of divine names is a purposeful device of one author. However, both the extreme artificiality by which meaning is assigned to the use of the names, as well as the constant need to adjust the theory in every succeeding section, does not evoke great confidence in this approach.

I tend to agree with Habel (ZAW 1965, p. 302) that, in spite of the presence of literary sources, there is more unity in the present text than has been generally recognized. First of all, the real tensions in the account are not to be found in vv. 1–6. This suggests that the common core was considerable and explains why a precise separation is difficult. The major tension which has been emphasized by Noth, concerns the relation of the flight from Egypt and the return (2.16 and 4.19) with the theophany at the bush and reflects a problem of oral tradition rather than literary sources (cf. Rudolph). The most obvious remaining tension is between the doublets in 7–8//9–12. The presence of two sources seems still to be the most obvious solution. The significant differences in the accounts would perhaps suggest the reason for the retention of both sources. There are some additional signs of literary reworking in ch. 4, but the roughness in vv. 5 and 8 are hardly to be accounted for by source analysis. The introduction of Aaron in 13–16 does appear to be secondary, and most probably entered on the literary level (cf. Westphal, ZAW 26, 1906, p. 227). The role of Aaron as spokesman remains in some tension with v. 11 and the subsequent activity of Moses himself in confrontation with Pharaoh.

C. *Form-critical and Traditio-critical Analysis of 3.1ff.*

The form of the call narrative has been thoroughly analyzed in recent years by Zimmerli, Habel, Kilian and most recently by Richter. In my judgment, the initial work of Zimmerli which Habel has developed remains the most insightful.

Habel outlines the call of Moses as follows: (i) the divine confrontation, vv. 1–3, 4a; (ii) the introductory word, vv. 4b–9; (iii) the commission, v. 10; (iv) the objection, v. 11; (v) the reassurance, v. 12a; (vi) the sign, v. 12. The striking parallels of Ex. 3 with Judg. 6 and Jer. 1 have long been noticed and confirm a stereotyped structure. Zimmerli (*op. cit.*) has contrasted the above form with a second type of call narrative which he finds in I Kings 22 and Isa. 6. In contrast to the first form which is a conversation between Yahweh and his appointed messenger, the second form has a setting in the heavenly council. The prophet overhears the deliberations. Habel's attempt (pp. 310ff.) to demonstrate that the basic structure of both types is common to both is not fully convincing, but he does show correctly some important areas of similarity which have been often overlooked. The primary significance of recognizing this formal structure lies in the aid which it affords the interpreter in assigning proper weight to the various elements within the passage. It prevents the psychologizing of the text by reading it as autobiographical.

The present section 3.1–4.17 is a greatly expanded form of the basic call narrative. The call ends with the giving of the sign in v. 12 (perhaps with vv. 16 and 17a). In its present form a series of objections has been appended which allows a variety of divergent traditions to be incorporated within the narrative framework. The questions reflect widely differing concerns and point to a development of tradition over a considerable length of time (cf. section on OT context).

The more difficult form-critical question arises when one seeks to determine the *Sitz im Leben* for the call narrative. Does the fixed form reflect the function of a particular institution or office which has shaped the material? Here the opinions diverge greatly.

1. Gressmann's analysis remains fundamental in being the first to pursue vigorously the problem of the history of traditions in the call narratives. His analysis of the call narrative remains one of the most brilliant sections in his entire book, and continues to exercise considerable influence (cf. Noth's dependence on it). Gressmann attempts to isolate three different levels of tradition. The first level in its Yahwist formulation is a mythological cult saga which functions etiologically to legitimize a holy place. The second level of development reflects a major shift in function. The local etiological saga has been transformed into a call narrative. Moses is summoned by Yahweh who has developed from a local numen into a national deity. According to Gressmann's classic formulation: 'The discoverer (*Entdecker*) has become the discovered (*Entdeckte*)'. The third

level is the Priestly account found in ch. 6 which is dominated by a philosophical concept of history.

Gressmann's important contribution lay in seeing the signs of local cult tradition in the bush narrative which were not constitutive of the call narrative and which functioned originally as the *hieros logos* to a sacred place. However, Gressmann's method failed to distinguish between genuine levels of Israelite tradition and his own theory of the development of tradition which formed the basis for his reconstructions. The etiological saga did not function as a primitive level for Israel but was incorporated into the call narrative only in the form of vestiges to perform a new role. The call narrative supplied the original nucleus of the story and made use of local tradition. The original setting, in other words, was not mythological.

2. Plastaras (*op. cit.*, pp. 6off.) has attempted to modify Gressmann's interpretation. He accepts his description of Ex. 3.1–6 as the *hieros logos* of a sacred place narrative and treats the passage separately from the call narrative for which he suggests a juridical setting. Plastaras replaces the mythological interpretation with a cultic one. He sees the closest parallels in the several examples of divine manifestation at a holy place (Gen. 12.7ff.; Josh. 5.13ff., etc.). However, the cultic function reflects a highly theological reworking of the older material. 'Thus the burning bush narrative presented Moses to the Israelites who were about to enter the sanctuary of God as their model. When man goes to meet God, he must be open to receive the word of revelation.' But Plastaras' compromise solution offers little actual help to the problem, and leaves the author exposed to the charge that his alleged theological reinterpretation is merely homiletical.

3. Habel has suggested a connection between the call narrative and the commissioning of a messenger or ambassador. Naturally the similarity in form between the *Botenspruch* of the messenger and that of the prophet has long been recognized. However, even this similarity must not be overdone. It is becoming increasingly difficult to subsume the prophetic office under the simple title of messenger. Too many other factors are involved. Habel's attempt to find the provenance of the call in the specific practice of commissioning messengers is artificial. The pattern of Gen. 24 is not the same in spite of allowing generous adjustments to the oral tradition.

4. In my opinion, the evidence points more convincingly toward seeing the setting of Ex. 3 in the prophetic office. This is not to suggest

that the form of prophetism which developed in the monarchial period was simply read back into the Mosaic period. Rather, the reverse movement seems closer to the truth. The tradition linked Moses' call as Yahweh's messenger with the later phenomena of classic prophetism. It recognized correctly that a new element entered with Moses which set it apart from the patriarchal period. The patriarchs received revelation in theophanies, but had no commission to transmit a message to others. Moses' call recounts the deep disruptive seizure of a man for whom neither previous faith nor personal endowment played a role in preparing him for his vocation. However, it is also clear that the later prophetic office influenced the tradition of Moses' call. Particularly in the expanded form of the present text, the series of questions raised by Moses in objection to being sent echo the inner and outer struggles of the prophets of Israel.

D. *A Form-critical Study of Ex. 3.12*

The problem of interpreting the sign in v. 12 has long been felt. The real difficulty of this verse lies in determining exactly the nature of the sign and how it functions in the narrative. To state the problem in grammatical terms, to what does the demonstrative 'this' (*zeh*) in v. 12 refer?

The attempt has often been made to see the antecedent in the preceding clause. Thus, for example, the translation of the NJPS: 'I will be with you and it shall be a sign that it was I who sent you.' However, this interpretation faces some weighty syntactical objections. Specifically the asyndetic connection with the infinitive construct *behôṣî'akā* speaks strongly against referring the demonstrative to the preceding clause. The NJPS translation is forced to supply a connective 'and', the lack of which in the text is precisely the problem. (But cf. Orlinsky, *Notes*, p. 153.) For the same reason, to refer the demonstrative to the burning bush runs into a similar difficulty grammatically. Others have suggested relating it to the preceding assurance 'I will be with you' (Seebass). Beside the grammatical difficulty, this stereotype does not have the function of a sign in the other call narratives.

For these reasons, the majority of modern commentators have sought to find the antecedent in what follows. The sign to Moses was that the people would worship Yahweh on the same mountain after the successful deliverance from Egypt. The strength of this interpretation lies in its grammatical consistency. The parallel construction in I Sam. 10.1 (LXX), I Sam. 2.34, Jer. 44.29, etc. certainly lends support to this interpretation. However, the difficulty of this view is that the sign would only confirm the word after the mission had been accomplished, which does not satisfy the biblical definition of a sign, in spite of frequent attempts to find a warrant for such an interpretation in Isa. 7.14 and II Kings 19.29f. Ordinarily, a sign takes the form of a concrete guarantee which follows the promise and yet precedes the fulfillment.

A final group of commentators have, therefore, rejected both of the major alternatives and have argued that the original sign must have fallen out of the present text. According to Noth the sign must have originally stood after v. 12a. Gressmann suggests a sign such as the appearing of the messenger of God in a pillar of fire and cloud which would lead them to Horeb. However, this remains an interpretation of desperation which can no longer make sense of the text.

In the light of this impasse we offer a fresh form-critical study with the hope of shedding some new light on this vexing problem. Enough work has already been done on the subject of signs in the Old Testament to have demonstrated the variety of usage. Keller's study, *Das Wort OTH*, Basel 1946, has sketched the Deuteronomic and Priestly use of sign with great clarity. Our concern is not to review this material, but to concentrate on one small area which bears directly on the Exodus passage.

We suggest that there are two patterns of sign-giving found in the early tradition of the Old Testament which have much in common, but diverge at important points. The first pattern (designated A) is found in I Sam. 2.34; I Kings 13.3; II Kings 19.29; 20.9; Jer. 44.29. In each case a threat or promise is pronounced by a prophet of God which is to take place in the future. Then a sign is offered as confirmation of the prophetic word by means of the formula: 'This is a sign to you' (*weẓeh leḵā hā'ôṭ*). The sign precedes in time the impending threat or promise. Moreover, the sign is a specific historical event which prefigures the fulfillment by the affinity of its nature. In I Sam. 2.30 the threat of destruction is pronounced against the whole house of Eli. The sign in 2.34 is that both sons, Hophni and Phinehas, would die on the same day. In Jer. 44.27 a threat is announced against all the men of Judah who have escaped to Egypt. The sign is then given in vv. 29f. Hophra, king of Egypt, will die. In I Kings 13.2 a threat is spoken by a man of God against the altar at

Bethel. Its priests will be killed and the altar fully desecrated. The sign in v.3 is that the altar will be first torn down and its ashes poured out. This feature of the prophetic sign as being a prefigurement of the fulfillment is closely connected with the symbolic action of the prophet, which is also designated as a sign (Isa. 8.18; 20.3; Ezek. 4.3). The sign functions in a causative relation to the fulfillment as a 'history creating word' (von Rad). In summary, a threat is made by a prophet. The sign is given to confirm the threat. It precedes the fulfillment, but participates already in the reality.

There is, however, a second pattern (designated B) which shares several features, but diverges strongly at critical points. In I Sam. 10.1 (LXX) Samuel anoints Saul to be prince over Israel with a promise that he would save his people. The sign is then given with the same formula as pattern A: 'This is a sign to you.' However, the sign serves to confirm the anointing, and does not relate directly to the promise. This function is explicitly stated by a *ki* clause in v. 1b, 'a sign that Yahweh has anointed you to be prince'. However, the sign is in the form of a series of astonishing events which serve as a sign in being highly unusual in character, but do not show a prefigurement of the prophecy.

In Judg. 6.14 the messenger of Yahweh announces to Gideon his role as deliverer of Israel (6.12), and extending an assurance of God's presence (16a) offers a promise of success over Midian (16b). Gideon requests a sign by means of a closely similar formula: 'Give me a sign.' This is followed by a relative clause which specifies the function of the sign: 'that it is you who speak with me'. Again, the sign serves to confirm the office to which Gideon has been commissioned. It is given in the form of an extraordinary event, demonstrating super-human power, which attests its divine origin, but it does not prefigure in kind the promised event.

Finally, Ex. 3.12 is another call narrative in which Moses is appointed deliverer of Israel. He is offered divine assurance (12a) and a sign. The formula is stereotyped: 'This is the sign for you.' It is followed by a *ki* clause which specifies its function: 'that I have sent you'. The sign functions to confirm the office and is not directly related to the promise. To summarize: in the call narrative the sign follows the appointing to an office. It serves to confirm the appointment by means of an extraordinary event which legitimates the authority of the one doing the appointing.

Keeping these two patterns in mind, we return to the problem of

Ex.3.12. Now the remarkable feature which emerges from this analysis is the fact that 3.12 does not fit smoothly into either of the patterns. In spite of our using the passage to delineate pattern B, a major difficulty arises in terms of the sign. According to the pattern and its own explicit statement, the sign is to confirm the office by legitimating the speaker's authority. One expects an extraordinary show of power to this end. Instead v.12 makes reference to a future event when the mission has been accomplished.

This lack of consistency with the pattern of B would suggest that the sign is much more closely akin to the A pattern. Indeed, it does seem to relate to the final promise rather than the office as in pattern B. Moreover, the return of the people to worship on the same mountain would indicate a basic element of affinity between the sign and its fulfillment. The place and the practice have been somehow prefigured at an earlier occasion. These features of the sign appear more akin to pattern A than B. But still there remains a difficulty. In pattern A the sign is clearly distinguished in time from the fulfillment, whereas in Ex.3.12 the sign and the fulfillment coalesce. In other words, the sign does not function consistently when read according to either pattern.

In the light of this apparent impasse, we suggest a thesis by which to unravel the tangle. The analysis demonstrated that Ex.3.12 shares several features with pattern B. It is a call narrative with a sign designated to test the authority of the one commissioning the prophet. According to the normal sequence the sign follows an initial objection and dispels it with an exhibition of power. The sequence of this pattern has been dislocated in the Exodus passage. The most likely explanation for this lies in the development of the tradition which made use of a local etiological narrative concerning the burning bush (cf. Gressmann). This older material was adapted to the biblical call narrative. But as a result the extraordinary demonstration of divine power which confirmed the authority of the sender preceded rather than followed the objection. The demonstrative adjective in v.12 normally refers to what follows, but in this case, because of the history of tradition, it was forced to find its antecedent in what preceded, namely in the burning bush. Once this connection has been seen, it is apparent that the burning bush does meet the requirements of the sign in pattern B. It serves to confirm the sender's authority by a show of extraordinary power.

However, a problem still remains in interpreting 12b. What is the function of Israel's return to Sinai in order to worship? It seems likely that in the formation of the call tradition, the theophany to Moses was read in the light of the subsequent events at Sinai. Then a typological relation between the burning bush on the holy mountain, and the devouring fire at Sinai was recognized. The sign to Moses was seen as a prefigurement of Israel's experience. Once this connection was made, it was natural that the pattern exemplified as A would have been a compatible vehicle for this theology. The sign of the bush now pointed to the fulfillment, rather than being directed to the office, and shared in its quality as prefiguring the characteristics of the promise.

In sum, the problem of the sign in Ex. 3.12 has arisen because of its history of tradition. Once this has been seen, the final form of the text becomes transparent. The point of the verse is as follows: this burning bush is a sign that it is I who send you, and it is your guarantee that when you have rescued the people from Egypt, you will worship God on this same mountain.

E. The Problem of Ex. 3.14 and the Divine Name

B. ALBREKTSON, 'On the Syntax of *'ehyeh *'ᵃšer *'ehyeh* in Exodus 3:14', *Words and Meanings: Essays presented to D. Winton Thomas*, ed. P. R. Ackroyd, Cambridge 1968, pp. 15–28; A. ALT, 'Ein ägyptisches Gegenstück zu Ex. 3.14', *ZAW* 58, 1940/41, pp. 159f.; W. F. ALBRIGHT, 'The Name Yahweh', *JBL* 43, 1924, pp. 370–8; *From the Stone Age to Christianity*², Baltimore and London 1957, pp. 15ff.; W. R. ARNOLD, 'The Divine Name in Exodus iii.14', *JBL* 24, 1905, pp. 107–65; F. M. CROSS, Jr, 'Yahweh and the God of the Patriarchs', *HTR* 55, 1962, pp. 225–59; O. EISSFELDT, *KS* IV, Tübingen 1968, pp. 193–8; D. N. FREEDMAN, 'The Name of the God of Moses', *JBL* 79, 1960, pp. 151–6; P. HAUPT, 'Der Name Jahwe', *OLZ* 12, 1909, pp. 211–14; S. HERRMANN, 'Der alttestamentliche Gottesname', *EvTh* 26, 1966, pp. 281–93; 'Der Name JHW³ in den Inschriften von Soleb', *Fourth Congress of Jewish Studies Papers* I, Jerusalem 1967, pp. 213–16; H. B. HUFFMON, *Amorite Personal Names in the Mari Texts*, Baltimore 1965, pp. 70–2; J. P. HYATT, 'Yahweh as "the God of my Father"', *VT* 6, 1955, pp. 130ff.; J. KINYONGO, *Origine et signification du nom Divin Yahvé*, BBB 35, 1970; J. LINDBLOM, 'Noch einmal die Deutung des Jahwe-Namens in Ex. 3.14', *ASTI* 3, 1964, pp. 4–15; E. C. B. MACLAURIN, 'Yahweh, the Origin of the Tetragrammaton', *VT* 12, 1962, pp. 439–63; R. MAYER, 'Der Gottesname Jahwe im Lichte der neuesten Forschung', *BZ*, NF 2, 1958, pp. 26–53; S. MOWINCKEL, 'The Name of the God of Moses', *HUCA* 32, 1961, pp. 121–33; A. MURTONEN, *A Philological and Literary Treatise on the Old Testament Divine Names*, Helsinki 1952; G. QUELL, 'κύριος', *TWNT* III, pp. 1056–80 = *TDNT* III, pp. 1039–98; C. H. RATSCHOW, *Werden und Wirken*, Berlin 1941; E. SCHILD, 'On Exodus iii 14—"I am that I am"', *VT* 4, 1954, pp. 296–302; R. DE VAUX, 'The Revelation of the Divine Name YHWH', *Proclamation and Presence. OT Essays in honour of G. H. Davies*, London and Richmond,

Va. 1970, pp. 48ff.; Th.C. VRIEZEN, *"ehje 'ašer 'ehje'*, *Festschrift Bertholet*, Tübingen 1950, pp. 498–512; W. ZIMMERLI, *Grundriss der alttestamentlichen Theologie*, Stuttgart 1972, pp. 12ff.

Few verses in the entire Old Testament have evoked such heated controversy and such widely divergent interpretations. The reason for the debate is easy to discover. From even a casual reading a whole battery of questions arise. First, why does Moses put the question of v. 13 in this way? 'If I say the God of your fathers sent me to you, they will ask me, what is his name?' Have the people forgotten the name of their God or was the God of the Fathers nameless? Again, is the question really a request for factual information, or rather a way of asking for the significance of the name? Finally, there is a logical problem to be considered. How does the giving of the name serve to validate Moses' claim to divine revelation? If the name were unknown how could it act as evidence for adjudicating the claim? (Cf. Maimonides, *Guide* I. 63.)

There is a second group of questions which turn about the interpretation of the answer (v. 14). Can one indeed speak of an answer to the question, or is v. 14 really a refusal of an answer? Again, is the response of v. 14a directed solely to Moses or to the people as well? Above all, how is the phrase *'ehyeh 'ašer 'ehyeh* (I am who I am) to be translated and what does it mean?

Finally, the literary connection of these verses poses a number of hard questions. How is 14a related to 14b? Then again, what is the logical sequence of v. 14 to 15 and 13 to 15?

Proposed Solutions

Although the majority of scholars tend to combine their literary solution with other questions which relate to the development of Israel's tradition, nevertheless certain characteristic patterns do emerge in the literary handling of these verses. First of all, we find a large group of scholars who suggest rearranging the sequence of verses or eliminating portions as secondary glosses. The major reasons which evoked this move are the threefold introduction to Yahweh's speech and the difficulty of finding logical continuity in the shift of persons in the use of the verb. Most frequently v. 14 is interpreted as a gloss which interrupts the original sequence of 13 and 15 (Eerdmans, Beer, Noth). Rudolph retains v. 14b and sees vv. 14a and 15 as later additions. Then again, Arnold argues that v. 14a is a midrash or gloss on v. 14b. A number of scholars retain vv. 13 and 14 as original while eliminating all or part of v. 15 (Holzinger, Bäntsch). In sum, the high degree of subjectivity reflected in these solutions would caution against a literary solution done in isolation from the history of the tradition of the text.

The second pattern by which scholars have sought to solve the literary difficulty is by emendation of the text. Wellhausen, citing Ibn Ezra, suggested emending the first person *'ehyeh* in v. 14b to third person (so also Holzinger). The LXX's reading ὁ ὤν is usually evoked as an additional warrant. Again Haupt, who argued for the hiphil stem form, suggested reading *'ehyeh 'ašer yihweh* to mean 'I cause to be what comes into existence'. Haupt's theory was accepted by Albright in his 1924 article. Cross, going beyond Haupt, reconstructs the third person for both verbs in the formula.

Closely related to the method of emendation is the third pattern of historical reconstruction. This approach has tended to focus on the formula in Ex. 3.14 and the problem of explaining the Tetragrammaton. The question remains a classic crux in Old Testament scholarship which has called forth dozens of solutions in countless articles (cf. the bibliographies in R. Mayer, *op. cit.*, F. M. Cross, *op. cit.*, and R. de Vaux, *op. cit.*).

Undoubtedly the most forceful recent argument toward a solution has been that of Albright. He sees the name YHWH to be a hypocoristic or abbreviated form of an original theophorous sentence name which he derives from the hiphil of the root **hwy > *hwh*. In recent years this position has been refined and buttressed by Freedman (*op. cit.*) and Cross (*op. cit.*).

Freedman begins by accepting Albright's derivation of the Tetragrammaton from the hiphil. He argues that the verb in Ex. 3.14 was orginally a hiphil with the meaning: 'I bring into being'. His concern is to improve on the Haupt-Albright interpretation of the formula which had emended the second *'ehyeh* to a third person to read: 'I cause to be what comes into existence'. Freedman, recognizing the parallel with the circular *idem per idem* construction in Ex. 33.19, renders the formula: 'I create what I create', or more simply 'I am the Creator'. Then he suggests that Ex. 34.6, which begins with the repetition of the Tetragrammaton, is really a prose adaptation of the original poetic formula. This supports his translation: 'God creates what he creates'.

In my judgment, Freedman's reconstruction encounters a number of difficulties. First, even if one were to assume on the basis of extra-biblical parallels that the name YHWH was originally derived from a proto-Semitic hiphil, there is no clear evidence that in the biblical tradition this connection with the hiphil was ever made. Freedman begs the question by his reconstruction. To regard the qal in the formula as secondary remains highly problematical (cf. the strong arguments of de Vaux against describing the verb as a hiphil). Secondly, to translate the *idem per idem* formula as 'I am the Creator' misses completely the force of the formula, which lies in its indefiniteness (cf. Vriezen). The force of 3.14 is different from 34.6 and the two cannot be related as Freedman suggests.

F. Cross, following a somewhat different tack, presents an elaborate case, supported by recent Ancient Near Eastern parallels, for a theory that Yahweh was originally a cultic sentence name of El, the creation deity, who split off from the El cult and eventually ousted him from his place of pre-eminence. Cross supports his theory by attempting to trace the development of the formula *'ehyeh 'ăšer 'ehyeh* from its proto-Semitic form. He argues that the formula was a sentence name, originally to be read in the third person since *'ăšer* replaced the relative particle *ḏū* toward the end of the Late Bronze Age in Ugaritic. Thus he reconstructs the formula: *yahwī ḏū yahwī*. He draws a parallel between *ḏū yahwī* and El's appellative in Ugaritic *ḏū yakāninu* ('He who creates'). He then postulates that *ḏū yahwī* was originally an epithet of El and suggests reconstructing the primitive formula as *'ēl ḏū yahwī*. Then the substitute of *yahwī* for *'ēl* in the first position would occur when Yahweh became the principal cult name.

Without attempting to explore all the issues involved in Cross's interpretation, certain difficulties can be sketched: (i) In my judgment, it seems highly unlikely that the *idem per idem* formula developed according to this elaborate historical hypothesis when there are close parallels elsewhere, such as Ex. 33.19 (cf. Vriezen). (ii) Cross's theory fails to explain adequately the presence of the first-person form in the formula. The alleged explanation that the deity addresses himself in the first person while the cult participant employs the third person form does not avoid the difficulty of its double occurrence. (iii) At best the theory remains highly tentative because of the lack of direct evidence to support the several hypothetical projections.

Over and above the historical and philological difficulties of Cross's theory, which historians and linguists will continue to debate, there remains a basic hermeneutical question in regard to the method of reconstruction employed by Cross and others. Cross has made out a strong case for connecting the name Yahweh originally with the Amorite causal verb. His evidence offers a major correction to the widespread opinion of Semitists such as Dillmann who argued that a hiphil of *hwh** was unprecedented. However, a critical problem arises in his use of a method which fails to distinguish between a reconstructed history of Israel's development on the basis of Ancient Near Eastern parallels, and Israel's own history of tradition.

Cross argues that the Tetragrammaton reflects a tradition of a creation deity analogous to the Ugaritic El which developed from the Canaanite religion. He tries to find support for this theory by a reconstruction of the tradition in Ex. 3. Only in this passage the name is plainly connected with the verb *hāyāh*, and then clearly in terms of the qal form. Cross is forced to argue that the conflict of his reconstruction with the tradition of Ex. 3 is only with a late, secondary layer of the present text. Evidence for this theory is not found in vestiges within the Israelite tradition, but only in a reconstructed history of development which, in its way, is as radical as that of Wellhausen or Gressmann. In other words, Cross does not trace the different levels within the tradition, but substitutes a reconstructed tradition by analogy with Ancient Near Eastern parallels. This assumes a degree of continuity between the Ancient Near East and the earliest levels of Israel's tradition which is, by and large, a theoretical projection.

An alternative solution is to take seriously Israel's own tradition when it interprets the divine name in a manner which is in striking discontinuity with the Ancient Near Eastern parallels. Such a view would certainly recognize the Ancient Near Eastern cognates of the divine name and even reckon with a long prehistory of the name before its entrance into Israel, but it remains open to the possibility that a totally new meaning was attached to the name by Israel. The fact that the biblical tradition itself retains none of the lines of continuity projected by Cross, but emphasizes the newness of the name to Moses, would support this latter approach to the problem.

A. *Form-critical analysis of Ex. 3.13–15*

We have criticized the attempt to solve the literary problems of the text apart from the oral tradition. Also we have objected to positing theories of early development without taking seriously the history of tradition of the passage. What can we learn from a form-critical analysis?

An initial observation regarding the form is that no one traditional pattern of oral tradition can be recovered. Rather, there is an extremely complex interweaving of elements from several patterns. Failure to recognize this complexity has called forth solutions which are supported in part by the text, but which are forced to discard or suppress other important features.

First of all, the theophanic appearance of the deity, who, often at a holy place, reveals himself by name in a self-revelatory formula, employs a form which has many parallels in the Old Testament (cf. Gen. 17.1; 26.23; 28.13; Ex. 3.6, etc.). God himself appears to one of the patriarchs, announces his name in the fixed formula of self-introduction: *'ᵃnî/'ᵃnōkî 'elōhê 'aḇrāhām* and renews a promise. The recipient of the theophany is not sent, as in the prophetic call, nor is he given a sign. Only in the case of Gen. 15.2 does Abraham raise objections to the promise offered him by God.

Secondly, there is another group of passages, which have been generally designated as theophanies, but which differ considerably from the first form (cf. Gen. 32.30; Judg. 13.17). Here the revelation is through the form of an intermediary. There is an initial encounter, the content of which varies considerably, but on the basis of which a divine promise or blessing is pronounced. However, the act of self-revelation does not initiate the encounter. Rather, the recipient inquires concerning the name of his protagonist. The context of Gen. 32 and Judg. 16 makes it clear that genuine information is sought since his name is unknown. As has often been observed, there is a characteristic oscillation between the angel of Yahweh being an intermediary and his being a manifestation of Yahweh himself. Nevertheless, the form is quite distinct from the self-revelation formula of the first pattern.

The third group of passages represents a call pattern which we have already analyzed in connection with Ex. 3.1ff. There is an initial appearance, usually by the angel of Yahweh, which leads to the introductory message and the commission. With the exception of Ex. 3.1 the divine messenger does not introduce himself nor is a revelation of a name involved. The focus of these passages falls on the commission with the subsequent objections, which leads to the giving of a sign. This pattern differs from that of the theophany in attributing little significance to the appearance of the deity or the place of revelation, or to acquiring the name of the commissioner, since this latter fact is assumed to be known.

Finally, there is a form reflected in a number of passages which arises from a question regarding the significance of some religious practice (Ex. 12.26; 13.14; Deut. 6.20; Josh. 4.6, 21; 22.24). Soggin (*VT* 10, 1960, pp. 341ff.) has characterized this form as a stereotype form of instruction. The form is of interest in this discussion in so far as it employs a question which is not enquiring after new information, but rather seeks to discover the significance of a practice which is known. The form is akin to the etiological form which Gunkel isolated. However, it differs in retaining its question form as part of the tradition rather than representing an earlier level which needs reconstruction in order to recover it (cf. Gunkel on Lot's wife).

The purpose in outlining these different forms is to see what perspective can be thrown on Ex. 3.13-15 from these traditional patterns. It is not suggested that the four patterns remained independent of one another, or necessarily reflect separate settings. Still a recognition of the stereotyped elements often aids in sorting out the complex interweavings which took place in the passage in Ex. 3.

We now return to a closer look at the text. Verse 13 is presented in the larger context of a series of objections on the part of Moses in the face of his call. It is important to note at the outset that the question of the name of God does not proceed directly from Moses as if he had said: 'What then is your name?' The request is couched as a question from the people. Even then Moses does not directly request the name. Rather he inquires how to answer the people when they ask for a name. Conceivably other possibilities are open than the actual giving of a name.

There is still another observation to make regarding the nature of the question. It is not posed as a hypothetical question (*'im*), but in a *hinnēh* clause: 'Agreed, I come to the people. Now when I say that the God of your fathers sent me, and they then say, "What's his name?" what shall I reply?' The response of the people to Moses' proclamation is not regarded as a remote reaction, but as the natural one which he is sure to expect. The question suggests that the verification of Moses' commission is integrally tied to the revelation of the divine name. How is this to be explained?

Can one find an antecedent for this connection in any of the four patterns which we have outlined? In the first theophany form the name of God is revealed in a self-revelatory formula to legitimate the revelation, but there is no connection with a commission. In the second form the question of the name is raised, but the issue turns on legitimating the revelation by an intermediary, and not in being commissioned for others. Again in the call narrative, it is not the revelation of the name which legitimates the commissioned one, but the signs serve this purpose. Finally, the etiological pattern inquiring after the significance does not serve to legitimate the one responding, nor is the answer a means of testing validity. Moreover, if the question were to be interpreted simply as asking the significance of the name: 'What does his name reveal regarding his intention toward us?', then the form of the objection is unsuitable. Moses already knows God's intention for Israel. We conclude, therefore, that none of the four patterns which we have examined provide a genuine antecedent for the question raised in v. 13. Even though elements of the question are represented, the actual form differs markedly from all of them.

Is it then possible to look elsewhere for an explanation of the peculiar elements of the question? One could argue that the request for the divine name was a necessity for the proper execution of the cult (Greenberg). Israel, like the rest of the Ancient Near East, required the divine name for its worship. While this connection between name and cult is valid, it does not solve the difficulty of the text. If Moses had immediately claimed a commission to hold a festival, the request for a name could be explained as a natural reaction arising out of cult practice. However, the issue is one of relating commission to name rather than cult.

Perhaps one could argue that the unusual juxtaposition of these two elements reflects the later problem of the prophet's claim to authority which, as we know, was frequently called into question (Amos 7.10ff.; Hos. 9.7, etc.). The prophet claims a commission from God; the people seek a test of this claim. The difficulty, however, lies in the nature of the text. The prophetic apology is neither evoked by a request for God's special name, nor is it ever answered in these terms. The classical prophets defend their claim to represent God by recounting the radical disruption of their ordinary life which occurred at the act of commissioning, and by their demonstrating their authority in delivering God's word. Again, a parallel to Ex. 3 cannot be sustained.

In the light of this failure to find an antecedent for the question in the traditional answers, a different solution must still be sought. When did the issue of the name of Yahweh become a means by which a messenger could be tested? Clearly the issue is one connected with the prophet's office. Who has a claim to this office and how is the claim to be validated? Deut. 13.1 cites the case in which a prophet arises, who not only can give signs and miracles, but can even make events come to pass. Against this threat of the false prophet who will lead Israel astray, there is one sure test of truth. If the prophet says: 'Let us go after other gods,' then he is certainly a deceiver. He has taught rebellion against Yahweh. Likewise, Deut. 18.20 addresses prophets speaking 'in the name of other gods'. The conflict between the prophets of Baal and the prophets of Yahweh climaxes in Elijah's conflict on Carmel (I Kings 18.19ff.; cf. II Kings 10.19ff.). However, even Jeremiah knew of prophets who prophesied in the name of Baal (Jer. 2.8; 23.13). Of course in the later period the issue of distinguishing true and false prophets entered a new crisis (cf. the literature to this discussion in the works of von Rad, Quell, Osswald, Kraus). Both true and false prophet claimed the name of Yahweh. Nevertheless, it is also clear that early in Israel's history the test for being a true messenger was linked to prophesying in the name of Yahweh.

Now according to the oral tradition preserved in E, the divine name of Yahweh was first revealed to Israel in the Mosaic period. Whereas the J tradition identifies Yahweh with the God of the Fathers, the E tradition, followed by P, marks a discontinuity in the tradition. A new name was revealed to Moses. I would like to argue that this E tradition, in the course of its transmission, was influenced by the later question of the true and the false prophet. In fact, the peculiar juxtaposition of elements in Ex. 3.14 which has proved to be so baffling to interpreters can best be explained by this hypothesis.

The E tradition has Moses approaching the people with the claim of being sent to them by the God of their fathers. The people inquire after the name of God. The problem has been how to explain this request. Had they forgotten God's name? How then could it be a test? The point of the inquiry is to elicit from Moses an answer which will serve as the ultimate test of his validity as a prophet. What is the name of the God who sent him? Verse 15 supplies the answer. *Yahweh* is the God of the fathers; this is his name forever! The effect of E's using this form as a vehicle for his tradition serves two purposes. First, the main testimony of the E tradition has been preserved which marked the introduction of the new name to Israel through Moses while at the same time preserving the continuity of God's history of revelation. Secondly, Moses' role as true prophet is reaffirmed in the light of the new situation which has arisen in Israel. Moses confirms his prophetic office by announcing God's one true name.

Still our analysis is not complete. How is one to explain v. 14? God said to Moses, "*ehyeh *ᵃšer *ehyeh*'. And he said, 'So you shall speak to the Israelites, "*ehyeh* has sent me to you."' The parallel between vv. 14 and 15 has long been observed. Both sentences are introduced as God's response to the question in v. 13. Nevertheless, the content of v. 14a is completely different from that of v. 15. One can question whether it is really an answer or rather the refusal of an answer. L. Koehler, along with a number of other Old Testament scholars, has interpreted it as an evasion of the question similar to Gen. 32 or Judg. 13. God is the *deus absconditus*.

In my opinion, there are several strong reasons which speak against this interpretation: (i) verse 14b certainly does not interpret it as a refusal, but as a positive response to the inquiry. (ii) The formula, 'I am who I am', does not mean 'It is not your concern' – note that the Hebrew is not *ᵃnî *ᵃšer *ᵃnî* – rather it is a paronomastic use of the verb *hāyāh*. Moreover, Vriezen has clearly shown that the formula is not simply an expression of indefiniteness, but emphasizes the actuality of God: '"I am who I am" means: "I am there, wherever it may be . . . I am really there!"' The parallel in Ex. 33.19 would confirm this interpretation.

What is the setting for such an answer? It is obviously quite different from that which has been suggested for v. 15. Verse 14 answers the question by offering a word play on the name Yahweh which is connected to the root 'to be'. This suggests that the question in v. 13: 'What is his name?' was understood as a request not for information, but rather for an explanation of the significance of the name. What does the name mean? Of course, the close connection between the name of the person and his character is common both for the Old Testament and the Ancient Near Eastern world. In other words, the question has been interpreted after the pattern of the etiological 'child's question'.

How is the shift in interpretation to be explained? One suggestion would be that once the identification of Yahweh with the God of the fathers had been completely taken for granted the original point of the question lost its meaning. When Moses reported that the God of the fathers had sent him, no one would think to ask what is his name. Therefore, it must be read in terms of the name's significance. What does Yahweh intend for us by this name? Although it is difficult to determine precisely when such a shift occurred, it appears most probable that it occurred on the literary level. Certainly the combination of the J and E sources completed the full identification of Yahweh with the God of the fathers, which further obscured the point of E's tradition respecting the name. The present form of the text also reflects literary activity rather than a fusion of oral tradition. Verse 14a appears as a parallel to v. 15, with 15b providing a literary bridge back to v. 13.

In summary: vv. 13–15 reflect a history of tradition which extended from the oral to the literary level, and offer a series of witnesses to the questions of prophetic office and divine purpose.

F. *Stylistic and Thematic Analysis*

Several interesting linguistic patterns can be observed in these chapters. First of all, the verses fall into groups each of which uses a different cluster of verbs formed from one Hebrew root. Notice, for example, that in vv. 2–7 the root 'to see' (*r'h*) appears seven times; in vv. 10–15 'to send' (*slḥ*) occurs five times; in 4.1–9 'to believe' (*he'emîn*) four times; in 4.10–17 'to speak' (*dbr*) seven times, and 'mouth' (*peh*) seven times. This clustering hardly represents a conscious technique since the choice of verbs is basically dictated by the subject matter. Still a pattern does seem clear.

Along with the tendency to cluster around one verb, there are several phrases which recur throughout the chapters to provide a thematic unity. The appearing of the God of Abraham, Isaac, and Jacob, which was first announced in 3.6, is again picked up in 3.15, 16; 4.5. The phrase 'I will be with you' occurs in 3.12 (cf. 3.14); 4.12, 15. Note also the frequency of such verbs as 'know' (3.7, 19; 4.14) and 'go' (3.10, 16; 4.12).

Of more importance is an appreciation of the stylistic achievement as a whole. After the initial description of the theophany a similar style continues throughout both chapters in the use of an extended dialogue. The contrast between the two speakers is remarkable. God's speeches are consistently long and often repetitious. At times this fact can be explained by the combination of sources, but not always. The length arises from God's speaking twice without a response from Moses (3.5–6). Often the continuing speech is marked by such phrases as 'again' (3.15; 4.6) or by some other connective such as 'and now' (3.9). In contrast, Moses speaks in short, often brusque, speeches.

The major characteristics of the speeches are not exhausted, however, by simply recognizing the difference in length, which is a formal device. Rather, the writer shows remarkable skill in sketching his portrayal of resistance. Moses raises five sets of objections to his commission. These are not logically connected, although they do begin with a personal focus. The progression of the dialogue is more visceral than rational. Each time in which the objection is fully met, a new one springs up, unconnected with the later. No visible gain is ever made. The picture emerges of one person trying to reason with another who is throwing up arguments, but basically whose will, not mind, is resisting the call. Moses' initial objection points to his own inability. Soon, however, his objection can flatly contradict God and attribute the worst to the people. In the end he is trapped and his real doubt emerges.

The speeches of God are portrayed with consummate skill. Each objection is carefully answered, usually with an assurance of aid over and above the explanation. In contrast to the disconnected objections, God's answers move solidly along the one track. In each response the writer has God taking up and repeating key phrases such as 'the God of your fathers', 'I know', and 'I am with you'. Moreover, each time God's speech concludes by urging Moses into action (3.10, 16; 4.12). Even when his patience ends with Moses' flat refusal to go, the biblical writer does not alter basically the pattern of God's dealing with his servant. He remains patient but resolute.

One final feature of the speech of God is the writer's use of anticipation. Almost every divine response goes beyond the immediate problem to describe and incorporate the future (cf. 3.12, 18, 21f.; 4.9, 15). The effect is to give his speech an atmosphere of great confidence and expectation which finally overcomes and absorbs the resistance of his messenger.

3. Old Testament Context

These chapters are characterized throughout by an interaction between the human and the divine. The section recounts a revelation of God to Moses. It issues in a divine commissioning of a messenger. It relates at length Moses' resistance to his inclusion in the divine plan. The intertwining of God's redemptive purpose for Israel with the reaction of his chosen vehicle forms the warp and woof of the call narrative.

[3.1–12] The initial encounter between God and Moses reflects a remarkable mixture of ordinary elements of human experience with the extraordinary. Moses is shepherding the flock of his father-in-law as always. The verbal form of v. 1 emphasizes the continuity in time with the past. The repetition of Jethro's name marks the continuation of his occupation. On his own initiative, and undoubtedly in search of fresh pasture, he arrived at Mount Horeb. There he notices a common desert bush on fire and decides to go over and look at it more closely. However, Horeb happens to be 'the mountain of God', holy ground. The phrase: 'the angel of Yahweh appeared to him in the midst of the bush', serves as an interpretative superscription to the entire description which then follows. The burning bush is not consumed by the fire. This is the 'great wonder' which causes Moses to turn aside. What began as just another day doing the same old thing, turned out to be an absolutely new experience for Moses. The old life of shepherding was ended; the new life of deliverer was beginning. The transformation is recorded in the interaction of God with Moses. The initiative is shifted from Moses to God. The ordinary experiences emerge as extraordinary. The old has been transformed into the new.

The biblical description of the theophany and the call as an interplay between Moses' initiative and God's has been explained historically as the fusion of two levels of tradition. Moses the 'discoverer of God' in the local etiology becomes the 'discovered by God' in the call. Whatever truth this analysis may or may not have, it cannot be used as a substitute for determining the significance of this interplay of elements within the present text. The diachronistic dimension serves its function in illuminating the synchronistic, not in destroying its integrity. The fact that the interplay of elements within the chapter is not simply the result of an artificial fusion of traditions is confirmed by the skillful design throughout the chapter which continues to weave together the elements of the divine and the human. In a real sense, each of the subsequent objections arises from the perspective of past experience (3.11, 13; 4.1, 10) and each of God's replies points him forward to the new reality of faith which has been promised (3.12, 14; 4.5, 11ff.).

The subtle dialectic of the chapter is certainly missed by commentators who would subsume the divine element within the category of the psychological. Moses' call then becomes the internal brooding of a man over the problems of his people and the mounting religious conviction that God wanted him to aid. The chapter is absolutely clear in seeing Moses' call along with the entire prophetic experience as being a radical break with the past, initiated by God, for which 'neither previous faith nor any other personal endowment had the slightest part to play in preparing a man who was called to stand before Yahweh for his vocation' (von Rad, *OT Theology* II, p. 57).

Conversely, the point of the call description lies in showing that there remains a human initiative and will which, far from being crushed, remains a constitutive element of the one who is being sent. The astonishing elements of the awe-inspiring theophany before which Moses cowered, suddenly recede into the background of the chapter and God addresses Moses as his chosen agent: 'I know their sufferings . . . I have come to deliver them . . . I send you to Pharaoh.' The divine will seeks to transform the human, but the messenger continues to resist even after he has been given the office. The prophet of God is not just a vehicle of communication in the Old Testament. Exodus 3 offers a classic description of the office as one which, even though initiated fully by God, incorporates a genuine human personality. The one called can drag his feet, even elicit a compromise in the divine plan (4.14), but finally he will speak for God in spite of himself (4.15ff.).

We have already characterized the second major portion of the call narrative as a portrayal of resistance. Again it is significant to notice that the different sets of objections, each of which reflects a history of tradition, nevertheless when read from the context of the chapter as a whole form a highly interesting narrative pattern. The lack of logical connection between the various questions, which fluctuate between portrayals of genuine modesty, fear of the unknown, reproach of the people, and excuse making, adds a tremendous richness to the scene. Some of the questions are genuine, others contrived. Some are worthy of a prophet, others are not. Each is handled by God with utmost seriousness. The objection is examined and then met with a divine promise. The fear from the past is not allowed to thwart the redemptive promise of the future.

The first objection, 'Who am I that I should go to Pharaoh and bring the Israelites out?' reflects the spontaneous response of Moses who senses immediately the gaping discrepancy between his own ability and the enormity of the task. It is the traditional answer of the one called (Jer. 1.6; I Sam. 9.21; Judg. 6.15). In Exodus the inverted credentials which demonstrate lack of prestige are omitted – he is a nobody from an undistinguished family (Judg. 6.15) – but the rural setting of the chapter is sufficient to make the point. What business has a shepherd with such a mission!

To this objection Moses is given an assurance and a sign. These are not identical but related. Moses is assured that God will accompany him. The grounds for his being sent do not rest on Moses' ability, but on his being a vehicle for God's plan. Then a sign is volunteered by God which is to confirm the act of commissioning. The real difficulty of the verse lies in determining exactly the nature of the sign and how it functions in the chapter. In the previous section we have argued for the need of a historical dimension in understanding this text. The demonstrative adjective in v. 12 refers, first of all, to the theophany of the burning bush. Here is a visible sign of God's power which breaks through the limits of human experience. Every one knows that bushes burn and are soon consumed. But here is one which burns and is not consumed. It is a great wonder reflecting the holiness of God which no man dare transgress.

However, the sign points in another direction and functions in two different ways. First, it serves as an overwhelming demonstration of God's power who commissions and equips his prophet for a divine purpose. The old question, 'Who am I?' dissolves before the new potential of the office. Secondly, the sign already participates in the future promise of a redeemed people worshipping God in his sanctuary. It functions as a foretaste of the future promise, the reality of which has already emerged in the call of Moses. His commission finds its ultimate meaning in the corporate life of the obedient people whom he is called to deliver in accordance with God's purpose.

[3.13–15] Then Moses raises a second objection. 'Assuming that I come to the people of Israel and say to them, "The God of your fathers has sent me to you," and they ask me, "What is his name?" what shall I say to them?' This question has evoked such a long history of scholarly controversy and has been approached with so many oblique questions that it is extremely difficult to hear the text any longer within its present context. Is this a genuine question? Was it something needful for Moses to know as God's messenger? The fact that it was not actually raised in the subsequent discussion with the people is not a decisive argument against its legitimacy.

Conversely, the fact that God took it with utmost seriousness and offered an elaborate answer is no evidence for seeing the question as a genuine response of faith. The same seriousness on God's part holds true for obvious evasions of responsibility by Moses. Finally, an evaluation of the question in its present context is only evaded when one appeals to a special Hebrew or Near Eastern mentality with its connection between name and reality as offering the exegetical key. It remains part of the exegetical question at issue to determine from the biblical context whether the question is a genuine one of faith or not. Its role here cannot be simply assumed on the basis of general analogy.

Certainly in its present context Moses' question is viewed as one in a series of objections. It is part of the prophet's resistance. The issue as to whether it reflects the genuine concern of a prudent man or an artificial pretext of the doubter has, therefore, been somewhat relativized. The question is colored by the others in the series which more and more reflect doubt and outright excuse-making. Clearly the present text does not view Moses' concern as something absolutely needful to his office which God inadvertently failed to clarify. The tremendous importance which modern scholars attribute to the answer should not obscure this point.

The literary and form-critical analysis (cf. above) confirmed the scholarly opinion that vv. 13ff. reflect the special tradition of one early witness which connected the communication of the divine name to Moses' commission. However, it is now our task to hear this testimony as it found its place within ch. 3. What is the import of the question in its present context? Moses conjectures that the people will respond with a query. They will react to the announcement of his commission with the question, 'What is his name?' The question contains both a request for information and an explanation of its significance. These are two aspects of the one question. Clearly the people want to know more about God's intention. By requesting his name, they seek to learn his new relationship to them. Formerly he related to them as the God of the Fathers. What will he be to Israel now?

In the answers which follow the major point of the original tradition which concerned the revelation of the divine name Yahweh has been modified by its new position within the larger narrative. God first directs an answer to Moses which is explicitly distinguished from the answer intended for the people in response to their hypothetical question. The answer addresses itself to the question of God's intention. The fact that this answer is directed to Moses indicates that the question is not taken simply at face value. It reveals as much of Moses as it does of the people. He has cloaked his own doubt as to God's intention in terms of the people's query. God deals first with his problem which again indicates the description of prophetic resistance is still being portrayed. God said to Moses, 'I will be who I will be.' The word-play on the name of God (*'ehyeh-yahweh*) confirms the connection between name and significance. The formula is paradoxically both an answer and a refusal of an answer. The tenses of the formula indicate that more than a senseless tautology is intended, as if to say, I am who I am, a self-contained, incomprehensible being. Moses is not simply refuted as was Manoah (Judg. 14.18). Rather God announces that his intentions will be revealed in his future acts, which he now refuses to explain. The paronomastic formula, which gives the answer its indefinite quality, also testifies that the reality of God will not be different from that made known in his revelation. The accent of the formula in 14a falls on the first verb, as is shown by 14b. God's intention for Moses is an expression of his being God and will be manifest according to his own plan. A positive answer is given to Moses, but one which neither condones his doubt nor satisfies his curiosity.

Next God addresses an answer to the people's query which was posed by Moses. 'Say this to the people of Israel: "I AM has sent me to you!"' Moses' answer to the people can only reflect what God has revealed to him. He knows no more of God's intention than has been revealed in the formula. The people also will experience God's purpose by what he does in their future. But the God who has made known his reality has sent his messenger as the medium through whom the divine purpose will begin to work. Once the significance of the name has been explained, the ineffable name itself is given in a sentence which parallels v. 14b: Yahweh is the God of the Fathers. He is the one who sent Moses. The people's question has been directly answered, but first the intention which it contained was carefully defined.

The final phrase of v. 15 indicated by its shift in person is again addressed to Moses: 'This is my name for ever and thus I am to be remembered throughout all generations.' God's answer began with Moses. It now draws the theological implications for the revelation far beyond the immediate concern of Moses' original question. God has revealed himself to Moses in his eternal name. This is the name which will then be cultically remembered by his people throughout the generations. The revelation of the name in Israel is not to satisfy curiosity, but to be the medium of continuous worship.

[3.16–4.9] Moses' second objection has been carefully answered. God now seeks to urge Moses into action. 'Go and gather . . . and say.' Moses is now fully equipped to begin and the same themes closely paralleled to the initial theophany are repeated (vv. 16//7ff.). Then God assures Moses of success with a second discourse which anticipates the future. The people will believe, the king will be hardened, the Egyptians will be plagued, the deliverance will occur, and finally the Egyptians will be despoiled! The author uses the speech to show that from God's perspective the way is clear. His whole plan unfolds before an open future. Each of the obstacles, which successively appear to grow in size, are all part of his plan.

The divine speech also functions to highlight the prophet's new form of resistance and to build a transition to the third major objection. God's speech has unfolded the future in a rapid projection of futile obstacles which he has promised to overcome. But the prophet stumbles on the first. Then Moses answered: 'They will not believe.' Again God must return to a point long since passed and address his prophet who stands fixed in doubt still unable to scale even the first hurdle.

Some commentators have tried to avoid the conclusion that Moses' third objection is a contradiction of God's assurance in v. 18: 'And they will hearken to your voice.' However, in its present context Moses' brusque response does come as a note of harsh dissidence which can hardly be avoided. The fact of the people's outright unbelief in respect to a prophet's word is reflected in the whole history of Israel. 'All the violent men said to Jeremiah: "You are telling a lie. Yahweh our God did not send you."' Now the front has shifted. Yahweh is certainly our God, but he did not appear to you! The prophet must legitimate his call from God.

The present narrative shows great skill in incorporating this theme within the framework of Moses' resistance. The same signs function in three different ways. First, Moses himself is addressed. As with the second objection, the people's question reflects his own state of uncertainty. The prophet must himself be convinced of God's power present in him. He casts down his rod and takes the writhing snake by the tail. He thrusts his hand into his bosom and then sees it restored to health. Again the same signs function to convince the people. Verse 5 makes this point specifically – 'that they may believe that Yahweh . . . has appeared to you.' The signs are demonstrations of divine power which have become the equipment of God's envoy. The power is a possession which can be used. These signs differ from the sign in v. 12 in that they are repeatable and are channeled through Moses. The use of the sign, however, is clearly restricted. It functions to confirm the prophetic office (v. 15) and cannot be used indiscriminately.

Finally, the signs function in demonstrating God's power to Pharaoh and the Egyptians. The phrase 'if they will not believe' (v. 8) picks up the vocabulary of vv. 1 and 5, but there is a subtle shift. The subject of disbelief has carried the writer beyond that of the prophet and the Israelites. The real locus of unbelief and resistance lies with Pharaoh and the Egyptians. Almost imperceptibly the subject of the verb has shifted. If they do not believe, then God has prepared the first plague. The seam in the narrative can be seen in the shift from sign to plague. The change of the Nile from water to blood cannot be repeatedly practiced. It occurs only once and evokes a disaster. God's reply to Moses began with the concrete objection, but it again ends on the note of anticipation, foreshadowing the events of the future. The fact that the first two signs were not used before the Hebrews, but are executed only before Pharaoh as an introduction to the plagues (cf. 7.8ff.) indicates a variety in the tradition. However, the present writer has skillfully adapted his material within his own narrative, enriching the portrayal of prophetic resistance, and pointing the reader toward the plagues in which material these signs were originally at home.

[4.10–17] The fourth objection moves more directly toward being an obvious excuse. It returns again to the messenger's personal qualifications and is more akin to the initial objection. 'O, my Lord, I am not eloquent . . .' The emphasis on the use of the word as the trade mark of the prophet reflects a major theme of the classical prophets (Jer. 1, etc.). The divine answer comes in the form of a wisdom saying closely akin to Ps. 94.9. In the classical prophets, wisdom sayings in the style of a disputational speech are also frequent (cf. Isa. 28.27ff.). The form adapts beautifully to the present narrative. The wisdom saying elicits an obvious answer which is then succinctly and powerfully supplied. 'Who made man's mouth . . . Is it not I, Yahweh?' The pattern reminds above all of Deutero-Isaiah in its exalted tone. The question evaporates before the reality of

Yahweh as the creator God. Both the form and content of this verse would caution against contrasting too strongly Yahweh's role as redeemer and creator. The point has been made, the objection dispelled with dispatch. Again the imperative is sounded (v. 12), again an assurance which reaches over and above that of the past: 'I will be with your mouth and teach you what you shall speak.' God's reply reflects the same careful, patient answer, but the tempo of the narrative has quickened.

Time has run out for Moses. There are no more reasons for delay which he can pose. Now he must either go or refuse. He does the latter: 'O, my Lord, please send somebody else.' The plea is diffident, but it is visceral and desperate. God's reaction of anger is likewise spontaneous. It is not described but merely stated. Then a concession is made. Aaron is appointed as spokesman. However, Moses is not relieved of his responsibility, simply the medium of communication has been altered. As Moses was agent for God, so now Aaron will be the mouthpiece for Moses. The arrangement is not up for discussion. Moses has been commissioned. The final sentence picks up the theme of the rod and the signs which had begun ch. 4. The rod is a gentle reminder that Moses is still God's vehicle of power for the coming deliverance.

Detailed Notes

3.1. 'Jethro, Moses' father-in-law'. Cf. note on 2.16.

'behind the wilderness'. A large literature has developed on the role of the desert in the Old and New Testament. Cf. U. W. Mauser, *Christ in the Wilderness*, SBT 39, 1963, for a full bibliography on the subject. Add the more recent article of S. Talmon, 'The "Desert Motif" in the Bible and in Qumran Literature', *Biblical Motifs*, ed. A. Altmann, Cambridge, Mass., and London 1966, pp. 31ff.

'mountain of God'. Although this expression is used proleptically in the present context, the expression may well reflect the earlier level of the original tradition. Cf. Gressmann, *op. cit.*

'Horeb'. The term appears to be a synonym for Sinai which is used in the Elohist and Deuteronomic strands of the tradition. The attempts to make a distinction in terms of different parts of the mountain remain without solid evidence. Cf. the discussion in ch. 19.

2. 'angel of Yahweh'. A divine emissary of Yahweh who assumes the form and speech of Yahweh himself. Beside the standard commentaries on Genesis, cf. von Rad, *TWNT* I, pp. 75f. = *TDNT* I, pp. 74f. Eichrodt, *Theology of the OT* II, pp. 23ff.; W. Baumgartner, 'Zum Problem des "Jahve-Engels"', *Schweiz. Theol. Umschau* 14, 1944, No. 5, pp. 97–102; R. S. Kluger, *Satan in the OT*, Evanston 1967, pp. 57ff.; F. Stier, *Gott und sein Engel in AT*, Münster 1934.

'appeared'. There has been much recent discussion of the verb *r'h* within the larger context of the debate on the nature of biblical revelation. Cf. R. Rendtorff, 'Die Offenbarungsvorstellungen im Alten Israel', *Offenbarung als Geschichte*, Göttingen 1961, pp. 23ff.; W. Zimmerli, 'Offenbarung im Alten Testament', *EvTh* 22, 1962, pp. 15ff.; J. Moltmann, *Theologie der Hoffnung*, Munich 1965, pp. 87f.; ET *Theology of Hope*, London and New York 1967, pp. 97f.

'bush'. Cf. A. Tourney, *VT* 7, 1957, pp. 410ff. where he argues for identification with the bramble on the basis of the only ancient parallel, namely, the Legend of Aḥiqar from Elephantine. Cf. also, M. A. Beek, *OTS* 14, 1965, pp. 155ff.

6. 'God of your father'. Cf. the parallels in Ex. 15.2; 18.4. The question of the historical background of the term and its close parallel in the plural 'God of your fathers' has been much discussed. Cf. the articles of Alt, 'The God of the Fathers', *Essays*, pp. 3ff.; J. P. Hyatt, *op. cit.*; F. M. Cross, *HTR*, *op. cit.*; W. Richter, *op. cit.*, with full bibliography; F. M. Cross, *TWAT* I, pp. 259–79.

7. 'my people'. On the subject of the 'people of God', cf. N. Lohfink, *Festschrift G. von Rad*, Munich 1970, pp. 275–305.

8. 'to deliver them out of the hand of the Egyptians'. There has been much work done on the significance of this formula, including essays by Humbert, Wijngaards, etc. Cf. the bibliography in Richter, *op. cit.*, p. 91.
'land flowing with milk and honey'. Cf. A. Musil, *Arabia Petraea*, Vienna 1907–8, Vol. III, pp. 156ff.
'Canaanites, Hittites, Amorites, Perizzites, Hivites, Jebusites'. Cf. the classic treatment of E. Meyer, *Die Israeliten und Ihre Nachbarstämme*, Halle 1906, reprinted Darmstadt 1967, pp. 328ff. and a modern Bible dictionary such as *IDB* or *BHH*.

14. Cf. the special excursus on this verse in the preceding section.

15. 'This is my name and this my memorial.' The 'memorial' (*zēker*) is often parallel to the 'name' (*šēm*). A distinction is difficult to discern. The *šēm* is the name which has been spoken, while the *zēker* denotes the act of utterance. Cf. O. Grether, *Name und Wort Gottes im AT*, BZAW 64, 1934; B. S. Childs, *Memory and Tradition*, p. 71; W. Schottroff, *'Gedenken' im Alten Orient und im AT*, pp. 292ff.

16. 'God of your fathers'. Cf. note on 3.6.

18. 'three days' journey'. Cf. 5.3.

4.3 'serpent'. Cf. the standard Bible dictionaries.

8. 'sign'. C. A. Keller, *Das Wort OTH*, Basel 1946, pp. 146ff.; F. J. Helfmeyer, *TWAT*, pp. 182–205.

14. 'Aaron, your brother, the Levite'. Cf. the latest treatment by A. H. J. Gunneweg, *Leviten und Priester*, Göttingen 1965, pp. 95ff.

15. Cf. parallel in 7.1.

4. New Testament Context

The New Testament makes several explicit references to the call of Moses. Ex. 3.6 is cited in Matt. 22.32 and in its synoptic parallels (Mark 12.26; Luke 20.37). The New Testament context finds Jesus in a controversy with the Sadducees who attempt to refute the claim for resurrection of the dead by the use of a story which reduced the doctrine to absurdity. Jesus rejects their illustration on two points (v. 29). They do not know the Scriptures, nor the power of God. Then the second point is expanded in v. 30 and the first in vv. 31–32.

In vv. 31f. Jesus cites Ex. 3.6 as a proof text for the resurrection of the dead. Now the point of the scriptural argument has often been characterized as midrashic, and described as a complete caricature of the original meaning of the Old Testament text. D. E. Nineham (*Saint Mark*, Harmondsworth 1963, p. 322) cites Wellhausen's well-known comment that the Old Testament's own deduction from these words would have been precisely the opposite of what the New Testament deduces, namely, that the dead are excluded from all relationship with God. Nineham himself comments that the original sense of God's words did not mean, 'I am the God with whom they *now* stand in relationship', but rather 'with whom they *once* stood in relationship.'

In my judgment, the evidence is clear that the synoptics are reflecting an exegetical tradition which shared many features of first-century Judaism. It has long been recognized, especially since the thorough description by John Lightfoot (on Matt. 22.32, *Works* XI, 1822, pp. 273f.), that there was a traditional rabbinic method of maintaining the resurrection by proof texts from the Torah (cf. B. Sanhedrin 90b, and other passages cited by Billerbeck I, pp. 892ff.). In Matt. 22.32 the various exegetical steps are omitted and only the conclusion, 'He is not God of the dead but of the living', follows immediately on the Exodus text. Now it has been suggested the warrant for the resurrection was found in the present tense of the verb (εἰμί). That this factor played a role is possible, although the failure of the verb to occur in the synoptic parallels considerably weakens the argument. (Bengel rejected the theory outright.) But certainly there is more involved in Matthew's use of the Old Testament than a mechanical reading of the present tense of the verb. Such a theory misrepresents both rabbinic exegesis as well as the New Testament's application of it.

First of all, Matthew complements his proof text with the words: 'You do not know the power of God.' This supplies a *Sachkritik* or material norm, an indication that Jesus is appealing to the reality of which the text speaks and is not limiting himself to an artificial reading of the written text apart from its substance. Again, while it is true that Matthew's use of the Old Testament as evidence for the resurrection goes beyond the Exodus passage, nevertheless, the real issue at stake is whether he has imposed a totally foreign meaning on the ancient text. Surely Nineham's comment is incorrect when he states that the original point of the Exodus passage was to demonstrate that Yahweh was formerly, in the past, the God of the Patriarchs. The entire witness of Genesis (17.4ff.; 28.13ff.; 31.42) focuses on the continuity of God's promises and his covenant which extend to the children of the fathers. Indeed, the fathers continue to live in their sons (Isa. 51.2).

Then again, Wellhausen's attempt to juxtapose a passage from the earliest level of Israel's faith with the New Testament fails to reckon with the development within the Old Testament itself. Such a passage as Ps. 73 is a clear witness to Israel's struggle with the nature of death and its confession that the believer in some way shares in the life of God. Certainly Schniewind (*Das Evangelium nach Matthäus*, Göttingen 1962, p. 223) is closer to the mark when he finds the basic issue in the controversy with the Sadducees to lie in the question of the reality of God. Seen from this perspective the revelation of God to Moses in the bush is a basic witness to this faith.

Acts 7.30 offers another use of Ex. 3 in the context of Stephen's speech (cf. the secondary literature cited on Ex. 2). The call of Moses is referred to in order to demonstrate how God's early messengers were rejected by Israel, whose disobedience culminated in the death of Christ. The use of the Old Testament passage again shows some sign of influence from Hellenistic exegesis. Verse 30 knows, for example, that forty years had passed in Midian (*Tanchuma* on Ex. 2). Moses is described as 'trembling' in v. 31 which is reminiscent of Heb. 12.21. But in general there is a rather free technique of paraphrasing the text which has rearranged the Old Testament sequence. The fact that the shoes are removed after the giving of the name hardly rests on a special exegetical tradition, but fits in more smoothly with the ongoing narrative of the chapter. This New Testament account also shares a feature with Philo and Josephus in playing down Moses' own resistance to God's call.

The New Testament's reference to the name formula of Ex. 3.14 is a complicated subject which goes beyond the scope of this commentary (cf. *TWNT* II, pp. 350ff.; *TDNT* II, pp. 343ff.). However, a few words are in order. Rev. 1.8 refers to God as the one 'who is, and who was, and who is to come' (ὁ ὢν καὶ ὁ ἦν καὶ ὁ ἐρχόμενος). Already within the Old Testament a two-member formula for God's name had been developed. He was the 'first and the last' (Isa. 44.6). Again, Deut. 32.39 and particularly II Isaiah had used the formula of divine self-address '*anî hû*' which the LXX rendered as ἐγώ εἰμι. The Jerusalem Targum certainly approached a three-member formula when paraphrasing Ex. 3.14. God who had once spoken at the creation, now speaks: 'I am He who is, and who shall be.' Rev. 1.8 shares in a similar development which arises from a natural continuation of Ex. 3 and II Isaiah. John's use of the familiar formula ἐγώ εἰμι appears to have had a somewhat different history.

It remains a more difficult question to assess to what extent ontological overtones were attached to the biblical formula. (Naturally much turns on the term 'ontological'.) However, it is of interest to note that at least the vocabulary of the LXX's rendering of Ex. 3.14 (ἐγώ εἰμι ὁ ὤν) was picked up in Rev. 1.8. Certainly Philo developed the Greek translation further in terms of existence: 'Tell them that I am He Who is, that they may learn the difference between what is and what is not and . . . further . . . that no name at all can properly be used of Me, to Whom alone existence belongs' (*Vita Mos.* I. 75). Although this vocabulary was not used in the New Testament, the note which Philo strikes has some real kinship with the witness of II Isaiah and cannot be dismissed as 'alien Greek thinking'.

Finally, it is important to consider the broader question of the New Testament's use of the call of Moses. It is surprising to note what a minor role this event does actually play, particularly since the call of God to both apostle and others is a basic theme of the New Testament (cf. *TWNT* καλέω). Particularly, in Paul's own letters as well as in Acts' description of Paul's call, the Old Testament does provide the background. Paul was set apart for God before his birth (Gal. 1.15; cf. Isa. 49.1ff.; Jer. 1.5). He has a promise of deliverance from 'the people and the Gentiles' which reminds of Jer. 1.18. He is sent to the Gentiles to 'open their eyes that they may turn from darkness to light' (cf. Isa. 42.6, etc.). In other words, it is the prophetic call, especially of Jeremiah and the servant of II Isaiah, which provides the framework for the New Testament. References to Moses' call appear only as they are reflected through the later prophetic experience. Various reasons undoubtedly contributed to this development. Moses' initial resistance to the call did not find a ready place in the New Testament's understanding of apostleship. Moses was called to deliver Israel from a physical slavery, whereas the mission of the servant of II Isaiah focuses largely on a 'spiritual' deliverance. But probably more important was the dominant motif of suffering in the prophets which made this form of the call tradition more suitable for the New Testament's appropriation.

5. *History of Exegesis*

AUGUSTINE, *On the Trinity* V.2f., CCL 50, MPL 42; JACOB BRYANT, 'A Dissertation upon the Divine Mission of Moses', *Observations upon the Plagues*, London 1810, pp.175ff.; J. BUXTORF, 'De nominibus dei hebraicis', *Dissertationes Philologico-theologicae*, Basel 1662, pp.247–281; J. CLERICUS, *Commentarius in Exodum*, Amsterdam 1735, pp.376–379; E. GILSON, *The Spirit of Medieval Philosophy*, London 1936, pp.42ff. and 433f.; CORNELIUS A LAPIDE, *Commentarius in Exodum*; MAIMONIDES, *Guide for the Perplexed* I, 63.

Early Jewish exegesis did not attribute unusual importance to Ex. 3. It saw in the burning bush incident an allegory on the life of Israel, who, although sorely oppressed, could not be consumed. Moses was the good shepherd who first learned how to tend a flock in preparation for his real mission. The revelation of the name revealed the divine attributes under which God would effect his deliverance from Egypt (cf. the typical midrashim collected by *Exodus Rabbah*). Only in the Middle Ages did the philosophical debate on the nature of being begin seriously to involve Jewish commentators (Maimonides, *Guide* I.63).

For the Christian church the situation was very different. Few passages lent themselves so admirably to the central theological concerns, of both the early and medieval church. As a result the number of treatises on ch. 3 are overwhelming in sheer number (cf. the bibliographical information in Lapide and Gilson). Most of the major church Fathers left at least one treatise on the subject. First of all, the whole christological problem emerged in the revelation at the bush. Who was this 'angel' who appeared in the fire in the lowly bush, who spoke for God in executing the redemption from Egypt? For most of the early Fathers the identity with the Son was completely obvious (Eusebius, *Praep. Ev.* XI, 9ff.; Justin, *Trypho* 59–60; Irenaeus, *Adv. Haer.* III.6; IV.10; Ambrose, *De fide* I.13).

However, the issue took a different turn with Augustine who continued to return to the problem throughout his life (cf. *De Fide et Symbolo* IV.6). Augustine was not adverse to the identification of the angel with Christ, but soon developed a more sophisticated trinitarian interpretation, particularly under the pressure of the Arian controversy. Identifying Christ directly with the angel led to the danger of seeing him as a created being. Therefore, the angel was regarded as only representing the Son and speaking in his name.

Finally, it was the philosophical implications of the passage which evoked such intense and lasting interest in Ex. 3.14. Obviously the LXX's translation of the verse aided in turning the discussion in this direction. It was, therefore, not too surprising for Eusebius (*op. cit.*) to argue at great length that Plato had borrowed his doctrine of being from Moses because Moses had already taught that God's being is eternal without beginning. Augustine developed his understanding of God as the only unchangeable essence. 'Other things that are called essences or substances admit of accidents. But there can be no accident of this kind in respect to God . . . who is the only unchangeable essence to whom certainly Being itself belongs' (*Trin.* V. 2: cf. Aquinas, *Summa Theol.*, Prima Pars, 13.11). Gilson summarizes the significance of Ex. 3.14 for the schoolmen: 'Exodus lays down the principle from which henceforth the whole of Christian philosophy will be suspended. From this moment it is understood once and for all that the proper name of God is being and that . . . this name denotes His very essence' (*op. cit.*, p. 51).

The Reformers continued to treat the passage within the exegetical tradition of the Middle Ages, but with some remarkable changes of emphasis. Luther offers, along with several sermons on Ex. 3, an explicit allegorical interpretation ('Allegoria oder geistliche Deutung dieses Andern Capitels', WA XVI, pp. 80–89). He passes over many of the traditional features of the older allegory, but then suggests that allegory is a useful device if it is firmly anchored in Christ. Clearly the christological emphasis lies at the heart of Luther's interpretation and it allows him to hang loosely on the traditional Christian exegesis. In the revelation of the divine name Luther hears the notes of the first commandment: 'I am God on whom you must fully rely and not trust on other creatures.' Human reason cannot discover God. He alone makes his name known (WA XVI, p. 49).

Calvin offers a highly sophisticated exegesis of Ex. 3. On the one hand, he affirms that 'the ancient teachers of the church have rightly understood that the eternal Son of God is so called in respect to his office as Mediator, which he figuratively bore from the beginning . . .' But on the other hand, Calvin is concerned to maintain the importance of the incarnation at which time only Christ assumed his office. In the end, Calvin moves toward an ontological interpretation of Christ's role in the Old Testament, insisting that the Old Testament saints 'never had any communication with God except through the promised Mediator'. Furthermore, in his interpretation of Ex. 3.14 Calvin focuses the meaning on God's divine glory, which is self-existent and eternal. He quickly distances himself from Plato's concept of divine being because it fails to do justice to God's power and governance of all things. 'All things in heaven and earth derive their essence from him who only truly is' (*Exodus, ad loc.*).

Finally, Zwingli (*Annot. in Exodum*) is significant in his attempt to hold firmly together God's attributes of Being with his role of creator of life and new being: 'qui omnibus tum *esse* tum *vita* est, omnia sustinet, omnia regit' (p. 211). Of particular interest is his citing of Isa. 40 as a commentary on Ex. 3.14. Clearly among the reformers the discussion of God's being as a philosophical problem has shifted to focus now on the function of God's being in ruling, governing, and redeeming his world.

The Post-Reformation period up to the rise of the historical critical school appears to have offered very little new in respect to this chapter. Reformed scholars, such as Piscator and Drusius, seem now to combine features from all the various previous periods of exegesis, including the arguments of the Greek Fathers and the classic Jewish commentators, but without either the philosophical interest of the medieval period or the theological cutting edge of the Reformers (e.g. Ainsworth, Patrick, Clarke). Often the burning bush is seen as an allegory on the church under fire. Christ, in some modified form, is identified with the angel and many of the traditional complexities of interpreting 3.14 are rehearsed. Jacob Bryant's learned treatise (*op. cit.*) stands as somewhat of an exception to the general trend in this period. He sees the formula in v. 14 as a polemic against the false worship of the Egyptians and offers an elaborate philological and *religionsgeschichtliche* defense of his thesis.

The critical period opened up a whole new set of problems by recognizing the historical dimensions of the text. Since these issues have already been discussed in an earlier section, it will not be necessary to review them again. However, there are certain characteristic theological interests which have emerged in the modern period deserving brief mention. Already J. Clericus (*ad loc.*) had warned against reading Plato's philosophy into Ex. 3.14. In the contemporary period it has become a hallmark of theology to reject, by and large, the history of exegesis as being misled by philosophical interests. Plastaras (*The God of Exodus*, pp. 94f.) offers a classic example of modern biblical theology when he writes: 'It is difficult to translate Exodus 3.14 into western language because in the process we inevitably impose upon the Hebrew text categories of being and essence which were quite foreign to the Hebrew mind. The ancient Greek and Latin translations of the Old Testament unconsciously but radically changed the meaning of the Hebrew text . . . in terms of essential being . . . In fact the name Yahweh "defines" God in terms of active presence.'

Plastaras reflects an important concern in his emphasis in recovering the original meaning of the text in its Hebrew setting. However, it remains a real question to what extent one philosophical stance has been substituted for another. Surely, it is not a self-evident historical fact that the ancient Hebrews had no concept of being, but only action (cf. Barr, *The Semantics of Biblical Language*, London and New York 1961, pp. 58ff.). A similar oversimplification to be avoided would be constructing a history of development from the early Hebrew meaning of God's name as 'becoming' to a later growth of a concept of being caused by the infiltration of Greek elements (cf. R. Dentan, *The Knowledge of God in Ancient Israel*, New York 1968, p. 131). Of course, once the simple contrast between Greek and Hebrew mentality is called into question, then the task of seeing the whole range of alternative interpretations throughout the history of exegesis takes on new significance.

6. *Theological Reflection*

The major witness of Ex. 3 lies in the revelation by God of himself to Moses as that divine reality who had already made himself known in the past to the Fathers and who promised to execute his redemptive will toward Israel in the future. The New Testament witness is an attempt to understand this same revelation of the divine reality in relation to the eschatological event of Jesus Christ. Both testaments reflect on the nature of God whose reality has not been discovered but revealed, and whose revelation of himself defines his being in terms of his redemptive work.

Both testaments are forced to speak of God in terms of his activity which encompasses both the past, the present, and the future. It is not an unknown God who encounters Moses, but the covenant God who has long since spoken to the Patriarchs. Even the name Yaḫweh points to the future orientation of God's relationship with his people. Who he is and what he does will emerge in the history which yet lies ahead. Likewise, God who has revealed himself in Jesus Christ is eschatological in character and his being spans the gap separating creation from new creation.

In the history of Christian theology most of the major theological problems have entered into the discussion of Ex. 3. In the early and medieval periods the interest focused on the issue of ontology and divine reality; in recent years on revelation as history or history as revelation. The amazing fact is how seminal this one passage continues to be for each new generation. It lies in the nature of dogmatic theology to go beyond the biblical witness and to draw out the critical implications of its testimony for the modern church in the language of its culture. Perhaps the biblical theologian can best serve in this case by attempting to sketch some of the parameters of the two testaments:

1. The being and activity of God are not played against each other, but included within the whole reality of the divine revelation. God's nature is neither static being, nor eternal presence, nor simply dynamic activity. Rather, the God of Israel makes known his being in specific historical moments and confirms in his works his ultimate being by redeeming a covenant people.

2. History is the arena of God's self-revelation, but history receives its definition in terms of what this God is doing. God's redemptive will for Israel is not tied to a philosophy of history, nor can the resurrection of Jesus Christ be encompassed within any overarching historical rubrics since his work is that of calling non-being into existence (Rom. 4.17). Thus the concept of history can be just as much a theological trap as ontology if it is divorced from the divine reality which appeared in its fullness in the incarnated Lord, who is both 'first and last'.

3. The divine reality of which this passage speaks encounters Moses as well as the writers of the New Testament in a particular historical situation and seeks to evoke a response of obedience within God's plan. The story of Exodus 3 is characteristic of the biblical approach in joining the act of God's self-disclosure with the call for commitment

from its recipient. Revelation is not information about God and his nature, but an invitation to trust in the one whose self-disclosure is a foretaste of the promised inheritance. The future for the community of faith is not an unknown leap into the dark because the Coming One accompanies the faithful toward that end.

THE RETURN TO EGYPT

4.18–6.1

Y. BLAU, 'The Ḥatan Damîm (Ex. 4.24–26),' (Hebrew) *Tarbiz* 26, 1956, pp. 1ff.; J. COPPENS, 'La prétendue agression nocturne de Jahvé contre Moïse, Séphorah et leur fils', *ETL* 18, 1941, pp. 68ff.; W. DUMBRELL, 'Exodus 4:24–26: a Textual Re-examination', *HTR* 65, 1972, pp. 285–290; G. FOHRER, *Überlieferung und Geschichte des Exodus*, 1964, pp. 45–9; J. FRISCHMUTH, 'De Circumcisione Zippore ad Exod. IV:24', *Thesaurus Theologico-Philologicus* I, Amsterdam 1701, pp. 208–95; H. GRESSMANN, *Mose und seine Ẕeit*, 1913, pp. 56–61; J. DE GROOT, 'The Story of the Bloody Husband', *OTS* 2, 1943, pp. 11–17; J. HEHN, 'Der Blutbräutigam', *ẔAW* 50, 1932, pp. 1–8; R. JUNKER, 'Der Blutbräutigam', *Nötscher Festschrift*, BBB 1, 1950, pp. 120–8; H. KOSMALA, 'The "Bloody Husband"', *VT* 12, 1962, pp. 14–28; E. MEYER, *Die Israeliten und ihre Nachbarstämme*, Halle 1906, p. 59; P. MIDDLEKOOP, 'The Significance of the Story of the "Bloody Husband" (Ex. 4, 24–26)', *South East Asia Journal of Theology* 8, 1966/7, pp. 34–8; J. MORGENSTERN, 'The "Bloody Husband"(?) (Exod. 4:24–26) Once Again', *HUCA* 34, 1963, pp. 35–70; C. F. NIMS, 'Bricks without Straw?', *BA* 13, 1950, pp. 22–8; J. M. SASSON, 'Circumcision in the Ancient Near East', *JBL* 85, 1966, pp. 473–6; H. SCHMID, 'Mose, der Blutbräutigam', *Judaica* 22, 1966, pp. 113–18; F. SIERKSMA, 'Quelques Remarques sur la Circoncision en Israel', *OTS* 9, 1951, pp. 136–69; S. TALMON, 'Ḥatan-Damîm' (Hebrew), *Eretz Israel* 3, 1954, pp. 93–6; B. UGOLINI, *Thesaurus Anti-quitatum Sacrarum*, Venice 1744ff.; Vol. XXII contains articles on circumcision by J. Spencer, S. Daylinger, J. Quandt, and H. B. Gedaeus; G. VERMES, 'Baptism and Jewish Exegesis: New Light from Ancient Sources', *NTS* 4, 1957–8, pp. 308–19.

4 [18]Then Moses returned to Jether, his father-in-law, and said to him, 'Let me please go back to my kinsmen in Egypt to see whether they are still living.' Jethro said to Moses, 'Go with my good wishes.' [19]And the LORD said to Moses in Midian, 'Go back to Egypt, for all the men who wanted to kill you are dead.' [20]So Moses took his wife and sons, mounted them on an ass, and went back to the land of Egypt. And Moses took the rod of God in his hand.

21 The LORD said to Moses, 'When you return to Egypt, see that you perform before Pharaoh all the marvels that I have placed within

your power. For my part I will harden his heart so that he will not let the people go. [22]Then you shall say to Pharaoh: "Thus says the LORD, Israel is my first-born son, [23]and I say to you, 'Let my son go that he may worship me.' If you refuse to let him go, then I will slay your first-born son."'

24 Then it happened, at an encampment on the way, the LORD met him and sought to kill him. [25]Then Zipporah took a piece of flint, and cut off her son's foreskin and touched his feet with it, saying, 'You are a blood-bridegroom to me!' [26]So he let him alone. At that time she said 'blood-bridegroom' in reference to circumcision.

27 The LORD said to Aaron, 'Go, meet Moses in the wilderness.' So he went and met him at the mountain of God and kissed him. [28]And Moses told Aaron about all the things with which the LORD had commissioned him and all the signs with which he had instructed him. [29]Then Moses and Aaron went and gathered together all the elders of the Israelites. [30]And Aaron repeated all the words that the LORD had spoken to Moses, and he performed the signs before the people. [31]The people were convinced. When they heard that the LORD had visited the Israelites and that he had seen their misery, they bowed in worship.

5 [1]Afterwards Moses and Aaron went to Pharaoh and said, 'Thus says the LORD, the God of Israel: "Let my people go that they may hold a feast for me in the wilderness"'. [2]But Pharaoh said, 'Who is the LORD that I should obey him and let Israel go? I do not know the LORD, and I will surely not let Israel go.[3]They replied, 'The God of the Hebrews has met us. We request to go on a three days' journey into the wilderness to sacrifice to the LORD our God, or else he will strike us with pestilence or the sword.' [4]But the king of Egypt said to them, 'Moses and Aaron, what do you mean by distracting the people from their work? Get back to your jobs!' [5]And Pharaoh said: 'They are already more numerous than the native population and you would have them stop their jobs!'

6 That same day Pharaoh ordered the overseers and their foremen, saying, [7]'You are no longer to supply the people with straw for making bricks as heretofore; let them go and gather straw for themselves. [8]But impose on them the same quota of bricks which they were making up to now. Do not reduce it for they are lazy. This is the reason why they keep crying: "We want to go and offer sacrifices to our God." [9]Let the work be intensified on the men and let them work at it and not pay attention to empty talk.'

10 So the overseers and the foremen of the people went out and said to the people, 'Thus says Pharaoh, "I will not give you any straw. [11]You are to go and get straw wherever you can find it; but there will be no reduction whatsoever in your work."' [12]So the people dispersed in all the land of Egypt to gather stubble for straw, [13]while the overseers kept after them saying, 'You must finish your work, the same amount

each day as when you had straw given you.' [14]Then the foremen of the Israelites whom Pharaoh's overseers had set over them were beaten, and questioned, 'Why have you not finished the prescribed number of bricks either yesterday or today?'

15 Then the Israelite foremen came and complained to Pharaoh, 'Why do you treat your servants like this? [16]No straw is supplied to your servants, yet you keep demanding of us: "Make bricks!" Thus your servants are being beaten and you wrong your own people.' [17]He replied, 'You are lazy, lazy! That's why you say, "We want to go and sacrifice to the LORD." [18]Now get on with your work. No straw will be supplied you, but you must deliver your quota of bricks!' [19]Now the Israelite foremen realized that they were in trouble, when they said: 'You are not to reduce your daily quota of bricks.' [20]Then as they were leaving Pharaoh's presence, they found Moses and Aaron, waiting to meet them, [21]and they said to them: 'May the LORD see and punish you for making us obnoxious before Pharaoh and his subjects – putting a sword in their hands to kill us.'

22 Then Moses returned to the LORD and said, 'O LORD, why have you brought evil on this people? Why did you ever send me? [23]For since I first came to Pharaoh to speak in your name, it has gotten worse for this people and you have done nothing to deliver your people.'
6 [1]Then the LORD said to Moses, 'You will soon see what I will do to Pharaoh. Because of a strong hand he will send them out, and because of a strong hand he will drive them out of his land.'

1. *Textual and Philological Notes*

4.18. 'Jether'. A variation in the spelling of the same proper name occurs elsewhere in the OT. Dillmann cites the reference to Neh.6.1, 6.

20. *bānāw*, 'sons'. Many commentators (Dillmann, Bäntsch, Driver) hold that a singular form was original (2.22; 4.25) which was later altered to account for 18.24. This explanation is possible, but the fact that this is a conjecture without support from the versions should be considered seriously when reaching a decision.

24–26. Cf. J. Hehn (*op. cit.*) for a detailed handling of the textual problems. The chief textual variations are as follows: v.24 LXX: ἄγγελος κυρίου = *mal'ak YHWH*; v.25, LXX: καὶ προσέπεσεν πρὸς τοὺς πόδας ('and she fell at his feet') for MT *wattagga* *l^eraglāw*; v.25, LXX: καὶ εἶπεν ἔστη τὸ αἷμα τῆς περιτομῆς τοῦ παιδίου μου ('and said "The blood of the circumcision of my son stood" '); however, A ΣΘ are all closer to the MT; cf. Σ: καὶ ἀψαμένη τῶν ποδῶν αὐτοῦ εἶπεν ὅτι νυμφίος αἱμάτων σύ μοι (cf. F. Field, *Origenis Hexaplorum* I, Oxford 1875, pp.87f.); v.26, LXX^A (>LXX^B): καὶ ἀπῆλθεν ἀπ' αὐτοῦ διότι εἶπεν ἔστη τὸ αἷμα τῆς περιτομῆς τοῦ παιδίου μου ('and he departed from him because she said: "The blood of the circumcision of my son stood" ').

24. NAB softens the Hebrew by its use of the subjunctive: 'would have killed him'.
25. *ḥᵃṭan-dāmîm* = 'blood-bridegroom'. Cf. the bibliography for the various attempts to explain the term. Most recently Kosmala (*op. cit.*) defends the view that the term is actually Arabic and therefore to be translated 'a blood-circumcised one'. Cf. the exegesis for the reasons why this is not possible.
26. Several conjectural emendations have been suggested which must be considered in the larger context of the exegesis. Gressmann and Ehrlich suggest reading *'āmᵉrû* instead of *'āmᵉrāh*. Also *lammûlîm* ('to the circumcised') instead of *lammûlōṯ* (cf. *BH*³). The variations among the modern translations of v. 26 are also significant (cf. AmTr, RSV, NJPS, NEB, NAB).
On the use of *'āz* with the perfect, G–K § 107c. On the use of the *lamed* in the final word with the meaning 'with reference to', cf. G–K §119u and König, *Lehrgebäude* III, §271c.
27. The difficulty in the sequence of the narrative cannot be avoided by reading a pluperfect tense for the initial verb. Cf. S. R. Driver, *Hebrew Tenses*³, §76; König, *Lehrgebäude* III, §142.
5.5. The logic of the MT is not fully clear: 'the people of the land are numerous and you would . . .' The LXX alleviates the difficulty by omitting reference to 'the land'. The Samar. reads *mēʿam*, 'more numerous than the people of the land'. The Samar. reading is supported by the meaning it gives to the technical term 'people of the land' which is consistent with the early pre-exilic period. Cf. R. de Vaux, *Ancient Israel*, pp. 70ff.
9. Instead of the MT *wᵉyaʿᵃśû* the Samar. (supported by the LXX and Pesh.) reads *wᵉyišᵉû* which some modern commentators accept as original (Bäntsch, etc.).
13. The versions improve the sense greatly by the addition of the phrase *nittān lāḵem* ('given you') which was probably original.
16. The last phrase in the MT is difficult. G–K §74g. interprets *ḥātā'ṯ* as a 2 sg. masc. verb, but then one would expect a preposition to follow. Dillmann apparently takes the verb as 3 fem., but then the sense is unclear. *Σ* reads the equivalent of *wᵉḥaṭṭā'ṯ ʿimmāḵ* 'the fault lies with you'. Probably the most satisfactory solution is to follow the LXX which reads ἀδικήσεις οὖν τὸν λαόν σου which is the equivalent to *wᵉḥāṭā'tā lᵉ ʿammeḵā* 'you sin against your people'.
6.1. It seems unwise to follow *BH*³ and to correct the text on the basis of the common Deuteronomic idiom.

2. *Literary, Form-Critical, and Traditio-Historical Problems*

A. *The Scope of the Unit*

The beginning and the ending of the larger sections in this portion of the book of Exodus are not immediately evident. The story moves along without sharply defined chapters. There is the danger of laying too much emphasis on determining the scope of the section which probably did not play too significant a role for the ancients. However, some suggested divisions are better than others and the alternatives should be briefly reviewed.

The problem of deciding where the preceding section ended has already been discussed in the previous chapter. The reasons for preferring to end the section at 4.17 have been presented, which resulted in the decision to assign the beginning of the new section to 4.18. Most commentators recognize a break at this point, although recently the NEB has proposed a division at v. 19. In terms of content the narrative turns its attention to Moses' return to Egypt which sets it apart from the revelation at the bush. But how far does the unit extend? In 5.1 Moses has arrived back in Egypt and begun his negotiations with Pharaoh. For this reason a majority of commentators start a new section in 5.1 and regard 4.18–31 as a short literary bridge. In my judgment, 5.1 should not be regarded as the beginning of a section. In approximately forty occurrences of the word $we^{,}ahar$ ('afterwards') in the Hebrew Bible, there is only one clear instance in which it marks an introduction to a new section, namely Ezra 7.1. But this one case can also be discounted as an example of a late Hebrew idiom which replaced the usual narrative introduction in pre-exilic literature (cf. Gen. 48.1; Josh. 1.1, etc.). In sum, the unit extends from 4.18 to the obvious break after 6.1 and includes the return to Egypt and the initial failure in achieving the release of the Israelites.

B. *Source Criticism*

The majority of critics find the two older Pentateuchal sources represented in the chapter, namely J and E. The presence of a rather clear doublet in 4.18 and 19 is evidence for the lack of complete literary unity. However, there is uncertainty as to the exact extent of each source. The sequence of the narrative in 4.18–27 is not fully in order, but does not seem easily disentangled by source criticism. Two major literary alternatives emerge. Either one attempts a rather detailed source division between J and E which often becomes extremely minute (cf. Bäntsch on 4.29–30 or 5.1–5), or one reckons with one major source, usually J, with secondary expansions accounting for the unevenness (Noth). The important exegetical issues in the chapter hardly seem affected by which alternative solution one chooses. Fohrer's attempt (*op. cit.*, pp.47ff.) to isolate a 'nomadic source' in these chapters has not called forth much positive response.

C. *History of Tradition*

In the present form of the narrative the section 4.18–6.1 separates the revelation of the divine name in Midian (3.1ff.) from the revelation in Egypt (6.2ff.). The section also brings Moses back to Egypt where he encounters the stubborn resistance of Pharaoh which calls forth the plagues (7.8ff.). In my judgment, this section does not reflect the most ancient layer of Exodus tradition such as that found in the revelation of the name and the plagues. Rather, it assumes its present shape in the process of forming a continuous narrative. However, at the same time it is important to recognize that precisely this section reflects a remarkably accurate historical knowledge of Egyptian slave-labor organization and its building techniques (cf. Nims, *op. cit.*). Moreover, the antiquity of such stories as that in 4.44-26 is unquestionable.

In his Exodus commentary Noth has attempted to isolate a more ancient tradition (5.3-19) in which Moses does not appear, but the Israelites themselves deal collectively with Pharaoh. He even finds a fragment of an older tradition which began the deliverance from Egypt with a meeting of Yahweh with his people in Egypt and which resulted in his summoning them to a feast in the wilderness. In my judgment, Noth's evidence for the theory is extremely fragile and reflects his tendency to assign the figure of Moses to a secondary level of the tradition whenever possible. Noth's method does not give adequate place to stylistic variations within a literary composition which would far better account for such things as the plural form in 5.3 than an alleged variant oral tradition.

D. *The Special Problems of Ex. 4.24-26*

Few texts contain more problems for the interpreter than these few verses which have continued to baffle throughout the centuries. The difficulties cover the entire spectrum of possible problems. First of all, the passage seems to have little connection with its larger context. Why should Yahweh suddenly seek to kill his messenger? No reason is given for the assault. Again, the reaction of Zipporah is without explanation. How did she know what to do? Furthermore, the lack of antecedents throughout the passage render it difficult to specify the agents involved. Whom did Yahweh seek to kill in v. 24. Moses or his son? Again, in 25 the antecedents to the prepositions are uncertain: 'she touched his feet and said, "You are to me a blood-bridegroom."' Is the same person intended throughout the verse and who then is meant? Then again, what is the meaning of the term *ḥ^atan dāmîm* ('blood-bridegroom'?), and how does it relate to the circumcision of the child? Finally, how is one to account for the irrational, almost demonic atmosphere of the passage in which the blood seems to play an apotropaic role?

The ancient versions offer the earliest attempts to solve these innumerable exegetical problems (cf. Vermes, *op. cit.* for a careful study of this material). Already in the LXX a clear tradition of interpretation had developed. First, Yahweh himself has been replaced by his angel as the one who did the attacking. Secondly, Zipporah's role has been altered. She falls at the angel's feet and announces that the rite has been performed with the words: 'the blood of the circumcision of my son stood (or is staunched).' Vermes emphasizes the sacrificial meaning of the words; the blood shed by his wife saved Moses' life. The Targum of Onkelos makes the sacrificial character of the circumcision even more explicit: 'Then she said, "Were it not for the blood of this circumcision, my husband would have merited execution."' Likewise the Fragmentary Targum: 'May the blood of this circumcision atone for the guilt of my husband,' and Neophiti I: 'How blessed is the blood of this (circumcision)!'

Rabbinic midrashim (*Mekilta*, Exodus Rabbah) developed the idea that Moses had failed to circumcise the child by the eighth day. Various reasons were offered for the omission – he had been prevented by his father-in-law (Targum Onkelos, Neofiti I, Jer. Targum); he had been negligent for an hour – but all focused on the seriousness of the failure to perform the rite which almost cost him his life. The classic medieval Jewish commentators continued, by and large, within this exegetical tradition, and they attributed the attack to a sin on Moses' part. The majority of Christian commentators right up to the nineteenth century followed in this same tradition, naturally with some minor variations (Lyra, Münster, Drusius, Calvin, etc.; but cf. Calmet for an adumbration of the later critical approach).

With the coming of the historical-critical period and the discovery that the passage reflected a long history of development prior to its present form, the traditional interpretation which had connected the incident with Moses' failure to circumcise his child was rejected as inadequate. It was argued that the sudden attack had not been clarified. Moreover, there was nothing in the text to allow the interpreter to postulate that Moses had disobeyed God, especially since the command respecting circumcision in Gen. 17 was now dated in the post-exilic period.

From the innumerable attempts to recover the original meaning of the passage which have been advanced during the last hundred years, several classic critical theories have emerged as the most serious options in understanding the history of tradition. First of all, Wellhausen (*Reste arabischen Heidentums*[2], Berlin 1897, p.175) argued that the story was an attempt to explain how circumcision, which was originally a puberty rite, was transferred from adulthood to childhood in Israel. Accordingly, Moses had not been circumcised and was therefore attacked. Zipporah circumcised her son as a substitute and established a permanent change in the rite by its successful outcome. Although this interpretation has a certain coherence and has been frequently accepted by other scholars, it is not without its problems. First, the theory that the tradition functioned originally as an etiology remains a reconstruction which can be posited, but not demonstrated from the text itself. There is simply no evidence by which to trace the history of circumcision within Israel. Again, the interpretation of 'bloody bridegroom' is not obvious from the theory in spite of the Arabic cognate *ḥatana* by which Wellhausen sought to join bridegroom and circumcision. *Ḥātān* never means husband in reference to a wife, but only in reference to one's in-laws (Greenberg, *op. cit.*, p.114).

There is a second attempt to explain the original meaning of the passage which was developed especially by E. Meyer and H. Gressmann along the lines of oral tradition following in the footsteps of Gunkel (cf. bibliography). Accordingly, the story originally concerned a local *numen* who claimed the *ius primae noctis* from a bride on her wedding night. When the woman recognized the peril, she circumcised her husband, touched the nakedness of the demon with the foreskin, and exclaimed 'You are my blood-bridegroom'. Thus she deceived the attacker into releasing her husband. The story was a cult etiology which explained the origin of adult circumcision as a sacrifice to the deity and a protection for the bridegroom. However, the elements of speculation with this theory are even greater than the previous hypothesis. Most of the key features are supplied by the theory itself, rather than from the biblical text. In fact, Gressmann is forced to make several major emendations to support his proposal (cf. his treatment of v.25). Moreover, the alleged manner by which the demon was deceived seems particularly unconvincing.

Finally, there is the Midianite theory of H. Kosmala which is compatible with proposals made by Morgenstern and Fohrer.

Accordingly, the circumcision story deals with the preservation of the first-born son. A Midianite deity sought to claim the child. Zipporah performed the blood rite and pronounced the formula, which according to its original Midianite – that is Arabic – meaning, designated the child as a 'blood-circumcised one'. The deity, on seeing the blood, disappeared and the first-born was saved. Again, several objections come to mind. First of all, the Arabic root *ḥatana* does not just mean 'circumcise' by itself, but denotes the act of circumcising the bridegroom which is an essential part of the verb. Secondly, from a history of traditions perspective there is no evidence to support such a Midianite tradition. What circle within Israel would have treasured a 'Zipporah cycle'? It is far from obvious that an Arabic word would have been transmitted in the way Kosmala suggests. In sum, the theory raises as many problems as it solves.

It seems quite obvious that a serious impasse has been reached in the effort to reconstruct the original meaning of the story. The attempts at tracing the earlier history have made some contribution to recovering certain dimensions of the prehistory of the text even when its complete recovery has not been successful. However, in my judgment, there have been several methodological errors. First, few have been willing to recognize the limits in their evidence when attempting to trace the history of tradition. As a result the speculative elements in the reconstruction run far beyond the historical evidence. Again, the dominant concern with the 'original' meaning has obscured the present function of the passage in the Exodus narrative. Failure to understand the redactor's intention with the text has resulted in the loss of this major witness.

What then can one say about the present function of this text in the light of its redaction? The passage is only loosely joined with what has preceded. The initial *wayyᵉhî* sets it off as a separate incident, but the antecedent to the pronoun 'him' in v.24 is left unspecified. It would seem most probable that Moses is to be understood as the one under attack, because the son is specified in the following verse, which otherwise would not have been necessary. However, the issue is not fully clear. Zipporah then circumcises the child and touches 'his legs'. Again the antecedent is unspecified. Next she speaks: 'You are to me a blood-bridegroom'. The significance of the words and to whom they are addressed remain enigmatic. What is clear, however, is the effect of her action: 'he let him alone.' That is to say, the attack by Yahweh on the life of the person ceased.

The story itself ends in 26a. The most significant redactional element is found in the statement of 26b. How one evaluates the entire passage hangs to a large extent on one's analysis of these final words: 'At that time (then) she said, "A blood-bridegroom" in relation to circumcision'.

There are several grammatical points to be observed. First, the adverb 'āz has a variety of meanings within the Old Testament. It can designate a time in the past (or future) by relating it to another event in terms of temporal sequence (Josh. 20.6; Judg. 8.3). Again, the adverb can denote a past time which is related to another event in terms of a logical sequence (II Kings 13.19; Ps. 119.6). Then again, the adverb can specify a time in the past which is not in a sequence. This reference can be to an indefinite time in the past (damals) as in Gen. 4.26. Or the adverb can refer to a definite time in the past. In Josh. 14.11 the 'āz designates specifically 'the day Moses sent me'. In Ex. 15.14 the adverb refers to the conquest of Canaan.

How is the adverb used in Ex. 4.26? It seems quite clear from the context that the word does not denote a temporal sequence as 'after this'. This would imply that Zipporah spoke the words a second time after the first utterance of the words had secured his release (v. 25). Grammatically one would expect we'āz. Also it is most unlikely that Zipporah repeated her words with an explanation 'because of circumcision'. Rather the clause in v. 26b is an editorial reference by the story's narrator to her words in v. 25b.

A more likely alternative is to see a logical sequence implied. Thus the LXX renders the sentence: 'He departed from him because (διότι) she said . . .' But for such a construction Hebrew normally uses the conjunction kî. Moreover, this interpretation has difficulty making sense of the additional element in the clause, 'because of circumcision'. The LXX omits this final word which seems, however, to contain the reason for the repetition of the enigmatic expression.

Another option is between interpreting the adverb as designating a specific time in the past, or as an indefinite one. However, a reference to an indefinite time in the past is only possible if one can translate the verb in a frequentative sense: 'At that time women used to say . . .' (cf. NEB margin). But since the verb is perfect and not in the plural, this does not seem possible. In sum, the adverb refers to a specific time in the past, namely 'at that time' when Zipporah had first said, 'You are a blood-bridegroom to me' in v. 25b.

The next grammatical problem turns on the function of the

preposition *le* in the word *lammûlōṭ*. Gesenius-Kautzsch (§ 119u) indicates the use of the preposition in the sense of 'in reference to' particularly after a *verbum dicendi* such as Gen. 20.13. Moreover, König (*Lehrgebäude* III, §271c.d) with specific reference to Ex. 4.26 offers several excellent Arabic parallels in which the preposition *le* carries the meaning 'in reference to' following a citation of a previous remark. The sentence, therefore, makes good sense and should not be emended as has been often proposed (Gressmann, *BH³*, etc.). The sentence reads: 'At that time she had said "blood-bridegroom" in reference to circumcision.'

What are the implications which can be drawn from this sentence? First, the sentence functions as a redactional comment and is not itself part of the story. It seeks to explain the meaning of the phrase which had been used within the story. When Zipporah used the term *ḥᵃtan damîm*, it was in reference to circumcision. In what way does this observation help? It seems evident that even when the story was being edited, the phrase 'blood-bridegroom' already presented problems. The comment does not attempt to paraphrase the terms in order to illuminate its meaning. Nor does it offer any explanation as to whom the phrase was addressed. Rather, it serves only to relate the enigmatic expression to the rite of circumcision. It is not at all clear that the redactor understood any longer what the phrase meant. His comment simply set it in relationship to the institution of circumcision. Whatever it meant, it belonged to the rite.

The effect of this redaction is twofold. It focused the whole emphasis of the passage on circumcision. Whatever Zipporah had done – she had cut off the foreskin, touched his 'feet', pronounced the words – comprised the act of circumcision, and this is what saved Moses. Again, the redactional comment served to eliminate other possible interpretations of what had transpired. Indeed all the elements which modern scholars have detected in the story, such as the apotropaic use of the blood, a puberty rite on the bridegroom, a sacrificial offering, are drained of their independent life and lumped together as part of circumcision. From the redactor's point of view, the story does not explain the origin of circumcision, but rather circumcision explains the meaning of Zipporah's action. This interpretation is, of course, the exact opposite of the etiological.

For almost a hundred years it has been commonplace to assume that the tradition of Ex. 4.24–26 functioned originally as an etiology. The theories of Wellhausen and Gressmann have this feature in common. Indeed the majority of modern translations have implied the etiological interpretation, often unconsciously. Nevertheless, on the basis of form-critical evidence there is no support for this interpretation unless one completely reshapes the text in order to bring it into line with a preconceived pattern. Of the some hundred examples of the occurrence of the adverb '$\bar{a}z$ in the Hebrew Bible, nowhere does it function as part of an etiological formula. Even when the adverb implies a logical sequence, the connection is completely different from the causal principle found in such a genuine etiological formula as '*al-ken* ('therefore') (cf. Fichtner, *VT* 6, 1956, pp. 372–396).

Finally, one can raise the question as to how the redactor understood the whole passage. As we have seen, the passage itself nowhere explains explicitly why Yahweh attacked Moses. It was only clear that what Zipporah did rescued him from death. The redactor's contribution was to subsume all of Zipporah's action under the rubric of circumcision. It was not the blood in itself which had power, nor the sign upon the legs, nor even the words which she had spoken. Rather all these elements were part of the rite of circumcision which was known to Israel. Nevertheless, the effect of this redaction is at least to imply that it was the failure of Moses to have the child circumcised which evoked the attack. Otherwise why would the circumcision of the child have spared his life? In sum, the traditional interpretation of the 'pre-critical' period reflects, to a large extent, the redactor's perspective. What is surprising is to recognize that circumcision had already attained such an importance within Israel at this early date.

4. *Old Testament Context*

[4.18–20] The section is closely joined to the preceding call of Moses. Moses has been ordered back to Egypt to deliver Israel in spite of his great resistance. Now he returns to take his leave from Jethro, his father-in-law. He informs Jethro that he wishes to visit his kinsmen to 'see whether they are still alive'. This seems to be a Hebrew idiom and includes the general welfare of a person (Gen. 45.3). Commentators have continued to puzzle over the fact that Moses does not communicate to Jethro his real reason for leaving. The medieval Jewish commentators speak of Moses' modesty. Cassuto tries to be more contemporary in his comment: 'diplomatic negotiations cannot be done openly' (p. 53). Calvin offers a more profound insight in suggesting that men have difficulty speaking of God, and talk more freely of just human emotions. However one decides, Moses secures Jethro's blessing. Jethro reappears in the narrative only after the deliverance from Egypt has been accomplished (Ex. 18) and their greeting confirms their mutual affection.

In v. 19 God again orders Moses to return to Egypt. The command seems redundant and offers some friction with the preceding verse. However, the second part of the sentence does supply an important element in the narrative by referring to the death of those who had once threatened Moses' life (2.15). It offers a reason why no mention is made of Moses' earlier life. When he returns to Egypt, he appears before Pharaoh, neither as the adopted son of the Egyptian princess, nor as a fugitive from the law. Rather, he makes his entrance only in his new role as leader of the Hebrews seeking their release. Accordingly, in v. 20 Moses returns to Egypt with his wife and sons – up to now mention had only been made of one (cf. 2.22; 4.25) – and with the 'rod of God'. Although the rod has only appeared so far in connection with the serpent (4.2ff.), its explicit mention anticipates its coming role in the great plagues upon Egypt (7.15; 8.12, etc.).

[4.21–23] The additional instructions which God here gives to Moses do not fit in with a strict chronological sequence, but this is not unusual for Hebrew narrative style. Cassuto cites Gen. 28.10ff. as a parallel. The admonition to perform 'all the marvels' then anticipates the resistance of Pharaoh and the consequent divine punishment as did 3.18–22. The formulation of the threat is of particular interest. It spans all the plagues and speaks immediately of the final one. In 11.1 the death of the first-born departs from the pattern of the earlier plagues – at least in the J account – since no warning is given. Here the final weapon is announced and as an unequivocal warning.

The form of the threat makes use of a subtle figure of speech. That Israel is Yahweh's first-born son is a metaphor which expresses the unique relation between God and his people (cf. Hos. 11.1), but then the threat moves immediately beyond the metaphor to speak in grim, realistic terms of Pharaoh's first-born. Of course, when reading from the perspective of the subsequent events, one tends to overlook the enormous leap in associating two totally different concepts. But far more is at stake than an artistic literary device. The conflict is over paternal power, and in the claim of the first-born the God of Israel and the king of Egypt have clashed in a head-on encounter. Later on in the narrative the slaying of the Egyptian first-born is attributed to 'the destroyer' (12.23b), but there was never any doubt within the tradition that Yahweh, the God of Israel, was the ultimate power behind that destruction.

[4.24–26] An exposition of some of the chief problems of these enigmatic verses has already been given in the introduction. The author of the Exodus narrative has done his best to fit this old tradition into his story. The incident takes place 'at an encampment on the way'. In the present context this can only imply on the journey back to Egypt, somewhere in the wilderness. Although the expression in the text is ambiguous, it seems most probable to assume that it was Moses whose life was threatened. The text gives no hint as to the form of the attack, but it is not possible to soften the unexpected harshness of the incident by suggesting that the expression is a Hebrew idiom for falling ill (Buber). Of course, the most difficult feature of the passage is to understand why God should now try to kill Moses whom he had only recently commissioned. Whatever one decides finally to be the author's understanding of this enigma, at this point in the story no reason whatever is offered.

Then Zipporah sprang into action. The fact that Zipporah took the lead in circumcising the child is another indication that Moses was under attack and incapable of responding. She did three things, which are related in quick succession. She circumcised the child, touched his feet with it, and spoke the words, 'You are a blood-bridegroom to me.' Of these three only the first is comparatively clear, although even here one could wonder why the child is designated 'her son'. In the second clause it is not clear as to whose 'feet' were touched with the foreskin, what part of the body was intended (cf. Isa. 6.2), or what was the purpose of the action. In my opinion, the redactor of the present narrative seemed to have understood the child as the recipient of the action. The smearing of the blood serves as a visible demonstration that circumcision had indeed been performed. Whether this was the original meaning of the action is uncertain.

The significance of Zipporah's words remains one of the most enigmatic parts of the story, and the attempts to unravel its mystery are almost legion. To whom were the words addressed? On the surface they seem to apply neither to the child nor to Moses, and assuredly not to Yahweh. The frequent suggestion of translating the phrase on the basis of Arabic to mean 'the blood-circumcised one' escapes some of the difficulties but cannot be sustained philologically. It appears probable that the term was a technical one and was intelligible at some earlier stage of the tradition. It is possible that elements from an older etiology were involved. But this dimension of the tradition has now been hopelessly, and perhaps consciously, blurred in the present story. In fact, it is a real question whether the author any longer attached any meaning to it. This impression is confirmed by the final comment which he joins to the story. 'At that time she said "blood-bridegroom" in reference to circumcision.' This comment does not even attempt to explain the meaning of the expression. What it does is to relate the phrase to the rite of circumcision. Whatever the details of this story meant – probably the final collector no longer fully understood – it belonged to circumcision which the author assumes to be a familiar institution and established within Israel. One thing which is completely clear in the passage is that Zipporah's action resulted in the release of Moses.

If one looks at the story as a whole in its present form, it serves to dramatize the tremendous importance of circumcision. Although the fact is never stated directly, the implication is certainly that Moses was held culpable for its omission. Indeed so serious was the offense as to have nearly cost him his life. When Zipporah righted the omission, he was released.

[4.27–31] Aaron is now brought into the story. His important role had already been discussed in the call of Moses (4.14). He is now commanded by God to meet Moses in the wilderness. The temporal sequence of this section is not presented very smoothly. Although it is quite possible in Hebrew to indicate prior time, which would require the pluperfect tense, this is not the case here, and the result is a bit awkward. The two brothers meet 'at the mountain of God' which would indicate that its site lay between Midian and Egypt. No particular significance is attributed to the meeting place by the author. The greeting is slightly reminiscent of that between Moses and Jethro in 18.7ff. Once this has been reported, the action of the narrative moves very fast. The author does not waste even a word on the trip back from the wilderness to Egypt, but describes immediately the gathering of the elders in Egypt, the giving of the signs before the people, which oddly enough were performed by Aaron, and their effect on the people. 'They believed . . . and worshipped.' At least at the outset things were progressing splendidly.

[5.1–9] Then Moses and Aaron went to Pharaoh. The connecting word 'afterwards' introduces this encounter as if it were just another in the series of quickly executed events which have been reported in the preceding verses. But almost immediately the author shifts his style with the introduction of extended dialogue as if to indicate a different kind of reaction.

Moses and Aaron address Pharaoh in the form of the prophetic oracle: 'Thus saith the LORD.' This form of expression, which is so common in the prophetic books, is surprisingly rare in the Pentateuch. With few exceptions the formula is restricted to Moses' encounter with Pharaoh during the plagues (4.22; 7.17; 8.1; 9.4, etc.). For this biblical author there is a parallel between Moses' confrontation with Pharaoh and the later ongoing battle between prophet and king (cf. pp. 145ff. for a detailed discussion).

The initial demand in the form of a divine oracle closely parallels 3.18. Moses requests a temporary respite from work in order to hold a religious festival in the wilderness. This request, which at first seems inconsonant with the real aim of Moses for complete deliverance, continues to play an important role in the later negotiations between Moses and Pharaoh (8.21ff. [EVV 25ff.]). At this point the request is flatly refused by Pharaoh who arrogantly replies that Yahweh is unknown to him. The theme of Pharaoh's not knowing Yahweh, which is introduced here for the first time, continues to be picked up and developed within the plague narrative. With considerable relish the biblical writer describes how Pharaoh comes to know who Yahweh is as he demonstrates his power over Egypt (8.18 [22]; 9.29; 11.8). The Jerusalem Targum paraphrases Pharaoh's reply: 'I have not found the name of the LORD in the Book of the Angels. I am not afraid of him, nor will I release Israel.'

The response by Moses and Aaron to this arrogant rebuff is surprisingly mild. In fact, the prophetic style is abandoned and quite a different line of argument is followed. Prefacing their reply with the particle 'I pray thee', they now argue in terms of their own experience with God and the dire consequences for them if they fail to hold a wilderness pilgrimage. But this tactic is hardly successful. Perhaps Pharaoh does tone down his arrogance somewhat, but only because he has won the day. He makes no concessions whatever, accuses Moses and Aaron of distracting the people from their work, and orders the work continued. The MT of v. 5 is not clear and the Samaritan text is preferable. The excuse for continued abuse is that Israel now outnumbers the native population and is a theme picked up from 1.9.

What then transpires offers a penetrating commentary on the tyrant in action. He has wrested the initiative easily away from Moses who is made to appear incredibly inept. Now he strikes while the iron is hot to make doubly sure that the disturbance among his slaves is fully eradicated. 'That same day' he sends orders down through his chain of command that the work quota be increased. The logic of totalitarianism is surprisingly consistent. Resistance is stamped out by utterly exploiting the energy of the slaves.

[5.10–21] Two things are of particular interest in the description of Pharaoh's plan to intensify the pressure on the Hebrews. First, the scheme to withdraw part of the essential materials by which bricks were made, thereby forcing the Hebrews themselves to supply it, is presented in a somewhat oversimplified manner – as if slaves were allowed to roam freely around the country finding straw where they could. But in point of fact, the picture reflects a good knowledge of ancient Egyptian building practice. The well-known pyramid paintings of brick making (cf. *BHH* III, cols. 2239f.) portray all too clearly the tedious work done by slaves who mix, mould, and carry the bricks under the watchful eye of the overseers. Secondly, the organization of a chain of command is highly realistic. Obviously the Egyptians maintained absolute control under the ultimate jurisdiction of the king. But they had employed Hebrews as overseers who were in direct contact with the slaves and who were forced to bear the direct responsibility for fulfilling the quota. Modern parallels from Nazi concentration camps come to mind. When the impossible quota failed to be achieved, then the Hebrew foremen were beaten. When they complained, the same old charge of idleness was simply rehearsed. The biblical writer succeeds brilliantly in picturing the utter sense of helplessness before the highly organized machinery of the system.

Perhaps the most diabolic side to the whole scheme was the calculated plan to divide the slaves into factions and sow inner discontent. Accordingly, the Hebrew foremen are pictured turning on their leaders with vicious resentment. Now Pharaoh does not have to discredit Moses directly. He is renounced by his own people, who would gladly trade the thought of freedom for a return to the earlier *status quo* which suddenly was made to appear quite tolerable.

[5.22–6.1] The last scene portrays the disastrous effect of the rebuff on Moses. In a complaint reminiscent of Jeremiah's, he accuses God of bringing evil on his people. He questions the meaning of his whole mission. And he points out that not only has God not succeeded in delivering his people, but he has intensified their problem. The divine answer is short and to the point. There is no reference whatever to the past failure, but only a word for the future. 'Now you will witness what I am going to do to Pharaoh which will force him to release the people.' Pharaoh had responded to Moses' request with the mailed fist. Yahweh will now demonstrate what real power is like.

Detailed Notes

4.24–26. Cf. the bibliography for the major treatments of this passage. A history of earlier exegesis is offered by Frischmuth and Vermes, and of the later period by Kosmala and Fohrer.

31. 'they believed'. On the vocabulary of believing cf. *TWNT* VI, pp. 182–97 = *TDNT* VI, pp. 174ff.; J. Fichtner, *Evangelische Kirchenlexikon*² I, pp. 1580f.; A. Jepsen, *TWAT* I, pp. 314ff.; E. Pfeiffer, 'Glaube im Alten Testament', *ZAW* 71, 1959, pp. 151–64.

5.1 On the problem of this early Hebrew festival, cf. J. Wellhausen, *Prolegomena to the History of Israel*, ET Edinburgh 1885, p. 88.

7. On the Egyptian method of constructing bricks, cf. Nims, *op. cit.*

22. On the subject of the curse, cf. now W. Schottroff, *Der israelitische Fluchspruch*, WMANT 30, 1969.

VI

THE RENEWED CALL OF MOSES

6.2–7.7

K. ELLIGER, 'Ich bin der Herr – euer Gott', *KS zum AT*, Munich 1966, pp.211–31; B. JACOB, *Das zweite Buch der Tora Exodus*, pp.48–52; G. FOHRER, *Überlieferung und Geschichte des Exodus*, 1964, pp.48–52; M. GREENBERG, *Understanding Exodus*, 1969, pp.130ff.; M. R. LEHMANN, 'Biblical Oaths', *ZAW* 81, 1969, pp.8off.; N. LOHFINK, 'Die priesterschriftliche Abwertung der Tradition von der Offenbarung des Jahwenamens an Mose', *Biblica* 49, 1968, pp.1–8; E. C. B. MACLAURIN, 'Shaddai', *Abr-Nahrain* 3, 1961, pp.99–118; J. A. MOTYER, *The Revelation of the Divine Name*, London 1959; M. OLIVA, 'Revelacion del nombre de Yahweh . . .', *Biblica* 52, 1971, pp.1ff.; G. VON RAD, *Die Priesterschrift im Hexateuch*, Stuttgart 1934, pp.43–5; M. WEIPPERT, 'Erwägungen zur Etymologie des Gottesnamens 'el šaddaj', *ZDMG* 3, 1961, pp.41–62; R. D. WILSON, 'Yahweh (Jehovah) and Exodus 6:3', *Princeton Theological Review* 22, 1924, pp.108–19; F. WIMMER, 'Tradition reinterpreted in Ex.6:2–7:7', *Augustinianum* 7, 1967, pp.405–18; W. ZIMMERLI, 'Ich bin Jahwe', *Geschichte und Altes Testament*, Tübingen 1953, pp.179–209 = *Gottes Offenbarung*, pp.11–40; *Ezechiel* I, Neukirchen-Vluyn 1955ff., pp.45ff.

6 [2]God spoke to Moses and said to him, 'I am the LORD. [3]I appeared to Abraham, Isaac, and Jacob as El Shaddai, but by my name YHWH I did not make myself known to them. [4]I also established my covenant with them to give to them the land of Canaan, the land in which they lived as sojourners. [5]Now I have heard the moaning of the Israelites whom the Egyptians have enslaved, and I have remembered my covenant. [6]Say therefore to the Israelites: "I am the LORD, and I will bring you out from under the burdens of the Egyptians and I will deliver you from their bondage and I will redeem you with an outstretched arm and with mighty acts of judgment. [7]And I will take you for my people, and I will be your God. You shall know that I am the LORD your God who has brought you out from under the burdens of the Egyptians. [8]I will lead you into the land which I swore to give to Abraham, Isaac, and Jacob, and I will give it to you for a possession. I am the LORD." ' [9]But when Moses spoke in this way to the Israelites,

they would not listen to Moses because they had become impatient from their cruel slavery.

10 The LORD spoke to Moses, saying: [11]'Go and tell Pharaoh, king of Egypt, to let the Israelites go from his land.' [12]But Moses responded to the LORD saying: 'If the Israelites have not listened to me, how then should Pharaoh heed me, especially since I am a halting speaker?' [13]But the LORD spoke to Moses and Aaron, and gave them their orders regarding the Israelites and Pharaoh, king of Egypt, to bring the Israelites out of the land of Egypt.

14 The following are the heads of their clans: the sons of Reuben, Israel's eldest son: Enoch, and Pallu, Hezron and Carmi; these are the families of Reuben. [15]The sons of Simeon: Jemuel, Jamin, Ohad, Jachin, Zohar, and Saul, the son of a Canaanite woman; these are the families of Simeon. [16]These are the names of the sons of Levi in their genealogical order: Gershon, Kohath, and Merari (the length of Levi's life being one hundred and thirty-seven years). [17]The sons of Gershon: Libni and Shimei, by their families. [18]The sons of Kohath: Amram, Izhar, Hebron, and Uzziel (the length of Kohath's life being one hundred and thirty-three years). [19]The sons of Merari: Mahli and Mushi. These are the families of the Levites in their genealogical order.

20 Amram married his father's sister Jochebed, and she bore him Aaron and Moses (the length of Amram's life being one hundred and thirty-seven years). [21]The sons of Izhar: Korah, Nepheg, and Zichri. [22]The sons of Uzziel: Mishael, Elzaphan, and Sithri. [23]Aaron married Elisheba, daughter of Amminadab and sister of Nahshon, and she bore him Nadab and Ahibu, Eleazar and Ithamar. [24]The sons of Korah: Assir, Elkanah, and Abiasaph. These are the families of the Korahites. [25]And Aaron's son, Eleazar, married one of the daughters of Putiel and she bore him Phinehas. These are the heads of the Levitical clans, arranged by families. [26]It was to this same Aaron and Moses that the LORD said, 'Bring out the Israelites from the land of Egypt according to their fixed groupings.' [27]It was they who spoke to Pharaoh, king of Egypt, about bringing the Israelites out of Egypt. These are the same Moses and Aaron.

28 When the LORD spoke to Moses in the land of Egypt, [29]the LORD said to Moses, 'I am the LORD; tell Pharaoh, king of Egypt, all that I say to you.' [30]But Moses responded to the LORD: 'I am a halting speaker, how then will Pharaoh listen to me?' 7 [1]Then the LORD said to Moses, 'Look, I will make you as God to Pharaoh, and your brother Aaron shall be your spokesman. [2]You shall speak all that I command you; and Aaron your brother shall tell Pharaoh to let the Israelites go out of his land. [3]But I will harden Pharaoh's heart that I may increase my signs and wonders in the land of Egypt. [4]When Pharaoh will not listen to you, I will lay my hand upon Egypt and lead out my hosts, my

people, the Israelites, from the land of Egypt by great acts of judgment.
[5]The Egyptians shall know that I am the LORD, when I stretch out my
hand over Egypt and bring out the Israelites from their midst. [6]And
Moses and Aaron did this. As the LORD ordered them, so they did.
[7]Moses was eighty years old, and Aaron was eighty-three, when they
spoke to Pharaoh.

1. Textual and Philological Notes

6.3. *be'ēl šadday*, 'as El Shaddai'. The preposition is a *beth essentiae* (G–K §119i) and
parallel to Ex. 3.2.

ûšemî, 'and my name'. The syntax of this noun remains controversial; however,
the text should not be emended as *BH*[3] suggests. König (*Lehrgebäude* III,
§328g) argues for an accusative of specification and cites Gen. 3.15 as a parallel.
G–K (§144l) describes it as a peculiar idiom in which there are two subjects,
one of the person and one of the thing.

'ēl šadday. The term occurs some 40 times in the Old Testament, with and without the *'ēl*. The LXX translates it παντοκράτωρ (almighty) or ἱκανός (sufficient)
and appears to reflect the early rabbinic attempt at an etymology (*še* + *day*
= self-sufficient). A great variety of hypotheses have been proposed, the most
popular of which is probably Albright's derivation from the Akkadian *šadu*, a
theory proposed earlier by Hommel and others. Cf. W. F. Albright, *From the
Stone Age to Christianity*,[2] Baltimore and London 1957, p. 188; E. C. B.
MacLaurin (*op. cit.*) and Weippert (*op. cit.*), F. M. Cross, *HTR* 55, 1962,
pp. 244ff.

nôda'tî 'I did not make myself known'. Cf. Jacob (*op. cit.*) for a detailed study of
all the parallel passages.

4. *gam.* C. J. Labuschagne, 'The emphasizing particle *gam*', *Studia Biblica . . .
Vriezen*, Wageningen 1966, pp. 193ff., argues that *gam* functions here as
emphasis rather than addition.

6. On the semantic range of *g'l*, cf. J. J. Stamm, *Erlösen und Vergeben im AT*,
Bern 1940, pp. 27ff.

9. *qōṣer rûaḥ.* LXX translates the phrase ὀλιγοψυχία (faint-heartedness); AV
'anguish of spirit'. The closest parallels in Mic. 2.7; Prov. 14.29; Job 21.4,
would rather denote impatience. Cf. the related idiom *qāṣar nepeš*, Num. 21.4.
The Sam. offers a textual addition to provide the antecedent for the complaint
in 14.12.

12. *hēn.* Cf. 4.1.

13. *'el-benê yiśrā'ēl* is missing in the LXX which matches the context far better;
cf. vv. 11f. and 7.1ff.

14. *bēṭ 'āb*, 'father's house, or clan'. Sometimes the term expresses a subdivision of
the tribe in the hierarchial order of the *bēṭ 'āb*, *mišpāḥāh*, and *šēbeš*. Cf. Josh. 7.14–
18. But generally the term is fluid and can comprise a larger or smaller grouping. Contrast Num. 3.24, 30 which is the larger clan, with the smaller family in
Ex. 12.3. Cf. de Vaux, *Ancient Israel*, pp. 7f.

20. Instead of the MT's *dōdātô* (aunt) the LXX reads θυγατέρα τοῦ ἀδελφοῦ τοῦ πατρὸς
αὐτοῦ (the daughter of his father's brother) which is clearly a dogmatic cor-

rection which reflects the later prohibition of such a marriage (Lev.18.12).
30. G. Fohrer, *Überlieferung*, p.49, cites v.30 (cf. 12) as a clear example of C. Kuhl's
    theory of 'Wiederaufnahme' (*ZAW* 64, 1952, pp.1–11).
7.1. Cf. the parallel tradition in Ex.4.15 where prophet = mouthpiece. Targ.
    Onkelos and Neophiti I render it 'interpreter', NJPS 'oracle'.

2. *Literary, Form-Critical and Traditio-Historical Problems*

There has been a wide consensus for over a hundred years in assigning
these verses to the Priestly source. The reasons for this judgment are
presented fully in the older commentaries (cf. Bäntsch, Driver), and
relate to characteristic vocabulary, Hebrew style, and theology.

A more difficult literary problem turns on the issue of evaluating
the role of the genealogy which has been inserted within the narrative
material (vv.14–25). The genealogy can hardly be called an interpolation because it has been given a literary framework which both
precedes and follows it (vv.13, 26–27). Verse 13 serves to introduce
Aaron into the narrative which is essential before his genealogy is
traced. Verses 26–27 interpret the purpose of the genealogy in the
narrative by relating the two main figures of the story to the Levitical
order. However, the genealogy clearly interrupts the narrative. The
objection of Moses in v.12 receives its answer from God first in 7.1.
Therefore, in order to pick up the broken thread vv.28–30 recapitulate the preceding account ('Wiederaufnahme'). Verse 30 is virtually
a duplication of v.12. This evidence would suggest that a priestly
redactor, and not the original Priestly writer, has carefully inserted
the genealogy within the narrative.

Another difficult question concerns the relation of 6.1ff. to the
earlier call narrative in 3.1–4.17. It has long been noticed by literary
critics that 6.1ff. offered originally a parallel account of Moses' call
and not a sequel. 6.1ff. shows no recognition of the earlier call
narrative in its content. Indeed, if there had been a prior rebuff by
Pharaoh, the *a priori* argument in 6.12 would hardly have been used.
Again, there is also a striking similarity in the form of the two
narratives (cf. Wimmer, *op. cit.*, pp.408ff.) which includes commission,
objection, divine response, and sign, which would confirm its parallel
role. However, the differences in the two accounts must not be overlooked. The setting for 6.1ff. is Egypt and not Midian. God reveals
himself by means of a self-identification formula and not in a
theophany.

The question of the historical relationship between the two

sources has been raised by Noth (*Exodus*, pp. 61f.). He feels the affinities are so close that one can assume that the Priestly writer knew the earlier narrative even in its expanded literary form. His main evidence is the reference to Aaron (7.1ff.) which is paralleled in 4.13–16 and which Noth had earlier judged to be a secondary expansion in the J narrative. In my judgment, the case for assuming a simple literary relationship is far from clear. First, in the rest of the book of Exodus the relation between the common elements in J and P appears to be usually on the oral level (cf. plagues, crossing, etc.). Secondly, Noth's analysis of the development of the earlier source can be questioned (cf. chs. 3f.). Finally, the nature of the similarities as well as the differences appears to me better explained by positing a common oral tradition with a long period of independent development.

There is another set of questions which arose in the history of exegesis, but which relates directly to the literary and traditio-historical problem of the text. The issue at stake is how to understand the statement in 6.3: 'I appeared to Abraham . . . as El Shaddai, but by my name YHWH I did not make myself known to them.' Since in the present form of the Pentateuch the name of Yahweh was known to the Patriarchs (Gen. 4.26; 15.2, etc.), it was assumed in traditional Jewish and Christian exegesis that the statement could only refer to the Patriarchs' failure to understand the fuller aspects of God's nature which the name Yahweh contained (cf. Rashi, Ibn Ezra *contra* Saadia, Calvin, Rosenmüller, etc.).

The critical theory which had emerged in the first half of the nineteenth century – Knobel already assumed its validity in 1857 – represented a sharp break with the traditional interpretation. These scholars (cf. Dillmann, Bäntsch) argued that the text in 6.2 does not speak of the *meaning* of the name being unknown, but of the name itself. Accordingly, the P writer had a concept of a development of Israel's religion and one which differed from that of the earlier sources. God had revealed himself in stages by means of different names. To the Patriarchs he appeared as El Shaddai, but only to Moses was the new name Yahweh made known.

This critical theory continued to call forth opposition from both conservative Jews and Christians (cf. D. Hoffmann, *Die wichtigsten Instanzen gegen die Graf-Wellhausensche Hypothese*, Berlin 1904; Jacob; Cassuto; E. W. Hengstenberg, *History of the Kingdom of God under the*

Old Testament I, ET Edinburgh 1871, pp. 258ff.; Keil). Their arguments focused on several points: (i) The formula 'I am Yahweh' is never used for mere self-identification of a hitherto unknown person. (ii) The verb *nôḏaʿtî* does not denote the imparting of information, but rather the revealing of one's character. (iii) Ezek. 20.5ff., which is the earliest commentary on Ex. 6, confirms the aspectual character of God's revelation of himself through his name (cf. the elaborate recapitulation of the conservatives' arguments by Jacob, *op. cit.*).

Now the purpose of reviewing this history of exegesis is to suggest that more recent scholarship has learned to approach the problem in a somewhat different way, which has broken this older impasse. On the one hand, a form-critical analysis of the formula 'I am Yahweh' by Zimmerli (*op. cit.*) has demonstrated the ancient, liturgical background to this traditional formula of self-revelation. Moreover, the widespread parallels of self-introduction in the Ancient Near East (cf. Greenberg) confirm its function as an elevated style of address which asserts the authority of the speaker of the name. To this extent the conservative opposition against understanding the formula as simply making known the hitherto unknown name of Yahweh has been fully justified. Moreover, if the context of the passage is taken seriously, it is apparent that the focus of the passage is not on the revelation of a new name. In fact, v. 3 appears almost as a parenthesis. Rather, the emphasis falls on the revelation of the character of God in the name of Yahweh which affirms the promise made earlier to the Patriarchs (Lohfink). The revelation of the name of Yahweh is at the same time a revealing of his power and authority. To this extent the aspectual side to the name-giving cannot be denied.

However, on the other hand, the traditional interpretation was clearly wrong in trying to avoid the implications plainly in the text that a new name was given to Moses. The fact that the Priestly writer recognizes a history of revelation by means of different divine names is an essential witness of the text. This explicit contrast of God's dealings with the Patriarchs and Moses sets Ex. 6 apart from Ezek. 20, which makes no reference to the Patriarchs, but combines the revelation of the name with the giving of the law. Moreover, the traditional aspectual interpretation of the name-giving fails to do justice to the major witness of the text which is to affirm the continuity between the various different periods of God's history of revelation. The revelation of the name Yahweh serves to confirm the divine promise of the land made to the Patriarchs in a covenant which he now fulfills in delivering them from Egyptian bondage and leading them to the land.

In the history of modern critical exegesis Ex. 6.3 has played an important role because it appeared to address the historical and history-of-religions question regarding the form of the religious worship of the Patriarchs. But although this text provides some material for the historical question to the extent that it sharply distinguishes between the Patriarchal and Mosaic ages, the historical question in its modern form is obviously foreign to the perspective of the biblical author and lies beyond the scope of a commentary (cf. ch. 3 for the secondary literature on the subject of the 'God of the Fathers').

Finally, what can one say about the redaction of this passage in its present form? Previously it was pointed out that 6.1ff. originally formed a parallel call narrative of the Priestly source to the earlier story of JE in 3.1ff. But in the present combined narrative of Exodus, the passage has been given another function. Already Dillmann had seen that the purpose of the passage lay in its confirmation of a past promise and was now viewed as a sequel, not a parallel to the call in Midian. Because the Priestly writer places the greatest weight on the covenant made between El Shaddai and Abraham in Gen. 17, this original call narrative could now serve as a confirmation of Ex. 3.1ff. without any major redactional changes.

3. Old Testament Context

[6.2–13] The previous section had ended with the harsh rebuff of Pharaoh in response to Moses' attempt to secure a release of the people. To Moses' complaint God had replied that shortly Pharaoh would feel his judgment. 6.2 introduces a further response of God. When read in the context of the larger narrative, it addresses one of the complaints of Moses: 'You have not delivered your people at all' (5.23). It does so, not by justifying his action, but by a fresh revelation of the nature of the covenant God.

The importance of the phrase 'I am Yahweh' for the entire passage emerges at the outset from its repeated usage (vv. 2, 6, 7, 8). It is the basic formula by which God identifies himself in an act of self-revelation. He does not merely inform Moses of his name, but by announcing the name he also makes known his essential character. Indeed, as Zimmerli has pointed out, in the divine name is encompassed the whole redemptive power of God. Ezek. 20.5 speaks of the revelation of the name as a solemn oath which God swore, committing himself to Israel as God.

The content of the divine name which is now revealed to Moses is made plain by reference to the history of God's revelation. Above all, Yahweh identifies himself as the selfsame God who had made himself known to the Fathers. The reference to God's revelation of himself as El Shaddai immediately calls to mind Gen. 17.1ff. and the covenant between Abraham and God. Verse 4 goes on to make explicit the reference to the covenant which contained the promise of the land. It is the validity of this promise which God now confirms. However, at the same time the revelation of the name of Yahweh to Moses is sharply contrasted with the revelation to the Fathers. Although it is the same covenant God, a decisively new element has entered into history: 'By my name Yahweh I did not make myself known to them.' The Fathers knew God only as El Shaddai. He had promised them a land when they were still sojourners. Now God reveals himself to Moses as Yahweh who remembers his covenant, and who moves to bring his promise to completion.

Modern Old Testament scholars have focused their interest on the revelation of the different names because it proved to be an avenue for penetrating into Israel's history of religion. But for the biblical writer the revelation of different names is important because it made known the character of God. He had made a covenant with the patriarchs as El Shaddai, but they had not experienced the fulfillment of that promise. Indeed Moses had complained that God had done nothing. Now God reveals himself through his name as the God who fulfills his promise and redeems Israel from Egypt.

The message which Moses is commanded to announce to Israel both begins and ends with the proclamation of the name: I am Yahweh. The content of the message which is bracketed by this self-identification formula, is actually only an explication of the name itself and contains the essence of God's purpose with Israel. First, there is the promise to deliver: 'I will redeem you with an outstretched arm.' Secondly, there is their adoption into the covenant as the people of God: 'I will take you for my people, and I will be your God.' Thirdly, there is the gift of the land which had been promised to the Fathers: 'I will give it to you for an inheritance.' The name of Yahweh functions as a guarantee that the reality of God stands behind the promise and will execute its fulfillment.

However, the contrast between the promise and the present situation is immediately brought home in the narrative by the reaction of the people to Moses' message. He had announced: 'You shall know that I am Yahweh' (v. 7). But when Moses spoke, the people did not listen. Because of the present hardship they had no time for Moses' words or for God's future. The effect of their unbelief was contagious. (Here the writer picks up the traditional motif from the call narrative.) Moses himself resists the command to speak to Pharaoh. 'If even the people will not listen, why should Pharaoh pay any attention to my stuttering?' In the earlier narrative this same objection of Moses had called forth a lengthy response (4.10ff.), which finally led to the appointment of Aaron. But this time the writer abruptly breaks off the discussion to make room for a genealogy and only when he has finished does he pick up the threads of Moses' objection.

[6.14–27] The introduction of a genealogy at this point in the narrative strikes a decidedly dissident note in the ears of a modern reader. It seems to serve as an unwanted interruption. But for the ancient Priestly writer the genealogy is anything but a superfluous interpolation. Rather it provides the historical setting for the figures in the narrative and serves for the P source a role parallel to the account of Moses' birth and early life in the J narrative. By placing Moses and Aaron in their genealogical order the author offers their true historical significance, which means that for him 'history' is determined in terms of the ongoing life of the established institutions and offices of the covenant people. The writer leaves no doubt as to his purpose in presenting the genealogy. In vv. 26f. he makes an explicit transition from his genealogy to the Exodus narrative. First, he connects Aaron and Moses – the order is significant – to the genealogy: 'These are the same men' whose lineage has just been traced. Then he designates their office in terms of a twofold function: they were given the message of God and they delivered it to Pharaoh.

Several things should be noted about the details of the genealogy. Its form shows that it is of mixed origin. That is to say, that the writer has not created the genealogy *de novo*, but joined together several traditional forms to serve his purpose. Therefore, although his interest focuses on Levi, the third son of Jacob, he does not begin here, but follows the traditional order of the twelve tribes, beginning with the eldest son (Gen. 49.3ff.). The simplest form of 'These are the heads of the clans . . .' is used for the background material, but the more detailed form is employed which includes the wife and age when the Levitical stem is traced (20ff.). One can also notice a complete introduction and conclusion to the Levitical stem (vv. 19–25).

Again, the choice of material is highly selective. At times the principle of selection is unclear, as for example, why of the four sons of Kohath only Hebron's lineage is left incomplete. However, the basic concern to establish the Levitical lineage of Aaron and Moses is obvious. Of the three sons of Levi only Kohath's line is traced beyond one generation, and of the four sons of Kohath only Amram's line is followed through to the third generation. Aaron's lineage is traced through Eleazar to Phineas, probably because of the later importance of both men, whereas Moses' sons are not mentioned (cf. Judg. 18.30). The principle of selectivity is also clear in comparing other genealogies within the Old Testament. So, for example, according to Ex. 6 Aaron and Moses belong to the fourth generation after Jacob, whereas from the lists in Ruth 4.18–20 and I Chron. 2.4–10, it would appear that Aaron's wife Elisheba, the daughter of Amminadab, belonged to the sixth generation. It is not fully clear why, for example, the lines of Izhar and Uzziel are traced in such detail except perhaps to place important men who were contemporary with Aaron and Moses.

There is an additional problem raised by the genealogies. According to Ex. 6 the period of captivity in Egypt extended over four generations (cf. 1.2) – Levi, Kohath, Amram, Aaron – and the ages of each is given. Elsewhere Israel's stay in Egypt is reckoned at 430 years (12.40). How are these two sets of numbers related to one another? Several different solutions have been proposed. One is to see the 430 years as a round figure. Others argue that the ages of the four men are artificial and are symbol variations of the number seven (Heinisch). More recently, Cassuto has argued with ingenuity and learning that the numbers are based on a sexagesimal system, and that one of the purposes of Ex. 6 was to reconcile these two traditions regarding the length of the sojourn in Egypt. Although his arguments are of interest, there is enough juggling of figures involved to leave some doubt regarding his harmonization.

[6.28–7.7] The genealogy had interrupted the narrative in v. 12. In order to pick up the broken thread the author, following a common Old Testament practice, recapitulates a bit of his story (28ff.) before continuing with his narrative. In the early call narrative the appointment of Aaron as Moses' mouthpiece reflected God's exasperation with Moses. In this account there is no note of irritation in the choice of Aaron, although the roles of the two brothers are described in a similar way. Moses is made as 'god to Pharaoh', that is to say, he is to function with divine authority before Pharaoh, and like God, make known his word through his prophet. Aaron is appointed the organ of the message, the description of which offers an important insight into the Hebrew understanding of the prophetic office.

The word which now follows from God outlines his intention with Pharaoh and serves as introduction to the plague stories. Moses is to demand the release of Israel. There is no suggestion of a temporary respite. But God will harden Pharaoh's heart and he will refuse. As a result God will multiply his signs and wonders in the land, and deliver Israel with great acts of judgment. The full implications of this theology are discussed at length in the next section, but it is clear that this biblical writer offers a highly sophisticated reflection on the theology of the plagues. Central to his understanding is that through the plagues the Egyptians will come to know that 'I am Yahweh'. This same formula which in 6.1 summarizes God's revelatory purpose with Israel is now used to encompass his plan for Egypt as well. For this writer because the entire redemptive history is compressed into the one great self-revelation of God, the same formula can apply to all the various manifestations of his power and authority.

This section ends with a note which recounts the ages of Moses and Aaron. Moses was eighty; Aaron three years older. Within the present narrative this note serves to recall how much time has passed since Israel had been afflicted in Egypt. Perhaps it also serves to demonstrate the maturity of Moses for the task which he now sought to undertake.

Detailed Notes

6.2. On the formula, 'I am Yahweh', cf. the two basic articles by Zimmerli (*op. cit.*) and Elliger (*op. cit.*).

3. 'I appeared' – N. Lohfink (*op. cit.*, pp. 2ff.) offers a study of this word in the Priestly theology. Cf. also F. Schnutenhaus, 'Das Kommen und Erscheinen Gottes im AT', *ZAW* 76, 1964, pp. 1ff. Cf. note on Ex. 3.2.

4. 'I established my covenant' – cf. Eichrodt, *Theology of the OT* I, pp. 45ff., for a classic study of covenant terminology. His work should be supplemented by the more recent studies of A. Jepsen, 'Berith', *Verbannung und Heimkehr. Festschrift W. Rudolph*, Tübingen 1961, pp. 161ff.; E. Kutsch, 'Der Begriff berît in vordeuteronomischer Zeit', *Das Ferne und Nahe Wort*, Berlin 1967, pp. 132ff.; G. Fohrer, *Studien zur altt. Theologie und Geschichte*, BZAW 115, 1959,

pp. 84ff.; L. Perlitt, *Bundestheologie im AT*, WMANT 36, 1969; M. Weinfeld, 'Berit', *TWAT* I, pp. 782–808.

5. 'I will remember my covenant' – cf. W. Schottroff, *'Gedenken'*, pp. 202ff.

7. Cf. R. Smend, *Die Bundesformel*, Zürich 1963, on this expression.

14ff. On the whole question of Old Testament genealogies within the context of the Ancient Near East, cf. Robert R. Wilson, *Genealogy and History in the Old Testament* (Yale Dissertation, 1972). The early literary-critical approach is represented in Colenso, *The Pentateuch and the Book of Joshua* I, London 1862, pp. 96ff.

7.3 On the sign cf. C. Keller, *Das Wort OTH*, Basel 1946.

4. Theological Reflection

The theology of the call of Moses has been treated earlier in connection with Ex. 3. Also the manner in which the Priestly account of the call was understood as a sequel to the first call has been developed in an earlier section (p. 114).

Perhaps the greatest theological significance of Ex. 6 in the context of the canon is the tremendous theocentric emphasis of the biblical author's understanding of the exodus. Although the shape of a call narrative is still present in ch. 6, interest in the manner of God's appearing or the human reactions to a theophany have receded to vanishing point. Rather, the whole focus falls on God's revealing of himself in a majestic act of self-identification: I am Yahweh. Although there is a history of revelation which includes a past and a future, the theocentric focus on God's initiative in making himself known tends to encompass all the various times into the one great act of disclosure. To know God's name is to know his purpose for all mankind from the beginning to the end. Ezekiel pursues this same line of thought even more consistently when he sees all of God's intervention into human history arising from his concern for his name (20.9). In his testimony that nothing in human history shares the glory which belongs alone to God, the writer reduces Pharaoh to a pawn on God's great chess-board, and Israel, far from being viewed as a partner in the plan of God, is judged for consistent disobedience and allegiance to the idols of Egypt (Ezek. 20.8).

In the New Testament, several writers develop aspects of this side of Old Testament theology. It is not by accident that Paul picks up the theme of Pharaoh's role in the exodus (Rom. 9.14ff.) to confirm his argument of God's absolute freedom in carrying out his plan for Israel and the nations. But perhaps it is John's gospel which elaborates the theology of Ex. 6 most thoroughly when he sees all of Israel's history centered in the great act of self-revelation in Jesus Christ. John does not have a concept of *Heilsgeschichte* in the sense of Heb. 1.1, but he understands the incarnation as an event encompassing past and present. In this selfsame Christ God made himself known in his glory to Abraham (8.58), to Isaiah (12.41), to his disciples (1.14) as the true light of the world, bringing life through his name (20.31).

VII

THE PLAGUES OF EGYPT

7.8–11.10

M. Buber, *Moses*, 1946, pp. 6ff.; G. M. Camps, 'Midraš sobre la historia de les plagues (Ex. 7–11)', *Misc. Biblica B. Ubach*, Montserrat 1953, pp. 97–113; G. W. Coats, 'The Traditio-Historical Character of the Reed Sea Motif', *VT* 17, 1967, pp. 253–65; F. Dumermuth, 'Folkloristisches in der Erzählung von den ägyptischen Plagen', *ZAW* 76, 1964, pp. 323ff.; H. Eising, 'Die Ägyptischen Plagen', *Lex Tua Veritas, Festschrift H. Junker*, Trier 1961, pp. 75–87; G. Fohrer, *Überlieferung und Geschichte des Exodus*, 1964, pp. 6off.; W. Fuss, *Die Deuteronomistische Pentateuchredaktion in Exodus 3–17*, Berlin 1972; E. Galbiati, *La Struttura letteraria dell' Esodo*, 1956, pp. 111–33; M. Greenberg, 'The Thematic Unity of Exodus III–XI', *Fourth World Congress of Jewish Studies* I, Jerusalem 1967, pp. 151–4; *Understanding Exodus*, 1969, pp. 151–92; H. Gressmann, *Mose und seine Zeit*, 1913, pp. 66ff.; G. Hort, 'The Plagues of Egypt', *ZAW* 69, 1957, pp. 84–103; ib. 70, 1958, pp. 48–59; B. Jacob, 'Gott und Pharao', *MGWJ* 68, 1924, pp. 118ff., 202ff., 268ff.; C. A. Keller, *Das Wort OTH*, Basel 1946, pp. 28ff.; S. E. Loewenstamm, *The Tradition of the Exodus in its Development* (Hebrew), Jerusalem 1965, pp. 25ff.; 'The Number of Plagues in Ps. 105', *Biblica* 52, 1971, pp. 34–8; B. Margules, 'The Plague Tradition in Ps. 105', *Biblica* 50, 1969, pp. 491–6; D. McCarthy, 'Moses' Dealings with Pharaoh: Ex. 7:8–10.27', *CBQ* 27, 1965, pp. 336–47; 'Plagues and Sea of Reeds: Exodus 5–14', *JBL* 85, 1966, pp. 137ff.; M. Noth, *Überlieferungsgeschichte des Pentateuch*, 1948, pp. 7off., ET *A History of Pentateuchal Traditions*, 1971, pp. 65ff.; J. Plastaras, *The God of Exodus*, 1966, pp. 117ff.; J. Schildenberger, 'Psalm 78(77) und die Pentateuchquellen', *Lex Tua Veritas. Festschrift H. Junker*, Trier 1961, pp. 231–56; C. A. Simpson, *The Early Traditions of Israel*, Oxford 1948, pp. 170–81; F. V. Winnett, *The Mosaic Tradition*, 1949, pp. 3ff.

Note: *The chapter and verse division is that of the Hebrew. In the English versions 7.26–29 becomes 8.1–4 and 8.1–28 becomes 8.5–32.*

7 ⁸The Lord said to Moses and to Aaron, ⁹'When Pharaoh says to you, "Produce your spectacle", then you shall say to Aaron, "Take your rod and throw it down before Pharaoh," and it will turn into a serpent.' ¹⁰So Moses and Aaron came before Pharaoh and did as the

LORD commanded. Aaron cast down his rod before Pharaoh and his courtiers and it turned into a serpent. ¹¹At this Pharaoh summoned the wise men and the sorcerers, and the Egyptian magicians did the same thing by their spells. ¹²Each one threw down his rod and these turned into serpents, but Aaron's rod swallowed up theirs. ¹³Still Pharaoh's heart was hardened and he did not listen to them, as the LORD had said.

14 Then the LORD said to Moses, 'Pharaoh's heart is hard; he refuses to let the people go. ¹⁵Go to Pharaoh in the morning on his way out to the river. Position yourself to meet him by the river's bank, and the rod – the one which turned into a serpent – take in your hand. ¹⁶And say to him, "The LORD, the God of the Hebrews, sent me to you to say, 'Let my people go that they may serve me in the wilderness. And, what is more, up to now you have not yet obeyed.' ¹⁷Thus says the LORD, 'By this shall you know that I am the LORD. See, I now strike the water with the rod which is in my hand and it will be turned into blood. ¹⁸Then the fish in the Nile will die and the river will stink and the Egyptians will find it impossible to drink the water from the Nile.'"' ¹⁹The LORD said to Moses, 'Say to Aaron, "Take your rod and stretch out your hand over the waters of Egypt – its rivers, its canals, its ponds, all its bodies of water – that they may turn to blood; and there shall be blood throughout all the land of Egypt, even in wooden bowls and stone jars."'

20 Moses and Aaron did just as the LORD commanded. He lifted his rod and struck the water in the Nile in the sight of Pharaoh and his courtiers, and all the water in the Nile was turned to blood. ²¹Then the fish which were in the Nile died and the river stank and the Egyptians were not able to drink the water from the Nile. There was blood throughout all the land of Egypt. ²²But the Egyptian magicians did the same with their spells. Still the heart of Pharaoh was hardened and he did not listen to them, as the LORD had said. ²³Pharaoh turned and went into his palace, and dismissed the thing from his mind. ²⁴But all the Egyptians had to dig all around the Nile for drinking water because they could not drink the water of the Nile. ²⁵Seven days passed after the LORD's striking of the Nile.

26 The LORD said to Moses, 'Go to Pharaoh and say to him, "Thus says the LORD, 'Let my people go that they may serve me. ²⁷If you refuse to let them go, then I will plague your whole country with frogs. ²⁸The Nile shall swarm with frogs, and they shall come up and get into your palace, into your bedroom and on to your bed, into the houses of your courtiers and your people, and into your ovens and kneading-troughs. ²⁹The frogs shall come up on you and on your people and on your courtiers.'"' 8 ¹And the LORD said to Moses, 'Say to Aaron, "Stretch out your hand with your rod over the rivers, the canals, and the ponds, and bring up frogs upon the land of Egypt."' ²So Aaron

stretched out his hand over the waters of Egypt, and the frogs came up and covered the land of Egypt. ³But the magicians did the same with their spells and brought frogs upon the land of Egypt.

4 Then Pharaoh summoned Moses and Aaron and said, 'Pray to the LORD to remove the frogs from me and from my people, and then I will let the people go to sacrifice to the LORD. ⁵Moses said to Pharaoh, 'Take the advantage over me of commanding at what time I am to set for you and your courtiers and your people that the frogs be removed from you and your houses and be left only in the Nile.' ⁶He replied, 'For tomorrow.' Then he said, 'Let it be as you say, that you may know that there is no one like the LORD our God. ⁷The frogs shall depart from you, your houses, and your courtiers, and your people; they shall be left only in the Nile.' ⁸Then Moses and Aaron left the presence of Pharaoh, and Moses appealed to the LORD concerning the frogs which he had put on Pharaoh. ⁹The LORD did as Moses had asked; the frogs died away from the houses, the courtyards, and the fields. ¹⁰They piled them up in one heap after another and the land stank. ¹¹But when Pharaoh saw that there was relief, he hardened his heart, and would not listen to them, as the LORD had said.

12 Then the LORD said to Moses, 'Say to Aaron, "Stretch out your rod and strike the dust of the earth, that it shall turn to mosquitoes throughout the land of Egypt."' ¹³And they did so. Aaron stretched out his hand with the rod and struck the dust of the earth and mosquitoes came on man and beast and all the dust of the earth became mosquitoes throughout all the land of Egypt. ¹⁴And the magicians tried to produce mosquitoes with their spells, but could not. And there were mosquitoes on both man and beast. ¹⁵Then the magicians said to Pharaoh, 'It is the finger of God!' But the heart of Pharaoh was hardened and he would not listen to them, as the LORD had said.

16 Then the LORD said to Moses, 'Rise up early in the morning and present yourself before Pharaoh as he is leaving the water and say to him, "Thus says the LORD, 'Let my people go, that they may serve me. ¹⁷For if you do not let my people go, then I will send swarms of flies upon you, your courtiers, your people, and your houses; and the houses of the Egyptians and even the ground on which they stand shall be filled with swarms of flies. ¹⁸But on that day I will set apart the land of Goshen where my people dwell so that no swarms of flies shall be there, that you may know that I am the LORD in the midst of the land. ¹⁹And I will make a distinction between my people and yours. Tomorrow this sign shall appear.'"' ²⁰And the LORD did so. Great swarms of flies came into Pharaoh's palace and the houses of his courtiers and in all the land of Egypt the land was being ruined by the flies.

21 Then Pharaoh summoned Moses and Aaron and said, 'Go and sacrifice to your God within the land.' ²²But Moses replied, 'It would

not be right to do this, for what we sacrifice to the LORD our God is an offense to the Egyptians. If we sacrifice before their very eyes what is offensive to the Egyptians, will they not stone us to death? 23We must go on a three days' journey into the wilderness and sacrifice to our God as he commands us.' 24Pharaoh said, 'I will let you go and sacrifice to the LORD your God in the wilderness, only you must not go very far away. Now intercede for me.' 25Then Moses said, 'As soon as I leave your presence I will intercede with the LORD that the flies depart from Pharaoh, his courtiers, and his people tomorrow; only let not Pharaoh trifle by not letting the people go to sacrifice to the LORD.' 26Moses left Pharaoh and interceded with the LORD. 27And the LORD did as Moses asked. He removed the flies from Pharaoh, from his courtiers, and from his people; not one was left. 28But once again Pharaoh hardened his heart and would not let the people go.

9 1The LORD said to Moses, 'Go to Pharaoh and say to him, "Thus says the LORD, the God of the Hebrews, 'Let my people go, that they may serve me. 2For if you refuse to let them go and continue to hold them, 3then the hand of the LORD will strike your livestock in the fields – the horses, the asses, the camels, the cattle, and the sheep – with a severe pestilence. 4But the LORD will distinguish between the livestock of Israel and the livestock of the Egyptians so that nothing shall die of all that belongs to the Israelites.' "' 5And the LORD set a time, saying, 'Tomorrow the LORD will do this thing in the land.' 6The next day the LORD did it; all the livestock of the Egyptians died, but of the livestock of the Israelites not a single animal died. 7Pharaoh inquired and discovered that not one of the livestock of Israel had died. But Pharaoh's heart was hardened, and he would not let the people go.

8 Then the LORD said to Moses and to Aaron, 'Take handfuls of soot from a kiln, and let Moses throw it into the air in the sight of Pharaoh. 9It shall become a fine dust over all the land of Egypt, and it will produce sores which erupt into boils on man and beast throughout the land of Egypt.' 10So they took soot from the kiln, and standing before Pharaoh, Moses threw it into the air and it produced sores, erupting into boils on man and beast. 11The magicians were not able to appear before Moses because of the boils, because the boils were upon the magicians as well as all the other Egyptians. 12But the LORD hardened the heart of Pharaoh, and he would not listen to them just as the LORD had said to Moses.

13 The LORD said to Moses, 'Rise early in the morning and present yourself before Pharaoh, and say to him, "Thus says the LORD, the God of the Hebrews, 'Let my people go, that they may serve me. 14This time I will send all my plagues against you, your courtiers, and your people that you may know that there is none like me in all the earth. 15By now I could have stretched out my hand and struck you

and your people with pestilence and you would have been wiped off the face of the earth. [16]But I have spared you for this reason: to show you my power, and to have my fame recounted throughout all the earth. [17]Yet you continue to trifle with my people, not letting them go. [18]Therefore at this time tomorrow I am going to send a heavy hail storm, such as has not been in Egypt from the day it was founded until now. [19]Now order your livestock and everything which belongs to you in the open to be brought under shelter. Every man and beast that is left outside and not brought indoors shall die when the hail comes down upon them.'''' [20]Then those among Pharaoh's courtiers who feared the word of the LORD rushed their slaves and livestock indoors, [21]but those who disregarded the word of the LORD left their slaves and livestock in the open.

22 The LORD said to Moses, 'Stretch out your hand toward heaven, that hail may fall in all the land of Egypt upon man and beast, and upon all the vegetation in the land of Egypt.' [23]So Moses stretched out his rod toward heaven, and the LORD sent thunder and hail, and fire streamed down to the earth. Thus the LORD rained hail down upon the land of Egypt. [24]There was hail with fire continually flashing in the midst of the hail, extremely heavy, such as had not ever fallen in all the land of Egypt since it had become a nation. [25]The hail struck down everything in the land of Egypt which was outdoors both man and beast, and all the vegetation of the field was crushed and all the trees of the field shattered. [26]Only in the land of Goshen, where the Israelites were, there was no hail.

27 Then Pharaoh sent and called for Moses and Aaron and said to them, 'This time I have sinned. The LORD is in the right and I and my people in the wrong. [28]Intercede with the LORD for there has been enough of God's thunder and hail. I will let you go; you need stay no longer.' [29]Moses said to him, 'As soon as I leave the city, I will stretch out my hands in prayer to the LORD. The thunder will cease and there will not be hail any longer that you may know that the earth is the LORD's. [30]But as for you and your courtiers, I know that you do not fear the LORD God.' [31](The flax and the barley were ruined for the barley was in the ear and the flax was in the bud; [32]but the wheat and spelt were not ruined for they came later.) [33]So Moses left Pharaoh's presence, went out of the city, and stretched out his hands in prayer to the LORD. The thunder and hail ceased, and rain no longer fell on the earth. [34]But when Pharaoh saw that the rain and the hail and the thunder had stopped, he sinned again, and hardened his heart, as did his courtiers. [35]So the heart of Pharaoh was hardened and he would not let the Israelites go, just as the LORD had said through Moses.

10 [1]Then the LORD said to Moses, 'Go to Pharaoh, for I have hardened his heart and the heart of his courtiers in order that I may

perform these signs of mine among them, [2]and in order that you may recount to your son and your son's son how I toyed with the Egyptians and how I performed my signs among them; so that you may know that I am the LORD.' [3]Moses and Aaron went to Pharaoh and said to him, 'Thus says the LORD, the God of the Hebrews, "How long will you refuse to humble yourself before me. Let my people go that they may serve me. [4]For if you refuse to let my people go, then tomorrow I am going to bring locusts into your country. [5]They shall cover the face of the land so that no one can see the land. They shall devour the residue which was left you from the hail and shall eat up all your trees growing in the fields. [6]They shall fill your palaces and the houses of all your courtiers and the houses of all the Egyptians, the like of which neither your fathers nor your grandfathers have ever seen from the day they appeared on earth until this day."' Then he turned and left Pharaoh's presence.

7 Pharaoh's courtiers said to him, 'How long is this man going to endanger us? Let the men go and serve the LORD their God. Are you not yet aware that Egypt is ruined?' [8]So Moses and Aaron were brought back to Pharaoh and he said to them, 'Go, serve the LORD, your God, but who exactly is to go?' [9]Moses replied, 'We will go with our young and old; we will go with our sons and daughters, our flocks and herds for we must observe a pilgrim feast to the LORD.' [10]But he said to them, 'I would just as soon wish God's blessing on you as to let your children go with you! Look, you have some evil design in mind. [11]No, let the men go and serve the LORD, for that's what you want.' Then they were driven out of Pharaoh's presence.

12 The LORD said to Moses, 'Stretch out your hand over the land of Egypt for the locusts, that they may come upon the land of Egypt and eat up all the vegetation in the land, whatever the hail has left.' [13]So Moses stretched his rod over the land of Egypt, and the LORD drove an east wind over the land all that day and night. When it was morning, the east wind had brought the locusts. [14]The locusts came up over all the land of Egypt and settled within the whole territory of Egypt, a thick mass of them; never before had there been such locusts nor will there ever be such again. [15]They covered the face of the whole land until the land was black; they ate up all the vegetation of the land, and all the fruit of the trees which the hail had left. Not a green thing was left on tree or plant in all the land of Egypt.

16 The Pharaoh summoned Moses and Aaron in haste and said, 'I have sinned against the LORD your God, and against you. [17]Now forgive my offense just this once and intercede with the LORD your God that he at least remove this death from me.' [18]So he left Pharaoh's presence and interceded with the LORD. [19]The LORD turned a very strong west wind which lifted the locusts and swept them into the Sea

of Reeds; not a single locust was left in all the territory of Egypt. [20]But the LORD hardened Pharaoh's heart, and he would not let the Israelites go.

21 Then the LORD said to Moses, 'Stretch out your hand toward heaven that there may be darkness upon the land of Egypt, a darkness that can be touched.' [22]So Moses stretched out his hand toward heaven, and there was a thick darkness over all the land of Egypt for three days. [23]People could not see one another and for three days no one could leave his spot; but all the Israelites had light where they dwelt.

24 Then Pharaoh summoned Moses and said, 'Go serve the LORD; only your flocks and herds shall remain behind; even your children may go with you.' [25]But Moses said, 'You must also provide us with sacrifices and burnt offerings to offer to the LORD our God. [26]Our livestock also must go along with us – not a hoof shall be left behind – for we have to take some of them to serve the LORD our God; and we do not know what we are to offer to the LORD until we arrive there.' [27]But the LORD hardened Pharaoh's heart, and he would not let them go. [28]Then Pharaoh said to them, 'Get out of my sight. Watch yourself. Never see my face again for in the day you see me, you will die.' [29]Moses replied, 'You are right! I will not see your face again.'

11 [1]Then the LORD said to Moses, 'Only one more plague I will bring upon Pharaoh and upon Egypt; after that he will let you go from here. Indeed, when he lets you go, he will drive you out bag and baggage. [2]Tell the people that each man should request from his neighbor, and each woman hers, objects of silver and gold.' [3] Then the LORD caused the Egyptians to look with favor on the people. Moreover, Moses himself was highly esteemed in the land of Egypt among Pharaoh's courtiers and among the people.

4 Moses said, 'Thus says the LORD: "About midnight I will be going forth among the Egyptians, [5]and every first-born in the land of Egypt shall die, from the first-born of Pharaoh who sits on his throne to the first-born of the slave girl who works the hand mill. [6]There will be a great cry in all the land of Egypt, such as there has never been, nor will ever be again. [7]But against any of the Israelites, whether man or beast, not so much as a dog shall bark," in order that you may know that the LORD makes a distinction between Egypt and Israel. [8]And all your courtiers shall come down to me, and shall bow low to me, saying, "Go away, you and all the people who follow you!" After that I will leave.' Then he left Pharaoh in hot anger.

9 The LORD said to Moses, 'Pharaoh will not listen to you in order that my wonders may be increased in the land of Egypt.' [10]Moses and Aaron had performed all these wonders before Pharaoh but the LORD had hardened Pharaoh's heart so that he would not let the Israelites go from his land.

1. Textual and Philological Notes

7.9 *tannîn*, 'serpent'. In Gen. 1.21 (cf. Isa. 27.1; Ps. 74.13) the term refers to a sea monster, but in Ex. 7.9, 10, 12 simply a serpent is denoted (cf. Deut. 32.33), which is parallel to *nāḥāš* Ex. 4.3; 7.15 in the earlier source. The LXX may have added to the confusion by rendering it δράκων = dragon.

11. *ḥarṭummîm*, 'magicians'. Most Egyptologists support B. Couroyer, *RB* 63, 1956, p. 487, in deriving the word from the Egyptian *ḥr-ṭp* = 'the chief of the priests', which in Assyrian became *ḥarṭibi*. Most recently, D. B. Redford agrees, *A Study of the Biblical Story of Joseph*, Leiden 1970, pp. 203f. However, some Egyptologists are not convinced of its derivation (cf. T. O. Lambdin, *JAOS* 73, 1953, pp. 150–1; J. Vergote, *Joseph en Egypte*, Louvain 1959, pp. 8off.).

13. On the vocabulary of 'hardening', cf. the excursus with its bibliography.

17. The problem that the subject of the divine speech changes from Yahweh to Moses lies in the nature of the material and cannot be avoided by means of artificial punctuation as the NEB attempts. For the use of *bᵉzō'ṭ* cf. the parallel in I Sam. 11.2.

18. It is characteristic of the Samar. text throughout the plague stories to expand the text in order to recount the actual delivery of a divine speech to Pharaoh which was only commanded in the MT. Thus 7.18b records the execution of the command ordered in 7.16. Cf. 8.19; 9.19; 10.2.

19. Cf. T. Meek, 'Result and Purpose Clauses in Hebrew', *JQR* XLVI, 1955, pp. 40f.

20. The subject of the striking is ambiguous in the Hebrew and has been debated at length by the classic Jewish commentators (cf. Jer. Targum, Rashi). The larger context would probably point to Moses; however, the evidence is inconclusive. Cf. 8.13.

25. It is not clear whether v. 25 goes to the narrative which precedes (AV, NEB) or which follows (RSV, NJPS, NAB). I tend to feel that the former has the stronger case form-critically.

28. The Hebrew reads *ʿam* with the preposition, whereas the LXX construes it as a genitive which is preferable.

8.5 (EVV 9). *hitpāer ʿālay*. The expression already caused the versions difficulty. The LXX has τάξαι πρὸς μέ 'Appoint for me'. Onkelos paraphrases it: 'Glorify thyself on account of me', which interpretation is reflected in the NJPS: 'You may have this triumph over me'. Rashi cites Ezek. 35.13 as its closest parallel, but cf. also Judg. 7.2 and Isa. 10.15. The RSV considers it to be a formula of politeness which has lost its original literal meaning. This conclusion does not seem to me right for two reasons: (i) The philological evidence consistently points to a meaning of 'obtaining an advantage over a person', whereas there is no clear philological evidence of its being merely a polite formula. (ii) The context, particularly in Moses' response in v. 6, demands far more content to it than a formal convention (cf. exegesis). Also cf. the discussion by C. Rabin, *Scripta Hieros.* 8, 1961, p. 397.

8. The syntactical problem turns on the question of the antecedent for the final phrase. Dillmann and the RSV refer the words to the promise of their removal and translate: 'as he had agreed with Pharaoh'. The other interpretation, referring the words to the noun, while somewhat redundant in content, has a

better grammatical warrant: 'which he had brought on Pharaoh', and is preferable.

9. The preposition *min* has a separative sense here (Brockelmann, *Syntax*, §111e) and should not be translated 'in' (NEB). The separative sense is also required by v.5.

13. The form of *kinnām* is contested. Dillmann suggested that it is a fem. collective, constructed by the Massoretes, because of the verb *teḥî*. Bauer-Leander (*Historische Grammatik der hebräischen Sprache*, Halle 1922, §61k¹, p.504) follows in this same direction (cf. *G–K* §85t). The word occurs infrequently in the OT (Ps. 105.31; Isa. 51.6(?)) and its meaning is not fully clear. The meaning of 'gnats' is represented in the LXX, Philo, and Origen, whereas Pesh. and Targ. Onk. render it 'lice'. NEB uses 'maggots'. Most modern commentaries prefer the term 'gnats', but hardly on philological grounds. Some argue that it is a parallel to the flies of the fourth plague (Noth). Others think that gnats are more characteristic of Egypt. The evidence is indecisive.

15. On the expression 'finger of God', cf. B. Couroyer, 'Le Doigt de Dieu', *RB* 63, 1956, pp.481–95. He has argued that this is a technical Egyptian magical formula, however, his parallels are not fully convincing. The older view is to understand the phrase as an example of synecdoche, referring to the divine power of his hands.

17. *ʿārōḇ*, 'flies'. Rabbinic literature has proceeded from the homonymous root 'to mix', and thus understood the noun to mean a 'mixture of wild beasts'. However, an insect is definitely intended. Exactly what variety of fly is meant, is difficult to say. Cf. G. Hort, *op. cit.* p.99.

19. *pedut*, 'distinction'? The meaning here is difficult. It would seem to be derived from the root *pdh* and mean 'redemption' as in Ps.111.9; 130.7. But this meaning does not fit the context and the LXX renders it διαστολή. Therefore several emendations have been suggested, but the problem remains unsettled. Cf. the most recent treatment of A. A. Macintosh in *VT* 21, 1971, pp.548ff.

22. F. Nötscher, 'Zum emphatischen Lamed', *VT* 3, 1953, pp.372–80, has suggested taking *lō* as an emphatic and translating, 'the Egyptians will certainly stone us'. This interpretation is possible, but not compelling.

25. *hāṭēl*. An Arabic cognate carries the connotation of 'act coquettishly'. The Hebrew means 'to trifle with a person' in a less than serious manner.

9.3. G. S. Ogden, 'Notes on the use of *hwjh* in Ex. ix:3', *VT* 17, 1967, pp. 483f., has pointed out that the participle of *hyh* occurs only once in the OT. Actually one would expect the imperfect or a nominal clause without the copula. Ogden attributes its use here to an attempt to conform to a larger pattern in the narrative in which the participle is consistently used (7.17, 27; 9.3; 10.4).

7. *yišlaḥ*, 'send' is here used elliptically as 'send to inquire'.

9. 'boils breaking out into pustules'. The noun *šeḥîn* has an Arabic cognate meaning 'to be hot'. The idea of heat may be implied in the soot taken from the kiln. The exact nature of the eruption and whether one specific disease is intended is not clear (cf. II Kings 20.7; Deut. 28.35; Lev. 13.18). Cf. G. Hort, *op. cit.*, p.101ff., for an attempt to identify the disease scientifically.

14. 'upon your heart'. S. R. Driver suggests emending the text by changing one letter to read *ʾēlleh beḵā* 'all these . . . on you'. But the MT is clear enough (cf. Dillmann).

18. Cf. B. Couroyer, 'Un égyptianisme biblique; "depuis la fondation de l'Égypte"', *RB* 67, 1960, pp.42ff.

28. *qōlōṯ 'elōhîm* is taken by D. Winton Thomas, *VT* 3, 1953, p.210 as a superlative: 'mighty thunderings'.

30. The expression 'Yahweh Elohim' is rare in the OT outside of Gen.2, but it is doubtful whether a special connotation is intended here.

10.6. On the idiom *'aḏ hayyôm hazzeh*, 'until this day', cf. Childs, *JBL* 82, 1963, pp.279ff.

10. The sarcastic idiom used by Pharaoh is misinterpreted by the NEB, in my judgment: 'Very well then . . . and the Lord be with you.' Cf. rather NAB: 'The Lord help you if . . .'.

12. The LXX has a considerably longer text which may be original.

15. 'was darkened'. The graphic Hebrew figure is in order and should not be emended according to the LXX.

21. There is not sufficient reason to suggest a corruption in the text as *BH*[3] does. Targ. Onkelos may have been led astray by seeing a parallel in Job 5.14.

11.1. The suggestion of reading *keṣillehû kallāh*, 'as one sends away a bride', was apparently first suggested by J. Coppens, *ETL* 23, 1947, pp.178f., and accepted by J. Morgenstern, *JBL* 69, 1949, pp.1ff. and D. Daube, *Studies in Biblical Law*, Cambridge and New York 1947, and NEB. The emendation is not very likely and leads to a straining of the text.

2. *š'l*, 'ask'. Cf. the excursus on 'Despoiling of the Egyptians' for a treatment of the verb.

3. The Samar. text makes a great many changes, both in person and order, adding sections from Ex.12.35; 4.22 in an attempt to smooth out the narrative.

7. Cf. F. C. Fensham, *VT* 16, 1966, pp.504f. for a discussion of the Hebrew idiom.

2. *Literary, Form-Critical, and Traditio-Historical Problems*

A. *Literary and Form-Critical*

The plague stories have long been considered an excellent section on which to demonstrate the role of sources. However, within recent years there has been a growing tendency in some circles to discount the importance or even the presence of the latter. The attack combines two arguments. First, some of the difficulties in terms of the inner consistency among the sources are pointed out. Secondly, and more important, the claim is made that a proper interpretation of the plague account reveals a clear and unified structure (cf. B. Jacob, *op. cit.*; Winnett, *op. cit.*, pp.3ff.; Cassuto, *Exodus*, pp.92ff.; Loewenstamm, *Tradition*, pp.76ff.).

The difficulty with this approach is that the description of that 'clear and unified structure' is never the same. Compare, for example, the analysis of Cassuto, Winnett, and McCarthy. Moreover, even when the demonstrations of patterns are convincing, the observations seldom bear directly on the issue of source criticism. Rather, they deal with the level of final redaction. Therefore, while fully acknowledging the need to examine the final form of the passage, we do not feel that the case against source criticism is at all convincing. The alleged subjectivity of the source critics is compounded by the advocates of simple literary unity. (Cf. below for a discussion of the final form of the narrative.)

The main lines of the source divisions had already been worked out by Wellhausen. The P material had been isolated earlier, although the analysis is still confused by Knobel, 1857. The largest portion of the remaining material was then assigned to J with small fragments given to E. In general, wide agreement has been sustained in respect to the Priestly source. The issue which was contested turned about the place of J and E. Wellhausen's divisions were accepted with slight modifications by Holzinger, Bacon, Bäntsch, and Gressmann. Smend and Eissfeldt opted for another source J¹/L, and Rudolph sought to eliminate E completely. The most impressive attack on seeing three sources, however, came from Noth, who argues for a basic J account which has been glossed and expanded, rather than for an E source. In my opinion, the recent analysis of Fohrer has successfully met Noth's arguments and sustained Wellhausen's three-source division. The decisive argument seems to be that the material which has been isolated apart from J and P does reflect a definite form-critical pattern. This would hardly have been the case if J had been only glossed. By including much of the E material under P Noth, in effect, blurs the clear Priestly schema. In addition to the three sources there is widespread agreement regarding several late glosses. We suggest the following divisions:

J: 7.14–15a, 16–17a, 17b*, 18, 21a, 24–25, 26–29; 8.4–11a, 16–28; 9.1–7, 13, 17–18, 23b, 24a*, 24b, 25b, 26–30, 33–34; 10.1a, 3–11, 13b, 14b, 15a*, 15b–19, 24–26, 28–29; 11.4–8.

E: 7.15b, 17b*, 20b, 23; 9.22–23a, 24a*, 25a, 35a; 10.12–13a, 15a*, 15b, 20, 21–23, 27; 11.1–3.

P: 7.1–7, 8–13, 19–20a, 21b–22; 8.1–3, 11b, 12–15; 9.8–12, 35b; 11.9–10.

Additions: 9.14–16, 19–21, 31–32; 10.1b–2*.

There remains considerable disagreement regarding the scope of the plague narrative. Driver and others (Fohrer, Plastaras) follow an older scholarly tradition by starting the section at 7.14. The logic of this division is that the P material is parallel to the JE account of Moses' call in 3.1–4.23. However, a strong case can be made for seeing 7.8–13 as the introduction to the plague story. Certainly the style and vocabulary is continuous with what follows in P, and the motif of the contest with the Egyptian magicians begins here (so Bacon, Bäntsch, Beer, Rudolph, Noth, McCarthy).

Although I am inclined to agree with this latter view, there is an additional problem which has not been given sufficient attention. As we saw earlier, the P redactor has broken off his account in 6.12 and summarized the remaining part in v. 13 in order to introduce a genealogy. One now has the impression that for this redactor the plague account began at 6.28. Of course, v. 7 continued to act disjunctively as a conclusion from P's original structure, but v. 3 presents in summary form P's major point. God will harden Pharaoh's heart in order that he can multiply his signs and wonders with the result that Pharaoh will not listen. This assertion by God runs like a red cord throughout the narrative following each of P's plagues, and is picked up in the phrase 'as God had said' (7.13, 22; 8.11, 15; 9.12, 35). Since 7.3 is the only possible antecedent to the phrase, the continuity would suggest seeing 6.28ff. as the introduction. Again, the P conclusion to the plague story in 11.9 not only summarizes the plagues after the ninth one, but clearly refers back to 7.3. Pharaoh had indeed hardened his heart in order 'to multiply signs in the land'. This evidence would seem to indicate that, although P began his account of the plagues with 7.8, the final redactional hand structured it to begin at 6.28. The earlier sources appear to have started it with the plague which turned water to blood (7.14).

Turning now to the ending, there is again a much debated issue. Clearly 11.9–10 serves as the conclusion to P. But what about the earlier sources? The problem is posed by 10.29. Pharaoh forbids Moses to reappear under a judgment of death. Moses agrees that he will not come again. But in 11.4 he is again in conversation with the king and only in v. 8 does he leave in anger. The earlier critical position objected to the attempted harmonization of the difficulty – Jacob still defends a pluperfect tense for *wayyō'mer* in v. 4 – and sought to connect 11.4–8 with 10.29 as being one continuous speech. Accordingly, the difficulty arose by the redactional position of E in 11.1–3 (so Dillmann, Bäntsch, Driver, Fohrer).

Against this position Gressmann voiced an objection: 'One doesn't pronounce such a judgment when heading out of the door!' (p. 97).

Recently, Noth has picked up Gressmann's case and further buttressed it. He noticed the inconsistency of the addressee within the passage and suggested that originally the passage was directed to Israel (vv. 4–6) and not Pharaoh. The remaining verses are removed as an 'ill-considered addition'. Fohrer has objected to Noth's position by pointing out the consistency of the passage with J's style. One can add to this that the same formal inconsistencies can be found in Plague V and there is no previous warrant for seeing Israel addressed in this manner. The elements of the disputation have dislocated the normal form and we conclude by agreeing with Fohrer in seeing a continuous speech in 10.29 and 11.1–8.

Finally, the difficulty has been overstressed which sees an irreconcilable problem in relating Moses' statement in 10.29 with his appearance before Pharaoh in 12.31 (cf. Dillmann, *ad loc.*). 10.29 is a type of pun which belongs to the disputation and makes a self-contained point. Pharaoh says to Moses: 'Don't appear again lest you die!' Moses responds: 'You are right. I'll not appear ever again.' The hidden implication is: I'll be gone. The fact that Moses does appear again to receive the release of the people is hardly an inconsistency arising from a source problem.

The frequent characterization of the patterns of the three sources allows our treatment of this to be brief (cf. Bäntsch, p. 55; Driver, pp. 55f.; Fohrer, pp. 63ff.). Moreover, there remains a number of other difficult literary questions which require further investigation.

The J source

The basic narrative pattern can be divided into three sections: (i) It begins with Yahweh's command for Moses to deliver to Pharaoh a message which contains both a demand for release of the people (7.14ff., 26, etc.) and a threat if he refuses (7.27; 8.17). (ii) The threat is then carried out by Yahweh (8.20; 9.6) and its effects described (7.21; 8.20, etc.). (iii) Pharaoh then summons Moses; a conversation ensues, often resulting in a concession; Moses intercedes, but Pharaoh's heart is hardened and he refuses to release the people (8.4ff., 21ff.; 9.27ff.).

Worked into this basic pattern are in addition a number of special motifs. It is not always clear whether these are *Sondermotiven* or belong to the pattern itself. I tend to regard the hardening motif as part of the basic structure because of its recurring formulae, while the separate themes lack fixed vocabulary. Among these special motifs are such themes as 'that you may know' (8.6, 18; 9.29; 11.7), the distinction between Israel and Egypt (8.18; 9.4, 7; 9.26; 11.7), and the series of concessions. The interesting problem is that in spite of the constant elements in J, there is a great variety and freedom both within the narrative pattern and in the use of the special motifs. In plague I there are no negotiations with Pharaoh or intercession. Plague V seems to be exceedingly short in length and also lacks negotiations and intercession. The final elements of the messenger speech also varies from the normal J pattern. Plague VIII reflects one of the most serious variations. Yahweh does not address a speech to Moses, but instead the actual delivery of the speech to Pharaoh is reported which is unique to J. Finally, the negotiations in 10.24 do not seem to have been originally attached to plague IX, but part of VIII.

How is one to account for such a large amount of variation within a rather rigid pattern of successive plagues? Certainly more than one factor is at work. A few of the examples cited are dislocations which resulted from the combination of sources. The introduction to plague IX (darkness) from the E source accounts most probably for the unusual character of J in this plague. It is difficult to determine just how much of the variation in plague I is due to source combination. With the exception of plague X, it is the only one with a combination of three sources. But it is also possible that the lack of an intercession goes back to J and was a device to show an initial lack of response. Noth has argued that plague V is a secondary element in the J account. Plastaras suggests, on the basis of a comparison with Ps. 78, that its original place followed plague VII. However, both theories remain quite speculative and do not afford much help.

The most extensive variation appears in plague VIII (10.1ff.). The passage starts with the usual J introduction, but changes over to a first-person Yahweh speech instead of a message to Pharaoh. In v. 3 the message is actually delivered with all the distinctive marks of a J speech. Only a few slight grammatical changes are necessary in v. 3 to give the scene its narrative setting. Usually commentators suggest that this dislocation has resulted from the interpolation in 1b–2, which is considered a late redactional development. Although this solution is to be taken seriously, it does not strike to the heart of the problem. Actually the issue is more deep-seated than a slight redactional adjustment and affords a good insight into J's use of his material.

The issue hangs closely together with the special theme of the concessions. Plague VIII needed to have the negotiations with Pharaoh *before* the plague because the conversation ended this time in an impasse. The plague *followed* as a result of the failure to agree. The device which the author employed to facilitate the movement of the narrative was an intercession on the part of Pharaoh's servants. But the writer needed to have the divine threat actually delivered in order to have evoked this response. Because J normally omitted the delivery of the message and passed directly to Yahweh's execution of the plague, the writer was forced to alter the announcement of the threat to Moses into the delivery of the message to Pharaoh by Moses.

The complexity of the concession motif has not usually been noticed. Two different types appear to be involved. In the first (schema A) a concession is made by Pharaoh which finally is acceptable to Moses (cf. 8.24=EVV 28; 9.28). On the basis of the concession, Moses offers intercession, and only because Pharaoh later reneges on his promise does the plague sequence continue. However, in the second instance (schema B) the concession is not adequate and the negotiations end in an impasse (10.8ff.; 10.24ff.). The transition from schema A to schema B comes in plague VIII. Both schemas play an integral part of J's narrative. Pattern B is dictated by the last plague. The negotiation breaks down with no further entreaty possible, and the final threat is announced (10.24ff.; 11.4ff.). The climax is prepared by having the breakdown in negotiations begin with plague VIII. In spite of Pharaoh's lack of a concession, but because of his indication of repentance in 10.17, Moses intercedes. Then the negotiations resume (10.24) only to end in a complete impasse. However, without schema A, it would have been impossible for the concession scheme to have been carried through a series. By the skillful use of the concession motif the author built up a gradual suspense. Pharaoh yields on *where* the people are to go, even *when* they are to leave (9.28), only to disagree violently on *who* is allowed to depart.

What emerges from a close analysis of the concession motif is an appreciation of the high degree of literary creativity in J. The change in the pattern is in this case not redactional but a conscious literary formation. In spite of traditional forces bearing on the writer which had determined in general the conclusion and the general structure of the narrative, the J writer shows tremendous freedom and imagination in fashioning his account.

Several other signs confirm this judgment. First, there is the interesting tension in J between the absolute demands of release repeated in the phrase, 'Let my people go', and the willingness to negotiate. The reader is left to wonder just what is involved in Moses' apparent acceptance of the stipulations only to leave the land for a short distance. Is this only a ruse to escape? The writer skillfully pursues the dual approach, until with a jar, the negotiations run aground. In the end, the two lines again meet and the irreconcilability of the two positions emerges sharply.

Again, the writer shows consummate skill in portraying the two protagonists in spite of the set roles which the tradition had assigned them. Moses is presented as an apt debater who continually counters Pharaoh's moves with clever arguments. 'The Egyptians will be offended if we sacrifice to our God in their land' (8.22). 'All the people must attend because it is a special feast (*ḥāg*)' (10.9). 'How can we leave our animals when we do not know what Yahweh will require?' Commentators have long debated the validity of these arguments, but the major point certainly lies in the effect they produce on Pharaoh. Frequently he chides the king, anticipating his duplicity (8.25). In the end his anger rises to match Pharaoh's and his departure is a masterpiece of subtle restraint (10.29).

The picture painted of Pharaoh is only slightly less impressive. The proud tyrant who is finally forced to yield belongs to the received tradition. But to J belongs the picture of Pharaoh who slyly spars with Moses, who passionately confesses his wrong, but with equal speed relents once the pressure has been removed. He can be violent (10.28) and sarcastic (10.10), almost to the extent of getting the best of the argument (10.11). He even seems to know Jewish law! Then when all is lost, the portrayal is not one of tragic despair, but of a sly fox still trying to salvage what he can (12.32). This interest in the figure of Pharaoh as a person is confined almost entirely to the plague narrative. Everywhere else, with the exception of ch. 1, he returns to his stereotyped role of the oppressor.

Finally, the interrelation between the various special motifs in J deserve attention. The phrase 'in order that you may know' (*lᵉmaʿan tēdaʿ kî*) occurs four times in J, not counting the redactional passages. Each time it is a speech addressed to Pharaoh and carried in the theme which was first introduced by Pharaoh in 5.2, 'Who is Yahweh? I do not know Yahweh.' In two cases the disclosure of the true knowledge of God is related to his separating Israel from the plague (8.18; 11.8.) But in two cases the phrase relates to his power to remove the plague at a specific time (8.6; 9.29). It would therefore seem that for this writer both the motif of Israel's distinction and the precise time of removal function in a similar way as signs of his power. This fact is of significance when we try to assess the theological import of Yahweh's special handling of Israel. (Note: J's hardening theme will be handled together with P in an excursus.)

The E source

The E source is preserved in a rather fragmentary form. In spite of this, there does appear to be a discernible pattern which would speak against its being considered as a series of glosses rather than a continuous strand. Again, the basic scheme contains three elements which are best seen in plague IX: (i) Moses is commanded to stretch out his staff (or hand) in order to bring a plague, which is then described. (ii) The command is carried out by Moses and the ensuing plague is described. (iii) The effect is reported with the hardening formula.

The schema is far briefer than either J or P, but does seem to be complete and not simply a torso. It appears to lack any special themes (10.23b may well be redactional). The basic movement of the narrative is closely akin to P and seems to reflect more the original tradition which was their common source. The plagues, which already combined elements of the miracle and the plague, come in quick series. They are mediated by Moses and have no effect on Pharaoh because of his hardness. Especially characteristic of the E source is Moses' role in producing the plagues. Still the difference in his role should not be exaggerated (cf. Gressmann). There are no grounds for seeing Moses in the role of a magician or the like. The differences lie in the idiom which has been chosen. At least in the joining of J and E there is no sign whatever of friction between Yahweh and Moses as instigators of the plagues.

Of some interest is the manner in which J and E have been combined. J and E together appear in plagues VII, VIII, and IX, with P in plague I. The technique employed in joining J and E is approximately the same in each case. The first section of E, the command to Moses, is inserted following J's initial section which consists of the message to Moses. The transition from Yahweh's executing the plague in J to Moses' being the agent is managed so smoothly as only to be noticed by the critical age. The execution of the plague and its description is then intertwined from parts of J and E. There then follows J's third section which deals with the negotiations between Pharaoh and Moses. E's formula of hardening usually ends the section. (An exception is in I where J's last section is missing.) The result of the combination is an expansion of J's basic schema. The most serious deviation from this pattern comes in plague IX. This was the only case in which J lacked a parallel plague. Part of J's negotiations in plague VIII was, therefore, taken and used with E's to round out plague IX. The effect is somewhat odd, but the general technique of source fusion is the same.

The method of intertwining of J and E is different from that used by the Priestly redactor. P is preserved in complete blocks wherever possible even though it meant the loss of some of the earlier source (plague II). Only in plague I is P divided into two sections to preserve the order of the narrative in its combined form. This would seem to be indirect evidence that P worked with a form of the tradition in which J and E were already combined.

The P source

The schema of P once again falls into three parts: (i) God commands Moses to instruct Aaron to stretch out his rod and thereby to effect the plague (8.1 [EVV 5] is a slight variation). (ii) The command is executed with a description of the ensuing plague. (The special theme of the contest with the Egyptian magicians appears at this point.) (iii) Pharaoh fails to react because of the hardness of his heart.

There are several important places in which the P account reflects a variant tradition from P. The first clear difference between P and J is the handling of the call narrative (cf. above). In P the call takes place in Egypt, not in Midian. The response of Pharaoh is predicted in advance to be negative. But perhaps the most important change is the over-all function of the section 6.28–7.7. Although it remains a part of the call narrative, yet it now functions to introduce and interpret the plagues. The purpose of the signs is set forth in 7.3f. and repeatedly picked up in the body of the narrative in the phrase 'as Yahweh said'.

Another important variation in P which reflects a different tradition is in beginning the plague account first with a contest between Moses and the Egyptian magicians. The J account of the signs belongs to the call narrative and is directed to the people rather than to Pharaoh. At this point Gressmann (p. 86) has suggested a distinction between the plagues and miracles, and on the basis of this has tried to reconstruct the development of the tradition. Certainly Gressmann has noted an important difference in function between the plague and the sign. However, his attempt to use this distinction as the main key for opening up the history of the plague tradition seems to have been less than successful. The problem lies in the fact that in P's schema Moses and the magicians compete in the performing of miraculous signs, yet the signs soon take on the characteristics of plagues, whereas the J source speaks initially of plagues, but these shortly function as signs. This would seem to suggest that the distinction played an important role in distinguishing two varying traditions, but at a very early stage the two functions had begun to merge.

The key to understanding the structure of P's plague narrative as well as its relation to the subsequent tradition of the passover and exodus seems to be given in 7.3ff. The passage contains several interesting features which have not as yet been closely enough observed. In 7.3 the writer interprets the function of the hardening. According to P the plagues were not the result of Pharaoh's hardness, but rather the reverse. Pharaoh was hardened in order that Yahweh might multiply his signs. Nor has it been noticed that P ends his sign narrative in 11.9–11 following plague IX. This has been thought to be a late redactional addition (cf. Bäntsch). However, the repetition of the identical vocabulary of 7.3ff. confirms a conscious pattern of the P writer in interpreting the function of the plagues. 11.9–10 conclude the plague account by confirming the prediction that Pharaoh would not listen, as Yahweh had said at the outset.

Closely connected with P's ending of the plague sequence in 11.1f. is the fact that for the P tradition the killing of the first-born is not seen as the tenth and final plague in a series. This interpretation has already been given from the structure of the plagues. Additional evidence now comes from the passover tradition. The death of the first-born has been incorporated within the passover tradition and transmitted as a separate tradition. Whereas both J and E introduce the death of the first-born as yet one more plague (11.1), P never once refers to the plagues in this regard. The passover tradition directs a blow against the first-born and all the gods of Egypt (12.12), but not in a sequence, nor as a sign. Actually the sign within the passover tradition functions to ward off the 'blow'. As a result of this blow Yahweh leads his people out of Egypt. A summary of this tradition is given in 7.4: 'Then I will lay my hand upon Egypt and bring forth my hosts, my people the sons of Israel, out of the land of Egypt by great acts of judgment.' Two points are worth making. Only in ch. 12 in the passover tradition is the smiting of the Egyptian gods referred to as executing judgment (12.12). Also only in P after the plague reference is there mention of the 'hosts' (12.41). These verses (12.40–42) function in a similar way for the passover tradition as did 11.9–11 for the plague tradition. They summarize the tradition and confirm the initial framework of P given in 7.3ff.

There is another tradition which P links in an unusual way to the plagues, namely the crossing of the sea. In a recent article ('Plagues . . .' *op. cit.*) McCarthy noted the strange continuity between the plague sequence and the crossing of the sea, which is completely missing in the passover of ch. 12. This continuity with the plagues is in striking contrast with the J tradition which links the crossing of the sea with the wilderness tradition rather than with the exodus from Egypt. However, in my opinion, McCarthy has drawn an incorrect conclusion from the similarity in P between the plague tradition and the crossing. A closer study of the distinctive P vocabulary and the structure of the narrative goes far to clarify the problem.

In the P narrative the victory of Yahweh over Pharaoh at the sea serves a clear purpose. Yahweh excites Pharaoh to pursue with the purpose of getting glory over him and that 'the Egyptians will know' that Yahweh is Lord (14.4). It is only in the crossing that the phrase 'Egypt will know . . .' occurs in P. Although it functions in J in connection with the plagues, P confines its use to the crossing. From what has already been said, it is evident that the plagues in P could not have the function of making Yahweh known to the Egyptians. Again in P, the passover blow is directed against the gods of Egypt, but the crossing is against Pharaoh and his hosts (14.4, 18). This third stage of the structure of P's narrative is indicated in 7.5 with the sentence: 'Then the Egyptians shall know that I am Yahweh, when I stretch forth my hand and bring the people from among them.' For the P tradition also the crossing is not part of the exodus from Egypt – Egypt had been left following the passover night – but it is a rescue from the Egyptian army.

An examination of the effect of combining the J(E) and P sources reveals some interesting changes. The original P sequence of the plagues as signs which climaxed in the defeat of the Egyptian magicians was subsumed within J's framework of the plagues. The contest became a subordinate theme. While fusion between signs and plagues seemed to have begun early in the oral stage, certainly the final merger occurred on the literary level. Now signs function as plagues and plagues serve as signs.

An even more important change occurred in terms of the relation of the J plague tradition to the P crossing tradition. The phrase 'that the Egyptians may know' served in J as a function of the plagues. The same phrase in P formed part of the crossing tradition. As a result of the fusion of the sources the special roles within the different strands became blurred. The effect was that in the combined narrative the crossing of the P source was read in the light of the J plague narrative. The crossing no longer retained the unique emphasis of P of making Yahweh known, since this role had already been assigned to J's plagues. The final effect of the combination was that the tradition of the crossing of the sea was drawn into closer proximity with the exodus tradition. This may account for the duality of the sea tradition which at times points to the wilderness tradition and at times to the exodus.

One final change effected by the combination was in terms of the relation of the plagues to the passover. In P the passover was clearly set apart, but through the combination assumed the schema of J. The effect was to bring the two traditions into closest proximity.

Lastly, a brief discussion is in order of the material which is later than the three sources, often designated as glosses. There is rather widespread agreement among the critical commentators in regarding the following as not belonging to the major literary strands: 9.14–16, 19–21, 31–32; 10.1b–2. However, there is little consensus as to how to interpret these verses since no one set of forces seems at work.

[9.14–16] These verses appear to contain a theological reflection on the basis of the JE material which is concerned to explain why God has allowed the plagues to continue so long. The P writer deals with the same question in a different way by his theology of multiplying signs. This writer emphasizes that God's long-suffering does not reflect his impotence – in fact, just the opposite. He has restrained himself by not exercising the full intensity of his might in order to demonstrate his power.

[9.19–21] The specific warning to Pharaoh and his servants is a unique feature in the plague sequence. Bäntsch notes that it does not fit with the usual solidarity between king and servants found in J. Noth suggests that it may be a type of midrashic attempt to explain why all the cattle were not destroyed by the previous plague. Indeed there are other signs that a later reader was concerned to harmonize some of the internal tensions in the sequence of the narrative (cf. 10.12b; 10.15b, etc.). However, the difficulty of the animal plague preceding the hail remains untouched. Plastaras has suggested an originally different order. Winnett explains the difficulty by restricting the term 'cattle'. Neither explanation seems too helpful. I am, therefore, inclined to follow Bacon who sees a didactic interest at work in distinguishing between the 'god-fearers' and the unbelievers, even among Pharaoh's servant. This provides a testimony that the solidarity of judgment against all Egypt could always be relieved by faith in God's word.

[**9.31–32**] Again there has been considerable discussion whether this gloss reflects simply a later archaeological interest or is a midrashic attempt to account for the continued presence of crops after the hail. The lack of a larger pattern makes it difficult to decide with any certainty. Since the date of the passover and final plague was fixed, it is possible that a learned calculation is being made and historical implications drawn for the story. But then is the agricultural time that of Egypt or of Palestine?

[**10.1b–2**] The final expansion is theological in character, and usually identified with a Deuteronomic redactor. The author uses the hardening vocabulary of J, but the theology of P. Any clear-cut distinction between sign and plague has also been lost. The expansion reflects the early interest in the actualization of the plague for a later generation. Here the Deuteronomistic interest is more didactic than liturgical (cf. Ex. 13.14f.; Josh. 4.21). The understanding of the plagues as a testimony to God's great power by which to make sport of mighty Pharaoh is at work.

B. *The Provenance of the Plague Tradition*

There is a strange atmosphere which surrounds the plague stories which differs from anything else in the book of Exodus. Some of the difference lies in the extravagant length of the story in comparison to the succinct and often rigidly controlled summaries of other traditions. But the problem of characterizing the peculiar flavor of this narrative lies deeper than mere length. It is the sense of historical distance which demands explanation.

The pervading quality of historical distance does not stem from the so-called 'supernatural' elements. Many other miracle stories, such as Elijah's contest on Carmel (I Kings 19), reflect a totally different atmosphere. Nor can one attribute it fully to the manner in which the characters are portrayed. In strange contrast to the rest of Exodus, Pharaoh emerges with a definite personality to oppose a vigorous Moses. Rather, the source of the problem lies in the continual linking of events in an artificial sequence, which runs counter to the normal reactions within history. The fact of this stereotyped, inflexible framework gives the account a flavor of historical unreality, and raises the fundamental traditio-historical question as to whether there are other non-historical forces at work which account for these peculiar qualities.

The problem is made complex once it is recognized that the final form of the narrative reflects a multiplicity of forces which have operated in giving the story its shape. One obvious reason for the protracted form lies in the literary fusion of sources, as has been shown. But this observation does not strike to the heart of the problem because already in the oral stage the various strands of the tradition all seem to share this quality which we are attempting to describe. Nor is the solution to be found in a novelistic love of embellishment (*Erzählungsfreude*), a characteristic which is attributed to ballad singers of all ages. Although on occasion such a factor may have played a role, the decisive question is whether there is one setting which is fundamental to the story and to which other forces have been joined. Or again, did the final form have no such foundation? Does it reflect the effect of a history of various traditional and literary forces which together account for its peculiar shape?

A brief glance at modern critical exegesis shows that there have been no lack of theories regarding the setting:

1. The attempt to pose an original mythological battle in a historicized form has been suggested, but can be dismissed as fanciful. More plausible is to see an occasional mythical motif entering, but even this is not obvious. The darkness of plague IX comes as a rather harmless anti-climax rather than as the terrifying sphere of the underworld. The striking contrast between the later apocalyptic use of the plagues (Enoch and Revelation) and its Old Testament form appears to be a decisive argument against the theory. Even the description of a 'battle' fails to do justice to the major movement of the narrative (*contra* Frey).

2. The theory which sees the didactic element as a major factor is based on the use of refrains, numbers, and stereotyped phraseology

which have distant parallels in wisdom literature. Although it is clear from Deuteronomy that the plagues later functioned didactically, the element does not seem to be a basic one.

3. Again certain elements of the disputation have entered and have played a significant role in the J source. Still few commentators would see this as more than a motif in the expansion of the story.

4. A cultic setting would suggest itself because of its connection with the passover, and perhaps because of its familiar function in the Jewish Haggadah, but few have been convinced of any thoroughgoing cultic theory.

5. There are some interesting elements which might point to a legal provenance. The parallels between the curses of Deut. 28 and the plagues is noteworthy, but still quite distant. Jacob (*op. cit.*, pp. 277ff.) has mounted a detailed argument for regarding the law against the rebellious son in Deut. 21.18–21 as being the legal pattern on what the plagues were patterned. However, the only really convincing parallel with the plague tradition lies in the common phrase: he refuses to hear.

6. Finally, an impressive case has been outlined by Buber (*op. cit.*, pp. 63ff.) for seeing in the plague story a representative situation which is recurrent throughout Israel's history of prophet versus king. The events are included within the causal nexus announced by the prophetic word, which explains its unique atmosphere. What is essential here, however, can only be that historical situation which recurs again and again from Samuel to Jeremiah, a situation in which the *nabi* penetrates into history. Buber's observation is illuminating, but not fully adequate to explain the formal features. The record of the prophet versus the king, when it occurs in the prophetic books, is completely different in form (cf. for example, Amos 7.10ff.; Isa. 7.3ff.; 14.4; Jer. 22.13ff.; Ezek. 28.1ff.). Buber has sensed somewhat the difficulty when he conjectures that the expansion of the tradition took place among the disciples of Elisha. Indeed, the real parallel to the plague story is found, not in the words and deeds of the written prophets, but in the genre of the prophetic legend. This is the thesis which we shall now examine further.

There are several obvious reasons for seeking a connection between the plague stories and the prophetic legend. (For a definition of this genre see K. Koch, *The Growth of the Biblical Literature*, New York 1968, London 1969, pp. 184ff.; A. Rofé, 'The Classification of the Prophetical Stories', JBL 89, 1970, pp. 427–40).

First of all, Moses was very soon identified in the tradition as the prophet *par excellence* (Deut. 18.18). It was natural that traditions of the exodus would be cultivated in a circle of prophets. We have already pointed out some signs of this influence at work in the call narrative. Again, the confrontation of Moses with the king of Egypt certainly was analogous to the repeated antagonism between prophet and king, as Buber correctly observed. Those prophetic circles which were so active later in preserving the traditions of such opposition would naturally have found great interest in the plague stories.

However, far more important than these general reasons are the formal parallels between the two literatures. The legend is transmitted in prose narrative style with a clear introduction and conclusion. Frequently the story is introduced with instructions of God to the prophet as to where to go, whom to meet, and what to say (I Kings 21.17ff.; II Kings 1.3, etc.//Ex. 7.15; 8.16, etc.). But of even more significance, and basic to the prophetic legend, is the message of Yahweh given to the prophet to be announced with a messenger formula: 'Thus says Yahweh' (I Kings 21.19; 14.7; II Kings 1.4; 9.3, etc.). Indeed, the parallel is clear: Moses is sent to deliver a message to Pharaoh with the same message formula throughout the plague account (Ex. 7.15; 8.16, etc.). Moreover it should be pointed out how seldom this messenger formula actually occurs in the Pentateuch outside of the plague stories. The importance of the prophetic word to the genre of the prophetic legend is further apparent by the concern of the narrative to report its fulfillment. The message was not only delivered, but was fulfilled exactly 'according to the word of the prophet' (I Kings 14.18; 17.16; II Kings 1.17; 2.22; 7.16ff.).

However, right at this point the first major difficulty with the legend parallel emerges. In spite of the frequent use of the messenger formula in the plagues, one searches in vain for any use of a concluding formula such as indicated above. Nowhere is the word of Moses fulfilled. Moreover, further reflection makes it clear that this formula was not omitted from an oversight, but failed because it had no proper place in the narrative. The pattern in Exodus is for God to announce the approach of the plague and then to execute it either directly or through his leaders. The sequence is immediate. The plague is produced by the direct action of Moses and Aaron, not by the prophetic word which is subsequently fulfilled. The power is not in a prophetic word which ultimately brings an event to pass, but in the prophet himself who possesses the charisma to unleash at will.

Moses' role is primarily to demonstrate divine power. Because the demonstration is then obvious to all, the narrative needs merely to describe the effect of the power without ever drawing a connection to the prophetic word.(The only reference to a 'word' is to God's word regarding Pharaoh's hardness, 7.13, etc.)

We have, therefore, in the plague stories a totally different picture of Moses' role from that of the legend in which the prophet is basically a messenger of the word.

In his treatment of the plague narratives, Gressmann noticed certain of these features of Moses' office. He sought to characterize Moses in the role as a magician or sorcerer, and saw an early level of tradition which was akin to magic in its basic orientation. In my opinion, Gressmann confused his basic insight by introducing the problem of magic. Subsequent research by other scholars has contested his interpretation of Moses as a magician (cf. Keller, *op. cit.*). The more important issue is rather the two different roles which the tradition reflects. In the one, the prophet is servant of the word. This understanding dominates the classical prophets and has left its deep impression on the prose tradition of the prophetic legend. Amos, Isaiah, Jeremiah are not remembered as men of charismatic power, but as men to whom the word of God came. In the other role, the prophet can unleash the divine power by what are often called signs. Pharaoh asks Moses to prove his office by working a wonder. A contest occurs between Moses and the Egyptian magicians to determine whose power is greatest. How different this test of divine authority is from that pictured in Jeremiah and his contest with Hananiah (Jer. 28; cf. Deut. 13.1). The picture of the prophet as possessor of power is also found in the prophetic legend. Elijah and Elisha can call down fire from heaven (I Kings 18; II Kings 1), split rivers (II Kings 2), and strike men with blindness (II Kings 7). However, this function of the prophet, although often ancient, was gradually replaced in the prophetic legend by the prophet's role as messenger. A few stories still retain a certain tension between the two concepts and indicate that the later picture had not fully absorbed the earlier (I Kings 2.19ff.).

Now what are the implications from this observation of the two different prophetic pictures on our analysis of the setting of the plague stories? Simply this, the attempt to see the prophetic legend as the setting which gave the plague stories their basic stamp must be seriously revised. The fact that the picture of the prophet in the legend is another from that in the plagues must be squarely faced. But does the prophetic legend play any role in the structuring of the plague narratives? It seems to me that the evidence points to an important secondary role. We turn briefly to examine this thesis.

First, we noticed the use of the messenger formula in the plague stories, which was also characteristic of the prophetic legend. Now it is important to note that, although this formula occurs hundreds of times in the earlier and latter prophets, its use is highly restricted in the Pentateuch. Of the ten times in which the formula comes in Exodus with Yahweh as the subject, eight of these are in connection with the plagues and all fall within the J source. From a purely statistical perspective, this would point in the direction of seeing the formula as a secondary feature to the tradition, rather than being primary since it occurs nowhere else in the Pentateuch. Moreover, if we examine its usage in J closely, this conjecture is further buttressed.

The formula introduces a Yahweh speech which contains a demand and a conditional threat in case of disobedience. 'Let my people go ... If not, then ...' The content of the demand is never varied, whereas that of the threat is. Now it is interesting to note that the message of the divine demand never contains any new content. It is therefore not a message in the strict sense, but rather constitutes the grounds of disagreement making up the conditional. 'Unless you let my people go, I will ...' In the same way, the conditional does not in fact function as a real conditional. No report of Pharaoh's reaction to the condition is needed. His refusal is simply assumed. The plague commences in an automatic sequence. In other words, the messenger formula imitates a function which it does not actually perform. The speech contains neither a genuine message, nor a genuine conditional. Its function in J is no different from that of P. It serves to announce the plague which is shortly to be executed. A basic pattern of the plague tradition underlies all the sources. Because of Pharaoh's resistance of God's will, a series of plagues are unleashed in quick succession. However, he remains unchanged in spite of these signs of power. We conclude that the messenger formula is a secondary adaptation of the form by J to an older tradition which originally functioned without it. The prophetic legend does not provide a primary setting, but rather a secondary influence.

There are several additional factors which would confirm this evidence that the genre of the prophetic legend has exercized a subsequent influence on the Yahwist source in his shaping of the plague tradition. The stylized repetition of phrases, while not absent from the P material, is certainly most pronounced in the J source. Among the prose material, this use of repetition finds its fullest development in the prophetic legend (cf. II Kings 1.5ff.; II Kings 2.1ff.; I Kings 19.9ff.; I Sam. 3.3ff.). The frequent report of the role played by symbolic numbers in the stories also reflects the same interest (I Kings 18.43 – 'go look again seven times'; II Kings 5.10 – 'wash in the Jordan seven times'; I Kings 18.34 – 'pour water three times'). Even more characteristic of the prophetic legend is the confrontation of the prophet and king which ends with the latter's being humbled. Proud Jeroboam is struck with paralysis and must beg the prophet to intercede with God on his behalf (I Kings 13.4ff.). Ahab repents humbly in sackcloth before his reprieve (I Kings 21.27). David is brought to his knees by Nathan's word (II Sam. 12.1ff.), and Saul by Samuel (I Sam. 15.20). In the plague account of J the theme of Pharaoh's entreaty is of major interest and carries over even after the final plague (Ex. 12.32). Again, the role of the servant as adviser to the king who suggests a concession has literary parallels in the legend (I Kings 20.31ff.; II Kings 5.13ff.; II Kings 6.11ff.; II Kings 7.13ff.). Finally, the theological interest of the legend of having a confession of Yahweh's uniqueness made by a foreigner (II Kings 5.15; II Kings 19.19) affords a striking parallel to J's interest that Pharaoh should know the character of Yahweh (7.17; 8.18). The fact that the features most characteristic of the prophetic legend appears in the special themes of J would confirm the theory that the shaping of the J narrative reflects the influence of the legend.

What implications can be drawn for the original question regarding the *Sitz im Leben* for the plague stories? So far the conclusions have been chiefly negative. The prophetic legend is not the primary force, but a secondary one, and in only one source.

Our study has shown that the picture of Moses as one possessed of power to perform miracles is found in the tradition prior to its receiving the prophetic stamp of J. This tradition also appears to be common to both E and P in spite of some variation. Essential to the tradition is the repetition of great signs of power on the part of Moses, which however did not succeed in forcing the Egyptian king to release the Israelites. In fact, this fundamental failure of the miracles to subdue Pharaoh accounts for the variety of reflections which sought an explanation. Pharaoh's heart was hardened; Pharaoh continued to renege on his promise; the magicians used magic to copy Moses. Only in the plague stories was a tradition retained in which such great miracles, constantly repeated, continued to fail. The fact that ultimately plague X did accomplish its end, did not remove the difficulty of the earlier one, nor explain the failure. The P tradition even continued to identify the final blow with the passover and not with the nine other plagues.

This line of argument would suggest that the ultimate strangeness of the plague narrative, the question with which the study began, cannot be accounted for by supposing the influence of some special sociological setting. The peculiar flavor which we have described as historical distance is not to be derived from its particular genre. Rather, a study of the tradition leads us back through its history of transmission to a primary, non-derivable stage. And at this level, we encounter the same contradiction. Indeed the sense of the mystery of Pharaoh's resistance lies at the root of the tradition. Now it is apparent that the essential problem with which we began is not ultimately form-critical in nature, but profoundly theological. The interpreter is still faced with the task of penetrating the mystery of God's power before human pride.

C. *The Redaction of the Sources*

It is a source of frustration common to most readers of commentaries that so much energy is spent on the analysis of the prehistory of a text as to leave little for a treatment of the passage in its final form. The complaint is certainly justified. Ultimately the use of source and form criticism is exegetically deficient if these tools do not illuminate the canonical text. Gressmann likened literary criticism to an archaeological excavation in which no responsibility is felt by the scientist for rebuilding the mound. The analogy is inappropriate and highly misleading. The text under study is not only a record of history, but – even at its minimal formulation – a piece of literature with its own integrity.

However, the synthetic task of understanding the final form of the plague account is a difficult one. The majority of scholars who have attempted it have not met with great success. Several reasons for the frequent failure can be noted:

1. Often the synthetic approach has been used apologetically against source criticism with little understanding of the different

levels of the text which are being discussed (cf. Jacob and Cassuto). However, to show a larger pattern which cuts across the sources does not disprove their existence.

2. Often certain formal elements are isolated which do exhibit a certain structure and balance, but which are made to be major pillars for supporting the whole structure (cf. Winnett, McCarthy).

3. Again it is difficult to determine how much sense for symmetry was intended by the final redactor and how much is accidental. Rashbam, followed by Abarbanel and Cassuto, has argued for a structure of three sets of three. Plagues I, IV, VII begin with the charge: 'Go to Pharaoh in the morning when . . .'. Plagues II, V, VIII all begin: 'Yahweh said to Moses, "Go and say . . .".' Plagues III, VI, IX begin with a command to the Hebrew leaders to do something which will begin the plague which occurs without previous warning to Pharaoh. While this principle of ordering the plagues is useful, it remains questionable to what extent it is more accidental than intentional. But perhaps the decisive question is not that of intentionality, but in what way this structural observation aids in illuminating the final composition. In my judgment, the major themes are not brought into any sharper focus by recognizing this pattern. The fact that Cassuto can find two different kinds of order, one in terms of form and one of content, would raise the question whether one can really speak of any one definite pattern in the final form of the narrative.

4. The fact that many times the suggested order of the plagues is homiletical rather than literary is not in itself a derogatory characterization. However, it is essential that the commentator have a measure of clarity regarding the nature of the claims being made.

In the light of this survey of recent theories, the more modest claims of M. Greenberg ('Thematic Unity . . .', pp. 151ff.) seem much more fruitful. Greenberg seeks to delineate the major themes of the entire passage, which analysis is not dependent on recognizing one final literary pattern. He sees the major theme of the plague story to revolve around the revelation by God of his nature to Pharaoh, to the Egyptians, and to all men. Even more important is recognizing how this theme fits into the movement of the book as a whole. The initial revelation of God's name met with human resistance and disbelief which created the tension of the narrative. The plagues function as a demonstration of God's nature which shattered the resistance.

When properly used, this approach has the additional advantage of being able to make use of the more technical analytic work as well. On the one hand, by incorporating the full richness and variety of the individual sources into the themes, one's understanding of the narrative can be enriched rather than impoverished by reductionist generalizations. On the other hand, the interpreting of the sources within the thematic framework of the whole passage prevents the exegesis from becoming unduly fragmented. For example, one can allow for the differences between J and P within the theme of Pharaoh's resistance. Even the tension between signs and plagues could help to sketch the full range of God's method of showing his power. The fact that at times Pharaoh is warned, and at times not, or that Moses can be both flexible and intransigent, provides tremendous possibilities for discovering new combinations and dimensions of the story.

3. Old Testament Context

[7.8–13] The previous section had reiterated God's commission to Moses in respect to Pharaoh. The passage had also outlined God's ultimate intention with Pharaoh. Because he was hardened, he would refuse to let Israel depart. Then God would increase his signs and wonders and bring out his people with great acts of judgment. Verses 1–7 point in both directions within the narrative. On the one hand, the commission relates directly to Moses' earlier complaint (6.12ff.). On the other hand, the words clearly form an introduction to the plague stories which follow.

The theme of Moses' conflict with the magicians of Egypt is presented as an initial attempt to convince Pharaoh of Moses' divine authority in seeking the release of Israel. When he failed with his demonstration of unusual power, the sequence of the plagues started. The miracle which he performed was in no sense a plague and even in its structure lay outside the sequence of the ten ensuing disasters. Nevertheless, the theme of the conflict with the magicians continues throughout several of the plagues (7.22; 8.14; 9.11), and culminates in their defeat by the power of Moses. It is possible that the theme once provided the major framework of the Priestly source for recounting the tradition of the plagues, but in its final form the theme is only one of the many which make up the rich and diverse pattern of the present narrative.

Whereas the later passages mention the role of the magicians almost in passing, this passage gives it a detailed coverage. Moses had been forewarned by God of Pharaoh's demand for proof of his authority and instructed on the suitable sign. Aaron was to throw his rod down upon the ground which would then turn into a snake (cf. 4.2ff.). But when Moses performed his miracle, Pharaoh forthwith called in his own magicians who executed the same trick. Even though Aaron's rod proceeded to devour the magicians' rods, Pharaoh refused to be impressed or comply with Moses' demand. Rabbinic commentators make much of the exact formulation of the text: Moses' *rod* devoured their *rods*. So great was Moses' power! But presumably in the context of the story the rods were both in their transformed shape.

Now the passage is of interest for several reasons. First of all, it is significant to note that this particular sign was given by God to Moses. The narrative does not suggest for a moment that Moses thought up the sign himself, and was therefore to be blamed for an unlikely choice. Rather, the genuine ambiguity of the situation emerges when one recognizes that it was God's choice of a sign by which he sought to legitimate his messenger that was duplicated by the magicians. Even though the narrative attributes to God Moses' ability to perform such a miraculous event, the miracle did not achieve its purpose. Now by introducing this element of ambiguity right at the outset, the author makes it clear that the witness of the plague stories does not lie just in a naïve display of supernatural fireworks. The issue at stake is on another dimension. How can Pharaoh be made to discern the hand of god? The so-called 'supernatural' element was in itself not enough. The divine sign is made to look like a cheap, juggler's trick which a whole row of Egyptian magicians can duplicate with apparent ease.

Older commentators spent considerable energy reflecting on the problem as to how the Egyptians could accomplish the same miracle (cf. history of exegesis section). How was one to understand the expression 'by their spells' or 'secret arts'? Many decided that their attempt at duplication of the miracle was simply a fraud. Only Moses was able really to change a rod into a snake. But this interpretation is a form of rationalism – of course, within the framework of orthodoxy – which misses the point of the conflict by attempting to remove its ambiguity. Indeed, the text implicitly rules out this possibility when it comments that Aaron's rod devoured the other serpents. The issue at stake is not fraud, but a genuine conflict of power. Josephus strikes this same note when he has Moses say to the king: 'I do not disdain the cunning of the Egyptians, but I assert that the deeds wrought by me far surpass their magic . . . it is from God's . . . power that my miracles proceed' (*Antiq.* II, 284ff.).

Finally, it is striking to observe how little interest the author shows in describing the psychological reactions of the two men. There is no mention of Moses' boldness, of the king's scorn, or of any surprise and embarrassment. Indeed, one of the most dramatic parts of the story, which was the initial demand of a sign, was not even described but presented in the form of prior instruction. This is a further indication that the formula, 'Pharaoh's heart was hardened' is not to be understood psychologically. Rather, its point is profoundly theological: God's judgment on Egypt is such that Pharaoh will not listen.

[7.14–25]   *First Plague: Water to Blood*

The first plague reflects a good number of unique features which sets it apart from the stereotyped patterns of the other plagues which follow. Its beginning on the note of Pharaoh's hardness is somewhat unusual (but cf. 10.1). Also its ending is somewhat unexpected since the issue is left completely unresolved. All the various earlier literary sources are involved which has resulted in a rich mosaic of different patterns.

The initial command which specifies that Moses was to meet Pharaoh 'in the morning, as he is going out of the water . . . by the river's bank' is not to be interpreted primarly as an indication of the author's interest in the historical background of the encounter. Rather, these expressions tend to be fixed and belong to the pattern of narration within the plague account which lays emphasis on Moses' role as a prophetic figure. God gives him exact instructions where he is to go, and what he is to say, just as he did to Elijah (I Kings 17.3) and to Isaiah (7.3), and others. The message itself, 'Let my people go,' which is the standard refrain throughout the plague story, is given in the prophetic style of direct address. Moreover, the purpose of the ensuing event is clearly stated. Pharaoh is to know 'that I am Yahweh' when the water turns to blood. This theme of knowing who Yahweh is through his great acts continues to appear in different forms throughout the plague narrative and is closely connected with the basic motif of the king's resistance to God's plan which he first expressed when he denied any knowledge of Yahweh (5.2). The transformation of the water is performed dramatically. By striking the water with the rod all doubt was to be removed as to where the real power lay.

The main lines of the story are clear enough, but some of the details remain unclear and show a certain lack of consistency. In v. 17 it appears to be only waters of the Nile which are changed, whereas v. 19 explicitly includes all the waters of Egypt, even water in vessels. The later description is difficult to reconcile with the Egyptian magicians subsequently changing more water into blood. Again, it is not fully clear whether the Egyptians could not drink the water because it had become blood, or because it had been made foul by dead fish. Although these details continued to bother later commentators, there is no sign at any level within the text itself that a redactor sought to harmonize the difficulties.

The explicit reference now to Pharaoh's reaction in v. 23, 'he went into his house and was unconcerned', would seem to emphasize the contrast with the rest of the Egyptians who had to search hard to secure water. Up to this point Pharaoh was personally unaffected. A Jewish midrash highlights this interpretation by having Pharaoh reply to Moses: '"You don't trouble me, for if I can't have water, I'll have wine",' whereas 'his people suffered and had to dig' (*Sekel Tob*, cited by Greenberg, *ad loc.*).

The later references to the plague tradition within the Old Testament are agreed in considering the changing of water into blood as the first plague (Ps. 78.44, etc.). Yet for many modern readers such a catastrophe presents a far more serious threat to human life than some of the later plagues, and makes it difficult to discern a pattern of increasing intensification within the whole series. Nevertheless the tradition itself seems to view the first plague more as a disgusting nuisance than as a fundamental threat to life. It lasted seven days, causing the Egyptians to dig for water, before the second plague was sent. Pharaoh himself did not take it seriously at all. To this extent there is a slight exegetical basis for seeing some relation between the tradition of the first plague and the natural seasonal reddening of the Nile, which modern critical commentaries never tire of citing.

[7.26–8.11 (EVV 8.1–15)]   *Second Plague: Frogs*

The sending of the frogs is likewise first announced as a warning in prophetic style, and then executed by Aaron. The text itself makes no causal link whatever with the preceding plague, although commentators have long since sought to connect the poluting of the Nile with the arrival of the frogs. In the long list of plagues which Moses evoked on the Egyptians, frogs would certainly be accounted among the least fearful. They do not bite or destroy property. Yet they are a dreadful nuisance, and highly offensive both in sight and sound. Calvin emphasizes the element of mockery in the plague; Jacob speaks of a bogey ('Kinderschreck'). The text focuses on the elements of nuisance and annoyance. The frogs entered the houses, climbed on the beds, into the kitchen and eating utensils. Even the most unlikely place to attract a frog, namely the dry oven, was not immune.

The new theme which enters is the element of concession by Pharaoh which he makes to Moses as a condition for the removal of the plague. This theme of the gradual weakening of Pharaoh's resistance to Israel's departure continues to grow until the final impasse is reached which culminated in the sending of the final plague. The fact that Pharaoh's resistance can indeed be weakened by means of a plague sounds a somewhat different note from the introduction in 7.3 which describes his hardening as intentional. Accordingly, the plagues are not given to soften his resistance, but to glorify God's power and authority. With some justification the literary critics assign these two different themes to separate sources. But in the final shaping of the plague narrative these two themes do not stand in a real tension. Rather, they contribute to the richness of the narrative and vary the pattern of the series to prevent the threat of monotony in recounting the long series. Because the concessions reach an impasse, in the final analysis there is no real conflict in terms of content between the two approaches to Pharaoh's resistance.

The negotiations between Pharaoh and Moses are particularly interesting because genuine human characteristics break through the dominant stereotyped forms of the larger narrative tradition. Pharaoh emerges as an extremely shrewd bargainer. His initial offer to let the people go to sacrifice (v.4) sounds like a complete capitulation, on which he subsequently reneged. However, in each subsequent negotiation Pharaoh picks up his earlier offer, which he then proceeds to interpret as only containing a partial concession. Thus in v.4 Pharaoh agrees to let the people go to sacrifice, but with great cleverness he still holds back his hidden cards as to the participants and location of the sacrifice.

For his part Moses is pictured as equally shrewd. While he remains above all God's messenger, this commission does not restrict his freedom to negotiate. This factor comes out in Moses' response to Pharaoh's first concession and helps explain the initial expression in v. 5. The RSV renders it as simply a polite expression, 'Be pleased to command me . . .'. But this does not do justice to the Hebrew or fit the context of the section. Rather, Moses responds to Pharaoh: 'I'll give you the advantage. Set the amount of time needed for removing these frogs.' When Pharaoh gives him only one day, then Moses replies: 'Just as you say – in order that you may recognize the authority of Yahweh.' Moses accepts a handicap, giving Pharaoh the advantage, to show him how much power is at his disposal. It is a classic example of 'one-up-manship'. Some commentators find a note of irony in the final comment that, even though the frogs were removed, they left their smell in the land – a bonus for which Pharaoh had not negotiated.

[8.12–15 (EVV 16–19)]   *Third Plague: Gnats*

The third plague strikes without warning and is concluded without the element of concession. The concluding phrase 'as Yahweh said' (7.13; 8.15; 9.12, 35), relates to the initial prediction that Pharaoh would remain hardened in spite of all the plagues (7.4). The exact nature of the affliction is not fully clear. Although some sort of insect is involved, scholars are divided on whether gnats or lice are intended. Of course, the term 'gnat' designates the stinging variety of mosquito.

The writer picks up the theme of the magicians again. They had been able to change water into blood and also to produce rival frogs. Now for the first time they are unable to bring forth mosquitoes. Rather, they confess that the hand of God is at work. This is the first explicit indication of how the author settles the question of the true and false miracle. The true overwhelms the false and the magicians themselves bear testimony to the fact.

[8.16–26 (EVV 20–32)]   *Fourth Plague: Flies*

The fourth plague returns to the style of the first, and for that reason has caused some commentators to see the plagues in cycles of threes. Again Moses is to meet Pharaoh at the water's edge and warn him in prophetic style. The message entails the threat of flies, and not that of wild beasts as one older exegetical tradition suggested (cf. Jer. Targum).

The new element which enters in the fourth plague is the setting of a distinction between the Israelites and the Egyptians. The land of Goshen is set apart and does not experience the flies. Commentators are divided as to whether the sparing of Israel from the plagues was intended from the start (cf. already Philo, *Vita Mos.* I. 143ff.). However one decides, the theme continues to grow in importance and culminates in the final separation of Israel with the mark of blood on the lintel which protects God's people from the last great blow.

The fourth plague results in a renewal of the negotiations between Moses and Pharaoh. Pharaoh picks up his earlier concession – the Israelites will be allowed to sacrifice to their God – but he then restricts it with the decisive stipulation 'within the land'. Moses' retort to this offer is somewhat surprising. The more obvious answer would have been to designate the land of Egypt as unclean for Hebrew sacrifice. Rather, Moses argues that their method of sacrifice would be offensive to the Egyptians and would call forth reprisals against his people. He then reiterates his demand for a three days' journey into the wilderness. It is not fully clear wherein the offense lay (Gen. 46.34). Was it that the Hebrews sacrificed cattle which were considered sacred by the Egyptians (cf. Targ. Onkelos)? Was it the offering of sheep (cf. Jer. Targ.), or did the offense lie in the manner of the whole offering? At any rate, Moses succeeded in winning his point. Pharaoh's final comment, 'but do not go very far', seems to be quite a meaningless restriction once he allows Moses to enter the wilderness, but suits admirably the picture of Pharaoh as clutching after every pretext in his rear action retreat. Moses' own suspicion of Pharaoh's motives is succinctly expressed in v. 25. He is shrewd enough not to trust him.

[9.1–7] *Fifth Plague: Animal Pestilence*
The fifth plague matches in its style that of the second, but is considerably shorter and adds no new themes. However, the earlier note of Israel's being set apart is picked up and developed further. Pharaoh sends messengers to confirm whether in fact Israel's cattle have been spared. Difficulty has been caused by the comprehensive extent of the cattle murrain. Verse 6 reports that 'all the cattle died', whereas cattle are again mentioned in the seventh plague. But the discrepancy is not a serious one, since the narrative style should not be overtaxed. Again, it is interesting to notice that the responsibility of Pharaoh for his active resistance is fully maintained (v. 2), and

not destroyed by the hardness theme which now frames each plague.

[9.8–12]   *Sixth Plague: Boils*

The account is extremely short; however, it brings to a conclusion the theme of the conflict of Moses with the Egyptians. Not only could they not produce boils, but they no longer could even appear in Moses' presence since they were sorely afflicted by boils themselves just like all the rest of Egypt. The idiom of Pharaoh's hardening is slightly varied in v. 12 – *God* hardens his heart – but the meaning is not really different from the earlier expressions. It simply functions to make the psychological interpretation of the hardening even less tenable.

[9.13–35]   *Seventh Plague: Hail*

In distinction from the brevity of the two prior plagues, the account of the hail is one of the longest descriptions in the entire story. This fact cannot be explained solely from a combination of several sources, but marks the build-up within the narrative leading to the final judgment. The pattern is varied in the beginning by an extended speech of Yahweh directed to Pharaoh. The speech puts into words the obvious reaction of every reader who has followed the long recital of plagues: 'By this time I could have wiped you off the face of the earth!' Then the reasons for the number of plagues is given. God has let Pharaoh live, first, in order to show him his power, and secondly, in order to declare his glory throughout the world.

What then follows comes as a welcome relief to the inevitability of the previous plagues. The next plague is announced but a genuine alternative is offered. Those who listen can save their slaves and cattle by bringing them in time under shelter. The writer describes the growing distinctions which have developed within the Egyptian people. These are those who stand in awe of Yahweh's word; they are spared. But those who disregard the warning, suffer the consequences of the hail storm. Shortly the writer will return to the theme of the 'God-fearers' within Egypt who will seek to persuade Pharaoh to yield.

The reaction of Pharaoh seems to strike a new level of intensity and signal a growing readiness for serious negotiation. Pharaoh said: 'I have sinned . . . Yahweh is in the right, I and my people in the wrong.' However, Moses' response dispels any hope that a real change has occurred with Pharaoh. He is willing to intercede to demonstrate God's control of the world, but he rejects the religious dimensions of the confession: 'As for you . . . I know that you do not yet fear the LORD God.'

Verses 31–32 interrupt the present narrative quite abruptly by offering a type of learned interpolation. The note distinguishes between the harvest season of two sets of crops. Flax and barley which were harvested in February–March in Egypt were destroyed by the hail. But the wheat and spelt which were harvested only in March–April remained undamaged. For the historical critical reader the note has assumed great importance by providing an unambiguous dating index. The significance for the biblical author is less obvious. It is possible that it served to harmonize the fact that crops remained after the hail storm which were then devoured by the locust, but this conjecture remains simply one theory (cf. 10.5, 15).

The account ends with a return to the familiar theme of Pharaoh's change of mind because of the hardness of his heart, but in addition the author joins the theme which Pharaoh had just introduced: 'once again he *sinned* in not letting the people go.'

[10.1–20] *Eighth Plague: Locusts*

The eighth plague is again described in considerable length caused by the introduction of new themes and the expansion of older ones. For the first time the purpose of the plagues is described explicitly as 'making sport' of Pharaoh which was to be recounted in the ears of the children (cf. Jewish Haggadah service). Again, the concession theme is introduced before the coming of the actual plague and connected with the intercession of Pharaoh's servants. This slight change in the structure of the story allows Pharaoh's reaction to be described both before and after the plague.

The negotiations are carried on in an extremely lively style. Now the issue turns on who is to be included in the desert pilgrimage. Moses is portrayed as growing in intransigence. He demands the right to take everybody, both young and old, along with the flocks. Pharaoh rejects his demand sarcastically and accuses Moses of double dealing. Moreover, he makes a rather good point. If Moses has in mind only a three-day sacrifice, why not just take the men, who alone participate in the cultic rite? But the issue is left hanging and Moses and Aaron are driven from the king's presence.

There follows the usual pattern. The locusts are summoned and destroy the country. The Pharaoh relents and calls for Moses to intercede. The sense that a climax is approaching is brought out in the phrase 'only this once'. The final showdown is obviously drawing near.

[10.21–29]   *Ninth Plague: Darkness*

Both the form and content of the ninth plague have caused difficulty for the interpreter. According to the form Pharaoh called Moses to negotiate after three days of darkness. But one is left to assume that the darkness was removed even though the negotiations broke down in a complete deadlock. Some commentators have also wondered whether the occurrence of mere darkness could really be considered an intensification of the judgment. Was it not an anti-climax after the disasters of the hail and locust? Others have sought to emphasize its elements of terror, and discovered a cosmic battle between light and darkness. But again many of these problems obviously escaped the attention and concern of the author. The plague of darkness is not inappropriate for the last plague but one, in that it foreshadows the ultimate judgment when the first-born was slain at night. But there is also a certain contrast between the deathly silence within a darkness which can be touched and the 'great cry' which was soon to break forth.

The last attempt at negotiation between Moses and Pharaoh bypasses completely the issue of the darkness, and focuses on the real issue at stake. Pharaoh makes his last concession: the Israelites can go and even take their children with them. Only their cattle must remain, obviously to insure their return. Moses refuses to budge or even to soften his demand. Everything must go. Not a hoof will remain! He does add a reason: he does not know which of the animals Yahweh will require, but it does ring a bit hollow. Both men now know that the complete freedom of the Israelites is at stake. Pharaoh threatens Moses with death if he ever sees him again. Moses in turn accepts the finality of this last meeting. 'Fair enough. You will not see my face again – I'll be gone!'

[11.1–11]   *Tenth Plague Announced*

The climax to the long series of plagues comes in the tenth plague. 'Yet one more plague . . . and he will drive you out completely.' Yet the complexity of the larger Exodus tradition has forced a restructuring of the normal pattern. This plague is first only announced to the Israelites but it takes place after the preparation of the passover (ch. 12). In other words, the slaying of the first-born is both the culmination of the plague narrative and the beginning of the passover tradition. Chapter 11 as a literary unit, therefore, points both backward and forward.

In the context of the announcement of their final departure from Egypt, Moses is ordered to instruct the Israelites to borrow items of silver and gold from their Egyptian neighbors. At this point in the narrative no motivation for the action is offered, but only its success guaranteed. Only later in the story is its purpose explained (13.36). Rather than offering a reason, the present narrative turns to comment on the stature of Moses, not only among his own people, but among the Egyptians as well. The comment does not fit very smoothly into the context and appears somewhat clumsy.

The most difficult problem in the chapter has to do with the speech of Moses which begins in v. 4. Moses announces in the familiar prophetic style the coming of the last plague. Yahweh himself will go forth through the land and the first-born in all of Egypt will die. Among the Israelites not a hair shall be touched. But the problem arises in determining the context of the speech. To whom is Moses speaking and at what time? The ending of the passage makes it clear that these words are addressed to Pharaoh. His courtiers will come shortly and entreat Moses to depart from the land (v. 8a). The final part of v. 8 fully confirms this judgment. When he had finished speaking, Moses went out from Pharaoh in hot anger.

Of course, then the problem arises of fitting the speech into the chronology of the chapter. In spite of its difficulties, the best solution, in my judgment, is to assume that ch. 11 has been constructed in topical and not chronological order (cf. literary analysis). Moses' speech to Pharaoh actually belongs at the end of ch. 10, and was displaced by the interjection of the instructions for despoiling the Egyptians (11.1–3). Therefore, in the context of the whole, even the last plague was not given without warning. However, the warning is now given with a new air of confidence and defiance. Israel will not sneak out of the land. Rather, the mighty of Egypt will prostrate themselves and beg them to leave.

The final two verses in ch. 11 formally bring the plague narrative to a conclusion by picking up the vocabulary of the introduction in ch. 7. Lest one consider the plagues a failure by not accomplishing their purpose of freeing Israel, the narrative begins and ends with a theological justification. It belonged to the judgment of God on

Pharaoh that he continued his resistance in order to allow God to multiply his signs and wonders. Only when this had been done would God stretch out his hand and bring Israel out of the land in triumph.

Detailed Notes

7.9ff. On the role of the serpent in Egypt, cf. L. Keimer, *Histoires des serpentes dans l'Égypte ancienne et moderne*, Paris 1948, and the article by M.-L. Henry, *BHH* III, cols. 1699ff.

14ff. The most detailed recent treatment which attempts a scientific explanation of the plagues and their historical sequence is offered by Greta Hort, *ZAW* 69, 1957, pp. 84–103; 70, 1958, pp. 48–59. Her attempt to explain the redness of the water in terms of an unusual physical phenomenon relating to the seasonal confluence of the White and Blue Nile is of special interest.

8.21ff. On the question of sacrifice in ancient Egypt, cf. the articles on 'Opfer' and 'Widder' by Hans Bonnet, *Reallexikon der Ägyptischen Religionsgeschichte*, Berlin 1952, pp. 547ff., 867ff.

9.3. The recent archaeological evidence on the domestication of the camel in the Ancient Near East is reviewed by F. C. Fensham (*Exodus*, p.40), who would set the date earlier than 1200 BC, the date defended by Albright.

4. New Testament Context

H. GUNKEL, *Schöpfung und Chaos*², Göttingen 1921; A. T. HANSON, *The Wrath of the Lamb*, London and New York 1957; LARS HARTMAN, *Prophecy Interpreted*, Lund 1966; H.-P. MÜLLER, 'Die Plagen der Apokalypse', *ZNW* 51, 1960, pp. 268–78; P. S. MINEAR, *I Saw A New Earth*, Washington 1968; A. VANHOYE, 'L'utilisation du livre d'Ézéchiel dans l'Apocalypse', *Biblica* 43, 1962, pp. 436–76.

The New Testament makes little use of the Old Testament plague tradition with two exceptions. First, the hardening of Pharaoh in Ex. 9.16 is cited by Paul in Rom. 9.17. Secondly, in the book of Revelation there is considerable reference to the plagues, especially in chs. 8 and 16. In the first case, Paul uses the example of Pharaoh's hardening in the context of his argument concerning the continuity of God's purpose in electing Israel as his chosen people. Paul illustrates God's unlimited freedom in terms of both his mercy and his judgment by citing the case of Pharaoh's hardening. However, the argument does not rest on an exegesis of the Exodus passage and the reference to Pharaoh only serves as one illustration among many in his total argument. Nevertheless it is significant to see that Paul follows the Old Testament text closely and, rather than avoiding the difficulties implicit in attributing Pharaoh's hardening to the work of God, actually develops the theme of God's freedom and power even beyond the Old Testament with tremendous boldness.

In the second case, there is more extensive use of the actual plague tradition within the three cycles of apocalyptic judgments. However, it is equally clear that the plague material has undergone considerable development beyond its Old Testament form. To be sure, the New Testament plagues have a sequence of plagues which clearly reflect Old Testament influence. Rev. 16 pictures the seven bowls of judgment in terms of boils, water to blood, death of fish, fierce heat, darkness, foul spirits like frogs, and lightning, thunder, and earthquake. Again, the repetition of the phrase 'they did not repent and give him glory' (16.9, 11) reflects the Exodus pattern. However, the New Testament context is quite different. The apocalyptic vision with its dimension of genuine terror and anguish has produced a different picture from that portrayed by the didactic repetition of the Exodus plagues. It seems highly probable that the author of the book of Revelation drew his material from a circle in which the exodus story had long since been given a new function with an apocalyptic framework (cf. Enoch). It also seems clear that this use of the Old Testament plague tradition was not typical for the rest of the New Testament which found its eschatological imagery elsewhere.

When one views the limited use made of the plague tradition even within the rest of the Old Testament, the New Testament development does not seem strange. The tradition found its major development within the Bible only with a few psalms (78, 105), and then for the purpose of rehearsing Israel's history of disobedience. In the prophets the Egyptian plagues played no significant role. Not that the prophets and apocalyptic writers did not use the imagery of pestilence, but they used it in a form uninfluenced by the Exodus tradition. Thus Joel can speak of the 'day of the Lord' as a locust plague with accompanying darkness and earthquakes (2.2ff.), but his material is unrelated to Exodus. In the same way, the visions of Isa. 13 which speak of cosmic desolation have nothing in common with the older plague tradition. Even Zech. 14 which speaks explicitly of Egypt is only remotely related.

There are several reasons which one can deduce to explain this development. First, the eschatological perspective which was central to the prophetic message was missing in the Exodus tradition, and therefore the material did not lend itself to their purpose. Again, the didactic framework in which the plague tradition was transmitted had removed much of the real element of terror which is characteristic of the prophetic imagery. Finally, one wonders whether the juxtaposition of the two nations, Israel and Egypt, in the plague tradition was compatible with use in the prophetic attack which focused on Israel itself.

As a result when Acts 2 speaks of the great signs and wonders of Pentecost it cites the prophecy of Joel. Likewise Matthew's apocalyptic picture of the end (ch. 24) reflects the judgment in terms of Daniel, Isaiah, and Zechariah. Finally, the gospel's description of the crucifixion as a time of darkness, earthquake, and resurrection draws its language from the Old Testament psalms and apocalyptic writers rather than from Exodus.

5. *History of Exegesis*

Early Hellenistic exegesis of the plague stories tended to retell the tradition in terms of the great triumph of Moses. Artapanus has Moses rendering the Egyptian king impotent and speechless by whispering the divine name into his ear (Eusebius, *Praep. Ev.* IX. 27). Philo described the initial encounter with the magicians as a complete rout in which 'the marvellous spectacle had refuted the scepticism in every ill-disposed person's soul' (*Vita Mos.* I. 94). Josephus recounts the story to demonstrate that 'Moses was not mistaken in even one of his predictions' (*Antiq.* II. 294; cf. *Jubilees* 48.6).

Soon the biblical description of the plagues was embellished in an effort to make real the terror of the punishment. The Wisdom of Solomon pictures the darkness with demonic overtones, and chilled its readers with the description of 'the passing of beasts and the hissing of serpents' (17.9). Artapanus has Moses unleashing hail and an earthquake which destroyed the houses and most of the temples. He also brought forth a winged monster which harassed the Egyptians (*ibid.*). Josephus let his imagination run wild in painting an incredibly plastic scene of the country saturated in 'their horrible slime; a stench intolerable and foul was everywhere of frogs dying, living, and dead' (*Antiq.* II. 297). Moreover in this early exegesis one can discern the attempt to find some larger pattern in the series of the plagues. Philo not only explains the number ten, but distributes them between the four elements of the universe – earth, fire, air, and water – which carried out the assault (*Vita Mos.* I. 96).

Perhaps most characteristic is the larger didactic framework going considerably beyond the Old Testament from which the tradition was interpreted and which became increasingly the model for later interpreters. Josephus felt that the plagues were instructive 'because it behoves mankind to learn to restrict themselves to such action as shall not offend the Deity nor provoke Him to wrath' (*Antiq.* II. 293). Philo drew the interesting observation that 'the Hebrews were not merely spectators of the sufferings of others . . . but learners of the finest and most profitable of lessons – piety' (*Vita Mos.* I. 146). But surely the most creative interpretation of the plague tradition is found in the Wisdom of Solomon (16ff.). This writer has felt free to inter-weave whole blocks of other Old Testament tradition with the plague stories in order to illustrate his point that God delivers the righteous, but destroys the workers of evil.

Some of the tendencies of early rabbinic exegesis can be readily seen reflected in the Targum of Onkelos, particularly that of clearing up ambiguous passages such as the offense of Israel's sacrifice in 8.22 (EVV. 26). The Mekilta solves the problem of where Pharaoh got the horses with which to pursue the Israelites since all the animals had died, by assigning them to the 'God-fearers' of 9.20. But more significant was the larger typological interpretation which was introduced. First, the ten plagues were a reward for the deeds of Abraham who withstood ten temptations (*Ex. Rabbah* 15.27; *ARN* 33.95). Secondly, each plague corresponded, measure for measure, to a crime committed by Egypt against the Hebrews (*Mek. Beshallah* 7).

Among the church Fathers most of the major lines for later inter-pretation were set by the lengthy and impressive interpretation provided by Origen (*Homilies on Exodus*). First of all, he showed unusual care in pointing out the various patterns within the story and marking the characteristic differences. Now although Philo (*Vita Mos.* I. 162) had already pointed out the relation between the law and the plagues, it was Origen who elaborated on this analogy at great length and so provided the framework for much of the subsequent allegory. The plagues were given so that the heaviness of the punish-ment made the Egyptians recognize their deviation from the divine law. Augustine elaborated on this scheme in his famous sermon 'On the Ten Plagues and the Ten Commandments' (MPL 46. 945), and established the pattern firmly for the later Fathers and Schoolmen (cf. Honorius, Isidore, Walafrid Strabo, etc.).

One also sees a concern, shared by both Jews and Christians, to reconcile some of the more obvious tensions within the narrative. Thus, for example, the question of where the magicians got the water to change into blood, after Moses had already transformed all the water, receives a variety of different explanations among the Fathers (Augustine, *Quaest. in Hept.* II. 23; Theodoret, *Quaest.* 20 (MPG 80. 248); cf. Rashi and Ibn Ezra). An even more important question was why God allowed the magicians the power to do miracles and what was the nature of their enchantments (Theodoret, *op. cit.*, 18). Rules were sought by which to distinguish the true from the false miracle (cf. summary in Lapide, *ad loc.*). Finally, each of the Fathers and the medieval Jewish commentators dealt with the problem of Pharaoh's hardening and usually ended up with a compromise position which combined God's power with man's free will.

The Protestant Reformers of the sixteenth century carried on much of the medieval exegetical tradition, but contemporized the story by picturing Moses as the bold and faithful preacher of God's judgment who successfully encountered the arrogance of the Egyptian king, the symbol of terrestrial government. The great wealth of material within the plague cycle allowed each of the Reformers classic passages on which to expound several of their favorite themes. For example, Luther contrasted with great eloquence the rude speech and appearance of God's messenger with the pomp and splendor of the Egyptian court, showing how in the end God destroyed the false prophets of Satan's kingdom. He emphasized Israel's experience of affliction as a lesson toward praying to God in moments of great adversity. Zwingli offered a rather straightforward literal exposition, but at several points went into detail to show that the language is metaphorical: Moses in 7.12 uses 'catachresis' – which is a literary technique akin to the gospel's use of 'hoc est corpus meum'! – and hyperbole in 10.21 (*Farrago Annot. Exod., ad loc.*). Calvin's exegesis is by far the most detailed and carefully done. He reconciled, in passing, some of the difficulties, such as the extent of the plague in 9.6, but his main emphasis fell elsewhere than on such details. Above all, he saw in the plagues a vindication of divine governance of the world against the might of impiety. God destroys men's idols and manifests his glory over this world's rulers. Obviously Paul's use of Pharaoh's hardening in the context of predestination afforded Calvin a warrant for expounding on the subject. His insistence in following the literal sense of the text, namely, that God was the author of Pharaoh's hardening, called forth the ire of subsequent Roman Catholic expositors (summarized in Lapide).

Further, the strong didactic and pastoral concern of Calvin's exegesis is striking. He consistently drew brief homiletical application for the shaping of the Christian life in terms of trust and patience.

The seventeenth century is of particular interest because of the new element of intensity and scientific concern for the exact details of the plagues. Scholars such as Samuel Bochartus, John Lightfoot, and Johannes Drusius attempted to describe each plague with precise accuracy. Bishop Ussher along with a host of others sought to determine the time interval between the plagues in terms of absolute chronology. All the older solutions of the alleged contradictions were re-examined and new ones offered (cf. Clericus on the changing of water to blood). The issue of the plagues as an example of Old Testament miracles *par excellence* entered into the philosophical and theological controversy with the English deists, and men like Edward Stillingfleet sought to bring new precision into distinguishing between true and false miracles (*Origines Sacrae* II.10, *Works* II, London 1709, pp. 210ff.).

Perhaps the beginning of the modern period can be best set with the publication of J. G. Eichhorn's classic essay *De Aegypti anno mirabili* (1818). Naturally many rationalistic arguments to explain the plagues had long been proposed (cf. Bertholdt), but no one had sought to explain the whole cycle so consistently from a rationalistic position in such detail before Eichhorn. He saw the whole affair as arising from natural annual occurrences which Moses exploited with some of his own sleight-of-hand tricks. Moses' initial display with the snake proved to be unsuccessful because he had forgotten that the Egyptian magicians knew the same trick. Then he sought to impress Pharaoh with the power of the Hebrew God by changing some water contained in a vase into a red color by means of some chemical contrivance which he accompanied with the threat against the Nile as well. Of course, Eichhorn's explanations were so forced and often so outrageous as to call forth dozens of rebuttals from men like Rosenmüller, Hengstenberg, and others.

The responses are of importance in showing the changing temper of the times. Hengstenberg, who best represented Lutheran orthodoxy in the first half of the nineteenth century, sought to defend the historicity of the plagues by demonstrating accurate acquaintance with Egyptian local color. However, he took a different tack in agreeing with Eichhorn that the plagues were closely akin to natural phenomena within Egypt. Then he argued that the best demonstration of the supernatural quality of the biblical account was the consistency between the natural and the supernatural. The two are in 'friendly alliance' and not violent opposition (*Egypt and the Books of Moses*, ET Edinburgh 1845, pp. 98f.). That not all the conservatives were happy with this line of argument can be seen in the note of the English editor who voiced his objection (p. 125).

Moreover, some mention should be made of the very learned book of Jacob Bryant (*Observations upon the Plagues* . . ., London 1794). He followed closely the lines of the classic English apologist. He argued for the 'great fitness and propriety' of the plagues chosen (p. 126). Moses adapted the signs of the Egyptian scene in a sense as if he were 'speaking their language' in order to make clear the nature of the judgment. Thus he used their sacred frog to ridicule it, the filthy lice to condemn their contemptible rites (pp. 37ff.). Bryant tried to demonstrate the supernatural quality of the plagues by showing their divergence from the normal season in which the natural phenomenon would be present, which was the reverse of the later approach of Hengstenberg. Thus frogs would normally appear in September after the Nile had subsided, but Bryant calculated the biblical plague occurred in January, the coolest month of the season (p. 79).

In many ways the attempt to defend an historical interpretation of the plagues by means of rationalistic arguments finds its most recent representative in the learned articles of Greta Hort (*ZAW* 68, 1957). However in the end, this genre of apologetic literature suffers from the strange anomaly of defending biblical 'supernaturalism' on the grounds of rationalistic arguments. As a result there is an ironical affinity between the arguments of Eichhorn and those of Hort.

The modern form-critical, history-of-traditions approach has tended to relegate the plague cycle to a minor role within the exodus material. Gressmann regarded the whole tradition as an 'artificial stylization' (p. 82), which prepared the death of the first-born. Likewise, Noth characterized the plague tradition as a comparatively recent, and novelistic expansion which was attached secondarily to the passover festival (*Überlieferungsgeschichte*, pp. 70f. = *Pentateuchal Traditions*, pp. 68ff.). However, it is certainly questionable whether one is doing justice to the biblical tradition when all the weight of the exodus is transferred to the crossing of the sea. It may be a legacy from past controversies that modern scholars find little of importance to say regarding these chapters.

6. *Theological Reflection on the Plagues*

The most striking thing which emerges from viewing the plague tradition from the context of the whole canon is the subsequent theological criticism which was exercised upon it. In contrast to the theme of deliverance from Egypt which continued to be celebrated by prophet, psalmist, and sage, the plague tradition was relegated to a minor role. Indeed, it was not used at all in the traditional form of the exodus narrative. Rather, it was either ignored or sharply reworked. Of special significance is the fact that the biblical tradition did not develop in the direction of later Hellenistic exegesis, both Greek and Rabbinic, which stressed such elements as the mockery of the Egyptians, the separation of Israel from punishment, and God's commitment to Israel's cause.

The theological reworking of the plague tradition took a variety of forms. Either the plagues were seen as God's special act of grace, which Israel then rejected because of her own sin (Pss. 78 and 105), and which thus in the end were given in vain, or the prophets passed over this tradition and chose other forms of cosmic disaster in which God wrought judgment on his own people. Perhaps the most radical reworking of the tradition is reflected in the apocalyptic interpretation. The book of Revelation is saturated with the imagery from the plague tradition, but in a completely different form. The plague tradition witnessed to the great battle between God and Pharaoh over the rule of his people, but this theme has become both a cosmological and eschatological battle between God and Satan. No longer is the battle a glorious memory in Israel's past history, but it still lies in the future with its impending threat. The struggle with evil has taken on a new dimension of anguish and terror. The people of God do not stand carefully protected in Goshen, but are called upon to participate in the battle unto death. All the terrors of Gog and Magog, of the dragon from the deep, of the beasts from Daniel's visions, are combined into a terrifying picture of the Antichrist.

The people of God are not measured in terms of their nationality, but of their faith. God's judgments are 'true and just' and directed against all the sin and corruption of Babylon. God then brings into his kingdom and he is worshipped by his saints (4.8) because he alone is worthy to receive 'glory and honor and power'. There is a new heaven and a new earth and God dwells with his people for ever (21.1ff.).

In sum, the Bible used its own theological criticism in taking an ancient Hebrew tradition and transforming it to become a far truer testimony to God's purpose with his world.

Excursus I: The Hardening of Pharaoh

H. Eising, 'Die Ägyptischen Plagen', *Lex Tua Veritas. Festschrift für H. Junker*, Trier 1961, pp.75–87; J. Gnilka, *Die Verstocking Israels*, Munich 1961; F. Hesse, *Das Verstockungsproblem im Alten Testament*, Berlin 1955; E. Jenni, 'Jesajas Berufung in der neueren Forschung', *TZ* 15, 1959, pp.321–39; Cornelius a Lapide, *Commentaria in Scripturam Sacram* I, *Exod.* ch.16; M. Luther, *Auslegungen über das zweite Buch Mosis*, WA XVI, 1899; O. Procksch, 'Verstockung', *RGG²* V, 1931, cols.1573ff.; G. von Rad, *Old Testament Theology* II, 1965, pp.151ff.; K. L. Schmidt, 'Die Verstockung des Menschen durch Gott', *TZ* I, 1945, pp.1ff.; with M. Schmidt, 'παχύνω' *TWNT* V, pp.1024ff. = *TDNT* V, pp.1022ff.; I. L. Seeligmann, 'Menschliches Heldentum und göttliche Hilfe', *TZ* 19, 1963, pp.385ff.; P. Volz, *Das Dämonische in Jahwe*, Tübingen 1924; W. Zimmerli, *Erkenntnis Gottes nach dem Buche Ezechiel*, Zürich 1954, pp.22ff. = *Gottes Offenbarung*, pp.61ff.

The difficulties connected with the subject are well known. In spite of the repeated efforts to illuminate the concept of hardness the results have been less than satisfactory. Much of the problem, of course, lies with the subject matter. Although there are some general parallels in the rest of the Old Testament, the problem of hardening is unique in Exodus. It emerges as if from nowhere and then vanishes. But it has become a gigantic stumbling block which has rendered the whole plague narrative opaque. With the introduction of the source critical method, it was once felt that the key to the problem of hardening had been discovered. Indeed, there is by and large a distinctive vocabulary which can be assigned to the different sources. But the hope has been frustrated and no major breakthrough has emerged (cf. Hesse).

One tendency of scholars is to turn to psychological ploys by which to solve the problem. Hardening is only an idiom used to describe the inner human reaction of resistance which once begun could no longer be reversed by the individual will. Another tack is to approach the issue as an expression of a theological or philosophical position. Hesse speaks of 'the almighty power of Yahweh and the sinful action of man in an unrelievable tension'. The difficulty of this approach is that the problem becomes immediately burdened by the history of the later discussion, which usually conceals the primary meaning of the text. Therefore it will be our endeavor to limit the investigation as closely as possible to the problem of the Exodus text. If we are successful on this level, the wider implications can be easily pursued in a suitable context.

The statistics of the hardness terminology have been treated so often by commentaries and monographs (cf. Hesse) that a repetition hardly seems necessary. However, a brief resume may be in order for this discussion. The verb *kābēd* to express hardness appears usually in the hiphil with Pharaoh as the subject and *libbô* 'his heart' as the object (Ex.8.11, 28; 9.34), one time in the qal with the 'heart of Pharaoh' as the subject (9.7), and once as a verbal adjective referring to the 'heart of Pharaoh' (7.14). Only once does *kābēd* appear in the hiphil with Yahweh as the subject (10.1). The verb *ḥāzaq* usually occurs in the piel with Yahweh as the subject, or 'the heart of Pharaoh' (4.21; 9.12; 10.20, 27; 11.10) or 'heart of the Egyptians' (14.17) as the subject. The verb also appears in the qal with 'the heart of Pharaoh' as the subject (7.13, 22; 8.15; 9.15). In 7.3 the hiphil *'aqšeh* appears with Yahweh as the subject, in 13.15 with Pharaoh as the subject.

A rather clear picture of distribution among the sources also emerges. The Yahwist always uses *kābēd*. The Priestly writer normally chooses *ḥāzaq*, but once *hiqšāh*. The E source choice is parallel to P. There are several redactional passages whose usage varies from these patterns and which will be discussed below (7.14f.; 10.1).

We turn first to the use of the verbs in the J source. It is significant to notice the position of the hardening phrase in the J pattern. One might have expected it to come after the threat of the plague, and as such to be the cause of the ensuing plague. However, the hardening phrase comes consistently at the end of the episode, in fact after the plague has been removed through Moses' intercession. This means that for the J writer the hardening does not function as the direct cause of the plagues. Rather, the hardening appears as a reaction to the plagues, or more specifically, to the removal of the plagues. This connection is made explicit in 7.11, 'When Pharaoh saw that there was a respite, he hardened his heart'. However, it is implicit in the other examples by virtue of its position in the narratives.

Because of the hardening, the plagues did not produce the response which was intended. However, the writer specifies repeatedly what reaction is expected. The signs function in order to reveal the knowledge of Yahweh to Pharaoh. In 5.1 this motif is introduced by

Pharaoh's failure to recognize Yahweh: 'Who is Yahweh? I do not know Yahweh.' The function of the plague is to make him known. The formula is 'that you may know that . . .'. On the one hand, the function of making known Yahweh is connected with the manner in which the plague is executed, and comes before the plague (7.17; 8.18; 11.7). The special treatment of Israel is the peculiar feature which reveals Yahweh at work. On the other hand, the special manner in which the plagues are removed also functions to make Yahweh known (8.6; 9.29). Here the specific time and unusual circumstance of the removal serve this purpose. The hardening serves to prevent the proper function of the plagues as a means for knowing Yahweh. One could perhaps infer that the sudden respite from the plague gave Pharaoh a reason for equivocating (7.11). Could the plague have been by chance after all? However, the writer attributes the failure of the plague to produce true knowledge to Pharaoh's being hardened. Hardness for J is not a state of mind, but a specific negative reaction to the signs from God.

We turn next to the P writer. Some very distinctive features emerge in his use of the hardening terminology. First of all, the parallelism of phrases is significant. The sentence pattern of 7.3, 4 is that of ab–abc. The two cola of v.3 parallel the first two cola of v.4. For this writer the expression 'I will harden Pharaoh's heart' is closely akin to 'Pharaoh will not hearken'. The closeness of meaning is further confirmed by a comparison of 11.9 with 7.3. In both verses, and only here, Pharaoh's resistance serves to 'multiply signs in Egypt'. However 7.3 describes the resistance as 'I will harden Pharaoh's heart' while 11.9 expresses it 'Pharaoh will not hearken'. Finally, it is significant to note that these same two phrases consistently make up the concluding formula for P: 'Pharaoh's heart is hardened, nor will he listen' (7.13, 22; 8.11, 15; 9.12).

Now the fact that two phrases occur in parallelism does not justify one's assuming that the phrases are identical in meaning. What is the nature of their similarity? The first suggestion would be that they are related in terms of cause and effect: 'Because I am hardening the heart of Pharaoh, he will not hearken to you.' But this relationship is not supported by the above parallelism, nor is it attested to elsewhere. Again, a proposal has been made to see the relation of the phrases in terms of objective and subjective effects. The one phrase is theological in character, the other psychological. But this sort of polarity is totally foreign to P. The two phrases function on the same level as grounds for multiplying the plagues. This means that for the P writer the plagues are not the result of Pharaoh's being hardened, but rather the reverse. Pharaoh is hardened in order to effect plagues. His refusal to hear results in the multiplying of the signs.

There is another aspect in P by which the motif of hardening is connected with the giving of signs. It is indicated by the position of the expression within the narrative pattern. The formula follows the contest of Moses with the Egyptian magicians, and concludes a unit. The hardness prevents Pharaoh from reacting positively to the signs. In P the role of the magicians parallels in function the concession motif in J. Both are means by which Pharaoh avoids the full impact of the signs. The signs fail in their function, but by design. Because Pharaoh does not hear, the plagues continue.

There is another pecularity to P's use of the motif which differs strikingly from that of J. The plagues do not function to reveal to Pharaoh the knowledge of Yahweh as in J. However, the same idiom 'that you may know' does occur in P, but in connection with the crossing of the sea. This is all the more striking since the terminology of J in this section is totally different from that of his plague narrative. The P writer appears to distinguish sharply between the function of the plagues and the catastrophe at the sea (7.5). The hardening allowed the plagues to be multiplied as a great judgment. The crossing served to make Yahweh known to the Egyptians (14.4).

In the light of these differing usages of the hardening motif, it is of interest to turn to the several secondary passages in the narrative. 10.1b–2 is usually attributed to the Deuteronomic redactor. The choice of the verb stems from J's use; the form and theology of the passage are however much more influenced by the P narrative. Yahweh is the agent of the hardening and he proposes to multiply the signs. Also parallel to P is the knowledge of Yahweh which Israel receives through the signs (6.7).

The interpretation of 7.14 is more difficult. Usually the entire verse is treated as belonging to the Yahwist. However, the second half of the verse which contains the phrase 'the heart of Pharaoh is hardened', has several peculiarities which would raise questions about its belonging to J. Formally the verses seems to be an interpolation when compared with the usual pattern of J (7.26; 8.16; 9.1). Again, the adjectival form is unique in the plague stories, and functions differently both in form and position from anything else in J. The hardening is not a definite reaction to the plagues, but the description of a state. Therefore, the suggestion seems possible that the phrase entered as a redactional connection with the fusion of the sources and has been influenced by the hardening formula of P in v. 13.

The important implication for our analysis of the two sources is in seeing that in both the hardening terminology is closely connected to the giving of signs. In J hardness prevents the signs from revealing the knowledge of God; in P the hardness results in the multiplication of signs as judgment. This means that all attempts to relate hardness to a psychological state or derive it from a theology of divine causality miss the mark. The motif of hardening in Exodus stems from a specific interpretation of the function of signs. Again, hardening did not function as a technical means to tie together originally independent plagues. Rather, the motif sought to explain a tradition which contained a series of divine signs but which continued to fail in their purpose. Hardening was the vocabulary used by the biblical writers to describe the resistance which prevented the signs from achieving their assigned task. The motif has been consistently over-interpreted by supposing that it arose from a profoundly theological reflection and seeing it as a problem of free will and predestination. It is clear that the P source extended the origin of hardening into the plan of God and thus went beyond J. But the polarity between hardening as a decision of Pharaoh and as an effect of God never was seen as a major issue. The occupation with this problem by commentators has contributed to their failure to determine its major role within the passage.

The only explicit reference to the hardening of Pharaoh in the rest of the Old Testament occurs in I Sam. 6.6 and supports its close relation with signs. The Philistines have been plagued by the ark and are confused as to what to do. The priests and diviners advise returning the ark with a guilt offering in order to determine why the God of Israel continues in anger. The problem for the Philistines is to determine whether the plagues came by Yahweh's power or by chance (v. 9). The reference to 'hardening your hearts as the Egyptians' (v. 6) refers to their refusal to learn from the clear divine signs.

Of course, the larger theological problem of divine causality did emerge in Israel. I Sam. 2.25 speaks of the will of Yahweh to slay Eli's sons, and the prophet in II Chron. 25.16 knows of God's determination to destroy Amaziah. I Kings 22 and Isa. 6 both testify to the prophet's task of closing men's minds to the will of God. Again, a later theological generation made use of the Exodus passage in their reflections on the wider problem, as Romans 9 demonstrates, Certainly the LXX translation had already moved in this direction. Nevertheless, this history of theological development must not obscure the sharp profile of the hardening motif as it first emerged in the plague narratives.

Excursus II: The Despoiling of the Egyptians

A. CALMET, *Commentaire littéral sur tous les livres de l'ancien et du nouveau Testament* I, Paris 1724, pp. 398ff. on Ex. 3.21; G. W. COATS, 'Despoiling the Egyptians', *VT* 18, 1968, pp. 450–7; D. DAUBE, *The Exodus Pattern in the Bible*, London 1963, pp. 55ff.; S. GOLDMAN, *From Slavery to Freedom*, 1958, pp. 194–206; E. W. HENGSTENBERG, *Genuineness of the Pentateuch* II, ET Edinburgh 1847, pp. 417–32; B. JACOB, *Das zweite Buch der Tora Exodus* (Microfilm, Jerusalem), dritter Teil, pp. 495–7; J. MORGENSTERN, 'The Despoiling of the Egyptians', *JBL* 68, 1949, pp. 1–28.

There are three passages within Exodus which record the tradition of Israel's despoiling of the Egyptians before the departure of the nation (3.21–22; 11.2–3; 12.35–36; cf. Ps. 105.37). The very close conceptual and linguistic formulation of the tradition lends itself to treating the passages together. Accordingly, Israel was commanded by God to 'ask' of their Egyptian neighbors on an individual basis objects of silver and gold. Then God caused the Egyptians to respond favorably to the Israelite's request. Two of the Exodus passages summarize the event as a 'despoiling' of the Egyptians (3.22; 13.36).

Few passages have provoked such an obvious embarrassment both to Jewish and Christian expositors as has this one. It is amazing to see the vigorous apologetic in defense of the tradition which began in Hellenistic times and continues up to the present. Of course, it should not be forgotten that the apology was often called forth by scurrilous attacks against the Jews (cf. Augustine's defense, *Contra Faustum* XXII.71; Lessing's *Wolfenbüttel Fragments*, Berlin 1786, p. 53). The issue at stake turns on whether or not Israel was guilty of deception in gaining an advantage, and how one is to explain the explicit command of God in effecting the despoiling. Since the attack on Israel's behaviour involved invariably an attack on the Old Testament and the God of Israel, Jews and Christians generally found themselves waging a common battle against agnostics and heretics. Only occasionally – at least until the nineteenth century – did Christians such as Marcion exploit the passage in order to contrast the 'higher ethics' of the New Testament.

It is remarkable to see the great variety of answers given by which to justify the despoiling. A few have continued to be used right through the modern period. First of all, it was argued that the despoiling compensated for Israel's legitimate wages of which she had been deprived as oppressed slaves (Jub. 48.18; Philo, *Vita Mos.* I. 140ff.; Tertullian, *Contra Marcion.* IV.24). Again, it was suggested that the Egyptians were not compelled, but gave of their own free volition even more than was requested (*Mekilta*). Josephus suggested that some gave gifts to speed Israel's departure, but others out of affection, 'neighbourly feelings toward old acquaintances' (*Antiq.* II. 35ff.). Augustine argued that Egypt had not made good use of their treasures and that it was better for these to be used in the service of truth (*Doct. Christ.* II.60). Still others interpreted the despoiling as evidence that God was forcing Egypt to send Israel free with the compensation which the Mosaic law demanded for any slave (Daube, Greenberg, p. 87). Then again, the borrowed jewelry was needed for the festive dancing in which Israel came forth as a bride (Morgenstern). Finally, it was God's way of providing the needed materials for the tabernacle and its furniture.

In considering this text it is important to distinguish, at least at the outset, between the descriptive task of understanding what the text meant in the context of the Exodus narrative, and the broader ethical and theological problems which involve the modern reader. In all three texts, the same verb appears to describe the manner by which the Israelites acquired the jewelry: 'Each woman is to "ask" of her neighbor'. The Hebrew root is *š'l*. The initial problem arises in that the verb can mean either 'to ask' or 'to borrow'. Thus, for example, in passages like Judg. 8.24; I Sam. 1.27, etc. one asks for something with no thought of return. However, in Ex. 22.13; II Kings 4.3; 6.5, the connotation is quite clearly that of borrowing for a temporary use. In other words, the same word has a semantic range which covers both meanings and it depends on the context to determine what is meant in a specific case. For whatever reason, the context for the despoiling in Exodus is not clear. There is no indication that a pretext was involved. The text does recognize that such willingness on the part of the Egyptians to comply with the request is highly unusual, but attributes this response to the intervention of God. In sum, the traditional way of putting the question – permanent gift or temporary loan – runs into an impasse which cannot be answered from the text itself.

A somewhat more fruitful entry into the intention of the tradition is provided by the summary statement found in 3.22 and 12.36: 'Thus they plundered the Egyptians.' The closest Old Testament parallel to this piel usage is II Chron. 20.25, which signifies the taking of spoils from a defeated army after a military victory. The point of the tradition focuses on God's plan for the Israelites to leave Egypt as victors from a battle. In striking contrast to the entire history of exegesis, the Old Testament text makes no attempt whatever to justify the act. Rather the concern of the text is to explain how it came about: 'God gave the people favor in the sight of the Egyptians', and the result of the action: 'they stripped Egypt clean'.

Turning now to consider the larger ethical question on which the subsequent history of exegesis has concentrated, the immediate danger to avoid is to isolate this one issue from the rest of the Old Testament. The tradition of the despoiling of the Egyptians is primarily a witness to God's complete solidarity with his people who are set over against the nations. He not only delivers Israel from Egypt, but intervenes in such a way as to effect a plundering of their treasures. But then is this identification of God with one people justifiable? Obviously the Old Testament has much to say about this issue. The whole prophetic polemic – not to speak of earlier evidence – called into question Israel's special election because of the sinfulness of the nation which was spelt out in terms of basic injustice to one's neighbor. In the end, the God of Israel destroyed the nation which he had once delivered. Seen in the light of the whole Old Testament, the despoiling of the Egyptians is another sign of Israel's election which constituted the faith of Israel (Gen. 15.14). This element was never explained rationally, but ultimately derived from God's inscrutable will (Deut. 7.7). God's relation to Israel was unique. The Old Testament is a testimony to his purpose for this people and for the world through this people. No one incident can, therefore, be extrapolated from its context within the history of redemption to form an ethical principle for all times.

VIII

PASSOVER AND EXODUS

12.1–13.16

E. Auerbach, 'Die Feste im alten Israel', *VT* 8, 1958, pp. 1–18; G. Beer, *Pesachim (Ostern). Text, Übersetzung und Erklärung*, Giessen 1912; A. Brock-Utne, 'Eine religionsgeschichtliche Studie zu dem ursprünglichen Passahopfer', *ARW* 31, 1934, pp. 272ff.; M. Caloz, 'Exode, XIII, 3–16 et son rapport au Deutéronome', *RB* 75, 1968, pp. 5ff.; J. Engnell, 'Paesaḥ- Maṣṣot and the Problem of "Pattern-ism"', *Orientalia Suecana* I, 1952, pp. 39–50, reprinted as 'The Passover' in *A Rigid Scrutiny*, Nashville 1970 (= *Critical Essays on the Old Testament*, London 1970), pp. 185ff.; G. Fohrer, *Überlieferung und Geschichte des Exodus*, 1964, pp. 79ff.; N. Füglister, *Die Heilsbedeutung des Pascha*, Munich 1963; G. B. Gray, *Sacrifice in the Old Testament*, Oxford 1925; E. Guthe, 'Passahfest nach Dtn 16', *Abhandlungen zur semitischen Religionskunde . . . Festschrift W.W. Baudissin*, Berlin 1918, pp. 217ff.; H. Haag, 'Pâque', *DBS* VI, 1960, pp. 1120–49; J. Hofbauer, 'Die Pascha-Maṣṣot- und Erstgeburtsgesetzte des Auszugsberichte Ex 12 und 13', *ZKTh* 60, 1936, pp. 188–210; J. Jeremias, 'Passa', *TWNT* V, pp. 895ff. = *TDNT* V, pp. 896ff.; *Die Passahfeier der Samaritaner*, BZAW 59, 1932; H. J. Kraus, 'Zur Geschichte des Passah-Massot-Festes im Alten Testament,' *EvTh* 18, 1958, pp. 47ff.; E. Kutsch, 'Erwägungen zur Geschichte der Passafeier und des Massot-festes', *ZThK* 55, 1958, pp. 1–35; P. Laaf, *Die Pascha-Feier Israels*, Bonn 1970; H. G. May, 'The Relation of the Passover and the Festival of Unleavened Cakes', *JBL* 55, 1936, pp. 65ff.; S. Mowinckel, 'Die vermeintliche "Passahlegende", Ex. 1–15', *Studia Theologica* 5, 1951, pp. 66ff.; J. Pedersen, 'Passahfest und Passahlegende', *ZAW* 52, 1934, pp. 161–75; L. Rost, 'Weidewechsel und altisraeli-tischen Festkalendar', *ZDPV* 66, 1943, pp. 205–16; J. B. Segal, *The Hebrew Passover*, London 1963 (with a full bibliography); R. de Vaux, *Ancient Israel*, 1961, pp. 484ff.; *Studies in Old Testament Sacrifice*, ET Cardiff 1964, pp. 1ff.; A. C. Welch, 'On the Method of Celebrating Passover', *ZAW* 45, 1927, pp. 24ff.; J. Wellhausen, *Prolegomena to the History of Israel*, ET Edinburgh 1885, pp. 83ff.

12 ¹The Lord said to Moses and to Aaron in the land of Egypt: ²'This month shall mark for you the beginning of the months; it shall be the first month of the year for you. ³Speak to the whole community of Israel and say that on the tenth of this month each of them shall take a lamb to a family, one for each household. ⁴But if the household is too

small for a lamb, let him share one with the closest neighbor in the number of persons. You shall make your count for the lamb according to what each can eat. ⁵Your lamb must be without a blemish, a male, one year old; you may take it from the sheep or from the goats. ⁶You shall keep it safely until the fourteenth day of this month when all the assembled community of Israel shall slaughter it at twilight. ⁷They shall take some of the blood and smear it on the two doorposts and the lintel of the houses in which they are to eat them. ⁸They shall eat the flesh that same night, eating it roasted, with unleavened cakes and bitter herbs. ⁹Do not eat any of it raw or cooked in any way in water, but roasted, both its head as well as its legs and entrails. ¹⁰You must not leave any of it over until morning; whatever is left from it until morning, you shall burn.

11 This is how you are to eat it: with your belt fastened, your sandals on your feet and your staff in your hand. You shall eat it in a hurry. It is the passover to the LORD. ¹²Then I will pass through the land of Egypt in that night and strike down every first-born in the land of Egypt, both man and beast; on all the gods of Egypt I will execute judgments: I am the LORD. ¹³The blood will serve as a sign for you on the houses where you live: when I see the blood, I will pass over you and no plague will destroy you when I strike the land of Egypt.

14 You shall keep this day as a memorial day and you shall celebrate it as a festival to the LORD. Throughout your generation you shall observe it as a perpetual ordinance. ¹⁵Indeed for seven days you shall eat unleavened bread; on the first day you must get rid of all leaven from your houses, for if anyone eats leavened bread from the first day until the seventh that person shall be cut off from Israel. ¹⁶On the first day you shall hold a sacred assembly, and on the seventh day a sacred assembly. No work can be done on them. Only what every man must eat, that alone can be prepared by you. ¹⁷You shall observe the feast of unleavened bread, for on this very day I brought your hosts out of the land of Egypt. You shall observe this day throughout your generations as a perpetual ordinance. ¹⁸In the first month, from the fourteenth day of the month at evening, you shall eat unleavened bread until the twenty-first day of the month at evening. ¹⁹For seven days no leaven shall be found in your houses for whoever eats what is leavened, that person shall be cut off from the community of Israel, whether he is a foreigner or native of the land. ²⁰You shall eat nothing leavened. In all your settlements you shall eat unleavened bread.'

21 Then Moses summoned all the elders of Israel and said to them, 'Go, select lambs for your families and slaughter the passover lamb. ²²Take a bunch of hyssop, dip it in the blood which is in the basin, and smear some of the blood from the basin on the lintel and the two doorposts. None of you shall go outside of his house until morning. ²³For

when the LORD passes through to slay the Egyptians, and sees the blood on the lintel and on the two doorposts, the LORD will pass over the door, and not let the destroyer enter your houses to slay you. 24You shall observe this as a rite for you and your children for ever. 25When you enter the land which the LORD will give you, as he has promised, you shall observe this service. 26And when your children say to you, "What do you mean by this service?" 27you shall say, "It is the passover sacrifice to the LORD, because he passed over the houses of the Israelites in Egypt when he struck the Egyptians, but saved our houses."' And the people bowed low in worship. 28The Israelites went and did just as the LORD had commanded Moses and Aaron.

29 In the middle of the night the LORD struck dead all the first-born in the land of Egypt, from the first-born of Pharaoh who sat on his throne to the first-born of the prisoner who was in the dungeon, and all the first-born of the cattle. 30Pharaoh arose in the night, he and all his courtiers, and all the Egyptians, and a great cry of anguish went up, because there was not a house where there was not someone dead. 31Then he summoned Moses and Aaron in the night and said, 'Up, go away from my people, you and the Israelites with you, and go serve the LORD as you said. 32Take also your flocks and your herds, as you said, and go; and bring a blessing on me too!'

33 The Egyptians put pressure on the people to speed up their departure from the land for they said, 'We shall all be dead.' 34So the people took their dough before it was leavened, their kneading bowls being wrapped up in their cloaks and slung over their shoulders. 35The Israelites had followed Moses' instructions, and asked the Egyptians for objects of silver and gold and for clothing. 36The LORD had caused the Egyptians to look with favor on the people so that they let them have what they requested. Thus they plundered the Egyptians.

37 The Israelites journeyed from Rameses to Succoth, some six hundred thousand men on foot, besides the dependants. 38Moreover, a large mixed assortment went up with them, and much livestock, both flocks and herds. 39With the dough which they brought out of Egypt they baked unleavened cakes, for it was unleavened because they had been rushed out of Egypt without time to prepare food for the journey.

40 The length of time that the Israelites lived in Egypt was four hundred and thirty years. 41At the end of the four hundred and thirtieth year, to the very day, all the hosts of the LORD went out from the land of Egypt. 42That was a night of vigil on the part of the LORD to bring them out from the land of Egypt. That same night belongs to the LORD, one of vigil for all the Israelites throughout the generations.

43 The LORD said to Moses and Aaron, 'This is the regulation for the passover: no foreigner shall eat of it, 44but any slave which a man has

purchased, once he has been circumcised, may eat of it. ⁴⁵No temporary resident or hired worker may eat of it. ⁴⁶It shall be eaten in one house. You shall not take any of the flesh outside the house, nor shall you break a bone of it. ⁴⁷The whole community of Israel shall offer it. ⁴⁸If a stranger who dwells with you would keep the passover to the Lord, every male of his family must be circumcised. Then he may approach to offer it. He shall be regarded as a native of the land. But no uncircumcised person may eat of it. ⁴⁹There shall be one law applying to both the native and the stranger who dwells among you.'

50 All the Israelites did just as the Lord had commanded Moses and Aaron. ⁵¹That very day the Lord brought the Israelites out from the land of Egypt, according to their tribal groups.

13 ¹The Lord said to Moses, ²'Consecrate to me all the first-born; the first birth of every womb among the Israelites is mine, man and beast.' ³Moses said to the people, 'Remember this day on which you came out of the land of Egypt, out of the state of slavery, how the Lord freed you by the strength of his hand; no leavened bread shall be eaten. ⁴This day you are going out, in the month of Abib. ⁵When the Lord brings you into the land of the Canaanites, the Hittites, the Amorites, the Hivites, and the Jebusites, which he swore to your fathers to give you, a land flowing with milk and honey, then observe this service in this month. ⁶Seven days you shall eat unleavened bread, and on the seventh day there shall be a festival to the Lord. ⁷Unleavened bread shall be eaten for seven days and nothing leavened shall be seen in your possession, nor any leaven be seen anywhere throughout your territory. ⁸You shall explain to your son on that day, "It is because of what the Lord did for me when I came out of Egypt." ⁹It shall serve you as a sign on your hand and as a memorial between your eyes, that the teachings of the Lord may be on your lips, for with a mighty hand the Lord freed you from Egypt. ¹⁰You shall therefore observe this institution at its proper time from year to year.

11 When the Lord has brought you into the land of the Canaanites, as he swore to you and to your fathers, and has given it to you, ¹²you shall set apart the first birth of every womb for the Lord. Every male firstling of your cattle belongs to the Lord. ¹³But every firstling ass you shall redeem with a lamb, or if you choose not to redeem it, you must break its neck. Every first-born child among your sons you shall redeem. ¹⁴And when in time your son asks you, "What does this mean?" you shall say to him, "With a mighty hand the Lord brought us out of Egypt from a state of slavery. ¹⁵And when Pharaoh stubbornly refused to let us go, the Lord struck dead all the first-born in the land of Egypt, the first-born of both man and beast. On account of this I sacrifice to the Lord the first male birth of every womb, but I redeem every first-born among my sons." ¹⁶It shall serve as a sign on your hand,

and as a symbol on your forehead that with a mighty hand the LORD brought us out of Egypt.'

1. *Textual and Philological Notes*

12.2. Cf. Cassuto, *ad loc.*, for the syntactical problem of the verse.

3. *l⁰ḇêt-'āḇôt*. The phrase can have a wide connotation of 'clan' (6.14), but also a narrower meaning 'family'. In v.3 the addition of the word *labbāyit* (household) makes clear this latter, restricted meaning. Cf. Kalisch's detailed arguments (*Exodus*) against Clericus for distinguishing the two terms sharply in v.3.

4. The syntactical problem turns on whether the phrase *b⁰miksat n⁰pāšôt* is to be construed with the preceding clause according to the accentuation of the MT, and rendered with the NJPS: 'the neighbor closest to this household in the number of persons', or whether one follows the LXX and relates the clause to what follows: '. . . the neighbor that lives near to him [that is, geographically] as to the number of souls, each one according to his eating . . .' Both renderings are syntactically possible. In terms of the context I think that the first choice is preferable. The selection of a neighbor is not in terms of geographic proximity, but size of the family. The final clause continues this thought with the additional modification respecting the amount eaten. But cf. Orlinsky, *Notes* (*ad loc.*) who suggests that the committee of the NPJS will change its translation in a new edition.

The verb *kss* refers to the computing of the number and not to the cost, as the NEB suggests. On the use of the *min*, cf. *G–K* §133c. C. Rabin's proposal of an alleged noun does not recommend itself (*Scripta Hier.* 8, 1961, p.394).

12.5. *ben-šānāh*, 'one year old'. Cf. de Vaux, *Studies in OT Sacrifice*, pp.4ff. for a discussion of the exact sense of the term.

6. 'between the evenings'. Cf. Ex.29.39; Lev.23.5; Num.9.3, 5, 11. The exact meaning has been much disputed especially in rabbinic discussion (*Mek., Sifra, Sifre; B.Pes.*58a). How is one to reckon the period of dusk? Cf. Driver (*ad loc.*) for the traditional explanation. He himself accepts the Talmudic interpretation which set the 'first' evening shortly after noon and the 'second' with the coming of actual darkness. Cf. F. M. Th. Böhl, '*bên hā'arbāyim*', *OLZ* 18, 1915, pp.321ff.

7. On the specialized use of '*al*, cf. Dillmann, *ad loc.*

8. *maṣṣôt*. Unleavened cakes are intended. The term appears elsewhere in other Old Testament rites, Lev.2.4; 7.12. Cf. the various Bible dictionaries for modern parallels.

m⁰rôrîm, 'bitter herbs'. Later Jewish tradition specified five species of herbs which would be included within this category (*Mishnah, Pes.* II, 6), and spiritualized its significance as a remembrance of the bitterness of life in slavery. What the original historical meaning was is not clear. Cf. G. Beer, 'Die Bitterkräuter beim Paschafest', *ZAW* 31, 1911, pp.152f.

9. *nā*', 'raw'. The word comes only once in the Old Testament. The prohibition probably includes half-cooked meat as well.

The inf. abs. serves to extend the range of prohibition to all forms of cooking with water. Cf. B. Jacob, *Das zweite Buch, ad loc.*, for an attempt to harmonize with Deut. 16.7.

11. The term $b^e\underline{h}ipp\bar{a}z\hat{o}n$ includes the sense of fear as well as haste. Cf. Deut. 20.3. *pesaḥ*, 'passover'. The etymology of the word and its meaning is much disputed. The noun designates both the animal offered (Ex. 13.21) and the festival itself (Deut. 16.1). The verb occurs very infrequently outside of Ex. 12. It appears in Isa. 31.5 with the connotation 'to protect'. In the remaining passages the verb means 'to limp' (II Sam. 4.4; I Kings 18.21, 26) which causes *BDB* to distinguish its root from that of the first. The attempt to derive all the meanings from a form of limping has not been successful. The Isaiah passage could already be dependent on the Exodus tradition. Again, there have been numerous other etymological explanations proposed, including derivations from the Arabic, Akkadian, and Egyptian. These attempts are reviewed and evaluated both by Segal, *op. cit.*, pp. 96ff. and P. Laaf, *op. cit.*, pp. 142ff.

13. *l^emašḥît*, 'destroy'. Cf. note on v. 23.

15. The particle *'a̱k* serves to emphasize, not restrict. Contrast its use in v. 16.

16. On 'sacred assemblies', cf. Num. 10.2ff. and Isa. 1.13.

17. The NEB repoints *maṣṣôṯ* as *miṣwōṯ* (commandments). Cf. LXX.

19. Cf. de Vaux, *Ancient Israel*, pp. 74ff., on the exact distinctions in the social terminology of *gēr*, *'ezrāḥ*, *tôšāḇ*, *śāḵîr* in the passover stipulations of this chapter.

20. The definite article on the noun 'passover' has often been thought significant (cf. Dillmann) since this is the first mention of the institution in the early source. But to what extent does it simply reflect its present position within an ongoing narrative?

22. On the term *sap*, 'basin', cf. A. M. Honeyman, *JTS* 37, 1936, pp. 56ff.

23. The term *hammašḥît* denotes 'the destroyer', which has its close parallel in the destroying angel of II Sam. 24.16. In contrast v. 13 pictures Yahweh himself striking the first-born dead and using the same root in a verbal sense. That v. 13 is a demythologizing of the earlier concept is possible, but not as obvious as some commentators assume.

27. *zeḇaḥ-pesaḥ*, 'passover sacrifice'. This term occurs only once, but cf. Ex. 23.18; 34.25.

32. The request 'pray for me also' does not seem to be intended sarcastically. Rather, now that Pharaoh has conceded all of Moses' original demands, he requests intercession as before, only no longer in reference to the removal of a plague.

35. Cf. Excursus II above for the sense of *š'l* = 'borrow'.

38. *'ēreḇ* 'mixed multitude'. Targum Onkelos makes a connection with Num. 11.4 which later midrashic exegesis expanded.

40. The LXX adds the phrase 'and in the land of Canaan' which alters the chronology (cf. the exegesis). It is probably an attempt at harmonization with Gen. 15.13.

41. The LXX joins the first word of v. 42 to v. 41.

42. Budde (*ZAW* 11, 1891, p. 200) argues with cogency that the observance is not 'for' Yahweh, but 'by' Yahweh for bringing Israel out.

49. The law is repeated with slight variation in Lev. 24.22; Num. 9.14; 15.15, 16, 29.

13.2. *peṭer*, 'first issue', is a technical priestly term coming in Ex. 34.19; Num. 3.12; 8.16; 18.15 etc.

3–16. M. Caloz (*op. cit.*) offers the most thorough study available of the Hebrew vocabulary of this chapter.

8. The use of *zeh* as a relative pronoun is unusual for prose, but need not indicate a textual corruption as *G–K* § 138h and *BH³* suggest.

12. Cf. Driver (*Exodus*, p. 108) on this unusual verbal usage.

16. The etymology of *ṭōṭāp̄ōṭ* is still uncertain. Cf. the note in the exegesis on the subject of phylacteries.

2. *Literary, Form-Critical, and Traditio-Historical Problems*

A. *The Problem of Sources*

There is a fairly general agreement among critical scholars respecting some of the source divisions within these two chapters. The Priestly source is most easily distinguished and to it is usually assigned 12.1–20, 28, 40–51; 13.1–2. Within the Priestly source different levels are sometimes distinguished. So Bäntsch sees a secondary redaction in 12.2, 14ff. Noth contests the presence of P in 13.1–2, but without sufficient evidence to upset the broad consensus. Most recently Laaf (*op. cit.*, pp. 10ff.) tried to solve some of the inner tensions within P in terms of a *Grundschrift* which underwent a history of priestly redaction. But with these variations in detail the broad lines respecting P seem well established.

Another source, usually designated as J, is recognized as a parallel strand to the Priestly. Some of the older commentators such as Driver assigned to J those verses which did not belong to P, but indicated the presence of Deuteronomic terminology which had entered into the J material. Starting with Bäntsch, the more recent commentators (Noth, Plastaras, Hyatt, etc.) have tended to distinguish the Deuteronomic redaction sharply from the J material. Nevertheless, there remain difficulties in simply identifying these Exodus passages with a seventh-century Deuteronomic writer, both in terms of vocabulary and conceptual similarity. Lohfink (*Hauptgebot*, Rome 1963, p. 121), followed by Caloz (*op. cit.*), has used the term 'proto-deuteronomic' in an attempt to identify the style as Deuteronomic without accepting a late dating. The issue has not been fully settled. Tentatively we propose assigning to J: 12.2–23, 27b, 29–34, 37–39. To D are assigned: 12.24–27a; 13.3–16. The E source may be present in 12.35–6.

There remains an additional problem which has been forcefully raised by Fohrer (*Überlieferung*, pp. 82f.; cf. earlier Smend and Eissfeldt). Within the source usually assigned to J there is considerable friction between the J plague narrative and the specific passover account of 12.21–24. For example, in the J plague account the motif of Yahweh's distinguishing the Israelites from the Egyptians is continued into the last plague (11.7), but without the need of the special protection of the blood ritual. Again, in J the Israelites are pictured as dwelling apart in Goshen (8.19; 9.26), whereas the passover blood ritual functions to distinguish between the Israelites and their neighbours who are mixed together. Fohrer argues for the presence of another literary source on the basis of this inner tension. His evidence for a N source appears far less convincing. Rather, in my opinion the problem cannot be solved on the literary level, but reflects a history of tradition which retains some inconsistencies.

One final matter calls for a response. It is unfortunate that the most recent and thorough English treatment of the passover by J. B. Segal (*op. cit.*) should feel constrained to reject the entire literary-critical analysis. Respecting Segal's criticism of source analysis, the following points should be made:

1. Segal argues that source analysis does not really aid in resolving the inner discrepancies. However, to substantiate this charge, he offers examples which do not hold up under scrutiny. On p. 72 Segal builds a case on the assumption that critics assign 12.31–32 to E, but actually Bäntsch, Bacon, Driver, and Noth assign these verses to J which undercuts the force of his argument. Again, to find a discrepancy between 12.34 and 39 (p. 72) is to construct a straw man. Segal consistently represents the source-critical hypothesis in its most extreme form in order to demolish it easily, but rarely, if ever, does he come to grips with the real force of the hypothesis as argued, for example, by Noth.

2. Segal assumes a historical knowledge of the post-exilic period which is highly questionable. He argues on the basis of the Mishnah's stipulation for the *pesaḥ* sacrifice to be performed only at the temple, that the P account (12.3ff.) of the passover as a family ritual would be impossible for the post-exilic period.

3. Segal's own positive literary suggestions hardly commend themselves. The claim that 'each document stresses some particular aspect of the ritual; they supplement each other' (p. 76) rests on dogmatic assumptions rather than literary evidence. Again the claim that 'in their present order, the Passover documents of the Pentateuch reflect

the picture of the evolution (*sic*) of the Passover as it was seen by the compiler' is without support and highly unconvincing.

B. *The History and Traditions of the Passover*

Few problems in the Old Testament have called forth such sustained scholarly research as has that of the passover. However, the focus of study and methods of investigation have tended to shift from period to period in the history of research. (Cf. for the older period the literature cited by Beer, *Pesachim*; for the recent period Segal's bibliography, *op. cit.*, and Laaf's, *op. cit.*)

1. Wellhausen's *Prolegomena* set the problem for the period which was dominated by the literary critical approach. By studying the festival calendars of the various sources (Ex. 23=J; Deut. 16=D; Lev. 23=P), Wellhausen attempted to reconstruct the history of Israel's cult. He noted that in the earliest period, represented by J, the Spring festival (*maṣṣôt*) was agricultural in character and was akin to the Canaanite practice. Later the Deuteronomic reform centralized the festival in Jerusalem, and combined *maṣṣôt* with passover in a historicized form which related the passover to the exodus from Egypt. Finally, the post-exilic Priestly writer removed the festival completely from its natural cycle, combined the two originally separate festivals with a rigid chronological framework, and returned it to the family setting. Wellhausen recognized the pre-Israelite origin of both the passover and *maṣṣôt* festival, which he derived from the pastoral and agricultural culture of early Palestine, but his major contribution lay in his attempt to reconstruct cultic history from source analysis.

2. By and large, the period dominated by the literary critical method continued to focus on the relation of passover to *maṣṣôt*, modifying and correcting Wellhausen's reconstruction, based often on fresh literary critical studies. Frequently the origins of the two festivals were assigned to different geographical areas, and a northern and southern provenance of passover and *maṣṣôt* were projected. But very little consensus emerged even respecting the broad lines. This lack of agreement on how to relate passover and *maṣṣôt* continues to reflect itself in the latest controversy between H.-J. Kraus (*EvTh* 18, 1958) and E. Kutsch (*ZThK* 55, 1958).

Kraus argued, chiefly on the evidence of Josh. 5.10–12, for an ancient festival, celebrated at Gilgal, in which elements of passover and *maṣṣôt* had already been fused into a unified ceremony and historicized in relation to the exodus and Jordan crossing. Kraus postulated a period of disintegration in which the family setting of the passover worked as a splintering force under Canaanite influence. The Deuteronomist sought to combat this disruption by binding passover to the central sanctuary. His program functioned to restore the old order rather than to initiate something new. Furthermore, the references to the passover under Hezekiah and Josiah are to be seen as a part of this same restoration program, rather than a tendentious literary retrojection.

The article of Kutsch strongly contests Kraus' position. Using the literary analysis of Horst on Deut. 16, Kutsch argues that the combination of passover and *maṣṣôt* belongs to the final Deuteronomic redaction and that *maṣṣôt* and passover did not originally belong together. In fact, the two were not joined until the exile. Josh. 5.10ff. is therefore post-exilic and offers no evidence for an early, unified festival from the period of the tribal league.

The above controversy illustrates the difficulty of reaching solid ground on these complex issues. Kraus' article is valuable in its attempt to overcome the fragmentation of the literary critical method, but far too much weight rests on unproven assumptions such as the early date of Josh. 5, and the purpose of the Deuteronomic reform. Kutsch depends too much on the overly refined literary analysis of Horst on Deut. 16 which hardly offers a solid basis for a historical reconstruction.

In sum, although it seems increasingly clear that both the passover and *maṣṣôt* traditions stemmed from pre-Israelite cultic practices and were later adapted by Israel for her own needs the process by which this historicization took place is not evident. Nor is the dating of the various stages at all settled. In my judgment, it is not likely that the passover material could have been transmitted for a long period within Israel in a non-historicized form. Recourse to a theoretical reconstructing of the historical process can hardly be avoided because of the nature of the material, but caution is in order lest too much certainty is claimed which the evidence does not support. Of course it remains part of the larger hermeneutical problem to decide to what extent an interpretation of the present form of the Exodus text is dependent on such historical reconstructions.

C. *Comparative Religion and the Problem of Passover*

Concurrent with the literary critical emphasis was the continual application of comparative religion data in an effort to unravel the complexities of the Hebrew passover. The fact that the passover was closely linked with two other cultic rites, the festival of unleavened bread and the first-born offering, encouraged scholars to seek some extra-biblical perspective which would illuminate the fragmentary biblical records and provide a unifying principle for comprehending the whole.

From the days of the ancient church parallels to the passover were frequently adduced, usually in a polemical setting, to disprove or prove the validity of the Old Testament account. However a whole new phase was introduced in the nineteenth century when comparative religion was developed into a systematic and scientific discipline. The insight that common laws governed the development of religious practice from primitive to higher forms was shortly applied to the Bible, particularly to the rite of passover and first-born. Wellhausen joined the two by suggesting an earlier stage in which the sacrifice of the firstling belonged to the primitive passover. However, he resisted the more radical theories of J. G. Frazer and W. Robertson Smith, who saw the sacrifice of animal first-born as a refinement of a more primitive claim on the human first-born. S. R. Driver (*Exodus*, pp. 411f.) was typical of English commentators in agreeing generally with Frazer regarding the actual roots of the Old Testament rite, but placing the emphasis on the transformation which the Hebrews effected in their usage of the older practice.

Beginning in the late thirties the history of research turned from the broad theories of Frazer and others to seek closer parallels in the Ancient Near Eastern material. Engnell (*op. cit.*) argued for an early *pesaḥ-maṣṣôṭ* festival which reflected the pattern of a Canaanite New Year's Festival in the spring. He suggested that the passover festival had a southern provenance, while the *maṣṣôṭ* he characterized as belonging to the north. The combination produced the Israelite passover. On the basis of Ancient Near Eastern parallels he thought he could describe the role of the king in a cult myth which encompassed Ex. 1–15.

Segal (*op. cit.*) followed a similar method, but in a much more comprehensive study. He also began with the assumption of an Ancient Near Eastern pattern of a New Year's festival, into which he placed the various elements of the Hebrew festivals. Some of Segal's parallels are impressive and of considerable interest. It is evident that rites such as blood manipulation, selection of sacrificial animals, calendar calculations, etc. arose from a common Near Eastern background. However, the weakness in both presentations is the failure to explain the peculiarities of the Hebrew ritual, which reflects itself in the loss of specificity right at the points which were central for the Hebrew rite (cf. Segal, p. 155). The effect of this consistently oblique reading of the text is that conjectures are made on why unleavened bread is used, or why the bones of the animal cannot be broken, but the inner relationship of the various parts of the tradition remains as enigmatic as ever. Again, it is surprising to see how static the patterns are which have not been able to work seriously with the developing history of tradition within Israel itself.

One of the most important contributions to the early history of the passover, which employs a method of comparative religion, was Rost's article on 'Weidewechsel' (periodic change in pasture) in 1934 (*op. cit.*). Rost attempted to describe the setting of the passover in the culture of the semi-nomads whose livelihood depended upon the successful alternation of feeding seasons between the cultivable land during the summer and the edges of the desert during the winter. The passover festival functioned to assure protection against the many dangers involved in the annual migration in the spring from the desert to the cultivable land. Then Rost conjectured that the passover right of the semi-nomads at the period of migration provided an analogy to the exodus from Egypt to the promised land. The annual cycle was historicized to commemorate the one event of passing from the dangers of Egypt to a new life in the land. Although Rost's theory remains hypothetical, it has the advantage of retaining a high level of historical and geographical specificity which differentiates it from the usual patterns of comparative religion, in which all festivals, whether spring or fall, begin to look alike.

D. *The Relation of the Passover Tradition to other Traditions*

In spite of the continuing interest in the above problems, much of the recent discussion of the passover among the last generation of scholars has focused on the problem within the broader framework which encompasses the study of the traditions of the entire Pentateuch. It is generally agreed that the historical problems connected with the passover are to be distinguished, if not separated, from the complex development which the other exodus traditions have undergone. Only occasionally does a modern scholar such as Jacob or Cassuto fail to understand the need for investigating the traditio-historical problem of the passover.

Certainly the impetus for the modern debate stems from the brilliant article of J. Pedersen, 'Passahfest und Passahlegende', of 1934. Although earlier scholars had suggested the important influence of the cult upon the narrative (Meyer, Bäntsch), Pedersen was the first who worked out a thorough-going cultic theory to explain the history of traditions. He argued that the entire complex of tradition of Ex. 1–15 should be understood as a cultic legend which had historicized in a story the various elements which constituted the original ceremony. Thus the victory over Pharaoh reflected the victory of order over the primordial dragon of chaos, which was followed by the mythical battle with the sea.

M. Noth (*Überlieferungsgeschichte*, 1948) accepted the basic features of Pedersen's hypothesis, but offered an important correction. Noth argued that the destruction of the Egyptians at the sea did not belong to the passover legend, but reflected an independent tradition which was non-derivable in character. However, Noth agreed with Pedersen in characterizing the plague tradition as secondary to the passover which in turn had its core in the death of the first-born. Noth's major contribution was his comprehensive study of the development of the Pentateuch. He placed the passover tradition within the major theme 'exodus from Egypt' and followed Rost in seeing the rite as a later historicization of a pre-Israelite cult festival of semi-nomadic herdsmen into the exodus tradition.

Within the last decade there have been several major attacks on Noth's reconstruction of the development of the passover tradition. Kutsch (*op. cit.*), Fohrer (*op. cit.*), and H. Schmid (*Mose*, pp. 44ff.) criticized Noth's theory, held in common with Pedersen, that the passover tradition is integrally related to the tradition of the first-born. One cannot derive the apotropaic protection of the passover from the first-born tradition. Therefore, it follows that if the passover and the first-born traditions were independent of one another, the entire history of exodus traditions was different from that envisioned by Noth. Fohrer goes on to propose seeing the death of the king's son as an 'Urplage' and the kernel of the plague complex. In my judgment, Fohrer's criticism of Noth is far more convincing than is his own positive alternative proposal.

In the light of this present lack of any consensus in regard to the traditio-critical problem of the passover, I would like to offer my own analysis of the problem. Any fresh attempt to unravel this complex history of traditions problem needs to reflect critically on the adequacy of the methodology employed. Obviously scholars continue to be at odds with one another and there is no sign that the next decade will bring a consensus nearer. The danger of atomizing the various traditions is inherent in the traditio-critical method. Yet conversely, there is little gained by over-arching categories, whether historical, literary, or theological, which simply harmonize the difficulties or subordinate the peculiarities of the text into a general pattern of Near Eastern parallels. Certainly apologetic endeavors, such as abound in Jacob's and Cassuto's commentaries, need to be eschewed when working historically. Particularly in the area of the history of traditions, it is wise to recognize the tentative, hypothetical nature of much of the work. To the extent that such projections do ultimately illuminate the text in its final stage, such research is justified.

First of all, the criticism levelled against the theory held by both Pedersen and Noth which derived the passover legend from the cult and placed the death of the first-born at its center appears to me basically correct. Both Fohrer and Kutsch have made a strong case in contesting a primary relation between the sacrifice of the first-born and the early passover tradition. Reference to the first-born is missing in 12.21–24. Again the verses in Ex. 13.1f., 11–16 do not relate to the passover. The result is that a crucial link in Noth's reconstruction has been removed.

Again, the evidence seems to confirm the theory that the passover tradition was originally independent of the plague tradition. The fact that the plague account in the early J strand stands in considerable tension with the plague sequence points in this direction. This independent life can be more easily explained in the oral tradition than by positing another literary source. Moreover, the theory that the passover rite stems from the pre-Israelite period is supported not only by parallels from comparative religion, but particularly from this literary evidence. Whether one accepts Rost's attractive hypothesis or not, it does seem likely that only later in the development was the ancient Semitic passover rite joined to the exodus traditions.

However, the task of determining the exact relationship between the passover traditions and the plagues is difficult and involves a complex development within the history of traditions. Once again, Pedersen's oversimplified reconstruction of the passover legend cannot be sustained. At the outset, it is of importance to note that in the J source the plague tradition is simply juxtaposed to the passover with no attempt to remove the tensions. In the J plague sequence

(11.4–8; 12.29–39) Yahweh distinguishes between the Egyptians and the Israelites without mention of a special sign, whereas in the passover the blood functions to protect. In the J plague account, Israel departs during the night, whereas leaving the house at night is prohibited in the passover tradition. In the J plague account the first-born is attacked (cf. also Ex. 4.23), whereas in the passover the distinction is made only between the houses of the Egyptians and those of the Israelites. Finally, the agent of judgment in the passover tradition, the so-called avenger, disturbs the normal plague sequence of Yahweh's battle with Pharaoh.

The fact that these two traditions still show a tension would attest to their original independence. It would also indicate that even up to the period of traditional history which is reflected in the J source, the plague tradition had not influenced the passover tradition to any great extent (contra Schmid, *Mose*, p. 45). However, the relation between the two traditions reflected by the P source has been considerably altered and points to a further development.

The first factor to be noticed is that the simple juxtaposition of traditions by J is no longer the case in P. Although P's passover tradition is clearly dependent upon the same tradition held in common with J, elements from the plague account have now been thoroughly integrated into the passover. The blood of the passover now protects the first-born; Yahweh assumes full responsibility as the avenger (note the syntactical changes in 12.13). The Israelites do not leave until morning (Num. 33.3). In P the hasty exodus of J has been ritually simulated within the passover ceremony (12.11) which removes the tension found in J between the passover preparation and the flight.

However, there is another remarkable change in the way in which P has related the passover traditions to the plagues which calls for an explanation. In the P passover account the motif of the slaying of the first-born, which the writer had inherited from the common tradition, has been incorporated into his narrative, but this has been accomplished by isolating the slaying of the first-born from the plagues. In other words, nowhere in the P account is the slaying of the first-born seen as the final plague within a series. Rather, the plagues are brought to an end in 11.9–10. Their lack of success in freeing the Israelites comes as no surprise, but had been God's intent from the start. In ch. 12 a new chapter begins, but now the slaying of the first-born belongs to the passover ritual and the successful freeing of

Israel from Egypt. In the P account there is no confrontation with Pharaoh. P simply records the end of the Egyptian sojourn and the exodus during the 'night of watching'. (12.40–42). Moreover P has now transformed the sea tradition (ch. 14) to function as a continuation of the plagues. Not only does he reintroduce the plague vocabulary from chs. 7–10, which is completely missing in J, but he transfers the confrontation and humiliation of Pharaoh to the defeat at the sea.

Of course, the basic question is to explain why P reflects such a different understanding of the relation between the passover and plague traditions. Although the answer remains highly tentative, certain reasons suggest themselves. First of all, the P account of the passover, although clearly dependent on tradition common to J, nevertheless shows an independent development far beyond that of the earlier stage. The Priestly writer's description of the passover in Egypt has been strongly influenced by the later cultic ceremony which has been projected back into the original night of the exodus. The lamb is selected at a specific period which has a specific calendar designation. The prescription for proper preparation is closely regulated, including the use of unleavened bread. Indeed the manner of eating which has become part of the rite simulates the original haste in departure rather than describing the actual events as did J. This means that the P account reflects a long history of oral tradition arising out of cultic practice, and is not simply a late literary variation from J.

Now it seems likely that the ongoing, independent development in the cultic use of the passover strongly influenced P's understanding of the other traditions relating to the Exodus. The variation between P's account of the passover night and J's is certainly striking. According to J the Israelites left at night, whereas P has them depart in the morning. In J the people are unprepared and hastily packed up their unleavened bread. In P careful preparation has been made for the feast throughout the night. The hasty departure is only acted out. Unleavened bread is not an accidental discovery, but part of the prepared ceremony. In J the death of the first-born culminated the long struggle with Pharaoh and resulted in his abject defeat and capitulation. In P the judgment is directed rather to the gods of Egypt (12.12) and Pharaoh plays no significant role.

The effect of P's variant account of the passover night certainly was a factor in the structuring of the larger narrative. First, the passover in the P tradition had assumed an independent role, which separated it from being simply the last step in the plagues. Therefore, the P writer structured the rite as something distinct and separate from the previous negotiations with Pharaoh. Secondly, the P writer could not accommodate his form of the passover to the J tradition of the ensuing events, particularly the negotiations with Pharaoh and the departure at night. Therefore, the P writer employed the sea crossing as the event in which Pharaoh was defeated and, by bracketing the passover, linked the crossing with the plagues.

It seems likely that P's version of the larger narrative took shape already in an oral stage, but that the decisive force which exerted the major force for the dislocation was the ongoing development of the passover ritual. The fact that the P tradition could vary so strongly from the J, especially in respect to the manner of relating the larger blocks of tradition, would indicate the fluid state of these traditions and offer additional evidence that the passover tradition functioned independently of the plague tradition for a considerable period of time.

As one would have expected, the cult was the bearer of the passover tradition. At an early date the passover was incorporated into Israel's tradition in historicized form to celebrate the exodus from Egypt. The manner in which the passover and plague traditions are juxtaposed in J would indicate that the passover cult did not provide the basic kernel of the exodus tradition, but was added to another body of tradition which had previously served to actualize the exodus. The P account reflects a period in which the passover had assumed a new importance. It was able to incorporate features from the plague tradition, as well as to assume an independent cultic significance in its own right. In other words, the shape of the literary sources points to a development within the cult, which continued to function as transmitter of the passover and plague traditions in celebration of the exodus. The change in the cultic significance of the passover resulted in an alteration in the passover narrative, especially in its relation to the other traditions closely associated with it.

E. *The Tradition of the First-Born*

The place of the first-born tradition requires a word. The above analysis has reached the conclusion that the sacrifice of the first-born was not integrally connected with the passover tradition (*contra* Pedersen, Noth). We would agree with H. Schmid (*Mose*, p. 44) in seeing it as an independent element of tradition with a setting distinct from that of the passover. The sacrifice of the first-born belongs to the pre-Israelite culture which prescribed special sanctity to the firstlings of animals and dedicated them to the deity as a special token of gratitude. The stipulations regarding the claims on the first-born in the early legal material (Ex. 22.29–30; 34.19) as well as the Deuteronomic (Deut. 15.19–23) and the priestly material (Ex. 13.1) indicate the originally independent character of these laws. The original motivation of the law has long been lost in antiquity. The later etiological explanation of the Deuteronomist (Ex. 13.14ff.) has tied it to the slaying of the first-born in Egypt. The connection is, of course, a natural one because of the common motif of the first-born in the ancient Canaanite practice and the plague tradition. The connection of the slaying of Pharaoh's first-born with Yahweh's claim on Israel which is made in Ex. 4.22 is also a secondary development, as our earlier form-critical study of the use of the messenger formula in Exodus demonstrated. Also the application to Israel in the formula 'Israel, my first-born' is derivative rather than primary.

The much discussed question as to what extent the claim on the first-born reflected a primitive practice of child sacrifice seems incapable of a definitive solution. Although it has become increasingly clear that child sacrifice was a part of ancient Semitic religion (cf. II Kings 3.27), the relation of the practice to Israel's tradition remains unclear. The story in Gen. 22 would indicate that the question did enter into the Hebrews' tradition (cf. Micah 6), but the abhorrence of Israel toward the practice at a very early age makes a study of the historical development of any such tradition impossible. The claim on the first-born of animals seems unconnected with any more primitive rite in the Canaanite culture at the time of its appropriation by Israel, but the possibility of latent connotations attached vestigially to such traditions is certainly conceivable.

3. *Old Testament Context*

The point has been frequently made throughout this commentary regarding the need to deal seriously with the final form of the text. The emphasis on the prior history of the biblical text by means of source and form criticism has often resulted in unwillingness and even inability to read the text in its present form. If for no other reason – and there are many important theological reasons in addition – the fact that the final redaction offers one of the first interpretations of the material justifies its close study.

The passover section has a clear introduction in 12.1; however, the conclusion of the section is not so easily discernible. Most commentators – note the early Jewish tradition – see a new introduction in 13.17 which would define the conclusion of the previous section at 13.16. Still the question remains open whether the section 12.1–13.16 has an internal coherence, or is simply a loose collection of appendices attached to an initial passover pericope. An outline of the material reveals immediately the basic elements of the formal structure.

Chapter 12.1–20 consists of a speech of instruction regarding passover made by God to Moses and Aaron which is to be conveyed to the people. Verses 21–27a then record Moses's speech to the people also giving instructions for the passover ritual. Verses 27b–28 describe in narrative style the response of the people. The speeches of instruction by God and Moses are then followed by a narrative section 29–42. Verses 40–42 serve as a summary. Verses 43–49 consist of another set of instructions by Yahweh to Moses. Verse 50, which parallels v.28, records the people's obedient reaction. Verse 51, which then parallels v.41b, is another narrative summary. 13.1–2 records Yahweh's speech to Moses while 13.3–16 brings a speech of instruction by Moses to the people.

[12.1–20] Once the formal structure of the passage in its final form has been outlined, the first task is to determine to what extent there is an inner coherence of the parts. Is the final form of the passage simply an incoherent jumble of disparate units which are unintelligible when read in their present order? If we now turn to the first formal unit 12.1–20, we are immediately faced with a problem. Verses 1–13 deal with the preparation for the passover while vv.14–20 are concerned with the feast of unleavened bread. There is no essential problem with the future tense in v.14 which parallels the preceding unit (cf. vv.6 and 13). Rather, the problem turns on the antecedent to the phrase in v.14, 'this day' (*hayyôm hazzeh*). To what does the demonstrative refer? Already Dillmann had made the point, which was accepted by Driver and most modern commentators, that there is nothing in vv.1–13 to which 'this day' can refer. It can only mean 15 Nisan, the day of the exodus, and not the 14th, the day of passover. He concluded that vv.14–20 cannot have been the original sequence and that perhaps something fell out which belonged between vv. 13 and 14.

In my opinion, these modern commentators have exaggerated the difficulty, which has not arisen simply because of a literary splicing of two disparate units, but lies in the nature of the material itself. Verses 1–13 described the preparation for the eventful night of delivery starting with 10 Nisan. The animal is to be slaughtered 'between the evenings' which separate 14 and 15 Nisan, the 15th beginning at sundown following the evening of the 14th. Then during the passover night of 15 Nisan Yahweh kills the first-born. Verses 1–13 describe the events into the night of the 15th. Then vv. 14–20 prescribe how this redemptive event is to be cultically celebrated. 'This day' of v. 14 is 15 Nisan, the day of exodus, but it includes the night of passover. The reference in v. 14 is to 'that night' (v. 12), but includes the entire day of the 15th. The apparent incongruence lies in the varying perspectives of the two passages. Verses 1–13 are describing the passover in terms of its chronological sequence, whereas vv. 14–20 are concerned with the length of time for the cult. It speaks of days and weeks. This accounts for the lack of a strict grammatical antecedent for the phrase in v. 14. Still there can be no real doubt how vv. 14–20 are linked coherently to vv. 1–13. The passage views passover and *maṣṣôṭ* as part of the one redemptive event. Here is an instance in which the scholarly concern with the prehistory of passover and *maṣṣôṭ* has obscured the real connection in the final stage of the text. We conclude that vv. 1–20 can be understood as a coherent whole.

The initial command of Yahweh to Moses and Aaron begins with a calendar stipulation. The month of the exodus is to mark the first month of the Hebrew year. Although there is considerable evidence to suggest that historically this form of the calendar marked a change from an earlier practice (cf. notes), the stipulation is given as a straightforward description of policy without emphasis on the element of innovation. Moreover, there is nothing to suggest a distinction between the civil and religious calendar. Rather, the new beginning of life for Israel is remembered by marking the beginning of a new year.

The instructions for the preparation of the passover meal are then set forth in the most precise language possible. The whole community of Israel is involved (v. 3) and the concern to include all Israel continues throughout the chapter as an essential feature. The lamb is to be selected on the 10th and kept until the 14th when it is to be slaughtered (v.6). The text itself does not explain the significance of selecting on one day and killing the lamb four days later, although later expositors have come up with a variety of possible reasons. The text focuses its attention first on stipulating who is to eat the passover. The prescribed unit is the family, which rules out individual celebration or arbitrary groupings of friends. Two families can unite if individually they are too small for an entire lamb. B. Jacob (*ad loc.*) makes a good point in observing that the law is not primarily concerned that there be too many people for a lamb, but that there be enough. The final phrase in v. 4b offers the normal eating capacity as the criterion by which the computation of participants is made. The very young and the very old would not count in the same way as the average adult.

The selection of the animal to be sacrificed is specified precisely. It is to be a perfect specimen, male, one year old, and either a sheep or a goat. When it is killed at sunset – the exact time is still contested – its blood is to be smeared on the doorposts and lintels of the houses. The significance of this move is explained in v. 13. The blood serves as a sign both to Israel and to Yahweh that no harm will befall the family during the night of destruction of the first-born. The manner in which the animal is cooked and eaten is stipulated. It is to be roasted whole. It is to be eaten in an attitude of haste and fear as if the community were ready for departure at a moment's notice. Nothing is to be left over until morning, all is to be burnt.

The ceremony of the passover night is described as that which was to take place in Egypt on the night before the exodus. The narrative describes the events which were shortly to transpire on that first passover night when Yahweh passed through Egypt to strike the first-born dead. From a historical point of view it seems quite evident that the narrator has combined elements of the later cultic celebration of the passover with his description of the first night. The actions by which Israel dramatized the passover night – the loins girt, sandals on the feet, eaten in haste – have been welded together into the one picture of the night of deliverance. For this biblical narrator the historical distinction between earlier and later passovers was lost. It is only because the first passover ritual was reported later in the narrative in its original form that one can reconstruct from the differences the historical sequence in the development of the tradition.

In the verses which follow (14–20), the same process of cultic remembrance continues, but in a form which has become increasingly distant from the events of the first passover. How could Israel be observing the feast of unleavened bread when they were thrust out of Egypt? The text itself seems to be somewhat aware of the problem when it stresses the command for perpetual observation. Still the redactor makes no real effort to ease the difficulty of passing from the first night to later celebrations of the festival and seems basically unconcerned with the exact historical sequence of events. What happened 'that day' is to be remembered in Israel throughout all generations in the festival of unleavened bread.

[12.21–28] The problem of relating the section which begins in v. 21 with the preceding section has caused much discussion among commentators. Two extreme positions are worth noting in delineating the issues at stake. On the one hand, Cassuto sees no problem whatever in relating Moses' instructions to the people regarding passover with the prior instructions of God. It is 'self-understood' that the essential elements of the festival as described in vv. 1–20 will be repeated and are to be taken for granted. Only the new points are stressed by Moses in his speech. On the other hand, Bacon (*Triple Tradition*, pp. 58ff.) stresses the utter incompatibility of Moses' alleged reiteration to the people of what Yahweh had previously told him. 'Moses ought at least to tell what he was told, and not something quite different.' He concludes that vv. 21ff. present a 'parallel' passover law which cannot be read in sequence with the preceding priestly account.

In my opinion, the controversy between the positions of Cassuto and Bacon lies in failure to clarify properly the context from which one is speaking. If one is addressing the historical issue of the development of passover, it is essential with Bacon to see the diachronistic dimension of the various texts in ch. 12. Surely he is right in seeing an original parallel relation between vv. 1–20 and 21ff. Nevertheless, Cassuto is correct in defending the coherence of the text when read from a synchronistic perspective. In the present form of the chapter, the redactor has understood Moses' speech in 21ff. as a transmission of the divine instructions. The fact that Moses' instructions differ from those he received cannot be used to contest the present coherence. It can be explained as a typical biblical style which has parallels in material which stems from one source. Or it can be understood as the redactor's interpretation of Moses' office and the implied freedom in his interpretation of the commands. However one moves at this juncture, a good case can be made for an inner coherence in the present structure.

Up to now the passover instructions have been given in the form of a divine speech to Moses and Aaron. Now Moses transmits these orders to the people. Of course his message is quite different from that given by God to him, as commentators have long since noted. But when read in its narrative context the major difference is one of length. The speech touches only on the selection of the lamb, its slaughter, and especially the manipulation of its blood on the house doors. There is no mention of a passover meal or of a ceremonial behaviour. Only those elements which relate to the last plague are selected and elaborated. The blood is to protect Israel from the destroying angel. The literary effect of Moses' speech is one of tremendous telescoping. The four days' preparation following the selection are ignored. The speech simply assumes the passover lamb is known, as if the definite article in v. 21 had its obvious antecedent in v. 11. The time of preparation is over. Moses has given the signal. The great event has started.

But once again, the narrative momentarily pauses, and turns briefly from the historical setting into a parenetic style. Because this rite is to become a permanent institution within Israel, later generations must need to know its significance. How does Israel transmit its faith to the next generation? The writer poses the questions in terms of a child's query. When your sons ask in time, what is the meaning of this ritual, then you will say: 'It is the passover offering to Yahweh through which we were redeemed.' This response is not simply a report, but above all a confession to the ongoing participation of Israel in the decisive act of redemption from Egypt.

According to our source analysis v. 27b belonged to the J account, whereas v. 28 formed P's conclusion to vv. 1–20. The use of these last verses in the final form of the passage is of interest. The people's reaction is separated from v. 20 to allow a place for Moses' speech of the J section rather than to supply a reaction before they had heard God's instructions. This evidence would thus confirm our theory that the redactor was consciously attempting a coherent sequence in his linking of God's speech to Moses.

[12.29–42] Up to this point the passage has connected the divine speech of instruction with Moses' reiteration of the orders and the concluding response of the people. Now the redactor inserts a large block of narrative material which describes the actual events of the passover night. This narrative picks up the same vocabulary of Yahweh's speech in v. 12, but now relates the events of the night from the perspective of the Egyptians, rather than of Israel. Only after they have been dismissed from the land does the departure of the Israelites assume the major focus of the account. The description starts with the extent of the judgment. It affected the very highest as well as the very lowest. There were no exceptions. 'Then Pharaoh arose in the night' – the contrast with his initial indifference is highlighted (7.23) – to share in the agony of all Egypt. Then he summoned Moses and Aaron. Some commentators have stressed the tension with 10.28f., in which Moses agrees with Pharaoh that this is his last visit. But the friction in the narrative is hardly a serious one because the point of the story is to portray Pharaoh's complete capitulation. His parting speech makes this fully clear. He requests them to leave with everything including the flocks and the herds. He even seeks from Moses a blessing which serves to underline Moses' complete victory.

Within this same context the insertion of the despoiling of the Egyptians adds the final evidence of the utter defeat of the Egyptians. The Israelites do not slink out of the country, but go as a victorious army who has plundered their oppressors. Verses 35f. break momentarily the forward movement of the story. By reversing the normal word order, the author picks up part of the events which preceded in time their departure in v. 34. The Priestly account of the passover night (vv. 40–42) now serves as an appropriate summary of the narrative section. It calculates Israel's total stay in Egypt, marks the very day of departure and concludes by returning to the theme of the earlier speeches by stressing the continual observance of this night 'for all generations'.

[12.43–50] The passover pericope has come to an appropriate ending. The fact, however, that the chapter continues has often been accepted as evidence of later additions. Moreover, the content of 43–50 points clearly to conditions connected with the settlement of the land. Even Cassuto considers what follows to be simply 'appendices' to the passover section. Although this judgment is probably correct in respect to the historical development of the text, it remains questionable whether it is an adequate analysis of the present function of these remaining verses.

Verse 43 once again introduces a divine speech to Moses and Aaron regarding the observance of the passover. The material is presented as 'the ordinance of the passover' (*ḥuqqaṭ happāsaḥ*) which indicates that the various laws are viewed as aspects of the one statute (cf. Ex. 29.9; Lev. 16.29; Num. 10.8 etc.). Indeed, the material is grouped around the subject of the prescribed qualifications of the participants. The summary in v. 49, when it is repeated in Num. 9.14, even substitutes *ḥuqqaṭ* for *tôraṭ*. Now it is not at all obvious why the passover ordinance has been assigned its present position. Occasionally one of the older commentaries conjectures a reason. For example, Kalisch suggests that these verses have been inserted here to bring them into closer connection with the sanctification of the first-born, but without enough evidence to convince. The one objective indication of the redactor's intention appears in the framework of the oracle. The oracle is introduced as a divine speech to Moses and Aaron which parallels 12.1. It concludes with the response of the people in v. 50 (cf. v. 28), and the exodus formula in v. 51 paralleling v. 41. The introductory messenger formula (v. 43) would indicate that the redactor understands the ordinance of passover as possessing the same divine authority as the early commands which instituted the Egyptian passover. These are not some later additions in the eyes of the redactor who had no sense whatever of historical development. Moreover the present position of the statute has significance for the biblical author. He has placed the passover ordinance after the departure from Egypt (vv. 42ff.) and yet he concludes the section in v. 51 with a repetition of the exodus formula of v. 42. The effect of this redaction is to suggest that the passover ordinance was not given until after the first passover celebration, but was commanded before the exodus had been completed.

Of course, it is possible that the inclusion of the ordinance following the narrative resulted from a hesitation to disturb the pattern in vv. 1–20 which was then duplicated in vv. 21–28. The style is certainly different. (Note the five prohibitions in vv. 43ff.) But there is a further reason which might be suggested. The present position following the exodus narrative may have arisen from the redactor's concern to specify at this point the qualifications for participation in the future feast, mentioned in v. 42. Moreover, the exodus of a large mixed multitude with Israel (v. 38), who had presumably not participated in the first passover, but now joined Israel would have made the issue of the non-Israelite role an acute one.

[**13.1–16**] The order of the concluding section is equally difficult to understand. Formally, the section parallels 12.1–20 in its two parts. 13.1–2 consists of a divine oracle giving instructions to Moses; then

3–16 recounts Moses' address to the people. The formal structure is particularly interesting because it disrupts the natural content units by separating the first-born stipulation in 13.2 from its detailed explication in vv. 11ff. There is an additional formal pattern to be observed in the section. Within Moses' speech there is a striking parallelism between the feast of unleavened bread (vv. 3–10) and the laws regarding the first-born (vv. 11–16). Both are related to the entrance into the promised land (5//11); both focus on the answer to the son (8//14); both require the visible sign of remembrance on the hand (9//16); both are grounded in the exodus formula (9//16).

In my opinion, these elements of a formal structure provide the key to the interpretation of this section according to its present order. Patterned after 12.1–20, section 13.1–2 is presented as a divine speech which is then interpreted by Moses in 13.3ff. The effect is that the divine address now serves as a superscription to the Moses address. The function of 13.1–2 is lost if one removes it from its present position and relates it to v. 11 because of its content. This move not only disregards its role as a divine word, but destroys the symmetry between the two parts of Moses' address.

But then the question arises how vv. 1–2 can possibly serve as a heading to be explained by Moses when the content has so little in common with what follows? First, we have already observed how closely the two sections of Moses' speech parallel each other in spite of the distinct topics dealt with in each. Moreover, this similarity is greatly enhanced because of an overriding concern which is shared by both sections. The center of both oracles focuses on the answer which the father gives the son in explaining the faith. The section 3–16 is characteristically different from the earlier laws because of the high level of homiletical intensity. The writer – usually he is named the Deuteronomist – is concerned, not only that the tradition be passed on to subsequent generations, but that the tradition be experienced. It is to be 'in your mouth' (v. 9), written 'on your hand' for a 'remembrance'. The effort to internalize the tradition allows the writer to ride roughshod over earlier fine distinctions. The writer historicizes both ceremonies, *maṣṣôt* and first-born, by means of the one exodus formula.

Now it is evident that the command of God regarding the first-born in 13.2 reflects an ancient cultic claim, which probably stemmed from pre-Israelite times. In other Priestly contexts the exact stipulations for the offering and redemption of the first-born are explained in detail. Verse 13 still reflects elements from the Priestly law. But it now seems evident that 13.1–2 have been assigned a different role in the present position. The initial point that God claims the first-born has been spiritualized. This claim has been extended from the first-born to all Israel. God has a special claim on his people: 'he belongs to me' (*hû' lî*). Understood in this way, it becomes clear that vv. 1–2 can serve as a superscription to vv. 3–16. The formal structure of a divine address demands the same authority as it did in the preparation of the passover. The setting of the address on the very day of the exodus (13.3) in the mouth of Moses anchors the claim in the basic redemptive event of Israel's faith. The address follows the narrative of the deliverance and draws its implications for future generations, not simply in setting up the later ritual practices of passover, but in calling for an ongoing experiential appropriation from the heart in response to what God had done. Far from being a clumsy appendix, the last section gives a major theological reflection on the tradition which it interprets.

Conclusion

There are some broader implications for understanding the passover pericope which arise from our literary analysis of the final form of the present text. If an expositor takes seriously the final redaction, he can recognize an important biblical testimony to the relationship between word and event in the redactor's manner of linking commands to narrative material. The biblical writer brackets the Exodus event with a preceding and a succeeding interpretation. He does not see the exodus as an 'act of God' distinct from the 'word of God' which explains it. In theological terms, the relation between act and interpretation, or event and word, is one which cannot be separated. The biblical writer does not conceive of the event as primary or 'objective' from which an inferential, subjective deduction of its meaning is drawn (*contra* G. E. Wright, *God Who Acts*, SBT 8, 1952). The event is never uninterpreted. Conversely, a theological interpretation which sees the subjective appropriation – whether described cultically or existentially – as the primary element from which an event may be reconstructed, is again introducing a theological scheme which has no warrant in the theology of the redactor.

Again, the richness and variety in the relationship between the event and its implications for Israel's faith, as we have found in the whole section, should keep us from over-emphasizing one pattern as normative. The frequent stress on the primacy of the indicative mood, followed by a secondary imperative as in Ex. 19.1ff., is certainly one biblical stance, but by no means the sole one. The frequent attempt to see the suzerainty treaty pattern as the major analogy to the biblical understanding of covenant runs the danger of distortion through over-emphasis. The Deuteronomic application which seeks to internalize afresh the claims of God upon each new generation of God's people, finds its best analogy, not in the Ancient Near East, but in the New Testament gospel.

Finally, the redactor's use of the dialectic between redemption as hope and redemption as memory has important theological implications. Those commentators who are disturbed over the detailed instructions for future celebration before the initial event has transpired have failed to see that far more is at stake in the text than chronological consistency. The interplay in vv. 1–20 and 21–28 between the now and the then, between what is to come and what has already happened, is not dissolved after the event, but once again picked up and maintained in a new dialectic between the past and the future. Israel remains a people who has been redeemed, but who still awaits its redemption.

There is one final question which might be briefly raised in connection with the study of the final form. In terms of the present text, how valid is the traditional rabbinic distinction between the 'Egyptian passover' (*pesaḥ miṣrayim*) and the 'later passover' (*pesaḥ dôrôt*)? Usually in critical commentaries the distinction is dismissed immediately. This impatience stems from the time when it was first recognized by historical criticism that the stipulations for the so-called 'Egyptian passover' were a reflection of later cultic practice which the P writer had read back into the original event. However, the question must again be faced if one deals seriously with the text in its final form. The issue can be phrased as follows: Is there evidence to support the claim that such a distinction between these two passovers was intended by the final redactor?

Certainly the rabbis were correct in seeing the distinction between the original passover in Egypt and the passover celebrated by later generations. The 'now/then' polarity is integrally built into the passage. However, the rabbinical distinction functions mainly to distinguish between statutes which applied only to the original passover and those which applied to its later observance. Used in this way, a legal category is introduced which goes much beyond the biblical movement and serves chiefly to harmonize the later Jewish practice of keeping passover with elements from the biblical tradition.

Detailed Notes

12.1. 'in the land of Egypt'; cf. 6.28. The use of this phrase caused considerable discussion in rabbinic exegesis; cf. for example, *Mekilta de-Rabbi Ishmael, ad loc.*, an issue which was picked up by both Jacob and Cassuto.

2. 'This month is for you the beginning of months; it is the first month of the year for you.' There are two major problems in this verse. The first turns on the syntactical relation of the two parts of the sentence. The second relates to the historical implications for the problem of the OT calendar. (i) Cassuto has pointed out the syntactical problem quite correctly. According to Hebrew usage, the verse offers a statement of an existing fact, not the introduction of a change in the calendar. The two halves of the verse state approximately the same thing. (ii) The issue at stake is whether an ecclesiastical year is being reckoned which is distinguished from the secular year, or whether in fact a historical change in calendar reckoning is reflected. The traditional view (Kalisch, Segal, Cassuto) defended the view that the Hebrew calendar had a double New Year, one on the first day of Tishri which was civil, and one on the first day of Nisan which was religious. The critical view, defended by Wellhausen and most scholars thereafter, saw in this verse the later post-exilic calendar practice of beginning the year in the spring, as did the Babylonians, in opposition to the old Hebrew system which began in the autumn. The issue is more complex than is often realized. Cf. H. Cazelles, *DBS* VI, 1957–60, and R. de Vaux, *Ancient Israel*, pp. 190ff. with an extensive bibliography.

5. On the various elements of *realia* connected with the passover ritual such as the selection, slaughter, blood manipulation, etc. cf. the monograph of J. Jeremias, *Die Passahfeier der Samaritaner*, 1932.

6. B. Jacob (*ad loc.*) develops in an interesting way the midrashic theory that the lamb was selected on 10 Nisan because of the darkness which preceded 14 Nisan.

8. *maṣṣôt* = cakes. Cf. article on 'bread' in *IDB*, and 'Massoth' in *BHH* II, cols. 1169f. Various reasons are adduced for unleavened bread from comparative religion parallels. Cf. Segal, *op. cit.*, pp. 179ff. The biblical tradition is itself divided. The J source offers an etiology on unleavened bread (12.34ff.). Deut. 16.3 calls unleavened cakes the 'bread of affliction', which already shows a symbolic understanding. For the P writer the unleavened bread is constituted part of the festival from the beginning.

9. 'nor boiled in water'. There has been much speculation on this stipulation. Cf. Segal, *op. cit.*, pp. 205ff.

13. On the question of 'signs', cf. especially C. Keller, *Das Wort OTH*, Basel 1946; B. O. Long, *The Problem of Etiological Narrative in the OT*, BZAW 108, 1968, pp. 65ff.; F. J. Helfmeyer, *TWAT* I, pp. 182–205.

14. 'memorial'. Cf. B. S. Childs, *Memory and Tradition*, pp. 66ff.; W. Schottroff, *'Gedenken'*, pp. 299ff.

26ff. On the etiological form, cf. A. Soggin, 'Kultätiologische Sagen und Katechese im Hexateuch', *VT* 10, 1960, pp. 341–7. Cf. also the interesting extra-biblical parallels offered by J. Loza, 'Les Catecheses Etiologiques dans L'Ancien Testament', *RB* 78, 1971, pp. 481–500.

32. Cf. the bibliography on 'blessing' in *TWAT* I, p.638.

35. Cf. the excursus on the 'Despoiling of the Egyptians'.

37. Cf. the following for a treatment of the number of Israelites in Egypt: G. Beer, *Exodus*, pp.68f.; A. Lucas, *PEQ*, 1944, pp.164ff.; R. Hentschke, 'Bevölkerungsverhältnisse', *BHH* I, cols.237ff.

37. Succoth is the well-known Egyptian Teku which is located at Tell el-Maskhutah in wadi Tumilat. Cf. the recent discussion in Hyatt, *Exodus*, on Ex.1.11.

40. For the chronological problem, cf. N. H. Tur Sinai, *Bibliotheca Orientalis* 18, 1961, pp.16f.

46. On the prohibition of breaking bones, cf. J. Henninger, 'Zum Verbot der Knochen zerbrechen', *Studia Orientalistici G. Levi Della Vida* (Rome, 1956), I, pp.448ff.; A. Scheiber, *VT* 13, 1963, pp.95ff.; R. de Vaux, *Studies in Old Testament Sacrifice*, pp.9ff.

13.2. 'first-born'. Cf. de Vaux, *Ancient Israel*, pp.443f. with bibliography.

13. E. Nielsen, 'Ass and Ox in the Old Testament', *Studia Orientalia J. Pedersen . . . dicata*, Munksgaard 1953, pp.263ff.

16. On phylacteries, cf. E. A. Speiser, *JQR* 48 (1957/8), pp.208–17.

4. *History of Exegesis*

The history of exegesis of the passover pericopes of chs. 12f. presents a variety of problems which are unique in the book of Exodus. In the first place, the scope of the problems in which these chapters played a significant role is immense. In Judaism its interpretation involves the entire development of the Jewish ritual and halachah in a period which extends from the early Hellenistic traditions to its Talmudic form. In addition, the entire range of Jewish thought, from orthodox Pharisees to the most radical sectarianism, exhibited an intense interest in the passover. In Christian thought, not only was the death of Christ set against the background of the passover in the gospels, but this imagery was immediately picked up by other early Christian writers and developed. Not only did the issue of the passover become a burning controversy in early Christian history, but the passover became a vehicle for almost every important Christian doctrine with the ensuing controversy from the early Middle Ages throughout the post-Reformation period. In the second place, the complexity of the problems are also unrivalled in the history of exegesis. The majority of the problems have continued to be debated by specialists without reaching a general consensus. One only has to recall the New Testament debate on the nature of the Last Supper to be made aware of the difficulty of the issues at stake.

Consequently in the light of this situation, it does not seem wise to attempt to sketch the history of exegesis in any great detail within the limited space of an Exodus commentary. Rather, the different problems will be merely outlined and some of the important secondary literature presented for further study. If the reader is at least made aware of the range of problems which arose at different historical periods in relation to this chapter, no further justification for this section will be needed.

A. *The Passover in Judaism*

In the Hellenistic period Jewish exegesis and religious practice set about developing and fixing the tradition of the passover ritual. The biblical tradition of Ex. 12 had established unequivocally the duty of a perpetual celebration of passover which was sharply distinguished from the first passover in Egypt. Moreover a multitude of details regarding the precise celebration of the rite had to be settled in terms of Jewish law. What herbs were to be reckoned as 'bitter herbs'? When precisely could the last meal with leavened bread be eaten? How was leaven to be disposed of? What was the relation of the obligation to celebrate the passover to the observance of sabbath? By the time of the Mishnah, if not well before, the major lines of the halachah had been set.

However, it would be a serious mistake to imagine that the interest in the passover focused only in the area of halachah. The haggadah service is eloquent testimony to the religious life of the community in striving for continual participation in the redemption of the past and intense longing for the deliverance in the future: 'This year here, next year in the land of Israel; this year as slaves, next year as free.'

There can be no doubt that there was a long and complex history of development before the tradition in its various forms merged in a relatively fixed shape. In some cases, as in the passover haggadah, many of the major lines of development can still be discerned (cf. Goldschmidt and Finkelstein below). In other cases, the history is far less certain. Moreover, the few fragments which stem from sources outside the main lines of Pharisaic Judaism (Elephantine, Qumran, Samaritan) testify to the sparsity of evidence in whole areas which have been virtually lost.

The primary rabbinic texts which bear on the subject are the

Targums, Tannaite midrashim, the Mishna, Tosephta, Megillat Ta'anit, Haggada, and Talmuds. The important non-rabbinic texts are the ostraca and papyri from Elephantine, Jubilees, Wisdom of Solomon, Philo, Josephus, Qumran, and the Samaritan ritual.

The following secondary literature is important:

G. BEER, *Pesachim (Ostern)*. *Text, Übersetzung und Erklärung* (Giessen, 1912); H. BILLERBECK, 'Das Passamahl', *Kommentar zum NT* IV, München 1928, pp. 41ff.; R. LE DÉAUT, *La nuit pascale* (Rome, 1963); M. DELCOR, 'Le sacerdoce, les lieux de culte de Khirbet Qumrân', *Rev. de l'Hist. des Rel.* 144, 1953, pp. 5ff.; A. DUPONT-SOMMER, 'Sur la fête de la Pâque dans les documents araméens d'Elephantine', *Revenue des études juives*, n.s. 7, 1946–7, pp. 39ff.; I. ELBOGEN, *Der jüdische Gottesdienst*[2], Frankfurt 1924; L. FINKELSTEIN, 'The Oldest Midrash: Pre-Rabbinic Ideals and Teachings in the Passover Haggadah', *HTR* 31, 1938, pp. 291ff.; 'Pre-Maccabean Documents in the Passover Haggadah', *HTR* 35, 1942, pp. 291ff.; 36, 1943, pp. 1ff.; T. GASTER, *Passover. Its History and Traditions*, Boston and London 1958; E. D. GOLDSCHMIDT, *Die Pessach-Haggada*, Berlin 1937; J. JEREMIAS, *Passahfeier der Samaritaner*, Berlin 1932; A. JAUBERT, *La Date de la Cène*, Paris 1957; H. LICHTENSTEIN, 'Die Fastenrolle. Eine Untersuchung zur jüdisch-hellenistischen Geschichte', *HUCA* 8/9, 1931–2, pp. 257ff.; J. NEUSNER, *The Rabbinic Traditions about the Pharisees before 70* I, Leiden 1969, pp. 231ff.; S. SPIEGEL, *The Last Trial*, New York 1967, pp. 54ff.; G. VERMES, *Scripture and Tradition in Judaism*, Leiden 1961, pp. 215ff.; S. ZEITLIN, 'The Liturgy of the First Night of Passover', *JQR* 38, 1947/8, pp. 431–60.

B. *Early Christian Interpretation of the Passover*

The basic New Testament problem arises from its ambivalent approach to the Old Testament-Jewish passover traditions. On the one hand, the early church continued in the observance of the rite, as had Jesus, and confessed its solidarity with Israel's past and future. The language of passover continued to be the appropriate vehicle for Christian faith (Paul, John). Yet on the other hand, the death, resurrection, and Messianic kingdom of Jesus Christ was soon understood as the bringing of the true content of the Old Testament passover which was consequently set over against the Jewish observance. This same theological tension is reflected in the difference between the synoptic tradition, which has Jesus eating the passover meal just before the crucifixion, and John's gospel, which pictures Jesus as being himself the slaughtered Lamb of God.

The Quartodeciman controversy of the second century provides further evidence that the church struggled at length to understand its relation to the Jewish passover. The earliest Christian homily of Melito of Sardis reflects not only a vigorous polemic against the Jewish observance, but also the strong eschatological hope associated with the passover in early Christianity. The two major theological traditions of the church regarding the passover emerge sharply within the schools of Origen and Hippolytus. At the same time, the lasting effect of the older Jewish tradition on Christian liturgy can be traced, although often with considerable uncertainty.

For the New Testament see the full bibliographies in:

J. Jeremias, '*Πάσχα*', *TWNT* V, pp. 896ff. = *TDNT* V, pp. 896ff.; H. Haag, 'Pâque', *DBS* VI, pp. 1120ff.; B. Lohse, *Das Passafest der Quartadecimaner*, Gütersloh 1953, pp. 143ff.; A. J. B. Higgins, *The Lord's Supper in the New Testament*, SBT 6, 1952; B. Gärtner, *John 6 and the Jewish Passover*, Lund 1959.

For the passover in the early church, cf.:

J. Blank, *Meliton von Sardes. Vom Passa*, Freiburg 1963; C. Bonner, *The Homily on the Passion by Melito, Bishop of Sardes*, London 1940; W. Huber, *Passa und Ostern: Untersuchungen zur Osterfeier des alten Kirche*, BZNW 35, 1969; B. Lohse, *op. cit.*; P. Nautin, *Homélies Pascales* I–III, SC 27, 36, 48, 1950–7; E. Preuschen, 'Passah, altkirchliches und Passahstreitigeiten', *RE*[3] XIV, pp. 725ff.

C. *Church Fathers, Schoolmen, and Reformers*

The main lines of the allegorical and typological exegesis which had emerged by the late fourth century in the schools of Origen and Hippolytus continued and were expanded in the centuries which followed. It is characteristic of medieval interpretation that the passover symbolism was joined with most of the basic Christian doctrines, including the passion, death, resurrection, baptism, eucharist, eternal life, final judgment, and Christian morals. At times considerable interest focused on the historical details of the exodus account (Theodoret, Nicholas of Lyra), while at other times the mystical interpretation lost complete contact with the literal sense of the Old Testament (Ambrose, Rupert of Deutz).

The Protestant Reformers did not offer a real break in the history of Christian interpretation in respect to the passover. Rather their characteristic emphases were simply joined to traditional themes. Luther related the passover to the eucharist and to the passion of

Christ very much along traditional lines. However, he introduced his sermons on Ex. 12 with a hermeneutical discourse regarding the limited role of the Old Testament for the Christian. Calvin's exegesis is impressive both in its attention to detail and in its penetrating theological summary of the passover as a 'recollection of past deliverance and nourishment for future redemption'. Equally interesting is his restraint in trying to offer explanations for certain elements of the ritual such as the prohibition to boil or break the animals bones. Zwingli is very traditional in first offering a brief, literal interpretation of Ex. 12 before beginning with a theological interpretation much along the lines first set out by Paul.

D. *The Post-Reformation Period*

In many ways the post-Reformation period is one of the most interesting and important periods in regard to the interpretation of the passover. New interest in the biblical text, coupled with tremendous learning, turned its full attention to exploring the historical background of the ancient Hebrew ritual. Beginning in the sixteenth century with such men as Fagius, Christian scholars turned to a minute examination of the Jewish passover traditions. The interest was ultimately theological in most cases, but this concern was pursued through the concrete historical *realia*. In a real sense, the groundwork for the modern critical era was laid by the diligent research of these men, particularly in the seventeenth century, who returned to the sources and who recognized most of the historical problems involved.

Cf. the extensive list of specialized studies on the passover in J. Le Long, *Bibliotheca Sacra* II, Paris 1723, p. 1066. The following are some of the most important treatments from a long and impressive list:

S. BOCHART, *Hierozoicon* I, London 1663, pp. 551ff.; J. BUXTORF, *Synagoga Judaica*, Basel 1603, ch. xviii; J. H. HOTTINGER, *Jus Hebraeorum*, section IV, 1651, reprinted in UGOLINI, *Thesaurus Antiquitatum Sacrarum*, Venice 1744ff., Vol. III; J. LIGHTFOOT, *The Temple Service, Works* I, London 1684, pp. 951ff. = *Works* IX, London 1822, pp. 128ff.; J. SPENCER, *De Legibus Hebraeorum Ritualibus*, Cambridge 1685.

E. *The Modern Period*

The essentially new element in the study of the passover which distinguishes the modern critical approach from the earlier period was a concept of historical development. Early writers had recognized many of the inner tensions of the text and sought to explain them in different ways. Some continued the traditional Jewish distinction between the Egyptian passover and the later celebration. Some followed the lead of Spencer in seeking an explanation of difficulties from comparative religions. Nevertheless well into the first quarter of the nineteenth century, even among writers who were often inclined toward rationalistic explanations (Michaelis, Rosenmüller), one finds very little sense of historical dimension in terms of a development within the Old Testament. Then quite suddenly a number of critical articles and monographs appeared which explicitly sought to recover an earlier stage of the passover ritual. Very shortly the literary problem of the Pentateuch entered into the picture and the modern period had begun.

The following were some of the early critical studies which finally culminated in Wellhausen's brilliant synthesis:

F. C. BAUR, 'Über die ursprüngliche Bedeutung des Passahfestes', *Tübinger Zeitschrift*, 1832, pp. 40–124; J. F. GEORGE, *Die älteren jüdischen Feste*, Berlin 1835; K. C. W. BÄHR, *Symbolik des mosäischen Cultus* II, Heidelberg 1839, pp. 627ff.; H. EWALD, *De feriarum hebr. origine ac ratione*, Göttingen 1841; H. HUPFELD, *Commentatio de primitiva et vera festorum apud Hebraeos ratione*, Halle 1853ff.

5. *Theological Reflection on the Passover*

The Christian confession of Jesus Christ as the fulfillment of the Old Testament prophecy effected almost immediately a different understanding of the place of the passover in the church from that of the synagogue. The change in approach reflected itself in a variety of fundamental issues of faith. What had been for Israel an unequivocal and straightforward memorial to the deliverance from Egypt became for the Christian church a mysterious and paradoxical sign within God's redemptive history of both the new and the old, of life and of death, of the future and the past. Both the New Testament and early church history testify to the struggle in coming to terms with a new understanding of the passover in the light of the gospel, which seemed both to confirm and to refute their Jewish heritage.

Judaism had developed a clear tradition on how the ancient passover rite was to be actualized for every new generation of Jews. Indeed the Old Testament itself offered an unequivocal warrant for involving Israel's sons in the great redemption out of Egypt. But for the church this direct, unbroken identification of deliverance was no longer possible. The weight of the tradition had been decisively shifted. What Israel thought was the substance of her freedom was only the foreshadowing of the hope. In the history of the early church one can see the growing sense of discontinuity with the traditional Jewish interpretation. Increasingly the sense of a reality hidden within the old form made direct participation in redemption through the passover impossible. Both in I Corinthians and I Peter one sees how sharing in the new life of Christ has taken the place of an unmediated access to freedom through the passover memorial. Now the Christian lives as a free man (I Peter 2.16) by sharing Christ's holiness, by love for the brethren, and by hope in the coming glory.

The effect of understanding the Old Testament passover traditions in the light of the New Testament is to affirm the hope of Israel in so far as it foreshadowed God's true redemption. But without the fullness of God's plan, the passover rite can lead to distortion. God's redemption is not simply a political liberation from an Egyptian tyrant, but involves the struggle with sin and evil, and the transformation of life. Similarly, the slaughtered lamb becomes a symbol of the cost to God of Israel's redemption, indeed, the redemption of the whole world. I Peter makes the move of bringing together the passover lamb with the suffering servant (2.22) which becomes a model for later Christian theology. The Christian testifies to his redemption by sharing in Christ's suffering for the sins of the world. The celebration of the eucharist likewise points to the dimension of new life as an identification with Christ's death and resurrection.

The Christian understanding of the passover has always been dialectical, but all too often the movement from the New Testament back to the Old Testament has been forgotten. The New Testament not only fulfills the Old, but equally important the Old Testament interprets the New. Certainly Melito of Sardis is guilty of this failure when he speaks of the passover once being of value, but 'today becoming worthless' (*Paschal Homily* 43). Rather, the New Testament provides adequate warrant for seeking to understand what the redemption in Jesus Christ is by means of the witness of the Old Testament passover. First, the ceremony of passover testifies to the redemptive nature of God's dealings with Israel. The New Testament's insistence that divine deliverance is a spiritual transformation does not abrogate the Old Testament witness that the physical is involved as well. In spite of its ambiguity, the political overtones of Israel's deliverance are part of the whole biblical message. Again, the passover ritual serves as a warning against overlooking the collective nature of God's intervention. He redeemed a people. Israel shared a meal in the night of deliverance as families, and went out of the land together. Individuals were destroyed, but a people was redeemed. Liberation was achieved when God overcame the powers of evil in a struggle and invited his people joyfully to share in the event. Finally, the eschatological dimension of redemption already found deeply embedded in the passover traditions of Judaism, must not be lost through an over-concentration on the death of Christ. The formal parallelism between the Jewish and Christian hope – both look to the past, both hope for the future – affirms the profound degree of solidarity which unites the two faiths together in a common testimony to God's final victory. Should there not then be a common sharing of God's joy which links the *seder* and the eucharist into common praise?

IX

THE DELIVERANCE AT THE SEA

13.17–14.31

G. J. BOTTERWECK, 'Israels Errettung im Wunder am Meer', *Bibel und Leben* 8, 1967, pp.8ff.; H. CAZELLES, 'Donneés géographiques sur l'Exode', *RHPR* 35, 1955, pp.51–60; 'Les Localisations de l'Exode et la critique littéraire', *RB* 62, 1955, pp.321–64; B. S. CHILDS, 'A Traditio-Historical Study of the Reed Sea Tradition', *VT* 20, 1970, pp.406–18; G. W. COATS, 'The Traditio-Historical Character of the Reed Sea Motif', *VT* 17, 1967, pp.253ff.; O. EISSFELDT, *Baal Zaphon, Zeus Kasios und der Durchzug der Israeliten durchs Meer*, Halle 1932; G. FOHRER, *Überlieferung und Geschichte*, Berlin 1964; L. S. HAY, 'What really happened at the Sea of Reeds', *JBL* 83, 1964, pp.297–403; S. HERRMANN, *Israels Aufenthalt in Ägypten*, Stuttgart 1970, pp.83ff., ET *Israel in Egypt*, SBT 2.27, 1973, pp.56ff.; J. P. HYATT, 'The Site and Manner of the Israelites' Crossing of the Sea', *Exodus*, 1971, pp.156ff.; A. LAUHA, 'Das Schilfmeermotif im Alten Testament', *Suppl. VT* 9, 1963, pp.32–46; S. E. LOEWENSTAMM, *The Tradition of the Exodus in its Development* (Hebrew), Jerusalem 1965; T. W. MANN, 'The Pillar of Cloud in the Reed Sea Narrative', *JBL* 90, 1971, pp.15–30; DENNIS J. McCARTHY, 'Plagues and Sea of Reeds: Exodus 5–14', *JBL* 85, 1966, pp.137ff.; E. MEYER, *Die Israeliten und ihre Nachbarstämme*, Halle 1906, reprinted Darmstadt 1967, pp.19ff.; M. NOTH, 'Der Schauplatz der Meereswunders', *Festschrift O. Eissfeldt*, Halle 1947, pp.181–90; W. J. PHYTHIAN ADAMS, *The Call of Israel*, London 1934, pp.137ff.; K. von RABENAU, 'Die beiden Erzählungen vom Schilfmeerwunder in Exod.13, 17–14, 31', *Theologische Versuche*, ed. P. Wätzel, Berlin 1966, pp.9–29; T. H. ROBINSON, 'Der Durchzug durch das Rote Meer', *ZAW* 51, 1933, pp.170–73; M. B. ROWTON, 'The Problem of the Exodus', *PEQ* 85, 1953, pp.46–60; E. A. SPEISER, 'An Angelic "Curse": Exodus 14:20', *JNES* 80, 1960, pp.198–200; J. R. TOWERS, 'The Red Sea', *JNES* 18, 1959, pp.150ff.

13 [17]When Pharaoh let the people go, God did not lead them by the way of the land of the Philistines, although it would have been nearer, for God thought: 'Lest the people change their minds when they experience war, and return to Egypt.' [18]Rather God led the people round about by way of the wilderness toward the Reed Sea. The Israelites went up armed out of Egypt. [19]Moses took the bones of Joseph with him who had made the Israelites take a solemn oath, saying: 'God will surely look out for you, and then you must take my bones up from here with you.' 20Setting out from Succoth they encamped at Etham on the edge of the desert. 21The LORD used to go in front of them, in a pillar of cloud by day to guide them along the way, and in a pillar of fire by night to give them light in order that they might travel by day and night. 22The pillar of cloud by day and the pillar of fire by night never moved from before the people.

14 1Then the LORD said to Moses, 2'Tell the Israelites to turn back and encamp before Pi-hahiroth, between Migdol and the sea, in front of Baal Zephon. You shall encamp facing it, by the sea. 3Pharaoh will say of the Israelites: "They are wandering aimlessly in the land; the wilderness has closed in on them." 4Then I will harden the heart of Pharaoh so that he will pursue them, and thus I will gain glory through Pharaoh and all his army, and the Egyptians shall know that I am the LORD.' And they did so.

5 When the news was brought to the king of Egypt that the people had fled, the mind of Pharaoh and his courtiers changed toward the people and they said, 'What is this that we have done in letting Israel go from serving us?' 6So he had his chariots made ready and took his army with him. 7He took six hundred picked chariots and the rest of the chariots of Egypt with officers in charge of them all. 8Then the LORD hardened the heart of Pharaoh, king of Egypt, and he pursued after the Israelites who were going forth defiantly. 9The Egyptians pursued them – all the horses and chariots of Pharaoh, his cavalry and infantry – and overtook them encamped by the sea, by Pi-hahiroth, in front of Baal Zephon.

10 Now as Pharaoh drew near, the Israelites suddenly caught sight of the Egyptians pursuing after them. Extremely terrified, the Israelites cried out to the LORD. 11They said to Moses, 'Was it because there were no graves in Egypt that you have taken us away to die in the desert? What have you done to us, taking us out of Egypt? 12Is not this what we told you in Egypt would happen, when we said, "Leave us alone and we will serve the Egyptians"? For it is better for us to serve the Egyptians than to die in the wilderness.' 13 But Moses said to the people, 'Do not be afraid; stand by and see the deliverance which the LORD will work for you today, for as you see the Egyptians today, you will never see them again. 14The LORD will fight for you. You only have to keep still!'

15 Then the LORD said to Moses, 'Why do you cry to me? Tell the Israelites to go forward, 16but you raise your rod and stretch out your hand over the sea and split it, so that the Israelites may go on dry ground into the sea. 17Then I will harden the heart of the Egyptians so that they go in after them, and thus I will gain glory over Pharaoh and all his army, his chariots and horsemen. 18And the Egyptians shall know

that I am the Lord when I have gained glory over Pharaoh, his chariots and his horsemen.'

19 The angel of God who was accustomed to go in front of the Israelite army, moved and went behind them. And the pillar of cloud shifted from in front of them and took its place behind them, 20and came between the army of Egypt and the army of Israel. And there was the cloud and the darkness and yet it gave light by night, and neither came near the other all night.

21 Then Moses stretched out his hand over the sea and the Lord drove back the sea with a strong east wind all night, and turned the sea into dry land. The waters were split, 22and the Israelites went into the sea on dry ground, the waters forming a wall for them on their right and on their left. 23The Egyptians pursued after them right into the sea, all of Pharaoh's horses, chariots, and horsemen. 24At the morning watch, the Lord looked down upon the Egyptian army in the pillar of fire and cloud, and threw the Egyptian army into panic. 25He clogged the wheels of their chariots so that they moved forward with difficulty. Then the Egyptians said, 'Let us flee from the Israelites for the Lord is fighting for them against Egypt.'

26 Then the Lord said to Moses, 'Stretch out your hand over the sea, that the waters may come back upon the Egyptians, upon their chariots and horsemen.' 27So Moses stretched out his hand over the sea, and as morning broke, the sea returned to its normal course, and as the Egyptians were fleeing before it, the Lord shook the Egyptians into the sea. 28The waters returned and covered the chariots and horsemen which belonged to the whole army of Pharaoh that had followed them into the sea, not one of them remaining. 29But the Israelites walked through the middle of the sea on dry ground, the waters forming for them a wall on their right and on their left.

30 Thus the Lord delivered Israel that day from the power of the Egyptians and Israel saw the Egyptians laying dead on the seashore. 31When Israel saw the great act which the Lord had performed against the Egyptians, the people feared the Lord and had faith in the Lord and his servant Moses.

1. *Textual and Philological Notes*

13. 17. The first *kî* introduces a concessive clause. The *Zürcher Bibel* seems to take it as an explicative clause, which is possible in some instances, König III §373a.

18. There is a syntactical ambiguity in respect to the relation of the 'wilderness way' to the 'sea'. Cf. Dillmann, *ad loc.* Meek (AmTr) joins them: 'in the direction of the desert and the Red Sea'. Kalisch insists on the construct state rather than the accusative of direction.

18b. Driver, *Hebrew Tenses*³, §161.2, understands the clause to be circumstantial.

$h^a mušīm$. The meaning of the term remains uncertain. The Targums (Onkelos and Jer.), followed by the Vulgate and Rashi, take it as 'armed with weapons', and find a warrant in Josh. 1.14. The LXX interprets it as 'the fifth generation'. Cf. the history of exegesis which is traced by Rosenmüller, Kalisch, and Dillmann.

14.3. $n^e\underline{b}u\underline{k}īm$. C. Rabin, *Scripta Hierosol.* 8, 1961, p.388, argues on the basis of an Arabic cognate that the verb means 'to be pressed'.

6. Cf. the parallels to *ye'sōr*: Gen.46.29; I Kings 18.44; II Kings 9.21. *'am* = 'fighting force' is an abbreviation for *'am haṣṣābā'* (Num.31.32) or *'am hammilḥāmāh* (Josh.8.1).

7. Meek's translation (AmTr) offers a more coherent meaning, but requires undue liberty with the text: 'six hundred chariots, picked from all the chariots of Egypt'.

10. The *hinnēh* clause expresses the suddenness and surprise of the discovery by the Israelites of the pursuit.

11. Meek's translation (AmTr) is striking: 'What a way to treat us', but it does obscure the parallel with 5b.

13. A controversial syntactical problem turns on whether the *'a^šer* should be understood as *ka'^ašer (quemadmodum vidistis)*. Against this interpretation are AmTr, RSV, NJPS; for the modal sense LXX, Kalisch, Dillmann, König, *Lehrgebäude* III, §388a.

17. *'ikkāḇ^edāh*. NJPS renders 'assert my authority over' which is an illuminating translation, although a bit free.

20. The textual problem of the second half of the verse is extremely difficult. The LXX has a strikingly different text: καὶ ἐγένετο σκότος καὶ γνόφος καὶ διῆλθεν ἡ νύξ = 'and there was darkness and blackness, and the night passed.' In general, three major approaches to the problem have been suggested: (i) One remains with the MT and tries to explain the text along the lines of the Targums: the same cloud produced darkness to the Egyptians and light for the Israelites. (ii) One tries to reconstruct a verbal form from the noun 'darkness' (so NAB), or makes some use of the LXX's ἦλθεν. Cf. Wellhausen, Gressmann, Noth. (iii) One seeks another root meaning of the verb *y'r* using the comparative philological method. Cf. Speiser, *JNES* 80, 1960, pp.198ff., which suggestion has been accepted by NJPS. But no wide consensus has emerged up to now.

21. Cf. the close parallel of expression in Ex. 10.13.

25. Most modern commentators prefer to read as the root *'sr* with several of the versions, rather than *swr* = 'to remove'.

28. For this use of the preposition *l^e*, cf. König III, §281a.

2. Literary and Traditio-Historical Problems

A. The Source-Critical Problem

The lack of unity in the account of the sea event has been recognized for well over a hundred years. The presence of clear duplicates, particularly in the manner of the crossing, offered the strongest evidence for a composite narrative. On the one hand, the crossing was made possible by Yahweh's driving the sea back by means of a strong east wind (v. 2). On the other hand, the crossing was effected by Moses splitting the waters, which formed a wall to the left and right of the fleeing Israelites. To this was added a whole series of other doublets which included the motivation for the detour (13.17–18a// 14.1–4), the pursuit (14.8a//9a), the overtaking (9a//10a), etc.

Quite early in the use of source criticism, these chapters were assigned to J and P with a few fragments designated to E. This initial source division has been accepted ever since by the majority of critical scholars (Dillmann, Bacon, Bäntsch, Gressmann, Driver, Noth). However, in spite of this apparent critical consensus there remain a number of unsolved questions which continue to call forth a strong minority report from other scholars. Wellhausen (*Die Composition des Hexateuchs*[3], p. 77) voiced reservation against the usual description of the Priestly material and pointed out a basic problem. What has usually been assigned to P deviates considerably from the Priestly style and vocabulary of the plague stories. Note, for example, that the form of the command in 14.15, 21, 26 has its closest parallel in 10.12, 13, 21, rather than in the P material of 8.1, 12. Again, the vocabulary of hardening uses a formula which, although close to P, reminds of E. The role of the 'rod' in relation to the 'hand' continues to cause difficulty in the division (Wellhausen, p. 77).

On the basis of these difficulties a group of influential scholars has proposed a different source division. Although the new division reflects a wide variation, there is nevertheless a broad similarity which binds the group together. Thus Smend, Eissfeldt, Fohrer dispense with P, by and large, and assign the material which had been previously his to either J[1], L, or N. There is also a general agreement on the scope of the J material.

In my judgment, this latter attempt has been more successful in criticizing the weaknesses of the older critical position in respect to the P source than it has been in establishing a substitute source theory. For example, Fohrer (p. 98) argues that P has no sea account, but ends the exodus at 12.40ff. But this is to confuse the traditions of the exodus from Egypt with the sea event and is not tenable (cf. below). The analyses of both Smend and Eissfeldt reflect an unusually high degree of subjectivity and disagree at several crucial points.

In spite of the difficulties of the older critical view which assigns a major role to P, this analysis appears to me still to have the most in its favor. The basic soundness of assigning the second source to P has been recently confirmed by the detailed study of von Rabenau (*op. cit.*). Noth has also accepted it. I am inclined to feel that the peculiarities of the P source in this section may well reflect his dependence on the E source which remains only in a few fragments.

I accept the following source analysis as a working hypothesis for the commentary:

J: 13.21–22; 14.5b, 6, 9aα, 10bα, 11–14, 19b, 21aβ, 24, 25b, 27aβb, 30, 31.
The argument for assigning 13.20 to P rather than J (Noth) seems to me fairly strong (cf. Bacon, p. 73; Bäntsch, p. 119). It is possible that 14.5a and b belong to J (so Bäntsch and Rabenau). The difference in Pharaoh's motivation has been over-emphasized, in my judgment. A phrase from J may be present in 14.7. The phrase 'they pursued after them' in v. 9aα has a clear duplicate in 8aβ (*contra* Bäntsch). Noth, following E. Meyer, falsely eliminates 11–12 from J. It is essential for the correct traditio-historical analysis that it be retained (cf. below). Von Rabenau's reasons for assigning vv. 13–14 to P are unconvincing. E is probably represented in v. 20, but the textual problem causes considerable uncertainty. The 'angel' and the 'cloud and pillar of fire' present a difficulty. Cf. vv. 19, 21, 22.

P: 13.20; 14.1–4, 8, 9aβb, 15–18, 21aαb, 22–23, 26, 27a, 28–29.
14.3 is certainly not typical of P and should perhaps be assigned to E (so Bäntsch). Nevertheless, P has probably incorporated the verse within his source. In spite of von Rabenau's argument (pp. 13ff.) for assigning the question in v. 15 to P, it does not fit well into P's account.

E: 13.17–19; 14.5a, 7, 19a, 25a.
I do not agree with Volz's attempt to eliminate the E source completely, but certainly little of it is left intact in this section.

There is some value in rehearsing the story according to each of the two main sources. However, the case will be made in the exegesis for the integrity of the composite account.

The J account
The Israelites depart from Egypt, led by the cloud and the pillar of fire by day and night. (It remains unclear whether they fled from the beginning or, having received permission for a desert festival, used this occasion to flee.) Pharaoh changes his mind about allowing the Israelites to depart. He gathers his army and pursues. As the Israelites

reach the sea, they suddenly see the Egyptians behind them. A fear breaks out among the people, and they turn in complaint to Moses who in confidence points them to the help which is to come from Yahweh. The cloud, instead of leading the way, moves behind the Israelites, and turning into darkness conceals the Israelites. (This interpretation is uncertain because of the state of the text.) The Egyptians are unable to approach closer because of the darkness. During the night a strong east wind lays the bed of the sea bare. (There is no account of the crossing in J, or of any movement for that matter by the Israelites.) Yahweh, in some way working through the cloud and pillar of fire, causes a panic in the Egyptian army. At the same time the water flows back into its old bed; the Egyptians, fleeing toward it, are met and overwhelmed. They are shaken off into the midst of the sea. The Israelites see the dead Egyptians and believe on Yahweh and Moses.

The P(E) account

When Pharaoh lets the Israelites depart, they do not take the main highway which leads along the coast, but they change their original direction. (The reason for the route differs in E and P.) Yahweh hardens Pharaoh's heart, and gathering his army, he pursues. He overtakes them as they are camped on the sea. (P has the exact geographical location.) The people see the approaching Egyptians and cry to God. He commands Moses to raise his staff over the water. (In E the angel of Yahweh moves from behind the Israelites to a position before the Egyptians to prevent them from approaching.) Moses executes the command, and the waters divide. There is a path through the sea with the waters standing as a wall on both sides. The Israelites go through followed by the Egyptians. (E speaks of the angel of Yahweh hindering the movement of the chariot wheels to slow up the Egyptians.) When the Israelites have crossed, Moses stretches out his hand, and the waters return, covering completely the horses and riders of the Egyptians. The Israelites proceed in safety.

B. *The Traditio-Historical Problem of the Deliverance at the Sea*

M. Noth's study of the pentateuchal traditions launched the modern discussion of the problem. He identified the heart of the exodus tradition with the crossing of the sea: 'It is the very act which was first and chiefly meant when Israel confessed Yahweh as "the

God who led us up out of Egypt"' (*Exodus*, p. 104). Moreover, Noth suggested that the tradition of the sea event was connected neither with the passover tradition nor with the plague tradition which he regarded as a secondary expansion of the passover. As a result the juxtaposition of the two traditions which recounted Israel's salvation, namely, the exodus tradition and the Reed Sea, remained unexplained for Noth. The sea event appeared unexpectedly in the narrative almost as a postlude.

Since Noth's monograph in 1948 there has appeared a steady stream of articles which have attempted to correct or to go beyond Noth. Of these the incisive article of G. W. Coats (*VT* 17, 1967, pp. 253ff.) is certainly one of the most important in respect to the history of traditions problems. Coats argued that the formula 'Yahweh brought us out of Egypt' does not refer to the sea event. Rather, the formula has reference consistently to the coming out of Egypt which preceded the sea event, and was caused by the death of the first-born. Coats then argued that the sea event does not belong to the exodus tradition (used in the narrow sense), but to the wilderness wanderings tradition. His major support for this thesis lay in the use of the *hôšî'* formula, the appearance of the murmuring tradition at the sea (J), and the sea-river pattern within the wilderness-conquest tradition.

Although Coats has made a major step forward, several important problems remain which have not been adequately explained by his thesis. Above all, Coats has not recognized that the Old Testament is inconsistent in its assigning the sea event to the wilderness tradition. Moreover, the lack of consistency reflects not some accidental confusion, but rather a complex development of tradition. For example, even within the various literary sources of the Pentateuch, the place of the sea event within the narrative framework is strikingly different. In JE the sea event is part of the wilderness tradition, but in P it rather functions as an integral part of the exodus traditions. In addition, the shift of imagery used to depict the event emerges as a major issue. For these reasons, the traditio-historical problem of the sea tradition needs to be re-examined.

In the J account the rescue at the sea follows the exodus from Egypt and the sea event clearly belongs to the wilderness tradition. But the history of traditions problem is sharply posed when one moves from the early stage to the later. There are several major changes which have taken place which seem to indicate that P views the event at the sea in connection with the exodus from Egypt. First, as Coats has correctly argued, P follows the JE tradition in having Israel's departure clearly precede the sea event. Ex. 12.41 is unequivocal. Nevertheless, this inherited chronology has been modified in a number of ways. If in 12.50 the people left Egypt, in 14.1 they are commanded to 'turn back'. Only when Israel crosses the sea does she enter into the wilderness. The wilderness wanderings do not begin until after the sea.

Secondly, the close connection between the crossing and the plagues confirms the point that the sea event is considered part of the exodus tradition. Whereas, in the JE accounts, the imagery associated with the plagues is entirely missing in the sea account, the reverse is true for P. The plague imagery clearly returns (14.4, 7, 18, 21). The sea event in the P source is no longer understood as part of the wilderness wanderings but brings to completion the plan of God which had begun with the plagues. The issue at stake is to explain the forces which influenced P in not following J's assigning of the crossing to the wilderness period.

First of all, the influence of the mythological language from the sea battle affected the transmission of the tradition of the Reed Sea. Particularly in the poetic passages the language of creation as a victory over the sea monster soon fused with the language of redemption at the sea. By the time of the Priestly writer the language of splitting the sea, of drying up the waters which were part of the myth, had become stereotyped vocabulary for describing the Reed Sea event.

Again, it seems highly probable that the language of the Reed Sea was influenced by the Jordan tradition of the river's crossing which introduced the language of a path through the sea and the river's stoppage. Thus the exodus as the 'going out of Egypt' and the conquest as the 'coming into the land' were joined in a cultic celebration of Israel's deliverance and transmitted together. This complex of tradition exerted a definite force toward pulling the Reed Sea event away from its original prose setting in the wilderness tradition and attracting it within the cycle of the exodus.

Finally, the new role which the passover assumed within Israel's cult in the post-exilic period affected strongly the shape of the sea tradition (cf. ch. 12). The passover became the major cultic vehicle for commemorating the deliverance which had begun with the plagues. The sea event therefore became the heart of the exodus story which was annually rehearsed in the passover ritual. By the end of the Old Testament period the Reed Sea event had been thoroughly identified with the departure from Egypt rather than marking the beginning of the wilderness wanderings.

3. *Old Testament Context*

The practice has usually been followed among critical scholars of dividing the chapter into various sources. Much attention has then been given in characterizing the differences between the sources. Although this method is useful in bringing the variety of the biblical witnesses sharply into focus by reconstructing the early levels and literary transmission, it remains unsatisfactory to the extent to which no attempt is made to deal with the passage within the context of the final form of the text. The final literary production has an integrity of its own which must not only be recognized, but studied with the same intensity as one devotes to the earlier stages. With this end in mind, we now turn to the text in order to understand the crossing when viewed from the combined witness of the final narrative.

The unit begins in 13.17 with an explanation of God's reasons for guiding the released people in an unexpected direction. He did not lead them along the obvious route which proceeded directly to the land of the Philistines, but he caused them to take the round about way. This initial theme of God's plan is narrated by the author who supplies God's reason for the decision as well. Since this reason is not directed to anyone specific, it belongs most naturally to a part of the divine self-revelation. The same theme of Yahweh's plan is further attested by the writer's recalling Joseph's predication of God's visitation. Verse 20 describes the route taken, while v. 21 in a circumstantial clause relates the manner of God's leading both day and night by means of the pillar of cloud and fire.

In spite of the fact that the verses which follow in 14.1ff. originally stemmed from a different literary source, in the present narrative the verses continue the initial theme of God's plan. 13.17 had introduced the theme of God's plan from the divine perspective. 'God did not allow . . . he thought . . . God led them round about . . . he went before them.' In 14.1ff. the human actors are brought into the plan by means of instructions issued to Moses for the people. 'Yahweh said to Moses, "Speak to the people . . ."'. The order to change route (14.2) now serves as the execution of the plan which had already been introduced in its broad lines in vv. 17–18.

Yahweh's plan is now announced to Moses. It is a plan which is set in direct confrontation with the intention of Pharaoh. Verse 3 relates that the change in route is to produce an effect on Pharaoh. He will think that the Israelites are hopelessly lost in the wilderness. Then Yahweh's plan for Pharaoh is revealed: 'I will harden his heart; Pharaoh will pursue; I will be glorified and the Egyptians will recognize that I am Yahweh.'

Next the writer turns to Pharaoh. His role as the major protagonist had been briefly introduced in 13.17. He had allowed them to leave. Pharaoh's change of mind is motivated by word that the Israelites had fled. The biblical writer makes no effort to relate this information more closely to his initial permission in 13.17, but he turns his attention to describing the formation and execution of Pharaoh's plan regarding Israel. Pharaoh regrets his former decision and prepares to follow with chariots and riders, the choicest of the Egyptian army. But Pharaoh's plan to pursue is also part of Yahweh's plan for him which he had previously announced. The contrast in perspective is further highlighted in the conflicting description of Israel. Pharaoh thinks that they are lost and imprisoned in the desert (v.3), but actually they are going forward 'equipped for battle' (13.18) and defiantly (14.8). The first section closes in 14.8 with the two conflicting plans—Yahweh's and Pharaoh's—fully under way. The stage is set for the struggle for supremacy with Israel sharing in the drama.

The second section begins in v.9. The verse serves both to recapitulate the events of the previous section and to describe the new crisis. The Egyptians pursued (v.8), with horses and riders (vv.6, 7); the Israelites were encamped at the sea (v.2) by Pi-hahiroth, in front, of Baal Zephon. The new element is introduced in the word 'they overtook them'. But in order to describe how this overtaking took place, the author shifts his perspective back to the Israelites. 'Pharaoh drew near' – for the biblical writer he is the opponent *par excellence* – and suddenly Israel saw the Egyptians. To their horror (*wehinnē*) all of Egypt was coming after them. In their terror they cried to Yahweh.

There now follow two speeches. The people address Moses (vv.11–12) and Moses responds to the people (vv.13–14). The people are in despair and complain to Moses. They recognize only Pharaoh's plan as having substance and, despairing of finding any other alternative, they attack their leader. The parallel in vocabulary between Israel's reaction and the Egyptians when hearing of Israel's escape is striking: 'What is this we have done that we have let Israel go from serving us?' // 'What is this you have done to us . . . in bringing us out of Egypt? . . . better to serve them.' The two reactions are parallel because neither reckoned with God's plan.

Moses replies by challenging Israel to respond to God's plan. His speech is directed to their initial reaction and not to their verbal articulation. 'Do not fear' – they had feared (v. 10). 'Stand and see the salvation of Yahweh today' – they had seen only the Egyptians approaching. Then this theme is repeated and expanded. 'As you see the Egyptians today (or the Egyptians which you see today) you shall not see them ever again ever' (cf. alliteration 'ôḏ 'aḏ 'ôlām). The people had cried to Yahweh; they are to be quiet. The battle – it is not just a flight as the Egyptians thought – will be fought by Yahweh for them.

The final section of the chapter begins in v. 15. The instruction formula repeats the form of address just used by Yahweh to Moses in v. 1: 'Yahweh said to Moses . . . "Say to the Israelites . . ."' But into the traditional formula has been spliced an interrogation. 'Why do you cry to me?' Within the present narrative only the people have cried to Yahweh (v. 10), and Moses' only response was of confidence in God's salvation. But God's plan is still unknown to him except in its broadest outlines. He only knows God's intention which issued in Egypt's pursuit. Had Moses prayed to God privately for instruction? (Traditional midrash moves in this direction.) However one wishes to understand this phrase within the present narrative, Yahweh quickly instructs Moses. First, a command is directed to the people 'to go forward' ('stand' is understood psychologically in v. 13). Then Moses receives his personal orders. He is to raise his hand and split the sea to form a path of escape for the people. Then the plan of God is repeated in respect to the Egyptians in the vocabulary of the initial revelation to Moses. 'I will harden . . . they will pursue. I will be glorified over Pharaoh . . . and they will recognize that I am Yahweh.'

Up to this point in the chapter the major movement of the story has arisen in the contrast between the two plans, Yahweh's and Pharaoh's. Now the writer ceases from portraying Pharaoh's plan as arising from independent action, but absorbs him completely within the divine plan of Yahweh. Moreover, the writer's attention now turns to portraying the two different levels in the execution of the divine plan. On the one hand, Yahweh's plan is announced to Moses and executed by him according to the announcement-fulfillment pattern in this section of the chapter. On the other hand, Yahweh acts directly against the Egyptians in a way not related to Moses' mediation. The biblical writer achieves this effect by skillfully splicing parts of the earlier sources into the Priestly narrative.

Thus the messenger of Yahweh and the cloud 'go forward' to stand between the advancing Egyptians and the Israelites. In v. 21 Moses executes the command to raise his arm and split the sea, but in between the raising and the splitting the writer again introduces Yahweh's direct action. He has caused a strong east wind to blow all night which dried up the sea. The Egyptians pursue the Israelites into the midst of the sea, while Yahweh impedes their chariots, and terrifies them into panic by means of the fiery pillar. Now the Egyptian reaction of fear is recorded, reversing the previous description of Israel's. The very promise of Moses in v. 14 is attested as true through the mouth of the Egyptians. They say: 'Yahweh' – they now even know his name – 'fights for them.' In v. 26 Yahweh instructs Moses to stretch out his hand again causing the waters to return to their normal channels and so drown the Egyptians. However, once more Yahweh's direct intervention against the Egyptians is recorded. They try to flee from the encroaching flood, but Yahweh shakes them into the sea. Verse 29 concludes the final section. In the repetition of the description of Israel's crossing – they went on dry land, in the midst of the sea, between the walls of water – the miraculous delivery is contrasted with the destruction of the Egyptians, not one of whom was left alive.

Verse 30 functions as an epilogue to the story. It summarizes the event, picking up the promise of v. 13: 'Thus Yahweh on that day rescued Israel from Egypt.' But, more than that, the effect on Israel is portrayed. Israel recognized it as God's act. This transformation appears in the new use made of an earlier theme. Now Israel fears Yahweh (contrast v. 10). They trust Moses, Yahweh's servant whom they had previously maligned.

What has been achieved by rehearsing the story according to the present form of the biblical text? First, it should now be evident that the final form of the story has an integrity of its own. It is not simply pieces of fragments put together, but it forms a meaningful composition which is different from the sum of its parts. Secondly, the present story offers its own testimony as to what transpired at the sea which is dependent on a reading of the story from the context of the whole chapter. Through failure to reckon with the final form, and dealing with the chapter only in its reconstructed forms, this major theological witness is lost.

It is of great importance to see how the actual crossing was viewed by the final author. For the modern critical reader the hermeneutical problem is posed by the earlier J account which stresses the effect of 'natural causes' (strong east wind, dry sea bed, panic among Egyptians), and the later P account which is 'supernaturally' oriented (splitting of the sea, wall of water, etc.). On the basis of this critical evidence the usual hermeneutical move is to suggest that the original crossing was viewed as resulting from a series of natural events, and that the later writer sought to articulate the theological *meaning* of this event by extending the imagery into the supernatural. This allowed the modern biblical theologian to speak of the great act of God at the exodus in delivering his people while at the same time to regard the event historically as little more than the accidental escape of some slaves across a treacherous marsh.

If attention is paid to the final witness of this passage, little warrant can be deduced in support of this sort of theological move. The biblical writer is aware both of the variety within the tradition and of the two levels of divine activity which combined ordinary and wonderful elements. The writer first brackets the entire episode within the framework of a divine plan which is in mortal conflict with another plan. Then the writer assigns to Moses as the human agent the execution of the wonderful elements. He is the catalyst for splitting the sea and causing it to return. At the same time the direct intervention of God is pictured in terms of 'natural' causes such as the blowing of the east wind, the impeding of chariot wheels, and the panicking of the Egyptian army.

The implication of this final redaction is to suggest that the alignment of the two levels of divine activity into a pattern of historical development runs counter to the intention of the final author. Likewise, the assigning of historical validity to the natural events and theological meaning to the supernatural is also a move which is entirely incompatible with the inner dynamic of the biblical witness.

To put the issue in another way, the canonical ordering of the various traditions functions as a critical norm. It prevents a false reading of the separate strands of the tradition. By joining together the parts in a particular way, the redactor succeeded in creating a story which was different from its separate parts. However, the parts in themselves did not present a story which was different in kind from the combined one. Indeed both sources (J and P) witnessed to Israel's redemption through the hand of God. Yet the historical critical method has demonstrated that the parts could be placed in a larger framework, namely that of historical development, which could read the parts as stories different in kind. The early level was natural; the latter was supernatural. The canonical redaction operates as a critical judgment against such a move and bears witness to how the separate parts which comprise the full tradition are to be understood.

Detailed Notes

13.17. On the difficult problem of the route out of Egypt, there is a large accumulation of secondary literature. Cf. the literature cited by G. E. Wright, *IDB* I, p.199 and by Y. Aharoni, *The Land of the Bible*, Philadelphia 1967, pp.178ff. O. Eissfeldt opened up a new phase of the discussion with his monograph of 1932 (*Baal Zaphon, op. cit.*). The most thorough general summary of the geographical evidence remains Cazelles' article ('Les Localisations . . .', *op. cit.*). Most recently M. Haran (*Tarbiz* 40, 1970–1, pp.113–43) has attempted to sketch three different routes which he finds portrayed by the different sources, E-Deut., J, and P. Haran's somewhat idiosyncratic handling of the source divisions has reduced the value of his very detailed analysis of the geographic traditions.

'the way of the land of the Philistines'. Cf. the classic essay of A. H. Gardiner, 'The ancient military road between Syria and Palestine', *Journal of Egyptian Archaeology* 6, 1920, pp.99–116.

18. 'sea of Reeds'. Cf. N. H. Snaith, *VT* 15, 1965, pp.395–8.

20. 'Succoth' is probably Tell el- Mashkutah; cf. Ex.1.11; 12.37. 'Etham.' The site is unknown, lying somewhere on the eastern frontier of Egypt.

21. On the 'pillar of cloud', cf. T. Mann's attempt to explain the imagery from Ugaritic parallels (*JBL* 90, 1971, pp.15ff.).

14.2. 'Pi-hahiroth'. A town situated in the East Delta which cannot be precisely located. Cf. W. F. Albright, *BASOR* 109, 1948, p.16, and the excellent discussion of the philological problems in *IDB* III, pp.810f.

'Migdol'. A word meaning tower in Hebrew. Its location is also uncertain, although it has often been placed at Tell-el-Heir between Qantara and Pelusium (cf. Aharoni, *op. cit.*, p.179). Cf. T. Lambdin, *IDB* III, p.377.

'Baal Zephon'. In a monograph published in 1932 Eissfeldt used the recently discovered Ugaritic material in an attempt to locate Baal Zephon. He argued that Mount ṣpn was identical with the peak in Syria known as *jebel 'el- 'akra'*, and in classical times as Mons Casius. Classical sources speak of a cult of Zeus Casius on this mountain and also of a cult of the same god on another Casius in Egypt. Postulating a continuity between the cults of Baal Zephon and Zeus Casius in Syria, Eissfeldt suggested that the biblical Baal Zephon in

Egypt must be the predecessor of Zeus Casius. Since its location was known to be near Lake Sirbonis, Eissfeldt felt that he could now locate the crossing in this region. Eissfeldt's argument has received wide acceptance (cf. Noth). However, in 1950 Albright published an article in which he disagreed with Eissfeldt's suggested location on the basis of Egyptian and Ugaritic texts ('Baal Zephon', *Festschrift Bertholet*, Tübingen 1950, pp. 1ff.). But Albright's evidence is not conclusive. Cf. especially the strictures of M. Pope in his handling of the key Ugaritic text (*JBL* 85, 1966, pp.455ff.).

11. Cf. G. W. Coats, *Rebellion in the Wilderness*, Nashville 1968, for a treatment of the murmuring motif.

31. 'believe in Moses'. Cf. note on 4.1.

4. *New Testament Context*

Cf. the bibliography cited by G. Te Stroete, *Exodus*, 1966, p.20. Add J. Plastaras, *The God of Exodus*, 1966, pp.313ff.; J. G. GAGER, *Moses in Greco-Roman Paganism*, New York 1972.

A. *Hellenistic Interpretation*

Because the New Testament interpretations of the exodus from Egypt reflect the milieu of its period, we shall begin by outlining the shape which the Old Testament tradition had acquired in the Hellenistic period.

1. Josephus' account of the exodus from Egypt (*Antiq*. II. 318ff.) is a highly significant handling of the biblical tradition. The actual crossing is reduced sharply. The miracle is effected by Moses striking the sea with his staff without mention of the east wind. Josephus does not attempt to rationalize it. However, the major impression of his account is certainly the strong rationalistic overtones of the larger account. Moses chose his route by means of a clever calculation. He encourages his disheartened followers in an exhortation which is strongly reminiscent of the speeches of Thucydides. But the most important element is the personal commentary of Josephus with which he concludes his account. He draws attention to a parallel event in the history of Alexander the Great who was also offered a passage through the sea. Josephus allows that it could have been 'by the will of God or maybe by accident'.

A more explicit example of the rationalistic tendency of the Hellenistic historian is the account of Artapanus (80–40 BC) which is preserved by Eusebius (*Praep. Evang.* IX.4). He attributes the crossing completely to natural causes. Moses, knowing the country and osberving the tide, took advantage of the low water and led the Israelites through it at low tide.

2. A very different handling of the tradition is found in Philo and the Wisdom of Solomon. Philo is, of course, fully acquainted with the biblical tradition and in his *Vita Mosis* (I.176ff.) recounts it in a rather traditional fashion. However, the more typical allegorical approach appears in other references to the crossing. In his *Legum Alleg.* II. 102 he interprets Ex. 15.1: 'He cast horse and rider into the sea' to mean 'God cast to utter ruin and the bottomless abyss the four passions and the wretched mind mounted on them. This is indeed practically the chief point of the whole Song.'

In the Wisdom of Solomon 10.15ff. the deliverance from Egypt is attributed to wisdom who delivered 'a holy people and blameless race . . . she gave to holy men the reward of their labors, she guided them along a marvellous way.' The repeated emphasis on the reward of the virtuous and the destruction of the evil is maintained throughout.

3. Finally, one can speak of the development of the midrashic traditions, although both Josephus and Philo share common elements of midrashic influence. The midrashic method was especially developed and preserved in the circles of rabbinic Judaism. Already the Targum of Onkelos had offered an interpretative translation which smoothed over certain of the difficulties in the MT. So in place of the puzzling 'Why do you cry to me?' (14.15), the Targum reads 'I have heard your prayer.' Again, the apparent textual difficulty in 14.20 has been nicely ironed out in the paraphrase.

Although the Jerusalem Targum now reflects a later form of the midrashic tradition which is subsequent even to the Tanaanite traditions of the *Mekilta*, nevertheless, there are some traditions preserved which give the impression of being ancient. Still the issue of dating is difficult to control. Interestingly both Targum Neofiti and the Jerusalem Targum share the interpretation that Israel left 'armed in good works'; Pihahirot is to play on the word licentious; Israel camps before the idol Zephon; there are four groups of Israelites at the sea; God assures Moses that Israel's prayers have anticipated his own intercession.

Even though the midrashic traditions of the *Mekilta* often reflect a development much later than that of the New Testament, some of its major features are significant in providing characteristic midrashic moves which maintain a remarkable consistency from the pre-Tannaite period to the Talmud. First of all, the *Mekilta* finds a warrant in 13.21, 'Yahweh went before them by day', for elaborating on the special protection of Israel. Some say there were seven clouds, others thirteen, which shielded Israel on every side. God himself went before his people to demonstrate to the nations 'how dear his sons were to him'. Indeed God chides Moses for crying to him. 'Is it not on behalf of my son? I am already reconciled to my sons' (*Beshallah*, ed J. Z. Lauterbach, II, Philadelphia 1949, p. 219). 'Will I not for this assembly of holy men turn the sea into dry land?' (p. 218).

A second major theme of the midrash is the emphasis that God redeems Israel because of his promise to the Fathers. The 'measure for measure' motif is worked out to parallel Abraham's acts of piety with God's corresponding deeds to Israel. The summary statement reiterates the doctrine succinctly: 'What was the cause of our attaining this joy? It was but a reward for the faith with which our fathers . . . believed' (p. 254).

Finally, there is the recurring theme that Israel came forth from Egypt in freedom. Moses commanded the people to turn back lest Pharaoh think that Israel fled. Moses said: 'It has been told to me by the word of God that you are free men' (p. 190). The theme of freedom is made explicit also in the Jer. Targum (14.18), and becomes the dominant theme in the haggadah. 'This year Jews are enslaved, may next year set them free.' Again, Israel prays to be led 'with head erect into the land'. The exodus was above all the formation of a nation of freed men who had been set free from oppression.

The Samaritan *Memar Marqah* shares a good number of midrashic features of the rabbinic tradition. So, for example, Pharaoh is pictured as worshipping Baal Zephon. However, the dominant Samaritan emphasis on Moses as Saviour is distinct from the rabbinic teaching.

B. *New Testament Interpretation*

The New Testament appropriation of the exodus traditions emerges out of this Hellenistic milieu, but in a form in which both shared these common features and which transformed them into something quite different.

At the outset, there are several references to the redemption from Egypt in the New Testament which use the Old Testament traditions in a sense of unbroken solidarity with Judaism. According to Acts 13.16ff. Paul speaks of 'our fathers' who were led out of Egypt. Again in Luke 1.67 Zachariah's praise to God for his deliverance consists of a catena of Old Testament passages which includes Pss. 18 and 106.

However, it is a striking fact how seldom in the New Testament this unbroken identification with the exodus from Egypt occurs. Occasionally commentators have sought to find an important reference to the exodus in Luke 9.31 (cf. F. F. Bruce, *This is That. The New Testament Development of some Old Testament Themes*, Exeter 1968, p. 32). However, the Greek ἔξοδος is obviously a reference to Jesus' departure in death and has no relation to the exodus tradition. The connection is only possible by means of an illegitimate semantic transfer.

Rather, it is characteristic of the New Testament to place the redemption of Egypt into a new context which radically alters its meaning and function for early Christianity. Matt. 2.15 makes reference to the exodus tradition of Hos. 11.1, 'Out of Egypt have I called my son'. But he cites the exodus as having been 'fulfilled' in the life of Jesus. Jesus not only participates in the history of the nation, but, as the true redeemer of Israel, he ushers in the messianic age which the original exodus from Egypt only foreshadowed.

Moreover, it is characteristic of the New Testament to shift the emphasis away from the first exodus to the 'second'. This is to say, the Old Testament exodus tradition has been heard primarily through its eschatological appropriation in Ezekiel and II Isaiah. The hymn of Zechariah speaks of the anticipated redemption with reference to Isa. 60.1, 2 and 59.8. Likewise, John the Baptist's role as herald of the coming salvation is portrayed completely in the eschatological language of II Isaiah (Luke 3.4ff.).

There is another characteristic usage of the exodus traditions which is strikingly different from the midrashic emphasis in the freedom won from Egyptian oppression. Paul's speech in Acts 13 begins with reference to the exodus from Egypt, but then concludes that Israel did not really achieve freedom. Only in Christ is there 'freedom from everything from which you could not be freed by the law of Moses' (v. 39). Likewise in I Cor. 10.1ff., which is the most extended reference to the Old Testament tradition, the exodus is given an initially positive interpretation. Paul employs an allegorical method akin to Philo in speaking of the Old Testament's 'means of grace'. 'Our fathers were all under the cloud, and all passed through the sea, and all were baptized into Moses in the cloud and in the sea . . .' The reference to the supernatural Rock which followed them reflects quite clearly a midrashic tradition (cf. Billerbeck, *Kommentar zum NT* III, München 1926, pp. 406ff.; J. Weiss, *Der erste Korintherbrief*, KEKNT 5⁹, 1910, p. 251). Yet the major point in Paul's argument was the failure of all of Israel to partake in the divine acts of mercy. 'With most of them God was not pleased.' Israel's failure to achieve salvation was given as a warning to Christians to take heed lest they also perish. In a similar way, Heb. 8 finds a warrant in Jer. 31.31ff. for emphasizing the inadequacy of the first exodus in achieving the intended goal. Because the first covenant proved obsolete, a new and better covenant was initiated.

Finally, there is a reference in Rev. 15.3 to the Christian saints singing the song of Moses and the song of the Lamb. The passage interrupts the announcement and execution of God's last judgment upon the earth before the end. The writer sees the saints, in anticipation of the victory, praising God for his acts of righteous judgment. There are certain parallel features between Ex. 15 and the hymn which follows. The crystal sea parallels the Red Sea, the elders with harps the victorious Israelites, the conquered beast the defeated Egyptian army. The hymn is made up of phrases from the Old Testament, frequently found in the Psalter. However, the striking similarity between the content of the hymn as praise to the just judgments of God parallels Moses' song in Deut. 32 far more closely than Ex. 15, and would therefore not be a direct application of the exodus tradition.

5. History of Exegesis

The Church Fathers took their lead in interpreting the exodus from Egypt from the New Testament, particularly from I Cor. 10, and extended the allegory to cover all the details of the tradition. Daniélou (*From Shadows to Reality*, ET London 1960, Westminster, Md. 1961, p. 171) speaks of a 'unanimous tradition which sees here a type of baptism'. Water became a type of judgment from which baptism provided an escape (Origen, Tertullian, Ambrose, cited by Daniélou). Even though Gregory of Nyssa recounts at some length the historical tradition of the crossing (*Vita Moysis*, MPG 44.309Df.) his major concern was to penetrate the symbolism of the language. The defeat of the enemy is a picture of the need to drown in the waters of baptism all of the sins of greed, pride, and anger which besiege the soul of the Christian. The exodus is a passing from earthly to heavenly things very much after the lines set by Philo. Again, it is of interest to see that Chrysostom follows another lead within the New Testament in contrasting the freedom from Egypt with the 'higher 'freedom' which is freedom from sin (cited by Daniélou, p. 192).

The Middle Ages called forth from Christian interpreters very little new over and above the major lines which had been set by the Church Fathers. Bede's *In Pentateuchum Commentarii* continues the allegorical tradition without much imagination or penetration. It had become an automatic reflex that 'Rubrum mare significat baptismum' (MPL 91. 310). Bernard shows considerably more flair in *Sermon 39 on Canticles* when he depicts the crossing at the sea as a type of battle with Satan and the desires of the flesh. Of course, throughout the Middle Ages, as was the case among the Fathers, the crossing of the sea and the destruction of the Egyptians served to illustrate a whole variety of other Christian doctrines (cf. Aquinas, *Summa* 2a2ae, qu. 108, 'De Vindicatione', Blackfriars ed. vol. 41, 1972, pp. 114ff.).

A much higher level of detailed exegesis was developed by the Jewish medieval commentators. Many of the directions of the early midrashim were continued and developed. Saadia describes Israel's going out 'openly' and not as thieves. Rashi sees a word play in Pihahiroth and reads $b^e n\hat{e}$ $h\hat{o}r\hat{\imath}n$ 'free men' (similarly Nachmanides). Whereas Christian commentators were generally critical of Israel's behaviour and stressed the elements of unbelief in 14.11f., Jewish commentators played down the disbelief. Usually only a small portion of the people (one of the four groups) is represented as voicing opposition. Rather, the emphasis is on the special handling and concern of God for his people 'taking them up in his arms'.

The most obvious characteristic of the Jewish commentators is the detailed exegetical concern with working out the tensions and difficulties within the text. Very early it was noted that in 13.20 Israel was encamped at Etham, yet according to Num. 33.8 they entered into the wilderness of Etham after the crossing. Ibn Ezra (with others) argued that Israel did not therefore cross the sea, but only went some way into it, and making a semi-circle, came out on the same side from which they had entered. (This theory was later accepted by many Christian interpreters of the sixteenth and seventeenth centuries. Cf. Poole, *Synopsis Criticorum*.) Although Jewish commentators were opposed to a rationalistic explanation of the crossing, Rashbam does observe that 'God acted in the usual way (*kdrk 'rṣ*) for the winds dry up and coagulate the rivers'. Many of the broader theological questions were also raised. Ibn Ezra and Abarbanel seek to explain why 600,000 Israelites should have been terrified by such a relatively small Egyptian force.

Luther and Calvin represent a decided break with the medieval exegetical tradition in respect to their interpretation of the exodus. Luther sees in the rescue at the sea an example of how Christian faith functions. God tests his people by putting them under pressure. Human reason can see no way of escape, but faith in God accomplishes the impossible (Sermon on Ex. 14.9–12; WA XVI, pp. 181ff.). Luther uses the passage then to elucidate the various aspects of faith. He notices the role of Moses' rod which in terms of reason is clearly superfluous because God himself effects the miracle. Luther then argues that this is characteristic of God's dealing with his people. He uses men in the proclamation of the gospel and through his word creates room. Luther has an explicit attack on the allegorical method at the conclusion of his sermon to emphasize that Paul's interpretation is not using the Scriptures figuratively, but homiletically as an example which rests on the real event of Scripture.

Calvin finds in the exodus an illustration of God's majestic power and gracious dealing with his people. He closes up all the ordinary ways of escape to demonstrate his power. He alone is the author of the miracle. Israel's disobedience only showed how necessary were God's repeated acts of intervention to bring us to salvation. Calvin speaks of the 'sacramental mode of speaking' in which God condescends to transfer his name to visible figures.

The seventeenth century saw the entrance of several new factors into the interpretation of the crossing. J. Clericus' famous essay appended to his Exodus commentary, 'Dissertatio de Maris Idumaei Trajectione' (1693), sought to demonstrate that the crossing could be explained by the movement of tides due to wind action. Although the theory had been suggested much earlier (Eusebius, *Praep. Ev.* IX.27), Clericus' essay was distinctive in terms of its unusual thoroughness and impressive erudition. Although Clericus maintained that his interpretation did not distract from the miraculous element, the tide theory was vigorously attacked by Calmet among the Catholics, and by Poole, Gill, Clarke among the Protestants. (Cf. also Kalisch's detailed rebuttal.)

Another factor which entered into the debate was the new interest during the eighteenth century in the geography of the Middle East which had been revived by fresh exploration on the part of travellers. Strabo and Diodorus Siculus had previously been the major ancient sources of geographical knowledge. But the new explorations of Thomas Shaw (1722), C. Niebuhr (1762ff.) and

G. H. von Schubert (1838) which climaxed in the reports of Edward Robinson (*Biblical Researches in Palestine*, 1841ff.) produced a whole new series of explanations of the crossing by the Hebrews. Robinson calculated that a path a half a mile in breadth would be needed in the sea for a column of one thousand abreast and two thousand in depth to have crossed in less than two hours.

The discovery of different sources within the account of Ex. 13–14 finally produced a new approach to the material which moved the discussion away from the impasse at which it had arrived by the end of the eighteenth century. Attention had first focused on Genesis, but by the early nineteenth century some of the implications for Exodus were being drawn. Ewald in his *Geschichte des Volkes Israel* (II², 1853, pp. 93ff.) distinguished between four different writers and compared and contrasted the different concepts of the event. In 1857 Knobel's learned commentary on Exodus appeared in the famous *Kurzgefasstes exegetisches Handbuch*, and offered a detailed source analysis. However, the sharp contours of the two different sources were still considerably blurred. Knobel reckoned 14.1–4, 8–9, 15–18, 21–23, 26–29 to the Elohist, which he thought was the earliest source, and noted signs of supernatural expansion in J, vv. 20, 24–25. However, by the time of Nöldeke the division between J and P had emerged which was to become generally accepted up to the present.

In recent years the focus of research on the crossing has fallen on analyzing the history of the tradition behind the various sources. The names of Gressmann, Pedersen, and Noth have been leaders in seeking a new way into the material. A recognition of the important role of the cult in shaping the tradition has been repeatedly emphasized, but the problem of relating the different levels of tradition to the event itself has produced very little agreement.

6. *Theological Reflection on the Exodus from Egypt*

1. God's miraculous rescue of Israel at the sea was remembered as the event by which God brought into being his people. Israel left Egypt as fleeing slaves, and emerged from the sea as a people who testified to God's miraculous deliverance. The tradition is unanimous in stressing that the rescue was accomplished through the intervention of God and God alone. He had provided a way of escape when there was no hope. In Isaiah the full implications of the radically new intervention is seen as the writer joins the redemption

from Egypt to the creation of the world (51.9ff.). Both in creation and exodus God wrought the impossible, and defeating the powers of the resisting enemy, brought forth new life. The New Testament, by tying the exodus through the sea to baptism, affirms the sharp discontinuity between the past and the present, the old age and the new. It acknowledges that the birth of the new was a miracle of incomprehensible dimension which emerged from the bowels of death by God's power alone. Surely Calvin was right in hearing the dominant note of the grace of God in a language which finds its clearest echo in the sacraments.

2. Again, the deliverance at the sea was effected by a combination of the wonderful and the ordinary. The waters were split by the rod of Moses, but a strong wind blew all night and laid bare the sea bed. The waters stood up as a mighty wall to the left and the right, and yet the Egyptians were drowned when the sea returned to its normal channels. Yahweh produced panic with his fiery glance, but it was the mud of the sea bottom which clogged the wheels of the heavy chariots. The elements of the wonderful and the ordinary are constitutive to the greatest of Old Testament events. There never was a time when the event was only understood as ordinary, nor was there a time when the supernatural absorbed the natural. But Israel saw the mighty hand of God at work in both the ordinary and the wonderful, and never sought to fragment the one great act of redemption into parts.

3. To the prose account which stressed the intervention of God in redeeming his people, there has been joined the response of the people. Already the prose account had concluded with the testimony to Israel's faith. In the Song of the Sea (ch. 15) the faith of the redeemed people is portrayed. It is fully clear that Israel was not saved because of her faith. Rather, Israel failed to believe right up to the moment before her deliverance. The faith of Israel did not provide the grounds of her salvation in any sense. Yet a faithful response was called forth. Israel broke out in praise to God. Indeed the language of joyful praise is constitutive of the redeemed. 'Together they sing for joy ... break forth into singing, you waste places of Jerusalem for the LORD has comforted his people' (Isa. 52.7–9). The sign of the redeemed is the joyful response of those who have been given a 'new song'.

4. But Israel did not remember. 'They did not keep in mind his power or the day when he redeemed them from the foe.' Already

within the Old Testament the inability of Israel to maintain itself as the new Israel was clearly recognized by the prophets. God must provide a new covenant, not like the one made with the fathers when he brought them from Egypt. Because there can be no full redemption from bondage until one is freed from sin and death, the people of God await with eager expectancy the final redemption from the world of evil. The exodus then becomes only a hint of what will come in full power at the end. The exodus from the bondage of Egypt serves as a foretaste of the final joys of life in the presence of God. Yet the exodus also serves as a warning. If Israel could have experienced the same signs of divine grace which were later made known to the church, how very real is the possibility of failing to respond! The church lives in the memory of the redemption from the past bondage of Egypt, and she looks for the promised inheritance. She now lives still in the desert somewhere between the Red Sea and the Jordan. 'Therefore let no one think that he stands lest he fall, but God is faithful and will also provide for us the *way of escape*.'

THE SONG OF THE SEA

15.1–21

A. Bender, 'Das Lied Exodus 15', *ZAW* 23, 1903, pp.1–48; B. S. Childs, 'A Traditio-Historical Study of the Reed Sea Tradition', *VT* 20, 1970, pp.410ff.; G. W. Coats, 'The Song of the Sea', *CBQ* 31, 1969, pp.1ff.; F. M. Cross, Jr and David N. Freedman, 'The Song of Miriam', *JNES* 14, 1955, pp.237–50; F. M. Cross, Jr, 'The Song of the Sea and Canaanite Myth', *God and Christ: Existence and Providence*, ed. R. W. Funk (*Journal for Theology and the Church* 5, New York 1968), pp.1–25; Judah Goldin, *The Song at the Sea*, New Haven 1971; N. Lohfink, 'Das Siegeslied am Schilfmeer', *Das Siegeslied am Schilfmeer* (Frankfurt 1965), pp. 102ff.; James Muilenburg, 'A Liturgy of the Triumphs of Yahweh', *Studia Biblica et Semitica T.C. Vriezen Dedicata*, Wageningen 1966, pp.238–50; Marc Rozelaar, 'The Song of the Sea', *VT* 2, 1952, pp.221ff.; Hans Schmidt, 'Das Meerslied. Ex.15, 2–19', *ZAW* 49, 1931, pp.59ff.; R. Tourney, 'Chronologie des Psaumes', *RB* 65, 1958, pp.335–57; J. D. W. Watts, 'The Song of the Sea – Ex.xv', *VT* 7, 1957, pp.371ff.

15 1 Then Moses and the Israelites sang this song to the Lord, saying:
I will sing to the Lord
For he is highly exalted,
Horse and driver he has hurled into the sea.
2 The Lord is my strength and song
He has become my salvation.
This is my God and I will praise him,
The God of my father and I will exalt him.
3 The Lord is a warrior;
The Lord is his name.
4 Pharaoh's chariots and his army
He cast into the sea;
And the pick of his officers
Are drowned in the Reed Sea.
5 The floods covered them,
They went down into the depths like a stone.

6 Thy right hand, O LORD, glorious in power,
  Thy right hand, O LORD, shatters the enemy.
7 In thy great majesty
  Thou breakest thy foes;
  Thou sendest forth thy fury,
  It consumes them like stubble.
8 At the blast of thy nostrils
  The waters piled up,
  The floods stood up like a hill,
  The deeps congealed in the heart of the sea.
9 The enemy said,
  'I will pursue, I will overtake,
  I will divide the spoil;
  My desire shall have its fill of them.
  I will draw my sword,
  My hand shall destroy them.'
10 Thou didst blow with thy breath,
  The sea covered them.
  They sank as lead
  Beneath the mighty waters.
11 Who is like thee,
  O LORD, among the gods!
  Who is like thee,
  Majestic in holiness.
  Awesome in splendor,
  Working wonders!
12 Thou didst stretch out thy right hand,
  The earth swallowed them.
13 Thou didst lead in thy love
  The people whom thou didst redeem;
  Thou hast guided them in thy strength
  To thy holy abode.
14 The peoples have heard and trembled,
  Anguish seized the dwellers of Philistia.
15 Indeed, the clans of Edom were dismayed;
  As for the tribes of Moab, trembling gripped them.
  All the dwellers of Canaan have melted away.
16 Terror and dread
  Fell upon them.
  Through the might of thy arm
  They were struck dumb like a stone.
  Until thy people pass by, O LORD,
  Until the people pass by whom thou hast purchased.
17 Thou wilt bring them and plant them

On the mount of thy heritage.
The place of thy abode,
Which thou hast made, O LORD,
The sanctuary, O LORD,
Which thy hands have established.
18 The LORD will reign for ever and ever.

19 When the horses of Pharaoh with his chariots and horsemen went into the sea, the LORD brought upon them the waters of the sea, but the Israelites walked on dry land in the midst of the sea. ²⁰Then Miriam, the prophetess, the sister of Aaron, took a timbrel in her hand, and all the women went out after her with timbrels and dancing. ²¹And Miriam sang to them:

Sing to the LORD
For he is highly exalted.
Horse and driver
He has thrown into the sea.

1. *Textual and Philological Notes*

The translation of the tenses in the Song of the Sea remains a difficult problem. Cross and Freedman (*JNES*, 1955) observed that the tenses function in a way more closely analogous to Ugaritic poetry than to ordinary Hebrew poetry. The sequence of affixed and prefixed verbal forms is characteristic of the early Canaanite epic style. It is typical to have a prefixed form in a series of affixed verbs, all of which seem to be best construed in the past (cf. vv.4–5) or an epic present. However, a future tense is clearly intended in v.9 which links six prefixed verbs together. The critical question arises then in the last half of the poem. From v.16 on there is again a series of six prefixed verbs (not counting the relative clauses). Is the 'entering the land' conceived of as a future or a past? In the 1955 article Cross and Freedman opted for the future tense after v.17. But in 1968, when Cross had decided on other grounds that the poet wrote from a perspective after the conquest, he translated all the verbs in the past with the exception of vv.9 and 18. From this analysis it is hard to discern what objective syntactical criteria are at work.

15.1. *rōḵebô*. Most all the ancient translations have taken it as a participle, translating it 'rider'. Frequently the emendation *riḵbô* = chariot has been proposed (cf. Cross-Freedman, *op. cit.*, for the rationale). But the term *rōḵēḇ*, which should be distinguished from *pārāš*, can also mean the rider in a chariot (Jer. 51.21).

2. *zimrāṯ* remains problematic. Cross-Freedman translate it 'protection, defense' on the basis of an alleged cognate with South Arabic, etc. But cf. the latest discussion initiated by S. E. Loewenstamm, *VT* 29, 1969, pp.464ff. who concluded that the word denotes 'the glory given to God in cultic song'. Then see the response of E. M. Good, *VT* 20, 1970, pp.358f., and especially that of S. B. Parker, *VT* 21, 1971, pp.373ff. who flatly rejects Loewenstamm's suggestion, and defends the meaning 'protection'.

2b. The AV translates the line 'I will prepare him a habitation' by mistakenly taking the root to be *nwh*.

6. On *ne'dārî* (glorious) cf. W. Moran, 'The Hebrew Language in its Northwest Semitic Background', *The Bible and the Ancient Near East: Essays in honor of W. F. Albright*, ed. G. E. Wright, New York and London 1961, p.60.

8. The translation of *nēd* remains a problem. The Arabic cognate meaning 'hill' has often been cited. Cf., however, NJPS 'stood straight like a wall', which follows the lead of Targ. Onk., Rashi, Ibn Ezra, etc. The occurrences of parallels in Ps.78.13 and Josh.3.13, 16 may well be dependent on Ex.15. Cf. the exegesis.

8. The meaning of the verb *qp'*, on the basis of the Old Testament and extra-biblical evidence, is clearly to 'congeal, thicken, and coagulate' (cf. Job 10.10). Cross and Freedman postulate an earlier meaning of 'churn' (p.246) which is the exact opposite connotation from that of congeal into a fixed position, and rests on a logical deduction rather than on linguistic evidence.

9. Cross and Freedman (p.246) follow Albright in suggesting an enclitic *mem* here and in the final colon of v.9. The suggestion is possible, but difficult to prove. There is no problem in translating the suffix in the MT in either case. For a discussion cf. H. Hummel, *JBL* 74, 1957, pp.85–107; David A. Robertson, *Linguistic Evidence in Dating Early Hebrew Poetry* (Yale Dissertation), 1966; James Barr, *Comparative Philology and the Text of the OT*, London and New York 1968, p.33.

11. Cross and Freedman (p.247) read *qedōšîm* and find a warrant in the LXX's ἁγίοις. Cf. also P. D. Miller, *HTR* 57, 1964, pp.241ff.

12. H. Gunkel, *Schöpfung und Chaos*, Göttingen 1895, first suggested *'ereṣ* be understood as the underworld. Accepted by Cross-Freedman.

13. The expression *neweh qodšekā* (holy encampment) is somewhat ambiguous. It can denote the whole land of Canaan (Jer.10.25; 23.3; Ps.79.7) or simply Zion (II Sam.15.25; Isa.27.10).

16. Cf. M. Dahood, '*Nādā* "To Hurl" in Ex.15, 16', *Biblica* 43, 1962, pp.248f.

16b. The verb *'br* can mean 'pass over' (Josh.3.17) or 'pass by' (Num.20.17). The choice depends on an exegetical decision respecting the proper context.

17. On the expression 'mountain of thy inheritance', cf. the discussion in the following section on dating the poem. The issue turns on the evaluation of a Ugaritic parallel.

2. *Literary, Form-Critical, Traditio-Historical Analysis*

In spite of the widespread form-critical interest in describing precisely the form of the Song, no consensus has emerged. The Song has been characterized as a hymn (Fohrer), enthronement psalm (Mowinckel), litany (Beer, Muilenburg), victory psalm (Cross-Freedman), hymn and thanksgiving psalm (Noth). Indeed, there do appear elements in the song which support each of the designations in part at least. The Song is filled with hymnic elements, especially the perorations on Yahweh's greatness (vv.6–11). The opening verses are typical of the thanksgiving psalm. Repetitions which appear to function as refrains (vv.6, 11) suggest a litany. Again a formula which is akin to the coronation psalms (e.g. 96; 99) appears in v.18, *YHWH yimlōk*. Finally, the setting of v.20 as well as the general content of the Song reflect clearly elements of a victory form. However, the chief form-critical problem is that no one form describes the entire song or does justice to the variety within the poem. It is, of course, possible that an original core such as a victory song was later expanded by virtue of a new and different function, but there is little formal evidence to support such a theory.

Surprisingly enough, little emphasis has been placed on the narrative sequence within the Song. It is less clear respecting the events at the sea, although its outline is preserved in vv.8–10. The later section then recounts in poetic form the conquest and possession of the land which culminate in the establishment of the divine sanctuary. The enumeration of the great acts of redemption which were celebrated in the Song appear to be a prototype of the historical recitals found in the Psalter (78, 105, 106).

In sum, the Song does not reflect any one genre in its form which would give the key to its function within the early life of the nation.

The traditio-historical problems of the Song are likewise difficult to assess and there has emerged no scholarly consensus. Nevertheless, in my judgment, several points are clear. First, although the event at the sea is described as a victory over the Egyptians and not as an exodus from Egypt, the sea tradition within the poem (1b–18) has been understood as belonging to the exodus tradition. The reasons are as follows: the wilderness tradition begins in v.13 with the fixed vocabulary of this cycle (*nāḥîṭā*). Again, the term *g'l* (v.13) functions as a stereotype in describing the victory at the sea as the decisive event which initiated Israel's redemptive history (Ex.6.6; Ps.77.16; Isa.52.9) and is not associated with the wilderness tradition. Also the characteristic elements of the wilderness tradition such as the pillar of cloud, the murmuring, and the path through the sea are missing.

Secondly, the sea tradition in the Song has been transmitted in conjunction with the conquest tradition. Verse 16 describes the crossing of the Jordan, v.17 the entrance into the land. In spite of the continued attempt of the Albright school to avoid this conclusion (Cross-Freedman, *JNES, op. cit.*, pp.237ff.), the conquest of the land is presupposed.

The description of the victory of the sea in the Song has evoked a variety of problems which relate to its traditional history. There is no mention of a crossing or a dividing of the sea. Scholars have tended to hold the view that this description of the sea event has little or nothing in common with that of the early prose account. But by assuming a totally different picture the essential features of the victory at the sea have been overlooked. First of all, the poem also describes a double action of the waters. With his breath Yahweh heaps up the waters (v. 8) and with his breath he covers the enemy (v. 10). Moreover, the effect of the wind is to congeal the waters into inaction. Finally, the poetic description contains the two elements which are now distributed between J and P, namely, the wind and the wall of water. Far from being a description totally independent of the prose account, the poetic tradition of Ex. 15 shares its basic features.

How is this common tradition to be explained? Some older scholars argued that Ex. 15 is a very late poem which has combined features of J and P. However, the linguistic arguments against this hypothesis seem decisive. Much more likely is the theory that would see a common tradition being shared by the early prose account of J and the early poetic tradition of Ex. 15. The fact that the sea was transmitted in the prose account with the wilderness tradition but in the poetic account with the exodus would point to the antiquity of the sea tradition. The common tradition preceded the period in which the prose tradition was transmitted within a larger traditional complex. In sum, Ex. 15 reflects a poetic tradition of the event at the sea, which, although as old as that in the J account, has been transmitted within the larger framework of the exodus and conquest traditions. In terms of the history of traditions, the poetic tradition represents initially a parallel development with the prose account rather than being a part of a linear development from J to P.

The evidence for determining an absolute dating of the poem remains much contested, even though many of the older arguments for a post-exilic dating such as those advanced by Bender (*op. cit.*) have collapsed. At present the clearest options seem to lie between German scholars, such as Noth, who regard the poem as relatively late, and American scholars, such as Cross and Freedman, who hold the poem to be very old indeed.

Cross and Freedman (*JNES*, 1955), and more recently Cross ('Song of the Sea', 1968) have outlined in considerable detail the arguments for an early dating. Of the various arguments brought forth the philological arguments carry the most weight. The cumulative evidence forms an impressive case for an early dating of the poem, particularly the tense system and the orthography. Of course, it remains possible to see these elements as conscious archaizing such as is found in II Isaiah. However, the overall consistency of the linguistic phenomena would rather point to genuine archaic elements.

W. F. Albright first defended a thirteenth-century dating in his *Archaeology of Palestine* (Harmondsworth, Middx. 1949, p.233). He was, however, forced to regard the reference to the 'inhabitants of Philistia' as an anachronism. Cross and Freedman, while seeking to buttress Albright's major arguments, dated the composition in the period between the twelfth and eleventh centuries. A major argument of Albright and his school for an early dating turned on their interpretation of the expression 'on the mountain of thine inheritance' (*b^ehar nah^alāt^ekā*) in v. 17. Previously this expression was thought to be a reference to the temple of Solomon in Zion and it was seen as a major reason for a date in the monarchial period or even later. Albright, followed by Cross and Freedman, argued on the basis of a close Ugaritic parallel that the phrase was a Canaanite formula and it specified the special seat of the deity.

Although the cogency of the Ugaritic parallel has been readily acknowledged, the implications which Albright and his students have drawn have met with resistance. (Cf. e.g. S. Mowinckel, *Der achtundsechzigste Psalm*, Oslo 1953, pp.73ff.; R. E. Clements, *God and Temple*, Oxford and Philadelphia 1965, pp.53ff. etc.) The decisive issue for dating a Hebrew poem is not the age of the original Canaanite formula, but its form and function within Israel's traditions. There is no traditio-historical evidence to support Cross and Freedman's reconstruction of a desert habitation of Yahweh. Rather, the closest parallels to the expression in the Old Testament have their setting either in the conquest or Zion traditions (cf. Jer. 25.30; 31.23; Deut. 3.25, etc.). As one would expect, both of these circles of tradition made wide use of Canaanite material. Although scholars continue to debate whether the expressions in Ex. 15.13, 17 refer to the whole land or specifically to Zion, at least the conquest of the land has been presupposed.

Again, there are a whole set of literary and redactional issues which continue to be debated without any real consensus having been reached. First of all, the relation of the Song of Miriam in v.21 to the Song of the Sea which Moses sang (vv. 1b–18) remains a problem.

German critical scholarship (Noth, Fohrer) sees the shorter poem of v. 21 as the oldest part of the chapter and the kernel out of which the later Song developed. However, Cross and Freedman, following Albright, have argued that v. 21 is not a different or shorter version of the song of the sea, but 'simply the title of the poem taken from a different cycle of traditions' (p. 237). Both hypotheses up to now rest largely on theories of composition which, for lack of conclusive evidence, remain projections. On the one hand, Noth's position has relied too uncritically on the assumption that shortness in length reflects antiquity, but clearly the opposite situation is true at times (cf. A. B. Lord, *The Singer of Tales*, New York 1968). On the other hand, Cross and Freedman have not at all demonstrated that titles function in biblical literature in the way suggested, nor has the theory of a different cycle of traditions been established.

The problem of sources is closely related to the previous one. A variety of solutions has been offered. Often v. 21 has been assigned to E and the larger poem to J or the redactor of D. But the evidence for source analysis is highly uncertain. Accordingly in recent times, many have ceased attempting to assign the traditional sources (Noth).

Then again the problem of determining a metrical form of the poem has long occupied scholars. (Cf. particularly Muilenburg's attempt, *op. cit.*) Certain obvious structural features have been often pointed out: the use of the first person in vv. 1b-2; the new subject matter after v. 13; the repetitions in vv. 6 and 11, the features of an appendix in v. 18. Nevertheless, the attempts to refine the analysis have not produced anything nearing a consensus. In my judgment, Muilenburg's essay is full of insights, but it remains a highly subjective reading of the text.

In regard to the problem of meter, Cross's analysis emerges as one of the more impressive attempts. His insistence on the predominance of 2'2' meter over against the older 4' analysis has been a genuine contribution. (Interestingly enough, Clericus had already argued for the 2'2' meter in the seventeenth century.) Cross has also recognized the shifts to 3'3' meter and the analogy in Ugaritic poetry to the extra colon in a line. In sum, the subject is still in great flux and needs further clarification. The division into strophes as a result continues to be a highly subjective enterprise which is chiefly determined by the content of the poem in spite of the claims for larger poetic patterns.

Finally a word regarding the redactional framework of the poem is in order. It has been argued by some older critics (Dillmann,

Bacon) that v. 1 must have stood in a literary source (usually assigned to J), since it is difficult to explain why the poem was attached to v. 1b rather than to v. 21 unless v. 21 had originally stood in another source (E). But several reasons speak against the suggestion. The tendency to ascribe an ancient poem to Moses would have taken precedence over Miriam's authorship. Again, most frequently the prose setting is secondary to the poetic piece (cf. Judg. 5 and Jonah 2). Lastly, it is not unusual for an expansion to precede rather than follow an earlier position in its final literary composition.

Perhaps of more importance is the role of the concluding prose summary in v. 19. Dillmann (p. 160) argued that this prose notice probably belonged to the book in which old songs were collected. The redactor of the chapter unwittingly included the prose setting as part of the song when he selected the poem. In my judgment, this theory is quite unlikely. The close parallel to the Priestly source – the last colon has been taken *verbatim* from 14.29 – would point rather to the work of the final Priestly editor. Was it added because he felt some tension between his own tradition of the crossing and that given in the Song? Perhaps, but more likely there was the need to bring the reader's attention back to the sea event in order to make the transition to Miriam's song.

3. *Old Testament Context*

The Song of the Sea is introduced by a type of superscription which fits the poem into the narrative. 'Then sang Moses . . . saying . . .' There are several parallels in the Old Testament to this method of setting a poem within a narrative setting (cf. Deut. 31.30; Judg. 5.1; I Sam. 2.1, etc.). Often the poem is earlier in date than its framework and originally served a different purpose in its independent state. Although it is a legitimate task of the traditio-historical method to trace these earlier stages before the development of its present literary role, an equally important and usually neglected exegetical task is to analyze the composition in its final stage. Regardless of its prehistory, the fundamental issue is to determine the effect of joining the poem to the preceding narrative.

First of all, the poem now provides the response of faith by the people who have experienced their redemption from the hands of the Egyptians at the sea. The narrative account had closed with the remark that the people 'feared Yahweh', and 'believed in him'

(v. 31). The content of this belief is now expressed by the song. It is a characteristic feature of Old Testament faith that the great acts of God are joined to the faith of the people which the event evoked. The redeemed people break forth in praise to the One who has done, and continues to do, great things on their behalf.

Secondly, the poem in its present setting offers an important interpretation of the event itself, and thereby affects the reading of the prose tradition which preceded it. Its role is not to add new information hitherto unknown, which is of course the historian's interest in the poem, but to supply Israel's response to her redemption. The poem praises God as the sole agent of salvation. Israel did not co-operate or even play a minor role. The figure of Moses is completely omitted. Yahweh alone effected the miracle at the sea. In the usual scholarly reconstruction, a growth in the sense of the supernatural is indicated. J had only an east wind; P had a wall of water. But from the perspective of the tradition, there never was a moment when God was not the all-dominating force at work with sovereign power over the floods and winds, the hosts of Pharaoh, and the inhabitants of Canaan.

Thirdly, the framework anchored the praise of God to a specific moment in history ('At that time Moses sang'), and yet did not destroy the inner tension of the poem which this fixing in time created. Early commentators had already noticed that the events which are praised extend far into the future beyond the period of Moses. The early commentators tried to solve the problem by understanding the preterite tenses as prophetic futures. The modern, critical scholars generally explain the difficulty as a reading back into the Mosaic period of a much later poem. But neither the traditional 'prophetic' interpretation, nor the critical historical explanation does justice to the present context of the Old Testament text. By taking seriously the synchronistic dimension of Ex. 14 and 15 a characteristic theological feature of the Old Testament emerges. God who has acted in Israel's history is the same one who is acting and will act. The chronological tension which continues to disturb modern commentators apparently did not provide a problem for the Old Testament redactor. The epic style allowed the writer to move back and forth from the past to the present without sacrificing the concrete quality of specific historical situations.

The poem begins in the first person: 'I will sing' (v. 1b). This usage extends through v. 2 and is never picked up again. Form critics (e.g. Noth) have tended at times to characterize this introduction as a feature of the 'individual song of thanksgiving', and distinguish it from the form of the hymn. However, the frequency of the first person introduction to the hymn would rather point to its being a stylistic feature of the hymn itself (cf. Deut. 32.1, 2; Judg. 5.3; I Sam. 2.1; Ps. 145.1). The poem shares the major features of the hymn throughout and shows striking parallels in form and content with those of the Psalter. Yahweh is praised for his greatness and strength (v. 6) which is then joined to his attribute of holiness (v. 13; cf. Ps. 89.14, 15). His specific deeds of redemption are without comparison (v. 11; cf. Pss. 77.14; 95.3). Above all, the display of divine power is to create for himself a people (v. 13; Ps. 77.16) before the astonished eyes of the nations (v. 14; Ps. 98.2) whose gods are proven to be worthless before the might of Yahweh (Ps. 96.5). Finally, he rules the world as king from his holy abode (v. 18; Pss. 93.1ff.; 96.7ff.).

The presence of these characteristic elements throughout Ex. 15 would support the essential unity of the whole poem in the one hymnic style in spite of the sharp shifts in content within the poem. The term hymn is also far more appropriate than victory song in distinguishing the form of Ex. 15 from Judg. 5. Whereas the latter celebrates a victory over Sisera and recounts the achievements of Deborah and Barak, Ex. 15 is directed completely to the praise of God and thus subordinates all the historical details of Israel's active involvement. Again, Judg. 5 has been given a setting 'to the sound of musicians at the watering places . . . repeating the triumphs of Yahweh', whereas Ex. 15 is much more cultically oriented. The poem is rehearsed at the sanctuary 'where Yahweh reigns forever'. The distinction is not an absolute one, but does reflect accurately the difference between a victory song and a hymn.

[15.1b–12] The first part of the hymn recounts Yahweh's victory at the sea. Two features stand out in the description and recur in a variety of ways. First, Yahweh is praised for his greatness and power (vv. 1b, 3, 6, 7, 11, 12). Often this description in praise of Yahweh is not directly related to the sea event, but in the hymnic style of the participle celebrates Yahweh's glory as 'fierce in action', 'doer of wonders' (v. 12). Even when the finite verb appears, the action is not confined to the Reed Sea event, but flows into a broader description of Yahweh's attributes which closely parallel the participial use. He is the one who 'smashes the enemy', 'destroys the foe', and 'sends forth his fury' (vv. 6–7). The victory at the sea simply illustrates those same attributes which are continually celebrated throughout the Psalter. Secondly, the specific and concrete elements of the victory at the Reed Sea are recounted, often in the past tense. The enemy is not the mythological sea (Hab.3.8f.), but the army of Pharaoh whom Yahweh drowned in the sea. The only verse which falls outside these two features of praise – called by Westermann declarative and descriptive praise – is v.9. Here the enemy is quoted in direct discourse which is a typical poetic device to intensify the threat (cf. Pss.35.12; 83.5, etc.).

The apparent lack of concern in the hymn to follow the chronological sequence of the event – already in v.1b he has overthrown the enemy – has led some commentators to discount elements of genuine sequence when such do occur. Verses 4 and 5 elaborate on the casting into the sea of Pharaoh's army which was first introduced in 1b. Then in vv.6 and 7 the hymn turns from the historical event to praise God declaratively in more general terms. In v.8 the writer returns to the sea victory and describes the effect of Yahweh's blowing the waters. 'The flood stood up in a heap, the deeps congealed.' Verse 9 then introduces the enemy, who seeks to pursue. In v.10 again Yahweh blows with his breath and drowns the enemy. Commentators have frequently claimed that the picture of the event in the poem is totally different from that of the prose, but the evidence does not support this argument. Far from being a reading back of the prose sequence into the poem, the poem itself follows an obvious sequence closely paralleling the prose. Of course, the sequence is not a major concern of the poet, as we have seen. In v.11 he again leaves the historical event to expand on Yahweh's power. Nevertheless, the poetic tradition of the event does not seem to be greatly at variance. Especially in the light of its poetic medium, it should not be flattened out and rationalized.

[15.13–18] The second part of the hymn begins in v.13. Not only is there a marked change in content with no further specific reference in the hymn to the sea, but v.13 offers an interpretation of the events which have preceded by its choice of vocabulary. The first half of the hymn described Yahweh's victory. Now v.13 interprets this event in relation to Israel. It was through this event that Israel was redeemed to become the people of God. Certain older commentators have suggested that this section is a later addition to an early poem concerning the sea rescue, however, again the evidence does not sustain the theory. Rather, whenever Israel's tradition the redemption at the sea is recounted, the subsequent leading of the redeemed people into the land is invariably included (cf. Isa. 63.11ff.; Ps. 77.15ff.).

The movement of the poem from the deliverance at the sea to the land interprets the significance of Yahweh's redemptive intervention. He not only redeems a people for himself, but he leads them into his land. Whereas the first part of the hymn revolved about Yahweh's victory at the sea, the focus of the second half is on Yahweh's sanctuary. He guides his people 'to his holy abode' (v. 13). He paralyzes the nations as his people cross through the land (vv. 14ff.). Yahweh brings them in, plants them on his mountain from where he rules his kingdom (v. 18). The poem ends with the ascription to Yahweh as king, so frequently found in the Psalter. Yahweh now rules; he is being praised by his people. In other words, the poem does not end by defining Israel's role in the land, but rather by reflecting Israel's function as the worshipping community. The concluding verses provide the cultic setting out of which the whole poem took its shape.

A certain parallelism has been noticed between motifs in the first and second parts of the poem. The danger from the Egyptians in vv. 1b–12 parallels the threat of the enemy in vv. 13–15. In both cases Yahweh renders the enemy helpless. The parallelism is emphasized in the Vulgate between the 'congealing' of the waters (v. 8, *congregatae*) and the 'becoming stiff' of the Canaanites (v. 15, *obriguerent*). Again, phrases such as 'like a stone' recur in both parts (vv. 5 and 16). Finally, there is a type of refrain in vv. 6 and 11. However, the elements of parallelism are so diverse in character as to make somewhat implausible the theory that conscious imitation was a force in shaping the latter section (N. Lohfink, 'Das Siegeslied', pp. 123ff.).

The hymn which recounts the redemptive history from the exodus, through the conquest, to the securing of Zion, is similar to many other hymns in omitting any reference to Sinai. The significance of this omission continues to be much debated (cf. ch. 19 for bibliography). Ex. 15 is also different from many other psalms in making no reference to Israel's later disobedience (cf. Pss. 78, 95, 105). Rather, the tone of the poem is closely akin to that of Joshua in celebrating the unbroken solidarity of Yahweh and his people which results in victory (Josh. 1.9; 2.9, etc.). The nations fall back in terror before God's leading. Only later in disobedience does Israel seek its own way to become a 'taunt to the nations' and a 'laughing stock among the people' (Ps. 44.15, 16). Likewise, only later does the need arise for the prophets to reinterpret eschatologically the meaning of Yahweh's kingship which Israel had early celebrated in her worship.

Detailed Notes

15.2. 'This is my God'. Cf. Eissfeldt, '"Mein Gott" im Alten Testament', *ZAW* 61, 1945/8, pp. 3–16.

2. 'God of my father'. Cf. Ex. 3.6.

3. On Yahweh as a warrior, cf. H. Frederiksson, *Jahwe als Krieger*, Lund 1945; G. von Rad, *Der Heilige Krieg im Alten Israel*, Zürich 1951; Frank M. Cross, 'The Divine Warrior in Israel's Early Cult', *Biblical Motifs*, ed. A. Altmann, Cambridge 1966, pp. 11–30; P. D. Miller, Jr, *Holy War and Cosmic War in Early Israel* (Harvard Dissertation), 1963.

4. O. Kaiser, *Die mythische Bedeutung des Meeres in Ägypten, Ugarit, und Israel*[2], Berlin 1962, gives a full bibliography on the role of the sea.

5. 'mighty waters'. Cf. H. May, 'Some Cosmic Connotations of *Mayim Rabbîm*, "Many Waters"', *JBL* 74, 1955, pp. 9ff.

11. Cf. C. J. Labuschagne, *The Incomparability of Yahweh in the Old Testament*, Leiden 1966, for a study of thèse expressions.

17. Cf. F. Dreyfus, 'Le thème de l'heritage dans l'Ancien Testament', *Rev. Science Phil. et Theol.* 42, 1958, pp. 3–49.

18. On the subject of Yahweh as king, cf. the lengthy bibliography cited by S. Szikszai, *IDB* III, p. 17; K. H. Bernhardt, *BHH* II, col. 981.

INTRODUCTION TO THE WILDERNESS
WANDERINGS TRADITIONS

R. BACH, *Die Erwählung Israels in der Wüste* (Diss., Bonn), 1951; C. BARTH, 'Zur Bedeutung der Wüstentradition', *Suppl. VT* 15, 1966, pp.14ff.; H. J. BOECKER, *Redeformen des Rechtslebens im Alten Testament*, WMANT 14, 1964; K. BUDDE, 'Das nomadische Ideal im Alten Testament', *Preussische Jahrbücher* 85, 1896, pp.57–79; H. CAZELLES, *VT* 21, 1971, pp.506–14 (review of Fritz's book); G. W. COATS, *Rebellion in the Wilderness*, Nashville 1968; 'An exposition for the wilderness traditions', *VT* 22, 1972, pp.288–95; S. DE VRIES, 'The Origin of the Murmuring Tradition', *JBL* 87, 1968, pp.51ff.; J. W. FLIGHT, 'The Nomadic Idea and Ideal in the Old Testament', *JBL* 42, 1923, pp.158–226; V. FRITZ, *Israel in der Wüste*, Marburg 1970; J. GRAY, 'The Desert Sojourn of the Hebrews in the Sinai-Horeb Tradition', *VT* 4, 1954, pp.148ff.; M. NOTH, *Überlieferungsgeschichte des Pentateuch*, 1948, pp.62ff., 127ff. = *History of Pentateuchal Traditions*, 1971, pp.58ff., 122ff.; P. RIEMANN, *Desert and Return to Desert in Pre-Exilic Prophets* (Diss. Harvard), 1964; F. SCHNUTENHAUS, *Die Entstehung der Mosetraditionen* (Diss. Heidelberg), 1958; S. TALMON, 'The "Desert Motif" in the Bible and in Qumran Literature', *Biblical Motifs*, ed. A. Altmann, Cambridge 1966, pp.31–63; A. C. TUNYOGI, 'The Rebellions of Israel', *JBL* 81, 1962, pp.385–90; F. V. WINNETT, *The Mosaic Tradition*, 1949, pp.121ff.

The term 'wilderness wanderings' attempts to encompass the great variety of material in the Old Testament which covers the period from the exodus out of Egypt until the entrance into the promised land. This material lacks both the formal and material unity of the traditions of the exodus and the conquest. There is even considerable debate as to where the wilderness cycle actually begins (cf. section IX above and G. W. Coats, *VT* 17, 1967, pp.253ff.). The traditions of the wilderness are now clustered into two major blocks, one of which precedes Sinai (Ex. 15–18), and one which follows (Num. 10ff.). The presence of striking doublets (cf. Meribah, Ex. 17//Num. 20; manna, Ex. 16//Num. 11) indicates that the present arrangement of the tradition reflects a complex history of traditional and literary development. The fact that the Sinai tradition is bracketed by parallel stories of the wilderness wanderings led both the literary critics (e.g. Wellhausen) and the form critics (e.g. von Rad) to see the present position of the Sinai tradition to be evidence for its secondary interpolation within the *Heilsgeschichte*. The traditions of the wanderings are extremely varied in content. They include stories of how Israel was maintained through lack of food and water, as well as how she overcame the dangers of attack from snakes, enemies, and internal rebellion. However, there is an increasing tendency within the Old Testament to unify the material within a larger conceptual framework and see it as a sharply defined period within the nation's history (cf. Pss. 78 and 106).

Much of the modern discussion of the wilderness traditions has taken its starting point from M. Noth's analysis in his well-known *Überlieferungsgeschichte des Pentateuch*. Noth describes the wilderness wanderings as one of the five main themes of the Pentateuch. However, he recognizes it as a minor one in comparison with the others. It presupposes the exodus from Egypt and the entrance into the land. In the brief summary lists of the traditions on which von Rad placed such emphasis, the theme of the wilderness wanderings is either passed over completely (Deut. 6 and 26), or briefly mentioned (Josh. 24). Nevertheless, the theme does tie the other two together and occasionally appears in its own right (Deut. 29.4). Actually Noth has remarkably little to say about this theme, and much of what he does say is directed against what he considers to be the excessive speculation of Gressmann and others. He feels that it is not certain at what stage in the development of the Pentateuch the wilderness wanderings traditions entered. He assumes that the stories originated among the southern tribes and in circles akin to those which treasured the stories of Abraham and Isaac in the Negeb. Moreover, he finds no evidence of a cultic setting nor any center of the tradition at Kadesh. When Noth turns to his section on the elaboration of the theme, he has more to say. He attributes much of the content of the stories to local tales, often etiological in character, which were brought in to fill out the tradition. Because of the complexity of this process, it will be necessary to examine individually in the proper place Noth's theories respecting each of the stories (cf. below). In sum, Noth's treatment tends to be dominated by his larger hypothesis regarding the development of the Pentateuch rather than resting on specific evidence from this tradition which offers very few leads.

Perhaps the most basic traditio-historical problem of the wilderness tradition has to do with the role of the murmuring motif, which, although it is completely missing from some of the stories (Ex. 17.8ff.; 18.1ff.), increasingly becomes the rubric under which these stories were interpreted (Deut. 9.22ff.; Ps. 78). The problem arises from the apparent divergence within the Old Testament in the understanding of the wilderness period (cf. von Rad, *Theology* I, pp. 280ff.). On the one hand, both within the Pentateuch and elsewhere, the wilderness period was condemned as a proof of Israel's early disobedience and repeated rebellion against God. On the other hand, there are strands within the Pentateuch (Ex. 16) and explicit references in the prophets (Hosea 2.16, EVV 14; Jer. 2.2) which give an apparently positive interpretation of the period. Indeed, it is characterized as a 'honeymoon' before the corruption of idolatry set in, caused by contamination with the Canaanites. In the light of this problem, several major attempts have been offered to explain the origin of the murmuring motif.

Again Noth offers the initial starting point for most recent discussion. He argues that the murmuring motif is often only loosely connected to the story itself, such as in the water stories (p. 136). However, in Num. 11.4ff. the theme of murmuring is firmly anchored to the popular etiology of the name Kibbroth-hattavah, meaning 'graves of craving'. This grave tradition then gave rise to the story of the sending of the quails in response to the murmuring of the people and subsequently spread to other stories throughout the wilderness tradition. By and large, this explanation has met with little enthusiasm and its several obvious weaknesses have been criticized by Schnutenhaus, Coats, De Vries, and Fritz. Coats, for example, has argued that there is no primary connection between the murmuring tradition and the etiology, which would make it highly improbable that this naming etiology would be the origin of the entire murmuring cycle.

Then Coats has put forth the thesis that the murmuring motif arose within the cult of Jerusalem during the early period of the divided monarchy and served as a polemic against the claims of the northern kingdom. Coats finds his major warrant for this pro-Judean flavor in Ps. 78 and suggests that this stance was projected back into the wilderness period. In my judgment, although Ps. 78 makes use of the murmuring motif in reference to the claims of Jerusalem, it does not follow that this inner conflict among the tribes was the origin of the tradition. The motif was continually used to explain different events in Israel's history. Ps. 106 relates it to the exile. Therefore, it is much more likely to see the conflict of the divided kingdom as a later application rather than the origin of the tradition. In the second place, there are many signs that the tradition is far older than Coats' explanation would allow. In my judgment, the same type of objections can be levelled against Fritz's theory (*op. cit.*) that the motif is an attempt to maintain the new won state independence of David.

Finally, Simon De Vries has more recently argued that the murmuring tradition arose out of the necessity of bringing a conquest tradition from the south into line with a tradition of the attack from the east. The murmuring tradition provided the needed time lapse to get Israel from the south to the east and also to offer an explanation for Israel's earlier defeat in terms of her sin. In other words, the murmuring tradition arose 'simply out of the theological reflex that faced the necessity of calibrating the southern conquest tradition with the already dominant tradition of the central amphictyony' (p. 58). Again, this theory appears to me unlikely. In my judgment, the murmuring tradition had long been in existence before its use in the spy traditions. Again this thesis does not adequately explain the content of the murmuring, particularly the repeated emphasis on the exodus.

My own interpretation of the origin of the murmuring tradition takes as its starting point the stereotyped language of the complaints, which has long been noticed. The fact of the close similarity in both form and content within these protests, and the lack of variation in quite different situations, would support the thesis that a set traditional language is being used. Coats has argued, chiefly on the basis of Begrich's and Boecker's form-critical work, that the formal structure of the murmuring has its setting in the pre-official stage of the trial. However, I wonder whether this theory has over-interpreted the evidence. Such complaints as 'Would that we had never left home', or 'You have led us out to kill us', are universal human reactions in times of adversity which are shared by all cultures. The fact that these same expressions appear in an actual trial situation is to be expected, but does not offer adequate reason for speaking of a *Gattung*. Such passages as Josh. 7.7ff. share the same form of complaint without being related to the murmuring tradition. Still we have yet to explain fully the forces at work in shaping the stereotyped form of the material.

Up to now in the discussion of the origin of the murmuring tradition within the wilderness cycle insufficient attention has been paid to the larger framework in which the murmuring language functions. Two distinct patterns can be detected in the structure of the stories which contain the murmuring theme. (I am indebted to a seminar paper of Paul Hanson for this original insight, which I have since developed along my own lines of research.) Pattern I is found in its clearest form in Ex. 15.22f.; 17.1ff.; and Num. 20.1–13. Accordingly, there is an initial need (15.22, 23; 17.1; Num. 20.2) which is followed by a complaint (15.24; 17.2; Num. 20.3), then by an intercession on the part of Moses (15.25; 17.4; Num. 20.6), which issues in the need being met by God's miraculous intervention (15.25; 17.6f.; Num. 20.11). In contrast to this, Pattern II is found in its clearest form in Num. 11.1–3; 17.6–15 (EVV 16.41–50); 21.4–10. Accordingly, there is an initial complaint (11.1; 17.6; 21.5), which is followed by God's anger and punishment (11.1; 17.10; 21.6), then an intercession from Moses (11.2; 17.45; 21.7), and finally a reprieve of the punishment (11.2; 17.50; 21.9).

There are some striking similarities and differences between these two patterns. The same stereotyped complaints appear in both patterns, and in both Moses intercedes for the people. However, the order of these elements differs in the two patterns and Pattern II has the additional elements of anger and judgment. The two patterns do not give the impression of being a literary creation, but stem from a particular situation already in the oral tradition. The relation between the two patterns is not easy to determine. First of all, the complaints function quite differently within the two patterns in spite of the same stereotyped language. In Pattern I there is always a genuine need – whether of food or water – which is made specific and calls forth the complaint, whereas in Pattern II the complaint is introduced without a basis in a genuine need, and it is usually explicitly characterized as an illegitimate murmuring: 'the rabble had a strong craving' (Num. 11.4), or 'the people became impatient', and called the manna 'this worthless food' (21.4).

It is possible that Pattern I originally functioned as a form by which to relate stories of the miraculous preservation of Israel in the desert as part of the recitation of the sacred history (*Heilsgeschichte*). The majority of the stories of this pattern relate to the miraculous gift of food and water and thus reflect the most pressing problem of sustaining life in the wilderness. Pattern II has a different emphasis.

These stories focus on Israel's disobedience in the desert and the subsequent punishment and eventual forgiveness which their unbelief called forth. However, it is most important to recognize that already in the oral stage the two patterns began to be closely joined and exercise a mutual influence. Originally the complaint in Pattern I had arisen from a genuine need, which was clearly not the case in Pattern II. Shortly the complaints in the two patterns were levelled and the identical set of stereotypes used in both instances. This suggests that both patterns began to serve an identical function. The later usage of the tradition in Deut. 9 and Pss. 78 and 106 offers a good insight into this function which continued with some variation throughout Israel's history. These stories lent themselves to a homiletical purpose and served as a warning against resistance to God's plan for the nation. The exodus and conquest cycles offered abundant proofs of God's great acts of deliverance, but the murmuring tradition offered a classic example for the preacher to address Israel in her failure to respond obediently to the divine mercy. This is not to suggest that there was a developed parenesis in the oral stage which already resembled the elaborate homilies of Deuteronomy. Rather, the parenesis was built into the narrative itself. By expanding on the subjective reaction of the people, the unjust nature of the complaint was brought home by the very recounting of how the need was met.

The signs that at a very early date Patterns I and II were levelled, and both became stories of similar murmuring, should not be interpreted to suggest that Pattern I was altered from a purely positive stance to that of a negative. Rather, it is much more likely that Pattern I had an element of negative complaint from the outset which was simply expanded by means of the fixed material from Pattern II. Pattern I was similar enough in its emphasis to be attached to Pattern II for a common parenetic function. At this point, C. Barth's strictures (op. cit.) are well taken that the negative interpretation of Israel in the wilderness was equally part of the oldest tradition and not a later transformation of an earlier stage of the tradition which was completely positive in character.

When one now turns to trace the development of the murmuring tradition within the literary sources, the manner in which the material is handled confirms our theory of the early age of the tradition. The tradition is found strongly represented in the J source. There are enough signs of tension within this early source to suggest that E may well have had the tradition also (cf. below), but the E source appears in such a fragmentary form as to prevent any solid conclusions from being drawn. Both of the two patterns which were described above appear in the J source (I = Ex. 14.11ff.; 15.22–27; 17.1–7; II = Num. 11.1–3; 21.4–10). This evidence would point to a prior role in the oral stage of development as we have suggested. It is difficult to determine what was the original order of the stories which originally must have been quite different from that of its present redaction. Within the J source the murmuring tradition has been adapted in various ways to fit into the ongoing narrative. For example, in Ex. 14.11ff. the murmuring of the people provides the device by which to contrast Moses' faith (v. 13) and the subsequent change in heart of the people (v. 31).

Of considerable importance in the development of the tradition was the further redaction of the J material. Several signs of change in the understanding and role of the tradition can be detected. In the first place, the arrangement of the J material within the Exodus narrative seems to have been influenced by the position of the golden calf incident. It is hardly by chance that the stories placed before the great apostasy are all of Pattern I, which stressed the help of God in overcoming a genuine need (Ex. 14.11ff.; 15.23ff.; 17.1ff.), whereas the stories following the golden calf incident are all of Pattern II (Num. 11.1ff.; 21.4ff.). Indeed, the J account of the manna story, which, like its parallel in P (Ex. 16.1ff.), must have once been formed on Pattern I, has now been reworked in order to include the element of unworthy complaint and divine judgment, which are characteristic of Pattern II. According to the redactor of J, Israel's rebellion and disobedience increased and intensified following the disaster with the calf.

There is another tendency to be discerned in the redaction of the J material. Traditions which arose in connection with Moses' office were joined to the murmuring tradition. There is some evidence to suggest that at a very early date a cycle of stories had collected about the office of Moses. Such stories as those in Ex. 33 and 34, Num. 11 and 12, appear closely related to the Mosaic office of covenant mediator and were attached to the tent of meeting (cf. ch. 19 for a full discussion). However, in the early oral stage of the murmuring tradition there was no connection with the office of Moses. Nor does even the J source appear to have joined these two cycles of stories. Not until one comes to the redaction of Num. 11.4ff. does one see traces of a combination. The author of the present chapter has combined the manna story with the tradition of Moses' prophetic office. The murmuring for food on the part of the people now issues in Moses' complaint that he cannot bear the burden of leadership alone and the bestowal of the prophetic spirit upon them. The redaction of Num. 16 is somewhat akin. Here an originally independent story which related to a challenge to Moses' leadership has been joined to the cycle of murmuring stories. Of course, the combination of the murmuring stories with those related to the Mosaic office is not surprising. Already in such stories as Num. 12, the element of complaint against Moses was present (v. 2), even if the issue at stake was clearly distinct from the stereotyped murmuring tradition.

The Deuteronomic use of the murmuring tradition is characterized, first of all, by an elaboration of the parenetic function of these stories. The homiletist found these wilderness stories ideal examples by which to admonish the people to obedience: 'Remember and do not forget how you provoked Yahweh your God to wrath in the wilderness.' Moreover, the Deuteronomic writer expands the scope of the murmuring tradition. The golden calf incident becomes the classic example of Israel's rebellion (9.6ff.). To this the writer adds an enumeration of rebellions from Taberah to Kadesh-barnea and draws the devastating conclusion: 'You have been rebellious against Yahweh from the day I knew you' (9.24). It is also noticeable that the Deuteronomist's great interest in the possession of the land causes him to lay unusual emphasis on Israel's failure to possess the land as a prime example of her rebellion, which he then urges should not be repeated (1.26ff.). In Ps. 78 one can see the parenetic use of the murmuring tradition under the influence of the Deuteronomic school developed into a historical principle of repeated disobedience by which to encompass the entire history of Israel up to the establishment of the Davidic monarchy.

Finally, the Priestly source witnesses to an important and often dramatic transformation of the murmuring tradition. Both oral patterns within the tradition have been retained (I = Ex. 16; Num. 20; II = Num. 13 and 17). Several of the stories in the Priestly source are also represented in J, notably the manna, water, and spy stories, but again there is much unique to P. The first strikingly new feature in the P material is the introduction of the theophany at the tent of meeting which appears in every story, excepting that of Aaron's rod (Num. 17.16ff.). In each case the glory of Yahweh appears, usually at the tent of meeting (Ex. 16.10; Num. 14.10; 16.19; 17.7; 20.6). This feature is introduced as a response to the murmuring of the people. In Pattern I the appearance of the glory offers Moses a chance to speak to God before the need is met (Ex. 16.11). However, in the more frequent cases of Pattern II, anger and judgment of God upon the rebellion follows.

The significance of the use of the theophany in the murmuring stories is closely related to the second place in which a change in the tradition can be discerned. In the Priestly writings the traditions of the Mosaic office have been joined to the murmuring tradition. Whereas, in the earlier J source, it was only in the later redaction that a secondary combination was made, in the P source the two traditions are closely joined. In Num. 16.3 the rebellion of Korah is directed against the office of Moses and Aaron: 'All the congregation are holy . . . why do you exalt yourselves above the assembly?' In Num. 20.1ff. the Priestly version of the Meribah story explains why Moses' office was cut off before his entering into the promised land. In Num. 17.16ff. Aaron's office is justified by the blossoming of his rod. This development in the murmuring tradition is not surprising from what we know of the Priestly interest in the Mosaic office and the tent of meeting. Indeed, the early tradition of the tent of meeting, such as those in Ex. 34.29ff., were treasured in Priestly circles.

Again, several of the stories within the P source have only secondarily been brought into the cycle of the murmuring tradition. This move confirms the later tendency already found in the Deuteronomist to expand the scope of the murmuring tradition. In the Korah incident of Num. 16, the story has been shaped by means of several of the stereotyped features of the murmuring tradition. There is the gathering against Moses, the complaint, the judgment, and the intercession. But the structure of the basic story appears quite distinct from either Pattern I or II. The central element is rather a contest between Korah and Moses which calls for a divine decision. Originally the story is more closely akin in its form to Elijah on Mount Carmel (I Kings 18) than to the murmuring stories. The parallel of the story in Num. 16 is also basically a contest, but lacks, by and large, the elements of the murmuring tradition. Again, it seems quite clear that P has fashioned the spy story tradition of Num. 14 into the form of the murmuring tradition. The earlier form of the J story assigns quite a different function originally to this material.

The Priestly writer does not follow the scheme of assigning stories of Pattern I to the period before the Golden Calf. However, there is a marked tendency to stress the element of rebellion in Israel's complaint. Both in the manna and Meribah stories the disobedience is emphasized, even though the basic pattern of divine aid in need is retained (Ex. 16.20; Num. 20.10).

Three other late usages of the murmuring tradition appear in Ezek. 20, Ps. 106, and Neh. 9 (cf. Coats' thorough discussion). All these passages share the Deuteronomic and Priestly tendency to expand the elements of rebellion and to make rebellion an overarching category by which to interpret the exile and other disasters. Certainly Ezekiel's use of the tradition which projects the rebellion and idolatry back into Egypt before the exodus is the most radical application of the tradition, but even here the message of the prophet issues in the preaching of forgiveness and the new exodus.

There is one final issue to consider, one with which we began the discussion of the murmuring tradition. How is one to understand the positive tradition of the wilderness which appears especially in such passages as Deut. 32.10ff.; Hos. 2.16 (EVV 14); 11.1ff.; 13.4ff.; Jer. 2.1ff.? The older explanation of a 'nomadic ideal' which influenced the prophets (cf. Budde, *op. cit.*, and Flight, *op. cit.*, for the classic presentation of this position) has not held up under closer scrutiny (cf. Talmon, *op. cit.*). More recently, R. Bach (*op. cit.*) has developed the thesis of a special 'Fundtradition' in which Israel's election stemmed from Yahweh's discovery of her as a foundling in the wilderness. Although von Rad and others have tended to accept Bach's theory as valid, it remains a real question whether the evidence is adequate for positing such a distinct tradition. I tend to feel that just as Ezekiel used his great freedom in intensifying the negative side of the murmuring tradition, other prophets, such as Hosea and Jeremiah, isolated the positive elements which had always been there for a particular purpose. In contrast to the national corruption which had set in through contact with the culture of the land, these prophets contrasted the uncontaminated life in the wilderness before the possession of the land. In my judgment, there is not sufficient evidence to suggest that an election tradition with just a positive interpretation of the wilderness ever existed by itself.

The chapters which immediately follow in Exodus, namely 15.22–17.7, are usually grouped together because of their related subject matter. The stories relate to the divine supply of water, bread, and meat. However, there are an amazing number of complex problems which caused Bacon to describe this section as affording 'the most difficult problems hitherto met in the analysis' (p. 80). Briefly to outline some of the initial problems:

1. The story of Marah contains a play on the word Massa, the account of which appears to come in ch. 17. However, in ch. 17 the water miracle is located at Massah-Meribah which would imply a duplicate name for one place. This is perplexing since Deut. 6.16 and 9.22 treat them as two different localities. In Num. 20.1–13 there is another water miracle story and the place is also called Meribah.

2. The chronology is also very confusing. Ch. 17 gives the impression that Meribah was reached before Sinai, but in Num. 20 it is associated with an event which followed. Again, 17.6 mentions Horeb before Sinai is reached, whereas certain features of the manna story would appear to place this story after Sinai (16.34).

Because of the complexity of these problems, the exegesis will attempt to deal with the wilderness wanderings stories on the level of both the early development and the final form of the narrative.

XI

THE WATERS OF MARAH

15.22–27

C. Brekelmans, 'Die sogenannten deuteronomistischen Elemente in Genesis bis Numeri: ein Beitrag zur Vorgeschichte der Deuteronomiums', *Suppl. VT* 15, 1966, pp. 90–96; G. W. Coats, *Rebellion in the Wilderness*, Nashville 1968, pp. 47ff.; O. Eissfeldt, 'Zwei verkannte militär-technische Termini', *VT* 5, 1955, pp. 235–8; V. Fritz, *Israel in der Wüste*, Marburg 1970, pp. 37ff.; H. Gressmann, *Mose und seine Zeit*, 1913, pp. 121ff.; H. Gunkel, *Das Märchen im Alten Testament*, Tübingen 1921, pp. 96ff.; J. Hempel, 'Ich bin der Herr, dein Arzt: Ex. 15, 26', *ThLZ* 82, 1957, cols. 809–26; B. O. Long, *The Problem of Etiological Narrative in the Old Testament*, BZAW 108, 1968, pp. 6, 12; E. Meyer, *Die Israeliten und ihre Nachbarstämme*, Halle 1906, reprinted Darmstadt 1967, pp. 100ff.; L. Ruppert, 'Das Motif der Versuchung durch Gott in vordeuteronomischer Tradition', *VT* 22, 1972, pp. 55–63.

15 ²²Then Moses had Israel set out from the Reed Sea and they went into the wilderness of Shur. They travelled three days in the wilderness without finding water. ²³Then they came to Marah, but they were not able to drink the water at Marah because it was bitter. That is why the place was called Marah. ²⁴So the people murmured against Moses, saying 'What are we to drink?' ²⁵He cried to the LORD and he directed him to a tree, and he threw it into the water, and the water became sweet.

There he made for them a statute and an ordinance and there he put them to the test. ²⁶He said, 'If you will really pay attention to the voice of the LORD, your God, and do what is right in his eyes, and give ear to his commandments, and keep all his statutes, I will not inflict upon you all the diseases which I have inflicted on the Egyptians; for I am the LORD, your healer.'

²⁷ Then they came to Elim, where there were twelve springs of water and seventy palm trees, and they encamped there beside the water.

1. *Textual and Philological Notes*

15.22. The Hebrew style of the first phrase is unusual with the hiphil form of the verb and the term Israel.

24. The term *lûn* (murmur) appears for the first time here, and with the exception of Josh.9.18 and Ps.59.16, is confined to the wilderness wanderings in Exodus and Numbers. The etymology of the verb is uncertain (cf. Coats, *op. cit.*, pp.22f. for the various suggestions). The word denotes a grumbling and muttered complaint. Coats' attempt to find in the word an overt, hostile reaction of rebellion tends to read the content of the larger context into the word itself.

25. *wayyôrēhû*, 'he directed him'. The MT understands the verb as a hiphil of *yrh*. The Samar. reads *wayyar'ēhû* and the LXX ἔδειξεν. Gressmann's insistence (*op. cit.*, p.122) that the sentence can only mean 'er lehrte ihn Holz' is grammatically too rigid and dictated by *religionsgeschichtliche* factors. The MT should be retained with the meaning 'point out, shew' as indicated by the parallel passages (Prov.6.13; Job 6.24).

Both NAB and Orlinsky (*Notes*, p.171) suggest the smoother translation 'a piece of wood', but this rendering does conceal a certain ambiguity within the Hebrew text. Thus Hyatt (*Exodus*, p.172) thinks only a shrub was intended.

25b. For the double use of *šām* cf. Mandelkern, *VT Concordantiae Hebr. et Chald.*, 1937, p.1189, for the frequency. In the majority of cases, a place name, which serves as the antecedent, precedes immediately. On the syntactical problem regarding the subject of the verb, cf. the discussion under 'literary problems'. H. Orlinsky (*Notes*, p.171) translates *ḥōq ûmišpāṭ* as a hendiadys: 'a fixed rule'. This move seems unwise in the light of the distinct nuances of both legal terms. Cf. the literature cited under 'Detailed Notes'.

Eissfeldt (*op. cit.*) has argued that the verb *nissāhû* is a hitherto undetected military term with the meaning of 'to train', but the theory is not supported by the context of the narrative.

2. *Literary and Traditio-Historical Analysis*

There are several difficult source-critical problems which have continued to puzzle commentators. Noth attributes the itinerary in vv.22aα and 27 to P, even though the initial formulae are strange to P. It is equally possible that the earlier source had elements of an itinerary. Verses 22b–25a stem from an earlier source, probably from J, even though there is some inner friction in v.23 caused by the etiology.

The majority of recent critical commentators feel confident in assigning vv.25b–26 to the Deuteronomist. They argue their case from the language and the poor syntactical connection between vv.25a and 25b. Indeed, it is not clear who the subject of v.25b is. However, there is enough evidence pointing in another direction at least to give one pause before going along with the consensus. First of all, as E. Meyer had already noted, the connection between the 'healing' of the water and 'Yahweh your healer' (v. 26) seems to be a very ancient one and not simply redactional. Secondly, the form of the speech in v. 26 is difficult to explain simply as a Deuteronomic addition. The verb 'to test' in v. 25 must have God as the subject and not Moses. Nevertheless, the oracle begins by addressing God in the third person as if Moses were the speaker, then it shifts to the first person. In Deuteronomic speeches there is frequently lack of consistency in the use of third and first person (cf. 7.4; 11.13; 17.3; 28.20; 29.5), but the pattern of this inconsistency is the exact reverse of this passage. Moses is the speaker, but he lapses into the first person. Here God is the speaker and the oracle begins with the third person. Finally, the theme of God's testing or proving Israel recurs quite frequently in the early sources of Exodus (16.4; 20.20) and is not necessarily Deuteronomic.

Although I would not agree with Rudolph (p. 32) in holding that the connection between vv. 25a and 25b is a smooth one, I think that there is evidence to suggest that the Deuteronomic writer has expanded a *Vorlage* which was present in the J account (so also Gressmann). In other words, the J source had already interpreted the healing of the water as a form of testing and made the connection with Yahweh as Israel's healer. The Deuteronomic editor tried to make more explicit the nature of the laws by which Israel was tested by his expansion in v. 26.

The traditio-historical problem of the passage is equally difficult. Theories based on comparative religion have tended to play as decisive a role as have those from form-critical research. E. Meyer and H. Gressmann both saw the passage as an early legend (*Sage*) in which God was a 'healer God'. Even less convincing were those who tried to find a tree cult in the original story (W. R. Smith). M. Noth envisioned a local etiological story at the base of the tradition which once related how bitter water had been made sweet. At a later stage the figure of Moses was attached to the etiology. G. Coats, in turn, has attempted to refine Noth's theory and to define more clearly how the original etiology was expanded and then joined to the murmuring tradition. In my judgment, neither Noth nor Coats has correctly analyzed the role of the etiology. The etiological form is limited to the naming of Marah (cf. Long). However, this element is not the primary tradition of the story, but a secondary expansion, closely resembling a gloss. The primary tradition is not etiological in form. If it had been, the name would have reflected the new state of the spring following the miracle, rather than the old.

There is no evidence that an original local tale formed the basis of the tradition. Rather, the story follows Pattern I of the murmuring tradition (cf. above) and relates the help of Yahweh in the face of dire need for water. However, it is also clear that a motif (not a tradition!) common to the Ancient Near Eastern world was employed (cf. II Kings 2.19ff.). Yahweh did not effect a miracle through his word; rather he instructed Moses in the use of a special tree by which to work the transformation. Of course, on the basis of the content several commentators have projected a local etiology, but there is no support for this theory from the form of the story itself.

There is one further problem which has played a significant role in the history of exegesis. In Ex. 17 the etiology of the name of Massah (v. 1) is clearly a secondary interpolation into the present Meribah story. But the name Massah is connected with the verb 'to test' (*nsh*) which occurs in v. 25b of the Marah story. Therefore, it has been reasoned, the Massah tradition has been somehow fused with the Marah tradition. Both Wellhausen and Bäntsch thought it to be of great importance that here was a fossil of an older law-giving tradition prior to that of Sinai (cf. Deut. 33.8ff.). This hypothesis cannot be ruled out of court, but there is insufficient evidence ever to settle the matter. In my judgment, the connection between the verb in v. 25 and Massah in 17.1 is probably accidental. The subject of the testing is certainly different in both passages. Rudolph's warning (p. 32) is well taken against the tendency to see subtle connections between all these various traditions.

3. Old Testament Context

The departure of the Israelites from the glorious rescue at the sea is effected with the minimum of words. The narrative plunges immediately into the new crisis, and there is no indication that the writer feels he is introducing a new type of material. A brief itinerary notice connects the Reed Sea with the Wilderness of Shur. After three days without water the disappointment in finding the water at Marah unpalatable is fully understandable. The people's discontent – it is certainly not a rebellion – is turned against Moses. Here for the first time the writer introduces the theme of the people's reaction with the term 'murmur' which is to become the stereotyped reaction throughout the wilderness wanderings. The entire action is related in the briefest possible manner. Moses cries to God. God directs him to a tree. He throws the tree into the water and the bitter water is transformed into sweet.

The story is reminiscent of certain features in the plague tradition, in which the miracle is effected by means of a particular use of an ordinary rod (4.2), or by changing a common substance into something uncommon (9.8). Older commentators (Clericus, Rosenmüller) debated the question whether the surprising transformation of the water had taken place because of God's direct intervention or by means of the tree which worked naturally once its properties were known. But the question arises out of the seventeenth-century conflict which contrasted the natural world with the supernatural. In the biblical story the fact that God provided water in time of great need was an evident sign of his ability to sustain his people. Nevertheless, the tradition is equally clear that the help was mediated to Moses in the form of a divine disclosure of the special properties of a tree. The writer of Exodus does not feel any tension in this means of meeting the need, nor did he show any inclination to pursue the modern, scientifically oriented question. Only at a much later period did a Hebrew sage explicitly seek to resolve the tension by suggesting that God had made 'water sweet with a tree in order that his power be known and he gave skill to men that he might be glorified in his marvellous works' (Sirach 38.5).

The interest in the biblical narrative rather falls on interpreting the significance of this event for Israel's faith. Old Testament scholars disagree among themselves as to whether the interpretation in vv. 25b–26 is of the same age as the first part of the story or stems from a subsequent editing (cf. the discussion in section 2). Indeed, the sequence of these verses does remain exceedingly difficult regardless of how one decides the critical question.

The initial difficulty is that v. 25b introduces a subject which has no apparent connection with the preceding story of the water except that it had the same geographical setting. The twice repeated 'there' is obviously Marah. But the writer does not disclose what he means by 'a statute and an ordinance'. The nature of the testing is somewhat clarified by what follows in v. 26, but again it does not seem to relate to anything in the earlier story. Perhaps one would be inclined to argue that vv. 25b–26 formed an independent unit without any connection with the water incident at all were it not for the reference to Yahweh as the healer. It would appear, therefore, that the redactor of the passage did see a link between the healing of the water and this title.

The biblical writer seems to be drawing a comparison between what happened with the water of Marah and the testing of the people, although this point is never spelled out. The connection is only made explicit in the final verse. Yahweh healed the water, but he now offers a far greater promise. He has revealed himself (I am Yahweh) as 'your healer' from all the diseases of Egypt. But the promise is made conditional on Israel's obedience to God's will, éxpressed in the statutes and ordinances. What then is the element of comparison provided by the first part of the passage? Perhaps it is that Israel had been tested and had responded in unbelief. The motif of murmuring is evidence that she had failed the test. The author does not belabor his point, but uses the story as a parenetic background for his renewed challenge to obedience and promise of healing.

Detailed Notes

15.22. On the problem of the Reed Sea, cf. 13.18.

The wilderness of Shur is the area which is on the eastern border of Egypt and is mentioned elsewhere in the Old Testament (Gen. 16.7; 20.1; 25.18; I Sam. 15.7; 27.8). In the itinerary of Num. 33.8 the wilderness is called Etham. The name has often been connected with the Hebrew *šûr* which means wall, but this derivation is very uncertain. The older theories are discussed in *HDB* IV, pp. 510. For more recent studies cf. *IDB* IV, p. 343, and Fritz, *op. cit.*, pp. 37f.

'three days'. Cf. J. B. Bauer, 'Drei Tage', *Biblica* 39, 1958, pp. 354–8.

23. Marah. The location is uncertain, although there have been many efforts on the part of travellers to suggest appropriate sites. Cf. the theories of Burckhardt and Palmer discussed by Driver, p. 142.

On the etiological formula cf. J. Fichtner, *VT* 6, 1956, pp. 372–96; B. O. Long, *op. cit.*, p. 6ff.

25. On the legal terminology cf. R. Hentschke, *Satzung und Setzender*, Stuttgart 1963, p. 29; G. Liedke, *Gestalt und Bezeichnung alttestamentlicher Rechtsätze*, WMANT 39, 1971, pp. 180ff.

26. On the diseases of Egypt, cf. Deut. 7.15; 28.21ff., 27ff. and the article by Hempel, *op. cit.*

XII

MANNA AND QUAILS

16.1-36

F. S. BODENHEIMER, 'The Manna of Sinai', *BA* 10, 1947, pp. 1–6; G. COATS, *Rebellion in the Wilderness*, Nashville 1968, pp. 83ff.; J. COPPENS, 'Les Traditions relatives à la manne dans Exode xvi', *Estudios Eclesiásticos* 34, 1960, pp. 473–89; V. FRITZ, *Israel in der Wüste*, Marburg 1970, pp. 42ff., 70ff.; E. GALBIATI, *La Struttura letteraria dell' Esodo*, 1956, pp. 164–75; P. HAUPT, 'Manna, Nectar and Ambrosia', *American Journal of Philology* 43, 1922, pp. 247ff.; A. HEISING, 'Exegese und Theologie der Alt- und Neutestamentlichen Speisewunder', *Zeitschrift für Katholische Theologie* 86, 1964, pp. 80–96; W. HERRMANN, 'Götterspeise und Göttertrank in Ugarit und Israel', *ZAW* 72, 1960, pp. 205–16; A. KAISER, 'Neue naturwissenschaftliche Forschungen auf der Sinaihalbinsel', *ZDPV* 53, 1930, pp. 63–75; A. KUENEN, 'Manna und Wachteln', *Gesammelte Abhandlungen zur biblischen Wissenschaft*, Freiburg 1894, pp. 276ff.; B. J. MALINA, *The Palestinian Manna Tradition*, Leiden 1968; G. VON RAD, *Die Priesterschrift im Hexateuch*, Stuttgart 1938, pp. 54ff.; K. WERNICKE, 'Ambrosia', in F. Pauly, G. Wissowa (eds.), *Real-Encyclopädie der classischen Altertumswissenschaft* I, Stuttgart 1894, pp. 1809–11; E. M. YAMAUCHI, 'The "Daily Bread" Motif in Antiquity', *Westminster Theol. Journal* 28, 1966, pp. 145ff.

16 [1]The entire community of the Israelites set out from Elim and came to the wilderness of Sin, which is between Elim and Sinai, on the fifteenth day of the second month after their departure from the land of Egypt. [2]The whole community of the Israelites murmured against Moses and Aaron in the wilderness, [3]and the Israelites said to them, 'If only we had died by the hand of the LORD in the land of Egypt, when we sat by the fleshpots and ate our fill of bread. For you have brought us out into this wilderness to starve this whole congregation to death!'

4 And the LORD said to Moses, 'I am going to rain bread from heaven for you, and the people shall go out and gather each day a day's portion, that I may test them, whether they will follow my instructions or not. [5]On the sixth day, when they prepare what they have brought in, it shall be twice as much as they have ordinarily gathered.'

6 So Moses and Aaron said to all the Israelites, 'In the evening you will know that it was the LORD who brought you out of the land of Egypt. 7And in the morning you will see the glory of the LORD because he has heard your grumblings against the LORD. For who are we that you should grumble against us?' 8And Moses said, 'When the LORD gives to you in the evening meat to eat and in the morning your fill of bread, because the LORD has heard the grumblings which you utter against him – what are we? Your murmurings are not against us, but against the LORD.'

9 Then Moses said to Aaron, 'Say to the entire Israelite community, "Draw near to the LORD for he has heard your murmurings."' 10But while Aaron was speaking to the whole Israelite community, they looked toward the desert, and suddenly the glory of the LORD appeared in the cloud. 11The LORD said to Moses, 12'I have heard the murmurings of the Israelites; say to them, "Between dusk and dark you shall eat meat, and in the morning you shall have your fill of bread; then you shall know that I am the LORD your God."'

13 In the evening quail came up and covered the camp and in the morning there was a layer of dew about the camp. 14When the layer of dew lifted, there appeared on the surface of the wilderness a fine flaky substance, as fine as frost, on the ground. 15When the Israelites saw it, they said to one another, 'What is it?', for they did not know what it was. Moses said to them, 'It is the bread which the LORD has given you to eat. 16This is what the LORD has commanded: "Gather as much of it as each of you requires to eat, an omer to a person, according to the number of persons there are, each man providing for those in his own tent."' 17The Israelites did so; they gathered, some more, some less. 18But when they measured it by the omer, those who had gathered much had nothing over, and those who had gathered little were not short. Each person had gathered what he could eat. 19And Moses said to them, 'No one is to leave any of it until morning.' 20But they did not listen to Moses; some left part of it until morning, and it bred worms and stank, and Moses was angry with them. 21Morning after morning they gathered it, each as much as he needed to eat; and when the sun grew hot, it would melt.

22 On the sixth day they gathered twice the amount of bread, two omers apiece; and when all the leaders of the assembly came and told Moses, 23he said to them, 'This is what the LORD has commanded: "Tomorrow is a day of sacred rest, a holy sabbath to the LORD; bake what you want to bake, and boil what you want to boil, and all that is left put aside to be kept until morning."' 24So they put it aside until morning as Moses had commanded them. It did not spoil, nor were there any worms in it. 25Then Moses said, 'Eat it today, for today is a sabbath to the LORD; today you will not find it in the field. 26Six day

you shall gather it, but on the seventh day, which is the sabbath, there will be none.' 27On the seventh day some of the people went out to gather and they found none. 28The LORD said to Moses, 'How long will you people refuse to keep my commands and my instructions? 29You see that the LORD has given you the sabbath. Therefore on the sixth day he gives you bread for two days. Let every man stay where he is; let no man venture out on the seventh day.' 30So the people rested on the seventh day.

31 The house of Israel named it manna; it was like coriander seed, white, and it tasted like a wafer made with honey. 32Moses said, 'This is what the LORD has commanded: "Let one omer be kept for future generations in order that they may see the bread with which I fed you in the wilderness when I brought you out of the land of Egypt".' 33And Moses said to Aaron, 'Take a jar, and put an omer of manna in it, and place it before the LORD, to be kept for future generations.' 34Aaron did as the LORD had commanded Moses, and placed it before the Testimony for safe keeping. 35The Israelites ate manna forty years, until they entered a land where they could settle; they ate the manna until they came to the border of the land of Canaan. 36(The omer is a tenth of an ephah.)

1. *Textual and Philological Notes*

16.2. 'they murmured'. The *kethib* points the verb as a hiphil, the *qere* as a niphal. In other places the reading of the *kethib and qere* is reversed as in Ex. 16.7 and Num. 14.36. The reason for this is unknown.

4. *leḥem*, bread. Although the Hebrew term for bread can have the wider connotation of food (cf. Judg. 13.16; I Sam. 14.24; Ps. 136.25), the narrow meaning of bread should here be retained (*contra* Ibn Ezra, Kalisch, Cassuto, etc.). Cf. the exegesis for the issue at stake.

5. *hēkînû*. Wellhausen suggested emending this verb to *kûl* which provides the somewhat better sense: 'to measure out'. NJPS tacitly emends in its translation 'apportion', in spite of alleged support from parallels for this wider semantic range (Orlinsky, *Notes*, p.71.)

The theory of Gressmann (p. 128) that the manna suddenly 'became' double in quantity is ruled out by the Hebrew, which would require the preposition *le*.

6. There is no significant difference in meaning between the two ways of saying 'at evening' in vv.6 and 8. Cf. *G–K* §112 oo for the use of the *waw* after a temporal expression.

7–8. The text of these two verses appears to have suffered a dittography. Moreover, v.8 is an incomplete sentence with a curious double use of the infinitive construct. However, the versions follow the MT and offer no assistance. Most commentators tend to eliminate v.8 either as a textual conflation or as a literary gloss. The evidence is inconclusive.

14. The term *meḥuspās* which is a *hapax* is uncertain. The older interpretation of 'round' is guesswork. It is usually related to an Arabic cognate meaning 'scale-like'. (Cf. *G-K* §55 k). There is no reason to suspect that the text is corrupt. The LXX does not offer a translation when it substitutes the phrase 'like white coriander seed'.

15. G. Vermes, 'He is the Bread' (see p. 293 below) claims that the Targum Neofiti reads: 'He (Moses) is the bread which the Lord has given you . . .' I agree with Meeks (*JBL* 91, 1972, p. 59) that this is not the case. A scribal error is involved. *mān hū'*. The etymology of the interrogative *mān* has been much discussed since it is a form unknown in Hebrew. The earlier attempts to link it with Arabic or even Egyptian have been rightly rejected. *Mān* means 'who' in Arabic and Aramaic, and not 'what'. The more recent attempt to relate it to Ugaritic as an old Canaanite form (Fensham, *Exodus*, p. 96) is similarly unconvincing. The term offers a popular etymology which is related by sound to the term being explained. Although syntactically the phrase could be understood as an indicative: 'It is manna', the context does not support this interpretation (*contra* Rashi, Ibn Ezra). Malina (*op. cit.*, p. 56) remains undecided whether Targum Onk. supports the indicative reading or not.

16. 'each according to his eating'. Cf. Ex. 12.4.

20. W. S. McCullough's conjecture (*IDB* IV, p. 878) that the worms are really 'ants' is not a philological judgment.

22. On the use of paronomasia in Hebrew, cf. T. Vriezen, *Festschrift für A. Bertholet*, Tübingen 1950, pp. 498–512.

30. Commentators are divided as to whether the verb should be translated 'they rested', or as a denominative, 'they kept the sabbath'. The latter usage is much clearer in Lev. 23.32.

31. The LXX and several Hebrew manuscripts read 'children of Israel' rather than the unusual expression 'house of Israel'. Still the MT is to be preferred.

33. *ṣinṣeneṭ*. The word is a hapax. The LXX renders it 'vessel', but the root *ṣnn* is cognate with the Aramaic *niṣṣā'* = basket.

2. *Literary and Traditio-historical Analysis*

A. *Source Criticism*

In spite of the several characteristic signs which indicate the presence of different sources in ch. 16, the exact division into sources has never been satisfactorily accomplished. At best one can claim to have traced the broad lines of the division. The literary problems of the chapter are as follows: (i) There are a variety of inner tensions, duplicates, and anomalies. Note vv. 6–8 in which Moses and Aaron deliver to the people a message from Yahweh which Moses then receives in vv. 11f. (ii) The relation of the manna to the quail seems strikingly different from Num. 11, but again with evidence of a complex, inner relationship between the stories. (iii) The gathering, preparation, and description of the manna seem difficult to harmonize into a consistent picture, particularly in relation to the Sabbath. (iv) There are several striking anachronisms (cf. v. 34).

The majority of critical scholars (Bäntsch, Gressmann, Driver, Noth) assign the main bulk of the chapter to P and the few fragments which remain to J. The argument turns on the fact that Ex. 16 shows many of the characteristic signs of the Priestly writer and is distinct from the JE account of Num. 11. At the same time, the earlier source in Num. 11 presupposes an account of the first giving of manna which is most probably to be found in Ex. 16. These scholars are basically agreed in assigning to J vv. 4–5 and 27–30, although admitting that the later verses do not show much friction in the present context (cf. Bäntsch, p. 154). There remains some disagreement whether or not J is also present in the etymology (vv. 13b–15, 31).

In spite of this agreement among a significant group of scholars, the fact that other scholars disagree radically must be taken into account. On the one hand, Kuenen, in an impressive article (*op. cit.*), made a case for seeing in the chapter only the P source with secondary reworking and glosses. On the other hand, Rudolph (cf. Smend and Eissfeldt) has argued for a basic J source with secondary glosses. The issue does not seem to be easily resolved. As a working hypothesis I accept the following source divisions as the most probable:

P = 1–3, 6–13a, 16–26, 32–35aα, b; J = 4–5, 13b–15, 21b, 27–31, 35aβ. Verse 36 is a gloss and can hardly be assigned to a source with certainty. The question of a Deuteronomic redaction in vv. 4b, 28 is discussed below.

In recent years there have been several attempts to solve the literary problems within Ex. 16 by denying the presence of sources. Benno Jacob (*Das Zweite Buch der Tora*, pp. 647ff.) begins with a sharp polemic against the critics who have 'cut up the chapter without understanding its intention'. But when Jacob offers his own alternative solution, it very much resembles a modern midrash. He attempts to avoid the difficulties in the sequence of vv. 1–12 by assuming a speech of Moses before v. 4. He interprets the verb in v. 11 as a pluperfect which he assigns to a period prior to v. 4. Finally, he suggests that the faulty Hebrew syntax in v. 8 is intentional in order to demonstrate that indeed Moses is not a good speaker and requires Aaron's help!

Cassuto's opposition to the theory of sources in the Pentateuch is well-known through his book, *The Documentary Hypothesis*. In his Exodus commentary he attempts to explain the present form of the chapter without recourse to sources, although he reckons with earlier traditions which the author of Exodus employed. His method is

hardly convincing. First, Cassuto resorts to the familiar, but questionable contrast between 'Greek and Hebrew mentality' to account for
inconsistencies. Next, he makes constant use of psychological sub-
terfuge by translating *wayyŏ'mer* in v. 8 as 'he thought to himself', or
interpreting vv. 11-12 as 'the Lord agreeing with Moses' thought'.
Lastly, he avoids many of the real difficulties by denying any significant relation between Ex. 16 and Num. 11.

A more interesting recent attempt at solving the chapter's problems without sources is that proposed by B. J. Malina (*op. cit.*).
Malina tries to analyze the component parts of the chapter by means
of an elaborate stylistic study. Initially he divides the chapter into
four narratives 'from the viewpoint of the cast of characters'. For
example, 'Moses, Aaron, and the whole congregation: vv. 1-2,
3c, 6-10', 'Moses and the children of Israel: 3ab, 11-18, 31, 35a', etc.
But these divisions are highly artificial and arbitrary. It makes little
sense to separate v. 3a into a 'Moses and the children of Israel'
narrative and v. 3c into a 'Moses, Aaron, and the whole congregation' narrative. As a result, obvious connections are pulled apart, and
disparate units joined in the analysis. Malina's stylistic analysis on the
basid of word patterns is even less convincing. Note in his analysis of
vv. 19f. the alleged parallelism between *'ªlēhem* in v. 19 and the
'ªlēhem in v. 20. Again, the loose categories chosen in analyzing
vv. 23-24 allow for no objective literary controls of the material.

We conclude therefore that these three attempts to solve the
literary problems of the chapter without the use of sources have not
proved successful.

B. *The Literary Problem of vv. 1-12*

The special problem of understanding the logical sequence of the
first twelve verses in the chapter has long been felt (cf. Rashi, Ibn
Ezra). Briefly stated, the problem is as follows: The initial response
of God to the people's murmuring for food makes no reference to the
complaint, but promises Moses bread from heaven. Moses and Aaron
then in vv. 6ff. inform the people that Yahweh has heard their
murmuring and that he will send flesh in the evening and bread in
the morning. Then in v. 10 Yahweh appears in a theophany and
informs Moses of a message which he is to pass on to the people.
However, it consists of an exact parallel to that which Moses has
already made known to them previously.

In the history of exegesis two major types of solution to the problem have been proposed. The first type attempts to retain the present sequence of verses and overcome the apparent anomalies by interpretation. Kalisch's attempt (*Exodus*, p. 292) is characteristic of the first approach. He argues that *leḥem* (bread) in v. 4 should be taken in its wider sense of food in general. This move seeks to bridge the sharp discontinuity between vv. 4f. and 6f. Then vv. 4f. become a promise to Moses concerning the manna and quail which was subsequently ratified by God in 10–12. But if the meat is included in v. 4, this would mean that it is promised as a continuous gift along with the manna. This implication is never drawn in Ex. 16 and raises enormous difficulties in relation to Num. 11. Cassuto's interpretation is similar with certain additional refinements.

Another elaborate attempt to avoid the logical difficulties of the passage by interpretation is offered by Galbiati (*op. cit.*). His approach is typical of a new type of literary patternism, which Catholic scholars, particularly in Rome, have developed (cf. Lohfink, *Das Hauptgebot*, Rome 1963, pp. 182, 195; B. J. Malina, *The Palestinian Manna Tradition*, pp. 3ff.). Galbiati's scheme for finding a unity in the passage is as follows (p. 167):

16.1–3, Preamble

A 4–5; Yahweh announces manna and gives *Instruction*

B 6–7: Moses and Aaron announce the two miracles with *unclear words*

C 8: Moses announces them with *exact words*

X 9–10: Theophany

C¹ 11–12: Yahweh announces the two miracles with *unclear words*

B¹ 13–15a: (no correspondence possible) fulfillment of miracle

A¹ 15b–21: Moses gives *Instruction*

In my judgment, Galbiati's pattern suffers from several major weaknesses. First of all, a rough correspondence between parts has been achieved by offering a conceptual abstraction from a verse, such as 'unclear words'. There is no indication whatever from the text that any contrast between clear and less clear was intended. Secondly, unessential features are set in parallel, while obvious parallels, such as the meat and bread of v. 3 and the theme of murmuring, are omitted. Finally, few of the genuine insights of the form-critical method have been exploited. There is no serious effort to relate form and function in this analysis.

The second major type of solution to the literary problems of the first twelve verses argues that the original order of the story has been disturbed and attempts to reconstruct the proper sequence by rearrangement of the verses. For example, Wellhausen proposed simply removing vv.6–8 as a disturbing interpolation. Kuenen, in turn, suggested a much more elaborate reconstruction of the order. His proposal for the original order was as follows: 1–3, 11–12, 9–10, 6, 7 (8 a gloss). In spite of its logical consistency there remain several problems with this approach. In the four close parallels in Numbers to the manna story (14.1ff.; 16.3ff.; 17.1ff. = EVV 16.26ff.; 20.3ff.), the speech of Yahweh to Moses (and Aaron) always *follows* the appearing of the glory, whereas in Kuenen's reconstruction Yahweh's speech precedes the theophany. For this reason, Bäntsch's subsequent modification (vv.4–5, 9–12, 6f.) is an improvement over Kuenen. However, none of the reconstructions attempts to explain how the dislocations occurred, nor is there a serious effort to understand the text in its final form.

How then is one to explain the disruption, if it is such, which brought about the disturbance in the logical order? One obvious explanation would be the combination of sources. As is generally recognized, vv.4–5 appear to be from an older source and stand isolated in their present position. The theme of bread from heaven does not link up with the cry of the people for bread and meat, nor is the subject matter of these verses picked up in what follows (vv.6–12). Nevertheless, these verses do introduce the theme of the sabbath and are, therefore, essential for a major element of the manna story. There is even an explicit reference to the promise in v.23. If the P writer wished to retain these verses, there is no better place in which they could be introduced than early in the narrative, even though the bread of 4f. does not match the meat-bread motif of vv.1–3, 6ff. One could then suppose that vv.9–12 were shifted from an original position following the murmuring to make room for vv.4–5. But right at this point, the theory of literary dislocation breaks down. There is no reason why the introduction of vv.4–5 should have affected the order of P. Logically vv.9–12 follow 4–5 better than 6–8. In sum, the problem of sequence lies within the P source and cannot be adequately explained by a multiple source theory.

To summarize the dilemma up to this point: the first approach has tried to find in the present order an intentional purpose of an author, but has not been able to mount a convincing case. The second approach has suggested that the present order is confused and arose from accidental damage to the text. Although this second proposal cannot be rejected out of hand, it is hardly satisfactory in that it cuts the 'Gordian knot', and does not succeed in untying it.

Is there any other alternative? In my judgment, the possibility that the order in Ex. 16.1–12 reflects a traditional sequence has not been adequately explored. In the introduction to the wilderness traditions certain traditional patterns were outlined. However, it is also clear that the Priestly writer has left his own stamp on the material, as is evident from those elements which are unique in his source. Accordingly, it is necessary to look first at the traditional patterns as they have been reflected in the Priestly source.

Num. 14 offers an interesting parallel to Ex. 16. There is the initial murmuring of the people (1–3), followed by a response by Joshua and and Caleb to the complaint (6ff.). Then the glory appears in a theophany (v. 10) and a divine oracle to Moses (and Aaron) is given (v. 26). Several formal elements in Num. 14 are of special interest. The response by Joshua and Caleb follows the murmuring and picks up elements within the complaint. The response resembles a disputation. Again, the theophany precedes the divine oracle to Moses. Finally, the form of the oracle consists in two parts. Yahweh first speaks to Moses (v. 27) and then he commissions Moses to address the people, 'Say to them'. The actual transmission of the message is not reported. In terms of its content the parallel between the divine oracles in Ex. 16 and Num. 14 is striking: 'I have heard the murmurings of the people of Israel' (16.12; Num. 14.27).

The parallels to the Priestly account of Korah in Num. 16 are equally impressive. There is the initial murmuring (v. 3), followed by Moses' disputation with Korah (vv. 5–7). Then the glory appears in a theophany (v. 19), and a divine oracle is given to Moses (v. 23). Most commentators feel that the Priestly account of Korah has been later expanded to include a subsequent debate within the Priestly tradition (cf. Noth). But these expansions follow the same pattern as the basic Priestly account, although in a fragmentary form which supplements the Priestly narrative. Notice the disputation of Moses which follows the murmuring (vv. 8ff.), then the speech of Yahweh to Moses (17.1 = EVV 16.36) which follows the theophany. Again the similarity in the content is remarkable. In his disputation with Korah (Num. 16.5), Moses also refers to the 'morning' (//Ex. 16.6) when 'Yahweh will show who he is' (// 16.6, 12).

The implications of this form-critical analysis of the P stories is evident. There is a traditional pattern shared by at least three stories which consists of a murmuring of the people, a disputation, a theophany and a divine word to Moses which instructs him to speak to the people. Moreover, the disputation picks up the major theme of the murmuring. Num. 14.26 parallels Ex. 16.11ff. in giving no explicit report that the oracle was delivered, but simply assumes it.

The traditional pattern of the Priestly source explains to a large measure the lack of logical sequence within Ex. 16.1–12. There is no warrant whatever for following Kuenen in placing the divine oracle to Moses (vv. 11–12) before the disputation (vv. 6–8). Nor is it any longer a disturbing factor that Yahweh's speech which climaxes the unit is addressed only to Moses. It is consistent for P that God only speaks through Moses (cf. Num. 16.40) and seldom is there an explicit mention of the actual delivery of the message.

The only significant friction which remains in the sequence of vv. 1–12 is the duplication between v. 8 and the divine oracle in v. 12. Verse 8 anticipates v. 12 in a way which is unusual in the Priestly pattern. Although it is not absolutely certain, this difficulty may lie in v. 8 which in its very syntax gives the impression of being a secondary comment on v. 7.

C. *The History of Traditions Problem*

Although the manna story of Ex. 16 reflects a complex literary history, the evidence is equally clear for a pre-literary, oral stage which did much to shape the tradition. The importance of investigating this level of the material emerges when one contrasts the purely literary research of Kuenen (1880) with the history of traditions approach of Gressmann (1913). Few would deny that a whole new set of questions have been opened up by the latter.

There is considerable evidence to suggest that at an early stage in the development of the tradition the manna and the quail stories circulated independently of one another. The relation of the two themes is clearly separated in Num. 11. Again, the quail theme has been worked into the manna story of Ex. 16 with considerable difficulty and is left in a fragmentary form (cf. 11.13). Moreover, the astonished reaction of Moses to Yahweh's promise of meat in Num. 11.18ff. would be quite inexplicable had the author of this story known of the gift of quail in Ex. 16.

The earliest tradition of the manna has not been retained in its full form. The tradition is presupposed in Num. 11 and a portion of it is included in vv. 7–9. Ex. 16 also probably has fragments of the early tradition in vv. 4f. and 14f. This early tradition seems to understand the manna as a gracious gift of divine sustenance. The form of the tradition appears akin to the structure which we have elsewhere designated as Pattern I (cf. Introduction to the wilderness wanderings). The people are in need; Moses intercedes and God supplies their want. It is not surprising that a parenetic note has already entered on this early level. God supplies Israel's need in the wilderness but Israel is being tested (v. 4).

But there is another early tradition, now found in Num. 11 (J), of the gift of quail. It is connected only loosely to the manna story. The people grow weary of the monotony of the manna and crave meat. Both the form and function of the quail story is different from that of the manna. The murmuring of the people calls forth God's anger. He sends the quail, but in the form of a judgment. In v. 20 the meat becomes loathsome from its sheer abundance; in v. 33 Yahweh strikes them with a plague. This frequent pattern of narrative we have designated earlier as Pattern II. Accordingly, the people murmur without a genuine need. God is angry and sends judgment. Moses intercedes and the punishment is abated.

Now it is interesting to observe that already in Ps. 78 – a psalm usually thought to precede the P tradition – the manna and the quail stories have been joined, but in a way different from the later P source in Ex. 16. In Ps. 78 both the manna and the quail stories are placed within the framework of Israel's disobedience (vv. 17ff.). Moreover, the Psalmist has combined elements from the two patterns. God is angry even when he sends the manna (Pattern II), but still it is a gracious gift (Pattern I). However, most significantly, the sending of the manna and the quail are set up as parallel events. In fact, God 'rains' both bread and meat (vv. 24 and 27).

When one now turns to the P account in Ex. 16, one again finds a combination of elements. The theme of the manna as a gracious gift has been retained. In fact, the theme has now been expanded by joining it with the quail theme. God's gift not only includes bread, but he sends meat in the evening and bread in the morning. Still one can see an unresolved tension in the text. The new P framework would imply that the quail was a continuous gift along with the manna, but this does not seem to be the intention of the redactor of the final chapter, for he does not pursue the quail theme further.

Still it is remarkable how far the P writer has moved from the tradition found in Num. 11 in seeing the quail as a gracious gift, which complements the manna and does not call forth judgment. Nevertheless the negative interpretation of the quail tradition which is reflected both in Num. 11 and Ps. 78 has left its mark on Ex. 16. The murmuring stems from rebellion against God (vv. 6ff.), but God is gracious in spite of unbelief.

Within Ex. 16 there are a variety of additional motifs which have attached themselves to the basic tradition. Especially the treatment of Gressmann brought out the variety of elements within the tradition. However, in my judgment, Gressmann's scheme of seeing numerous independent *Sagen*, slowly evolving from a primitive level to a more sophisticated stage, does not hold up under scrutiny. For example, it is very unlikely that there ever existed an independent story of how the shrewd Moses 'discovered the sabbath'. Rather, around the basic tradition there developed different motifs which elaborated on the story, such as the etiology of the name (v. 15), the differing descriptions of the manna (14.31), its relation to the sabbath (22ff.), and its preservation for future generations (32f.).

There is one more important aspect to the development of the tradition which has to be taken into consideration. Ever since ancient times (cf. Josephus) it has been known that there was a natural substance found in the wilderness of Northern Arabia and elsewhere which had a certain resemblance to the biblical manna. From the beginning of the nineteenth century closer attention was paid to this phenomenon (e.g. by J. L. Burckhardt, *Travels in Syria and the Holy Land*, London 1822; G. M. Ebers, *Ägypten und die Bücher Moses*, Leipzig 1867–8), until in the early decades of the twentieth century a completely modern scientific investigation accurately described the nature of the phenomenon (Kaiser, Bodenheimer; see note on v. 13, p. 292 below). There forms from the sap of the tamarisk tree a species of yellowish-white flake or ball, which results from the activity of a type of plant lice (*trabutina mannipara* and *najococcus serpentinus*). The insect punctures the fruit of the tree and excretes a substance from this juice. During the warmth of the day it melts, but it congeals when cold. It has a sweet taste. These pellets or cakes are gathered by the natives in the early morning and, when cooked, provide a sort of bread. The food decays quickly and attracts ants. The annual crop in the Sinai peninsula is exceedingly small and in some years fails completely.

The similarity in the description of the biblical manna and the natural desert substance certainly suggests some historical connection. The biblical tradition seems to reflect knowledge of desert 'manna' which has exerted an influence in shaping the tradition. In other words, the tradition shares the local color of the Egyptian wilderness which has remained basically unchanged up to the present time. This conclusion is not particularly surprising when one remembers other examples within the Exodus tradition (cf. plagues) which have made extensive use of local color. The description of the arrival of the quail is another example which matches well the environment of the Sinai peninsula. Reports of migratory birds flying up from Africa and arriving exhausted in the peninsula have been repeatedly verified in modern times. (Cf. the earlier accounts of the seventeenth and eighteenth century cited by Clericus and Rosenmüller.)

In itself the fact that elements of local color have a genuine, physical basis does not aid directly in establishing the age of the material or the historical reliability since these factors are continuous in the Sinai peninsula and adjoining areas. Nor do the modern parallels contribute anything essential in determining the genre of literature in which the tradition has been transmitted. In sum: although the modern parallels are of limited value for the history of traditions problem, they do pose basic philosophical and theological problems which will be dealt with in the final section of the exegesis.

3. Old Testament Context

[16.1–3] The section begins with an itinerary notice which links these various stories of the wilderness in a precise geographical and chronological sequence. The time is measured in terms of the departure from Egypt, the distance in terms of the goal of Sinai. The itinerary in Num. 33.9 mentions an extra stage on the Reed Sea between Elim and the wilderness of Sin. Travellers in the Near East have often attempted to determine the route of the Israelites. Because many felt that Burckhardt's identification of Elim in the Wadi Gharandel was convincing, the direction of the itinerary from Elim to Sinai has continued to pose an interesting problem. On the one hand, there were those who defended a northern route which led along the Wadi Ḥamr to an upland plain toward Jebel Musa. On the other hand, others proposed a coastal route, which proceeded along the plain of el-Markha, and up the Seiḥ Sidreh, and along the Wadi Mukatteb into Wadi Feiran. (Cf. Driver, *Exodus*, p. 145, for a map with the detailed suggested itinerary). However, it remains a real question how helpful these attempts are in bringing the biblical narratives into sharper focus. Not only is the location of Elim completely open to guesswork, but the fact that the location of Sinai itself is uncertain poses tremendous problems for the whole issue of the geography.

In spite of the fact that it remains impossible for the modern reader to trace the route with any certainty, it should not be forgotten that the biblical writer was extremely concerned to offer an itinerary. Indeed, the question as to why he maintained this interest in the exact itinerary is not easy to answer. It could be that the author had inherited an itinerary tradition which he simply included with his other material. Others have suggested the more sophisticated theory that interest in exact geography offered evidence for the author's concern to be writing history. In my judgment, the author's use of the itinerary stems from a modest, but deeply theological purpose. The tradition never tires of stressing the point that God *led* Israel through the wilderness. Israel did not just find its way. The concern with an exact itinerary bears witness to this divine guidance which lay at the heart of the tradition. Ex. 17.1: 'Israel moved by stages . . . according to the command of Yahweh.'

The motif of murmuring provides a major theme of the wilderness wanderings. Although the basic form of the complaint against Moses and Aaron is quite stereotyped (cf. Ex. 17.3f.; Num. 20.2ff.), the specific content of grumbling relates to some need which is dealt with within the story. In this chapter the murmuring focuses on the lack of food. Of course, it is beside the point to calculate with the midrashic commentators how many meals Israel had eaten from her supplies since leaving Egypt. Nor can the subsequent mention of cattle in Ex. 17.3 be made to play a significant role for this chapter. It is more important to recognize that the story does not begin with a genuine need as does 15.22 and 17.1. Rather, the author begins with the grumbling and thus casts the complaint immediately in a negative light. Israel is not presented as starving to death and crying out for bread. Instead, the people long for the 'fleshpots of Egypt' and for 'bread aplenty'. Num. 11.4 and Ps. 78.30 explicitly condemn the desire on the part of the people for meat as an illegitimate craving. Since the eating of meat was a rare delicacy for the common person in the Ancient Near East, the same negative judgment toward Israel's request is implied in Ex. 16. The theme of meat and bread which the murmuring introduces is then picked up in v. 6 and continues through the first half of the chapter.

The murmuring also introduces immediately the theme of the exodus from Egypt into the narrative. Usually the complaint is couched in the stereotyped question: 'Why did you bring us out of Egypt?' (17.3; Num. 11.20; 20.5, etc.). Here Moses is accused of causing the death of the nation by leading them out into the wilderness. In times of adversity it is a natural emotion to regret having ever undertaken such an enterprise. 'Surely we had it better in Egypt' (Num. 11.18). Yet is not more involved in the question than simply a natural reaction to difficult circumstances? The manner in which this complaint is taken up and dealt with in the subsequent narrative would suggest that the author did not take the complaint lightly. If God had made himself known in the deliverance from Egypt, then Israel's repudiation of this deliverance obviously struck at the heart of the relationship. Neh. 8.17 speaks of their disobedience as seeking 'to return to the bondage of Egypt' (cf. Acts 7.39). In short, the people's complaint is not a casual 'gripe', but unbelief which has called into question God's very election of a people.

[16.4–5] The reader is at first surprised to find that God's address to Moses takes only indirect notice of the people's craving for meat and bread. The sense of apparent disregard by God is strengthened when one sees the direct and even passionate reaction to the murmuring by Moses and Aaron in the verses which follow (vv. 6ff.). Nevertheless, these verses, even in their initial isolation from the immediate context, are essential for understanding the movement of the whole chapter. The promise of manna, the theme of testing, and the sabbath, are not only picked up again, but are skillfully intertwined into a coherent narrative. Verses 15f. appear to be an explicit reference to the earlier promise, even though most critics find different literary sources to be involved.

The promise is for 'bread to be rained from heaven'. Some commentators (e.g. Cassuto) have attempted to connect this promise of bread with the motif of meat and bread in vv. 3 and 18 by interpreting the bread (*leḥem*) in a wider sense as food. However, this move is not possible, and there is no indication that the later biblical tradition ever so understood it (cf. Ps. 78.24f.). Deut. 8 tends to contrast the manna with bread. God sent manna to teach Israel that 'man does not live by bread alone'. Ps. 78.25 characterizes the manna as the 'grain of heaven . . . bread of the angels'. Ex. 16 initially identifies the heavenly manna simply with bread (v. 15), but soon its miraculous quality is discovered. Two other elements of the promise of bread are added. The people are to gather a portion each day. It is given as a daily bread. Then on the sixth day the amount is doubled in preparation for the sabbath.

One final element in v. 4 is of importance. Along with the gift of bread goes a test: 'that I may prove them, whether they follow my instructions or not'. Because of the emphasis in Deut. 8 on manna as a test, most critical scholars (Bäntsch, Noth, etc.) have eliminated this phrase as a secondary expansion and alien to the earliest source. The historical critical issue is, however, certainly debatable. In my own judgment, a strong case can be made for seeing a parenetic element already in the earliest literary level (cf. the introduction to the wilderness wanderings). Be that as it may, the motif of God's testing his people certainly plays an essential role in the final form of the narrative. In v. 4 it is not stated precisely wherein the testing consists. Some commentators connect it with the immediately preceding command to gather a day's portion, while others would place it in conjunction with the following instructions relating to the sabbath. Actually the two directives belong together. In the narrative which follows, the people's disobedience involves both the failure to collect only one day's portion (v. 20) and seeking to collect on the sabbath (v. 27).

The theme of God's testing his people in vv. 4–5 has a wider significance for the whole chapter. The narrative begins with the people's finding fault. They think to put Moses, and ultimately God, to the test. The complaint in Ex. 17.7 makes the issue even more explicit. 'They put Yahweh to the test saying, "Is Yahweh among us or not?"' But vv. 4–5 make clear that Israel misunderstands what is really at stake in the gift of bread. Not God, but Israel is being tested. The critical point was made earlier that vv. 4–5 stand contextually isolated, both from what precedes and follows. Moreover, this lack of connection probably stemmed originally from the use of material from two different literary sources. But the effect of the verses, that is to say, their function within the present narrative, is to convey a hearty unconcern on God's part for Israel's complaint. God gives his gift on his own initiative and it carries with it its own conditions. Only later in confirmation of Moses' statement to the people does God graciously address himself to Israel's complaint.

[16.6–8] Most critical commentators feel that these verses have been displaced and should follow the command in vv.9–11 (so most recently Hyatt). In the preceding section the case has been made for maintaining the present sequence. It belongs to a traditional pattern for the disputation between the murmurers and the covenant officers to precede the theophany. The speech of Moses and Aaron which begins in v.6 is clearly a direct response to the people's murmuring. In a polemical style it takes up the issues raised point by point. First, the people had accused Moses of an ill intent in leading them into the desert. Moses replies that they would soon experience God who brought them out of Egypt. In vv.6 and 7 the emphasis does not seem to fall in the two separate times or the two separate verbs. Rather, the two verses are parallel and make one point. Shortly – evening and morning are used idiomatically – you will experience the power of God. But then, v.8 adds an appendix which seeks to function as a further clarification. God will make himself known specifically when he gives meat in the evening and bread in the morning. The reference to the two times and to the two signs are clearly distinguished.

Next Moses and Aaron take up the issue of the murmuring itself. The importance of the murmuring emerges clearly from the fact that it is referred to seven times in the next eight verses. The people had murmured against their leaders. Moses and Aaron throw the charge back in their faces. The people are fighting with God, not them. Of course, the real issue is that Israel was not unaware of this, but tried to conceal its unbelief in God by directing it to Moses. Moses will have none of this and strips away the pretext. 'Why us? Your fight is with God.'

[16.9–12] Following the disputation of Moses and Aaron with the people, Moses instructs Aaron to assemble the people 'to approach Yahweh' (*qirḇû lipnê*). The term is a technical one and refers to an encounter at a sanctuary (27.21; Num.16.17, etc.) Here the tent of meeting is undoubtedly meant (Num. 14.10; 16.19). While Aaron was still speaking to the congregation, the glory of God appeared in the cloud. The clause 'they looked toward the wilderness' has struck some commentators as strange since the people were already in the wilderness. But probably this is too logical a reaction. The expression is a somewhat clumsy indication of direction and should not be pressed for greater precision. Benno Jacob's comment: 'Man is never in the wilderness when he encounters God' (p.656), is a lovely thought, but an over-interpretation of this text. The real point of the verse is the sudden divine manifestation. In all the wilderness stories the people complain, men dispute, but finally God himself appears and brings the matter to a halt with a decisive judgment.

The address of God to Moses climaxes the section. He affirms that he has heard the people's murmuring. Their desire for meat and bread is still described as 'grumbling'. It is not acknowledged to be a real need. Yet the remarkable response is that God honors the murmuring anyway. He promises meat in the evening and bread in the morning. Nevertheless, he meets their request, not to satisfy their grumblings, but in order that Israel may learn who God is through this gracious act of sustenance.

One of the major difficulties in understanding God's speech to Moses has been that its content has been anticipated already in the earlier disputation with the people (vv. 6–8). But the point of the speech is not to provide new information, but rather to confirm what Moses has already promised. If in v. 4, it did not seem that God had heard the complaint, now he makes clear that he has. Moses' point has been confirmed: God is the one being accused and God is the one who will make himself known by his supplying Israel's need.

[**16.13–21**] The verses which follow report the fulfillment of the promise of food. 'In the evening' the quail came, and 'in the morning' the manna lay around the camp. But once the double wonder has been recorded to match the promise, all further concern with the quail disappears and the story goes on to treat the manna alone. The abrupt handling of the quail leaves the narrative in somewhat an unresolved tension which reflects the complex history of tradition behind the story. The balance between meat in the evening and bread in the morning at first leads the reader to picture both gifts alternating in a continuous cycle. Ps. 78 even extends the parallelism by having both the meat and the bread 'rained' from heaven (vv. 24 and 27). Although the text is never explicit and a certain ambiguity remains, the larger context does indicate that only the manna was understood as a continuing gift.

A description of the manna now follows. According to the Old Testament, dew was conceived of as falling from heaven (Deut. 33.28; Hag. 1.10), and therefore the manna came with it (Num. 11.9). Although the major adjective (*meḥuspās*) in v. 14 occurs nowhere else in the Old Testament, and is therefore uncertain, the term seems to denote a thin scaly substance which the writer compares with frost.

Then, much to the frustration of the scientifically-minded reader, the writer's attention shifts quickly from his brief description to offer an explanation of its name. The people react to the new phenomenon by saying to one another '*mān hû*'', which probably means 'What is it?' The additional comment: 'the people did not know . . .', indicates that the author understood the phrase to be a question which called to mind the Hebrew interrogative. This form of explaining a name is frequent in the Old Testament (cf. Gen. 3.20, etc.) even though it has little in common with the modern philological concept of historical etymology. It should be noted that some older commentators have tried to translate the people's reaction as a statement: 'It is manna.' The implications of this translation would be that the people at first wanted to identify the heavenly bread with a natural desert substance known to them as manna. However, in spite of its ingenuity, the interpretation cannot be maintained unless one disregards the context.

Moses reacts to the confused surprise of the people by identifying the manna with God's gift of bread. He then proceeds to relay the earlier command of God in more detailed form. Each man who gathers for his tent is commissioned to collect 'what each man could eat in a day', that is, 'an omer apiece'. Some commentators have found difficulty in relating the two expressions as if the first allowed one freedom to collect according to one's eating capacity, whereas the second limited everyone to an omer (cf. Gressmann). But the discrepancy is only apparent, and both expressions function in the same way in designating a given quantity. Actually this stipulation is mentioned here to introduce an unexpected surprise. When the people went out to gather the manna, some collected more than others. But when it was measured with the omer to determine an individual's portion, the one who had gathered much found he had no excess, and the one who had gathered little found that he was not lacking. The point is neatly summarized in v. 18: each man had gathered just the amount of food he needed. That this miracle had a purpose for Israel to learn is made clear in Moses' explicit prohibition from storing the manna. When some disobeyed and kept a part for the next day, it immediately spoiled, bred worms, and stank. So Israel was taught that this bread came 'morning by morning', in God's time, according to his plan. It could not be stored 'just in case . . .'. If one came too late, it had vanished with the heat of the rising sun.

[**16.22–30**] There was one great exception to the rule. It was not an afterthought, but built into the essential structure of the gift from the start (v. 5). God had made allowance for Israel's rest on the sabbath. In the earlier verse the promise had been simply stated to Moses that on the day preceding the sabbath twice the amount of manna would fall. But in v. 22 the execution of the promise is given a delightful twist. The people are not informed of the plan. They go blissfully out on the sixth day, gathering a day's portion as usual, and to their amazement, they gather twice the normal amount, two omers apiece. When they come to Moses, he exploits their surprise to instruct them in the nature of the sabbath. Certainly Gressmann (*op. cit.*, pp. 127f.) has missed the point when he finds in this narrative a 'discovery legend' (*Entdeckungssage*) which relates how Moses alone was clever enough to figure out what was afoot from the abundance of manna. Nor can one seriously imagine that the Old Testament tradition derived all the sabbath commandments from its relation to the giving of manna. Rather, the existence of the sabbath is assumed by the writer. But his was a natural question. If the manna fell every day and could not be stored, what happened on the sabbath? The story answers this question. Long before the reader wondered, God had made provision. The motif of the people's discovery adds one more charming element to the joyous wonder of the manna. God gives Israel, as it were, a surprise party.

In the verses which follow Moses explains in detail the nature of the sabbath and what it entails. It stems from a command of God; it is a day of special rest; it is set apart from the ordinary and dedicated to God. In anticipation for this special day, Israel is encouraged to be prepared. The manna can be baked or boiled – its properties are indeed wonderful – and kept in any form desired. When the people took Moses' advice, it did not spoil or become rancid. There is a festive ring in Moses' speech which continues in v. 25. The sabbath is not a day to go hungry and mourn. Rather Israel is to eat, for 'today' is God's special day. Later tradition expanded greatly on the theme of the joy of the sabbath, but the kernel of the theme is already present in the manna story.

Christian commentators have traditionally stressed the joy of the early concept of the sabbath which is surely correct. But the restrictive side of the day set aside to God belongs to the same tradition and cannot be dismissed. Not all the people were enjoying the sabbath. Some were out hunting for manna. Once again, the theme of God's testing the obedience of the people recurs. 'How long will you refuse to keep my commandments?' God gives them a double portion of bread, but he demands a different way of life.

[16.31–36] The concluding paragraph brings together a variety of different themes dealing with the manna. Again the naming of the bread as manna is given, which is a sure sign that the author has collected his material from several different sources. Again the writer offers a description of manna both in terms of its appearance and taste. Its shape was that of coriander seed, but white in color, and it tasted like wafers made with honey. The rabbinic midrashim pondered long on the taste of manna, and were puzzled how the description in Exodus could be reconciled with the 'taste of cakes baked in oil', which Num. 11 recounts. In the end they concluded that its wonderful properties allowed it to change at will and suit every man's taste to a delicacy.

Verse 32 introduces a new element. God commands Moses to preserve an omer of manna in a jar in order to bear witness to the future generations of God's sustenance of Israel throughout the period in the wilderness. It is to be 'an omer', that is, one day's portion, placed 'before God' and preserved. Once again the term 'forever' appears. The Hebrews measured time in terms of unbroken generations. Commentators have debated regarding the significance of preserving the manna. Some have suggested that it imports a concept which is alien to the function of manna as a daily provision which cannot be stored. However, the specification of one omer for preservation confirms that this message has not been forgotten. By preserving the manna forever Israel was made to remember how dependent she was on God for her life.

The jar of manna was to be placed 'before Yahweh', 'before the Testimony' (v. 34). Commentators (cf. Rashi) have long noticed the anachronism because the ark had not yet been built. Vatablus (*Critici Sacri, ad loc.*) reflects the traditional 'pre-critical' interpretation when he remarks: 'Everything at the end of the chapter is said by way of anticipation, as if the temple and the tabernacle had been built.' Historical critical scholars have been often quick to dismiss the reference to the ark as an oversight. However, such 'oversights' are hardly characteristic of the precise intention of this author whose chronological inconsistencies usually reflect definite theological concerns. It is much more likely that also here there is a theological point which caused the writer to override the chronological sequence.

A jar of manna which is the sign of God's sustaining mercy is kept alongside the tablets of the law. Indeed, the sign of divine grace preceded the giving of the law of Sinai! Still the emphasis of this passage does not fall on establishing the priority of the manna, nor should the chronology be pressed. Rather, the point of the text focuses on the testimony that the manna and the tablets belong together before God. In New Testament terminology, the gospel and the law cannot be separated.

The final verses record that Israel did not always live on manna. It ceased after forty years when Israel reached the promised land. This last verse is significant in revealing the perspective of the whole manna story. It has been compiled by one who now inhabits the land and looks back in memory to the time when God fed his people with food which rained from heaven.

Detailed Notes

16.1. On the itinerary, cf. the bibliography cited in Ex. 13.17. 'On the fifteenth day of the second month'. In recent years there have been several attempts to show that the Priestly writer employed the same calendar tradition as the book of Jubilees. Cf. especially A. Jaubert, *La Date de la Cène*, Paris 1957; P. Skehan, 'The Date of the Last Supper', *CBQ* 20, 1958, pp. 192–9; B. J. Malina, *The Palestinian Manna Tradition*, pp. 18ff. This hypothesis has been criticized by E. Kutsch, 'Der Kalender des Jubiläenbuches und das Alte und das Neue Testament', *VT* 11, 1961, pp. 39–47. In terms of Ex. 16 I fail to find the evidence convincing that the chapter covers an exact week. The crucial chronological points on which the theory rests seem to me to be supplied by the theory itself rather than arising from the text.

10. 'the glory of Yahweh'. Cf. C. Westermann, 'Die Herrlichkeit Gottes in der Priesterschrift', *Wort–Gebot–Glaube. Festschrift W. Eichrodt*, Zürich 1970, pp. 227–49.

12. 'in the morning'. Cf. J. Ziegler, 'Die Hilfe Gottes "am Morgen"', *Alttest. Studien F. Nötscher*, BBB 1, 1950, pp. 281–8.
'you shall know that I am Yahweh'. Cf. W. Zimmerli, *Erkenntnis Gottes nach dem Buche Ezechiel*, reprinted in *Gottes Offenbarung*, pp. 58ff.

13. On the description of the quail, cf. *BHH* III, col. 2123. The scientific description of the physical properties of the desert 'manna' is presented in A. Kaiser, *ZDPV* 53, 1930, pp. 63ff. and F. S. Bodenheimer, *BA* 10, 1947, pp. 1–6.

20. On the variety of worms, cf. *IDB* IV, p. 878.

23. Literature on the question of the sabbath is cited on Ex. 20.8.

35. On the problem of the connection between the manna and the passover which emerges in Josh. 5.10–12, cf. H.-J. Kraus, *EvTh* 18, 1958, pp. 54ff.

36. 'omer', 'ephah'. Cf. R. B. Y. Scott, 'Weights, Measures, Money and Times', *Peake's Commentary on the Bible*, ed. M. Black, London and New York 1962, pp. 37–41.

4. New Testament Context

P. Borgen, *Bread from Heaven: An Exegetical Study of the Concept of Manna in the Gospel of John and the Writings of Philo*, Leiden 1965 (cf. L. Martyn's review, *JBL* 86, 1967, pp. 244f.); B. Gärtner, *John 6 and the Jewish Passover*, Lund 1959; A. Heising, *Die Botschaft der Brotvermehrung*, Stuttgart 1966; U. W. Mauser, *Christ in the Wilderness*, SBT 39, 1963; R. Meyer, 'Manna', *TWNT* IV, pp. 466ff. = *TDNT* IV, pp. 462–6; B. J. Malina, *The Palestinian Manna Tradition*, Leiden 1968, pp. 94ff.; G. Vermes, 'He is the Bread', *Neotestamentica et semitica: Studies in honour of Matthew Black*, eds. E. E. Ellis and M. Wilcox, Edinburgh 1969, pp. 256–63.

The New Testament's handling of Ex. 16 cannot be fully understood without recognizing its dependence on Jewish exegetical tradition of the Hellenistic period. As one would expect, the New Testament shared both in its form and content elements of Jewish and Greek environment.

Jewish rabbinic exegesis, both in the midrashim and targums, worked seriously at combining all the Old Testament stories of the manna into a harmonious whole, while at the same time they found that the gift of manna provided an excellent vehicle with which to illustrate God's continual care for his people at times of difficulty. First of all, the midrash sought to bring into sharpest focus the description of the manna by combining the various reports in Ex. 16, Num. 11, and the Psalms. Since the taste of manna was pictured differently in Exodus and Numbers, the midrashic interpreters reasoned that manna did not have a fixed taste, but assumed whatever flavor one most wanted to experience (*Mekilta*, Ex. 16.23; cf. Wisd. 16.20). The rabbis went on to calculate how much manna fell in a day, at what time it disappeared, and how it appeared on holidays other than the sabbath. The reference to preparation in v. 5 naturally brought to mind the setting of sabbath limits (*Mekilta*, Pseudo-Jonathan). The midrash was in deadly earnest with the *realia* of the Bible because it was through the concrete situation that God had made himself known. Therefore, the rabbis conceived that the function of exegesis was to sharpen the focus as much as possible by the use of reason and insight.

Secondly, they were concerned to see in the manna stories the particular relation of God to Israel. God showed clearly in the provision of heavenly food his special love for his people which did benefit the nations as well (*Mekilta* on Ex. 16.21). The manna had been one of the things created on the eve of the sabbath (*Mek.*,

Ex. 16.32), and hidden away (Pseudo-Jon. v.4; cf. Ginzberg, *Legends of the Jews*, Philadelphia 1925, vol. V, p. 109 for all the rabbinic sources). Why did only Israel receive the manna? Certainly Israel did not deserve it. God did it because of his love for the Fathers. In fact, the whole manna story is foreshadowed in the life of Abraham. In Gen. 18 he did for God what God, in turn, was to do for Israel. Abraham found his visitor hungry; he spread a table and provided bread. In turn, God acted the gracious host for Abraham's posterity. In other words, rabbinic exegesis, especially in the post-Tannaite period, used typology to link the particular historical event with a broader, more general category.

Finally, the manna story illustrated for the rabbinic tradition man's natural disobedience and the need for the law. Yet in spite of this, his covenant is never shattered. God had provided the machinery of repentance for its repair. God's special love for Israel carried with it the assurance that he would never reject his miraculous maintenance of his people (cf. the development of this theme in the medieval exegesis of *Exodus Rabbah*).

There were several other directions which the interpretation of the Old Testament manna stories took within Judaism. The contrast between the rabbinic midrashic exegesis and Josephus, for example, is striking. Although Josephus' handling of the tradition shows many midrashic details, his overriding concern in the discussion of the manna incident is to make the account seem genuine to his readers by rationalizing as much of the tradition as possible (*Antiq.* III, 26ff.).

Another major alternative to rabbinic exegesis is represented by Philo. In one passage in *Vita Mosis* II. 258ff. Philo can paraphrase the story as a typical Greek homily which follows closely the main lines of the biblical narrative. But the chief use of the manna stories appears in several extended references (*Mut.* 258-260; *Leg. All.* III. 162ff.). Since P. Borgen has offered an exhaustive analysis of these passages in his study *Bread from Heaven*, his results will be briefly summarized. Borgen argues that Philo is dependent on a common homiletical pattern, but he applies the fragments of inherited haggadic tradition within the context of a Greek conflict between philosophy and encyclical education. The Greek educational concepts of 'virtue and wisdom' were substituted for manna which illustrated the contrast of the two concepts of learning. Manna was received 'without toil or trouble', and therefore became a symbol of the self-taught virtues of philosophy in contrast to the toil involved in the encyclical education. Manna was the heavenly wisdom sent from above on souls which shed the prudence of seeking knowing through earthly sources. Philo used Israel's daily dependence on God to warn against those in his own community who aspired for social and political success, and he pointed to the cosmic principles of the spiritual world by which God cares for the Jews, both now and in the future.

The New Testament likewise offers a variety of interpretations of the manna story. At times, the New Testament's use is more akin to the typical rabbinic midrash (I Cor. 10.3; Rev. 2.17); at times it shares the spiritualizing tendency of Philo (John 6). Nevertheless, there are several characteristic features in the Christian understanding of the manna stories which distinguished it from its Hellenistic environment. Basically, the New Testament regarded the gift of manna from both a negative and a positive perspective. On the one hand, the manna was incapable of supplying the Israelites with genuine life. On the other hand, the manna was a gift of saving grace which was then identified in some way with Christ. As a result of both of these directions, the New Testament had little interest in the concrete features of the manna, but focused on the divine reality of which the manna was only a sign.

The account of Jesus' temptation in the wilderness according to Matthew and Luke makes explicit reference to the manna story by its citing of Deut. 8.3: 'Man shall not live by bread alone . . .' There is an obvious analogy drawn between Israel and Jesus. As Israel wandered hungry for forty years in the wilderness and was tested by God, so Jesus the Messiah hungers for forty days and nights in the wilderness and is also put to the test. In the form of a disputation with Satan, Jesus rejects the temptation to misuse his messianic power. He acknowledges the true nature of the gift of food and cites Deut. 8 as a testimony to his faith that God can sustain by his Word even without food. Thus Jesus discerns the reality to which the miracle points.

Again, there is an implicit reference to the manna tradition in the synoptic account of the feeding of the five thousand (Mark 6; Matt. 14; Luke 9), although the form of the story has been influenced by the literary form of II Kings 4.42. The people are still wandering hungry in the wilderness. The deliverance through Moses is not complete, but only a foreshadowing of what Jesus does as the new Moses, signalling the coming messianic age. The emphasis is on the passive role of the people; the action is on the side of God. The miracle consists in feeding the people with ordinary bread and fish, but which were miraculously multiplied.

Then again, Paul makes use of the manna tradition. In I Cor. 10.1–13 he finds an analogy between Israel and the church in the great redemptive events of the old covenant. The Israelites were 'baptized into Moses . . . ate the same spiritual food and drank the same spiritual drink'. The parallel between the situation lies in the lesson that God's saving grace, which both experienced, can be forfeited and lost. The church has not reached the promised land, and must not succumb to temptation. Again in II Cor.8.15 Paul makes a homiletical reference to the manna, and finds in the equality of the divine gift a warrant for the church's responsibility to share its wealth with the needy.

Finally, the most extensive and profound use of the Old Testament manna tradition appears in John 6.31–58. Borgen has made out a strong case for John's use of a common homiletical tradition, closely akin to Philo. The evangelist also presupposes the giving of the law at Sinai as God's gift of life to the world. But the importance of John lies in the radical transformation of the tradition. First, he transfers the traditional role of the law to the bread from heaven (6.33). Then he identifies the heavenly bread with Jesus and draws the implications from this move. Those who have not accepted Jesus have failed therefore to heed God's voice given in the Old Testament (5.37ff.; 6.41ff.). Again, Jesus as the heavenly bread performs the function of Old Testament wisdom and sustains with food and drink those who 'come to him' (cf. Borgen, p. 154ff.).

Borgen (pp. 172ff.) has made a particularly illuminating exegesis of the Johannine dichotomy between the external and spiritual bread which was given to Israel. His contrast is not just between an earthly and a spiritual gift, as is often suggested. Rather, John places the events of the past in the external sphere and those of the present in the spiritual. The Fathers ate the external manna and died, but the man who eats of the spiritual bread from heaven never dies, but has eternal life. Thus Israel is divided into two groups. 'Jews' are those, both past and present, who partake of the external bread of Moses and fail to obtain life. 'True Israelites', both past and present, are those who eat the true bread from heaven and live for ever. John's interpretation is so radical because it moves the whole discussion on to a different plane entirely. The failure to understand resulted in death. The real purpose of the manna story is to raise the issue of life and death. Faith brings life; unbelief which is blindness brings death. John testifies that only in Jesus Christ, God's gift from heaven, do we have eternal life.

5. History of Exegesis

J. BUXTORF, 'De Manna', *Exercitationes ad Historiam*, Basel 1659, reprinted in B. UGOLINI, *Thesaurus Antiquitatum Sacrarum*, Venice 1744ff., VIII, pp.587–640; S. DEYLING, 'De manna in deserto, Exod.16', *Observationes Sacrae*, III[3], Leipzig 1735, pp.70ff.; L. DIESTEL, *Geschichte des Alten Testamentes*, Jena 1869, pp.585ff.; E. W. HENGSTENBERG, 'Supplementary Remarks . . . on Manna', *Dissertations on Daniel*, ET Edinburgh 1847, pp.561–9; RICHARD B. KENNEY, *Ante-Nicene Greek and Latin Patristic Uses of the Biblical Manna Motif* (Yale Diss.), 1968; E. F. C. ROSENMÜLLER, *Handbuch der biblischen Alterthumskunde*, IV, Leipzig 1831, pp.316–29; J. F. STAPELIN, 'Dissertatio de Vocula Man ad Exod.xvi: 15', Wittenberg 1664; reprinted in *Thesaurus Theologico-Philologicus*, Amsterdam 1701, pp.308ff.; G. B. WINER, *Biblisches Realwörterbuch* II[3], Leipzig 1847, pp.53–4.

The manna stories were frequently used by the early church Fathers as a homiletical vehicle for a great variety of themes. However, generally this use of the Old Testament did not reveal very much originality or insight. Ignatius identified the heavenly bread with the eucharist which prepared one for the higher life of martyrdom (*Romans* 7.3). Melito of Sardis elaborated homiletically on the parallels between the passover, manna, and the eucharist (*Paschal Homily*). Justin employed the theme polemically against the Jews who worshipped the golden calf while all the time partaking of the heavenly bread (*Dialogue with Trypho*, 20.4). Likewise, Cyril of Alexandria contrasted at length the carnality of the Jews who craved meat with the Christians who were taught by the foreshadowing of the manna (*umbram ac typum*) regarding the discipline and gift of Christ who offers the spiritual food of life (*De Manna et Coturnice*, MPG 69. 450ff.) Cf. also Origen, *In Exod. Hom.* VII.5 (SC 16, pp.176ff.); Augustine, *Quaest. in Hept.* II.62; Theodoret, *Quaest. in Ex.* 30–32.

The rabbinic midrash continued to find in the manna story an endless source for its homiletical reflection. The collection of midrashic traditions in the Babylonian Talmud (Yoma, 75–76), and *Exodus Rabbah* gives an impression of late baroque architecture with endless variations on earlier motifs. The supernatural properties were extended, and all the delights of heaven were encompassed in the miraculous outpouring of loving care for Israel. Indeed, the more difficult the times became for Jews, the more fantastic was the picture of heaven on earth.

The first real break in the history of exegesis came in the high Middle Ages and first made its impact felt on Jewish exegesis. The issue turned on the question as to whether the manna was totally new in the experience of the world, or whether it was in some way akin to the familiar desert food which shared many of its properties and which was continually being described by travellers to the Middle East. Ibn Ezra (died 1174) offered a vigorous polemic against those who sought to identify the biblical manna with the common food. He took a line of defense which was to become the classic rebuttal of the orthodox from then on. He pointed out in great detail those elements in the manna which were unique – its great abundance, its duration, its weekly cycle – and minimized the elements in common. Abarbanel (died 1508) followed a similar line with even more details, and attacked those who had tried to gain some philosophical support from Maimonides for holding to the unchanging laws of the natural universe.

It was obvious that before long Christian exegesis would also be engaged with the same problem. Already Calvin felt it necessary to offer an extended rebuttal 'to the idle talk . . . that the manna falls naturally in certain countries', and he follows the lines of defense set forth by Ibn Ezra, though unconscious of his dependence. However, full recognition of the Jewish contribution was made by the learned essay of J. Buxtorf the Younger in his *Exercitationes* of 1659, who felt that no better defense of the orthodox position regarding the supernatural qualities of manna could be found than those offered by the classic Jewish commentators.

The commentary of J. Clericus once again began to point in a new direction for Protestant exegesis. Regarding the issue of the nature of manna, Clericus found an earlier, little known interpretation, compatible with his own approach, which he cited at length. The French scholar Claudius Saumaise (died 1652), who had himself been dependent on a fifteenth-century Jewish rabbi, Isaac ben Meir Aramah, had argued that there was nothing new or strange in the substance itself, as if it came only once and afterward disappeared. Rather the miracle lay in its daily arrival, in its quantity, and its continuation throughout the year. The fact that the quail was a species common in that area was an additional warrant for seeing a strong continuity between the biblical story and the natural produce of the land. Clericus' role lay not only in popularizing this view, but in buttressing it with further arguments.

In the period which followed, various modifications of this mediating position were developed. Kalisch (*Exodus*, 1855) is typical when he tries to distinguish between two different kinds of natural manna, an 'air manna' and a 'tree manna', both of which share elements of the biblical story and caused the confusion between Exodus and Numbers. However, he still affirmed that 'God applies natural means for His great deeds . . . and that here a *miracle* is narrated' (p. 290).

It is an interesting commentary on the relation of biblical exegesis to the temper of the times to realize that, although no new scientific evidence appeared directly bearing on the manna, by the end of the nineteenth century the great majority of critical commentators simply took it for granted that the biblical manna was a natural substance. The miraculous element was attributed to the imagination of the Hebrew writers (Knobel, Vatke, Stade, etc.). By 1900 even cautious British scholars such as McNeile and Driver appear to assume a similar critical position, even though it is cloaked in a language which seeks to soften the impact. Manna for Driver has become 'a beautiful symbolic illustration' (p. 154). (Cf. C. Rylaarsdam, G. H. Davies, J. P. Hyatt, and R. E. Clements.)

6. Theological Reflection in the Context of the Canon

There are two separate problems which should be distinguished at the outset, although their solutions affect one another. The first turns on the problem of relating the witness within the canon to extrabiblical evidence. The second turns on the issue of relating the variety of witnesses respecting the subject of manna within the canon.

A. The Relation of the Canonical Witness to the Extra-Biblical

There are two traditional approaches to this first problem, both of which, in my judgment, are inadequate. The first is the 'supernaturalistic' viewpoint. According to this position the biblical witness is the normative, and therefore historically accurate, record of the event in accordance with which the extra-biblical evidence must be corrected and controlled. This position suffers in that it seeks to employ categories taken from outside the Bible, such as historicity, objectivity, and the like, and yet to retain without criticism the content of the canonical witness. It seeks to guarantee a reality testified to in the canon by means of dogmatic controls employed outside the area of faith. The second position, which is that of rationalism, represents the opposite extreme. It seeks to determine the truth of the biblical testimony on the basis of critical evaluation according to rational criteria, based on past human experience. It suffers from assuming that its criteria are adequate to test all reality, and it eliminates the basic theological issue by definition. In terms of the manna story, the supernaturalists claim that the exodus story is a historically accurate report of a unique miracle which is unrelated to any natural food of the desert. The rationalists conversely claim that the exodus story is an imaginary (or poetic) projection into the supernatural sphere of a natural phenomenon of the desert which can be fully described scientifically.

In my judgment, a correct understanding of biblical theology in the context of the canon allows one to break out of this old impasse. First of all, the theological concept of canon is a confession. It is a testimony of the Christian church as a community of faith that God has chosen the vehicle of sacred scripture through which to make himself known to the church and the world, both in the past, present, and future. It serves a unique function in the relation between God and his people. It points to a divine activity which only has its testimony in the witness of the prophets and the apostles. In other words, scripture is not simply one means among several others of testifying to a unique self-disclosure of God in Jesus Christ. To take the concept of the canon seriously is to assign to scripture a normative role and to refuse to submit the truth of its testimony to criteria of human reason. However, the concept of the canon lays no claim to universal knowledge or to a theory of infallibility, and thereby sets itself apart from supernaturalism. Specifically in terms of the manna story, the confession of canonical scripture does not seek to attribute to the biblical witness a quality of historicity which can be controlled objectively, that is, outside the community of faith. However, it rejects the suggestion that the biblical witness arose simply as a projection of human imagination. The integrity of the canon is maintained without calling into question legitimate areas in which the judgment of human reason is appropriate.

But can one isolate these two areas in this way? Is there not a genuine relation between the canonical witness to an event and extra-biblical evidence? Indeed there is, and the fact of an essential relationship lies at the heart of the problem. First of all, the canonical witness shares all the features common to human language. It is not written in a 'heavenly tongue', but in a common language of a given people in a specific period within history. Therefore, in order even to understand the testimony of the canonical writings, one must assume a continuity between experience inside and outside the canon. Specifically, the biblical witness speaks of manna as 'food' which satisfies 'hunger'. The gift of manna serves as food, but it has a very special function as well to which only the canon bears witness. It is by means of the manna that Israel came to know the power of God (Ex. 16.12).

Secondly, the area of common ground between the canonical witness and the extra-biblical extends to the content of both in all its aspects. The two share thought patterns, institutions, and experiences of ordinary human life. The canonical writings testify to God's dealing with his people, but the witness is not purged of its human frailty. The canonical writings function as God's vehicle specifically in its human form. There is no way to extract the purely 'divine' elements.

Of what importance is it then to recognize this relationship for understanding the testimony of the canon? It seems to me at this point very difficult to generalize on its value. At times the recognition of a relationship between the 'inner' and 'outer' shape of the witness appears most significant; at other times it appears less so, or not at all. Certain events are testified to in a similar way inside and outside the canon, such as the destruction of Jerusalem in 587. Other events, such as the redemption at the Reed Sea, are witnessed to only in scripture in the context of faith. How one moves from the area inside the canon to that outside remains a puzzlement, perhaps one should say a mystery. Attempts to construct assured hermeneutical bridges – whether philosophical, historical, or linguistic – tend to obscure the witness and dissolve the tension in the text.

The fact of the continuing tension between the biblical witness and the perspective outside the canon is a reminder that the witness of faith does not function as a rival philosophy of history. As a canonical testimony it points to God at work in a community of faith. The purpose of the manna story does not lie in measuring the depth of the supply to see how far the usual laws of nature can be stretched, but in discerning God's work in putting Israel to the test. The canonical witness loses its essential role if it is isolated from the reality to which it alone points. Extra-biblical evidence continues to play a role by offering another explanation without the need of faith or the community. If for this reason alone, it must be continually heard.

Again, the fact of a relationship between the perspectives inside nd outside the community of faith is recognized as important by the Bible itself. The redemption of God, as testified to in both the Old and the New Testament, is not confined to Israel and the church, but extends to the world. Although the gospel proclaims a complete 'newness of life', a movement from the church to the world is demanded of Christians. The message of life is not to a secret group of initiates, but to all men. The fact that the gift of manna fell only to Israel does not hide the diverse reaction to it. By some it was rejected in unbelief and judged as worthless (Num. 11.6). Even 'heavenly food' could be judged common.

Moreover, every reader, both ancient and modern, shares in himself both perspectives. He is constantly tempted to understand life completely within the confines of human experience. The function of the canon is to bear testimony to God's work which cannot be once and for all accepted, but must be responded to in a renewed commitment of faith. The controversy of John 6 over the understanding of manna turns on this issue. The manna – no matter how great a miracle – in itself cannot sustain life. It must point to God's true work which provides eternal life.

The biblical exegete is forced to hear testimony from inside and outside the community of faith because he lives in both worlds. He dare not destroy the canonical witness by forcing it into the mold of the 'old age', nor dare he construct out of the canonical witness a world of myth safely relegated to the distant past. Rather, he confesses his participation in the community of faith by 'searching the scriptures'. He seeks to share the bread of life with the church through the testimony of scripture. He remains open in anticipation to those moments when the Spirit of God resolves the tension and bridges the gap between faith and history.

B. *Understanding the Variety within the Witness to the Manna*

The great variety within the Old Testament's description of the manna has long been recognized, but certainly this feature has been highlighted through the critical study of the text over the last hundred years. The diversity in perspective does not just lie in the descriptions of Exodus and Numbers – does manna taste like oil or honey? – but in the broad framework into which the material has been shaped by Deuteronomy and the Psalter. Deut. 8 appears to contrast the manna with bread and to suggest that Israel learned humility through the eating of this food. The Priestly writer emphasizes the exact matching of the individual need. Each day every person received just what he required; no one had too much nor too little. For the Psalmist the failure to respond to the gift of manna provides a major testimony to Israel's unbelief which leads to judgment. Of course, when one adds to this variety the New Testament passages which speak of manna, the nature of the problem is even intensified.

In the light of this situation the midrashic method provides one clear option for handling the diversity. The material is placed within a large homiletical framework which serves to harmonize difficulties and render the material pliable for fresh practical application. It is theologically significant to note that basically the New Testament does not follow this lead in its handling of the manna stories, although it does make considerable use of midrashic tradition. Rather, it finds its warrant in the Old Testament for selecting certain themes from the variety and elaborating on these. The gift of manna is above all a gracious sign of God's care which sustains a rebellious, murmuring people and seeks to point them to an apprehension of the real meaning of provision through this divine favor. Because this selective process already operates within the Old Testament, the New Testament approach does not provide a sharp contrast, as is frequently the case; rather, it extends and develops the direction taken by Deuteronomy and the Psalter. Even John's use of the tradition, which marks the furthest extension of the Old Testament in the direction of Philo's exegesis, begins with themes which are firmly anchored in the Old Testament. Indeed, his christological interpretation moves far beyond the Old Testament text, but retains the central theme of 'heavenly bread which brings life to those who eat'.

The New Testament has chosen to reflect on only a portion of the whole Old Testament witness to the manna. The danger of selecting in this way emerges in the later history of Christian exegesis where the process of extending the New Testament themes has led to a virtual separation from its Old Testament base. The manna has become the heavenly food confined to the eucharist whose qualities are limited to higher spheres of spiritual attainment. It is an essential function of theological reflection within the canon to continue to sound the full range of notes from both the Old and the New Covenants. Particularly in our modern culture, the Old Testament witness to God's concern to satisfy the physical hunger of his people offers an essential foundation on which the New Testament's testimony to Jesus Christ as the 'bread of life' must be built.

XIII

WATER AT MASSAH AND MERIBAH

17.1-7

G. Coats, *Rebellion in the Wilderness*, Nashville 1968, pp. 53ff.; V. Fritz, *Israel in der Wüste*, Marburg 1970, pp. 10ff., 48ff.; H. Gressmann, *Mose und Seine Zeit*, 1913, pp. 145ff.; S. Lehming, 'Massa und Meriba', *ZAW* 73, 1961, pp. 71–77; M. Noth, *Überlieferungsgeschichte des Pentateuch*, 1948, pp. 127f. = *History of Pentateuchal Traditions*, 1971, pp. 115ff.; E. Meyer, *Die Israeliten und ihre Nachbarstämme*, Halle 1906, reprinted Darmstadt 1967, pp. 51ff.; H. Seebass, *Mose und Aaron, Sinai und Gottesberg*, Bonn 1962, pp. 61ff.

17 ¹The entire Israelite community set out from the wilderness of Sin by stages according to the command of the LORD. They camped at Rephidim, but there was no water for the people to drink, ²and the people quarreled with Moses and said, 'Give us water to drink.' Moses said to them, 'Why do you quarrel with me? Why do you test the LORD?' ³But the people thirsted there for water, and the people murmured against Moses, saying: 'Why did you bring us out of Egypt with our children and our livestock to let us die of thirst?' ⁴Moses cried to the LORD, 'What am I to do with this people? They are almost ready to stone me.' ⁵Then the LORD said to Moses, 'Move on ahead of the people, and take with you some of the elders of Israel and the rod with which you struck the Nile, and go. ⁶I will be standing there in front of you on the rock at Horeb. Strike the rock, water will pour out of it, and the people can drink.' Moses did so in the sight of the elders of Israel. ⁷He named the place Massah (test) and Meribah (quarrel) because the Israelites had quarreled and because they had tested the LORD, saying, 'Is the LORD in our midst or not?'

1. *Textual and Philological Notes*

17.2. Some Hebrew mss., the Samar., and the versions read a singular verb instead of *tᵉnû*. Many mss. read *ûmah*.

3. The versions read a 1st pl. suffix for the MT sing.

2. Literary and Traditio-Historical Problems

Commentators are generally agreed that the P source is represented by the itinerary note of v. 1abα. The remaining narrative does not seem to be of one piece, but the criteria by which to decide are uncertain. The main evidence for a multiple sources is found in the double name, Massah and Meribah, and the doublet in v. 1bβ-2 and v. 3. The older attempt of Gressmann, and more recently of Hyatt, to find two complete literary strands is unconvincing. Noth attributes the story to J with the exception of v. 3, which he assigns to E, admittedly without objective evidence. Certainly Fritz's attempt to attribute it to P is improbable because, in every other instance of P, Aaron is included with Moses. Rudolph finds only J, but at the cost of extensive rearrangement. Coats is unconvinced by the literary solutions and feels that the tension stems from the oral tradition. The question cannot be decided with any degree of certainty.

There is such a variety in the Old Testament's use of the Meribah tradition that one can suspect a complex history of tradition lying behind the present narrative. Unfortunately the evidence for tracing this development is no longer available, and one is left with a variety of hypotheses which have little chance of being established or disproved. The lexicographical evidence shows that Massah appears alone in Deut. 6.16; 9.22. Meribah (in slightly variant forms) is alone in Num. 20.13; Deut. 32.51; Pss. 81.8; 106.32. Massah and Meribah are paralleled but not identified in Deut. 33.8 and Ps. 95.8. The most widely accepted explanation of the relationship (e.g. Noth) is that Massah is a Deuteronomic element which has been secondarily introduced into the present narrative on the basis of the earlier poetic parallelism. Certainly the narrative in Ex. 17.1-7 focuses primarily on Meribah, but when and how Massah entered can only be speculated. It is probable that Massah and Meribah had a much earlier connection in the tradition. The fact that at times in the tradition the people dispute with Yahweh (Deut. 6.16; Ps. 95.8), and at times Yahweh tests the people (Deut. 33.8; Ps. 81.8) only adds to the complexity of the problem.

The story in Ex. 17.1-7 bears an obvious relation to that of Num. 20.1-13. Not only is the basic form and content very close, but the name of Meribah is preserved in both. Num. 20 differs chiefly in focusing the story on a tradition which attached to Moses' office. It is very difficult to say anything certain about the original position of this story in the narrative, although Wellhausen had already noticed how the two Meribah stories now enclose the Sinai tradition.

It is usually thought that the earliest level of the Meribah story represented a local place etiology, which sought to explain the name as a place in which disputes were settled. Von Rad writes: 'Massa and Meribah . . . imply that legal cases were investigated and decided by ordeal there' (*Theology* I, p. 12). At the same time, others want to see in the story an etiology which explained the presence of a spring which flows from a rock (Gressmann). The problem with the etiological explanation is that the etiology itself does not relate to the water from the rock, but to the dispute. Therefore, in order to avoid this difficulty Coats (pp. 53ff.) has to reconstruct three levels in the story's development. The first offered a play on the word 'dispute'; the second introduced the miracle of water; the third brought in the murmuring motif. In my judgment, the assumption that the etiology functions in this way within the tradition is extremely doubtful and needs re-examination. (Cf. the beginning made by B. O. Long, *The Problem of Etiological Narrative*, 1968.)

The Meribah story of Ex. 17 reflects an oral pattern which has appeared elsewhere within the wilderness traditions (cf. Pattern I in the Introduction to the Wilderness Traditions, pp. 258ff. above). Accordingly, the people are in need; they murmur against Moses; he intercedes with Yahweh and the need is met. In my opinion, this pattern is found in the earliest level of the tradition. The etiological elements, such as the word play on the name of Meribah, came in at an early period to fill out and expand the primary tradition. The tradition did not develop from the etiology, but the etiology subsequently attached itself to the tradition of Yahweh's aid in the wilderness.

3. Old Testament Context

The story of the water at Meribah follows a familiar pattern. Israel is on the move from the wilderness of Sin to Mount Sinai. The incident takes place at Rephidim, a place of unknown location, but according to the tradition not far from Sinai (19.2). Rephidim has no water and the people quarrel with Moses. There appears to be a duplication between vv. 1b–2 and 3. In both, the people thirst and find fault with him. Nevertheless, the effect of the present expanded narrative is that of creating out of stereotyped complaints a form which resembles a genuine controversy. Seldom does the dispute against Moses reflect such a real give-and-take. The use of the term 'dispute' (*rîb*) in v.2 is, of course, picked up finally in the naming of the place Meribah.

The seriousness of the murmuring comes out in Moses' address to God: 'What am I to do? Much more of this and they will stone me!' Moses is then instructed to go ahead of the people, taking as witnesses some of the elders and his rod. This latter is one of the few references within Exodus to the previous events of the plagues. Still it would be difficult for any writer acquainted with the whole tradition to mention Moses' rod without some reference to the event which first brought it into such prominence. Moses is to meet God on the rock at Horeb. The mention of Horeb is unexpected since the sacred mountain is not reached until ch. 19. It hardly seems possible to avoid the difficulty by suggesting that a larger region be included within the same terms. Some commentators (Jacob, Cassuto) suggest that the writer is making an explicit reference to earlier events in which God demonstrated his power. The rod recalls the plagues, Horeb the scene at the burning bush (ch. 3). However, the latter reference seems forced and lacks a warrant in the text itself. The remaining narrative reveals no further connection with Horeb.

Some commentators (Gressmann, Bäntsch) have speculated on why God stood on the rock if Moses was to strike it. Certainly it is completely arbitrary to suggest because of this clause that at one point in the development of the story God himself was pictured as striking the rock. The author clearly felt no tension between God's exercise of his power and Moses' role as his agent. Again, it seems fruitless to rationalize the story as Cassuto does by citing modern parallels of water breaking through the crust of rock in the desert. The whole point of the story turns on the gracious and surprising provision of God who provided water for his people when none was available.

Although it is possible that the names Massah and Meribah may once have denoted a place of legal decision, the names have entered the tradition in relation to the murmuring motif. God provided water for a contentious people who challenged his presence among them. Ps.95 speaks of Israel's hardness of heart when putting God to the test, even though they had repeatedly seen his great work.

Detailed Notes

17.1. 'Rephidim'. The location is unknown although a variety of different localities have been suggested. Cf. the suggestions in Driver's *Exodus*, pp. 155f. and in *BHH* III, col. 1551.

5. 'elders of Israel'. Cf. Ex. 24.1.

6. 'Horeb'. Cf. Ex. 3.1.

7. 'Meribah'. Most commentators locate Meribah at Kadesh because of Num. 20.13. H. Clay Trumbull, *Kadesh-Barnea*, 1884, claimed to have been the first to have identified Kadesh with ꜥēn qdēs, although this has been recently contested by Fritz. V. Fritz, pp. 49ff. reviews the evidence for identifying Kadesh with either ꜥēn qdēs or with ꜥēn el-qdērāt. Elliger (*BHH* II, col. 917) and the majority of modern geographers defend the former identification. But cf. Aharoni, *The Land of the Bible*, Philadelphia 1967, p. 184.

XIV

WAR WITH THE AMALEKITES
17.8–16

M. Buber, *Moses*, 1946, pp.90–3; V. Fritz, *Israel in der Wüste*, Marburg 1970, pp.55ff.; R. Gradwohl, 'Zum Verständnis von Ex. xvii, 15f.', *VT* 12, 1962, pp.491–4; H. Gressmann, *Mose und seine Zeit*, 1913, pp.155ff.; J. H. Grønbaek, 'Juda und Amalek. Überlieferungsgeschichtliche Erwägungen zu Exodus 17, 8–16', *Studia Theol.* 18, 1964, pp.26–45; E. Meyer, *Die Israeliten und ihre Nachbarstämme*, Halle 1906, reprinted Darmstadt 1967, pp.389ff.; K. Möhlenbrink 'Joshua im Pentateuch', *ZAW* 59, 1942/3, pp.14–58; M. Noth, *Überlieferungsgeschichte des Pentateuch*, 1948, pp.131ff. = *History of Pentateuchal Traditions*, 1971, pp.119ff.; T. Nöldeke, 'Über die Amalekiten', *Orient und Occident* II, 1864, pp.614–655; H. Schmid, *Mose. Überlieferung und Geschichte*, 1968, pp.62ff.

17 8Then Amalek came and fought with Israel at Rephidim. 9Moses said to Joshua, 'Pick some men for us and go out to fight with Amalek. Tomorrow I will stand on top of the hill with the rod of God in my hand.' 10Joshua did as Moses told him and fought with Amalek, while Moses, Aaron, and Hur went up to the top of the hill. 11Now whenever Moses held up his hand, Israel gained the advantage, but whenever he lowered his hand Amalek gained the advantage. 12When the hands of Moses grew tired, they took a stone, and put it under him, and he sat upon it. Then Aaron and Hur supported his hand, one on either side. Thus his hands remained steady until the sun set. 13Joshua disabled Amalek and its people with the edge of the sword.

14 Then the Lord said to Moses, 'Write this as a memorial in a book, and recite it in the ears of Joshua: I will utterly exterminate the memory of Amalek from under heaven.' 15Moses built an altar and named it, 'The Lord is my banner'. 16And he said, 'A hand upon the banner of the Lord. The Lord will be at war with Amalek throughout the generations.'

1. Textual and Philological Notes

17.9. The question of whether the adverb 'tomorrow' belongs to v.9a or 9b was already debated in the Tannaitic period. Cf. *Mekilta, ad loc.* Modern translators continue to be divided. Compare RSV and JNPS with AmTr and NEB. I prefer to relate it to the second part of the verse as offering a more logical sequence. The Massoretic accents provide an additional warrant.

11. The verbs are frequentative. The versions and the Samar. read the MT's *yāḏô* as a plural, but this is a secondary harmonization with v. 12.

13. 'disabled'. The basic meaning of the root *ḥlš* is 'to weaken'. In the context of Ex. 17.8ff. Israel's defeat of Amalek was not an annihilation. NJPS prefers the less literal rendering 'the people of Amalek'.

14. Orlinsky (*Notes*, p. 172) argues for the looser term 'documents' rather than 'book' which he claims is anachronistic in this passage. On the force of *zikkārôn*, cf. W. Schottroff, *Gedenken*, pp. 299ff.; B. S. Childs, *Memory and Tradition*, pp. 66ff.

16. The difficulty of understanding the text of this verse has long been felt. It already appeared as a problem in the versions and continued to be debated throughout the subsequent history of exegesis. There are two major aspects of the problem which are closely related: (i) What is the meaning of the word(s) *kēsyāh* in v. 16? (ii) What is the function of 16 in relation to 15?

In respect to the first problem the LXX reads ἐν χειρὶ κρυφαίᾳ ('with a secret hand'), which suggests the same consonants as the MT, but pointed as a verb *kᵉsuyāh*. The Samar. reads *ks'*. This interpretation of the word as 'throne' is followed by Onkelos, Pseudo-Jonathan, Neofiti I, and the medieval Jewish commentators. The Vulg. also reads 'throne', but reinterprets the Hebrew syntax: *quia manus solii Domini*. Occasionally the attempt has been made to retain the MT but derive the noun from a different Hebrew root, such as *kss* = 'to plan' (Cassuto). But certainly the most widespread theory is the textual conjecture of J. Clericus in the seventeenth century, and accepted by many scholars thereafter, of emending *kēs* to *nēs* ('banner').

In respect to the second problem the function of v. 16 is equally contested. The targums, Rashi and AV understand the sentence as an oath which God swears. Others interpret it as an oath which Moses swears (Dillmann, B. Jacob, NEB). Moreover, opinions vary whether the subject of the hand is God, Moses, or even Amalek (Clericus, AV margin). The translation of the NJPS: 'it means', interprets v. 16 as offering an explanation of the name in v. 15. Finally, Gressmann (*Mose und seine Zeit*, p. 159), and more recently Gradwohl (*op. cit.*, p. 494) have proposed the theory that the hand in v. 16 is a reference to a votive hand on the scepter of God to guarantee continual war against Amalek. Obviously a decision in regard to the first problem strongly affects the second.

My concern is not to offer a startling, new interpretation which differs from all those listed, but rather to suggest criteria for evaluating the evidence and reaching a degree of certainty in arriving at a solution. The starting point is with the naming formula in 15b: 'he called its name *YHWH nissî*.' J. Fichtner (*VT* 6, 1956, pp. 372ff.) and B. O. Long (*Etiological Narrative* [see p. 265 above] pp. 4ff.) have made it clear that there are two distinct etiological patterns used in the giving of a name. In Form I the giving of the name precedes its etiology; in Form II the giving of the name follows the etiology. Only Form I is of immediate concern. Three stereotyped elements are significant: (i) In regard to the sequence, the name is first introduced with the verb *qr'* (call), and then the etiology is offered (Gen. 41.51; Ex. 2.22). (ii) Some element in the name is picked up and repeated as a word play in the etiology: 'He called his name *mᵉnaššeh* because God made me forget (*naššanî*) . . .' (iii) The etiology is related to a word which was spoken: 'He called his name NN because he *said* . . .' Even when the verb is missing, the use of the direct quotation goes to prove unequivocally that the verb 'to say' is assumed (Gen. 4.25; 32.31; 41.51). When the verb '*mr* is used, it can be either preceded by a *kî* (Gen. 16.13; Ex. 2.22), or followed by a *kî* (Gen. 26.22; Ex. 2.10).

Now the point of this analysis is to demonstrate that Ex. 17.15f. clearly shares the elements of this etiological form. The name of the altar is first introduced with the verb *qr'*. Then the etiology follows, which is derived from a spoken word. The sequence *wayyō'mer kî* has its exact parallel in the etiologies in Gen. 26.22 and Ex. 2.10. The only element which is missing is the play on words between the name and the word spoken. The structural parallels offer a strong warrant for accepting the conjectural emendation by reading *nēs* for *kēs*, and thus completing the full etiological form.

There are several implications which arise from reconstructing the original etiological form. Verse 16 obviously functions as a causal explanation of the name in v. 15. Since the subject of the two verbs in the etiological form are the same – there are only a few exceptions – the traditional interpretation of God's pronouncing an oath is eliminated (Rashi, AV). Again, recognition of the etiological form rules out the interpretation which understands v. 16a as a new element, and connects it with 16b (NEB). Moreover, Gradwohl's theory of the votive hand is weakened in that it disregards the etiological connection of the hand with the first person suffix in the name. The most plausible alternative left is to understand the phrase 'hand on YHWH's banner' as a rallying cry of Moses which was directed to Israel.

Finally, what is the function of the *kî* in v. 16? The history of exegesis reveals a great uncertainty as to its force. It is often translated as a causal conjunction: 'because' or 'for'. Others interpret it as an asseverative: 'truly', '*fürwahr*' (Gradwohl) or even as an oath particle. Still others understand it to be a *kî recitativum*, parallel to the Greek ὅτι, which is used to introduce a direct quotation.

The full formula is represented by a double use of *kî* as in Gen. 29.32: *kî 'āmᵉrāh kî*. Here it is clear that the first *kî* is causal while the second is recitative. When only one *kî* appears and precedes the verb as in Ex. 2.22, it can only have a causal meaning. The same holds true when *kî* appears alone without any verb (Gen. 41.51). But what is the force of the *kî* when it follows the verb as in Ex. 17.16? The evidence strongly favors understanding it as recitative. The second *kî* has retained its function from the full form and the causal force of the first *kî* has been assumed by the *waw* consecutive (Gen. 26.22; 29.33; Ex. 2.10). In sum, the *kî* in v. 16 is recitative. The causal element is not contained in the word which is spoken but supplied by the etiological framework.

2. *Literary and Traditio-Historical Analysis*

There is general agreement on the unity of the section. The older commentators tended to assign it to E, chiefly because of the staff. But, as Noth and others have pointed out, the staff does not play an important role and could well be secondary (also Grønbaek). Noth, therefore, assigns it to J. Several modern commentators also regard v. 14 as a Deuteronomic expansion.

In respect to the history of traditions problem several factors have to be taken into consideration. The basic story of the victory over the Amalekites by means of Moses' uplifted hands certainly gives the impression of being ancient. The motif has its closest parallel in the oracles of Balaam whose curse effected a defeat in battle (Num. 22.1ff.). There is nothing in the story to connect the raised hands with prayer. Again, the story of the victory over the Amalekites is connected to the naming of an altar, which would suggest an early localization of the tradition. Although it remains doubtful whether one can actually join the tradition to Kadesh as has been often attempted (Sellin, *Geschichte des israelitisch-jüdischen Volkes* I, Leipzig 1924, p. 69; Grønbaek), there is nothing improbable in seeing in the tradition a historical memory from the wilderness period (also Noth).

A problem, however, arises in understanding the conclusion of the story which vows perpetual enmity against Amalek. How is this enmity to be explained, particularly in the light of the victory of the Israelites according to Ex. 17? The tradition in Deut. 25.17ff. casts a somewhat different light on the problem. There the vow of perpetual enmity is tied to a humiliating defeat of Israel by the hands of Amalek. The failure to spare the weak and defenseless was an act of barbarism and provided a motivation for Israel's continued hatred. A similar picture is reflected in I Sam. 15, when Saul was ordered to exterminate the Amalekites. Grønbaek's interpretation of the evidence is illuminating when he suggests that elements from the subsequent history between Israel and the Amalekites have been appended to the older wilderness tradition. It is more doubtful how much of a detailed reconstruction of this later history can any longer be recovered.

3. Old Testament Context

The geographical setting for the battle with the Amalekites is shared with the previous story, namely, Rephidim. The connection of this site with Kadesh remains contested, but it is not difficult to imagine that Israel fought with the Amalekites at some desert oasis. The Amalekites were a nomadic tribe which biblical tradition derived from the genealogy of Esau (Gen. 36.12). The tribe inhabited the Sinai peninsula in the region of Kadesh (Gen. 14.7) as far to the south as Shur (I Sam. 15.7; 27.8), from where they made raids on the settled population of southern Palestine (Num. 13.29; I Sam. 27.8ff.). Commentators have found it strange that the Amalekites were so far south as Rephidim, which assumes that the site was close to the traditional location of Sinai. However, the geographical uncertainty respecting both Rephidim and Sinai, as well as our ignorance of the detailed life of the Amalekites, makes this sort of speculation rather fruitless. Certainly for the story itself it is of little consequence.

Joshua appears for the first time in the Pentateuch, and his identity and importance are assumed (contrast Ex. 33.11). Joshua is to lead the army, which is not a professional body but an *ad hoc* selection of men. Moses for his part is to stand on the top of the hill overlooking the battle. The definite article (*the* hill) again suggests that the location was well-known. Moses takes the 'rod of God' (4.20) in his hand. The plan of Moses and his instructions to Joshua are not described as stemming from a direct oracle of God.

The battle in the valley is briefly described, but the interest of the writer focuses on Moses. The outcome of the battle depends on what Moses does. As long as Moses held up his hands, Israel gained the advantage in battle, but when he lowered his hand, Amalek prevailed. Therefore, when Moses' hands grew weary, he was seated on a stone and his hands were supported on either side by Aaron and Hur. Thus victory was assured for Israel.

The initial difficulty of this story lies in understanding Moses' activity. At the outset, there is a certain tension in the story, which the versions have sought to eliminate, between Moses' rod, his hand, and his hands. The famous rod of Moses is introduced, but plays no further role. It cannot be connected with the banner of v. 14 because of dissimilarity in respect to both its vocabulary and function (*contra* Gressmann). It is possible that the rod was in the uplifted 'hand' of v. 11. But shortly the plural term is used, which indicates that both hands were raised and both needed supporting.

Both Jewish and Christian commentators have been quick to assume that Moses's stance was that of prayer. What else would he be doing? However, there is no indication whatever in the text which would confirm this. No words are spoken, but the battle is decided simply by the raising and lowering of his hands. The same effect results from Moses' stance even when his weary arms are physically supported by others. Gressmann and Beer have described the scene as magical, with Moses playing the role of the cult magician. Additional parallels from the Ancient Near East have been suggested (T. H. Gaster, *Myth, Legend, and Custom in the OT*, New York and London, 1969, p. 233). Without discussing at length the validity of these extra-biblical parallels, certainly the Old Testament offers the closest parallel in the figure of Balaam (Num. 22.1ff.). He is hired to curse Israel, and the point of the narrative turns on the automatic effect of a curse (or a blessing) which, once it has been unleashed, continues relentlessly on its course. In Ex. 17 the hands are the instruments of mediating power, as is common throughout the Ancient Near East (cf. the Hebrew idiom in Gen. 31.29). This amoral element of the unleashing of power through an activity or a stance is still reflected in the story. Nor can it be rationalized away, as already in the *Mekilta*, by assuming that Moses' role was essentially psychological. His uplifted hands encouraged the Israelites to exert themselves fully, whereas without the encouragement they slackened in battle.

However, the remarkable thing in the passage is the clear attempt to understand this old tradition of an impersonal exercise of power as a sign of the direct intervention of God himself. The interpretation of the meaning of the event is a twofold one. In v. 14 Yahweh commands Moses to record in a book his purpose to wipe out the name of Amalek. This is the first reference to Yahweh so far in the story, but it serves to confirm and extend the action which Moses has taken. It is likely that this verse reflects a continual history of warfare between Israel and Amalek which is justified traditionally on the basis of this first encounter in the desert (cf. Deut. 25.17ff.).

In vv. 15ff. Moses commemorates the victory with an altar which he named 'Yahweh is my banner'. There is nothing within the tradition which would connect the altar with the stone on which Moses sat (v. 15), nor is the connection between the altar and the banner very clear. It is possible that some etiology was once involved which now escapes notice. But certainly the point of the naming is to bear witness to Yahweh's role in the battle. Yahweh is the standard beneath which Israel rallies. The explanation of the name in v. 16a is not fully clear: 'a hand upon the banner of Yahweh' (cf. philological notes). However, the point seems to be that a battle cry directed to Israel is offered as an explanation of the name. The final sentence summarizes the whole story. The war with Amalek will continue from generation to generation because Yahweh willed it so.

Detailed Notes

17.8. Cf. the standard Bible dictionaries for the history of the Amalekites: *HDB* I, pp. 77ff.; *IDB* I, pp. 101f.; *BHH* I, cols. 77f.
11. Beer's attempt (*Exodus*, p. 93) to relate Moses' uplifted hands to a pre-Christian 'sign of the cross' seems dubious and unsupported by his alleged parallels.

4. History of Exegesis

Early Jewish exegetes found little of difficulty in the story and, as if by reflex, read it as an example of the power of prayer (*Mekilta*, Rosh Hashana 29). Added to this piety was also a touch of rationalism which understood the function of the banner to be a means of stirring the Israelites to vigorous combat.

The early Christian interpreters continued to view the story along with the Jews as a prayer of Moses, but turned their attention to allegorical elaboration of the details. Philo (*Vita Mosis* I. 214ff.) had already assigned a symbolic value to the uplifted hands, which taught the superiority of heaven over earth. Origen (*In Exod. Hom.* XI. 3) saw Jesus foreshadowed in the name Joshua. The raised hands signified his cross and the defeat of the Amalekites the victory over evil. These early typologies shortly became stock in trade and continued to be elaborated on throughout the Middle Ages (cf. Lapide for citations from the Fathers). A particularly popular theme was the identification of Amalek with the threat arising from the flesh.

A very different application emerged in the debate between Faustus and Augustine. Ex. 17 became one of Augustine's warrants by which to defend the theory of the 'just war' (*Contra Faustum* XXII.5).

For both Luther (*Predigt über 2 Mose*) and Zwingli (*Farrago Annotationum in Exodum*) the story was primarily a mirror of the Christian life and illustrated its struggle. Luther was puzzled that so many Israelites (600,000) would have had trouble with a few beduin, but concluded in the end that it showed how demoralized and weakened Israel had become through disobedience.

Calvin developed a somewhat different theme which was taken up in succeeding Reformed circles. He saw in the story an example of how God delegates his authority through his ministers who function as his instruments of power. Bishop Joseph Hall (*Contemplations*) interjects the Puritan note with his usual charm in writing: 'In vain shall Moses be upon the hill, if Joshua be not in the valley. Prayer without means is a mockery of God.' Moreover, even Karl Barth (*Church Dogmatics* II.2, ET Edinburgh 1957, p. 375) found in Ex. 17 a lesson of God's working through man in a delicate balance which neither impaired God's will nor destroyed man's genuine activity.

One of Luther's less fortunate typologies was his equating Amalek with the Jews who fought against Christ. Much closer to the spirit of the story is the sentiment of R. de Pury (*Der Exodus*, Neukirchen 1961, p. 48), who commented on the passage: 'The enemy of Israel is the enemy of God . . . An attack on Israel is an attack on God himself. This still holds true for today.' When seen in the religious context to which it was addressed, the statement would find many defenders among Christians. However, when understood as political strategy, one could scarcely find a greater abuse of the Old Testament.

THE VISIT OF JETHRO

18.1–27

W. F. ALBRIGHT, 'Jethro, Hobab and Reuel in Early Hebrew Tradition', *CBQ* 25, 1963, pp. 1ff.; E. AUERBACH, *Moses*, Amsterdam 1953, pp. 98–104; K.-H. BERNHARDT, *Gott und Bild*, Berlin 1965, pp. 119ff.; C. BREKELMANS, 'Exodus xviii and the Origins of Yahwism in Israel', *OTS* 10, 1954, pp. 215–24; M. BUBER, *Moses*, 1946, pp. 94ff.; A. CODY, 'Exodus 18, 12: Jethro Accepts a Covenant with the Israelites', *Biblica* 49, 1968, pp. 153ff.; F. C. FENSHAM, 'Did a treaty between the Israelites and the Kenites exist?', *BASOR* 175, 1964, pp. 51–4; A. H. J. GUNNEWEG, 'Mose in Midian', *ZThK* 61, 1964, pp. 1ff.; C. HAURET, 'Moïse était-il prêtre?', *Biblica* 48, 1959, pp. 516ff.; S. HERRMANN, 'Mose', *EvTh* 28, 1968, pp. 301ff.; R. HENTSCHKE, *Satzung und Setzender*, Stuttgart 1963, pp. 30ff.; E. JUNGE, *Der Wiederaufbau der Heerwesens des Reiches Juda unter Josia*, Stuttgart 1937; R. KNIERIM, 'Exodus 18 und die Neuordnung der mosäischen Gerichtsbarkeit', *ZAW* 73, 1961, pp. 146ff.; B. MAZAR, 'The Sanctuary of Arad and the Family of Hobab the Kenite', *JNES* 24, 1965, pp. 297–303; E. MEYER, *Die Israeliten und ihre Nachbarstämme*, Halle 1906, reprinted Darmstadt 1967, pp. 66, 97ff., 498ff.; M. NOTH, *Überlieferungsgeschichte des Pentateuch*, 1948, pp. 150ff., ET *History of Pentateuchal Traditions*, 1971, pp. 136ff.; H. H. ROWLEY, *From Joseph to Joshua*, London 1950, pp. 149ff.; H. SCHMID, *Mose. Überlieferung und Geschichte*, 1968, pp. 74ff.; W. H. SCHMIDT, *Alttestamentlicher Glaube und seine Umwelt*, Neukirchen-Vluyn 1968, pp. 61ff.; H. SEEBASS, *Mose und Aaron, Sinai und Gottesberg*, Bonn 1962, pp. 83ff.; R. DE VAUX, 'Sur l'origine Kénite ou Madianite du Yahvisme', *Eretz Israel* IX, *W. F. Albright Vol.*, ed. A. Malamat, Jerusalem 1969, pp. 28ff.; F. V. WINNETT, *The Mosaic Tradition*, 1949, pp. 57ff.

18 ¹Jethro, the priest of Midian, Moses' father-in-law, heard all that God had done for Moses and for Israel his people, how the LORD had brought Israel out of Egypt. ²So Jethro, Moses' father-in-law, took Zipporah, Moses' wife who had been sent away, ³and her two sons. The name of the one was Gershom (for he said, 'I have been a stranger in a foreign land'), ⁴and the other Eliezer (for he said, 'The God of my father was my help, and delivered me from the sword of Pharaoh'). ⁵Jethro, Moses' father-in-law, came to Moses with his sons and his

wife in the wilderness where he was encamped at the mountain of God. ⁶And he sent word to Moses, 'I, your father-in-law Jethro, am coming to you with your wife and her two sons.' ⁷Moses went out to meet his father-in-law, bowed low to him and kissed him. When they had greeted each other, they went into the tent.

8 Moses then recounted to his father-in-law everything that the LORD had done to Pharaoh and to the Egyptians for Israel's sake, all the hardships that had met them on the way, and how the LORD had delivered them. ⁹Jethro rejoiced over all the good that the LORD had done to Israel in delivering them from the Egyptians. ¹⁰Jethro said, 'Blessed be the LORD, who has delivered you from the hand of the Egyptians and from the hand of Pharaoh. ¹¹Now I know that the LORD is greater than all gods, because he delivered the people from under the hand of the Egyptians when they dealt arrogantly with them.' ¹²And Jethro, Moses' father-in-law, brought a burnt offering and sacrifices to God; and Aaron came with all the elders to share a meal with Moses' father-in-law in the presence of God.

13 The next day Moses took his seat as magistrate among the people, while the people stood about Moses from morning until evening. ¹⁴But when Moses' father-in-law saw all that he had to do for the people, he said, 'What is this that you are doing for the people? Why do you act alone and all the people have to stand about you from morning until evening?' ¹⁵Moses replied to his father-in-law, 'The people come to me to inquire of God. ¹⁶When they have a dispute, they come to me and I arbitrate between one man and another, and I let them know the laws and teachings of God.'

17 But Moses's father-in-law said to him, 'What you are doing is not wise. ¹⁸You will certainly wear yourself out, as well as the people with you. Surely the task is too heavy for you; you cannot do it alone. ¹⁹Now listen to me. Let me advise you and may God be with you. You represent the people before God and bring their cases before God, ²⁰and instruct them in the laws and the teachings, and make known to them the way they should go and the things they should do. ²¹Moreover, you should search for capable men from all the people, who fear God, men of integrity and incorruptible; and set these over them as officers of units of thousands, hundreds, fifties, and tens. ²²Let them act as judges for the people at all times; let them refer every major dispute to you, but decide for themselves every minor case. Make it easier for yourself, and let them share it with you. ²³If you do this – and God so commands you – you will be able to stand it, and all these people will go to their homes content.'

24 So Moses listened to his father-in-law and did just as he had said. ²⁵Moses chose capable men from all Israel and appointed them heads over the people, officers over units of thousands, of hundreds, of fifties,

and tens. [26]They acted as judges for all the people at all times. Hard cases they brought to Moses, but all the minor matters they would decide for themselves. [27]Then Moses let his father-in-law depart, and he went back to his own country.

1. Textual and Philological Notes

18.1. *ḥōtēn mōšeh*, 'father-in-law of Moses'. The meaning of the Hebrew *ḥōtēn* is clearly father-in-law. The term cannot be made to denote brother-in-law, as some have attempted. The difficulty of the verse lies in reconciling the various names given and establishing the relationship between them (cf. the exegesis below). Albright (*CBQ* 25, 1963, p.7) follows Bäntsch, Beer, Rudolph, and others in emending *ḥōtēn* to *ḥātān* (son-in-law), but in effect this cuts the Gordian knot of the exegetical problem.

2. The syntax of the sentence is difficult. The RSV, NEB, etc. follow an old exegetical tradition in supplying a pluperfect to avoid the difficulty in the chronology of the narrative. However, an imperfect consecutive cannot designate an earlier period of time in this manner. Cf. S. R. Driver, *Tenses*[3], §76; König, *Lehrgebäude* III, §142. NJPS and NAB are closer to the mark.

The noun *šillûḥîm* denotes both a 'dismissal' as well as a 'dowry'. The latter meaning does not fit the context, although some have suggested it. The *Mekilta* understands the dismissal as a divorce and cites the parallel in Deut. 24.1.

4. *beʿezrî*. The preposition is a *beth* of identity before a substantial predicate. R. J. Williams, *Hebrew Syntax*, Toronto 1967, §563.

5. 'mountain of God'. The syntactical connection is somewhat hard, but cf. *G-K* §118g.

6. It is difficult to know whether to prefer the reading of the Samar. and LXX, *hinnēh* = 'behold' (so RSV, NEB). The close parallel in Gen. 48.2 speaks in favor of the LXX, although the MT is fully intelligible. The preceding verb does not present any real problem.

9. *wayyiḥaddeʿ*. The MT retains two traditions of pointing. The LXX reads ἐξέστη, which is either from the Hebrew root *ḥrd* or *ḥtt*.

10. 10b is missing in the LXX. Its content is very similar to 10a, which suggests a secondary gloss. The proposal of BH[3] has been accepted which transfers 10b to 11b.

11. Targ. Onk. interprets the comparative as a monotheistic formula: 'there is no god but he . . .'.
There is a textual problem in 11b. The MT is an anacoluthon. The LXX avoids the difficulty by disregarding the *kî*. The rabbinic tradition interpreted the verse as implying a 'measure for measure' reaction on the part of God (Onk., Pseudo-Jon.). It may be that a part of the verse has been lost, or that the missing verse is found in 10b, as suggested. On the meaning of the verb *zādû*, cf. Ex. 21.14; Neh. 9.10.

12. *wayyiqqaḥ* = 'he took'. The conjectural emendation of BH[3] *wayyaqrēḇ* 'offered' assumes too great an exegetical freedom with the text.

15. 'to seek God'. For a study of the idiom, cf. C. Westermann, 'Die Begriffe für Fragen und Suchen im AT', *Kerygma und Dogma* 6, 1960, pp. 2ff.
16. The LXX reads a plural for the sing. verb of the MT *bā'*. This provides a somewhat better sense in this context; however the subject of the verb could be the 'thing'. Cf. Ex.22.8. *ḥōq* = 'statutes'. For the semantic range of this word, cf. R. Hentschke, *op. cit.* pp. 28ff.; P. Victor, *VT* 16, 1966, pp. 358ff. For the most recent, thorough treatment of *šāpaṭ* = 'rule, judge', cf. G. Liedke, *Gestalt und Bezeichnung alttestamentlicher Rechtssätze*, WMANT 39, 1971, pp. 63ff.
19. The suggestion of A. Geiger (*Urschrift und Übersetzungen der Bibel*, Breslau 1857, p. 328) that *mûl hā'elōhîm* (before God) was a later correction of an original *lē'lōhîm* (for God) is badly off the mark. Cf. the exegesis.
21. 'men of integrity . . .' On the terminology cf. Knierim, *op. cit.*, p. 149. The opposite quality would be in Hebrew *'anšē benê-beliyya'al* (Judg. 19.22; I Sam. 2.12).
25. The Samar. text adds the passage from Deut. 1.9–18.

2. *Literary and Traditio-Historical Analysis*

There is general agreement among critical scholars that ch. 18 is basically a unified narrative. Attempts, such as that of Gressmann, to find two complete strands have remained extremely unconvincing. Only occasionally are there signs of duplication. The interchange between the two divine names (twelve times Elohim; six Yahweh) has often been thought to indicate at least parts of two sources; however, the content of the narrative might also have accounted for the variation. Most commentators assign the chapter to E (cf. Elohim, mount of God), but detect some J influence in the repetitious phraseology of vv. 1–12.

The two places in the account where the narrative shows apparent expansion reveal different sorts of problems within the text. Verses 2–4 appear to reconcile variant accounts of Zipporah and her children (cf. 4.20). The syntactical difficulty of v. 2 would point to a later, redactional hand. However, the problem in vv. 15ff. has to do with the different concepts of Moses' office. At times he is deciding disputes; other times he is declaring statutes, or acting as mediator between God and the people. This problem, therefore, lies deeply embedded in the oral tradition and does not reflect different literary sources.

Commentators have long been aware of the problem of the chronological order of ch. 18 within the Exodus narrative. Both Ibn Ezra and John Lightfoot (*Gleanings out of . . . Exodus*, Works II, London 1822, pp. 379f.) explained in great detail why they considered the original place of the chapter to be after the Sinai chapters. Thus, for example, no tabernacle nor altar for sacrifice had yet been built. Moses did not yet know the statutes of God. Deuteronomy (1.9ff.) places the incident at the close of the Israelites' sojourn. Occasionally scholars have attributed the displacement to a topical arrangement in which Jethro's friendship is contrasted with the hostility of Amalek in ch. 17 (Cassuto). In my judgment, the problem lies at a deeper level, and cannot be solved by chronological adjustments.

Chapter 18 also presents a series of extremely difficult problems in relation to the history of traditions. It is not surprising that the chapter has been for so long such a center of controversy. Attention first focused on Jethro's visit in the first half of the chapter. Already the classic medieval Jewish commentators had been bothered by Jethro's role in the story. What was a foreign priest doing sacrificing to the God of Israel unless he had become a proselyte? Later historical critics offered another option for the same question. Jethro could offer to Yahweh because he had always been a Yahweh worshipper! In fact, the story suggests that he took the lead and it was the Israelites who were initiated into his cult. The famous 'Kenite theory' was an attempt to elaborate and systematize these earlier insights from the side of the history of religions. In Germany the theory received its classic formulation from Budde, in England from Rowley.

Since the hypothesis is readily available in numerous textbooks, there is no need to rehearse it in detail. It is an attempt to reconstruct the history of Israel's early religion through inference from certain hints given in the biblical narrative. For example, Jethro, who was called a Kenite elsewhere, meets Moses at the 'mountain of God', and takes the lead in the cult. Later in the chapter he instructs Moses in the administration of justice which was considered a religious practice. Moreover, the name of Yahweh was 'discovered' by Moses while in Midian, living with Jethro. Was he not then already a Yahweh-worshipping priest? The later history of friendship between Israel and the Kenites would suggest a continuing sense of kinship. However, in spite of the ingenuity of the defenders of the hypothesis, the theory suffers from serious problems, and in its classic form, has few present-day defenders (cf. the criticism of Brekelmans, *op. cit.*, and de Vaux, *op. cit.*). First of all, the method of investigation predates form criticism. It makes no attempt to trace a history of tradition, but pieces together bits of information from the Old

Testament which originally functioned in a variety of different ways. Moreover, the method attempts to deduce historical information from sources which were often silent in the very areas of highest interest. The result was a logical construct which went far beyond the available evidence. In sum, the theory raised some important questions, but was itself a brilliant cul-de-sac.

A more promising approach was that of Gressmann who explained the tradition of Jethro as a cult etiology which attempted to locate the introduction of the Yahweh worship in Kadesh. Gressmann was fully aware of the different levels within the tradition and sought to trace a development. In recent years, there has emerged considerable agreement in seeing a very early tradition at the heart of the passage, which reflects a common cult between Israel and Midian. The preceding verses are then a secondary elaboration of this basic core of tradition. Of course, the nature of this early tradition remains contested. Conservative scholars such as Fensham (*op. cit.*) have argued that the tradition rests on an historical treaty between Israel and the Kenites, which treaty can only be posited by analogy in lieu of sufficient historical evidence (cf. also Cody, *op. cit.*). Others, such as Knierim (*op. cit.*), would be closer to Gressmann in seeing a Levitical, cultic etiology without historical continuity. However, v. 12 is not etiological in its present form and must also be posited to support this interpretation.

Perhaps more important for exegesis is the recognition that there are tensions within the text which reflect the history of traditions, but that there are also attempts within the text at the resolution of the tension. The chapter retains many elements from the oldest level of the tradition. Jethro is a priest and of a foreign nation, Midian. The meeting is at the sacred mountain of God and there is a common cult meal with the Midianite taking the lead. However, this old material has been given a different focus in its reworked form. First of all, the climax of the chapter now comes in v. 11 with the confession of Jethro. Verse 12 now forms the final element in a series of acts which proceed from hearing, rejoicing, blessing, confessing, and sacrificing. Moreover, the tradition did not resort to the device of a 'conversion story' by which to render the older elements harmless (cf. exegesis). Jethro is nowhere pictured as a heathen who becomes a Yahwist. The contrast with Naaman (II Kings 5) is striking in this regard. Rather, Jethro is described praising the God of Israel in the language of faith and following the pattern of Ps. 135. In sum, there are tensions within the text which scholars have rightly seen, pointing to a development within the growth of tradition. However, the tradition itself has gone its own way toward resolving them, but in a manner which often fails to satisfy those whose concern with the text is chiefly historical.

The second part of the narrative (vv. 13ff.) is equally complex. The nature of the traditio-historical problem was perceived in part by both Meyer and Gressmann, but the basic study was provided by Knierim in 1961 (*op. cit.*). Knierim recognized that the story presented an account of the reorganization of Israel's juridicial structure and derived its sanction from Moses' office. When he then pursued the question as to the setting for such a reorganization, he found the key in the military formulae which constitute the new juridical structure and pointed to the period of Jehoshaphat. Following an exhaustive form – critical study Knierim characterized the tradition as an etiology which sought to legitimate a monarchial institution of civil judges in terms of a decentralization of the original Mosaic office.

Although I agree in part with Knierim's penetrating analysis, it seems to me that there is other evidence to be considered which would allow quite a different picture of the earlier stages of the history of traditions. In particular, I doubt that the etiological factor was the decisive factor in the formulation of the tradition; rather, it functioned only in giving shape to the final form of the tradition.

First of all, there are elements within the description of Moses' role as 'judge' which point to an older tradition of the Mosaic office. The people come to Moses when they seek 'to inquire of God'. The parallel to Ex. 33.7ff. is striking. The setting appears to be that of the tent of meeting and Moses is pictured as discerning the will of God through an oracle or by means of the sacred lots (v. 19). Again, he is represented in v. 19 as a mediator, not between two dissenting individuals, but between God and Israel. Obviously, the issue is not that of civil disputes, but relates to issues affecting the covenant (cf. ch. 19 for a full discussion of the Mosaic office).

Now the Pentateuch contains another story in Num. 11 which relates to the decentralization of this charismatic, prophetic office. Although the story has an etiological point in 11.26ff., the basic tradition is independent of this application. The connection of Num. 11 with Ex. 18 is assured by the common theme of Moses' inability to carry the load of the entire people and a means being provided for sharing the responsibility. In Num. 11 the office is still conceived of as charismatic and the gift of the spirit qualifies the seventy elders to perform Moses' function. Deut. 17.18ff. and 19.15f. offer a further extension of this same tradition. The Levites serve as judges in both cases involving both civil and religious matters. Again, a distinction is made between easy and difficult cases and the Levite offers instruction (tôrāh, v. 11) and decisions (cf. H.-J. Kraus, *Die prophetische Verkündigung des Rechts*, Zürich 1957, pp. 12ff.).

Ex. 18.13ff. reflects an even later stage in the history of the juridical office which Knierim has described. This history is now reflected in the tension in vv. 15ff. which portrays the role of Moses. The problem has long been observed that the terminology of 'statutes and instructions of God' (v. 16) does not match the description of adjudicating civil disputes (cf. Hentschke, *op. cit.*, pp. 30ff.; Schmid, *op. cit.*, pp. 78f.). But the very fact of this tension is evidence against Knierim's theory that the major force in forming the tradition was an etiology which arose from a monarchial institution. Ex. 18.13ff. reflects a final stage in the transformation of the tradition which bears the stamp of the monarchial period and the organization of the professional army. Certainly Knierim is correct in seeing the effect of the monarchy on the present form of the tradition. The royal judges still combine elements from the civil and religious sphere which had not separated, but the weight now falls on civil adjudication. Nevertheless, the tradition connects this office with the original Mosaic one and finds therein a warrant for demanding covenant responsibility in the administration of justice.

The final problem turns on the issue of how to understand the role of the whole chapter within the exodus tradition. Gunneweg (*op. cit.*) has argued that there is a layer of Midianite tradition consisting of 2.15–4.20 and ch. 18, which functioned in an unusual way in relation to the dominant Sinai tradition. On the one hand, the Midianite element in the tradition was original and cannot be derived from another cycle. On the other hand, the Midianite complex of tradition functions as a secondary connecting link between the exodus and Sinai traditions. Gunneweg's own solution for this problem is to suggest that the name Yahweh was originally not connected to the exodus tradition, but only with Sinai. The Midianite tradition served to introduce Yahweh into the exodus tradition and only later was subordinated to its present position when it rivalled the Sinai tradition.

Although Gunneweg has made some very acute observations, it is unlikely that his theory will rally much support. The attempt to separate the name Yahweh from the exodus remains highly speculative, nor is the evidence available by which to confirm the displacement of the Midianite layer by Sinai tradition (cf. the incisive criticism by S. Herrmann, *op. cit.*, pp. 324ff.). In my judgment, one can hardly speak of a Midianite layer of tradition. Rather, there are two foci of the tradition which are connected with Midian, the revelation of the name, and the common cult. The connecting of these two points in the narrative arose at a later date in the history of tradition in which the connection between Exodus and Sinai had already been well established. Knierim has argued that the two parts of ch. 18 were already connected in the oral tradition, but certainly the second part of the chapter is much more loosely joined to the Midianites. The omission of Jethro's role completely in Deut. 1.9ff. would confirm this observation.

In sum, it is doubtful whether one can successfully penetrate very far behind the earliest levels of Israelite tradition to recover the history of pre-Yahwistic tradition. Rather, the lines of development begin to emerge clearly in the course of Israel's own reflections on her tradition in the light of the ongoing history of the nation.

3. Old Testament Context

[**18.1–12**] The introduction of Jethro, priest of Midian, Moses' father-in-law, carries the reader back to the earliest period in the Exodus narrative. His name, his occupation, his country, and his relation to Moses, all serve to recall the beginning of the story. It reminds of that period of exile before Moses had begun his task of deliverance. The fact that the author intended to make this connection is further attested by the explicit reference in vv. 2ff. to Zipporah and her two sons (cf. Acts 7.29). Zipporah had last been heard of in the strange story of the circumcision in 4.24–26. Now suddenly she reappears with Jethro. The author of the present story is aware of the sudden disappearance of Zipporah, and therefore he tries to pick up the lost thread by adding a note. She had been earlier sent back to her father. Still this reference to this earlier incident does not fit in too well with the ongoing narrative. The mention of two sons also shows some tension with the earlier story which had Moses setting off to Egypt with only one. Apparently the writer had a different tradition at his disposal which he now seeks to work into his account. The rather periphrastic style of rehearsing the naming of the children interrupts the smooth flow of the narrative, but it serves an important function nevertheless. The first child had been called 'stranger in a foreign land'. In the name Moses testified to his future mission. His life was with his people. The second name, 'My father's God was my help,' now gave witness to the mission which had been accomplished by God's power. The name reminded, moreover, of the revelation at the bush when God had first made himself known to Moses as 'the God of your father' (3.6).

In spite of the complex history of traditions problems which lie behind the Midian stories, these chapters now perform a simple and straightforward function within the Exodus narrative. Chapter 2 pictures the quiet period of preparation. Moses pastures sheep for forty years in the wilderness. It is the quiet before the storm which erupts in ch. 3 and drives him back to Egypt. Now ch. 18 functions as a concluding scene. Once again the writer pictures an idyllic family scene, reminiscent of the patriarchs in Genesis. In ch. 3 Moses had received the sign that he would not only deliver the people, but that he would worship with them on the holy mountain (3.12). Ch. 18 comes to a climax with the common meal which was led by Jethro and shared by Aaron and the elders of the people. The first part of ch. 18 offers a moment of grateful remembrance. It looks back at what has happened and what God has done for Israel. Not yet at least is there any hint of the momentous event of Sinai which lies just ahead. Just for a moment the writer pauses in the story to look backward and to rejoice.

The writer achieves his effect by slowing the pace of his narrative. Jethro, Moses' father-in-law, appears and is announced. The repetition of his kinship with Moses seven times in twelve verses produces an atmosphere of polite formality. Then Moses' reaction is described in great detail. Up to this point in his story the writer has scarcely paused to speak of Moses as a man, particularly since he arrived back in Egypt. He is either a prophetic figure stalking fearlessly before Pharaoh, or the harassed leader of a murmuring mob interceding before God. In ch. 18 the writer returns to Moses, the man. The reader is made to experience the spontaneous outburst of family affection. (Naturally in the Ancient Near East the affection falls on the father-in-law, not the wife!) Moses goes out to meet him, treats him as the one of higher station in doing obeisance. Still the writer tarries with his description. They kiss one another; they ask about each other's welfare. Only then does Moses lead Jethro back to his tent. (Naturally he has his own tent, but up to this point in the story the writer has not bothered to mention it.)

Then Moses relates to his father-in-law all that has happened. He does not chant him a creed or rehearse a *Heilsgeschichte*. There is nothing whatever formal about it. Rather, the story exudes the genuine enthusiasm of Moses as he tells him the story of the deliverance starting with the plagues – 'all he did to Pharaoh' – and brings him through the trials of the wilderness before they reached the safety of the mountain. But Moses did not simply relate a story. He bore testimony to 'all that Yahweh had done . . . for Israel's sake', and 'how he had delivered them from the hand of the Egyptians'. The author leaves no doubt as to where the emphasis of the story falls.

Jethro responds with the same enthusiasm which had characterized Moses. Indeed the same vocabulary is repeated. He rejoiced at all the good which Yahweh had done for Israel in delivering them from the Egyptians. But Jethro did more than just reflect spontaneous joy. Indeed his response follows the pattern which the Psalmist outlines for the faithful of Israel to praise God (cf. Ps. 135). First, Jethro 'blesses Yahweh', that is, he praises God for his great deeds of deliverance. To bless God entails a special sort of praise. It acknowledges in thanksgiving that one's trust in God's care (*ḥeseḏ*) has been fully vindicated (Gen. 24.27; Ruth 4.14; I Chron. 29.10).

Then Jethro offers a confession in which he employs the well-known formula: 'Now I know . . .' (I Kings 17.24; II Kings 5.15). The content of the confession 'that Yahweh is greater than all gods' has aroused considerable controversy. Some older commentators, such as Calvin, thought that the confession still smacked of polytheism, and that Jethro had not reached the point of pure monotheism. Yahweh was indeed the greatest, but nevertheless, among other gods. But this is to misunderstand the Old Testament idiom by being too literal. Surely when the Psalmist praises God with such words as: 'Yahweh is great . . . our Yahweh is above all gods' (135.5), there is no vestige of polytheism left (cf. C. J. Labuschagne, *The Incomparability of Yahweh in the Old Testament*, Leiden 1966, p. 99.). Others have taken the confession to mean that Jethro now announces his conversion to Yahweh and renounces his pagan past. But this interpretation also has its difficulty. Certainly the idiom in 18.11 is different from that used by Naaman: 'There is no God in all the earth except in Israel.' The latter confession contains an obvious polemic aimed at establishing the exclusive claim of Yahweh in the mouth of a pagan.

The problem of whether Jethro's confession implies a conversion to Yahwism cannot be decided alone on the basis of the formula *'attāh yāḏa'tî* (now I know), as has often been attempted. Certainly Zimmerli is right when he stresses that this sort of knowledge involves an act of acknowledgement as well (*Erkenntnis Gottes nach dem Buche Ezechiel*, Zürich 1954, p. 43). The confession is an acknowledgement of a new understanding of God which has resulted from his action. But the acknowledgement does not determine the status of the speaker before his confession. His new understanding can be a deepening of a prior knowledge (I Kings 17.24) or a totally new understanding which is fully discontinuous with the past (II Kings 5.15). In other words, from the formula alone Jethro's confession could indicate either that he was a previous worshipper of Yahweh, or that he was a new convert.

There remains a certain tension in the text which, of course, has called forth this discussion. The fact that Jethro is a priest from a foreign country who does not belong to the people of Israel is an essential part of the tradition. Nevertheless, Jethro acts throughout the story as a faithful witness to Yahweh. He is not treated as an outsider, not does he act as one. He rejoices with Moses because of what Yahweh has done for Israel, and offers him praise in the language of Israel's faith. The sacrifice which Jethro offers is the final stage in a series of acts of worship. There is no hint in the text that he has won the right to participate in the cult because of a recent conversion. Rather, he bears witness to the greatness of the God of Israel by praise, confession, and sacrifice. It is possible that behind v. 12 lies an old tradition of a covenant treaty between Midian and Israel (cf. introduction), but according to the present form of the text, the sacrifice flows naturally from Jethro's response to the story of Israel's deliverance.

[18.13–27] There is a historical dimension to the second portion of the chapter which once again reflects a long period of development. A whole series of historical changes in Israel's legal structure are mirrored in the story through the variety of vocabulary used as well as in the concepts of the Mosaic office. But once again the problem is to determine the present function of the story within the Exodus narrative.

The story has a chronological connection with the preceding

incident. It happened on 'the next day', and arose as if by accident. Jethro observed Moses acting alone as a magistrate, while crowds of people stood waiting for their cases to be heard. The description of Moses' activity 'from morning until evening' suggests that Jethro only posed his query at the end of the day. Jethro's question to Moses, 'What is this thing you are doing?' obviously did not arise out of the need for information. Clearly Jethro knew precisely what was happening, but rather he sought to elicit from Moses himself his own explanation of his role. Moses' apparent straightforward answer contains a number of problems. Verse 15 suggests that the people have come to him 'to inquire of God'. This is a technical expression, used often in the Old Testament, which has its historical setting in the dispensing of oracles. Usually the sanctuary is the place designated for the practice. Particularly in times of perplexity or embarrassment, a person sought a divine oracle (I Sam.9.9; II Kings 22.18; Jer.37.7). Ex.33.7ff. mentions Moses' role in connection with the tent of meeting when it served as a sacred place outside the camp to which people went 'to seek Yahweh'.

However, it is clear from v.16 that the ancient idiom has lost its original meaning of acquiring an oracle. The people now come to Moses when they have to settle a dispute with one another. Because God continued to be regarded as the ultimate judge of all of Israel's laws, the retention of the old vocabulary was not inappropriate. Verse 16 concludes, 'I make known the statutes of God (*ḥuqqê hā'elōhîm*) and his instructions (*tôrōṭâw*).' Now the problem arises that these technical legal terms are normally not used to designate decisions in a civil case, such as seem to be intended in v.16a. Rather, the *ḥuqqîm* are either priestly declarations which are centered in the cult (Lev.10.11ff.), or summaries of the will of God used in a Deuteronomic homily (Deut.7.11; 8.11, etc.). In Isa.10.1 the prophet attacks 'iniquitous decrees' (*ḥiqqê-'āwen*) which appear to be legal sanctions by the local court for oppressing the poor. In Ex.18.20 the 'statutes and instructions' recur as providing the content of Moses' teaching. Moreover, Moses is to instruct the people in the 'way in which they must walk and what they must do'. Once again the description of Moses' role moves from that of an arbitrator in civil cases to a preacher of the divine will. Indeed, in v.19 Moses functions as a mediator, not between disputing Israelites, but between God and Israel.

It does not seem possible to sort out precisely the various different roles of Moses which are now combined into one account. Clearly there is a historical dimension involved which has combined a developing understanding of the juridical office into one account. He gives oracles, he decides disputes, he proclaims and teaches the divine will, and he mediates between God and Israel. Later on in the period after the settlement of the land, Israel accommodated her legal practice to the common procedure of having civil cases decided by arbitration before the elders at the gate (cf. L. Köhler, *Hebrew Man*, ET London and New York 1956, pp. 149ff.). At a still later period of the monarchy royal judges were appointed (II Chron. 19.4ff.). Ex. 18.13ff. is significant in its finding a warrant for the variety of different procedures already in Moses' own office. The intermingling of a variety did not divide sharply between a religious and a civil sphere.

The same concern for justice under God emerges in Jethro's advice on the choosing of qualified men to share Moses' responsibility. The judges are to be 'God-fearers, trustworthy, and men of integrity'. The division of the people into units of thousands, hundreds, fifties, and tens reflects the military organization of the nation (I Sam. 29.2; II Sam. 18.1, etc.). In the division of labor 'every great thing' is brought to Moses for his personal decision, that is to say, cases of major importance. The less important cases are decided by the appointed judges. In Deut. 1.9ff. the principle on which the division of labor is made appears to be slightly different, and relates to the difficulty of the case. Obviously the major cases would usually prove to be the most difficult, and would call for Moses' direct attention. Verse 26 includes both criteria and combines the difficulty of the case with its intrinsic importance.

Jethro concludes his advice with a commendation that Moses follow his instructions. He even adds the surprising comment that it is God's command that he do so. The reorganization will result in preserving Moses' strength and in establishing peace among the people. Moses accepts the advice of his father-in-law and carries out the new scheme in detail. The chapter closes with Jethro's departure back to his own country.

Now it has long puzzled commentators that Moses, who had spoken 'mouth to mouth' with God and was his mediator *par excellence* should have depended on the practical advice of a foreign priest, albeit his father-in-law, for such an important element in the life of the nation as the administration of justice. Later exegetes developed a number of theories by which to explain the problem (cf. History of Exegesis below). Yet the remarkable thing is that the Old Testament itself does not seem to sense any problem on this issue. The narrative moves back and forth with apparent ease between advice offered on the level of practical expediency (vv. 17f.) and statements about God's will which supports the plan (vv. 19, 23). No tension appears between these two poles because both are seen to reflect the divine will to the same extent. Because the world of experience was no less an avenue through which God worked, the narrative can attribute the organization of a fundamental institution of Israel's law to practical wisdom without any indication that this might later be thought to denigrate its importance in the divine economy.

Detailed Notes

18.1. 'Jethro'. I am inclined to agree with R. de Vaux (*op. cit.*, pp. 28f.) that the confusion in the names involves a variety of traditions, rather than with Albright (*op. cit.*), who harmonizes the diversity by means of textual criticism. Cf. the two articles for a full bibliography on the problem. Mazar (*op. cit.*) makes some interesting observations on the Kenites' association with Arad on the basis of Aharoni's excavation in 1962–3.

7. Cf. I. Lande, *Formelhafte Wendungen der Umgangssprache im AT*, Leiden 1949, pp. 2ff., for the Hebrew idioms of greeting.

10. On the blessing formulae, cf. W. Sibley Towner, *CBQ* 30, 1968, pp. 386–99.

12. On the problem of the nature of the sacrifice, cf. the articles of Brekelmans, Fensham, and Cody, cited in the bibliography.

16ff. On the juridical terminology, in addition to the monograph of R. Hentschke (*op. cit.*), cf. H. J. Boecker, *Redeformen der Rechtsleben im AT*, WMANT 14, 1964; I. L. Seeligmann, 'Zur Terminologie für das Gerichtsverfahren', *Suppl. VT* 16, 1967, pp. 251–300; G. Liedke, *Gestalt und Bezeichnung altt. Rechtssätze*, WMANT 39, 1971, pp. 62ff.

21ff. E. Meyer (*op. cit.*, pp. 49ff.) offers a basic study of the military organization of Israel, which should be supplemented by E. Junge, *Der Wiederaufbau des Heerwesens des Reiches Juda und Josia*, Stuttgart 1937. Albright discusses the historical background of the judicial reform of Jehoshaphat in *Alexander Marx Jubilee Volume*, New York 1950, pp. 61ff.

4. History of Exegesis

Different sets of questions have tended to cluster about the first and second half of the chapter, which is natural in the light of the great difference in subject matter.

Jewish exegetical tradition has been consistent from the beginning in its treatment of Jethro's visit. From the early Tannaitic times through the modern era Jethro is understood as a pagan who is converted to the faith of Israel, that is, to Judaism. Onkelos para-phrased Jethro's confession in order to bring out his pure monotheism: 'There is no God but He.' Pseudo-Jonathan has Jethro coming as an announced proselyte (cf. the *Mekilta*). On other detailed problems within the biblical text there was considerable variety of interpreta-tion, such as explaining why Moses was not mentioned in v. 12 as also participating in the sacred meal (contrast Ibn Ezra with the *Mekilta*).

This traditional Jewish interpretation was frequently accepted uncritically by Christian writers, but the conversion of Jethro was then applied in a different manner. Thus Cyril of Alexandria viewed Jethro as a foreshadowing of the Christian faith in being converted from an older, inferior faith to the new, superior. Both Bede and Nicholas of Lyra followed a similar line, especially in seeing in the text a concern for the Gentiles which adumbrated the gospel.

Although this approach continued to be maintained by many throughout the nineteenth century as the accepted Christian inter-pretation, other important scholars turned in quite a different direction. Calvin thought that Jethro's confession was still tinged with vestiges of polytheism and that he had not attained to a pure faith. J. Tirinus (died 1636) argued that Jethro came as a believer in the true God and not as a pagan. He pointed out that he could not have lived forty years with Moses and not come to know the God of Israel.

It is of interest to note that very little new was introduced into the interpretation until the middle of the nineteenth century. Both Clericus and Rosenmüller follow the same traditional lines. The introduction of a history of religions perspective which slowly developed into the Kenite theory (cf. section 2) had the immediate effect of undercutting all the so-called pre-critical exegesis, whether Jewish or Christian. Only in recent years, as a result of a growing disaffection with the Kenite hypothesis, have some of the studies of Ancient Near Eastern covenants returned to certain of the traditional questions, albeit from quite a different starting point.

When we turn to the second part of the chapter, it is natural to expect that interest would focus immediately on the details of the new juridical organization. Jewish exegesis combined the notice of the size of the nation in Ex. 12.37 with the number of officials, and arrived at the figure of 78,600 (cf. *Mekilta*, *B. Sanh.* 19a). Interest focused on understanding how the early judges performed their duties, such as by delegating the legal responsibility through the proper channels, and the like. Christian biblical scholars continued very much along the same lines. Particularly noteworthy was the famous study of the English legal historian and orientalist, John Selden, who studied the juridical organizational structure of Israel from a broad historical perspective in which he exhaustively reviewed all the available Jewish sources (*De Synedriis et Praefecturis Juridicis Veterum Hebraeorum*, 3 vols. 1650–55; cf. I, 15f. for Selden's treatment of Exodus 18). Likewise, J. D. Michaelis, in his *Laws of Moses* (1770–75), continued to treat the chapter as a straightforward historical source for Israel's legal history (I §49–50).

Along with the historical problem in Ex. 18 went a very significant theological interest in the chapter. Josephus (*Ant.* III, 66ff.) spoke early of Moses' great integrity in not concealing his debt to Jethro for such an important innovation. But particularly Origen (*In Exod. Hom.* XI.6) and Clement (*Strom.* VI.66.5) reflected at length on the significance of Moses learning divine truths from a pagan priest. They found in this openness a warrant for seeking knowledge from non-Christians, who likewise had access to divine truths. Augustine (*Quaest. in Hept.* II.67) saw in Jethro's advice a good example of natural law and reasoned that Moses was able to recognize a wise plan as being from God however it may have originated (*Doct. Christ.* proem., §7, MPL 34.18).

In the Reformation period the reference to Jethro was widely employed to address the relation of church and state. Particularly Luther preached at length on the subject of the 'weltliche und geistliche Regiment' from Ex. 18. He found it amazing that Jethro taught Moses about law when Moses was 'full of the Holy Spirit' and he drew the lesson that God had established secular kingdoms according to principles of rationality. Zwingli (*Annot. in Exod., ad loc.*) compared taking Jethro's advice with the spoils of Egypt which could be made to adorn God's temple. He relegated Jethro's role to the external side of the law and argued that Moses had an internal criterion by which to evaluate the truth of Jethro's advice. Finally, Piscator (*Commentarius in Exodum*) developed from the chapter the typical Reformed emphasis on the role of the secular magistrate under the rule of God.

5. *Theological Reflection*

In my judgment, the most fruitful theological dimension of this text for today lies in extending the insights first seen by the Greek Fathers, and later developed by the Reformers. They saw the witness of the text to lie in the relation of God's will as revealed through divine communication to his prophet and God's will as discovered in the wisdom of human experience. Certainly the intensity of this problem has increased in the modern world.

The very fact that the Reformers found it a problem to explain why Moses should have bothered with practical advice when he had access to direct, divine communication would indicate that the concept of revelation in the sixteenth century was no longer identical with that of the Old Testament where there seemed to be no tension felt at this point. It is of great significance that this openness to the world which emerges in the relation with Jethro is found already deeply within the Pentateuch and is not a later development which occurs from the spread of wisdom literature. In a sense, the basic problem of relating the divine law as given in the Pentateuch with the knowledge of God as found in wisdom has already been posed within Ex. 18.

Ex. 18 offers a classic example of the delicate theological handling of the issue within the Old Testament. The execution of the will of God for his people in the fundamental area of law is viewed from two different sides, and yet in a way which does not leave the two areas hopelessly tied up in tension. What Jethro advises from his world of experience, that Moses share the burden of administering justice with men of judgment and integrity within the community according to their natural abilities, fits in harmoniously not only with the concept of justice within the Pentateuch, but certainly with the prophets as well. Conversely, there is no attempt made at philosophical generalizations which would identify revelation and experience into an all-encompassing category.

It is also significant to observe that the so-called secular and religious areas of life are kept in close contact without attempting to separate them. Moreover, the relationship cannot simply be dismissed with the historical observation that Ancient Israel did not know of a separation between church and state. The Old Testament is filled with examples of tyrants and kings who understood how to exercise power and sought to capture the state by sealing off the 'religious elements'. The prophetic movement offers a classic Old Testament rejection of the separation of the secular from the religious.

Finally, the advice of Jethro is presented as if it arose from a completely accidental situation. 'On the next morning Jethro happened to see Moses sitting . . .' The advice which Jethro offered was directed to a particular historical situation within the life of Israel. Nevertheless, the *ad hoc* quality of his suggestion does not cause any great friction within a concept of an eternal and universal divine law. Ancient Israel did not fall into the theological trap of polarizing the accidental and the eternal. Jethro's advice was deemed expedient at that moment in Israel's history and, therefore, from God. Deut. 1.17 summarizes the tradition of Ex. 18 with the concluding statement: 'You shall not be partial in judgment . . . for the judgment is God's.' It was this conviction which afforded Israel both its continuity with the past and the creativity for the future.

INTRODUCTION TO THE SINAI TRADITIONS

K. Baltzer, *Das Bundesformular*, WMANT 4, 1960, 2nd ed. 1964; H. B. Huffmon, 'The Exodus, Sinai and the Credo', *CBQ* 27, 1965, pp. 101–13; N. Lohfink, 'Zum "kleinen geschichtlichen Credo" Dtn 26, 5–9', *Theologie und Philosophie* 46, 1971, pp. 19–39; D. J. McCarthy, *Treaty and Covenant*, Rome 1963, 2nd ed. 1972; G. Mendenhall, 'Law and Covenant in Israel and the Ancient Near East', *BA* 17, 1954, pp. 26ff., 50ff.; E. W. Nicholson, *Exodus and Sinai*, Oxford 1973; M. Noth, *Überlieferungsgeschichte des Pentateuch*, 1948, ET *A History of Pentateuchal Traditions*, 1971; G. von Rad, *Das formgeschichtliche Problem des Hexateuch*, Stuttgart 1938, ET *The Problem of the Hexateuch and Other Essays*, Edinburgh and London 1966; A. Weiser, *Introduction to the Old Testament*, London (= *The Old Testament: Its Formation and Development*, New York), ET 1961, pp. 83ff.; A. S. van der Woude, *Uittocht en Sinaï*, Nijkerk 1960.

From the wide variety of problems connected with the growth of the Sinai traditions one problem has dominated the scholarly discussion during the period of the last thirty years. Briefly stated, the issue turns on establishing the relationship between the exodus and Sinai traditions.

In one sense the problem had been long recognized. The classic literary critics such as Kuenen and Wellhausen described quite accurately the loose connection between the departure from Egypt and the events at Sinai, and sought to solve such problems as the encampment at Meribah both before and after Sinai (Ex. 17.7; Num. 20.13) with theories of source criticism. However, the modern issue was sharply posed for the first time in the brilliant monograph of von Rad (*op. cit.*) in 1938. Taking his impetus from Mowinckel and Alt, von Rad argued his now famous thesis that form-critically one could distinguish two distinct traditions in the Old Testament, the exodus and Sinai, which derived from two distinct settings. They had been separately transmitted through different cultic functions and had been only secondarily joined together at a relatively late period within the traditional history of Israel. The thesis was greatly enhanced by its general acceptance in Europe by such leading scholars as Alt and Noth.

Opposition to the thesis arose soon from several sources. Weiser (*op. cit.*) expressed a sharp criticism of von Rad's use of the alleged credal formulations as providing an avenue into the earliest pentateuchal traditions. Again, scholars who continued to emphasize the literary approach (Eissfeldt, Pfeiffer) seemed basically unconvinced. But the major opposition came from the American archaeological school associated with Albright. These scholars rallied around Mendenhall's 1954 essay (*op. cit.*) regarding the Hittite suzerainty treaties as providing the evidence by which to refute von Rad and to establish the historical connection between the two traditions.

It is not necessary to rehearse the two decades of scholarly debate on the subject since the issues have been adequately reviewed many times (cf. McCarthy, Huffmon, Nicholson). In my judgment, there has been no final clarification of this extremely complex problem. The strengths and weaknesses of von Rad's original proposal have been repeatedly pointed out. Likewise, the difficulties of any direct application to the Old Testament of Hittite parallels have become increasingly apparent. Obviously it is impossible within the scope of an Exodus commentary to unroll fully all the issues of the debate. Nor is it likely that much that is new can be presented in terms of the present lines of the debate.

Perhaps the most disappointing side to the recent controversy has been in seeing how little genuine contribution has emerged for the actual exegesis of the book of Exodus as a result of the controversy. On the one hand, recent continental scholarship has often radicalized von Rad's form-critical approach in an endless search for earlier forms and alleged traditions. As a result, the present biblical text has been atomized and hopelessly blurred by hypothetical projections of the traditions' growth. On the other hand, American scholarship has tended to impose Ancient Near Eastern patterns upon the biblical traditions with a heavy hand which has only succeeded in smothering the text, or it has fallen back into rationalistic harmonizations and reductionistic theories of 'what really happened'. Both approaches have failed to deal seriously with the present form of the biblical text and have focused their major interest on some phase of the prehistory.

In my judgment, the study of the early development and historical background of the present text can be exceedingly useful to the extent in which the final form is illuminated, but there is no guarantee or necessity that such research will always, in each instance, play this decisive role. In fact, the history of research has often demonstrated how effectively the study of the prehistory has functioned in obscuring the biblical text through false parallels and mistaken ideas of historical development. Specifically in terms of the present impasse regarding the relation of the two biblical traditions, one can await the results of further research with an open mind. It may be that new and genuine insights will emerge which will have to be reckoned with. Conversely, it is possible that the investigation will collapse from its own weight and thus call for a fresh set of questions. However this may be, the challenge of interpreting the canonical text in its own integrity remains. It is even possible that by focusing more closely on the final form of the biblical text one may find some indirect aid in unravelling the mysteries of the earlier stage of the exodus traditions.

XVI

THE THEOPHANY AT SINAI

19.1–25; 20.18–21

G. Auzou, *De la Servitude au Service*, Paris 1961, pp. 243ff.; K. Baltzer, *Das Bundesformular*, WMANT 4, 1960, pp. 37ff.; J. B. Bauer, 'Könige und Priester, ein heiliges Volk (Ex. 19, 6)', *BZ*, NF 2, 1958, pp. 283–6; W. Beyerlin, *Origins and History of the Oldest Sinaitic Traditions*, ET Oxford 1965; W. Caspari, 'Das priestliche Königreich', *ThBl* 8, 1929, pp. 105–10; B. D. Eerdmans, *Das Buch Exodus*, Giessen 1910; O. Eissfeldt, *Hexateuch-Synopse*, Leipzig 1922; *Die Komposition der Sinai Erzählung, Exodus 19–34*, Berlin 1966; G. Fohrer, '"Priesterliches Königtum", Ex. 19, 6', *TZ* 19, 1963, pp. 359–62; reprinted in *Studien zur altt. Theologie und Geschichte*, Berlin 1969, pp. 149–53; H. Gressmann, *Mose und seine Zeit*, 1913, pp. 180ff.; M. Haelvoet, 'La Théophanie du Sinaï', *ETL* 29, 1953, pp. 374ff.; J. Jeremias, *Theophanie*, Neukirchen-Vluyn 1965, pp. 100ff.; R. Klopfer, 'Zur Quellenscheidung in Exod. 19', *ZAW* 18, 1898, pp. 197–235; H.-J. Kraus, *Worship in Israel*, ET Oxford and Richmond 1966, pp. 93ff., 179ff.; Dennis J. McCarthy, *Treaty and Covenant*, Rome 1963, pp. 152ff.; G. E. Mendenhall, 'Covenant Forms in Israelite Tradition', *BA* 17, 1954, pp. 50ff.; W. L. Moran, 'De Foederis Mosaici Traditione', *Verbum Domini* 40, 1962, pp. 3–17; 'A Kingdom of Priests', *The Bible in Current Catholic Thought*, New York 1962, pp. 7–20; S. Mowinckel, *Le Décalogue*, Paris 1927; J. Muilenburg, 'The Form and Structure of the Covenantal Formulations', *VT* 9, 1959, pp. 347–65; Murray Newman, *The People of the Covenant*, Nashville 1962; L. Perlitt, *Bundestheologie im Alten Testament*, WMANT 36, 1969, pp. 156ff.; W. Rudolph, *Der 'Elohist' von Exodus bis Joshua*, Berlin 1938; R. B. Y. Scott, 'A Kingdom of Priests, Ex. xix, 6', *OTS* 8, 1950, pp. 213–19; J. Wellhausen, *Die Composition des Hexateuchs*[3], Berlin 1899; H. Wildberger, *Jahwes Eigentumsvolk*, Zürich 1960; E. Zenger, *Die Sinaitheophanie*, Würzburg 1971.

19 ¹On the third new moon after the Israelites had gone forth out of the land of Egypt, on that very day, they entered the wilderness of Sinai. ²Having set out from Rephidim, they entered the wilderness of Sinai and camped in the wilderness. There Israel camped in front of the mountain, ³while Moses went up to God. Then the LORD called to him from the mountain, saying, 'Thus you shall say to the house of Jacob, and announce to the children of Israel: [4]"You have seen what I did to the Egyptians, and how I bore you on eagles' wings and brought you to myself. [5]Now then, if you will really hearken to my voice and keep my covenant, you shall be my special possession among all peoples (for all the earth is mine), [6]and you shall be to me a kingdom of priests and a holy nation." These are the words which you shall speak to the Israelites.'

[7] Moses came and summoned the elders of the people and put before them all the words which the LORD had commanded him. [8]All the people answered together, saying: 'All that the LORD has spoken we will do.' Moses reported the people's words to the LORD. [9]The LORD said to Moses: 'I am now coming to you in a thick cloud in order that the people may hear when I speak with you and then may trust you for ever.' Moses reported the people's words to the LORD. [10]Then the Lord said to Moses, 'Go to the people and let them prepare themselves today and tomorrow and let them wash their clothes [11]and be ready by the third day; for on the third day the LORD will come down upon Mount Sinai in the sight of all the people. [12]You must set boundaries for the people round about, saying, "Beware of going up the mountain or even touching the edge of it. Whoever touches the mountain shall be put to death. [13]No hand shall touch him, but he shall be either stoned or shot; whether beast or man, he shall not live." When the horn sounds a long blast, they shall come up to the mountain.' [14]Moses came down from the mountain to the people and had the people prepare themselves and they washed their clothes. [15]And he said to the people, 'Be ready by the third day; do not go near a woman.'

[16] On the third day, when morning came, there were peals of thunder and flashes of lightning, and a dense cloud upon the mountain, and a very long blast of the horn, and all the people who were in the camp trembled. [17]Moses led the people out of the camp toward God and they took their stand at the foot of the mountain.

[18] Now Mount Sinai was completely enveloped in smoke, for the LORD had come down upon it in fire. Its smoke rose like the smoke from a kiln, and the whole mountain trembled violently. [19]As the sound of the horn grew louder and louder Moses was speaking and God was answering him in a voice. [20]And the LORD came down upon Mount Sinai, on the top of the mountain; and the LORD called Moses to the top of the mountain; and Moses went up. [21]The LORD said to Moses, 'Go down and warn the people not to break through to the LORD in order to gaze, lest many of them perish. [22]The priests also, who approach the LORD, are to sanctify themselves lest the LORD break out against them.' [23]But Moses said to the LORD, 'The people cannot come up to Mount Sinai, for you yourself warned us saying, "Set bounds on the mountain and sanctify it".' [24]Then the LORD said to him,

'Go down and come back bringing Aaron with you; but do not let the priests or the people break through to come up to the LORD, lest he break out against them.' [25]Moses went down to the people and spoke to them.

[20.1–17; cf. the next chapter for a separate treatment.]

18 Now as all the people were perceiving the thunder and lightnings, the blast of the horn and the mountain smoking, the people became afraid and fell back, and stood at a distance. [19]They said to Moses: 'Speak to us, and we will listen, but let not God speak to us, lest we die.' [20]Moses answered the people, 'Do not be afraid, for God has come in order to test you and in order that the fear of him may be present with you to keep you from sinning.' [21]So the people stood at a distance, while Moses approached the thick cloud where God was.

1. Textual and Philological Notes

19. 1. *baḥōḏeš haššelîšî*. The word *ḥōḏeš* can mean either 'month' or 'new moon'. It has long been debated which of the two senses is intended here. Since the phrase 'on that very day' (v. 1) refers back to *ḥōḏeš*, the reference to new moon seems easier, and has been generally accepted by commentators (RSV, NEB, NJPS; not NAB). However, difficulties do remain with this interpretation. Dillmann points out that one would expect the expression *beʾeḥāḏ laḥōḏeš* (cf. Num. 1.1; 18; 29.1). Other examples of *baḥōḏeš* expressing the first day of the month are less convincing. Bäntsch and others argue that the exact date has fallen out and was probably removed intentionally to aid the later tradition in relating the giving of the law to the feast of weeks. However, statistics indicate that the expression *bayyôm hazzeh* or *beʿeṣem hayyôm hazzeh*, which is common to P, can follow either an exact date formula (Gen. 7.13) or also refer to a specific day without the precise formulation (Gen. 17.23; Ex. 12.17).

3. The LXX reads εἰς τὸ ὄρος τοῦ θεοῦ, which could be original (cf. 3.1). The LXX[B] reading of ἐκ τοῦ οὐρανοῦ, however, is secondary and a corruption of ἐκ τοῦ ὄρους (Rudolph, p.42). The inverse word order can best be explained by a change of subject. The Hebrism 'sons of Israel' should be retained because of the obvious parallelism. On the emphatic use of *ʾattem*, cf. Ex.20.22; Deut.29.1.

6. *mamleḵeṯ kōhⁿnîm*. The syntax and meaning of the expression has been much discussed (cf. bibliography for the articles of Scott, Bauer, Moran, Fohrer). There seems to be at least some consensus in respect to the linguistic parallelism within the verse. 'Priests' is an attribute of 'kingdom' as 'holy' is an attribute of 'nation' (cf. Moran, p. 7). Moreover, Moran seems to have established his point that *mamleḵeṯ kōhⁿnîm* is not to be regarded as a synonym of *gôy qāḏôš*, but a separate entity, 'priestly kings', which forms a totality with the people.

10. *qiddaštām*. The difficulty of the meaning has been felt at least since Targ. Onk. (*tzmnwn* = prepare). Cf. Rashi, Rashbam. From the context it is clear that Moses did not 'consecrate' the people, but had them prepare themselves. Cf.

Meek in the AmTr: 'go through a period of consecration', and NJPS: 'warn them to stay pure'. Still one would have expected the hithpael as occurs in 19.22.

12. The Samar reads *bāhār* for the MT *hāʿām*. Cf. 19.23. The Samaritan reading is accepted by NEB, but the MT should be retained as seen from the context.

13. The second half of the verse is difficult. *hayyōḇēl* is usually identified with the blast from the ram's horn of Josh. 6.5. However, the narrative in 19.16, 19 speaks rather of the *qōl šōpār*, which is hardly the same. The LXX reads: ὅταν αἱ φωναὶ καὶ αἱ σάλπιγγες καὶ ἡ νεφέλη ἀπέλθῃ ἀπὸ τοῦ ὄρους = 'when the voices and trumpets and cloud depart from off the mountain', which is an interpretative expansion. The use of the permissive sense of the verb *yaʿalû* ('they may go up' – Driver), while grammatically possible, does not remove the logical difficulties in the chapter.

17. *liqraʾṯ* frequently functions as a preposition (*BDB*, p. 896), but cf. the close parallel in Gen. 14.17.

18. Verse 18b has almost a circumstantial force, represented by the inverse order and finite verb.

LXX reads λαός for the MT *har* (cf. 16). Some nine Heb. mss. also read 'people'. The MT is probably to be preferred, although Dillmann's point that the subject of the verb is nowhere else an inanimate object carries some weight. There are many conceptual parallels to the MT (Judg. 5.4; Ps. 68.9, etc.) which are of limited value in deciding the textual problem.

19. The frequentative sense of the two verbs should be observed. In my judgment, the *NEB* translation is inadequate.

beqōl = 'in a voice'?; LXX φωνῇ; Vulg. *voce*. Although there has been a wide consensus among recent translators in rendering the Hebrew *qōl* as 'thunder', the problem is not so simple as imagined (cf. Rashi, Kalisch). There is no doubt that in certain poetic passages the 'voice of God' (*qōl YHWH*) is identified with thunder (cf. Pss. 18.14; 29.3, etc.). However, the issue at stake is whether this is the meaning of Ex. 19.19. The problem is as follows: ordinarily in Hebrew a clear distinction is made between a 'sound' (*qōl*) and a word (*dāḇār*), the latter being a semantic unit. In Ex. 19 thunder which is a specific sound is expressed by the plural form *qōlōṯ* (v. 16). Now Ex. 19.9 which anticipates v. 19 clearly refers to Yahweh's 'speaking'. This promise is fulfilled in v. 19. However, the difficulty arises because God is pictured in v. 19 as answering, not in words, but *beqōl* 'in a voice'. What is meant? The text leaves its meaning undetermined, without specification. On the one hand, to assume that God was speaking in an audible language is artificially to supply exactly what is missing. On the other hand, to render the word by 'thunder' is to determine arbitrarily what sound is intended, as if a thunderstorm was really what the chapter was about anyway!

Significantly this ambiguity has disappeared in Deut. The author is concerned to emphasize that Israel saw no form (4.12), but only heard a sound (*qōl*). Yet the lengthy description which precedes and follows consistently identifies the sound 'out of the fire' with speech and words. It was a voice which spoke words (4.10ff., 33ff.; 5.4, 22ff.). This move seems to be a conscious attempt of the writer to distance himself from the older language of the Psalmist which he did not feel appropriate for Sinai.

20.18. An initial circumstantial clause. Cf. Deut.4.12; Judg.13.19. Cassuto emphasizes correctly the simultaneous quality of the action. The Samar. has altered the text toward a more logical sequence,
The Samar., LXX, Vulg. read the plural for the MT's *wayyar'*. So also BH³, Driver, and many modern translations. Dillmann argues to retain the MT, as does the *NJPS*. The confusion between the two Hebrew roots is quite frequent in the MT (cf. I Sam.23.15; I Kings 19.3). The singular reading would seem to be mistaken in any case. An additional reason for emending is the reference in v.20 (cf. Judg.6.23; Isa.7.3).

20. *nassôt*. Greenberg (*JBL* 79, 1960, pp.273f.) argues for a factitive sense of the verb meaning 'cause to have experience of'. In my opinion, he has not established his case from the parallel usages of the piel. The issue at stake is rather exegetical than lexicographical. Cf. Kalisch for a full discussion of the rabbinic interpretation. Also the excellent formulation of Clericus (*ad loc.*).
yir'ātô. An objective genitive (*G-K* §135m).

21. The Samar. adds the following verses from Deut.:5.25; 18.18–22; 5.27–28.

2. *Literary and Traditio-Historical Analysis*

The extreme difficulty of analyzing the Sinai pericope has long been felt. In spite of almost a century of close, critical work many of the major problems have resisted a satisfactory solution. Even from a cursory reading of Ex. 19 one can observe tensions in the text which have caused the perplexity. Moses is pictured as ascending and descending Mount Sinai at least three times without any apparent purpose. At times the people are pictured as fearful and standing at a great distance from the mountain, whereas at other times there are repeated warnings which are intended to prevent any of them from breaking forth and desecrating the sacred mountain. Again, the description of God seems to fluctuate between his actually dwelling on the mountain and only descending in periodical visits. Finally, the theophany is portrayed both with the imagery of volcanic smoke and fire as well as with that of the clouds and thunder of a rainstorm.

Efforts to interpret this chapter have tended to fall into two major approaches, which in recent times have merged more and more, namely, the literary-critical and the traditio-historical. A brief review of some of the major attempts may help in bringing the problems into focus.

A. *The Literary-Critical Approach*

Wellhausen's literary analysis of the Sinai pericope (*Composition des Hexateuchs*, 1876; 1899³) was an early attempt to unravel the problem. He took as his initial lead the fact that in 19.10–19 Moses was with the people during the theophany while in 19.20–25 he was alone with Yahweh receiving a communication. He found three major strands in addition to the Priestly source (Q). To J he assigned 19.20–25, the Book of the Covenant 21–23, and 24.3–8. To E he gave 19.10–19, the Decalogue (20.1–19), and 24.1–2, 9ff. Ex. 34 he designated an independent source. However, after Kuenen's criticism, Wellhausen accepted in his second edition the evidence that the Book of the Covenant did not belong to J. This insight cleared the way for him to assign ch. 34 to J as the parallel to E's 'ethical decalogue'. He also accepted Kuenen's suggestion to transpose 20.18–21 before 19.15–19, which rearrangement has been generally followed by his successors.

The generation of scholars which followed built largely upon Wellhausen's analysis. It agreed basically on the extent of the P source, the independence of the Book of the Covenant and the J parallel in ch. 34 to E's Decalogue. However, Wellhausen's broad analysis of the J and E sources in ch. 19 called forth a far more critical and detailed analysis. Particularly men such as Bäntsch (*Exodus*, 1903) focused on the multiple inconsistencies within Ex. 19, and proposed a much more detailed division between J and E. Bäntsch assigned to J vv. 9, 11–13a, 15, 18, 20, 21, 25. To E (and E[1]) he attributed vv. 2b, 3a, 10, 13b–14, 16–17, 19. He followed Wellhausen in assigning vv. 3–8 to a Deuteronomic editor. If one analyzes Bäntsch's division, it becomes clear that the use of the divine names played an important role initially. The only three occurrences of Elohim in the chapter (vv. 3a, 17, 19) determined for him the basic division of sources respecting the theophany. The major remaining problem then turned about the sorting out of sources during the preparation period which preceded the theophany. However, the divine names could no longer function as the criterion since only the name Yahweh appeared. Therefore, Bäntsch employed conceptual distinctions, and the presence of alleged duplication as a guide. In J Yahweh 'descended' (v. 11a) upon Sinai, and sealed off the mountain (vv. 12–13a), whereas in E the people were to be sanctified in order to ascend the mountain.

Bäntsch recognized that the task of determining the continuation of sources through the legal material was even more involved: 'a complete tangle' (p. 177). He admitted straightaway that the normal source divisions did not work with the material and spoke of the need of sorting out different levels (*Schichten*) within each source.

He assigned the Decalogue to E, but then argued that E had provided only a secondary framework to an originally independent piece. The connection between the theophany and the giving of the law he saw as highly problematic. In 24.8 the connection was with the Book of the Covenant and not with the Decalogue, but here again the relation was regarded as redactional. From the Book of the Covenant he was able to isolate only a portion (*Horebdebarim*) as original. Finally, Bäntsch followed Wellhausen in seeing two different sources in ch. 24 which recounted the sealing of the covenant (vv. 3–8 and 1, 2, 9ff.). Whereas Wellhausen had assigned vv. 3–8 to E, and vv. 1, 2, 9ff. to J, Bäntsch sensed more sharply the difficulty of finding a place for J and assigned both accounts to different levels of E, in spite of the contradictory evidence of the divine names in this chapter.

In spite of its difficulties, Bäntsch's detailed source division of Ex. 19 approaches as near as possible to what might be called the 'standard' literary analysis. The same division with minor variations is found in Klopfer, Beer, Wildberger, Auzou, etc. Among the English commentators McNeile and Driver follow basically the same division, although there is more variation when it comes to analyzing the preparation for the theophany. Noth's view is generally accepted in respect to the actual theophany, but he assigns most of vv. 10–15 to J, reducing E to a minimum. Surprisingly enough, even Eissfeldt follows the main lines of Bäntsch's division and goes his own way only in assigning vv. 12 and 18 to L.

However, a much more serious disagreement was voiced by Gressmann (*Mose*, pp. 18off.). He felt that it was essential to a correct understanding of the chapter that v. 9a ('. . . that the people may hear when I speak with you') be joined to Moses' subsequent speaking to God in v. 19. This move, however, implied a complete disregard for the divine names. But Gressmann was prepared to assign almost the entire chapter to E leaving only v. 18 as original to J. Again in Te Stroete (*Exodus*, pp. 134ff.) the breakdown of the source division proposed by Bäntsch has become acute. His analysis of vv. 9–15 reverses almost completely the role of J and E, and at least demonstrates the possibility of a completely different scheme of source division. Then again, in the studies of Haelvoet (*op. cit.*) and Beyerlin (*op. cit.*) there is the tendency to seek a literary solution in a fragmentary hypothesis and abandon the classic theory of strands of narrative. Both of these writers designate a number of key verses as independent tradition and see no connection with either of the major sources.

Although few scholars have been convinced by the attempts of Eerdmans and Rudolph to salvage only one basic narrative in ch. 19, the effect of their criticism has been to heighten the uncertainty of the previous critical work. Particularly Rudolph was able to demonstrate with considerable impact how precarious the various linguistic and conceptual criteria were in analyzing the sources. Rudolph's own solution represented the opposite extreme from Gressmann and eliminated the E source entirely. However, his reconstruction seemed to suffer from arbitrary rearrangements of verses and equally subjective harmonization. Nor did Cassuto's repeated assurances that the literary critics were basically mistaken in denying the lack of unity to ch. 19 offer any viable alternative.

B. *The Traditio-Historical Approach*

At the beginning of this century scholars had begun to suggest that the solution to the problems of Ex. 19ff. did not lie on the literary level. Gressmann's study of 1913 was a first bold move to bypass the deadlock by an appeal to oral tradition. He sought to reconstruct a history of oral tradition behind each source and postulated different stages of development behind each of the literary strands. In spite of its brilliance and ingenuity Gressmann's theory suffered from uncontrolled speculation and few were entirely convinced. Mowinckel's study of 1927 (*op. cit.*) provided a much more solid basis for further research and certainly signalled a major breakthrough. He was the first to have clearly identified the cultic background of the Sinai pericope and tied it convincingly to a ceremony of covenant renewal. He found a basic oral pattern, common to both J and E, which reflected the cult and which progressed from the initial preparation to the theophany, giving of the law, acceptance by the people, and sealing of the covenant. Of course, this was the insight which von Rad took up and developed in his stimulating monograph (*Das formgeschichtliche Problem des Hexateuch*, 1938). Von Rad brought much greater precision to bear in delineating the cultic tradition. He suggested that a basic cultic pattern not only could be recognized in Ex. 19ff. but was also reflected in the whole of Deuteronomy. The pattern of historical recitation, reading of the law, promise, and sealing of the covenant roughly approximated to that of Mowinckel's.

However, in spite of the genuine insights found in this development which began with Mowinckel's traditio-historical approach to Sinai, certain major problems remained. The covenant pattern did not really illuminate ch. 19. At best it worked for 19.3–8 which Mowinckel regarded as secondary, but for the rest of ch. 19 Mowinckel's study offered no new insights beyond Gressmann, especially for the source-critical problem. Again, the covenant pattern did not really emerge from what was regarded as the J material and the important element in the pattern of the sealing of the covenant was lacking completely in ch. 34. In this respect the covenant pattern worked out by von Rad was no more helpful than Mowinckel in shedding light on the tradition and sources behind ch. 19.

Oddly enough, the discovery of the Hittite parallels to the covenant form (Mendenhall, *op. cit.*) confirmed the inadequacy of the pattern worked out by Mowinckel and von Rad in providing an understanding of Ex. 19. The suzerainty treaties offered a striking parallel to the broad covenant pattern which had been suggested for Ex. and Deut. But the repeated attempts of Mendenhall, Baltzer (*op. cit.*), and above all of Beyerlin (*op. cit.*) to find in the treaty covenant form the basic pattern underlying Ex. 19 has proved itself more and more untenable. Certainly McCarthy (*op. cit.*) is correct in denying that Ex. 19 reflects the covenant form. Not only is there no hint of a curse-blessing section in the Decalogue, but, even more central, the fundamental role of the covenant mediator of ch. 19 has no parallel in the treaty pattern. Indeed, the whole point of ch. 19 seems to lie elsewhere. It would seem, therefore, that Gressmann was correct in suggesting that the covenant form in 19.3–8 reflects a secondary development within the Sinai tradition which received its clearest expression in Deuteronomy. Regardless of how old its roots may be in Israel – the dating of vv. 3–8 is uncertain – it did not play the central role which it has been assigned. Nor does it provide the key to understanding the traditions behind Ex. 19.

In the light of the difficulties in the text and the apparent impasse in critical research it seems in order to attempt once again to assess the evidence. We begin with the literary-critical problem of the chapter. In spite of the wide divergence of opinion regarding the source divisions of ch. 19 as a whole, it would give a false impression to imply that the disagreement is absolute. Indeed in respect to the actual account of the theophany itself there is considerable agreement on some points. Commentators as divergent as Dillmann, Bäntsch,

Gressmann, Noth, Beyerlin, and Te Stroete concur in assigning vv. 18, 20 to J and vv. 17, 19 to E. Accordingly, the same commentators generally agree that J pictures Yahweh as descending on the mountain, causing it to smoke like a volcano, and forbidden to all but Moses, whereas E understands God as dwelling on the mountain, concealed in thunder clouds, and summoning the people to meet him at the foot of the mountain. It is on the basis of this limited area of agreement that many scholars continue to feel confident about sources in ch. 19, even though there is lack of consensus elsewhere.

In my judgment, the basic problem begins right at this point of greatest agreement, which has contributed to a beclouding of the issue. First of all, the divine names are not a reliable guide to sources in the chapter, even though this criterion continues to be employed in establishing the consensus on vv. 17—20. Thus, for example, in cases where a clear duplicate appears, such as vv. 9a and 10a, the same divine name is used. Again, in v. 3b Yahweh calls to Moses from the mountain, which implies the idea of God's dwelling, which is a concept attributed elsewhere to E. Then again, vv. 9a and 19 conceptually belong together, and yet because of the different divine names are assigned to different sources.

There are several additional problems with the consensus. The clear division made between J's imagery of the smoke and E's imagery of the rain cloud cannot be sustained throughout the chapter. In v. 9, which is attributed to J because of the divine name and Yahweh's visiting Moses, the image is of a cloud, not smoke. Or again, in 20.18–21, which is usually assigned to E, the image of thunder, lightning, trumpets, and smoke are combined in one verse. Then again, even in vv. 17–20 the sequence of events in the two strands is not in order. In the J account v. 18 assumes a burning mountain because of Yahweh's prior descent, whereas v. 20 reports the descent for the first time. One is obliged to posit a more complex literary development to support the two sources even at the portion of greatest agreement.

The point of this criticism is not to suggest that there are no literary tensions in the text, but rather that the traditional source division is unable to cope with them in this chapter. It seems quite clear in the earlier part of the chapter that there is repetition – one thinks of the preparation, washing, third day – but the elements of the duplication are so similar as to prevent a sharp division. This leads one to suggest that different traditions were already combined in the oral stage of transmission which accounts for much of the tension. Moreover, even if two literary strands, such as J and E, are present in ch. 19 they share so much of the same oral tradition that a separation is unlikely and without great significance.

Moreover the preoccupation with literary criticism has tended to obscure certain of the important differences within the Sinai tradition undoubtedly arising from the oral tradition which did not break according to source division. On the one hand, Moses is pictured as leading the people out to meet God in order to conclude a covenant with him. This theme is picked up in 19.3–8 and again in ch. 24.3ff. with the account of the actual ratification of the covenant. However, the people are terrified by the theophany and retreat to a distance. They implore Moses to act as mediator (20.18–20), which responsibility he assumes. The law is then given to him and accepted by the people. On the other hand, a different sequence is also described. At the outset God informs Moses that the purpose of the theophany is to legitimate him in the eyes of Israel (v. 9). This then takes place with Yahweh conversing with Moses in the sight of the people (v. 19). Moses is called up to the mountain, hears the law, and makes a covenant with God for Israel. In my judgment, two different forms of the Mosaic office are reflected here (cf. Section C on the Mosaic office). However, already at the oral level the two forms of the tradition have been joined, which accounts for much of the tension within the chapter.

The two patterns in the oral tradition of the Mosaic office also continue to be reflected throughout the whole Sinai pericope. The dominant pattern is found in chs. 19, 20, 24. The law is given, accepted, and the pattern culminates in Moses' cultic ratification of the pact. The minor pattern is confined mainly to chs. 19 and 34, which lack any covenant ceremony and focus alone on Moses' role. Although these two oral forms of the tradition were joined before the literary stage, generally speaking, the E source represents the dominant pattern, whereas the J source reflects the minor pattern.

The present sequence in the text of chs. 19–24 also gives evidence of an important pre-Deuteronomic redaction which established the major lines of the tradition. By moving 20.18–20 from its original position before the giving of the law to after the Decalogue, a place was made for the Book of the Covenant, which was ancient, but originally independent of Sinai (cf. exegesis). Moreover, this redactional move established a sharp distinction between the Decalogue and the Book of the Covenant which appears again in 24.3, 12.

C. *The Mosaic Office and the Sinai Tradition*

There is a striking discrepancy in Deut. 5.4–5 which has long been observed by commentators. Verse 4 reads: 'Face to face Yahweh spoke with you at the mountain out of the midst of the fire', whereas v. 5 states: 'while I was standing between Yahweh and you at that time to declare to you the word of Yahweh'. The verses occur in the context of Moses' speech which introduces the Decalogue and recounts the theophany at Sinai. Verse 4 is a finite sentence, introduced by an adverbial phrase to supply the emphasis, while v. 5 is an asyndetic circumstantial clause, which is subordinate to the preceding sentence. Although the subordination of v. 5 serves to soften somewhat the harsh disparity, it cannot hide completely the tension between the two verses. Verse 4 speaks of Yahweh's direct communication of the Decalogue to the people. The phrase 'face to face' emphasizes especially the lack of any mediation, whereas v. 5 suggests just the opposite. Moses acted as mediator. Moreover, the motivation clause in v. 5b supplies the reason for Moses' role by recalling the people's plea from Ex. 20.18ff. However, in Ex. 20.18ff. the people's request occurs *after* the receiving of the Decalogue.

How is one to explain the discrepancy between direct communication to all and mediation by Moses? This situation is striking because the Deuteronomic pattern is fully consistent elsewhere. Yahweh indeed spoke the Ten Commandments directly to Israel (4.36; 5.22; 9.10). Only after the Decalogue had been given did the people request Moses to intercede on their behalf (5.23ff.).

Ever since Kuenen's suggestion of almost a hundred years ago, most literary critics are agreed that the solution to the difficulty lies in a history of redaction which the present text of the Pentateuch has undergone. Kuenen suggested that in the original sequence of the Sinai events Ex. 20.18–20 belonged before the giving of the Decalogue, not after it. He argued that v. 18 explicitly states 'when the people perceived the thunderings and the lightnings and the sound of the trumpet and the mountain smoking', namely after the theophany of ch. 19, they besought Moses to act as their mediator: 'You speak to us . . . but let not God speak to us lest we die.' The passage was moved to its present position in order to make room for the introduction of the Book of the Covenant. A sequence of

events was constructed in which God first appeared in a theophany
(ch. 19), pronounced the Decalogue to all the people (20.1–17),
established Moses as mediator because of the people's fear (20.18–20),
and finally delivered the remaining laws of the Book of the Covenant
to Moses to be subsequently delivered to the people (20.21ff.).
Additional evidence for this theory is that in the original account the
covenant was sealed on the basis of the Decalogue alone (24.3ff.).
Only subsequently were the additional laws included as covenant
stipulations.

According to the theory Deuteronomy took as the basis of his
understanding of the Sinai events the Exodus account in its redacted
form, that is to say, after Ex. 20.18–20 had been shifted to its present
position after the giving of the Decalogue. For this reason, Deuteronomy understood the Decalogue to have been delivered by God
directly to all the people. This concept comes in Deut. 5.4 and
elsewhere. Only in 5.5 has the older tradition been retained which
still reflects the original sequence.

Of course such a literary theory has not been universally accepted,
and a good number of alternative theories have been proposed to
explain the difficulty in the verse. First, there are a variety of
harmonistic devices by which to reconcile the tension. Driver (*ad loc.*)
suggests that the people heard the 'voice' of God, but did not understand his words. However, this distinction does not seem at all evident
in the rest of Deuteronomy. Lohfink (*Das Hauptgebot*, Rome 1963,
pp. 145ff.) argues that a different office of Moses is suggested in 5.5
from that in 5.28ff. Earlier Dillmann (*ad loc.*) had moved in a similar
direction by trying to connect Ex. 19.9, 19 with an early role distinct
from Deut. 5.5. However, both of these attempts appear untenable in
the light of the obvious parallel between 5.5 and 5.22ff., Ex. 20.18ff.
Conversely, Ex. 19.19 has another function within the theophany
which is unconnected with the giving of the Decalogue, and cannot
be used to harmonize the verses in Deuteronomy.

Again, a large number of commentators simply remove Deut. 5.5
from the text as a later gloss (Hempel, *Schichten des Deuteronomiums*,
Leipzig 1914, pp. 104f.; Welch, *Deuteronomy: the Framework to the
Code*, London 1932, p. 18). However, the difficulty lies in their
explanation that the gloss was introduced to 'harmonize' Deut. 5.4
with Ex. 19. Actually the effect is just the opposite since v. 4 as it now
stands is in harmony with Exodus and Deut. 5.22ff., whereas the
alleged gloss causes the difficulty.

A much more serious alternative is that suggested by G. E. Wright (*IB* II, *ad loc.*). He argues that lying behind Deut. 5.4 is an ancient body of tradition which portrayed a different sequence at Sinai. Deuteronomy is simply reflecting two different but equally old traditions in these two verses. Although Wright is unable to make any concrete suggestions on the nature of this alternate tradition, his suggestion is of significance and needs to be tested. On the face of it, an explanation which is based on a comprehensive history of traditions analysis is to be preferred to a strictly literary explanation. What then can one say in respect to the Mosaic office, particularly in relation to his role as mediator of the law at Sinai?

We turn first to a closer analysis of the whole Sinai tradition as it is found in Exodus. Indeed, a rather clear picture of Moses' function emerges. If we leave open for the time being the question of the original position of 20.18–20, at least the intent of the passage is clear enough. The people are terrified by the thunder and lightning and request Moses to serve as mediator. God accepts the proposal and mediates the (remaining) law through him. Then on the basis of the divine commands Moses leads the people in a ceremony in which the covenant is ratified (24.3–8). The ritual consists in a rehearsal of the law, a commitment by the people, and a rite involving blood manipulation which seals the pact. The stereotyped nature of this covenant pattern has been fully confirmed by the flood of recent monographs and articles on the subject (von Rad, Muilenburg, Baltzer, Beyerlin, etc.). A large consensus has emerged which agrees that more than simply a literary narrative is involved, but that the text reflects an ongoing religious institution of covenant renewal going back far into Israel's early pre-monarchial history.

Within the structure of the covenant ceremony, Ex. 20.18–20 functions as a legitimation of the Mosaic office. It derives the special role of Moses from the people's request that he mediate the divine commands. The lines of this tradition can also be traced back into the theophany of ch. 19. The people are commanded to prepare themselves for the day in which they are to encounter God (19.10ff.). On the morning of the third day the theophany begins with thunder, lightning, and the sound of a trumpet. Then Moses leads the people out of the camp 'to meet God' and they stand at the foot of the mountain. It is at this point that the connection with 20.18–20 seems most plausible. The people are unable to stand the terrifying sights at the foot of the mountain and flee to a distance before seeking Moses' mediation.

However, Exodus also contains a different form of the Sinai tradition with a corresponding different understanding of the office of Moses. This sequence likewise begins with a period of instruction and preparation. However, there is the striking difference that the focus of the whole theophany here falls on the divine legitimation of Moses before the people (v. 9). Moses' special prerogative is planned from the outset and does not arise because of the subsequent fear of the people. When the theophany begins which terrifies the people, Moses is seen conversing with God as predicted (v. 19). Then Yahweh comes down upon the mountain and calls Moses up to meet him, away from the people. Ex. 34 continues the sequence in this form of the tradition. Moses alone is given the commandments and on the basis of these laws God makes a covenant with Moses on behalf of Israel (34.27). In this tradition the people do not participate in a covenant ceremony of ratification but are simply informed by Moses of the covenant (34.32). Central to this pattern is that God's direct revelation – face to face – adheres to Moses alone and not to the people.

If we now attempt to relate these two different forms of the Sinai tradition to the literary sources of the Pentateuch, there is considerable agreement that the first pattern in chs. 19, 20, 24 is represented by E, and the second pattern in chs. 19 and 34 by J. However, in my opinion, the evidence would suggest that already in the oral tradition lying behind the literary stage the two forms of the Sinai traditions had been fused (*contra* Newman, *People of the Covenant*). Moreover, this process occurred in a manner in which the first form, found chiefly in the E source, had tended to absorb the second form, now represented in the J source. This joining of the two forms of the tradition at the pre-literary stage would account for the great difficulty of separating sources in ch. 19. For example, the confusion which relates to Moses' frequent trips up and down the mountain cannot be successfully separated into two (or three) continuous strands, but stems from an attempt to join elements of Moses' different roles into one narrative. A similar tension within the text occurred from including Moses' special legitimation in the theophany before the people in vv. 9, 19a along with an explanation of his covenant office in 20.18ff. Again, the motif of sealing off Sinai for all except Moses continues to offer friction with the dominant theme of E which has Moses leading all the people to the foot of the mountain. In sum, although one can at times still distinguish between two literary sources, J and E, there is every reason to suspect that the real tension in the narrative arose from a complex history of tradition lying behind and reflected in both literary strands.

It is necessary to pursue the matter a step further. Assuming that there is some evidence of two forms of the Sinai traditions, especially in relation to the office of Moses, can one delineate with any precision the origin and function of these two traditions? In what historical period did the traditions live and who were their bearers? In short, what is their *Sitz im Leben*? In recent years, based primarily on the work of Mowinckel and von Rad, a growing consensus has emerged which recognizes a particular office in connection with Moses' role as covenantal mediator. Especially in such passages as Ex. 20.18–20 and Deut. 18.15ff., that which is being described is not simply a historical event, but rather an etiology for the establishment of something institutional and ongoing. Moses' role as covenantal mediator in the Sinai tradition has a decided cultic stamp which seems to point to an office within an institution. At this juncture, our purpose is not to press this hypothesis any further or to pursue the subject of the cultic prophet. Certainly the lack of evidence would caution against building too elaborate a reconstruction. However, the broad lines of the hypothesis respecting an office of covenant mediator seem plausible enough. Moreover, the office seems to be closely tied to that body of material which underlies the E source. This form of the Sinai tradition had its setting in the covenant renewal festival in which Moses functioned as the prototype of covenant mediator between God and the people. Particularly in Deuteronomy the profile of the ceremony and the office emerge in some sharpness.

However, our thesis is that there seems to be evidence for a different concept of Moses' office and one which is related to the material which underlies chiefly the J source. It is characteristic of this material that the Sinai theophany serves to legitimate Moses' special prerogative from the outset. At the height of the theophany, as the sound of the horn grew louder and louder, only Moses was conversing with God (v. 19). Then Moses alone is called up the mountain and God 'stood with him there' (34.5).

It is of great interest to observe in this form of the tradition that there is no account of a covenant ceremony (cf. the exegesis of

Ex. 24.1ff.). Rather the return of Moses to the people is related in the story of Moses' shining face (34.29ff.). Several things have long been observed about this passage. First of all, what is being described was not intended even by the biblical tradition to represent an isolated historical incident. The frequentative tense of v. 34 indicates clearly that a practice was here begun which continued. In short, an office is being described which is attributed to Moses. Moreover, the connection of this passage with Ex. 33.7ff. is evident to all. Again the tradition itself makes quite clear that an ongoing practice is being portrayed in which capacity Moses continually functions in mediating the will of God to Israel.

What can one say about the origin of this tradition of the office? In Ex. 33 Moses' office is closely connected to the tent of meeting. Moreover, there is a clear parallel between the sequence of Yahweh's appearance over the tent and the events of the Sinai theophany. In both accounts only Moses approaches God who is outside the camp. The people stand at a distance. Then the cloud descends and Yahweh speaks 'face to face'. The same tradition is reflected in Num. 12.1ff. Yahweh descends in a pillar of cloud, and stands at the door of the tent of meeting to confront those who contest Moses' sole prerogative. Then Moses' special office is confirmed. 'With him I speak mouth to mouth, clearly, and not in dark speech, and he beholds the form of Yahweh.'

More loosely associated with this tradition of the office is that cluster of stories which have to do with the revelation of the 'face of God'. In 33.14 Moses is promised that God's face will accompany Israel. Again in 33.17ff. Moses is hidden in a cleft of a rock and allowed to see God's glory, but not his face. Because of the mediacy of the office Moses needs a veil to hide his shining face (34.35).

In the E form of the tradition Moses functioned as the covenant mediator and sealed the covenant with Israel on the basis of the laws which he communicated to the people (24.3ff.). But in the J form there is no place for such a covenant ceremony. Rather, Moses functions as continual vehicle of the will of God in his office before the tent of meeting. His is a continuous medium of revelation. The covenant is based solely on the Ten Commandments, but understood in the context of Moses' ongoing role as recipient of the living will of the covenant God.

Another feature in this form of Moses' office is his function as intercessor. Already in the initial theophany at Sinai in 34.7 God is revealed as the forgiving God 'merciful and gracious, slow to anger . . .' from whom Moses immediately requests forgiveness for the sins of the people (v. 9). It is a consistent feature of J that Moses' role of intercessor is closely connected to the tent of meeting. In Num. 12 Moses intercedes before the tent for Miriam who has been stricken with leprosy. Again in the cluster of stories belonging to the murmuring tradition a consistent pattern emerges. Moses intercedes before the tent of meeting after the rebellion in Num. 14.4ff., again when Korah's uprising threatens total destruction (Num. 16.20ff.), and once again in Num. 17.10 (EVV 16.45). It is also clear that this element within Moses' office is not confined to the J source. In the golden calf incident (32.11ff.), particularly in the Deuteronomic interpretation (Deut. 6.6ff.), the intercessory role has been greatly broadened and detached from its close connection with the tent of meeting.

Finally, the office of Moses in the J tradition is related to a gift of the divine spirit. In Deut. 31, which already shows a mixture of the two forms of the office, Joshua is commissioned to replace Moses before the tent of meeting in which Yahweh appeared in the pillar of cloud. A similar tradition is reflected in the story of the seventy elders who share the spirit of Moses. Again the context is the tent of meeting and the cloud. However, in the following story of Eldad and Medad other elements related to the phenomenon of charismatic prophecy are involved.

Up to this point we have attempted to present the case for suggesting two different, traditional forms of Moses' office which were rooted in varying cultic institutions within ancient Israel. Yet it would be a mistake to characterize E's understanding of the office as prophetic, and J's as priestly. This schematization is not only an over-simplification, but it misrepresents the essential nature of the polarity. Although the covenant mediator of Sinai in the E form of the tradition does provide the prototype for the later prophetic office (Deut. 18.18), it is likewise true that the office shared from the outset many priestly functions, as is obvious from Moses' role in the offerings of Ex. 24.3ff. Conversely, the Mosaic office in J, while certainly reflecting some priestly functions, which continued to have the special interest of P (34.29ff.), is equally concerned with the prophetic function of the proclamation of the divine will and intercession (cf. M. Haran, *JSS* 5, 1960, pp. 56ff.). The major distinction between the two concepts of the Mosaic office rather stems from the different institutional roots of the traditions. The one was anchored in the covenant renewal ceremony, the other in the tent of meeting.

What can now be said about the subsequent history of the two forms of the Sinai tradition? First of all, it seems quite clear from recent research that the tent of meeting was a desert institution which persisted into the period of the settlement. However, there seems little doubt that its role declined in importance in the early period of the tribal league and that the function of the ark in the central sanctuary overshadowed the earlier institution (cf. A. Kuschke, *ZAW* 63, 1951, p. 91). Kuschke may be correct in suggesting that the tradition of the tent was treasured by a southern constituency which sensed a Canaanite threat from the side of the ark tradition. There is also considerable evidence that the covenant renewal ceremony became dominant in the tribal league, and through this institution preserved the Sinai tradition. These developments had some important implications for the history of the traditions. With the decline in importance of the tent of meeting went also the weakening of the J traditions which had attached the Mosaic office to the tent. In contrast, the growth in importance of the E form of the tradition was natural in a situation in which the covenant renewal ceremony flourished. The evidence is too scanty to speculate whether the tent tradition had a southern provenance which tended to be lost in the predominantly northern tradition of the covenant renewal. (Certainly Newman, *op. cit.*, has overshot the mark.) However, it does seem plausible that along with the pressure on the old tent tradition arising out of the settlement of the tribes, was the additional factor that priestly traditions began increasingly to absorb the tent tradition and to develop them in conjunction with Aaron's office in a different direction from its original one (cf. Ex. 25.8; 29.42; 30.36). In sum, the form of the Sinai tradition connected with the tent of meeting very shortly showed signs of dissolution.

As is well-known, a major development in the history of the tradition took place when the cultic forms of the amphictyonic traditions were worked into narrative form. Noth has developed an impressive case for postulating a *Grundschrift* (basic document) lying behind the later literary developments of the two oldest sources. We have already argued that there is considerable evidence to suggest that the two forms of the Sinai tradition had been joined in the oral stage. The effect of the fusion was that the form which had been connected with the tent of meeting was almost completely absorbed by the form of the covenant renewal ceremony. This dominant form of the tradition has given the over-all structure to the present Sinai narrative in Exodus 19–24. It is represented chiefly in the E source. However, as has been pointed out, tension within each of the two sources suggests that both oral patterns have left some mark on the sources.

By the time in which the book of Deutronomy was written the two forms of the Sinai tradition had been so closely fused as to have eliminated most of the tension found in J and E. The dominant covenant renewal form of E continued to be expanded by Deuteronomy and to overshadow completely the tent tradition. In fact, the absence of the tent is striking in Deuteronomy and the motif of the 'glory' has all but disappeared in favor of the name theology. The Mosaic office of covenant mediator (Deut. 18.18) conforms completely to the E form of the tradition with its focus falling on the prophetic role of mediating the word of God. Nevertheless, the Deuteronomic concept of the office has also been enriched by elements from the tent tradition. A major feature of Moses' function is his intercession for the people (9.13ff., 25ff.). Although this element is not foreign to the original concept of the office in E, it is rooted more closely to the tent tradition.

Finally, in the Priestly theology one can trace another development of the two forms which in many ways diverges from the direction pursued by Deuteronomy. The vocabulary of the old tent of meeting tradition has been, by and large, absorbed into the Jerusalem theology. The tent has become identified with the tabernacle (miškān). Yahweh now dwells in the sanctuary and the cloud and glory reflect the permanent divine presence. Nevertheless, the priestly school retained its sense of continuity with the older tent tradition and continued to afford a channel for preserving traditions of Moses' office which were found in the tent tradition, such as the shining face of Ex. 34.29ff.

We have now reached the point in the investigation in which we can return to the original question. How is one to explain the tension between Deut. 5.4 and 5? Does it stem from a literary development caused by the fusion of sources or is Deuteronomy dependent on some early tradition in which the law was given directly to the people? It is clear from our analysis that, although there were two early traditions of the Mosaic office, both understood Moses as mediator of the law. There is no evidence to suggest any other early tradition of a direct transmission of the law to the people. In the light of this evidence, the literary explanation of the tension remains the most plausible. Verse 4 is a reading of the tradition after the redaction of J and E placed the Decalogue in its present position within the narrative. Verse 5 represents accordingly an earlier tradition of the mediatorial office of Moses.

D. *Special Literary Problems in Ex. 19*

Two passages require a separate treatment because of peculiar problems.

1. *19.3b–8*

It has been generally recognized that these verses have a compositional integrity of their own. Indeed, the unit is a remarkable example of poetic symmetry and artistic beauty. The passage now serves as a topical introduction to the chapter, although the actual literary connection remains somewhat loose. The passage actually anticipates by way of summary the action of the next chapters, and presupposes the ratification of the covenant which only comes in 24.3ff.

Commentators remain sharply divided on assigning a date and author to these verses. One group of scholars (Muilenburg, Wildberger, Beyerlin) argue for an early date and assign the passage to E. Another group (Noth, Haelvoet, Perlitt, Hyatt) argue for a much later date, assigning the passage to the Deuteronomic editor or even later. In my opinion, the evidence is not absolutely conclusive for either side (cf. Baltzer's caution). The passage certainly reflects the older covenant tradition of Moses as a covenant mediator, which is most often found in the E source. Again, the poetic form appears old, and the vocabulary is not typical of Deuteronomy, as is the case for many obvious Deuteronomic expansions (32.9–14). However, the present position of the passage certainly appears to be redactional with an eye to summarizing the whole Sinai pericope. Again, the vocabulary is closely akin to Deuteronomy in some places. Moreover, the theological formulation of Israel's election appears more developed than one finds in the Elohist source. Finally, the formulation in v. 5, 'obey my voice and keep my covenant', appears to reflect, not the original sequence of the Sinai tradition, but the later version which has been expanded with the inclusion of the Book of the Covenant. Israel is to 'hearken to God's voice', which suggests with

Deuteronomy that the people heard the Decalogue directly, and 'obey his covenant', which are his other stipulations.

In sum, although the passage contains old covenant traditions, probably reflected through the E source, its present form bears the stamp of the Deuteronomic redactor.

2. *Ex. 19.20–25*

This section is almost universally held to be secondary. Haelvoet has closely analyzed the use of language and feels that it is untypical of the pentateuchal sources. Therefore, he agrees with the consensus in assigning it to a late redactor. But the major problem arises from the content of these verses. Right at the apparent climax of the theophany, the scene is interrupted and Moses is again called back up the mountain for further instruction. And what strange instructions! He is to warn the people 'from breaking through' lest they seek to gaze on God. Moses reacts in surprise, reminding God that such a command is unnecessary because God himself had already given the order which restricted the people.

Commentators have tried to get around the difficulties in several ways. McNeile suggests moving vv. 11b–13 after v. 24, but this literary rearrangement hardly helps with the interpretation of v. 23. The most widespread solution is to consider that vv. 20–24 arose as a sort of 'midrashic' expansion (so Rudolph, Haelvoet, Beyerlin) and assign it to a late redactor. Dillmann had long ago noticed that the execution of the command to seal off the mountain, given in vv. 11ff., is not reported in the chapter. On the basis of this observation commentators have reasoned that vv. 20ff. arose in an attempt to fill in this omission.

However, the midrashic theory suffers from several problems. First of all, a midrashic expansion arises in order to explain a difficulty in the text. But the difficulty alleged to have evoked the midrash, namely the failure to mention the carrying out of the orders in vv. 11bff., would hardly have been seen as a problem by late Jewish interpreters. Its execution would have been simply assumed, as is the case in parallel instances throughout the Old Testament. The perspective which senses a problem here is distinctly modern and not ancient. Secondly, even if a problem had been felt at this point, it would have been quite unthinkable to solve it by having Moses 'instruct' God in this way. For these reasons, whatever its age, the purpose of v. 23 must have been quite different from that of a midrash.

The immediate difficulty of arriving at a more satisfactory solution arises from the lack of close parallel passages. To my knowledge, there is no other instance within the Old Testament in which an earlier command of God's is cited as evidence that a later command of his is unnecessary. Nevertheless, there is reason to review the logic of Moses' argument (v. 23) in the light of other Old Testament usage which offers an indirect parallel.

Moses contests God's command: 'The people cannot come up to Mount Sinai', and he cites as his evidence an earlier command: 'You yourself charged us saying, "Set bounds about the mountain."' The form in which an earlier statement is cited is quite frequent within the Old Testament. One can cite a prior statement in the first, second, or third person (Ex. 14.12; II Sam. 1.16; Gen. 20.5). Invariably, the prior statement is given in the form of direct address, most frequently introduced by the infinite $l\bar{e}$'$m\bar{o}r$. At times the subject of the statement is emphasized by the addition of the separable preposition: 'he himself said . . .' ($h\hat{u}$' '$\bar{a}mar$ $l\hat{i}$). There is an additional formal characteristic to be noted. The citation of a prior statement, although given as direct address, is often in fact a rather loose paraphrase of the actual statement made. The slayer of Saul is cited in II Sam. 1.16 as having said 'I have slain Yahweh's anointed', whereas one can gather from the actual report of the slaying that this is a tendentious formulation. Likewise in Gen. 20.5 Abimelech's report on the conversation is at least an expansion of the account narrated earlier in the chapter.

There are several functions which citing a prior statement can perform. First, the citing of what has been said in the past can serve as direct evidence for establishing the truth or untruth of a statement in the present. For example, in Gen. 20.4 Abimelech defends his innocence by citing the prior remark of Abraham: 'Did he not himself say, "She is my sister"?' Abraham's remark provides evidence which directly relates to Abimelech's claim of innocence (cf. II Sam. 1.16).

This first usage can be distinguished from a second. An event in the present is cited as confirming the truth or untruth of a statement made in the past. The event provides evidence which proves or disproves a statement's validity. In I Kings 1.17 Bathsheba put her case before David: 'Adonijah has become king, whereas you said earlier, "Solomon shall reign."' The alleged fact that Adonijah reigns proved the untruth of the prior statement of David (Jer. 4.10; Ps. 89.20, 29). This second usage provides essentially the form in which the argument of prophecy is made. For example, in Num. 26.63ff. the former judgment on the wilderness generation has been confirmed by the subsequent events of history. Not a man has survived, except Caleb and Joshua.

A third usage can be distinguished which is a variant of the second. An event or a situation in the present is cited as indirect evidence for confirming the truth or untruth of a prior statement. For example, in Num. 11.21 Moses draws to God's attention the huge number of people, 600,000, which appears to call into question the truth of God's earlier promise of supplying meat to all for a whole month. Moses' reference to the large number involved did not prove the statement false as would occur in the second usage, but provides material from which one can deduce a conclusion of untruth. As in the case of the second usage, the prior statement is being tested, rather than the prior statement serving as a means for supporting the truth of another statement.

We now return to the analysis of Ex. 19.23. The formal characteristics are similar to the common Old Testament pattern of citing a prior statement within the context of mounting a case. The citation is in direct address, introduced by *lē'mōr* with the emphatic use of the separable pronoun. Moreover, the cited statement is a loose paraphrase of the actual command given in vv. 10ff. In v. 12 'the people' are to be sealed off; in v. 23 it is the 'mountain'. In the original narrative 'sanctification' precedes rather than follows the setting of barriers. The function of v. 23 is clearly akin to the first of the usages outlined. The prior statement is cited as evidence for the truth of another statement. Moses claims that the people are unable to come up to Mount Sinai and quotes for evidence a prior statement of God.

The fact that the use of the prior statement can function in different ways would speak against trying to establish a particular *Gattung* with a specific *Sitz im Leben*. Its usage occurs within a variety of genres. It appears within a speech of defense (Gen. 20.4ff.), a disputation (Ex. 33.12; Jer. 4.10), a complaint (Num. 11.11ff.), and a sentence of death (II Sam. 1.16). What actually emerges is a stereotyped pattern of speech which functions as a logical device in a variety of ways in order to support a case. The invariable features of the pattern arise from the inherent logic of the human mind, rather than from particular sociological forces.

Nevertheless, there are several implications which one can draw respecting the interpretation of Ex. 19.20ff. by the recognition of the logical pattern involved. First, the citing of a prior command is not a peculiar midrashic feature in which God is strangely corrected, but a common practice of argument appearing throughout Israel's history. Second, the loose paraphrase of the command is not necessarily a sign of being secondary, but again belongs to the pattern being employed.

3. Old Testament Context

Introduction

The major exegetical problems of ch. 19 relate to the issue of understanding how the various parts of the chapters fit together in the narrative. Such basic decisions determine to a large extent how one pictures the movement of the whole passage and properly locates the various themes. Very early in the history of exegesis there have been efforts made to rearrange the sections in ch. 19 in relation to chs. 20 and 24. Among the Jewish sages Akiba regarded Ex. 24.15f. as a repetition of the account in Ex. 19f. (cf. J. Goldin, *The Fathers according to Rabbi Nathan*, New Haven 1955, p. 175). Likewise, Rashi (Ex. 19.11) cited the rabbinical hermeneutical principle, 'There is no "earlier" and no "later" in Scripture,' as a warrant for identifying the covenant ceremony of ch. 24 with the action in 19.3–8. Interestingly enough, recent form-critical studies on the covenant forms (Muilenburg, Baltzer, Beyerlin) have followed unknowingly the rabbinic lead in identifying the action of 19.3–8 with that of ch. 24 because of the formal similarities.

Again, at least since Nachmanides – in critical scholarship since Kuenen – the suggestion has been put forward that the section 20.18ff. has been displaced and really belongs after 19.19. This displacement theory has now been so widely accepted that its validity is seldom even debated (cf. Beyerlin, p. 12). In my judgment, the present chapter shows every sign of having undergone a complex historical development. Moreover, the possibility that 20.18–21 once occupied a different position in the narrative is strong (cf. the discussion in section 2). Nevertheless there is great need not to allow evidence from the earlier development of the text to undercut dealing seriously with the final stage of the text. This does not mean that the modern exegete can operate with the present text midrashically. (Cassuto often slips into this danger.) One must be aware of a depth dimension and of the variety of forces which have been at work, while at the same time concentrating one's efforts in interpreting the biblical text before one. Because these various displacement theories respecting Ex. 19 seriously affect one's understanding of the movement of the chapter, they must be critically examined in the light of the explicit intention of the final form of the narrative.

An outline of chs. 19–24 may be useful in gaining a perspective of the whole.

1. Israel's arrival at Sinai and encampment, 19.1–2
2. God's covenant with Israel announced
   (*a*) Conditions of the covenant, 3–6
   (*b*) Israel's response of acceptance, 7–8
   (*c*) Moses' special role defined, 9
3. Preparations prior to the third day
   (*a*) Instructions for purification for two days, 10–11
   (*b*) Guarding the people from the mountain, 12–13a
   (*c*) The signal for approaching the mountain is set, 13b
   (*d*) Commands executed by Moses, 14–15
4. Preparations on the third day
   (*a*) The beginning of signs and the people's reaction, 16
   (*b*) Moses leads the people out to the foot of the mountain, 17
   (*c*) Further signs increasing, 18
   (*d*) Moses speaking with God, 19
   (*e*) Moses summoned for further instructions, 20–24
   (*f*) Instructions reported to the people, 25
5. Proclamation of the Decalogue, 20.1–17
6. Establishment of Moses' covenant office
   (*a*) The people's reaction of fear, 18
   (*b*) The request for intercession addressed to Moses, 19
   (*c*) Moses explains the manner of revelation:
      (i) Do not fear, 20aα
      (ii) God comes in order to test, 20aβ
      (iii) God comes in order to establish obedience, 20b
   (*d*) Moses accepts mediatorship for the people, 21
7. Further stipulations of the covenant, 20.22–23.33
8. Sealing of the covenant, 24.1–18

Certain implications can be provisionally drawn from the outline in regard to the present structure of the chapters. First, the theophany in 19.16ff. is closely tied to the people's reaction which is reported in 20.18ff. The passages must therefore be treated together as part of one narrative. Secondly, the extended preparations of ch. 19, especially in the light of vv. 20ff., focus on the giving of the law in 20.1ff. and are not to be handled as relating to a bare theophany. Third, a clear distinction in the sequence of events is maintained between the various acts of preparation (19.1ff.) and the sealing of the covenant (24.1ff.).

[**19.1–9**] The passage begins with a verse which serves as a superscription to the many chapters which follow and forms a sharp break with the history which has led up to the arrival at Sinai. The goal of the journey from Egypt has been reached. It is marked as a special day to be remembered ('on that very day'). Then the writer in v. 2 returns to pick up the traditions of the itinerary, which serves to reinforce the impression of a goal having been reached.

The first indication of a major theme of the chapter emerges in the contrasting juxtaposition of the people with Moses: the people camp, while Moses ascends the mountain (vv. 2b–3a). The midrashim and Cassuto find here an occasion to expand homiletically on Moses' faithfulness, but, as we shall see, the concern of the chapter to single out Moses is of fundamental importance for the chapter.

Immediately, without any delay, the purpose of God's bringing Israel to Sinai is announced to Moses (vv. 3–8). The elevated style of the prose, which approaches poetry in its use of parallelism and selected vocabulary, has attracted much attention in recent years (cf. bibliography). Form-critical work has discovered in its structure a stereotyped pattern of covenant renewal. Muilenburg speaks of a 'special covenantal *Gattung*' and goes so far as to characterize it as being '*in nuce* the *fons et origo* of the many covenantal pericopes which appear throughout the Old Testament' (*VT* 9, 1959, p. 352). Indeed there is a set form which proceeds from the proclamation of God's mighty deeds (v. 4), to the conditions of the covenant (vv. 5–6), and then to the response of commitment (vv. 7–8). (Cf. the parallels in Josh. 24.2ff. and I Sam. 12.1ff.) Moreover, there is considerable evidence to show that at an earlier stage in the development of the Sinai traditions, the material was treasured in a cultic form which was periodically re-enacted. Still, the discovery of how the material once functioned does not in itself solve the exegetical problems involved in the present narrative, nor does the recognition of a general pattern do full justice to the unique features of the text.

The invitation to a covenant is predicated on the great divine acts of the past which Israel has herself experienced. Above all, the reference is to the deliverance from Egypt, phrased in v. 4 in terms of the negative effect on Egypt (cf. Deut. 11.3ff.). Moreover, God has continuously cared for his people and like a great bird watched over his fledglings until he brought them safely to his dwelling. The picture is of God's bringing his people to Sinai rather than his going forth from Sinai (Ps. 68.7ff.). Then the promise is offered, announced with the decisive 'and now'. If Israel will obey God's will by being faithful to his covenant, then a special relationship is promised. Three terms spell out Israel's uniqueness: a special possession in distinction from all the peoples (*s^egullāh mikkol-hā^cammîm*), a kingdom of priests (*mamleḵeṭ kōh^anîm*), and a holy nation (*gôy qāḏôš*). The poetic balance of the sentence has been distuıbed by a parenthetical remark – surely all the world is mine – but the three are all to be interpreted in relation to one another (*contra* Moran). Israel is God's own people, set apart from the rest of the nations. Israel as a people is also dedicated to God's service among the nations as priests function with a society. Finally, the life of Israel shall be commensurate with the holiness of the covenant God. The covenant responsibility encompasses her whole life, defining her relation to God and to her neighbors, and the quality of her existence.

The conditions of the covenant are reported by Moses to the elders and transmitted to the people. Then all the people answered as with one voice: 'All that Yahweh has spoken will we do.' This, of course, is a similar response to that given by the people in 24.3, 7, and herein lies the problem. How can the people agree to accept as the grounds of the covenant 'all that Yahweh has spoken', when God's will has not yet been revealed to them? This observation lies at the basis of interpretation which would identify the covenant invitation of ch. 19 with the reading of the law and the sealing of the covenant in ch. 24. But in spite of the form common to both, the larger context of 19.8 in its present position provides a different nuance to the people's reply. A covenant has been offered; the people respond with enthusiastic acceptance, but the whole section only anticipates what is to follow. Israel will shortly learn what God's will is to which she has committed herself. In a real sense, the rest of chs. 19 and 20 unfold the full implications of the covenant and the nature of the covenant God, thereby casting the people's eager response in a new light. From the perspective of the whole passage Israel has not sealed the covenant, but rather only begun her period of preparation.

The invitation to enter into a covenant is addressed to corporate Israel (vv. 3–8) and the people as a whole replied. But before the preparation begins, and as an integral part of the divine purpose, a special word is addressed to Moses (v.9). From a literary point of view it is set aside from the covenant invitation by a fresh introduction: 'And Yahweh spoke to Moses . . . "I am coming to you (sing.)".' The message concerns Moses and is not a message to be simply transmitted further. Yahweh is coming in a thick cloud in order that (ba'aḅûr) Israel may hear God speaking with him and thereby acknowledge in trust his special office (14.31). The form-critical work has pointed out how significant the office of Moses was in shaping the material. This same recognition of the centrality of Moses' function in the covenant is fully sustained in the final stage of the narrative. Not only does the emphasis on the distinctiveness of Moses' role over against that of the people's run as a red thread throughout the entire narrative, but right at the outset it is given a special significance in the total purpose of God with Israel at Sinai. This verse testifies that the mediatorship of Moses did not arise as an accidental afterthought, but was intended from the start. How the writer combined this motif with that of 20.18ff. – Moses was appointed only because of Israel's fear – we shall discuss below.

[19.10–24] A new section begins in v.10. God's intention has been stated and the conditions for the covenant have been set forth and accepted. Now God demands of Moses that he prepare the people for the event which will take place on the third day when God descends upon the mountain. The need for elaborate preparation had not been anticipated up to now in the narrative. There is, of course, a connection between the promise of becoming a 'holy nation' (qāḏôš) and the demand to 'purify oneself' (qiddaštām), but the more profound connection between the people and God who has laid claim upon them begins to emerge in the process of preparation. Moses receives his instructions. He is to prepare the people by means of a period of consecration today and tomorrow. They are to wash their clothes, an act which traditionally precedes a great and solemn happening (Gen.35.2; Josh.3.5). Secondly, the people are sealed off from the sacred precinct. The severest punishment is enjoined upon transgressors lest the people be infected from one person's misdeed (v.13b). When the horn blast continues to sound, then the people are to move up toward the mountain.

Once again the narrative takes time to report Moses' execution of the divine command. He initiates the required sanctification, summarizing the commands with a specific, concrete injunction.

'Do not go near a woman!' Christian interpreters have traditionally had difficulty with such priestly material and sought to spiritualize it. The external restrictions symbolize the proper inner life of separation from the world and it is this side which is important (Heinisch, Frey, etc.). But the biblical author is certainly not focusing on the inner life. Nor is he seeking to draw a moral lesson as if abstinence were a training against sensuality (Maimonides, *Guide* III. 33). Rather, he employs a priestly language which is concerned with the external act. The holy God of the covenant demands as preparation a separation from those things which are normally permitted and good in themselves. The giving of the covenant is different from an ordinary event of everyday life. Israel is, therefore, to be prepared by a special act of separation. Cassuto (p. 230) is correct in insisting that Moses' formulation of the command in v. 15b should not be viewed as a supplement of his own, but as an elucidation of the command of sanctification (cf. the *Mekilta* and Lauterbach's footnote, Philadelphia 1949, II, pp. 217f.).

Verses 16ff. commence with the arrival of the third day. Early in the morning there is thunder, lightning, a heavy cloud, and increasing sound of the shophar. Two of the elements have been previously introduced, albeit in a somewhat different form, the cloud (v. 9) and the *yōḇēl* (v. 13). The author once again contrasts sharply the reaction of the people with that of Moses. All the people tremble, but Moses leads them out to stand at the foot of the mountain. (Obviously Moses is carrying out his prior instructions, which also serves to interpret for the reader the meaning of v. 13.) Once the people are positioned, the writer again returns to describe the effect of God's presence on Sinai. The imageiy is somewhat different (v. 18), with smoke and fire dominating. But the effect in the narrative is that of heightening the awe and terror, and increasing the surprise. Again, the reaction: now the whole mountain trembles. The climax to the whole scene comes in v. 19. When the sound of the horn has reached its greatest intensity, Moses is seen talking with God and God is heard answering in a voice. Moses had indeed been legitimated as God's special instrument, just as he had promised (v. 9).

[19.20–25] This section is generally considered a dismal anti-climax which disturbs the ongoing movement of the chapter (cf. above section D). Right at the apparent climax of the theophany, the scene is interrupted and Moses is called back up the mountain for further instruction. He is to warn the people from 'breaking through' in order to gaze on God. Even Moses objects, reminding God that such a command is unnecessary because God had already given the order which restrained the people.

Yet the essential difficulty of this section arises out of a basic failure to understand the passage and its role within the chapter. For those commentators who separate ch. 20 sharply from ch. 19, and find the purpose of the latter chapter to be the revelation of the bare theophany, the interruption of these additional instructions is extremely disturbing. But, as we have argued, the purpose of ch. 19 is to recount the preparation for the deliverance of the law. The inclusion of vv. 20–25 is clear evidence that the narrator (or redactor) understood ch. 19 as preparation for the main event. The preparations which were executed in the two previous days, and which preceded that moment on the third day, were still not considered adequate by God. Moreover, even Moses objected to the fresh command. In 19.5–8 the people expressed themselves ready for the covenant, but then learned of the required preparation. Now even Moses thought the people ready, only to learn that more was required. The motif of Moses' resisting God already emerged in ch. 3 and continues to be developed throughout Exodus.

The point of the preparation emerges from the repetition of phrases. 'Warn . . . lest they break through' (v. 21, 24), and lest he 'break through upon them' (vv. 22, 24). The issue at stake is not whether God is a stuffy monarch, who does not think enough honor has been shown him. This picture is a total misunderstanding. Rather, the warning is given for the sake of the people, who have no experience as yet of the dimensions of divine holiness, and lest warned will destroy themselves. Moses argues by citing the earlier command. But God overrules his mediator and insists on a further warning. Not even the priests who normally have access into God's presence are permitted to approach. Aaron alone is allowed to approach (cf. 24.1ff.). Only after the command has been executed is the period of preparation over.

[20.1–17] Then God delivers the law to the people, called by Ex. 34.28 and Deut. 4.13 'the ten words' (*ᵃśeret haddᵉḇārîm*). Because of their importance a separate section within the commentary is devoted to a detailed interpretation of these verses. Here the concern is to indicate the significance of their position within the larger narrative.

The commandments are preceded by a prologue which has

Yahweh introducing himself as Israel's redeemer from Egyptian bondage. The connection with 19.3ff. is obvious. Also the stipulations of the covenant are preceded by reference to what the God of the covenant has already performed on Israel's behalf. The covenant is an invitation arising from the divine initiative, but it entails a commitment from the side of Israel. Again there is a further parallel: 'Now if you will obey my voice . . . and keep my covenant' (v.5); 'God spoke all these words . . .' The Decalogue supplies the detailed content for the covenant obedience required in v.5. It makes known the will of God which the people have agreed to accept. In the theophany Israel begins to experience the nature of her God. In the law she hears the clear expression of God's will which the covenant demanded. A deliberate profile of the 'holy nation' has been sketched with the ten words of the divine will.

[20.18–21] The section which follows the Decalogue is essential for an understanding of the whole (cf. above). The initial participial form of the verb indicates that a circumstantial clause is intended. The people's reaction which is described did not first emerge after the giving of the Decalogue, but runs parallel with the whole theophany. When they perceived – the Hebrew says 'saw' – the thunder, lightning, and thick darkness, the people became terrified. They fled from the base of the mountain and stood afar off. Once again a major theme of the chapter is re-introduced. Moses has a role set apart from the people. The people beseech him that he act as mediator. 'Let God speak through you. We are no longer able to bear God's speaking lest we perish.'

Several things are striking in this request. First, there is a contrast in the behavior of the people before and after the divine revelation. The people who had said, 'All that Yahweh has spoken we will do,' now reply, 'Let not God speak to us lest we die.' The contrast does not imply a condemnation of the original response, as if it were flippant, but it does highlight a movement of the chapter in which Israel is educated into the fuller dimension of God's will.

More significant is the formal establishment of Moses' office as covenant mediator. The form-critical analysis suggested that there were two different forms of the tradition of the office. The narrator has been able skillfully to combine the two forms into his story in such a way as to reduce tension to a minimum. Up to this point, Moses had been set aside by God's choice (19.9) and legitimated in his office by God's speaking (19.19). Now we learn how his office was confirmed from the side of the people. He is not simply God's mouthpiece speaking to the people, but he represents Israel before God. More and more in the narrative the role of Moses as suffering mediator of the nation unfolds, reaching its first climax in the golden calf story, and culminating in his death outside the promised land because of the sin of the people (Deut. 1.37; 4.21, etc.). The formal establishment of Moses' office in Exodus prepares the way in the subsequent narrative for Moses not only to receive the remaining part of the law (20.22), but particularly to act as mediator in the sealing of the covenant (24.1ff.). The writer of Deuteronomy, reflecting on the office, makes completely explicit the divine confirmation of the people's request of Moses: 'They have rightly spoken' (5.28).

Moses moves immediately to execute his office. He accepts his position by exercising it: 'Do not fear.' God's intention is not to crush his people with commands, but to enter into a covenant. Moses then picks up the initial themes of 19.3ff. God has a purpose for his people. What has happened at Sinai is directed to this goal. It is on account of this that God has revealed himself. In a real sense, v. 20 provides the narrator's own key to his understanding of chs. 19 and 20. In two parallel clauses, both introduced by the preposition 'on account of' (ba'ª*ḇûr*) Moses explains the meaning of God's revelation at Sinai.

First, 'God has come to prove you' (*nassôṭ*). For those commentators who separate the theophany in ch. 19 from the delivery of the law in ch. 20, this verse is quite incomprehensible (cf. M. Greenberg, *JBL* 79, 1960, pp. 273ff.). How could the bare theophany actually test Israel? At this juncture, critical scholars usually disregard the present sequence of the narrative, and rearrange the sequence according to an alleged earlier (and correct) position. In my judgment, this move is not to take seriously the final form of the narrative. It simply cuts the Gordian knot and fails to understand what the text means in its present state. The point of the present sequence is to emphasize that the theophany and the giving of the law belong together. In spite of the probability that theophany and Decalogue circulated independently of one another during a long history of development of the tradition, the author of the present narrative wants the two chapters understood as part of one event. The people are terrified from the thunderings and lightning, but especially from the speaking of God. Similarly Moses' reply clearly includes God's word along with the theophany. God has come to prove Israel. The people who committed themselves to the covenant in 19.3ff. have been put to the test. How do they respond to the God who reveals himself both in word and deed? Deuteronomy provides the best commentary. 'Yahweh our God has shown us his glory and greatness, and we have heard his voice out of the midst of the fire' (5.24). Again, 'out of heaven he let you hear his voice that he might discipline you'. The revelation at Sinai carried with it a critical judgment which arose from being confronted with the clear proclamation of God's will.

Secondly, 'God has come . . . that the fear of him may be before your eyes to keep you from sinning.' If the first reason focused on the critical testing of the revelation, the second supplies the positive function of the law. The 'fear of God' in the Old Testament refers specifically to obedience to God (cf. L. Köhler, *Old Testament Theology*, ET London 1957, p. 110). It has nothing to do with the mystical sense of the deity described by R. Otto. God provides in his law a means of obeying God and keeping his people from sin. Again Deuteronomy provides the best commentary on the significance of Sinai: 'Gather the people to me, that I may let them hear my words, so that they may learn to fear me all their days . . .' (4.10).

The basic point of this verse is misunderstood when one combines the general concept of fear with the technical biblical term 'fear of God'. Indeed the people have feared before the theophany and are comforted by Moses. But the issue at stake is whether God came in order to evoke such an emotion. Calvin, followed by most modern exegetes, sees the purpose of the theophany to lie here: 'in order to inspire you with the dread of offending him' (Driver, p. 201). However, it is very doubtful whether the passage carries this meaning. The fear of God is not a subjective emotion of terror, but the obedience of God's law. The glory and holiness of God calls forth man's fear (cf. Isa.6), but the end is not the emotion, rather the deed.

Detailed Notes
19.1. The location of Sinai is a classic problem over which there is no consensus among modern scholars, in spite of intense research. The various geographical options are outlined in detail in Driver, pp. 177ff., Hyatt, pp. 203ff. and in every standard Bible dictionary. Cf. the article of G. I. Davies, *VT* 22, 1972, pp. 152ff., for a bibliography of the most recent literature. Especially to be noted are the several articles of J. König, in *RHPR* 43, 1963,

pp. 2–31; 44, 1964, pp. 200–35; and H. Gese, in *Das Ferne und Nahe Wort. Festschrift L. Rost*, BZAW 105, 1967, pp. 81–94.

3–8. There is much recent literature on these verses which handles the full range of problems. Cf. the bibliography above, and the articles of Muilenburg, Haelvoet, Wildberger, and Beyerlin.

5. *berîtî* 'my covenant'. In Deut. the covenant is synonymous with the Ten Commandments (4.13). Cf. the bibliography for the recent discussions, and the additional studies of A. Jepsen, in *Verbannung und Heimkehr*, Tübingen 1961, pp. 162ff.; E. Kutsch, in *Das Ferne und Nahe Wort*, pp. 133ff.; G. Fohrer, *Studien zur altt. Theologie und Geschichte*, pp. 84ff.; W. Zimmerli, 'Erwägungen zum "Bund"', *Wort–Gebot–Glaube. Festschrift Eichrodt*, Zürich 1970, pp. 171–90; M. Weinfeld, 'Berit', *TWAT* I, pp. 782–808.

5. Cf. M. Greenberg, 'Hebrew *segullā*: Akkadian sikiltu', *JAOS* 71, 1951, pp. 172ff.

6. *mamleket kōhanîm*, 'kingdom of priests'. The most significant, recent article is that of Moran (*op. cit.*). Moran has argued that the *mamleket kōhanîm* is not to be regarded as a synonym of *gôy qāḏôš*, but as a separate entity, priestly kings, which forms a totality with the people. Fohrer (*op. cit.*) generally accepts his interpretation. Moran has established the probability of *mamleket* occasionally carrying the meaning of 'king', although some of his examples are hardly convincing (II Chron. 32.15). However, the parallelism of the three Hebrew terms speaks against seeing an expression of totality in only the last two. Moreover, his actual interpretation of the priestly role appears to me most unlikely in the context of Ex. 19 and conflicts with the theology of the chapter as a whole.

9. The repetition in v. 9b of Moses reporting the people's answer to Yahweh presents a problem for the narrative. God had spoken directly to Moses. Why should he then report again to him the words of the people? Several solutions to the difficulty have been proposed. Critical commentators simply eliminate v. 9b as a gloss which has crept into the text from v. 8b (Bäntsch, Driver, Beer, etc.). More conservative commentators have tried to avoid the difficulty by seeing in v. 9b a repetition of the answer in v. 8b, used perhaps for a literary effect, but not intended as a double answer (Kalisch). Finally there is the midrashic interpretation. 9b can only mean that Moses reported the message of v. 9 to the people, who then responded, and it was this response which Moses reported back to God. The *Mekilta*, followed by Rashi, interprets the people as requesting to hear God's words directly and not through Moses. B. Jacob and Cassuto attempt to modernize the midrashic approach with some new observations on biblical style, but basically they follow the midrash in inferring a prior conversation between Moses and the people on the basis of v. 9b.

An important methodological issue is at stake. Does the effort to take seriously the final stage of the text imply that one must return to the midrashic method in order to interpret coherently the present text? In my opinion, this need not be the case. The danger of employing modern midrash can be met both by a critical evaluation in the light of the whole intent of the narrative, as well as by a recognition of the historical dimensions of the text. First of all, the word to Moses does not call for the people's response. It is not parallel to the covenant commitment. Faith in Moses will be evoked when they experience Moses' role. It is not an issue for prior consent. Again, the issue at stake is Moses' office, and not the manner of delivering the commandments. Note the idiom and order in v. 19. Moses was speaking and God was answering. Finally, another descent and ascent between vv. 9 and 10 seem out of place in the narrative. For these reasons we reject the midrashic interpretation as not doing justice to the whole text, and accept as more likely the critical explanation that the verse has arisen as a misplaced gloss from 8b.

12. Compare the formula in v. 23.

15. For parallels in the history of religions, cf. Clericus (Rosenmüller, Kalisch seem fully dependent on him), W. R. Smith, *Religion of the Semites*[2], London 1901, p. 455.

22. The mention of 'priests' is an old crux, since the sons of Aaron had not yet been assigned to the priestly office. The rabbis had early suggested a translation of 'first-born sons' (cf. Rashi). The most obvious explanation is to see here an historical anachronism (cf. McNeile, p. lxvi).

20. 21. This verse belongs to the unit 18–20 (so NJPS, NEB), and not to what follows (RSV). Note the parallel vocabulary in v. 18.

4. *New Testament Context*

O. Betz, 'The Eschatological Interpretation of the Sinai-Tradition in Qumran and in the New Testament', *Revue de Qumran* 6, 1967, pp. 89ff.

The New Testament use of the Sinai tradition tends to focus on several aspects of the Old Testament tradition. The first focal point is decidedly negative in emphasis and stresses the inadequacy of the Sinai event to establish a proper covenant. The most typical move for the New Testament is to view the covenant at Sinai from the perspective of Jer. 31.31ff. which contrasts the inadequacy of the old covenant with the promise of the new (Matt. 26.28 and parallels; Heb. 8.8ff.; 10.16f.). The most elaborate contrast of the two covenants which makes detailed use of Ex. 19, however, occurs in Heb. 12.18ff. (cf. below). In Acts 7.38ff. Israel's failure to obey the commandments is stressed and the golden calf incident is interpreted as immediately following the 'living oracle' of Sinai. Gal. 3.19ff. understands the giving of the law at Sinai as a concession to human sinfulness which adumbrated the promised mediator, while Gal. 4.24 uses Sinai as a symbol of slavery in contrast to Jerusalem which symbolizes freedom from the law.

The second focal point, although not completely without some negative overtones, stresses the continuity between the Old Testament promise and the New Testament church. Especially frequent is the application of Ex. 19.5f. with its reference to a 'kingdom of priests, a holy nation'. In I Peter 2.9 this verse is given a setting not unlike the first focal point by its combination with Isa. 28.16 and Hos. 2.25 (EVV 23). Further allusion to the Exodus verse occurs in Rev. 1.6 and 5.10ff. Again the imagery of the Sinai epiphany recurs in passages like Rev. 14, in which Mount Zion experiences the heavenly voice, the white cloud, and the saints who 'have not defiled themselves with women'.

Of all these various usages, clearly the most detailed and extensive reference to Ex. 19 occurs in Heb. 12.18ff. In addition to its length the passage contains a host of exegetical problems which arise from this one type of New Testament interpretation. First of all, as one would expect in Hebrews, Ex. 19 and Deut. 5 have been heard basically through the Greek translation. However, this observation needs some modification since the New Testament writer shows considerable freedom in diverging from the LXX (cf. the paraphrase of v. 20). More important is the writer's creativity in fusing together passages from Exodus, Deuteronomy, Ps. 68, and Hag. 2, 6. Again, there are several indications that the Sinai tradition employed has developed beyond the Old Testament. The common tradition of Hellenistic Judaism that God employed angels at Sinai, which apparently went back to the LXX's reading of Deut. 33.2, is assumed in v. 22, as it is in Gal. 3.19 and Acts 7.38ff. Also the reference to the 'heavenly assembly' and to the 'spirits of just men' has strong Hellenistic parallels (cf. Käsemann, *Das wanderende Gottesvolk*, FRLANT 55, 1938, p. 28). Finally, both in form and content the New Testament writer has copied the Jewish haggadic style of exegesis. He relates Moses' subjective response to the theophany (v. 21) by an apparent inference from Deut. 9.19 (LXX). Further, he pictures the Sinai event in highly eschatological language which reflects the common Jewish perspective (cf. Odes of Solomon 33.8 and I Enoch 1.4ff., cited by E. Lohmeyer, *Offenbarung*, HNT IV. 4, 1926, p. 116). In a similar way, the Qumran community portrays itself standing before the coming final judgment in the language of Sinai (cf. Betz, *op. cit.*, pp. 89ff.). Lastly, although the origin of the term 'first-born' ($\pi\rho\omega\tau\sigma\tau\acute{o}\kappa\omega\nu$) in v. 23 has been much debated, there is considerable evidence to connect it with the targumic reading of Ex. 24 which has substituted the term for the anachronistic 'priests'.

The reference to the Sinai theophany in Heb. 12 is set within the context of the writer's exhortation for steadfastness in the Christian faith (v. 12ff.). He contrasts the position of Christians before God with that of Israel at Sinai. Point by point, although not in exactly full symmetry (*contra* Bengel, *Gnomon of the NT*, ET Edinburgh 1877, and Delitzsch, *Hebrews*, ET Edinburgh 1883, *ad loc.*), he juxtaposes the giving of the old covenant with that of the new. The old was before a 'material mountain', accompanied by terrifying sounds and sights, frightening to both Moses and the people, and transitory in its effect. But the new covenant takes place in the 'heavenly Jerusalem', before an angelic assembly. Free access to this unshakable covenant is made possible by the new and better mediator (Heb. 8.6). The one represents the terror of the law; the other the freedom of the gospel.

Yet the writer of Hebrews goes to great lengths to show that it is the same God who once addressed Israel and now is addressing (v. 25) the Christian. Indeed – and here is the point of the parenesis – if Israel did not escape judgment in refusing to obey the earthly covenant, how much more terrifying is the thought of disobeying the heavenly warning. The mode of his revelation has changed, but God has not. He remains a consuming fire. There is a new revelation and a new access, but the promise of the final end remains. The author then connects the shaking of Sinai with the eschatological shaking. In that day only the spiritual, that which is unshakable and eternal, shall endure. Christians as the wandering people of God live by faith in this promise and respond in gratitude with acceptable worship.

Although it is clear that the writer of Hebrews shares with Paul and Luke–Acts a strong emphasis on the inadequacy of the old covenant, his method of working out the contrast does sharply diverge. The polarity between the material and the spiritual covenants as the transitory and the unshakable does not appear in Paul in this form. Rather, the law-gospel dialectic appears just as clearly within the Old Testament itself in Paul's argument. Nevertheless, the frequent tendency to interpret Hebrews in idealistic terms hardly does justice to the dominant eschatological thrust of its whole message. Again, although the stress on Israel's disobedience does not appear in the *heilsgeschichtliche* framework of Acts, it sounds the same note of prophetic judgment. The church can take no comfort in the failure of the early covenant, but must herself stand before the same threat of rejection. Finally, the understanding of the covenant as the ultimate encounter with the same terrifying God whose demands cannot be side-stepped with legalistic compliance or trivialized into philosophical speculation is fully in line with Pauline thought.

5. History of Exegesis

The history of the interpretation of Ex. 19 is of particular interest in showing the rise and development of a variety of new questions which are only indirectly connected with the biblical account itself. However, to dismiss the later developments as unscientific 'eisegesis' is to fail to see the importance of understanding the changing contexts in which the Bible has functioned over the last two thousand years.

Already early in the Hellenistic period one can observe the emergence of certain new emphases in the interpretation of the Sinai theophany, which have developed beyond the Old Testament accounts. In the first place, much interest focused on understanding exactly how the transmission of the law took place. The book of Deuteronomy had developed the theme that no form was seen, but only a voice, and God's words spoke out of the midst of the fire (4.36). But what was the nature of the voice? In what language was the Decalogue spoken, and how was it heard? Aristobulus argued that one could not understand the theophany literally, and he sought a deeper sense in the biblical story. The divine voice could not speak common human words, but must include within its speech the deed as well (cited from P. Riessler, *Altjüdisches Schrifttum ausserhalb der Bibel*, Augsburg 1928, p. 182). Moreover, the descent by God could not be a special one because God is everywhere (*ibid.*). Again, Philo expanded in the same direction on the nature of the divine voice which was 'equally audible to the farthest as well as the nearest' in illuminating each individual present (*De Decalogo*, 32ff.; cf. also Josephus, *Antiq.* III. 89f.). Remarkably enough, the interest in exactly how the Decalogue was delivered was picked up and further developed in the modern critical period (cf. below).

Then again, the early Hellenistic interpreters continued to reflect on the excellence of the law which Moses had received. Josephus had a strong apologetic interest in stressing its excellence to a Gentile audience (*Antiq.* III, 89f.). Likewise Philo described it as the 'best law' which required a divine transmission (*Quaest. Exod.* II.42). But particularly in the *Letter of Aristeas* the writer goes to great length to defend the Jewish law by showing the rationality which underlies its stipulations (121ff.). IV Maccabees even identifies the law with reason (2.6ff.).

Finally, one can detect the influence of Greek rationalism when these Hellenistic writers seek to show that the law of Moses was not an invention of man, but was rather a genuine oracle from God. Philo stresses that the laws were openly circulated, and not concealed in any recess (*Quaest. Exod.* II.41). Again in the sustenance of the desert Israel received the 'clearest evidence' that 'the laws were the pronouncements of God' and were not 'inventions' (*Dec.* 15ff.). Particularly in the Middle Ages and later this apologetic was developed by both Jewish and Christian philosophers against the allegation that the Jewish law was a creation of men and not divine in origin (cf. Judah Halevi, *Kuzari* I.87; J. Clericus, *Comment. in Ex.* 19.9, who cites Maimonides, *Fundam. Legis* viii.2, as having made the same point).

In rabbinic interpretation the giving of the law (*mattan Tôrāh*) obviously played a central role from the outset. Although it is impossible to trace all the nuances of their exegesis in a limited space, certain characteristic emphases can be sketched which make up a common midrashic tradition.

Much attention is given to describing Moses' covenant office with particular emphasis on the piety and faithfulness of Moses in the execution of the task. 'To teach us that Moses did not turn to his business, nor go down to his house, but went directly from the mountain unto the people' (*Mekilta*, ed. Lauterbach, II, p.215; *ARN*, ch.6). Later Jewish commentators develop at length the nature of Moses' prophetic inspiration (cf. Maimonides, *Guide* II. 33), and why his virtuous life equipped him with special insight (cf. Abarbanel, Ex.19, question 14, and Nachmanides, *ad loc.*). Again, the obedience of all Israel is a dominant note in the midrashic interpretation of Ex.19. In v.19 God spoke only after Moses told him: 'Speak, for thy children have already accepted' (*Mekilta* II, p.223). There is continual stress on the solidarity of Israel in accepting the covenant: 'If only one of them had been missing, they would not have been worthy of receiving the Torah' (*ibid.*, p.212). The Jewish tradition seems to move in two seemingly opposite directions when discussing the reasons for Israel's election. At times one hears of the 'excellence of Israel' (*šebāḥān šel yiśrā'ēl, ibid.*, p.230) whose action stood in striking contrast to the other nations. At other times, Israel is pictured as not having a free choice, but deriving the election solely from the hidden purpose of God: 'The Holy One . . . suspended the mountain over Israel like a vault and said to them: "If ye accept the Torah, it will be well with you, but if not, there will be found your grave"' (*B. Abodah Zar.* 2b–3a).

Certainly one of the most characteristic developments of the Jewish exegetical tradition is the midrash that the Torah was at first offered to all the nations, but when they heard its contents, they refused (*Mekilta* II, pp. 234f.). Only Israel agreed to accept (*qbl*) the law of the covenant. At times the implication is drawn of Israel's special worth, but more frequently the midrash is used to combat the charge that God was unfair in preferring Israel over the nations (cf. the different interpretation in *Pseudo-Philo*, ch. 11).

Christian commentators have taken their lead, by and large, from Heb. 12 and Jer. 31.31ff., and then have expanded their own interpretations in different directions. The old covenant is seen as fundamentally inadequate and in need of the new (Ps.–Cyprian, *De Montibus Sina et Sion*, MPL 4.909ff.). At times the emphasis fell on the enigma of the old covenant represented by Sinai. The signs of the cloud, darkness, and smoke symbolized 'seeing through a glass darkly' (Nicholas of Lyra, *ad loc.*). Augustine (*Spirit and Letter* XVII.29) contrasted the old and new law: 'there on tables of stone . . . here on the hearts of men. There it was outwardly registered . . . here it was inwardly given . . .' Others stressed the element of Israel's disobedience which caused the old to fail, thus calling for the new (Justin, *Dialogue*, 67).

The period of preparation preceding the theophany was often criticized as being only the externality of outward washing (Theodoret, *ad loc.*), whereas God called for spiritual purification. However, many saw the old covenant seeking to lead Israel by rites of purification from the mundane preoccupations to a higher, spiritual life demanded by God (Bede, Lapide, Piscator). Occasionally doubts were expressed about the sincerity of Israel's response of obedience (Cocceius, *Opera Omnia* II, p. 144). Luther writes in this same vein: 'Fahret schön, liebe gesellen, es ist zu hoc hund zu viel vermessen' (*Zweite Buch Mosis, ad loc.*, WA XVI, p. 409). More frequently the Christian commentator judged that Israel acted out of ignorance of God's real demands (Calvin).

Christian commentators often reflected on the cause of Israel's election in their treatment of Ex. 19. Generally the answer was given in terms of a special mission to the world. Israel failed in not bringing salvation to the world. There was a universal purpose even in the Sinai covenant which Israel was to have mediated (Theodoret, *Quaest. in Ex.*, 35). Thomas Aquinas follows the consensus in attributing Israel's election to the promise to the Fathers that Christ was to be born of them (*Summa*, 1a2ae, 98.4, Blackfriars ed., vol. 29, 1969, p. 19). Very early in Christian tradition the promise of Christ and the giving of the Spirit was seen adumbrated in the giving of the law at Pentecost. Just as the giving of the law followed fifty days after the passover sacrifice, which was the traditional Jewish interpretation of Ex. 19.1, so the Spirit came to the disciples on Pentecost (Augustine, *Quaest.* II. 70; Bede, *Quaest. super Ex.*, MPL 93.373).

The Protestant Reformers emphasized the majesty of God's revelation at Sinai which destroyed all human presumption of merit. Luther cited Ps. 139 as a parallel to the all-encompassing majesty of God before whom no man can flee. Calvin stressed that God shook the earth in order to arouse men's hearts and to correct their pride. The law was given in the context of divine terror to add to its authority and to drive men to the need of the gospel (Exodus, *ad loc.*).

Many of the critical theories of the modern period grew out of the earlier observations found in the classic commentators of both Jews and Christians. The parallels, in relation to ritual purification before the theophany, between the Old Testament and other religions, had naturally been observed, but a different conclusion began to be drawn in the seventeenth century and later. J. Clericus, after citing a wealth of parallels from classical sources, argued that the Jews must be imitating pagan religions. The traditional solution of explaining the similarity on the basis of pagan corruption of a pristine divine commandment was deemed unsatisfactory (*Comment in Exod.* 19.15; cf. also Rosenmüller, *ad loc.*). Very shortly this history of religions perspective was joined to the classic Christian emphasis on the inadequacy of Sinai, and then given a completely new twist. Sinai was conceived of as primitive, mythological and crude. Indeed, it stood on the same level with pagan religion. It was argued that only rarely in the Old Testament (Elijah in I Kings 18), but chiefly in the New Testament, the evolution of a more spiritual concept of revelation developed (Bäntsch, etc.).

Again it is significant to note how the early Greek interest in the exact mode of communication at Sinai was developed in the critical period. If the Old Testament description of God's actual speaking to

Moses, accompanied by manifestations of thunder and lightning, was considered primitive, then the real communication must have been of a different sort and only symbolized by these images. God's speaking to Elijah, not in thunder and storm, but in a 'still, small voice', was used as a warrant for psychologizing Ex. 19. Driver's comment is a classic example of Protestant liberalism: 'The literal truth was that God spoke to the heart of Moses: the poetic truth was that He spoke in thunder and lightning from the crest of Sinai' (*Exodus*, p. 177; cf. also Plastaras, *God of Exodus*, p. 204, for a typical mediating position).

Finally, for the last twenty years the dominant theological move has been to interpret the Sinai covenant according to the pattern found in the Hittite vassal treaties (Mendenhall). Theologically the effect has been to offer a compromise position between the controversial issues of classic Christian theology. God's initiative as the suzerain is stressed, but Israel's response as vassal is likewise considered essential (cf. D. N. Freedman, *Interpretation* 18, 1964, pp. 419ff.). In a somewhat broader context, Plastaras (*op. cit.*, p. 252) even draws a parallel between the covenant theology of J and E and the tension between Catholic and Protestant theology. He suggests a similarity between the charismatic theology of the northern prophetic tradition and the theology of the Reformation, which he contrasts with the hierarchical emphasis of Catholicism. Likewise, Buber's existential interpretation of Sinai – the covenant is 'not a contract, but an assumption into a life relationship' – tends to blur many of the older points of contention between Jew and Christian (*Moses*, p. 103). But the extent to which this modern ecumenical spirit has made any real exegetical contribution will have to await the later judgment of history.

6. Theological Reflection in the Context of the Canon

Certain important points respecting the covenant emerge with clarity from both testaments. First, the law and the covenant belong together. Regardless of the critical problems involved in respect to the original relation of ch. 20 to ch. 19, seen from the context of the canon there can be no separation theologically between the two. It is abundantly clear that the two have been joined in the final stage of the text's development and so read by the subsequent tradition. Theologically the close juxtaposition guards against a legalistic interpretation of the law apart from the covenant, on the one hand,

and, on the other hand, against an alleged covenant of grace conceived of without a content.

Secondly, the law defines the holiness demanded of the covenant people. The promise of the 'holy people' of Ex. 19.5 is specifically linked with the preparation for the theophany and interpreted as a testing by God (20.20). Likewise the New Testament picks up this promise as directed to the church and still providing a claim of obedience. The measurement of holiness in terms of God's own nature prevents the covenant claim from being given a moralistic interpretation or from the sectarian danger of a group set apart in its purity from the world. The covenant people are called to reflect the holiness of God to the world while rendering to God 'acceptable worship'.

Thirdly, the covenant at Sinai remains a witness for all ages of the ultimate seriousness of God's revelation of himself and his will to the world. God comes as an act of grace to join to himself a people, but his unveiling likewise brings with it a judgment. The New Testament is fully in accord with the Old in testifying that the God made known in Jesus Christ is not different in character from the consuming fire of Sinai. His covenant claim lays hold on man to demand full commitment on the central issue of life and death. Election by God brings no comfortable special status, but an invitation both to share the redemption of God to the world and to bear witness to his final judgment of sin.

Beside these common features of both testaments, the New Testament witness offers a theological judgment on certain features of the old covenant. Finding its warrant within the Old Testament itself, the apostles witness to the inadequacy and failure of the old covenant at Sinai to accomplish God's will for his people. The prophetic criticism focused on Israel's failure to keep God's covenant, but then pressed on to envision a new form of the same covenant, with an implied criticism of the old (Jer. 31.31). The point at issue is not simply the externality of the old, as if Jesus' function was to internalize the covenant relation. Rather, the dimension of human sin requires a complete transformation of a people. There can be no true covenant apart from the kingdom of God. Therefore, the New Testament links the Sinai theophany with the New Jerusalem and the ultimate eschatological consumation of God's will.

Again, the eschatological dimension of the Christian life determines the true shape of obedience to the will of God. The Christian lives by the promise of the gospel, as one who has been freed from the curse of the law which condemns without the power to deliver. He senses the radical claim for divine obedience which can only be filled by God's own power in a new act of creation. The radical nature of the New Testament witness remains a warning against the deceptive compromise of all forms of synergism, ancient and modern, as if man could find a good life with a little help from God!

Finally, the New Testament provides an additional corrective already found in the Old Testament against limiting election forever to Israel. God plays no favorites, but he has chosen instruments which he uses in particular ways through the course of history. Therefore, whether it is by means of Israel or the church the ultimate goal of God's will is directed to all men. Jesus Christ has provided the door of free access to God outside the established channels of religion.

Equally important for theological reflection within the context of the canon is the Old Testament's critical corrective of the New. Exodus 19 remains as a witness that God did enter a covenant with a historical people at a particular time and place. He formulated his claim on them in terms of commandments which they understood: 'Thou shalt not kill', 'Thou shalt not commit adultery'. This biblical witness remains a warning against spiritualizing the covenant and the demands of the law. Detached from the Old Testament, the witness of the letter to the Hebrews can lead the church along the path of Philo and the Gnostics to seek some philosophical concept of perfection, divorced from any concrete expression of response in human terms. Nor can the eschatological dimension of Hebrews be linked to forms of human dissatisfaction with the *status quo*. The thunder of Sinai continues to address the church in terms of obedient acts to one's fellow humans, done in response to God's claim, and measured by God's criteria. The externality of God's revelation at Sinai guards the church from encapsulating God within the good intentions of the religious conscience. Thus Ex. 19 provides the major content to the New Testament's witness that God is a consuming fire. The weakness of the Old Testament is not in creating a primitive concept of God, but in the failure of Israel to respond in righteousness. The new covenant is not a substitution of a friendly God for the terror of Sinai, but rather a gracious message of an open access to the same God whose presence still calls forth awe and reverence.

XVII

THE DECALOGUE

20.1–17

A. *Bibliography to Old Testament Law*

A. ALT, 'The Origins of Israelite Law', *Essays on Old Testament History and Religion*, Oxford 1966, pp. 81–132 (New York 1967, pp. 103–71); 'Zur Talionsformel', *ZAW* 52, 1934, pp. 303–5 = *KS* I, 1953, pp. 341–4; K. BALTZER, *Das Bundesformular*, WMANT 4, 1960; W. BEYERLIN, *Herkunft und Geschichte der ältesten Sinaitraditionen*, Tübingen 1961, pp. 16ff., 59ff., ET *Origins and History of the Oldest Sinaitic Traditions*, Oxford 1965, pp. 12ff., 49ff.; M. BUSS, 'The Covenant Theme in Historical Perspective', *VT* 16, 1966, pp. 502ff.; D. DAUBE, *Studies in Biblical Law*, Cambridge and New York 1947; K. ELLIGER, 'Das Gesetz Leviticus 18', *ZAW* 67, 1955, pp. 1–25; Z. W. FALK, *Hebrew Law in Biblical Times*, Jerusalem 1964; F. C. FENSHAM, 'The Possibility of the Presence of Casuistic Legal Material at the Making of the Covenant at Sinai', *PEQ* 93, 1961, pp. 143–6; G. FOHRER, *Studien zur alttestamentlichen Theologie und Geschichte*, Berlin 1969, pp. 84ff.; E. GERSTENBERGER, 'Covenant and Commandment', *JBL* 84, 1965, pp. 38–51; *Wesen und Herkunft des 'apodiktischen Rechts'*, WMANT 20, 1965; S. GERVITZ, 'West Semitic Curses and the Problem of the Origins of Hebrew Law', *VT* 11, 1961, pp. 137–58; H. GESE, 'Beobachtungen zum Stil alttestamentlicher Rechtssätze', *TLZ* 85, 1960, pp. 147–50; G. GURVITCH, *Sociology of Law*, London 1947; I. HEINEMANN, *Untersuchungen zum apodiktischen Recht* (Diss. Hamburg), 1958; A. JIRKU, *Das weltliche Recht im Alten Testament*, Gütersloh 1927; R. KILIAN, 'Apodiktisches und kasuistisches Recht im Licht ägyptischer Analogien', *BZ* 7, 1963, pp. 185–202; *Literarkritische und Formgeschichtliche Untersuchung des Heiligkeitsgesetzes*, Bonn 1963; D. J. McCARTHY, *Der Gottesbund im Alten Testament*, Stuttgart 1966; *Treaty and Covenant*, Rome 1963; G. E. MENDENHALL, 'Law and Covenant in Israel and in the Ancient Near East', *BA* 17, 1954, pp. 26–46, 49–76; J. MORGENSTERN, 'The Oldest Document of the Hexateuch', *HUCA* 4, 1927, pp. 1ff.; M. NOTH, *Die Gesetze im Pentateuch*, Königsberg 1940, ET *The Laws in the Pentateuch and Other Studies*, Edinburgh and Toronto 1966, pp. 1–107; J. VAN DER PLOEG, 'Studies in Hebrew Law', *CBQ* 12, 1950, pp. 248–59, 416–27; *CBQ* 13, 1951, pp. 28–43, 164–171, 296–307; K. RABAST, *Das apodiktische Recht im Deuteronomium und im Heiligkeitsgesetz*, Berlin 1948; H. GRAF REVENTLOW, *Das Heiligkeitsgesetz formgeschichtlich untersucht*, WMANT 6, 1961; W. RICHTER, *Recht und Ethos*, Munich 1966; H. SCHULZ, *Das Todesrecht im Alten Testament*, Berlin 1969; J. M. P. SMITH,

The Origin and History of Hebrew Law, Chicago 1931, Cambridge 1932; R. DE VAUX, *Ancient Israel,* London 1961, pp. 143ff.; V. WAGNER, *Rechtssätze in gebundener Sprache und Rechtssatzreihen im israelitischen Recht,* Berlin 1972; E. WÜRTHWEIN, 'Der Sinn des Gesetzes im Alten Testament', *ZTK* 55, 1958, pp. 255–70; W. ZIMMERLI, *The Law and the Prophets,* ET Oxford 1965, New York 1967.

B. *Bibliography to the Decalogue*

H. CAZELLES, 'Les Origines du Décalogue', *Eretz Israel* IX, 1969, pp. 14ff.; W. EICHRODT, 'The Law and the Gospel', *Interpretation* 11, 1957, pp. 23–40; H. GESE, 'Der Dekalog als Ganzheit betrachtet', *ZTK* 64, 1967, pp. 121–38; J. P. HYATT, 'Moses and the Ethical Decalogue', *Encounter* 26, 1965, pp. 199–206; A. JEPSEN, 'Beiträge zur Auslegung und Geschichte des Dekalogs', *ZAW* 79, 1967, pp. 277–304; A. S. KAPELRUD, 'Some Recent Points of View on the Time and Origin of the Decalogue', *Stud. Theol.* 18, 1964, pp. 81–90; W. KESSLER, 'Die literarische, historische und theologische Problematik des Dekalogs', *VT* 7, 1957, pp. 1–16; L. KÖHLER, 'Der Dekalog', *ThR,* NF 1, 1929, pp. 161–84; J. L. KOOLE, *De Tien Geboden* (Kampen 1964); H. KREMERS, 'Dekalog', *Evangelisches Kirchenlexikon* I, 1956, pp. 852–54; N. LOHFINK, 'Zur Dekalogfassung von Dt. 5' *BZ,* NF 9, 1965, pp. 17ff.; S. MOWINCKEL, *Le Décalogue,* Paris 1927; 'Zur Geschichte des Dekaloge', *ZAW* 55, 1937, pp. 218ff.; E. NIELSEN, *The Ten Commandments in New Perspective* ET, SBT 2.7, 1968; R. H. PFEIFFER, 'The Oldest Decalogue', *JBL* 43, 1924, pp. 294–310; A. C. J. PHILLIPS, *Ancient Israel's Criminal Law,* Oxford 1970, New York 1971; H. GRAF REVENTLOW, *Gebot und Predigt im Dekalog,* Gütersloh 1962; H. H. ROWLEY, 'Moses and the Decalogue', *BJRL* 34, 1951/2, pp. 81–118; H. SCHMIDT, 'Mose und der Dekalog', *Eucharisterion, Festschrift H. Gunkel,* FRLANT 36, 1923, pp. 78–119; S. SPIEGEL, 'A Prophetic Attestation of the Decalogue–Hos. 6, 5 with some observations on Psalm 15 and 24', *HTR* 27, 1934, pp. 105–44; J. J. STAMM, 'Dreissig Jahre Dekalogforschung', *ThR,* NF 27, 1961, pp. 189–239, 281–305; with M. E. ANDREW, *The Ten Commandments in Recent Research,* SBT 2.2, 1967; E. ZENGER, 'Eine Wende in der Dekalogforschung?', *ThRe* 3, 1968, pp. 189–198.

20 ¹God spoke all these words, saying,

2 I am the LORD your God who brought you out of the land of Egypt, out of the house of bondage.

3 You shall have no other gods before me.

4 You shall not make yourself an image, or any likeness of what is in heaven above, or on earth below, or in the water under the earth. ⁵You shall not bow down to them nor serve them; for I, the LORD your God, am a jealous God, visiting the guilt of the fathers upon the children, upon the third and upon the fourth generation of those hating me, ⁶but showing steadfast love to the thousandth generation of those who love me and keep my commandments.

7 You shall not abuse the name of the LORD your God, for the LORD will not leave unpunished the one who abuses his name.

8 Remember to keep the sabbath day holy. ⁹Six days you have to

labor and to do all your work; [10]but the seventh day is a sabbath to the LORD your God; you shall not do any work, you, your son or daughter, your male or female slave, or your cattle, or the stranger who is within your gate. [11]For in six days the LORD made heaven and earth, the sea, and all that is in them, and rested on the seventh day; therefore the LORD blessed the sabbath day and declared it holy.

12 Honor your father and your mother, that you may live long in the land which the LORD your God is giving you.

13 You shall not kill.

14 You shall not commit adultery.

15 You shall not steal.

16 You shall not testify against your neighbor as a false witness.

17 You shall not covet your neighbor's house; you shall not covet your neighbor's wife, or his male or female slave, or his ox or his ass, or anything that is your neighbor's.

1. *Textual and Philological Notes*

A specific textual problem respecting the Decalogue has arisen in connection with the Nash Papyrus. Cf. the literature on the problem: N. Peters, *Die älteste Abschrift der zehn Gebote, der Papyrus Nash*, Freiburg 1905; W. F. Albright, *JBL* 56, 1937, pp. 145–176; F. Horst, *RGG*[3], pp. 69–71; J. J. Stamm, *ThR*, NS 27, 1961, pp. 197f.; A. Jepsen, *ZAW* 79, 1967, pp. 277ff.

20.1. In the Hebrew text the Decalogue has a double accentuation. One system divides the commandments into ten parts for liturgical purposes, the other according to the division of the verses. Cf. *G-K* §15p; A. Geiger, *Urschrift und Übersetzungen der Bibel*, Breslau 1857, p. 373; Kalisch, *op. cit.*, p. 342.

2. The AmTr, NJPS, NAB translate *'ānōḵī YHWH 'elōhêḵā* with 'I the LORD am your God'. This translation, which is syntactically possible, seems less likely after Zimmerli's exhaustive form critical study ('Ich bin Jahwe', *Gottes Offenbarung*, pp. 11ff.). For the syntax of the relative clause which follows the person of the main sentence, cf. *G-K* §138d; Brockelmann, *Syntax*, §153a.

3. The translation of the expression *'al-pānay* ('before me'?) has occasioned much debate. Cf. the exegesis for a discussion of some of the options.

4. *pesel*, RSV: 'graven image'; NJPS: 'sculptured image'; NEB: 'carved image'; NAB: 'idols'. The parallel text in Deut. 5.8 fails to have a waw after the noun *pesel* which affects the syntax of the sentence. The asyndetic text of Deut. understands the clause as an apposition which further specifies the nature of the image. However, the Exodus text, which has a *waw*, understands the following clause as an addition over and above the prohibition of the image. Cf. Nielsen, *op. cit.*, p. 36.

The sequence *pesel weḵol-temûnāh* is syntactically extremely difficult to interpret. *'ašer* is attached as a relative to the absolute form of the noun which then reads, strictly speaking, 'any form which is in heaven'. However, one expects the relative clause to modify *kol*. Several suggestions to alleviate the difficulty have been made: (i) to emend the text in accordance with Deut. 4.16,

25 (cf. *BH*[3], but Zimmerli's criticism, *op. cit.*, p. 235). (ii) To read the sequence as a construct *tᵉmûnaṯ kōl*, but cf. Dillmann's objection, *ad loc.* (iii) To end the sentence after *tᵉmûnāh* (so Dillmann), but this suggestion lacks all textual support from the versions and creates an artificial construction for the *'ᵃšer* clause.

5. Deut. reads *wᵉᶜal-šillēšîm*. Cf. on the translation of *'ēl qannā'* H. A. Brongers, *VT* 13, 1963, p. 269.

6. There is disagreement on how to translate *'ᵃlāpîm*, whether in close parallel to v. 5 as the 'thousandth generation', or with unrestricted sense. The former option is preferred by the AmTr, NJPS, and NAB; the latter by RSV, NEB, Driver, Noth (cf. Ex. 34.7.). Deut. 7.9 makes the thousandth generation explicit. The issue is exegetical rather than strictly grammatical. I prefer the first option as better providing the intended contrast of the commandment.

7. *ṭiśśā' 'et-šēm . . . laśśāw'*. The versions vary considerably in rendering this expression. The LXX: ἐπὶ ματαίῳ, 'thoughtlessly'; Pesh.: 'deceitfully'; Vulg.: *in vanum*. Onkelos translates the MT literally as does Targum Neofiti I (but cf. the variant tradition of 'swear falsely' in mss. M). Also H. Orlinsky, *Notes*, pp. 175f.

8. Deut. reads *šāmôr*, 'observe', in place of *zākôr*, and adds a clause 'as Yahweh your God commands you'. On the force of the final clause, König, *Lehrgebäude* III, §407a.

11. Deut. has the much longer text with the significant addition 'that your male and female slaves may rest as well as you'. The motivation clause in v. 11 varies completely in Deut.

12. Deut. has in addition the clause 'that it may be well with you'.

13. The order of the 'sixth' commandment and the succeeding prohibition of adultery fluctuate considerably in the various textual traditions. The order of the Massoretic tradition is supported by Samar., Josephus, a Qumran copy of Deut., and rabbinic literature. The reversing of the sequence is found in the LXX, Philo, Nash Payrus, and the NT. (For a full discussion, cf. D. Flusser, *Textus* 4, 1964, pp. 220ff.)

15. For a study of the Semitic cognates of *gnb*, cf. L. Knopf, *VT* 8, 1958, p. 169.

16. Deut. reads *ᶜēd 'āwš*, which is clearly secondary to the Exodus text. *ᶜēd sāqer* is a technical term and better translated 'lying witness' than the more general 'false evidence'. Cf. Stoebe, *Wort und Dienst* 3, 1952, pp. 108ff.

17. Deut. reverses the order of 'house' and 'wife' and reads *tiṯ'awweh* in place of *taḥmōd*. The Samar. text inserts at this point Deut. 27.2, 5–7 in its altered form and part of Deut. 11.30 on the location of Gerizim.

2. *Literary and Traditio-Historical Problems*

A. *The History of Modern Research in Old Testament Law*

The study of the historical development of the traditions which comprise the Decalogue is closely tied to the whole modern discussion of Old Testament law in general. Because there are several reliable guides to the history of research, this survey can be extremely brief (cf. bibliography above).

Recent critical scholarship on Old Testament law has been dominated, by and large, by form-critical questions. This is not to suggest that only this aspect was considered important since significant work continued to be done in other areas. One thinks of the continued interest in comparative studies of Near Eastern law (cf. the bibliography in *Orientalisches Recht, Handbuch der Orientalistik, Ergänzungsband* III, Leiden 1964), and such fresh, independent studies as that of David Daube (*Studies in Biblical Law*, 1947) among others. Nevertheless, even these studies seemed to have been brought into the main streams of scholarship in so far as they could be used to enrich and correct form-critical work. Certainly form-critical research provided the major impetus for the study of Old Testament law and supplied the framework in which much of the critical investigation operated.

The fundamental study was, of course, Alt's essay of 1934, translated as 'The Origins of Israelite Law'. Naturally Alt was dependent on earlier studies, particularly those of Mowinckel, Jirku, and Koehler. Alt began by distinguishing sharply between two forms of law which he designated casuistic and apodictic. The former was characterized by a conditional style which defined specific legal cases, usually with an elaborate differentiation of subordinate circumstances (Ex. 21.1ff.). The latter was characterized by an unconditional, imperative style, usually in the second person, expressed in the negative without an explicit stipulation of punishment (23.1ff.). Alt argued that casuistic law grew out of the normal legal procedure of secular, lay justice which was administered at the gate. In contrast, he linked apodictic law to an original cultic setting which had its place within the covenant renewal celebration (cf. Deut. 31.10ff.). Moreover, Alt argued that although casuistic law was common to the Ancient Near Eastern culture (Canaanite), apodictic law was unique to Israel and provided 'true Israelite law' (*genuin israelitisch*).

Alt's essay with its rigorous form-critical analysis seemed to bring order into a field which had been up to then increasingly characterized by widely varying theses and much uncontrolled speculation (Bäntsch, Pfeiffer, Morgenstern, J. M. P. Smith, etc.). It was accepted by the majority of Old Testament scholars and further refined by a series of illuminating essays and monographs (cf. Jepsen,

Noth, von Rad, Zimmerli, Elliger, Cazelles, de Vaux, etc.). Particularly in von Rad's *Old Testament Theology*, vol. I, the theological implications of the law were expounded in a way which fully exploited Alt's insights. Whereas for Alt the characterization of apodictic law as 'genuine Israelite' was primarily a historical judgment, certainly its popularity in wider Old Testament circles was sustained by its theological application.

A new phase of the discussion of Old Testament law was opened up in 1954 with Mendenhall's essay on 'Law and Covenant' (*op. cit.*). The author argued for a similarity of form and content between the Old Testament covenant texts and a group of Hittite state treaties, the so-called suzerainty treaties. Mendenhall felt that the origin of the biblical covenant pattern was to be found in the Ancient Near Eastern treaty, particularly in the historical prologue. Furthermore, it provided the setting for Israel's apodictic law. Again Mendenhall's thesis was refined and buttressed by a veritable flood of articles (Baltzer, Beyerlin, Heinemann, Hillers, Moran, Huffmon, etc.) These scholars generally regarded Mendenhall's thesis as having broadened and modified Alt's thesis, but also as having sustained his major distinction. At the same time, opposition to the alleged Hittite parallel continued to be strong (Gese, Nötscher, Gerstenberger, etc.; cf. McCarthy's *Treaty and Covenant* for a survey).

The next major development was clearly the brilliant dissertation of Gerstenberger (*op. cit.*). Although few were willing to accept Gerstenberger's thesis in its entirety, certainly there was a growing consensus that he succeeded in delivering a major blow to the original hypothesis of Alt. First of all, following a lead of Gese, the author was able to show quite conclusively that the category of apodictic law was far from being a unified style. The sharp distinction between casuistic and apodictic needed to be greatly modified. Secondly, Gerstenberger argued for a 'prohibitive' style which lay at the base of all so-called apodictic law. Moreover the prohibitive was not unique to Israel, and even more significant, did not have its setting in a cultic (covenantal) ceremony. At best the Israelite cult – not to speak of the Hittite treaty – was a secondary usage of the prohibitive. Gerstenberger then argued – in my opinion less convincingly – for a 'clan ethic' (*Sippenethos*) which was reflected in wisdom literature as being the source of the prohibitive. In sum, it is clear from the literature subsequent to Gerstenberger's dissertation that he had succeeded in ushering in a new phase of the debate by opening up a whole new set of form-critical and *religionsgeschichtliche* questions (cf. especially Kilian, Fohrer, Richter, Schulz, Knierim [see p.385 above], etc.).

The over-all effect has been to emphasize the diversity of early Hebrew law. Lying behind the stylized series of apodictic commands such as the Decalogue was a long history of development. Only at a more advanced stage did it seem possible for originally disparate laws to have been given a unified function in the Israelite cult. The relation of law to the wider problems of moral sanctions in Ancient Israel which now emerged in a fresh way has not been adequately treated as yet. Moreover, it is likely that the tools of such a field as the sociology of law are needed which will carry the research far beyond the narrow limits of Old Testament study (cf. e.g. Gurvitch, *Sociology of Law*).

B. *Traditio-History of the Decalogue*

Again it is hardly necessary to review in detail the history of scholarship in relation of the Decalogue (cf. in the bibliography especially the surveys of Koehler, Stamm, and Stamm-Andrews). At the outset certain observations can be made on the basis of several generations of critical study. First, there is a wide consensus that the present form of the Decalogue is the product of a long historical development. The present form of the commandments gives evidence at times of being expanded greatly beyond its original formulation (20.8), while at other times of being contracted (20.13ff.). This is to say that one has to reckon with a period of oral tradition in which both the form and function of a commandment were different from its function within the Decalogue. Again, one has to reckon with a further development even after the formation of the Decalogue, as a comparison between Exodus and Deuteronomy demonstrates.

Secondly, the forces which gave the Decalogue its present shape were rooted in the institutional life of Israel. The religious usage of the Decalogue in the worship of the community, in its liturgy, preaching and teaching, certainly must be reckoned with. The changing function of the Decalogue within the development of Israel's life reflected itself in different layers of tradition which are now combined. However, it remains difficult to trace with certainty the nature of all the forces at work and the exact history of its growth.

Thirdly, the relation of the Decalogue to the larger narrative setting of Sinai in which it is now found has become increasingly problematic. On the literary level, the tensions between the Decalogue itself and its framework have long been pointed out (cf. most recently Gerstenberger, *Wesen und Herkunft*, pp. 90ff.). Moreover, the emphasis on the covenant renewal setting of the chapter has not done much to establish a closer connection between the cult and the Decalogue itself. It would seem that however one may understand the historical development, the present relation of the Decalogue to Sinai stems from a later redactional activity.

As a consequence, much of the recent study of the Decalogue has been an attempt to make use of the historical dimension to open up new insight for interpretation. Reventlow is typical when writing: 'The decisive exegetical question of the Decalogue is its original meaning . . .' (*Gebot und Predigt*, p. 9). The results of this approach have been mixed, to say the least. On the one hand, a whole new set of questions have emerged which have often brought penetrating insights to bear on the text. Zimmerli's study of the second commandment (cf. below) is a classic example of a genuine advance in interpretation. On the other hand, the dangers of exegesis being built on ill-founded hypothetical projections have increased dramatically during the last half-century. As a result, few passages have suffered such divergent interpretations as has the Decalogue.

The confusion in approach applies to questions of both form and content. In respect to the form, some have attempted to reconstruct the original series by excising alleged secondary commandments (H. Schmidt). Others have assumed that the length of each commandment must be metrically uniform and they have reconstructed a shortened and a lengthened form to match the hypothesis (Rabast). Others have taken for granted that the original form was negative in formulation and have therefore seen in the two positive commandments a later development (Alt). Some continue to defend the originality of the number ten (Mowinckel), while others have suggested seeing smaller units as original (Nielsen).

The same uncertainty applies to the study of the original function of the commandments. The generation of literary critics tended to understand the development of the Decalogue as first belonging to the Elohist source with subsequent Deuteronomic and Priestly expansions. In reaction to this, some form critics have sought to abandon all reference to sources and speak only of changing liturgical roles (Reventlow). Again the attempt to work from a projected cultic *Sitz im Leben* has produced widely differing suggestions (Mowinckel, Beyerlin).

Even more frustrating has been the continual attempt to establish a date for the Decalogue (cf. Rowley's survey). Often this has meant working from a prior concept of Israel's religious development, such as the assumption that an ethical consciousness was first introduced into Israel by the prophets! More recently the criteria for dating have stemmed from extra-biblical evidence (Beyerlin) or from form-critical observations (Alt).

Perhaps the primary lesson to be drawn from this history of research is the need for greater caution both in the construction and the use of an alleged historical dimension. The least which one should expect is that the distinction be maintained between a critical hypothesis about the text and the text itself.

C. *The Present Form of the Decalogue*

There is another aspect to the traditio-historical problem of the Decalogue which has not been adequately recognized. If one assumes, as I do, that a major purpose of biblical exegesis is the interpretation of the final form of the text, the study of the earlier dimensions of historical development should serve to bring the final stage of redaction into sharper focus. Indeed the recognition of different layers of tradition, both on the oral and literary levels, can have exegetical importance even though the factors which produced them often remain unclear. The fact that the present text of the Decalogue reflects a certain profile, regardless of the reasons why, can provide a basis for understanding what the commandments came to mean to Israel. An essential aspect of a critical analysis is to describe the features of the Decalogue itself and then to relate them to the laws in the rest of the Old Testament.

The following analysis attempts to work from the form of the present text while at the same time seeking to remain open to the historical dimensions of the text.

1. The introductory formula of Ex. 20.1 which frames the passage ('God spoke all these words, saying . . .') is a unique feature of the Decalogue. In Deut. 5.5 the formula has been reduced to the absolute minimum in order to accommodate the narrative framework. However, the Book of the Covenant (Ex. 20.22) is introduced as a speech of God *to Moses* for the people. Likewise in Ex. 34.32, in the Holiness Code (Lev. 17.1ff.), and in Deut. 6.1, the divine words of

commandment are mediated through Moses, and not directly by God himself.

2. The self-introductory prologue which follows in v. 2 (//Deut. 5.6) is closely paralleled in both form and function in other legal collections (Ex. 34.6; Lev. 19.2, etc.)

3. The Decalogue consists of a majority of negative commands; two, however, are in positive form (vv. 8, 12). The juxtaposition of positive and negative laws in a series is a characteristic feature of all Old Testament law (cf. Ex. 34.14ff.; Lev. 19.14ff.; Deut. 14.11ff.). There is no apparent inner tension between these two types nor is there any evidence which demonstrates the historical priority of the negative.

4. The individual commandments vary greatly in length from the extremely long commandments (vv. 4ff., 8ff.) to the extremely short (vv. 13, 13, 15). One can conclude that at least in the final redaction of the Decalogue metrical pattern has been completely disregarded. However, there is evidence to indicate that at an earlier stage similarity in either length or meter did once play a role. Parallel commandments in the Book of the Covenant (20.22ff.) and the Holiness Code (Lev. 19) show clusters of similar structured laws. Again, the bare prohibitive clauses reveal a fairly consistent length. However, Eichrodt's move to draw an immediate theological implication seems premature: 'This partial loss of the usual form was obviously (sic) not caused either by chance or by neglect; rather, it was dictated by a deep interest in the content' (Interpretation 11, 1957, p. 27).

5. The clauses which join the basic commandments show great variation in style and content, including a variety of motivation clauses (vv. 7, 11, 13), additional specifications (vv. 10, 17), participial ascriptions (vv. 5f.), etc. It is not by chance that most of the variations which Deuteronomy's form of the Decalogue exhibits, are to be found here.

6. The Decalogue is not consistent throughout in employing the first person pronoun for the speaker, but after v. 7 addresses God in the third person. Such a variation is a characteristic feature of other laws as well (Ex. 34.19, 23; 22.26, 27; Lev. 19.5, 8, 12, 19). The reason for this variation in the Decalogue is not immediately apparent.

7. The Decalogue is consistent in its use of the second person singular for the addressee, which is a feature not often found in a

legal series. Usually there is considerable variation from singular to plural (Ex. 34; Lev. 19). At times the consistent usage of the plural makes probable a different level of tradition from that using the singular.

8. The exact enumeration of ten commandments within the Decalogue is not obvious, as the variation in the later ecclesiastical tradition shows. The reference to 'ten words' does not appear in Ex. 20, but first in Ex. 34.28; Deut. 4.13 and 10.4. Although there is indication of other series of tens (Lev. 19), the same difficulty of isolating this number persists in these cases also. This would seem to suggest that the number ten became a model for law codes within Israel, but probably not at an early stage.

9. The division of the Decalogue into two tablets does not occur in Ex. 20, but in Ex. 34 and Deuteronomy 5. Nowhere in the biblical tradition is there indication of how the commandments were to be divided.

10. The order of the commandments does not follow a strictly logical sequence as, for example, in Lev. 18. In this respect, the lack of a rigorous order is a consistent feature of most Old Testament law. Nevertheless, there are some signs of design in the sequence. The initial command would indicate its importance in the series. Again, the grouping of commands in the beginning of the series which refer solely to God stands in contrast to the following commands which relate to one's fellows. Parallels elsewhere in the Old Testament would indicate that certain features of the Decalogue's sequence could be traditional (Lev. 19.3f.). The asyndetic relation between the commands of vv. 13ff., which is not represented in the Deuteronomic parallel, is of note, but its significance is unclear. The influence of parallelism between commands does not seem apparent (*contra* Gese, *op. cit.*).

11. The Decalogue employs a consistent 'apodictic' style. That is to say, the casuistic style of case law is not represented. This is an unusual feature of the Decalogue. In the other law codes the two styles are invariably mixed (Ex. 22.15ff.; Lev. 19.3ff.). The closest parallel in respect to consistency of style is the series of curses of Deut. 27.15ff. In Ex. 20 the casuistic style of law follows the Decalogue in the Book of the Covenant. This sharp separation could be accounted for on either the level of oral tradition, redactional activity, or both.

12. In respect to the content, there are parallel laws elsewhere in

the Old Testament to each of the commandments within the Decalogue, but there is no parallel to the whole series. Again, the parallelism is in terms of content rather than exact formulation. A close dependence such as that between the Book of the Covenant and Ex. 34 is not found to the Decalogue.

13. There are no sanctions to the commandments; however, elsewhere in the Old Testament similar commands carry the death penalty when disobeyed, Ex. 21.15ff.; 22.19; 31.12ff.; Lev. 20.6ff.; Deut. 27.15ff. (cf. Schulz, *Das Todesrecht*). In any case, the Decalogue is consistent in touching upon only those areas of extreme importance for the life of the community.

14. There is no distinction made between 'cultic' and 'ethical' laws. The contrast between the 'ethical decalogue' of Ex. 20 and the so-called 'cultic decalogue' of Ex. 34 introduces an unfortunate dichotomy nowhere found in Old Testament law. The fusion of both aspects is characteristic of Old Testament law from the earliest level of tradition.

15. The commandments are marked by their stark objectivity and apparent unconcern with inner motives. However, the process of internalization cannot be fully dismissed and stands on the edge of the commandments. Although the term 'covet' in v. 17 seems to have an original connotation of action and not simply intention (cf. below) the relation of this commandment to v. 15 moves its interpretation in the direction of intentionality. This move become explicit in Deut. 5.21. Cf. also Deut. 5.15, 12. While perhaps a case could be made that internalization of the commands increased in the later history of Israel, it does not ever seem to have been completely absent within Israel (cf. Gen. 39.9; Lev. 19.18; Deut. 8.11ff.; Prov. 6.27ff.).

16. The Decalogue is distinguished from most series of Old Testament laws in having little or no reference to a specific historical period such as post-settlement, or to particular institutions, such as a central sanctuary. The commandments deal with issues which remained central to the life of the nation from the beginning to the end. This observation, however, should not lead one to regard the Decalogue as being merely timeless principles. Nevertheless, the contrast of the Decalogue with the laws of the Book of the Covenant, the Holiness Code, and Deuteronomy which assume an agricultural society, or reflect seventh-century centralization, is striking and highly significant. The efforts to fix a date for the Decalogue on the

basis of certain laws – as if the sabbath law must be post-exilic – are certainly doomed to failure.

It is now our task to draw some implications from these observations and to offer an interpretation of the final form of the Decalogue viewed as a whole before turning to a detailed study of each separate commandment.

The Decalogue shows every sign of having been given a special place within the Old Testament tradition. The evidence that it was assigned a unique place of importance by the Old Testament itself, and not just by subsequent Jewish and Christian interpreters, is manifold. The commandments have a special name, the 'ten words' (^{a}seret hadd^{e}bārîm) (cf. also Ex. 31.18; Deut. 4.13; 9.9, etc.). Again, they are repeated in Deuteronomy as providing the foundation for the new promulgation of the covenant. The narrative framework of Exodus, but particularly of Deuteronomy, stressed the finality of the commandments: 'These words Yahweh spoke . . . and added no more' (Deut. 5.22). Finally, the reflection of the commandments in the prophets (Hos. 4.1ff.; Jer. 7.9ff.), and in the Psalms (50 and 81) testify to their influence upon Israel's faith.

Moreover, the reason for the Decalogue's centrality emerges clearly from the tradition itself. The commandments are tied inextricably to God's revelation at Sinai. The special character of these laws, in distinction from all others, finds expression in the specific formula which points to direct, unmediated communication of Yahweh himself: 'God spoke all these words, saying . . .' However much the modern interpreter finds signs of growth and development in the formation of the Decalogue, the tradition remained unequivocal in linking together the revelation at Sinai and the giving of the law. There is furthermore every indication that the redactor of the final form of the narrative sought to work out the inner logic of this received tradition. The commandments were not arbitrary stipulations which had unwittingly assumed an importance. Rather, they reflected the essential character of God himself. Both the manner of delivery and the effect upon reception makes this clear. The reaction of the people's terror stems both from the majesty of God and from the revelation of his will, which fall together.

The Decalogue is set apart from the other laws which follow. All of Israel's laws were from God, but the Decalogue had a special place. In what respect exactly the ten commandments differed from the

Book of the Covenant in terms of content is nowhere explicitly stated. In the final redaction the sealing of the covenant (Ex. 24) involved both sets of laws. Nor are the usual modern reflections on the Decalogue's being universal in character, or ethically oriented, based on solid evidence. Still there are some hints given within the tradition which relate to the specific content of the Decalogue. As we observed above, the Decalogue in contrast to the casuistic laws of the Book of the Covenant contains no stipulation for violators. Yet the seriousness of offense against the commandments is apparent from the punishment of death which is assigned elsewhere as the sanction. However, it makes considerable sense to suggest that the redactor understood the covenant framework of the narrative to function as the sanction. The Decalogue provides the basis for the covenant with all of Israel. In the same way the sanction of the covenant relates to the whole people and it is inherent in the claims of loyalty. The curse for disobedience is constitutive to these laws. Certainly the prophets drew this consequence from breaking the covenant.

Much has been made of the fact that the Decalogue contains both positive and negative laws. Since there is no clear evidence of a development at this point, the significance would seem to lie in the juxtaposition of these two types of law. The predominance of prohibitions concerning the most extreme examples of wickedness would first of all demonstrate an essential role of the Decalogue in charting the outer limits of the covenant (von Rad). One who breaks these commands sets himself outside the established life of God's people. To transgress is not to commit a misdemeanor but to break the very fibre of which the divine-human relation consists. Nevertheless, the presence of the two positive commands would reveal another function of the commandments. The Decalogue serves not only to chart the outer boundary, but also to provide positive content for life within the circle of the covenant. The Decalogue looks both outward and inward; it guards against the way of death and points to the way of life.

How is one to interpret the fact that the final form of the Decalogue reveals considerable evidence of expansion over and above its earlier form? The variation in the Deuteronomic recession amply illustrates the tendency to alter and expand elements within the commandments. Moreover, the different styles of writing attributed to a Deuteronomic or Priestly editor would further confirm the presence of several layers of historical development within the present form. The final form with its apparent expansions affords a good indication of how the Decalogue functioned within Israel. It obviously served as the basis for homily, exhortation, and instruction. The non-metrical expansions of basically parenetic material would also indicate that, whatever cultic usage it once had, this role had greatly receded. Another indication of the flexible parenetic usage of the Decalogue appears in the tendency within the later stages toward internalization which began to open up a whole new dimension to be subsumed under the authority of the will of God.

We noticed that the final form of the Decalogue lacked consistency in the manner by which God as the speaker was referred to. Great emphasis was laid on God's direct communication of his commands: 'God spoke all these words... "I am Yahweh... no other gods before me..."' Yet shortly God is referred to in the third person: 'You shall not take Yahweh's name in vain... Yahweh will not hold him guiltless...' Whatever historical reasons one can advance to account for this phenomenon, the shape of the final form would suggest that no apparent tension was felt by the redactor through this inconsistency. In the subsequent usage of the Decalogue the divine commandments were always heard through a human mediator. That the grammatical perspective was influenced by this usage appeared to raise no problems nor diminish the divine origin of the commands. This tendency within the tradition would again demonstrate the nature of the flexibility felt toward the Decalogue, which at the same time retained its special place as the foundation of the covenant.

Finally, there is need to reflect on the effect of the selection of commandments which comprise the Decalogue. On the one hand, we have observed that no single commandment can claim a unique status, either in form or content. Each finds its parallel within the rest of the Old Testament law. Yet on the other hand, the Decalogue has achieved a special status within the tradition, and as a series finds no parallels to match its completed shape. Rather than speculate on why this particular selection took place, a more fruitful approach would be to investigate the effect of the selection in its present form.

First of all, one is struck by the stark simplicity of the series. The apodictic style has contributed to this effect. Even when the command contains considerable specification (as vv. 8ff.), the initial thrust of each single command is retained. The Decalogue is not addressed to a specific segment of the population, to the priestly class, or a pro-phetic office within Israel, but to every man. It has no need of legal interpretation, but is straightforward and immediately manifest in its meaning.

Again, there is a comprehensiveness to the commands which sets the Decalogue apart from other series such as Ex. 34 or Lev. 19. The tradition testified to this quality of the Decalogue in insisting on the Decalogue's completeness. 'He added no more' (Deut. 5.22). This is not to suggest that every important aspect of Israel's legal tradition has been included, but rather to indicate the remarkable breadth of the selection. The element of comprehensiveness has been achieved both by expanding and by contracting the commands. The expansions in vv. 8ff. extend the prohibition of working on the sabbath to its farthest limits, and end by tying the commandment even to the primordial act of creation itself, whereas vv. 13ff. by shortening the command-ment to its bare verbal component ('not kill, not commit adultery, not steal') have extended its scope to cover every possible contingency. Moreover, there is an obvious balance, suggested by the order, between commands directed primarily to God and those affecting one's fellows. Yet these two aspects of the divine law belong together, as the various motivation clauses make explicit (Ex. 20.12; Deut. 5.15).

Lastly, the lack of a specific historical setting apart from that provided by the tradition in the narrative framework has long been observed. Those expositors who have sought to supply a reconstructed, original context have been singularly unsuccessful. This character-istic feature of the Decalogue has encouraged others to see in the Decalogue a summary of timeless ethical principles or a set of im-mutable divine laws. Yet the understanding of the tradition itself which emerges from the usage leading up to its final form would surely point in a different direction. The Decalogue was given a concrete historical setting in the Sinai covenant. Yet the covenant obligations allowed for a variety of applications in the ongoing history of the nation because the law was always seen as the living will of God himself. In the law one had to do with the self-manifesta-tion of God himself: 'I am Yahweh', who in his word and deed made known his claim on Israel. The commands were not a passing phase in an ever-changing process. The expression of God's will in the Decalogue was commensurate to his nature. The Old Testament never recognized a hiatus between his revealed and actual nature. The commands were best understood when kept in closest relation to the God of the covenant who laid claim upon a people and pointed them to a new life as the people of God.

3. Old Testament Context

[20.2] *Prologue*

K. ELLIGER, 'Ich bin der Herr, euer Gott', *KS zum AT*, Munich 1966, pp.211–31; H. G. REVENTLOW, *Gebot und Predigt*, pp.25ff.; W. ZIMMERLI, 'Ich bin Jahwe', *Geschichte und Altes Testament*, Tübingen 1953, pp.179–209, reprinted in *Gottes Offenbarung*, pp.11–40.

The Ten Commandments are introduced by a prologue, 'I am Yahweh your God . . .' Zimmerli, in his basic study, designated it as a 'self-introductory' formula. God makes himself known through his name. The prologue serves as a preface to the whole law and is not tied to the first commandment. It makes absolutely clear that the commands which follow are integrally connected to God's act of self-revelation.

The revelation of God's name serves as a prologue to the Decalogue, but also as a recapitulation and summary of the chapters which have preceded. In Ex.6.2 (cf. 3.14) the revelation of God's name to Moses was tied to the promise that he would deliver Israel from Egypt. Indeed, in his intervention on Israel's behalf God's actual nature would first become manifest. When Israel learned to know God's name, she would understand the nature of his redemption and his purpose for his people. Zimmerli writes: 'All that Yahweh had to say and proclaim to his people appears as a development of the basic announcement: I am Yahweh' (*Gottes Offenbarung*, p.20). Now the promise of redemption has been fulfilled. Israel has been delivered. The introduction of the formula at this place in the narrative points back to this history of redemption, but it also points forward to a new stage in the relation between God and his people.

The commandments are prefaced by the formula to make clear that they are understood as the will of Yahweh who has delivered his people from bondage. Yahweh has identified himself as the redeemer God. The formula identifies the authority and right of God to make known his will because he has already graciously acted on Israel's behalf.

The giving of the law, however, does not stand in direct line with the deliverance from Egypt. It is not simply another of the gracious acts of redemptive history. Rather, the giving of the law presupposes the deliverance from Egypt while at the same time serving another function. God made himself known in his name. Now he will enter into a covenant with his people. The Decalogue reveals the other side of God's nature which now lays a claim upon Israel. The law expresses the will of God for Israel. It spells out what God requires from a covenant people whom he delivered without demanding a prior commitment.

The much used expression, 'God revealed himself in history,' can be misleading in this context. Does not God rather reveal himself in his law? Actually in the Old Testament God reveals himself neither in history nor in law in some general sense, but in his special covenantal history with Israel. In the act of creating a people for himself history and law are not antagonistic, but different sides of the one act of divine self-manifestation.

[20.3]   *The First Commandment*: 'You shall have no other gods before me.'

A. ALT, 'The God of the Fathers', *Essays*, Oxford 1966, pp. 3ff.; W. EICHRODT, *Theology of the Old Testament* I, p. 222; R. KNIERIM, 'Das erste Gebot', *ZAW* 77, 1965, pp. 20ff.; N. LOHFINK, *Das Hauptgebot: Eine Untersuchung . . . zu Dtn 5–11*, Rome 1963; G. VON RAD, *Old Testament Theology* I, pp. 203ff.; W. H. SCHMIDT, *Das erste Gebot*, Munich 1970; W. ZIMMERLI, *Grundriss der alttestamentlichen Theologie*, Stuttgart 1972, pp. 100ff.

The first commandment is given in the short imperative style of the prohibitive. The recent attempt to read the verb as an indicative (Reventlow) cannot be sustained either on grammatical or form-critical grounds (cf. Knierim, *op. cit.*, pp. 26f.).

The initial problem turns on the translation of the much debated phrase *'al-pānay*. A wide variety of translations have been suggested in addition to the traditional rendering 'beside me' of the AV: 'in defiance of me', 'to my disadvantage', 'over against me'. However, the issue cannot be solved purely in terms of Hebrew grammar, but involves wider exegetical decisions. The preposition has such a wide use that almost every suggested translation can find some biblical warrant. Even the translation of Rashi, 'so long as I exist', which at first sight appears completely arbitrary, has striking support in such verses as Num. 3.4. The fact that the preposition can often carry a hostile tone (Gen. 16.12) has been noted in several of the renderings. Some commentators continue to stress the literal meaning 'before my face' as providing the original setting which prohibited setting up idols in the presence of Yahweh. The traditional translation 'beside me' can be faulted for carrying the connotation 'except me' which is foreign to the original sense of the text. Perhaps the somewhat neutral rendering 'before me' remains the most useful one in the light of the above difficulties.

Equally important for the interpretation is to note what is not being said. The claim for Yahweh's exclusiveness in the sense that Yahweh alone has existence is not contained in the first commandment. The contrast in idiom between Ex. 20.5 and that of II Isaiah is striking: 'There is no other god besides me' (45.21), 'none except me' ('ayin zûlâtî, 45.21), 'no one else' ('ên 'ôd, 45.6), 'no other gods' ('epes 'elōhîm, 45.14). However, in the first commandment the pro-hibition describes the relation of Yahweh to Israel by categorically eliminating other gods as far as Israel is concerned. The use of the singular (lō' yihyeh lekā) emphasizes the restricted nature of the reference.

The relation of the first commandment to the several parallel commands has been frequently discussed (cf. Knierim, op. cit., pp. 23ff.). The following passages in particular show a similarity: Ex. 22.19; 23.13; 34.14; Deut. 13.2ff.; Ps. 81.10. Von Rad (op. cit., p. 204) regards the formulation in the Decalogue as 'the most general and least detailed of all the versions', and would, therefore, see this verse as a later stage in the development in respect to Ex. 22.19. However one may judge the relationship between the passages – and it is not an obvious one – the close connection between the prohibition of other gods and their worship emerges as an essential element.

Considerable attention has been given to determining the age and provenance of this commandment. For some time it has been recognized that the older way of putting the question, namely in relation to the rise of monotheism, misses the mark. Rather, the issue at stake is whether one can isolate a particular function for this commandment within Israel's earliest traditions. There is a general consensus that Israel's adherence to one God alone is reflected in the earliest level of tradition. Israel did not gradually progress to a belief in one God, but this confession was constitutive to the covenant faith from the outset. Alt's important historical essay on patriarchal religion served to support the theological arguments.

However, the question whether the particular formulation of the first commandment can be traced to this early stage of tradition is not so easily answered. Specifically, how is one to explain the delineation of God's claim on Israel in negative terms against other gods? Two basic options have been offered by way of solution. On the one hand, Eichrodt is representative of a group of scholars who argue that the intolerance of Yahweh respecting other gods is an essential part of the Mosaic religion and can be deduced from the covenant itself. His answer attempts to speak to the substance of the issue, but avoids thereby the form-critical question. On the other hand, Knierim's essay (*op. cit.*) is representative of a group of scholars who argue that the particular formulation must be handled apart from the larger theological question. The formulation must have arisen from a concrete situation within the history of tradition. Knierim himself derives the formulation from the covenant at Shechem and the threat of rival Canaanite deities. His answer is supported by the literary evidence, but it remains a question whether this kind of evidence is adequate for the question which it seeks to answer. In sum, the choice between the two approaches involves a methodological decision which can hardly be reached in relation to only this one issue.

[20.4–6]   *The Second Commandment*: 'You shall not make yourself an image . . .'

K. H. BERNHARDT, *Gott und Bild*, Berlin 1956; W. L. MORAN, 'The Ancient Near Eastern Background of the Love of God in Deuteronomy', *CBQ* 25, 1963, pp. 85–7; H. W. OBBINK, 'Jahwebilder', *ZAW* 46, 1929, pp. 264ff.; G. VON RAD, *Old Testament Theology* I, p. 212ff.; L. ROST, 'Die Schuld der Väter', *Festschrift R. Herrmann*, Berlin 1957, pp. 229ff.; S. SEGERT, 'Bis in das dritte und vierte Glied', *Communio Viatorum* I, 1958, pp. 37–9; W. VISCHER, 'Du sollst dir kein Bildnis machen', *Antwort. Festschrift K. Barth*, Zürich 1956, pp. 764ff.; W. ZIMMERLI, 'Das zweite Gebot', *Gottes Offenbarung*, pp. 234ff.; 'Das Bilderverbot in der Geschichte des alten Israel', *Schalom: Studien . . . A. Jepsen*, Berlin 1971, pp. 86ff.

There are several exceedingly difficult problems involved in these verses which have long puzzled interpreters. It is generally agreed that the prohibition of making a *pesel* refers, first of all, to an image carved from wood or stone, but which later came to include metal figures as well (Isa. 40.19; 44.10). But how does the prohibition of an image relate to the phrase which follows 'and every form which is in heaven' (*wᵉkol-tᵉmûnāh ᵃšer baššāmayim*)? The difference between Exodus and Deuteronomy is not decisive at this point because in both readings the *'aʸšer* clause is attached in a clumsy way to the noun (cf. textual notes). In spite of the syntactical problem the meaning is fairly clear. To the prohibition of an image is attached a further specification which broadens the prohibition to include every representation. The term *tᵉmûnāh* designates the form or outward shape of an object (cf. Num. 12.8; Deut. 4.12, 15, 16, 23, 25; 5.8; Ps. 17.15; Job 4.16). It does not denote a mental concept as some have suggested from the Job parallel.

There is an even more difficult problem. How is one to interpret the plural suffix of v. 5 'them', when its antecedent, 'image', is in the singular? Some have attempted to avoid the problem by defending a *constructio ad sensum* which combined both nouns in v. 4 into a general concept of idols. That this move does not solve the problem has been demonstrated convincingly by Zimmerli (*op. cit.*, pp. 237f.). He points out that the vocabulary 'bow down and serve' is a stereotyped Deuteronomic expression which refers without exception to worshipping 'strange gods', and never has an image as its object. Moreover, Zimmerli, on the basis of this observation, has been able to make the most illuminating suggestion toward a solution yet proposed. He notes that v. 5 not only refers syntactically to the 'other gods' of v. 3, but also carries the major motivation clause for not worshipping strange gods. This interpretation means that in its present redaction the second commandment of v. 4 has been incorporated within the framework of the first commandment. Although from a form-critical point of view the second commandment emerges as an originally independent command, in the later redaction an interpretation has been given which casts it within the shadow of the first.

The ground of the prohibition of serving other gods is offered in a *kî* clause in v. 5. The sentence is a catena of older formulae. First, the self-introductory formula of v. 2 is repeated, but with the addition of the formula 'jealous God' (*'ēl qannā'*). The parallel passages again show this formula to be connected with the worship of false gods (Ex. 34.14; Deut. 6.14f.; Josh. 24.19). In the Old Testament Yahweh's zeal is very closely related to his holiness (Josh. 24.19). He will not tolerate reverence due to him being ascribed to another, but his zeal as his holiness burns like a 'devouring fire'. Moreover, the execution of his zeal is further described in the set terminology of the ban (cf. Rost; Ex. 34.7; Num. 14.18ff.). His judgment does not rest with the perpetrator, but extends four generations to the great-grand-children. However, in contrast to this stern judgment the mercy of God continues for a thousand generations.

In an important essay, Obbink (*op. cit.*) defended the thesis that the images which were being prohibited did not refer to images of Yahweh, but rather to images of foreign gods, whose use was rejected in the Yahweh cult. Obbink's strongest argument was the reference to Yahweh's jealousy. How could Yahweh be jealous before a picture of himself? Was it not more likely to arise before the worship of false gods which is indeed the setting of the formula? However, the reasons against Obbink's thesis appear quite decisive. First, Zimmerli's study has demonstrated the secondary nature of the connection between the second commandment in v. 5 and its justification in v. 5. The fact that the jealousy of God refers to strange gods does not touch on the original meaning of 'image'. Again, von Rad's study of the oldest formulation of the commandment in Deut. 27.15 (*OT Theology* I, pp. 215f.) would confirm the evidence that originally the prohibition concerned Yahweh images. Thirdly, the general picture of pre-monarchial Hebrew religion seems to confirm the judgment that images of Yahweh were forbidden, even though contraventions are recorded. Finally, the need to distinguish between the issues involved in the first and second commandments has not been met by Obbink's artificial distinction between cultic prohibition (II) and the worship of foreign gods in general (I).

The second commandment provides a good example of how the recognition of a historical dimension leading up to the development of the final form of the text can bring the interpretation of the latter into sharper focus. First, the syntactical difficulties in v. 4 can best be explained by seeing a secondary expansion of an original short prohibition with the intent of making the commandment more inclusive. It is certainly possible that the expansion which encompasses the outer limits of the earth's habitation in its interdiction arose in response to a fresh challenge from Canaanite religion. Even more important is the recognition that the Deuteronomic interpretation of the Sinai event – only God's word was perceived, not his form (4.9ff.) – appears to have been a force in shaping the present text. Second, the redactional enclosing of the second commandment within the first points to the earliest level of interpretation, and explains in a most illuminating fashion the reason behind the later ecclesiological diversity in understanding the sequence of the Decalogue. At the same time one must be cautious not to overstate the certainty with which the different levels of tradition can be distinguished (cf. Lohfink's criticism of Reventlow, 'Zur Dekalogfassung', *op. cit.*).

The final and most difficult question to be considered turns on the original theological intent of the second commandment. The initial problem to be recognized is that the reason which lies behind the commandment is never fully explained. The stress lies on the bare prohibitive. When the grounds for the commandment are given, they are in terms of the intense anger which is aroused in God. From this one can deduce that the worship of images is understood as encroaching on a prerogative of God, but precisely how is not stated.

Nevertheless, there are some indications within the rest of the Old Testament which do shed some light on interpreting the commandment. First, it seems clear that the second commandment must originally have served a function distinct from the first commandment which prohibited the worship of other gods. This assumption provides at least a negative control. Secondly, there are numerous parallels to the command scattered through the Pentateuch (cf. Ex. 20.22f.; 34.17; Lev. 19.4; 26.1; Deut. 27.15, etc.). However, the parallels repeat and expand the prohibition without aiding greatly in explaining the fundamental reason lying behind the command. The holiness Code is consistent with the Decalogue in tying the prohibition to the self-introductory formula, 'I am Yahweh your God'. God's right as Yahweh is somehow at stake. Again such passages as the Golden Calf episode (Ex. 32) reiterate the intolerance against images, most probably in an earlier and later level of tradition, without addressing the question of the ground for the command.

Perhaps the most helpful parallel is the Deuteronomic account of Sinai, 4.9ff. Here there is an actual attempt to probe into the reason behind the prohibition. The author argues that because God did not reveal himself in a form, but only in a voice, Israel should beware of making a graven image. Images are prohibited because they are an incorrect response to God's manner of making himself known which was by means of his word. While this passage is extremely important for our question, it should also be recognized that this is not the only interpretation possible and certainly not the earliest. Von Rad called it 'only a substantiation from history and not an explanation' (*OT Theology* I, p. 217). Num. 12.8 stresses that Moses did in fact see the form of God. The stress on the word is particularly characteristic of

Deuteronomy, although it is a stress which the prophets also share (Jer. 23.23ff.).

Another avenue of approach toward understanding the original significance of the commandment has been through the insights of comparative religion. K. H. Bernhardt's *Gott und Bild* in particular provides a detailed survey of the relevant comparative material from the perspective of both primitive religion and Ancient Near Eastern religions. He has made the point very forcibly that even on the most primitive level, the image was not identified with the deity itself. Rather, the image served simply as a vehicle for the divine spirit to function. Nor did its efficacy depend on the exactness of the plastic representation but on the extent to which the deity became present through the image. In the light of this research much of the traditional contrast between crude primitive materialism and spiritual religion seems misplaced.

Within recent years there have been several notable attempts to take seriously these insights from the history of religions while at the same time seeking to discover the earliest significance of the commandment. Both Zimmerli (*op. cit.*) and von Rad (*Theology* I, pp. 212ff.) agree in rejecting the idea that Israel's imageless cult was an expression of a special 'spirituality'. Von Rad argues that the issue at stake in the command was how the deity was pleased to reveal himself. The image failed to deal adequately with the nature of Yahweh 'by whose hidden action in history she was continually held in suspense' (p. 218). Because the freedom of God to relate himself to his world was encroached upon by the image, it was forbidden. Zimmerli (pp. 245f.) likewise relates the command to the issue of God's self-revelation. God has chosen to make himself known, not in a 'static' image, but in the ambiguity of dynamic history. The commandment protects God's entry to the sphere of human life by guarding against an abuse which seeks to exploit his revelation for one's own use.

Although there is considerable force in these modern explanations, certain aspects of the problem do not seem fully convincing. First of all, the issue of how to use the evidence of comparative religion for determining the significance of the image for Israel is extremely complex. Even if one were to assume that the image was regarded by the pagan devotee as only a vehicle, it is uncertain to what extent this view was shared or even understood by Israel. Y. Kaufmann (*The Religion of Israel*, ET Chicago 1960, London 1961) makes an important point in stressing that paganism was consistently misunderstood within Israel. The polemic of the prophets against idols as lifeless non-entities (Isa. 40.18ff.; 44.9ff.; Jer. 10.1ff.; Hab. 2.18ff., etc.) has often been judged to be a late, rationalistic criticism within Israel which developed after paganism had become a threat. However, the handling of images does not seem basically different in the earlier tradition (Ex. 32; Judg. 18; I Sam. 5). At least there is little evidence to show that Israel took the significance of images to be their function as a 'vehicle of the spirit'.

Then again, it remains a question whether the recent emphasis on history as the vehicle of revelation is not misplaced in this instance. Reventlow (op. cit., pp. 32f.) makes a point in criticizing Zimmerli's theory of history in relation to the commandment as being overly subtle. Again, von Rad's interpretation, which focuses on the element of suspense in history as the ultimate ground for the commandment, is far from being obvious. Although I would agree that the issue of how God reveals himself is involved, the full weight of the command does not fall on God's revelation, but rather on Israel's response to God in the light of his revelation. The central issue is the nature of legitimate worship. The reason why images are forbidden in Israel is not because they are a 'vehicle of the spirit'. Nor is there a polarity here between dynamic history and static picture which can be sustained. Rather, the issue turns on Yahweh's testimony to himself set over against man's. The prohibition of images is grounded, in the self-introductory formula, 'I am Yahweh', which summarizes God's own testimony to himself. The contrast to this true witness, the substitution of an image – regardless of whether spiritual or crass – is judged to be a false witness, hence a delusion. The Deuteronomic interpretation is a particular extension of this same argument. God testified to himself in a voice which is fully sufficient (4.2). An image is a rival human witness, and therefore false. Moreover, the prophetic use of the commandment, while employing homiletical freedom suited to a new historical situation, continues basically the same fundamental objection to images which Israel had learned from the beginning.

[20.7] *The Third Commandment*: 'You shall not abuse the name of Yahweh your god . . .'

O. GRETHER, *Name und Wort Gottes im Alten Testament*, BZAW 64, 1934; F. HORST, 'Der Eid im Alten Testament', *Gottes Recht*, Munich 1961, pp. 292ff.; M. A.

KLOPFENSTEIN, *Die Lüge nach dem Alten Testament*, Zürich 1964; S. MOWINCKEL, *Psalmenstudien* I, pp.50ff.; J. PEDERSEN, *Israel I–II*, pp.245ff.; W. E. STAPLES, 'The Third Commandment', *JBL* 58, 1939, pp.325–9.

The third commandment has been usually regarded as straightforward and giving little evidence of the complexity found in the majority of the other commandments. Nevertheless, there remain some difficulties in understanding the original significance of the commandment. The first problem turns on how exactly to translate the verse. Specifically the issue is posed by the translation of the NJPS which follows an ancient rendering found already in the Targum Jonathan and the Peshitta: 'You shall not swear falsely by the name of the LORD your God.' At first sight this translation seems to be an arbitrary departure from the traditional rendering of 'taking the name in vain'.

Nevertheless the reasoning behind the translation is impressive. First, it is argued that to 'lift up the name' is a synonym for taking an oath. In swearing an oath the name of Yahweh is called upon (Lev. 19.12; Deut. 6.13; 10.20; I Sam. 20.42). The formal quality of the idiom reflects the solemnity of swearing which is reinforced by the personal sanction of God himself (v. 7b). Indeed, the closest parallel to the Decalogue actually speaks of swearing: 'you shall not swear by my name falsely' (Ex. 23.1). Moreover, the use of *šāw'* in this verse seems to favor the meaning 'false report'. Again, the term *'ēd šāqer* (false witness) in Ex. 20.16 appears in the Deuteronomic parallel as *'ēd šāw'*. At least at the time of Deuteronomy the two terms, falsely and vainly, seem interchangeable. Finally, the later allusions to the commandment in the Old Testament seem to reflect an interpretation of 'swearing falsely' (cf. Hos. 4.2; Ps. 24.4; Ezek. 13.8, etc.).

Nevertheless, there are some difficulties with the translation of NJPS which, of course, is not an innovation, but reflects an old Jewish exegetical tradition (cf. *Mekilta*, Rashi). Dillmann long ago protested against the identification of *šāw'* with *šāqer*. He argued that the meaning 'to speak falsely' or 'to lie' was contained in the word *šāw'* but not exhausted by it. Indeed the etymology of *šāw'* seems to confirm his point. The root meaning is 'to be empty', 'groundless'. Because something without substance was considered worthless, the term almost always carries perjorative overtones. Still the point seems well taken that a usage closer to the meaning of empty does appear which is not immediately related to false swearing. Isa. 1.13 speaks of worthless offerings (*minḥaṭ šāw'*). Idols are called *hablê šāw'*

(Ps. 31.7), because they are without substance and mere vanity. To flatter a person is to speak *šāw'* (Ps. 12.3). Such words are false because there is no truth or substance to support them. Ezekiel condemns the visions of the false prophets as 'a vision of delusion'. They mislead the people, saying, '"Peace" when there is no peace'. They whitewash the reality; their words will never be fulfilled. The issue at stake is not conscious deception, but prophesying out of their own minds (13.2). It is a 'lie' in Old Testament thought, not because of the intention to deceive, but because objectively it is without any reality, and therefore false.

Incidentally, the strictly adverbial use of *laššāw'* seems confined to the book of Jeremiah (2.30; 4.30; 6.29; 18.15; 46.11). In each case the word precedes the verb and carries the meaning 'to no purpose', or 'vainly' (Jer. 18.15 is the only case with another option possible). However, in Ps. 24.4; 139.20; Ex. 20.7; and Deut. 5.11 *laššāw'* follows the verb and retains its original substantive meaning.

Some years ago Mowinckel (*op. cit.*) objected to deriving *šāw'* from a root meaning such as 'empty' or 'false' and defended the view that the basic meaning was rather 'that which brought evil or disaster' (*das Unheilstiftende, Verderben Bringende*). He then suggested that the original usage referred to evil caused by magical use of the name. One of his strongest arguments was the parallel usage between *'ēn* and *šāw'* which he claimed established his case. However, a closer look at the alleged parallels in Isa. 59.4; Hos. 12.12; Zech. 10.2, etc. are hardly convincing. In Isa. 59.4 the real parallel is with *tōhû* and not *'ēn*. Again in Zech. 10.2 the parallelism with *hbl* points more in the direction of 'worthless' or 'empty'. Although Mowinckel's theory cannot be simply ruled out of court, his evidence is far from conclusive.

To summarize the problem up to this point: On linguistic grounds the actual formulation of the third commandment cannot be identified with swearing falsely, but had a wider semantic range. Nevertheless, at a very early period and throughout the rest of the Old Testament the commandment was interpreted primarily in terms of the narrower connotation of swearing falsely. How is one to explain this situation?

It is clear from a study of the Old Testament that the use of the name of God played an important role in Israel's faith from the beginning (cf. Grether, *op. cit.*). On the one hand, one 'called' on the name (*qr'*, Gen. 4.26), 'prophesied' in the name (*dbr*, Deut. 18.19;

nb', Jer. 11.21), 'blessed' the name (*brk*, Ps. 72.19), 'praised' (*hll*, Ps. 69.31), 'trusted' (Isa. 50.10), 'sought refuge in' (Zeph. 3.12), etc. Yet on the other hand, the misuse of the name remained a continuing threat. It was forbidden to 'profane' his name (*hll*, Lev. 20.3), to 'blaspheme' (*nqb*, Lev. 24.16), to 'curse' (*qll*, II Kings 2.24), to 'defile' (*tm'*, Ezek. 43.8), to 'abuse' (*tpś*, Prov. 30.9), to 'swear falsely' (*śb' lśqr*, Lev. 19.12), etc.

There is also a wide consensus that the use of the name was firmly anchored in the Israelite cult long before Deuteronomy developed a more sophisticated theology around the concept of God's name. The early prohibitions of the misuse of Yahweh's name were an attempt to protect the divine name, which of course was identified with God's being itself, from abuse within and without the cult. The command in Lev. 19.12, 'you shall not swear by my name falsely', seems to reflect most clearly the earliest level of tradition. The prohibition focuses on the one concrete abuse of using the name to support a false oath which had the intent of inflicting evil upon another. Mowinckel's suggestion that a magical usage was involved may also have been involved. At the same time it is also clear that oaths in general were not forbidden, but continued in use.

The wording of the third commandment of the Decalogue lacks the specificity of the early parallels. The use of the idiom 'to lift the name' (cf. Ps. 24.4) is infrequent in the Old Testament. The semantic range of *śāw'*, as we have seen, is also much wider than the term *śeqer*. It would seem therefore that there was an effort made in the formulation of the commandment to broaden its application beyond its original concrete setting. What specific issues were at stake seem difficult to assess accurately. In spite of the attempt to cover a large scope, the later tradition continued to apply the commandment in its narrower function. This seems quite clear from the Deuteronomic interpretation of 5.20. In sum, although the Decalogue formulation allowed for a much wider application of the commandment, it remained for the post-biblical period to exploit the inherent possibilities of the text.

[20.8–11] *The Fourth Commandment*: 'Remember to keep the sabbath holy . . .'

G. J. BOTTERWECK, 'Der Sabbat im Alten Testament', *Theologische Quartalschrift* 134, 1954, pp. 134–47, 448–57; W. W. CANNON, 'The Weekly Sabbath', *ZAW* 49, 1931, pp. 325ff.; H. CAZELLES, *Études sur le Code de l'Alliance*, Paris 1946, pp. 92ff.;

A. R. HULST, 'Bemerkungen zum Sabbatgebot', *Studia Biblica et Semitica . . . Vriezen*, Wageningen 1956, pp. 152ff.; E. JENNI, *Die theologische Begründung des Sabbatgebotes im Alten Testament*, Zürich 1956; S. T. KIMBROUGH, 'The Concept of Sabbath at Qumran', *Revue de Qumran* 5, 1966, pp. 483–502; FELIX MATHYS, 'Überlegungen zur Entwicklung und Bedeutung des Sabbat im Alten Testament', *TZ* 28, 1972, pp. 242–62; T. J. MEEK, 'The Sabbath in the Old Testament', *JBL* 33, 1914, pp. 201–12; J. MEINHOLD, 'Zur Sabbathfrage', *ZAW* 48, 1930, pp. 121–38; J. MORGENSTERN, 'Sabbath', *IDB* IV, pp. 135–41; R. NORTH, 'The Derivation of Sabbath', *Biblica* 36, 1955, pp. 182–201; W. RORDORF, *Sunday*, ET London and Philadelphia 1968, with full bibliography; G. SCHRENK, 'Sabbat oder Sonntag?', *Judaica* 2, 1946, pp. 169–89; R. DE VAUX, *Ancient Israel*, 1961, pp. 475ff.; E. VOGT, 'Hat Šabbat im Alten Testament den Sinn von Woche?', *Biblica* 40, 1959, pp. 1008–11.

In the history of the critical study of the Decalogue over the last hundred years certainly more attention has been devoted to this commandment than most of the others. The reasons for this concentration of interest are evident. The commandment is the longest in the Decalogue, showing many signs of growth and expansion. Moreover the parallel passage in Deuteronomy is strikingly different in its formulation. The commandment seemed to many to provide an important link in the development of a major Old Testament institution. Finally, possibilities of extra-biblical parallels from the Ancient Near East appeared to offer a solution respecting the actual historical origins of the commandment.

It is not my present intention to unroll all the problems involved in the larger subject of the sabbath, but to focus on the commandment within the Decalogue. However, a brief summary of some of the traditional questions related to the sabbath is in order in terms of background.

1. The etymology of the term sabbath remains unsettled (cf. Cazelles and Botterweck). Most probably in Hebrew the noun *šabbāṭ* is derived from a verbal form meaning 'to rest, cease from work', rather than the alternative suggestion of seeing the nominal form as primary. The relation of Hebrew *šabbāṭ* to the Akkadian *šabattu/šapattu*, although much discussed, has not issued in any certainty. It is possible that a common West Semitic root lay behind both words, but a satisfactory explanation has not been forthcoming.

2. Several classic theories have been proposed respecting the origin of the sabbath, but no consensus has emerged. The attempt to derive the sabbath from the Babylonian *šapattu* (Meinhold *et al.*), which in the earlier texts designated a festival of the full moon, has

never satisfactorily explained the sabbath's independence from the lunar calendar. Again, the theory which connects the sabbath with a taboo day adapted from the Kenites (Eerdmans, Köhler, Rowley) rests on the scantiest possible evidence, and fails to explain the totally different function of the Hebrew sabbath. By and large, these hypotheses of origin have raised more problems than they have solved.

3. The problem of dating the beginning of the sabbath as an institution within Israel hangs together with the larger question of how one understands the development of Israel's religion, and how one handles the Old Testament sources. Over against the classic position of Wellhausen, there is general agreement that the sabbath has very early roots in the tradition, but that it did undergo considerable transformation throughout its history. Scholars are not agreed on how to evaluate the Deuteronomic and Priestly redaction of the commandment on the question of dating.

We turn now to a closer study of the commandment itself. The form of the commandment reflects a developed prose style. Verse 8 introduces the positive command by means of an infinitive absolute which functions as a strong imperative. Verses 9–10 describe the manner of hallowing the sabbath, first in terms of permitted work prior to the day, then in terms of a prohibition of work. The agents involved are enumerated in detail. Verse 11a provides the motivation clause (*kî*) for the command in terms of Yahweh's six days of work and his resting on the seventh. Verse 11b is an independent sentence, joined by a connective result particle, which draws the implications of Yahweh's action: 'he blessed and hallowed it.'

The elaborate structure of the commandment has spurred interpreters to seek an earlier original form of the law. Indeed, the parallel passages provide numerous examples of a much shorter form (cf. Ex. 23.12; 31.13ff.; 34.21). Two elements emerge as constants from the shorter formulations. There is the positive command: 'Six days you shall work but on the seventh you shall rest' (Ex. 23.12; 31.15; 34.21; Lev. 23.3). Then there is the negative command: 'You shall not work on the sabbath' (Ex. 20.7; Lev. 23.7; cf. Jer. 17.22). The issue at stake is to determine how to relate the two formulae, and thus to reconstruct if possible an earlier level of the sabbath tradition.

Reventlow (*op. cit.*) has argued in a very imaginative way against seeing either of these expressions as forming an original apodictic command. He feels that the first positive command: 'Six days you shall work', stems from priestly Torah and that the sabbath command was a specification of a particular festival within the liturgical calendar. Indeed, the parallels in the priestly Torah to this stereotyped positive formula are striking. However, it seems to me that Reventlow has overshot the mark in denying any element of an original prohibition. Schulz (*op. cit.*) is here closer to the truth in showing that the sanction of the death penalty for sabbath violation in Ex. 31.14, 15 clearly presupposes an original prohibition, which would approximate to the second stereotype: 'You shall not work on the sabbath.'

Actually there seems little point in debating whether the negative or positive command had priority. The evidence for either one is not likely to be conclusive. These are really two sides of the same coin. Far more important is the fact that both formulations testify to an early Israelite tradition which gave the sabbath a special sanction. Moreover, the earliest tradition did not carry a particular motivation with it. Rather, the command to observe, or not to desecrate, the sabbath was the bare datum of the tradition. To this basic command a variety of different reasons were added, but no one ever became fully normative, as the continual fluidity demonstrates. It is of great interest, therefore, to examine closely the different theological interpretations which were developed about the sabbatical command in seeing how the sabbath functioned in Israel.

The commandment in vv. 8–11 gives every indication of having been formed from composite elements. It combines both the positive and negative formulations. Its initial phrase is strongly homiletical in flavor. Moreover, the terminology of v. 11 is clearly dependent on the Priestly creation tradition of Gen. 1. Nevertheless, the present shape of the commandment is a carefully constructed unit which reveals a clear structure. To assume from the fact of a historical dimension that the final form is a patchwork of incoherent bits and pieces is basically to misunderstand the text (cf. Lohfink, *op. cit.*, pp. 22f.).

The command begins with an exhortation to 'hallow' the sabbath; it concludes by providing the reason for its hallowing. In between the introduction and conclusion a parallel is drawn between what Israel is obliged to do and what God has already done in his creation. Six days you shall work and on the seventh day you shall not work 'because' for six days God worked and he rested on the seventh. Several implications can be drawn from this structure. First, the major thrust of the command falls on the verb 'to hallow'. The piel form is a factitive use having the connotation 'to make holy'. The command to hallow is not identified simply with not working or resting, but over and above both of these is the positive action of making holy. It presupposes the cessation of the normal activity of work in order to set aside the sabbath for something special. The nature of the special quality is not spelled out, but briefly characterized in the phrase: 'the sabbath belongs to Yahweh your God'. Again, the sabbath command is tied to the act of creation. Indeed v. 11 provides an etiology for the sanctification of the sabbath, which was rooted in the creation tradition. The etiology grounds the sanctity of the sabbath in the creative act of God; it is built into the very structure of the universe. The sabbath commandment is not given to Israel for the first time at Sinai (cf. Ex. 16.22ff.), but at Sinai Israel is only exhorted to remember what had been an obligation from the beginning.

A comparison of Ex. 20.8ff. with Gen. 2.1ff. reveals quite clearly that the Exodus formulation is dependent on a common tradition with that of Gen. 2. In the Genesis account the entire creation story of ch. 1 focuses on the sanctification of the seventh day, the last part of which only has been used in Exodus. However, it is equally important to recognize that the sabbath command was not a creation of the Priestly writer. Rather, the influence was from the reverse direction. The present shaping of Gen. 1 on the pattern of seven days presupposes the prior tradition of the sabbath. The Priestly writer's contribution lay in working out a profound theology of the sabbath which grounded the day in the act of creation itself.

The fact that the Priestly theology was capable of quite a different emphasis respecting the sabbath can be seen by comparing Ex. 31.12ff. In this passage the emphasis falls on the sabbath as a sign of the covenant. Israel is commanded three times to observe the sabbath. The sanction of the death penalty for violators is made specific. Again, the terminology of sanctification occurs, but this time in reference to God's sanctifying Israel, the sign of which is preserved in the sabbath. The sabbath as the 'ôṯ (sign) is a reminder both to God and Israel of the eternal covenantal relationship which was the ultimate purpose of creation.

A strikingly different grounding for the sabbath commandment is given in the Deuteronomic parallel to the Decalogue (5.12ff.). Moreover, the difference does not lie only in substituting the Exodus tradition for that of creation. Rather, the whole structure of the commandment has been shifted in focus. To the introduction:

'Observe the sabbath to keep it holy,' has been added the somewhat clumsy clause, 'as Yahweh your God commanded you' (*siww^ekā*). Similarly the conclusion repeats the same word: 'therefore Yahweh commanded you to keep the sabbath'. The basic reason for observing the sabbath is that it has been commanded. But within the framework the Deuteronomic writer has incorporated a specific motivation. No work is to be done on the sabbath 'in order that your servant . . . may rest as well as you'. Commentators have frequently interpreted this motivation as reflecting a characteristic humanitarian concern of Deuteronomy. Still one should recognize that he is following a very old tradition in tying the sabbath to a social function (cf. Ex. 23.12).

The chief motivation clause, however, comes in v. 15: 'You shall remember that you were a slave in Egypt, and Yahweh brought you out . . .' How does Israel's memory of her redemption from slavery relate to the sabbath command? The syntax of the sentence makes it clear that Israel's memory does not act as the motivation for allowing slaves to participate in the observance of the sabbath. In such a case one would have expected the sentence to read: Remember that you were a slave and keep the sabbath. But this frequent interpretation does not adequately explain the subsequent clause: 'therefore he commanded you' of v. 15b. Memory does not serve to arouse a psychological reaction of sympathy for slaves, rather quite a different theology of memory is at work. Israel is commanded to observe the sabbath in order to remember its slavery and deliverance. This connection is even more explicit in Ex. 16.3. The festival arouses and excites the memory (cf. Jenni, *op. cit.*, p. 17). The Deuteronomist's concern is not primarily humanitarian, but theological. He is basically concerned that 'all Israel' participate in the sabbath. This is only a reality when the slaves also share in its observance. Israel's memory functions to assure the proper celebration of the sabbath by remembering the nature of the sabbath in Egypt at the time of the Exodus (cf. Childs, *Memory and Tradition*, pp. 52ff.).

[20.12] *The Fifth Commandment*: 'Honor your father and your mother . . .'

J. GAMBERONI, 'Das Elterngebot im Alten Testament', *BZ*, NS 8, 1964, pp. 161–90; H. KREMERS, 'Die Stellung des Elterngebotes im Dekalog', *EvTh* 21, 1961, pp. 145–61.

The fifth commandment is often thought to be a bridge connecting the obligations toward God in the first four commandments (*fas*) with those toward one's fellows (*jus*) in the last five. The major support for the suggestion arises from the fact that although the commandment concerns primarily one's fellow human beings, nevertheless the commandment contains reference to 'thy God', a phrase which otherwise only occurs in the verses concerning obligation to God (vv. 2, 5, 7, 10). If this theory has any substance, it is only in respect to the final form of the Decalogue. However, the reference to God appears in the commandments in which there has been a homiletical expansion and is missing, not only in the last command, but also in the first.

The commandment, like the sabbath, has a positive formulation and is followed with a promise rather than a theological reason (cf. Eph. 6.2). The closest parallels in the Pentateuch are found in Ex. 21.15, 17; Lev. 20.9; and Deut. 21.18ff. Because of the predominance of the negative style in these parallels, Alt and others have argued also for a negative command as the original form within the Decalogue. The most frequent suggestion is the formulation: 'You shall not curse your father and your mother' (Rabast, *Das apodiktische Recht*, p. 38). Against this theory Gerstenberger (*op. cit.*, pp. 43ff.) has made a strong case for the originality of the positive command as well. Indeed, his theory that the commandment arose from the general area of clan instruction receives its strongest support from this example. The large number of references to the honoring of parents within wisdom literature would certainly point to this area of Israel's life as being equally influential in the formulation of this commandment (Prov. 1.8; 15.5; 19.26, etc.). It seems most probable that the problem of the right of the parent was a concern which emerged out of a variety of different situations and was controlled through several means (court, cult, household). Lying at the heart of the original prohibition was a command which protected parents from being driven out of the home or abused after they could no longer work (cf. Ex. 21.15; 21.17; Lev. 20.9; Deut. 27.16).

The present positive formulation to 'honor thy father and mother' clearly reflects an intention to expand the area covered by the commandments as widely as possible. The choice of the term 'honor' carries with it a range of connotations far broader than some such term as 'obey'. To honor is to 'prize highly' (Prov. 4.8), 'to show respect', to 'glorify and exalt'. Moreover, it has nuances of caring for and showing affection (Ps. 91.15). It is a term frequently used to describe the proper response to God and is akin to worship (Ps. 86.9).

Moreover, the parallel command in Lev. 19.3 actually uses the term 'fear, give reverence to' (*tîrā'û*) which is otherwise reserved for God. Frequently in the past this commandment has been interpreted to mean that parents are the visible representatives of God for the exerting of his authority. While this interpretation has tended to go far beyond the biblical text, nevertheless, it can lay claim to a certain biblical warrant. The promise attached to the commandment speaks of an extended life in the land promised by God. The idiom, 'that your days may be long . . .', which is found chiefly in Deuteronomy, not only envisages a chronological extension of time, but points to the rich blessing of the society which is in harmony with the divine order. To this extent the command does touch on the relation of authority and order between God and his representative within the life established by the command.

[20.13] *The Sixth Commandment*: 'You shall not kill.'

D. FLUSSER, '"Do not commit adultery", "Do not Murder"', *Textus* 4, 1964, pp. 220–4; A. JEPSEN, 'Du sollst nicht töten! Was ist das?', *Evang. Luth. Kirchenzeitung* 13, 1959, pp. 384f.; H. SCHULZ, *Das Todesrecht im Alten Testament*, Berlin 1969, pp. 9–15; J. J. STAMM, 'Sprachliche Erwägungen zum Gebot "Du sollst nicht töten"', *TZ* 1, 1945, pp. 81–90.

The sixth commandment begins the series of the shortest formulations within the Decalogue. Parallels to the commandment against the taking of life are found elsewhere in the Pentateuch in a longer form (cf. Ex. 21.12; Lev. 24.17; Deut. 27.24). Particularly in Lev. 19.17ff. the scope of the command has been internalized to cover also hating one's brother in one's heart. Lying behind the prohibition to kill is the very ancient sanctity of life, which was understood as contained in the blood: 'Whoever sheds the blood of man, by man shall his blood be shed' (Gen. 9.6). The particular difficulty of the sixth commandment lies in understanding precisely the meaning of the verb 'to kill' (*rṣḥ*). It has long been recognized that a special type of killing is intended. The verb appears rather infrequently in the Old Testament (46 times) in comparison to the other common verbs employed (165 for *hrg*; 201 for *hmyt* – cited from Stamm-Andrew, *op. cit.*, p. 98). The verb has often been translated, 'thou shalt not murder' (so NJPS), which avoids the difficulty entailed in reconciling the broad prohibition of killing with the frequent taking of life in war and capital punishment throughout the Old Testament. However, it was soon recognized that the basic distinction between murder and killing, namely the factor of intentionality, cannot be sustained for the verb *rṣḥ*. Although *rāṣaḥ* often does refer to actual murder, it is also used to describe one who kills another unintentionally (Deut.4.41f.; Josh.20.3, etc.). Köhler, in his summary of critical research on the Decalogue in 1929, felt that a precise understanding of the term was no longer possible and contented himself with a conjecture that it probably originally forbade taking the law into one's own hands (*op. cit.*, p.182).

The first genuine illumination of the commandment in recent times was offered in an article of J. J. Stamm in 1945 (cf. bibliography). Stamm argued in a detailed word study that 'what *rāṣaḥ* means in contrast to *hārag* and *hēmît* is illegal killing inimical to the community; ... the life of the Israelite was protected in this way from illegal impermissible violence.' When Alt then accepted Stamm's interpretation as further evidence of the original covenant setting for the Decalogue, the issue seemed settled in the eyes of many.

However, in recent years Stamm's interpretation has been subjected to some criticism which at least has had the effect of eroding somewhat his precise definition of *rāṣaḥ*. The study of Reventlow (*op. cit.*, pp.71ff.) in particular has taken the lead in suggesting a modification of Stamm's thesis. Reventlow observed that the large majority of the occurrences of the verb relate clearly to the area of blood vengeance and the role of the avenger (*gōʾēl*; Num.35; Deut. 4.41ff.; Josh.20). Both the initial slaying and the retaliation are covered by the same verb. Moreover in such an instance as Num. 35.30 the verb *rāṣaḥ* is used for the execution of a murderer who has been tried by a court which would appear to contradict Stamm's distinction of illegal and legal killing (Stamm did recognize this exception). Reventlow, therefore, suggested understanding the verb as originally denoting killing which fell in the area of blood vengeance. This suggestion, which actually does not upset Stamm's thesis, but rather modifies it, has much to commend it. However, it is also clear that this original meaning was later altered and does not apply to many of the later instances of the use of the verb.

Moreover, it is precisely this later broadening of the term which is decisive for interpreting the sixth commandment. Perhaps the clearest indication of a shift in the meaning of the verb can be detected in Num.35. There are two clearly distinguishable meanings of *rāṣaḥ* which correspond to two different levels of tradition. In vv.16, 17,

18, 21 there is an old *môṭ yûmaṭ* series describing the various acts which constituted *rāṣaḥ* by means of the declarative formula: 'He is a *rōṣēaḥ*' (murderer). In this usage the verb has an objective sense of blood-shedding devoid of the question of motivation and delineates acts of violence which call forth the vengeance of the *gō'ēl* (avenger). Although all such acts are included under the category of *rāṣaḥ* regardless of motivation, nevertheless an exception is made in respect to the punishment. Cities of refuge are set aside for the *rōṣēaḥ* who has committed a killing unintentionally, but he is still called a *rōṣēaḥ* (v. 16ff.).

However, there is another level – undoubtedly later – within the same chapter which has shifted the meaning of the verb. In v. 20 a new definition of *rāṣaḥ* is offered, which has been interjected between the third and fourth elements of the *môṭ yûmaṭ* series. This time a *rōṣēaḥ* is one who kills out of enmity, deceit, or hatred. The term has now become equated with murder. The motivation behind the act has become the decisive factor. These two levels of meaning are further included in the description of the punishment. In v. 25 the older meaning is preserved. The slayer is called a *rōṣēaḥ* even though he slew unintentionally and thereby escapes the judgment of the blood avenger. However, in v. 24 he is termed simply the 'one who struck' until the intention behind the act was determined by a court.

In the later period, especially seen in the prophetic and wisdom literature, the term invariably carries the connotation of intentional and evil violence (Isa. 1.21; Hos. 6.9; Job 24.14; Prov. 22.13; Ps. 94.6). In the two instances in which a series of transgressions are mentioned which closely parallel the Decalogue (Hos. 4.2; Jer. 7.9), the verb *rāṣaḥ* has doubtlessly this same meaning.

In summary, the verb *rāṣaḥ* at first had an objective meaning and described a type of slaying which called forth blood vengeance. In order to protect innocent blood, an escape was provided in cities of refuge for the unintentional slayer, but this exception did not alter the objective context of the verb itself. However, at a somewhat later period – at least before the eighth century – a change in meaning can be observed. The verb came to designate those acts of violence against a person which arose from personal feelings of hatred and malice. The command in its present form forbids such an act of violence and rejects the right of a person to take the law into his own hands out of a feeling of personal injury.

[20.14] *The Seventh Commandment*: 'You shall not commit adultery'.

W. KORNFELD, 'L'adultère dans l'Orient Antique', *RB* 57, 1950, pp. 92–109; W. L. MORAN, 'The Scandal of the "great sin" at Ugarit', *JNES* 18, 1959, pp. 280–1; A. PHILLIPS, *Ancient Israel's Criminal Law*, pp. 110–29; J. J. RABINOWITZ, 'The "Great Sin" in Ancient Egyptian Marriage Contracts', *JNES* 18, 1959, p. 73; H. SCHULZ, *Das Todesrecht im Alten Testament*, pp. 15–36.

There are no major linguistic problems involved in this commandment. The verb *nā'ap* means to commit adultery, i.e. *Ehe brechen*, and the prohibitive is directed toward maintaining the sanctity of the marriage. The verb can have the man or the woman as subject. The verb is distinguished from others which are related in meaning such as 'sleep with' (*škb*), and to 'commit harlotry' (*znh*).

It has often been observed that according to the Hebrew idiom 'the man can only commit adultery against a marriage other than his own, the woman only against her own' (Stamm-Andrew, p. 100). Moreover, the punishment for adultery is death (Deut. 22.22), while seduction or violation of a virgin requires the man either to marry the girl or offer a money equivalent (Ex. 22.15; Deut. 22.28f.). It is clear from this evidence that throughout the Old Testament adultery was placed in a different category from fornication. The command relates specifically to the former. B. Stade once argued that intercourse of the man outside the marriage with an unmarried and unbetrothed women gave no offence within Israel (Gen. 38; Judg. 21.16), and the seduction of an unbetrothed daughter was simply an offence against property (cited from Stamm-Andrew, p. 100). Against this thesis Reventlow (*op. cit.*, p. 78) has mounted a good case to show that this latter instance was judged as a moral offense ('shameful'), and not just as a property violation.

Perhaps the best commentary on the seriousness with which Israel viewed adultery is reflected in the several narratives which relate to the subject. Abimelech reacts in horror at his near escape and accuses Abraham of bringing on him and his kingdom 'a great sin' (Gen. 20.9). Joseph rebuffs Potiphar's wife lest he 'do this great wickedness and sin against God' (Gen. 39.9). Even the king, David, falls under the death sentence for his adultery with Bathsheba. In the other portions of the Old Testament adulterers are commonly linked with murderers (Job 24.14f.) and treacherous men (Jer. 9.2) who misuse God's name (Jer. 29.23) and oppress the widow (Mal. 3.5). The instruction of the sages goes to great length to caution the simple youth against the wiles of the 'strange woman' whose path leads to

Sheol and death (Prov. 5.1ff.). (Cf. Phillips, *op. cit.*, for a good treatment of the broader legal problems of adultery in the Old Testament.)

[20.15] *The Eighth Commandment*: 'You shall not steal'.

A. ALT, 'Das Verbot des Diebstahls im Dekalog', *KS* I, 1953, pp. 333–40; M. H. GOTTSTEIN, 'Du sollst nicht stehlen', *TZ* 9, 1953, pp. 394–5; F. HORST, 'Der Diebstahl im Alten Testament', *Festschrift Paul Kahle*, Leiden 1935, reprinted *Ges. Stud.*, Munich 1961, pp. 167–75; H. SCHULZ, *Das Todesrecht im Alten Testament*, pp. 36–40.

The prohibition of stealing is the third in the series of commandments which consist of two words, and lacks an explicit object. The verb 'to steal' (*gnb*) can have as its object either a person or an object. The particular nuance of this word which distinguishes it from other types of misappropriation such as *lqh* or *gzl* is the element of secrecy. The act of taking by stealth is used in both a good and a bad sense within the Old Testament (II Kings 11.2; Hos. 4.2).

There are several problems which arise in an attempt to understand the original meaning of this commandment. First, how does this prohibition relate to the tenth commandment, a prohibition which seems to overlap? What was the original form and did it ever have a concrete object? How does the command relate to the preceding two which share the same short formulation?

Again it was A. Alt who broke new ground with his article in 1949 (*op. cit.*). Alt argued that the eighth commandment had originally contained a concrete object and that it was directed specifically against kidnapping, that is, the stealing of persons. He supported this thesis particularly with reference to Ex. 21.16 and Deut. 24.7, both of which refer to stealing a man who is a citizen of the community. Further support came from the larger context. In both the preceding two commands the prohibitive functions to protect in a specific way a basic right of the covenant community. Although stealing in general was punished in Israel, it was often done by means of a fine or the like (21.37ff.). Alt's interpretation moves the eighth commandment into a situation which parallels in seriousness the preceding commandments. All are deemed worthy of the death penalty.

Although Alt's thesis is illuminating for the prehistory of the text, it is very clear that the present form of the commandment reflects a different emphasis and has gone through an alteration in its meaning. Alt felt that the change could be closely tied to a development in interpreting the tenth commandment. However, the historical development of the tenth commandment is not fully clear either (cf. below). The sharp distinction suggested by Alt between stealing a man and stealing his property cannot be easily sustained. Perhaps it is wiser at this point not to rest too much on a projected development. It does seem clear that the shortened form of the eighth commandment without an explicit object had the effect of expanding the scope of the prohibition beyond its initial concrete object. It is possible, but by no means obvious, that this development was aided by an interpretation of the tenth commandment which laid increasing stress on the impulses behind the act of misappropriation of another's possessions.

[20.16] *The Ninth Commandment*: 'You shall not testify against your neighbor as a lying witness.'

M. E. ANDREW, 'Falsehood and Truth: Ex. 20:16', *Interpretation* 17, 1963, pp. 425–38; J. FICHTNER, 'Der Begriff des "Nächsten" im Alten Testament', *Wort und Dienst* 4, 1955, pp. 23ff.; M. A. KLOPFENSTEIN, *Die Lüge nach dem Alten Testament*, Zürich 1964; L. KÖHLER, 'Justice in the Gate', printed as an Appendix to *Hebrew Man*, London 1958; A. PHILLIPS, *Ancient Israel's Criminal Law*, pp. 142ff.; H. J. STOEBE, 'Das achte Gebot (Ex. 20, v. 16)', *Wort und Dienst* 3, 1952, pp. 108ff.

The ninth commandment contains several technical legal terms which point quite clearly to its original significance. The term '*ēd šāqer* (lying witness), which in the Deuteronomic formulation appears as '*ēd šāw*', arises out of the concrete legal procedure of Israel, a procedure which was common in the whole Ancient Near East. A man testifies against another in a court of elders (cf. Köhler, *op. cit.*). He can be a true witness (Prov. 14.25) or a lying witness (Deut. 19.18; Prov. 6.19). The verb '*nh* (answer) likewise reflects a legal background and points to the reciprocal response of the parties in a trial. Again, the term 'neighbor' (*rēa*') refers to the full citizen within the covenant community. The commandment is directed primarily toward guarding the basic right of the covenant member against the threat of false accusation. The original commandment is, therefore, not a general prohibition of lying, but forbids lying which directly affects one's fellow.

The importance of maintaining a true witness runs throughout the Old Testament. The law attempted to guard against the abuse of false witnessing by stipulating that 'no person shall be put to death on the testimony of one witness' (Num. 35.30; Deut. 19.15). Nevertheless, the story of Naboth's vineyard (I Kings 21) is a terrifying example of the results of false testimony. The frequent complaint of the Psalmist (27.12, etc.) against the accusation of deceitful witnesses would confirm how widespread the abuse could become. Deut. 19.19 specifies that if a witness is proven false, 'you shall do to him as he had intended to do to his brother'. Likewise, the Code of Hammurabi specifies that in capital cases the false witness shall be put to death.

The ninth commandment stands in close relation to both the third and the eighth commandments of the Decalogue. In Ex. 22.10 a man takes an oath in the name of Yahweh that he has not stolen. In Lev. 19.11 the prohibition of swearing falsely is closely tied to not stealing, dealing falsely, and lying to one another. The Deut. formulation of the third commandment makes explicit the connection between lying and swearing. The prophetic passages which most clearly reflect the Decalogue, namely Hos. 4.2 and Jer. 7.9, show how the inner connection between the commands were heard (but cf. Phillips' objections, *op. cit.*). The reference in Hos. 4.2 to *khš* (lying) would indicate that a broadening of the original ninth commandment had taken place which went beyond the false testimony in court. But already such passages as Lev. 19.16 would show an early concern within Israel to protect the reputation of one's fellow against any abuse, such as idle rumours, which would cause him injury.

[20.17] *The Tenth Commandment*: 'You shall not covet your neighbor's house . . .'

J. R. COATES, 'Thou shalt not covet', *ZAW* 52, 1934, pp. 238–9; C. H. GORDON, 'A Note on the Tenth Commandment', *JBR* 31, 1963, pp. 208–9; J. HERRMANN, 'Das zehnte Gebot', *Sellin-Festschrift*, Leipzig 1927, pp. 69–82; W. L. MORAN, 'The Conclusion of the Decalogue (Ex. 20, 17 = Dt. 5, 21)', *CBQ* 29, 1967, pp. 543ff.

The form of the tenth commandment has certain features which distinguish it from all the preceding commandments. The verb in the initial prohibitive is repeated in an independent clause, but with a different object. This is the factor which led the Roman Catholic and Lutheran traditions to see v. 17b as an independent command. Again, the verb appears to denote a subjective emotion whereas all the preceding prohibitions were directed against an objective action.

In 1927 J. Herrmann (*op. cit.*) presented the thesis that the verb *ḥmd* (covet) does not denote simply an emotion, but in addition included the action which stems from the emotion. To the impulse of the will is added the necessity of a corresponding action. His strongest evidence seemed to be from such passages as Ex. 34.24 and Ps. 68.17 in which the emotion of desiring included the act of taking possession. Herrmann's thesis received additional confirmation when it was accepted and further buttressed by Alt in 1949. Alt introduced a reading from the Karatepe inscriptions in which the verb *ḥāmad* expressed once again an emotion and a corresponding action. Herrmann's thesis was widely accepted in Old Testament circles, particularly by Köhler and Stamm, and was only occasionally resisted (Procksch, Volz).

Within recent years this thesis has received a major attack from William Moran (*op. cit.*). Moran's chief argument was as follows: 'The mere fact that a verb like *ḥāmad* occasionally clearly implies some act of seizure or the like, is not to be understood in the sense that such an act belongs to its proper denotation' (p. 548). Moran supported this point in reference to *ḥāmad* by three lines of argument. First, he argued that there are cases in which the verb is not followed by a corresponding action (cf. Prov. 6.25). Secondly, he tried to demonstrate that the verb *hiṯ'awweh* (desire), which is the parallel used in Deuteronomy (5.21), carries also the meaning of an emotion plus an action, which would destroy the suggested contrast between the two verbs. Thirdly, he argued that almost all verbs of desiring in Semitic are related to subsequent action, but without influencing the denotation proper of the verb itself.

Moran's arguments are of different weight, in my judgment. The first point is well taken, although a possible interpretation of Prov. 6.25 had already been made by Herrmann. The second point is less convincing. Moran's prize example, Prov. 23.6, when seen in its larger context, does not stand up to scrutiny. The verse contrasts the emotion of craving with the bad end to which it leads. Indeed, when one examines all the instances of *hiṯ'awweh*, the overwhelming emphasis of the verb falls on the emotion of craving, frequently related to the *nepeš*, which is usually distinguished sharply from any subsequent action. 'The sluggard craves, yet gets nothing' (Prov. 13.4). Again, David craved for water which he could not obtain (II Sam. 23.15). The Israelites in the desert longed for the rich food of Egypt (Num. 11.4, 34). Although there is an area of common denotation in both verbs, nevertheless, the stress on the emotion of the soul is certainly peculiar to *hiṯ'awweh* in distinction from *ḥāmad*. Finally, the impact of Moran's third point should not be exaggerated. Indeed, there are many other verbs of emotion which also are linked with subsequent action, but this does not mean that all such verbs are thus linked. There does seem to be a characteristic difference which belongs to its denotation between *ḥāmad* and *hiṯ'awweh* specifically in this regard. Moreover, Herrmann did not fall into the common error of confusing semantic range with Hebrew mentality, as was the case with Pedersen and Boman (cf. Childs, *Memory and Tradition*, pp. 20f.). Oddly enough, one of the strongest arguments against Herrmann's thesis was not used by Moran. It has to do with the fact that in closely paralleled passages relating to the Zion tradition (Pss. 68.19; 132.13f.), *ḥāmad* and *hiṯ'awweh* are used interchangeably without any significant difference in meaning.

What conclusions does one draw from this evidence? Certainly Moran has succeeded in eroding the sharp distinction suggested by Herrmann. However, in my judgment, there does remain a significant distinction between the semantic range of *ḥāmad* and *hiṯ'awweh* in spite of an area of common denotation. The emphasis of *ḥāmad* falls on an emotion which often leads to a commensurate action, whereas the focus of *hiṯ'awweh* rests much more on the emotion itself.

If we now turn to the question of the tenth commandment, this conclusion would mean that Herrmann was not justified in playing down the emotional denotation of the verb *ḥāmad*, even though it probably carried in addition the element of subsequent action. The original command was directed to that desire which included, of course, those intrigues which led to acquiring the coveted object. The Deuteronomic substitution of the verb *hiṯ'awweh* did not mark a qualitative difference of approach which had the effect of internalizing a previously action oriented commandment. Here a false interpretation of Israel's religious development is also at work. Rather, the Deuteronomic recension simply made more explicit the subjective side of the prohibition which was already contained in the original command. Moran has provided a good check against basing an interpretation of a commandment too much upon a reconstructed historical transformation, the different stages of which have been exaggerated.

Moreover, one of the most important contributions of Moran's article is his evidence that the second part of the tenth commandment reflects a traditional type of list, common to the Ancient Near East. There is every possibility that the list of Deut. 5.12 is equally as old as that of Ex. 20.17, and one can conclude nothing about a changing status of women from the different sequence. The function of the list is to be all-inclusive and to rule out any ambiguity as to the extent of a man's property.

4. *The Decalogue and the New Testament*

B. W. BACON, 'Jesus and the Law', *JBL* 47, 1928, pp.203–31; G. BARTH, 'Matthew's Understanding of the Law', in *Tradition and Interpretation in Matthew*, ed. G. Bornkamm, ET London and Philadelphia 1963; KLAUS BERGER, *Die Gesetzesauslegung Jesu*, WMANT 40, 1972, pp.258ff.; G. BORNKAMM, 'Das Doppelgebot der Liebe', *Neutestamentliche Studien für R. Bultmann*, BZNW 21, 1954; G. BORNKAMM, *Jesus of Nazareth*, ET New York and London 1960, pp.96ff.; B. H. BRANSCOMB, *Jesus and the Law of Moses*, New York 1930; C. E. CARLSTON, 'The Things that Defile (Mark vii. 14) and the Law in Matthew and Mark', *NTS* 15, 1968, pp.75ff., with full bibliography; W. D. DAVIES, 'Matthew 5:17–18', *Mélanges bibliques rédiges en l'honneur de A. Robert*, Paris 1957, pp.428–56; P. DELHAYE, *Le Décalogue et sa place dans la morale chrétienne*[2], Bruxelles 1963; R. M. GRANT, 'The Decalogue in Early Christianity', *HTR* 40, 1947, pp.1ff.; H. GROTIUS, 'Explicatio Decalogi ut Graece exstat, et quomodo ad Decalogi locos Evangelica praecepta referantur', Appendix in *Annotationes in Libros Evangeliorum*, Amsterdam 1641; W. GUTBROD, 'νόμος', *TWNT* IV, pp.1016ff. = *TDNT* IV, pp.1022ff.; R. HUMMEL, *Die Auseinandersetzung zwischen Kirche und Judentum im Matthäusevangelium*[2], Munich 1966; H. LJUNGMAN, *Das Gesetz erfüllen: Matt. 5, 17ff. und 3, 15 untersucht*, Lund 1954; C. F. D. MOULE, 'Fulfilment-Words in the New Testament', *NTS* 14, 1968, pp.293ff.

There are several difficulties which one encounters immediately when attempting to deal briefly with the subject of the Decalogue and the New Testament. First of all, the problem of the use of the Decalogue is not clearly distinguished in the New Testament from the larger issue of Old Testament law in general. Again, there is much variety in the New Testament's approach which tends to be lost when one moves away from detailed exegesis of specific passages to a summary. Quite obviously Paul's approach to the Decalogue differed from that of James, as did the historical situations which called forth the different New Testament witnesses. But in particular, recent New Testament research has concentrated on pointing out the redactional differences in the gospels and have brought into sharpest focus their various theological emphases. Therefore, to do full justice to this rich variety lies beyond the scope of this commentary. Still, this dilemma hardly justifies doing nothing at all.

A traditional approach to the New Testament's use of the Decalogue has been to comb the New Testament for imperatives which resemble the ten commandments, and seek to find a general correspondence between the two testaments (cf. Grotius, *op. cit.*). Indeed, one can find parallel commandments, if not specific reference to most items of the Decalogue itself, in the New Testament. Nevertheless, this method runs the risk of missing the major problems which are at stake. To what extent did Jesus fit his teaching within the Old Testament law? Was his attack on the Pharisees directed simply against their interpretation of the law or did it touch on the substance of the law itself? In what sense did Jesus bring a 'new law' (*lex nova*) which replaced the old? Finally, how does life in the spirit as the norm of the Christian life relate to the law?

A clear profile of Jesus' attitude toward the law emerges from the synoptic gospels in spite of the variety of redactional emphases. First, it is evident that Jesus regarded the Decalogue as the revealed will of God and in this respect did not differ from the Judaism of his age. To the rich young ruler (Matt. 19.18ff. and parallels) who sought eternal life, Jesus simply quoted the ten commandments as the expressed will of God. He attacked the Pharisees for their hypocrisy in subverting the divine commands, specifically the fifth commandment, and substituting their own human tradition (Matt. 15.4ff.). Nor is there any indication that Jesus made any distinction in his use of the Decalogue between the moral and ceremonial aspects.

Yet it is equally evident that Jesus retained a complete freedom toward the law. Not only did he antagonize the Pharisees by healing on the sabbath and disregarding food laws, but he struck at the root of the Pharisaical interpretation by proclaiming that 'the sabbath was made for man' (Mark 2.27), and that 'nothing outside a man which goes into him can defile him' (Mark 7.15). Moreover, by his various summaries of the law both in terms of Deut. 6 and Lev. 18 (Mark 12.29) as well as the double commandment of love (Matt. 22.34ff.), Jesus moved in a direction strongly opposed by rabbinic Judaism. The law was not to be viewed as a series of stipulations all on the same level (cf. the typical passages from rabbinic sources cited by G. Barth, *op. cit.*, p. 78). Rather, behind all the laws lay the one will of God, the intent of which could be summarized in the command to love God and neighbor.

Particularly in Matthew's Sermon on the Mount the antithesis between the old and the new in respect to the law is highlighted. Jesus radicalizes the law of Sinai, however, not in the sense of replacing it with another, but of bringing its original intent to fulfillment (cf. Moule, *op. cit.*). He is presented as the true interpreter of the

Old Testament law which is eternally valid, but which has been obscured by the sinful devices of men. For Jesus, the Messiah, the law of Sinai is still unquestionably the will of God for Israel and for his disciples.

The theology of Paul in respect to the Decalogue is presented in quite a different form from the gospel. Indeed, his complex dialectical style has continued to call forth a variety of conflicting interpretations. Certainly the frequent attempt to undercut the seriousness of Paul's theology by claiming that it was directed only to a distorted form of Hellenistic Judaism is basically in error (*contra* H. J. Schoeps, *Paul*, ET London and Philadelphia 1961, pp.213ff.). Nor can one succeed in penetrating his thought by aligning him with the gnostic enthusiasts who rejected the law in terms of a call to spiritual freedom.

For Paul the law was good and from God (Rom. 7.7ff.). It performs the function of rooting out sin, not as a code of morals, but by revealing the will of God to mankind. Paul quotes specifically the ten commandments as the means of uncovering sin (Rom. 7.7). Yet the law which became the pride of Israel was the means of Israel's undoing before God. Although given by God for life, it was made to function as a curse (Gal. 3.13) in executing death. The covenant of Mount Sinai became the symbol of slavery and stood in opposition to the freedom of Jerusalem (Gal. 4.24ff.). But what the law could not do, God accomplished in the death of his Son 'in order that the just requirement of the law might be fulfilled in us who walk not according to the flesh, but according to the Spirit' (Rom. 8.3f.). Christ is therefore 'the end of the law' (Rom. 10.4).

Now the crucial issue at stake is how to understand what role the law plays for the Christian in the theology of Paul. Obviously the law as a means of salvation is rejected throughout his epistles with consistent vehemence. Faith and works are inexorably opposed. Moreover, he denies unequivocally the claim of the Judaizers that the Jewish Christian is still obliged to follow the law (Gal. 3.2). He contrasts 'life in the Spirit' with 'life in the flesh', which is identified with the law (3.2ff.)

Yet once this has been said, there seems to be another context in which Paul has a positive word to say about the function of the law. Indeed the rigor of his argument should indicate that his shift in perspective does not arise from inconsistency, but is an intentional shift in the light of a different frame of reference. The most detailed usage of the Decalogue occurs in the hortatory section of Rom.

13.8ff. in which four commandments from the second tablet are cited. Yet the new framework in vv. 8 and 10 indicates unequivocally that the commandments are now seen in the light of the imperative to love one's neighbor which fulfills the law. The gospel cannot become law again. There are several other references to the Decalogue in the Pauline corpus, such as Eph. 6.2, which again make reference to the Old Testament law in the context of shaping the Christian life. Yet nowhere is there an explicit directive instructing Christians to follow the law in order to live the obedient life, as was the case especially in later Reformed dogmatics. The closest he comes to this stance is the reference to fulfilling the 'law of Christ' (Gal. 6.2). Thus when Paul admonishes his churches to obedience to the will of God, a form of commandment emerges which is closely akin in fact to Matthew's christological interpretation of the law. It was not by chance that later Christian theologians found little difficulty in joining the Sermon on the Mount with the Pauline polarity of spirit and letter of the law.

Finally, reference should be made to several other New Testament usages of the Decalogue, particularly those in James 2.11; Heb. 4.4, 10 (cf. Col. 3.5ff.). It is also possible that several of the lists in the Pastorals reflect elements of the Decalogue (I Tim. 1.8ff.).

5. History of Exegesis

H. BORNKAMM, *Luther und das Alte Testament*, Tübingen 1948, pp. 103ff.; P. DELHAYE, *Le Décalogue et sa place dans la morale chretienne²*, Bruxelles 1963; J. GEFFCKEN, *Der Bilderkatechismus des 15 Jahrhunderts*, Hamburg 1853; *Über die verschiedene Einteilung des Decalogus und den Einfluss derselben auf den Kultus* (Hamburg 1838); E. R. GOODENOUGH, 'Philo's Exposition of the Law', *HTR* 27, 1923, pp. 109ff;. R. M. GRANT, 'The Decalogue in Early Christianity', *HTR* 40, 1947, pp. 1ff.; B. JACOB, 'The Decalogue', *JQR*, NS 14, 1923-4, pp. 141ff.; BOAZ COHEN, 'Letter and Spirit in Jewish and Roman Law', *M.M. Kaplan Jubilee Vol.*, New York 1953, pp. 109-35; J. MANN, 'Changes in the Divine Service of the Synagogue due to Religious Persecution', *HUCA* 4, 1927, pp. 241-310; B. REICKE, *Die zehn Worte*, Tübingen 1972; H. RÖTHLISBERGER, *Kirche am Sinai*, Zürich 1965; H. SCHNEIDER, 'Der Dekalog in den Phylakterien von Qumrân', *BZ*, NS 3, 1959, pp. 18ff.; H. L. STRACK, H. BILLERBECK, *Kommentar zum Neuen Testament aus Talmud und Midrasch* I, Munich 1922, pp. 622-30; R. J. THOMPSON, *Moses and the Law in a Century of Criticism since Graf, Suppl. VT* 19, 1970.

The Decalogue has played such an enormous role, not only in theology, but in the history of the Western world, that it is quite impossible to do justice in a brief way to a history of its interpretation. The reader is, therefore, referred to the bibliography of secondary literature for pursuance of the subject. I shall only attempt to draw a few broad lines from this history in pointing out several of the more important interpretations, and in illustrating representative positions.

As early as the second-century, certain clear options emerged for the Christian church respecting the use of the Decalogue (cf. Grant, *op. cit.*). First of all, in the second-century catechetical work, *De Doctrina Apostolorum*, and in the *Didache* (1.3ff.), the Decalogue appeared along with excerpts from the Sermon on the Mount and other New Testament material to form a practical code of ethics. The *Shepherd of Hermes* likewise provides a list of twelve ethical rules for guidance which overlap to some extent with the Decalogue. In spite of reference to a specifically Christian emphasis on the new role of the spirit, there is a strong legalistic tendency in its use which serves to support a general Hellenistic morality.

Secondly, very early in the Christian era the treatment of the Decalogue was tied to the concept of natural law (cf. Delhaye, *op. cit.*, pp. 66ff.). Particularly in Justin, Irenaeus, and Tertullian the concept of natural law served an important theological end. It supported the right of Christians to drop the old Jewish law since Christ had fulfilled the eternal law of God. Again it functioned as a convenient polemic against the Jewish claim for the superiority of the Old Testament law. One could now argue that the value of their law lay in those elements which God had revealed to all men. Only these elements of the Decalogue concerned the Christian.

A far profounder theological approach was expressed by Augustine. To be sure, his emphasis on the freedom of the spirit as providing a new context for the whole law had been adumbrated in Origen's *Homily VIII.1 on Exodus*. However, in his remarkable treatise *On the Spirit and the Letter*, Augustine rejects the distinction between the law of works in Judaism, and the law of faith in Christianity. Rather, he develops a Pauline distinction in stressing that the law is good and was killed by sin. The law of the Spirit secured by faith liberates the Christian to perform the fruits of charity. The Decalogue, therefore, become the Christian's charter of freedom and is made wholly new in its function (cf. also *Contra Faustum* X.2). God's law is therefore love (*Spirit and Letter* XVII.29).

Aquinas developed at length his understanding of the Decalogue in the *Summa Theologica* (1a2ae, 98ff.; Blackfriars ed. vol. 29). He works out with great precision the scholastic distinction between the moral, ceremonial, and judicial precepts of the old law. Certain of the commandments are obvious from the law of nature, such as not killing and stealing. Others are understood only by careful consideration of the wise, while still other actions are such that the human reason needs divine instruction about the things of God, such as not making a graven image. The claims of the moral law still rest on the Christian as upon all men, while those of the ceremonial and juridical precepts, in different ways, have been largely abrogated. Certainly, for Catholic theology and beyond, a vulgarization of Aquinas' position became the dominant Christian approach, and still is represented in textbooks up until today (cf. Delhaye, pp. 30f.).

The impact of Martin Luther's interpretation of the Decalogue for the subsequent history of Protestantism can hardly be exaggerated. By giving it a central role in both his larger and smaller catechism he assured that it entered into the blood stream of the church. Luther's exegesis gave to the Decalogue a profoundly comprehensive role, covering every area of life, which has seldom been matched. At the same time he clothed it with such a concrete form of flesh and blood that it carried a tremendous impact in shaping the Christian life. Nevertheless, the theological reflection of Luther on the role of the Decalogue arose out of a complex dialectic which lay at the heart of his understanding of gospel and law (cf. especially Bornkamm, *op. cit.*, pp. 103ff.). At the outset Luther makes it absolutely clear that for the Christian the law has been completely abrogated. 'Moses is dead.' The law is a purely Jewish code of its own period and as such has nothing to say to Christians. Inasmuch as the Decalogue contains natural law also, Christian responsibility does not rest on Moses' law, but on a divine law for all men. Nevertheless, this law condemns him, leads him to death, and is the antagonist of the gospel which frees him. Conversely, for the Christian who has been justified by faith the law has a different face. When viewed from this side of the cross, Moses has become the herald of Christ. Indeed the Decalogue offers the clearest instruction in the new life of freedom. In the first commandment lies the heart of the gospel: 'that we should fear, love, and trust God above all things.'

Calvin's interpretation of the Decalogue (*Institutes* II. viii) was of a different sort from Luther's, but hardly less impressive. Calvin placed his emphasis on the 'third use' of the law, namely as instruction for the Christian life, and offered a brilliant hermeneutic in defense of his position. The Old Testament law when used by the Christian must be directed to the end for which it was given. It must reach to the substance of the precept. It must be expanded to enjoin the opposite of that which is prohibited. The result of his approach produced a rich and profound theological reflection which gave the Decalogue a remarkable centrality within his whole frame of thought. Likewise Melanohthon provided a hermeneutic along with his interpretation (*Melanohthon on Christian Doctrine: Loci Communes* 1555, tr. and ed. C. L. Manschreck, New York 1965, ch. VII), and provided a model for later Lutheran theology in the 'third use' of the law. As one might expect, the historical and theological relation of Melanohthon's interpretation to that of Luther's has been much debated in modern times.

In the post-Reformation period the exposition of the Decalogue became a standard section of Christian systematic theology (cf. Chemnitz, *De Lege Dei*, vii; J. Gerhard, *Loci*, I. xii, §53; J. Wollebius, *Christianae Theol. Compend.* II; J. Cocceius, *Summa Theologiae*, §89). In addition, a steady stream of detailed exposition emerged, such as the well-known *Five Decades* by H. Bullinger and the *Praelectiones in cap. XX. Exodi* of Rivetus. Invariably one could expect an introductory essay on the subject: 'An lex decalogi ad nos pertineat?' An English exposition which had an important influence on Puritan England and America was that of Bishop Lancelot Andrewes, *The Moral Law Expounded* (London 1642). Andrewes stated categorically: 'The Law is changed in nothing, but only the ceremonies are taken away by Christ and his truth' (p. 73). His own set of rules by which the commandments were to be 'enlarged and restricted' can surely be reckoned among the most able and learned examples of theological casuistry ever developed. A much more practical, yet likewise influential Scottish Calvinistic exposition was that of James Durham, *A Practical Exposition of the Ten Commandments* (London 1675) who could catalogue sleeping in church and talking during the sermon as clear violations of the Decalogue (p. 76). During this period much attention focused on the prohibition of images in the polemic against Rome, and called forth vigorous counter-attacks from such Catholic champions as Bellarmine. The prohibition to kill seldom provided difficulty for commentators in supporting unreservedly the need of 'killing of men in lawful war . . . or execution of malefactors by the hands . . . of the civil magistrate' (J. Gill, *Exodus, ad loc.*).

Before turning to the modern period, it is necessary to backtrack and review briefly the history of Jewish exegesis which paralleled in time and often in content the history which has just been sketched. Philo's estimate of the pre-eminence of the Decalogue (*De Decalogo*, 154) is shared by Jewish writings of the Mishnaic period. The fact that the reading of the Decalogue was incorporated into the liturgy of the morning service (Tamid V.1) demonstrates its central role in Judaism of this period. Moreover, the discovery of the Nash Papyrus and the phylacteries of Qumran which contained the Decalogue along with the other traditional biblical passages confirms its important role. It is also evident that this use of the Decalogue in the service was discontinued at a later period. The theory has generally been held that this move was evoked by the emphasis which Christianity placed on the Decalogue (cf. G. F. Moore, *Judaism* I, Cambridge, Mass. 1927, p. 291). However, the evidence from Qumran has suggested that a liturgical development within Judaism might have played a role as well (cf. Schneider, *op. cit.*).

Within Judaism a certain ambivalence regarding the Decalogue continues to reflect itself. On the one hand, it was accepted as the very heart of the divine revelation at Sinai, which was given by God himself. It contained in essence all the laws of Torah. Rashi speaks of it as the 'fountain head of all' (Ex. 24.12). It is 'the rare jewel of ten pearls' (Ex. R.44). Its homiletical popularity is eloquently attested by the delightful *Midrash on the Ten Words* (A. Jellenek, *Bet-ha-Midrasch* I, Leipzig 1853, pp. 62ff.). On the other hand, there is an apology directed against using the Decalogue at the expense of the other laws (*Sifre* on Deut. 1.3). Maimonides in his *Sefer Ha-Mitzvoth* simply includes the commandments of the Decalogue within the larger categories of the negative and positive commandments which make up the 613 precepts of the law. Likewise, Nachmanides fits the Decalogue into the framework of this halachic category. Benno Jacob (*Das Zweite Buch Mose*, p. 186) certainly reflects the same basic Jewish attitude when he first praises the Decalogue as being uniquely given by God himself, but then adds, 'though all the laws are God-given and require the same amount of obedience'.

Other features should also be noted in the history of Jewish exegesis. Many of the later exegetical 'discoveries' of the historical critical period were already clearly seen by the rabbis, as for example, Rashi's referring the prohibition of theft to 'stealing a man', or Ibn Ezra's understanding of false witness. Nor were the classic Jewish commentators uninfluenced by the philosophical discussions of their times; they also entered into the discussion of the role of natural law and human reason (cf. Judah Halevi, *Kuzari*, Part II).

The entrance into the modern period was foreshadowed by several penetrating studies of the seventeenth century. Certainly the commentaries of Grotius and Clericus marked a break from the main stream of post-Reformation exposition. Clericus in particular offered a detailed historical interpretation of the Decalogue with considerable philological precision, in which he stressed the particular Hebrew form of laws which he found paralleled elsewhere in the world. But to this new historical sense he added a theological perspective as well. The Decalogue was historically conditioned and therefore not to be regarded 'as the clear voice of God given to the whole assembly of mankind'.

Goethe's brilliant study of the Decalogue raised the fundamental question of later critical study, but made little impact, as is apparent from Wellhausen's total ignorance of the essay until a student pointed out to him the similarity of his hypothesis with that of Goethe's (cf. *Composition des Hexateuchs*[2], 1889, p. 328). By the year 1780, in his famous *Einleitung*, J. G. Eichhorn still held to the Mosaic authorship of the Decalogue while recognizing some elements of later expansion. In turn, Ewald cited the archaic form of the series as proof of its antiquity and characterized it as comprising 'the highest truths' by 'no other master-mind than Moses himself' (*History of Israel*, ET 1867, I, p. 443). But by the middle of the nineteenth century the attempt to reconstruct the original Decalogue was fully under way in the monograph of E. Meier, *Die Ursprüngliche Form des Dekalogs* (1846), and A. Knobel's *Exodus* (1857).

However, the decisive break with the tradition came with Wellhausen (and his school), who rejected completely the Mosaic authorship of the Decalogue and saw it as an eighth-century product of prophetic influence. Wellhausen argued that the 'universal moral code' could only be late and that a prohibition of images would have been unthinkable in early Israel (*Composition*, pp. 331ff.). The flood of conservative rejoinders from men such as Delitzsch and Öhler did little to restore the traditional view. Moreover, it was now felt necessary to defend such a case by providing evidence for a genuine historical setting rather than by appealing to the tradition. In this regard, the fact that Wellhausen's position has been seriously eroded by the form-critical work of Alt in 1934 ('The Origins of Israelite law', in *Essays*) and others, was in no way a return to the older, so-called uncritical position. Nor did Alt's early dating of apodictic legal material do much to restore the significance of the Decalogue. In some ways, Alt's work marked the completion of a process begun in the seventeenth century which removed the Decalogue from its elevated position as the epitome of divine law to a secondary compilation of laws about which one could say very little.

Certainly it remains a haunting question for anyone who has followed this history of exegesis whether one can really describe it as a history of steadily increasing insight. Perhaps a chart of rising and falling lines would be more appropriate. Certainly, the modern critical period has brought a new dimension of philological and historical precision to bear. Yet to the extent to which the scholar now finds himself increasingly estranged from the very substance which he studies, one wonders how far the lack of content which he discovers stems from a condition in the text or in himself.

6. *Theological Reflection in the Context of the Canon*

K. BARTH, *Church Dogmatics* I/2, ET Edinburgh 1956, pp. 76ff., 310ff.; M. BUBER, 'What are we to do about the Ten Commandments?', *Biblical Humanism*, New York 1968; A. DE QUERVAIN, 'Das Gesetz Gottes', *Theol. Existenz Heute* 34, 1935; 39, 1936; W. EICHRODT, 'The Law and the Gospel: The Meaning of the Ten Commandments in Israel and for Us', *Interpretation* 11, 1957, pp. 23ff.; H. RÖTHLISBERGER, *Kirche am Sinai. Die Zehn Gebote in der christlichen Unterweisung*, Zürich 1965; J. SCHREINER, *Die Zehn Gebote im Leben des Gottesvolkes*, Munich 1966; A. R. VIDLER, 'On Resuscitating the Decalogue', *Theology* 48, 1945, pp. 25ff.

One of the ironical things which emerges from reflecting on the history of the interpretation of the Decalogue is that the actual exegesis of the Ten Commandments consistently appears to belie the claim of its eternality. Although the Decalogue has been continually treated as if it, at least, were timeless and unchanging in value, the cultural conditioning of the interpretation appears with the greatest clarity right at this point. No one can read the Reformers' interpretation of the commandment to honor one's parents as a warrant for obedience to the state without sensing that an inherited, cultural concept of government played a role in shaping the exegesis. Nor does the Puritan stress on sobriety and modesty in dress seem to many moderns a self-evident deduction from the seventh commandment.

Conversely, the force of the categorical prohibition against killing would seem today for many moderns to have been all too easily disregarded by the conscience of our fathers.

However, the fact that every interpretation reflects a large amount of cultural conditioning should not be misunderstood. It is not evidence to justify a theory that all exegesis is purely a subjective endeavor anyway and that 'anything goes'! Rather, it belongs to the essential function of biblical interpretation that it does share the thought patterns and language of its age, while at the same time, if it is worthy of the name of exegesis, seeking to shape these patterns through an encounter with the biblical text. The mistake lies in assuming that there is such a thing as a timeless interpretation. The challenge to hear the Old Testament as God's word in a concrete definite form for one's own age carries with it the corollary that it will be soon antiquated. The fact that the church continues to tap an abundant source of life in its use of the Decalogue in order to shape its life for each new generation only demonstrates the function of the canon. Scripture is different in kind from the church's reflection upon it. Therefore, that one generation's understanding of the law differs from the next does not call into question the place of the Decalogue in the life of the church, but bears witness to the 'scandal of particularity' in which the Christian lives his life in the call to obedience.

The preceding bibliography lists several contemporary interpretations of the significance of the Ten Commandments. However, rather than offer yet another, it seems to be of more value for a commentary to reflect on some of the exegetical controls which have emerged from a study of the Decalogue and which should aid in testing the validity of each fresh attempt to deal seriously with the text.

1. The commandments are given by God as an expression of his will for his covenant people. They are not to be seen as simply moral directives apart from the living authority of God himself, who has made himself known.

2. The commandments are given by God to his people in the context of a covenant. Whatever broader implications the commandments may have, their primary function is directed toward shaping the life of his chosen community.

3. The commandments are addressed to the church both as a gracious gift pointing to the way of life and joy, and as a warning against sin which leads to death and judgment.

4. The intent of the commandments is to engender love of God and love of neighbor. These two sides cannot be fused into one command, nor can either be used at the expense of the other. The church cannot love God apart from service to neighbor; however, there can be no true service of neighbor apart from the love of God.

5. The church strives to be obedient to the will of God through the gift of the Spirit of Christ, which continues to open up new and fresh avenues of freedom. This transformation of the law through Jesus Christ guards against both a deadening legalism and an uncharted enthusiasm in which the life of the church in and for the world is endangered.

The theological challenge for the church today is to give to the divine commandments a form of 'flesh and blood' which not only strives to be obedient in the hearing of his word, but is equally serious in addressing its imperatives with boldness to the contemporary world. The church must speak to a thoroughly secular age which no longer understands the meaning of a divine word. It must seek to regain the significance of covenant responsibility in the context of a romantic, sentimental understanding of the religious life. It must bear witness to the divine will in a man-centered society to the end that man may be freed to fulfill his authentic role. Finally, it must reinterpret with new power the imperative to love one another before the threat of technological dehumanization. It is senseless simply to repeat parrotwise an interpretation of the past, but one can gain insight from its history in seeing how faithful wrestling with God's commandments promises to form the life of the church.

XVIII

STATUTES AND ORDINANCES
OF THE COVENANT

20.22–23.33

A. Alt, 'The Origins of Israelite Law', *Essays on Old Testament History and Religion*, Oxford 1966, pp.81–132 (New York 1967, pp.103–71); 'Zur Talionsformel', *ZAW* 52, 1934, pp.303–5 = *KS* I, 1953, pp.341–4; B. Bäntsch, *Das Bundesbuch Ex XX.22–XXIII.33*, Halle 1892; W. Beyerlin, 'Die Paränese im Bundesbuch und ihre Herkunft', *Gottes Wort und Gottes Land, H. W. Hertzberg Festschrift*, Göttingen 1965, pp.9–29; P. A. H. de Boer, 'Some remarks on Exodus XXI 7–11', *Orientalia Neerlandica*, Leiden 1948, pp.162–6; E. Bickermann, 'Two Legal Interpretations of the Septuagint', *RIDA*, 3. série, 3, 1956, pp.81–104; K. Budde, 'Bemerkungen zum Bundesbuch', *ZAW* 11, 1891, pp.99–114; H. Cazelles, *Études sur le code d'alliance*, Paris 1946; 'Loi israélite', *DBS* V, 1952–3, pp.497–530; D. Conrad, *Studien zum Altargesetz: Ex 20:24–26* (Diss. Marburg), 1968; D. Daube, *Studies in Biblical Law*, Cambridge and New York 1947, pp.74–101; R. le Déaut, 'Exode XXII 12 dans la Septante et le Targum', *VT* 22, 1972, pp.164–75; A. S. Diamond, 'An Eye for an Eye', *Iraq* 19, 1957, pp.151–5; O. Eissfeldt, *The Old Testament: An Introduction*, ET Oxford and New York 1965, pp.219ff.; Z. Falk, 'Exodus 21:6', *VT* 9, 1959, pp.86–8; F. C. Fensham, 'Aspects of Family Law in the Covenant Code in Light of Ancient Near Eastern Parallels', *Dine Israel*, ed. Z. W. Falk, vol. I, Jerusalem 1969, pp.v–xix; 'Clauses of Protection in Hittite Vassal-Treaties and the Old Testament', *VT* 13, 1963, pp.133–43; ''D' in Exodus XXII 12', *VT* 12, 1962,pp. 337–9; 'Exodus XXI:18–19 in the Light of Hittite Law §10', *VT* 10, 1960, pp.333–5; 'Maledictions and Benedictions in Ancient Near Eastern Vassal-Treaties', *ZAW* 74, 1962, pp.1–9; *The Mišpāṭîm in the Covenant Code* (Diss. Johns Hopkins), 1958 (not seen, but cited in his *Exodus* commentary); 'New Light on Exod.21:6 and 22:7 from the Laws of Eshnunna', *JBL* 78, 1959, pp.160–1; T. H. Gaster, *Myth, Legend, and Custom in the Old Testament*, New York 1969, pp.243–9; H. Gese, 'Beobachtungen zum Stil alttestamentlicher Rechtssätze', *TLZ* 85, 1960, cols.147–50; S. Gevirtz, 'West-Semitic Curses and the Problem of the Origins of Hebrew Law', *VT* 11, 1961, pp.137–58; C. H. Gordon, '*Elohim* in its Reputed Meaning of Rulers, Judges', *JBL* 54, 1935, pp.134–44; M. Greenberg, *The Ḥab/piru*, New Haven 1955; J. de Groot, *Die Altäre des salomonischen Tempelhofes*, Stuttgart 1924; M. Haran, 'The Book of the Covenant' (Heb.), *Encyclopaedia Biblica* V, Jerusalem,

1968, pp. 1087–91; J. HOFTIJZER, 'Ex XXI 8', *VT* 7, 1957, pp. 388–91; H. HORN, 'Traditionsschichten in Ex 23, 10–33 und Ex 34, 10–26', *BZ*, NF 15, 1971, pp. 203–22; J. L'HOUR, 'L'Alliance de Sichem', *RB* 69, 1962, pp. 5–36, 161–84, 350–68; B. JACOB, *Auge um Auge*, Berlin 1928; A. JEPSEN, '*Amaʰ und Schiphchaʰ*', *VT* 8, 1958, pp. 293–7; 'Die "Hebräer" und ihr Recht', *AfO* 15, 1945–51, pp. 55–68; *Untersuchungen zum Bundesbuch*, Stuttgart 1927; A. JIRKU, *Das weltliche Recht im Alten Testament*, Gütersloh 1927; R. KILIAN, 'Apodiktisches und Kasuistisches Recht im Lichte ägyptischer Analogien', *BZ*, NS 7, 1963, pp. 185–202; E. KÖNIG, 'Stimmen Ex 20, 24 und Dtn 12, 13f. zusammen?', *ZAW* 42, 1924, pp. 337ff.; H. J. KRAUS, *Worship in Israel*, ET Oxford and Richmond, Va. 1966; W. KREBS, 'Zur kultischen Kohabitation mit Tieren im Alten Orient', *Forschungen und Fortschritte* 36, 1962, pp. 373–75; I. LEWY, 'Dating the Covenant Code Sections on Humaneness and Righteousness', *VT* 7, 1957, pp. 322–6; S. E. LOEWENSTAMM, 'Biblical Law' (Heb.), *Encyclopaedia Biblica* V, Jerusalem 1968, pp. 614–37; O. LORETZ, 'Ex 21.6; 22.8 und angebliche Nuzi-Parallelen', *Biblica* 41, 1960, pp. 167–75; J. W. McKAY, 'Exodus XXIII 1–3, 6, 8: a decalogue for the administration of justice in the city gate', *VT* 21, 1971, pp. 311–25; I. MENDELSOHN, 'The Conditional Sale into Slavery of Free-born Daughters in Nuzi and the Law of Ex. 21:7–11', *JAOS* 55, 1935, pp. 190–5; J. MORGENSTERN, 'The Book of the Covenant', Part I, *HUCA* 5, 1928, pp. 1–151; Part II, *HUCA* 7, 1930, pp. 19–258; Part III, *HUCA* 8–9, 1931–32, pp. 1–150; Part IV, *HUCA* 33, 1962, pp. 59–105; E. NEUFELD, 'The Prohibitions against Loans at Interest in Ancient Hebrew Laws', *HUCA* 26, 1955, pp. 355–412; R. NORTH, 'Flesh covering, a Response, Ex. XXI 10', *VT* 5, 1955, pp. 204–6; S. M. PAUL, *Studies in the Book of the Covenant in the Light of Cuneiform and Biblical Law*, Leiden 1970; C. PERROT, 'La lecture synagogal d'Ex 21:1–22:23', *A La Recontre de Dieu, Mémorial Gelin*, Le Puy 1961, pp. 223–39; R. H. PFEIFFER, 'The Transmission of the Book of the Covenant', *HTR* 24, 1931, pp. 99–109; J. VAN DER PLOEG, '*Šāpāṭ et Mišpāṭ*', *OTS* 2, 1945, pp. 144–55; 'Studies in Hebrew Law', *CBQ* 12, 1950, pp. 248–59, 416–27; 13, 1951, pp. 28–34, 164–71, 296–307; M. H. PRÉVOST, 'Bibliography of Biblical Law', *RHD* 45, 1967, pp. 529–32; 46, 1968, pp. 530–5; 47, 1969, pp. 525–34; J. J. RABINOWITZ, 'Exodus XXII 4 and the Septuagint Version thereof', *VT* 9, 1959, pp. 40–6; M. RADIN, 'The kid and its mother's milk', *AJSL* 40, 1923–4, pp. 209ff.; E. ROBERTSON, 'The Altar of Earth (Ex 20, 24–26)', *JJS* 1, 1948, pp. 12–21; L. ROST, 'Das Bundesbuch', *ZAW* 77, 1965, pp. 255–9; J. W. ROTHSTEIN, *Das Bundesbuch und die religionsgeschichtliche Entwickelung Israels*, Halle 1888; S. SCHELBERT, 'Exodus XXII 4 im palästinischen Targum', *VT* 8, 1958, pp. 253–63; R. SCHMID, *Das Bundesopfer in Israel*, Münich 1964; G. SCHMITT, *Du sollst keinen Frieden schliessen*, Stuttgart 1970, pp. 13–24; H. SCHULZ, *Das Todesrecht im Alten Testament*, Berlin 1969; A. VAN SELMS, 'The Goring Ox in Babylon and Biblical Law', *AfO* 18, 1950, pp. 321–30; J. M. P. SMITH, *The Origin and History of Hebrew Law*, Chicago 1931, Cambridge 1932; E. SPEISER, 'Background and Function of the Biblical *Nāśi*', *CBQ* 25, 1963, pp. 111–17; 'The Stem PLL in Hebrew', *JBL* 82, 1963, pp. 301–6; J. J. STAMM, 'Zum Altargesetz im Bundesbuch', *TZ* 1, 1945, pp. 304–6; J. A. THOMPSON, 'The Book of the Covenant, Ex. 21–23 in the light of modern archaeological research', *Australian Bibl. Review* 2, 1952, pp. 97–107; R. DE VAUX, *Studies in Old Testament Sacrifice*, ET Cardiff 1964; V. WAGNER, *Rechtssätze in gebundener Sprache und Rechtssatzreihen im israelitischen Recht*, Berlin 1972; 'Zur

Systematik in dem Code Ex.21:2–22:16', *ZAW* 81, 1969, pp.176–82; J. WELL-HAUSEN, *Prolegomena to the History of Israel*, London 1885, pp.28ff.; D. H. WEISS, 'A note on *'ašer lō'-'ōrāśāh'*, *JBL* 81, 1962, pp.67–9; H. M. WIENER, 'The Altars of the Old Testament', *Beigabe OLZ* 30, 1927; *Studies in Biblical Law*, London 1904; R. YARON, 'The Goring Ox in Near Eastern Laws', *Jewish Law in Ancient and Modern Israel*, ed. H. H. Cohn, New York 1971, pp.50–60.

NOTE: *The chapter and verse division is that of the Hebrew. In the English versions 21.37 becomes 22.1 and 22.1–30 becomes 22.2–31.*

20.22 The LORD said to Moses, 'Thus you shall say to the Israelites: "You yourselves have seen how I spoke with you from heaven. [23]You shall not make gods of silver alongside of me nor shall you make for yourselves gods of gold. [24]An altar of earth you shall make for me, and sacrifice upon it your burnt offerings and your peace offerings, your sheep and your cattle. In every place where I reveal my name I will come to you and bless you. [25]But if you make for me an altar of stones, you must not build it of cut stone, for if you use your chisel upon it you profane it. [26]You must not ascend my altar by steps so that your nakedness may not be exposed upon it.

21 [1]These are the laws that you shall set before them: [2]When you buy a Hebrew slave, he shall serve six years, and in the seventh year he shall go free without payment. [3]If he comes in single, he shall go out single; if he comes in married, his wife shall go out with him. [4]If his master gives him a wife and she bears him sons or daughters, the woman and her children shall belong to her master and he shall go out single. [5]If the slave should state plainly: 'I love my master, my wife, and my children; I do not wish to be freed,' [6]then his master shall bring him before God and he shall bring him to the door or the doorpost, and his master shall pierce his ear with an awl, and he shall remain his slave for life.

[7] When a man sells his daughter as a slave, she shall not go out as the male slaves do. [8]If she does not please her master who had designated her for himself, then he must let her be ransomed; he does not have the right to sell her to a foreign people, since he broke faith with her. [9]If he designates her for his son, he shall show her the rights of a free-born woman. [10]If he takes another wife, he shall not withhold from the first her food, her clothing, or her conjugal rights. [11]If he does not do these three things for her, she shall go free without any payment.

[12] Whoever strikes a man and kills him shall be put to death. [13]However, if he did not do it intentionally, rather it happened by an act of God, I will assign you a place to which he can flee. [14]But if a man schemes against another to kill him treacherously, you shall take him away even from my altar to be put to death. [15]Whoever strikes his

father or mother shall be put to death. ¹⁶Whoever steals a man shall be put to death, regardless of whatever he has sold him or he is still in his possession. ¹⁷Whoever curses his father or his mother shall be put to death.

18 When men quarrel and one strikes the other with a stone or his fist, and the man does not die but is laid up in bed, ¹⁹if he recovers so as to be able to walk about outside with his cane, the one who struck him shall be cleared, except that he must pay for his loss of time, and shall see that he is thoroughly cured. ²⁰When a man strikes his male or female slave with a stick, and the slave dies on the spot, he must be avenged. ²¹But if he survives a day or two, he is not to be avenged since he is the other's property. ²²When men scuffle and injure a pregnant woman so that she has a miscarriage, but suffers no further harm, the one responsible shall pay whatever the woman's husband demands in accordance with an assessment. ²³But if there is further harm, then you must give life for life, ²⁴eye for eye, tooth for tooth, hand for hand, foot for foot, ²⁵burn for burn, wound for wound, lash for lash. ²⁶When a man strikes the eye of his male or female slave and destroys it, he shall let him go free on account of his eye. ²⁷If he knocks out the tooth of his male or female slave, he shall let the slave go free on account of his tooth.

28 When an ox gores a man or a woman to death, the ox shall be stoned, and its flesh shall not be eaten, but the owner of the ox shall be free of liability. ²⁹But if the ox has had a record of previous gorings, and its owner has been warned, but has not kept it under control and it kills a man or a woman, the ox shall be stoned, and its owner also shall be put to death. ³⁰If ransom is laid upon him, he shall pay whatever is imposed on him for the ransom of his life. ³¹If the ox gores a boy or a girl, he shall be dealt with according to the same principle. ³²If the ox gores a male or female slave, the owner shall give to their master thirty shekels of silver and the ox shall be stoned.

33 When a man uncovers a cistern, or digs a well leaving it open, and an ox or an ass falls into it, ³⁴the owner of the cistern shall make restitution; he shall pay the price of the owner, but shall keep the dead animal.

35 When a man's ox injures the ox of his neighbor so that it dies, then they shall sell the live ox, and divide its price and the dead animal as well. ³⁶Or if it is known that the ox has had a record of previous gorings and its owner has not kept it under control, he must restore ox for ox, but shall keep the dead animal.

37 When a man steals an ox or a sheep and slaughters it or sells it, he shall pay five oxen for the ox, and four sheep for the sheep – 22 ¹If the thief is caught in the act of house-breaking and is fatally injured, there is no bloodguilt in this case. ²But after sunrise, there is bloodguilt in that case – he must make full restitution; if he lacks the means, he

shall be sold to pay for his theft. ³If what he stole is found alive in his possession – whether an ox or ass or sheep – he shall pay double.

4 When a man causes a field or vineyard to be used for grazing, or lets his livestock loose and it feeds on another man's field, he shall make full restitution from his field according to its yield, but if all the field has been grazed over, he shall make restitution from the best in his own field and from his own vineyard.

5 When a fire is started and catches brushwood so that stacked grain, or standing grain, or a whole field is destroyed, the one who started the fire must make restitution.

6 When a man gives to another money or goods for safe-keeping and they are stolen from the man's house, then, if the thief is caught, he shall pay double; ⁷if the thief is not caught, the owner of the house shall be brought before God to determine whether he has not laid hands on the property of his neighbor. ⁸Concerning every case of misappropriation whether for an ox, an ass, a sheep, a garment, or any other lost thing of which a claim is made, 'This is it,' the case of both parties shall come before God; the one whom God declares to be in the wrong shall make double restitution to his neighbor.

9 When a man gives to another an ass, an ox, a sheep, or any other animal to keep, and it dies or is injured or is driven away without there being a witness, ¹⁰an oath before the LORD shall be made between the two of them to decide whether the one has not laid hands on the property of the other. The owner must accept this, and no restitution shall be made. ¹¹But if it has been stolen from him, he shall make restitution to its owner. ¹²If it has been severely torn by beasts, he shall bring it as evidence; he shall not make restitution for what has been torn.

13 When a man borrows anything from another, and it is injured or dies while the owner is not with it, he shall make full restitution. ¹⁴If its owner was with it, he shall not make restitution; if it was hired, it was reckoned in its hire.

15 If a man seduces a virgin who has not been engaged, and lies with her, he must pay the marriage price for her, and make her his wife. ¹⁶If her father absolutely refuses to give her to him, he must pay money equivalent to the marrage price of virgins.

17 You shall not allow a sorceress to live.

18 Whoever lies with an animal shall be put to death.

19 Whoever sacrifices to a god other than the LORD alone shall be executed under the ban.

20 You shall not wrong or oppress a stranger, for you were strangers in the land of Egypt. ²¹You shall not mistreat any widow or orphan. ²²If you mistreat them, and they cry out to me, I will be sure to hear their cry, ²³and my anger will be aroused, and I will slay you with the

sword, and your own wives shall become widows and your children orphans.

24 If you lend money to any of my people, to the poor among you, you shall not act toward him as a money-lender and charge him interest. 25If you take your neighbor's garment as security, you must return it to him before the sun sets, 26for it is his only clothing. It is the cloak with which he covers his body. In what else can he sleep? If he cries to me, I will respond, for I am compassionate.

27 You shall not revile God, nor curse a ruler of your people. 28You shall not hold back your first yield from the wine press. You shall give me the first-born from your sons. 29You shall do the same with your cattle and your sheep. They shall stay with the mother for seven days; on the eighth day you shall give them to me.

30 You shall be men holy to me. You must not eat flesh torn by animals in the field. You shall throw it to the dogs.

23 1You must not spread false rumours. Do not join forces with a wicked man to act as a corrupt witness. 2Do not side with the majority for evil, and do not distort the evidence in a dispute by favoring the majority. 3Do not show preference to a poor man in his case.

4 If you come across your enemy's ox or ass going astray, you must take it back to him. 5If you see the ass of your enemy lying helpless under its load, you must by no means abandon him. You must help him with it.

6 Do not pervert the justice due your poor in his dispute. 7Keep away from a false charge, and do not cause the death of the innocent and guiltless, because I will not acquit the guilty. 8Do not take a bribe, for a bribe blinds clear vision and perverts the cause of the just.

9 You shall not oppress a stranger, for you know what it feels like to be a stranger, having yourselves been strangers in the land of Egypt.

10 For six years you may sow your land and gather in its crops, 11but in the seventh year you shall let it rest and lie fallow that the poor among your people may eat of it, and what they leave let the wild animals eat. You shall do the same with your vineyards and olive groves.

12 For six days you are to do your work, but on the seventh day you must abstain from work in order that your ox and your ass may rest, and your house slave and the stranger may be refreshed.

13 Pay attention to all that I have told you. Do not invoke the name of other gods; do not let them be heard on your lips.

14 Three times a year you shall keep a festival to me. 15You shall observe the festival of unleavened bread, eating unleavened bread for seven days as I commanded you, at the appointed time in the month of Abib, for in it you came out of Egypt. None shall appear before me empty-handed. 16Keep the feast of harvest, of the first fruits of your work, of what you sow in the field, and the festival of ingathering at the

end of the year when you gather in the fruits of your work from the field. ¹⁷Three times a year all your males shall appear before the LORD God.

18 You shall not offer the blood of my sacrifice with anything leavened, or let the fat of my festal offering remain until morning.

19 The choice first fruits of your ground you shall bring to the house of the LORD your God.

You shall not boil a kid in its mother's milk.

20 Now I am sending an angel before you to guard you on the way and to bring you to the place which I have prepared. ²¹Pay attention to him and obey him. Do not defy him, for he will not pardon your offenses, because I will manifest myself in him. ²²But if you will really obey him, and do all that I say, I will be an enemy to your enemies, and a foe to your foes. ²³Then my angel will go before you, and bring you to the Amorites, the Hittites, the Perizzites, the Canaanites, the Hivites, and the Jebusites, and I will annihilate them. ²⁴You shall not bow down to their gods, nor serve them, nor do according to their practices, but you shall utterly eradicate them, and shatter their pillars to pieces. ²⁵You shall serve the LORD your God, and I will bless your bread and your water and I will remove sickness from your midst. ²⁶None shall miscarry or be barren in your land. I will complete the full number of your days.

27 I will send my terror before you, and I will throw into panic all the people against whom you will come, and I will put to flight all your enemies before you. ²⁸I will send the hornet before you and it shall drive out the Hivites, the Canaanites, and the Hittites before you. ²⁹I will not drive them out before you in a single year, lest the land become desolate and the wild beasts multiply against you. ³⁰Little by little I will drive them out before you until you have increased and possess the land. ³¹I will establish your borders from the Reed Sea to the sea of the Philistines, and from the wilderness to the Euphrates, for I will deliver the inhabitants of the land into your power, and you will drive them out before you. ³²You shall make no covenant with them and their gods. ³³They shall not stay in your land lest they cause you to sin against me – namely by serving their gods – for this would be a trap for you.

1. *Textual and Philological Notes*

20.23. This is an extremely difficult verse. The initial problem lies with the *'itti* which according to the Massoretic accentuation is without an object. The LXX substitutes ὑμῖν and divides the sentence after 'gods of silver'. Philo (*Spec. Leg.* I.22) supports the MT. The sequence ʿ*ŝh 't* is infrequent in the Old Testament and usually demands an object (II Kings 18.31; Jer.5.18; cf. Ps.109.21). Several different solutions have been proposed. The majority of translations

(RSV, NJPS, NEB) go against the MT accentuation and assign the phrase 'gods of silver' as the object of the first sentence, and 'gods of gold' to the second. This solution finds its warrant in the chiasmic structure of the sentence, but disregards the usual Hebrew idiom by dividing the silver and gold into separate objects. Another solution (Bäntsch, Beer, AmTr) completes the first colon with the expression 'other gods' or its equivalent (NAB). The first solution is probably preferable although hardly a satisfactory solution. The preposition may carry a local sense and be an allusion to the sanctuary. Cf. Cazelles *ad loc.*

24. *bᵉkol-hammāqôm*; Samar. *bammāqôm* (in every place?). Cf. the parallels with a distributive sense in Gen. 20.13; Deut. 11.24. The passage has played an important role in the history of critical scholarship in relation to the question of the alleged centralization of the cult in Deuteronomy (cf. E. König, *ZAW* 42, 1929, pp. 337ff.). *G–K* § 127e, following Merx, takes the use of the definite article as a 'dogmatic correction of *bᵉkol-hammāqôm* in *every place*' to avoid the difficulty that several holy places are here authorized. The article designates 'the whole place' as the temple. In my judgment, this hypothesis is unnecessary in the light of the above-mentioned parallel passages in which the article does not alter the distributive sense of denoting a plurality of places.

'ᵃdāmāh means basically 'soil' or 'earth', but it can also refer to clay, Isa. 45.9. The exact meaning of *šᵉlāmîm*, traditionally rendered 'peace offerings' with the LXX, is uncertain. Cf. the articles on sacrifice in *IDB* and *BHH*, and the recent monograph of R. Rendtorff, *Studien zur Geschichte des Opfers im Alten Israel*, WMANT 24, 1967, pp. 132ff. Rendtorff agrees with L. Köhler in deriving the word from the intensive stem *šlm* with the meaning of 'complete'. The *šᵉlāmîm* are the 'last sacrifice'.

The Syriac reads *tazkîr*, but this reading is clearly secondary. The real problem is how to interpret the hiphil of *zkr*. Most likely the idiom *hizkîr haššēm* means to 'proclaim the name' and is a denominative use (Isa. 26.13; 12.4; Ps. 45.18). Cf. Stamm, *op. cit.*, pp. 304f.; B. S. Childs, *Memory and Tradition*, pp. 12f.; W. Schottroff, *'Gedenken' im Alten Orient*², p. 247.

21.1. 'Hebrew'. The exact significance of the term has been long debated. There is general agreement that it is not an ethnic term but refers to a disadvantaged, social class during the second millennium. The whole question has been discussed by Greenberg, *op. cit.*, among others.

'slave'. Later Jewish law softened the term to mean 'hired man', and restricted its role. *Mekilta, ad loc.*, 'one sold into bondage for stealing'.

2. *ya'ᵃbōd*. Samar., Pesh., LXX read *ya'abdekā*. This is probably correct and certainly the form which one would expect in the legal texts.

hopšî, 'free'. Cf. discussion below. This is a technical term used for one who has been freed from slavery but appears still not to have reached the full rights of the free citizen (Noth).

3. *bᵉgappô*. Although the meaning of 'single' appears clear from the context, the word is rare and the Hebrew root is contested. Gesenius-Buhl connects it with the stem *gwp* and relates it to 'body'. Cazelles suggests that it could have an Egyptian derivation.

6. 'He shall bring him to God, he shall bring him to the door.' Cf. the syntactical analysis of B. Jacob (*Das Zweite Buch, ad loc.*), who demonstrates why Hebrew

grammar does not allow the two phrases to be equated, as often suggested. S. Paul (*op. cit.*, p.50) takes the reference to God as originally referring to symbols of the private house gods.

7. *'āmāh*, 'female slave'. In Genesis the term always means 'concubine' (20.17; 21.10, etc.).

8. *'ašer lō' ye'ādāh*. These words are much contested. The Greek versions vary greatly. The easiest solution is to follow several Hebrew mss, Qere, LXX[B], T. Onk., Vulg. by reading *lô* (to him). Budde (*ZAW* 11, 1891, pp.99ff.) argued that the text was far more corrupt than usually thought and he suggested emending to *ye'dā'āh*. (BH[3], NEB). However, this remains a conjecture without textual support from the versions. Cf. de Boer's criticism of Cazelles' solution (*op. cit.*, p.165). The most recent attempt of Hoftijzer (*op. cit.*) to translate the clause: 'he does not take the decision about her' is in my judgment not convincing.

9. 'to treat as a free-born woman' is a technical expression. Cf. the parallel Ancient Near Eastern texts cited by S. Paul, *op. cit.*, p.55.

10. *'onātāh*. The meaning is uncertain. 'Conjugal rights' is a traditional conjecture made chiefly on the basis of the context. S. Paul's suggestion of 'oil, ointment' (pp.59f.) on the basis of extra-biblical parallels is impressive, but not conclusive.

13. 'act of God'. Cf. parallel in *CH* §266.

16. The LXX inverts the order of vv.16 and 17.

17. 'curse'. Cazelles (*ad loc.*) makes a good case for reckoning with a wider semantic range in the light of the versions and Near Eastern parallels. Cf. also H. C. Brichto, *The Problem of 'Curse' in the Hebrew Bible*, Philadelphia 1963, pp. 132–5.

18. *'egrōp* (fist?). The meaning is uncertain. The traditional translation given here follows the LXX, Vulg., *Mekilta*. It is supported by the parallel word structure of *'esba'* 'finger', *'ezrôa'*, 'arm', etc. The alternative interpretation of 'shovel' (NEB) finds its warrant in the Arabic cognate (cf. Judg.5.21). However, the context of Exodus speaks probably in favor of the former.

20. The LXX translates the Hebrew *nāqōm yinnāqēm* with δίκη ἐκδικηθήτω = 'he shall be avenged by legal action'. The Vulg. reads *criminis reus erit* = 'he shall be required to make answer on a criminal charge'. Cf. B. Cohen, *Jewish and Roman Law* I, New York 1966, p.5 for the influence of Roman legal terminology on the Latin translation.

21. Jepsen (*Untersuchungen, op. cit.*, p.3) eliminates the phrase 'it is his property' as a gloss, but without sufficient evidence.

22. The rare term *biplilîm*, "assessment"(?) is an old crux. Cf.Job 31.11; Deut.32.31. The traditional translation 'judge' which fits in the Job passage does not fit the context of Exodus especially well. Cazelles understands the term to refer to a third party who arbitrates a settlement, which is possible. Budde emends the text to *nepilîm*. E. A. Speiser (*op. cit.* p.303) argues for a basic meaning of 'to estimate, to assess, calculate'.

23. 'eye for eye'. A more literal rendering of the preposition would be 'eye in the place of eye'.

30. 'ransom' = price of a life. Cf. the parallel in Gen.32.21 and the treatment of Stamm (*op. cit.*).

34. *šlm*, 'recompense'. Cf. D. Daube, *op. cit.*, pp. 134ff., and W. Eisenbeis, *Die Wurzel šlm im Alten Testament*, Berlin 1969.

37. The syntactical and exegetical problem arises from the fact that 22.1–2b interrupts the order of the sentence beginning in v. 37 and continuing in 2b. Whether the problem is best dealt with by rearrangement of verses is discussed below.

22.4. There are two different ways in which this verse has been translated by modern scholars which reflect in part two ancient textual traditions. The initial difficulty arises from the verb *b'r* which is homonymous in Hebrew: (i) to burn, (ii) to graze over, LXX καταβόσκειν. Cazelles (*ad loc.*) seeks new support for the later sense from Ugaritic, but the evidence is not fully clear. Cf. W. Baumgartner, *Hebräisches und Aramäisches Lexikon*[3], Leiden 1967, s.v. The fact of a homonym makes unnecessary the suggested emendation of Bäntsch and Driver.

An additional difficulty is found in the longer text of the LXX and Samar. texts which appears after the *'atnah* in v. 4: 'he shall make full restitution according to its yield and if the whole field is grazed over . . .'. Bäntsch judges this to be a secondary textual expansion arising from the initial confusion over the root *b'r*. The reverse is more likely. The LXX reflects the original text which explains the severity of the required restitution because no judgment can be formed as to the quality of the entire crop which has been destroyed. For further details on the issues cf. Cazelles, *op. cit.*, p. 65; E. Bickerman, *op. cit.*, and J. J. Rabinowitz, *op. cit.*

'before God'. cf. the parallel *mahar ilim*, *CH* § 23, 240, etc. Cf. P. Humbert (*VT* 12, 1962, pp. 383 ff.) for a study of the idiom 'lay hands on . . .'.

8. *kî* has an asseverative force here (*G-K* § 159ee) rather than being simply the sign of direct discourse.

14. There is another possible interpretation which has been widely accepted Geiger, *Urschrift* [see p. 321 above], pp. 191f.; Bäntsch, Cazelles, Noth, etc.). Accordingly *śākîr* designates the day laborer (Ex. 12.45). 'If he is a hired man (who caused the damage) it will come out of his wage.' Grammatically one can make out a strong case for this translation. However, the context speaks against it. The translation assumes a new subject matter distinct from v. 14a, which would certainly have required some indication. Cf. the discussion in S. A. Cook, *The Laws of Moses and the Code of Hammurabi*, London 1903, p. 224; D. Daube, *Studies in Biblical Law*, pp. 16ff.; S. Paul, pp. 94ff.

15. Cf. the note of D. H. Weiss, *JBL* 81, 1962, pp. 67–69.

16. On the subject of the *mōhar*, 'marriage price', cf. R. de Vaux, *Ancient Israel*, pp. 24ff., and the full bibliography on pp. 521f.

19. The textual traditions vary considerably. The Samar. and LXX[A] read 'other gods'. Moreover, the Samar. ends with v. 19a. Some commentators (Bäntsch, etc.) suggest that *'aḥērîm* fell out through haplography, requiring therefore an additional clause. However, one could argue in the reverse direction that the Samar. reading has replaced the unique text with a more common parallel.

20ff. The notable fluctuation in the MT between the singular and plural, along with considerable variation in the versions, seems to point to an expanded text. The easiest solution, first proposed by Meyer-Lambert, *REJ* 36, 1898, p. 203, and accepted by Bäntsch and Cazelles, is to rearrange the verses in the order

20a, 22b, 21, 22a, and 23. According to this theory, the original order was confused by a secondary expansion in 20b.

22. Cf. *G-K* § 163c for the use of *kî 'im*. On the inf. abs. following *'im*, cf. the parallel in 21.5 (*G-K* § 113m).

24. The first colon of the MT text is not smooth and appears to be conflated from a possible gloss. The LXX reads 'to thy poor brother'. Rashi understands it as an anacoluthon.

28. The exact significance of the first two words is difficult to determine because of the infrequency of use. Both appear archaic. *mᵉlē'āh* 'fulness' comes in Deut. 22.9 and Num. 18.27. In the latter instance it is clearly related to grapes and distinguished from the produce of the threshing floor. This would seem to rule out the traditional rendering 'harvest' here. *demaᶜ* occurs only here. The root suggests 'trickling', and denotes fresh juice extracted from the grape. Both terms, therefore, relate to grapes. The two words may well be a hendiadys and denote the first juice of the grape. Cf. NJPS: 'You shall not put off the skimming of the first yield of your vats.' Ibn Ezra: *mᵉlē'ātᵉkā = tîrôš; dimᵉᵃkā = yiṣhār.* 'first-born'. In the light of the difficult content, Jepsen (*Untersuchungen*) follows Klostermann in suggesting the word be emended to 'cattle'. However, this is most unlikely (cf. Ex. 13.1).

30. The syntax of the words *bāśār baśśādeh ṭᵉrēpāh* is difficult. One would have expected either a relative or a different order for *baśśādeh*. Ryssel (*Exodus*[3]) rejects Dillmann's appeal to Deut. 28.36; Jer. 41.8 as offering a parallel construction. Budde (*op. cit.*, pp. 112f.) removes *baśśādeh* as a dittography. He is apparently supported by the omission of the word in the LXX. However, the word is not superfluous in the law and should probably be retained in spite of the contracted Hebrew.

23.2. The text is extremely difficult and gives evidence of several grammatical oddities: (i) the double occurrence of *rabbîm*; (ii) *lᵉrā'ōt*, the plural form with the preposition instead of the singular is unusual; (iii) *ta'ᵃneh 'al-rib*, the use of this preposition is rare and then with a different meaning (cf. II Sam. 19.43); (iv) the double occurrence of *nāṭāh*, in spite of I Sam. 8.3, is suspicious; (v) *lᵉhaṭṭōṭ* appears to need an object. Nevertheless, the versions support the consonantal text in the main. The textual corruptions appear to be very old. Therefore, there seems to be little possibility of restoring the original text by conjecturing several major emendations as does Budde (*op. cit.*, p. 113).

3. Knobel's emendation of *dāl* to *gāḏōl* (great) has been followed by Bäntsch, Jepsen, etc., but rejected by Driver and Cazelles with good reason.

5. The last half of the sentence is difficult (cf. W. F. Albright, *Yahweh and the Gods of Canaan*, London and New York 1968, p. 104). The two uses of the verb *'zb* seem to require opposite meanings from the context. The first construction *wᵉhāḏaltā mē'ᵃzōḇ* follows the normal usage for a negative consecutive clause and means 'cease from abandoning' (König, *Lehrgebäude*, III, § 406y). This leaves the difficulty of the last phrase which BH[3] emends to *'zr* to obtain the required meaning. However, this move is unnecessary. One can either defend the view that *'zb* can mean 'let loose or free' (*BDB*, p. 737), or one can seek a homonymous root cognate with the Arabic (so Cazelles; cf. G. R. Driver, *JQR* 28, 1937–8, p. 126). J. D. Michaelis, *Commentaries on the Laws of Moses* I (ET, 1814), pp. 47f. argued for a proverbial usage behind the antithesis which had been

inherited by the writer. NJPS cites Neh. 3.8, 34 as parallels to its translation of *'zb*, 'to raise up', following Rashi. However, its translation of the previous clause 'and would refrain from raising it', runs counter to the normal Hebrew syntax. Cf. Deut. 22.4 for the closest Old Testament parallel.

6. Cassuto's attempt to find a homonym to *'ebyôn* (poor) with the meaning 'adversary, opponent', is not convincing on the basis of his evidence.

15. *yērā'û*. Cf. 34.20. According to the Massoretic pointing of the niphal, *pānay* is to be understood either as a locative (cf. König, *Lehrgebäude* III, §330k) or as the subject. Cf. I Sam. 1.22; Ps. 84.8. However, the fact that the qal form appears (e.g. Isa. 1.12; cf. Ps. 42.2) has led many commentators to conjecture that the qal was original and only later softened. Cf. the thorough discussion in Dillmann-Ryssel, p.276. The Akkadian has a corresponding expression: *amâru pân ili*, 'to see the face of God'.

20. *mal'āk*. The Samar., LXX, Vulg., read a first person suffix (cf. v.23) which supplies a much smoother reading. However, see Num. 20.16.

21. *tammēr* from the root *mārāh*, not *mārrar*. G-K §67y therefore suggests pointing it *temer*.

22. 'I will be an enemy to your enemies.' Fensham finds a parallel formula in the vassal-treaties, *VT* 13, 1963, pp. 133ff.

25. *bērak*. Read the singular with the LXX. The inconsistency in persons runs through this verse, possibly caused by the expansion in vv. 23b–25a.

27. NJPS offers the excellent translation, 'make all your enemies turn tail'; cf. II Sam. 22.41; Ps. 18.41.

28. *haṣṣir'āh*. Deut. 7.20; Jos. 24.12. The article is generic. G-K §126t. The word has traditionally been translated 'hornet', following the LXX's σφηκίας = wasp. However, the meaning is uncertain. NJPS renders it 'plague' on the basis of its Hebrew cognates. NEB, 'spread panic', is less convincing. L. Köhler, *ZAW* 54, 1936, p.291, argues for the meaning 'depression'.

31. *gēraštāmô*. Samar., LXX, Vulg., read first person which involves a repointing (cf. BH³).

33. The double *kî* makes for a clumsy translation. The first is best rendered as an explicative. Cf. Ex. 34.11ff.

2. Historical-Critical Problems

A. *Literary, Form-Critical, and Traditio-Historical Analysis*

1. *Title*

The complex of laws 20.22–23.33 has traditionally been entitled the 'Book of the Covenant' in the light of the reference in 24.3. The earlier literary critics, such as Riehm (*Einleitung*, §15), saw in the double reference in 24.3 to 'all the words of Yahweh' (*debarim*) and 'all the ordinances' (*mishpatim*) a clear distinction being made between the Decalogue and the Book of the Covenant. In modern times the distinction has been retained, although usually for different reasons.

2. Sources

At the height of the literary-critical period much attention was given in determining to what literary sources the Book of the Covenant was to be assigned. Wellhausen at first assigned it to the J source in contrast to the 'ethical Decalogue' of E (*Composition*, 1st ed. 1876), but retracted his opinion in 1889 in the light of Kuenen's criticism. Others attempted to assign the book to E (Jülicher). However, from the time of Bäntsch's monograph of 1892 a growing consensus had emerged that the Book of the Covenant was an older collection of laws which was independent of the usual critical sources. Usually it was thought that the secondary framework into which it had been placed was that of E.

3. Form criticism

In more recent times the interest has shifted away from the question of literary sources and focused rather on the question of analyzing the different forms in which the laws of the Book of the Covenant appear. Certainly the different literary forms within the Book of the Covenant had long been noticed. However, it was only after the rise of the form-critical method that the full implications of the stylistic observations were drawn. Literary critics, such as Bäntsch, tended to distinguish between the *mishpatim* (ordinances) in 21.1–22.16 and the *debarim* (words) in 20.22–26; 22.27–29; 23.10–16. The *mishpatim* had the casuistic form of case law, and regulated the secular affairs of an economic and social order. In contrast, the *debarim* were given in a direct, apodictic style, and dealt with matters of a cultic and moral nature. Bäntsch felt that the Deuteronomic redactor had combined the two forms of law.

A much more detailed study of the legal forms within the Book of the Covenant was undertaken by A. Jirku, *Das weltliche Recht* (1927). Jirku distinguished ten different formulations of legal material within the Pentateuch, only five of which occurred in the Book of the Covenant. The initial effect was that Jirku was able to refine Bäntsch's two larger categories into significant subheadings. He distinguished the singular and plural forms of the apodictic laws (22.17; 22.20; 22.27 and 22.21; cf. 20.18). He isolated the characteristic conditional formulation of the *mishpatim* (21.7–11; 21.14 etc.). Further, he recognized the important participial formulation (Ex. 21.12, 15, 16, 17) which was later to play such an important role in the discussion. Finally, he designated a 'when you . . .' formulation which appeared to combine elements of the casuistic with those of the apodictic (21.2; 22.24f., etc.). But Jirku's study proved in the end to be somewhat disappointing because it never got beyond the detailed analysis. In the same year A. Jepsen's book *Untersuchungen zum Bundesbuch* went far deeper into the analysis of certain of the forms, but again failed to rid itself of a predominantly literary approach. It did not prove to be qualitatively different from Bäntsch.

It remained for A. Alt to overcome this deficiency of his predecessors by establishing an organic connection between literary form and historical function. Alt was able to open up a new avenue into the study of Israelite law (*op. cit.*). In a sense Alt first simplified Jirku's classification by retaining only two major categories of casuistic and apodictic law. Then he suggested that the casuistic formulation of the conditional form had its setting in the secular case law of the Ancient Near East, whereas the apodictic formulation of the direct imperative arose out of the unique covenantal setting of early Israel. For Alt the subsequent fusion of legal material, far from being a late literary activity, reflected the institutional life of Israel during the early period of the Tribal League in which Israel appropriated common Ancient Near Eastern law from the Canaanites and brought it under the control of her unique covenantal law.

More recent form-critical work has tended to return to a more complex analysis of the forms than that proposed by Alt (cf. Gese, Gerstenberger [see p. 385 above], Kilian, Schulz). Particularly the need has been felt to distinguish the participial form from the imperative within the rubric of the apodictic. However, the basic insight of Alt in combining form and function in seeking to discover a *Sitz im Leben* for a law has provided a sound methodology for critical research.

4. Book of the Covenant and Sinai narrative

One of the most difficult questions, which has persisted from the beginning of critical scholarship turns on the relation of the Book of the Covenant to the Sinai narrative. It involves the large questions of form, unity, and historical setting of the Book of the Covenant. By and large, modern critical scholars have reached a consensus that the Book of the Covenant was not originally a part of the Sinai tradition, but only secondarily spliced into the narrative. The chief reasons for this conclusion are as follows:

(*a*) The Book of the Covenant interrupts the narrative sequence of 20.18–21; 20.1–17; 24.3, which is thought by many to be the original outline of events.

(*b*) The reference in 24.3 to the Book of the Covenant is redactional. The phrase 'all the words' which formed the basis for the covenant ceremony originally referred only to the Decalogue.

(*c*) The inner structure of the Book of the Covenant shows an independent history of development and redactional history distinct from the Sinai tradition.

(*d*) The content of the Book of the Covenant shows no original relation to the covenant, but points to a settled life long after Sinai.

In my opinion, these arguments are only valid in part. They tend to confuse the different levels in the history of the development of the text and on the basis of literary tension to draw historical implications which do not necessarily follow. For this reason the whole issue needs re-examination.

There are at least two distinct levels on which the problem of the present position of the Book of the Covenant has to be examined, namely, the literary and the oral level. If we turn first to the literary level, it is clear that the present position of the Book of the Covenant in the Exodus narrative shows many signs of redactional activity. First of all, the transition from the Sinai narrative in 20.22 shows every sign of being a secondary connection which was strongly influenced by Deuteronomy (*contra* Beyerlin, *Festschrift Hertzberg*, *op. cit.*, pp. 13f.). Again, the present order of the laws is due to a redactional ordering and is not original. This judgment is clearly sustained from the two different sorts of material which have been spliced together. The *mishpatim* begin in 21.1 with an obvious superscription. This collection continues through Ex. 22.16 in a strictly uniform style. The other material in a different style partly precedes and partly follows the *mishpatim*. Within the body of the *mishpatim* only once has there been a serious interpolation, namely in 21.12–17. This series of participial clauses was connected originally to 22.18, which is the only other example of this participial style within the Book of the Covenant. The conclusion to the Book of the Covenant, 23.20–33, is also a secondary parenetic addition and did not belong to the original layer of the laws. Finally, there is a series of Deuteronomic glosses which have entered into the text secondarily (22.20b, 23; 23.9b, etc.).

Now it is clear that this redactional activity on the literary level is highly significant in understanding the later stage in the development of the text. However, it is our contention that this evidence does not touch the heart of the issue at stake. The question as to whether the present position of the Book of the Covenant in relation to the Sinai narrative was a late creation of a redactor which was unknown to the original tradition cannot be decided on this level. The above evidence does not reveal the state of the tradition before the subsequent redactional activity.

It is, therefore, necessary to turn to the oral tradition in an effort to answer the question at issue. The strikingly different forms which are revealed in the two different blocks of material which make up the Book of the Covenant have already been mentioned. On the one hand, there is the section of *mishpatim* introduced in 21.1 and extending to 22.16. The style is uniformly casuistic. On the other hand, the rest of the material beginning at 22.17 has a predominantly apodictic style. We shall concentrate our attention first on this second block of material, and only later return to discuss the casuistic law of the *mishpatim*.

Several things can be said immediately in regard both to the form and function of this material. The form is dominated by the second person singular imperative. In addition, there is one block of a participial form in a series which deals with cases of capital punishment. Finally, there is the mixed form of 'when you . . .' which combines elements of apodictic and casuistic. The initial reaction to follow Alt's lead and see a connection with Israel's cult is supported by the content of the initial altar law as well as the final section on the festival calendar. The larger question as to whether the cult actually provided the original force in structuring the apodictic form can be set aside for the time being (cf. Gerstenberger). Rather the issue is whether there are signs pointing to a cultic *use* of the apodictic material in the Book of the Covenant.

First, a case has been made above for seeing an integral connection between the Book of the Covenant and the Mosaic office of the covenant mediator. Moreover, in this form of Sinai tradition the additional laws which were transmitted to Moses after the giving of the Decalogue formed the grounds for the covenant renewal ceremony. The apodictic form of the laws lent itself admirably to cultic recapitulation. God in the first person addresses his people as 'thou' (20.24). Likewise the content of the laws is permeated with covenant theology, a fact which is in striking contrast to the *mishpatim*. God has revealed his name to his people and therefore requires legitimate worship

(20.24). His name is not to be reviled (22.27). Sexual license is strictly forbidden (20.26; 22.18). Idolatry and the worship of other gods is punished by the ban (22.18). Moreover, the weak are to be protected (22.20) and justice is to be maintained (23.2, 8).

Again, there are secondary parenetic additions to this section of the Book of the Covenant which give further evidence of a cultic usage within a covenant context. Beyerlin (*op. cit.*) has made a good case for regarding the majority of these additions as pre-Deuteronomic in nature. For example, the command in 20.23 which is formulated in the plural sets the older altar law of 20.24–26 within the framework of Yahweh's personal address, and interprets the law as an instance which grows out of the first commandment. Conversely, 22.30 is again a parenetic addition, formulated in the plural with the first person for divine address. It summarizes the preceding commands by supplying a covenantal motivation: 'Men of holiness you shall be to me.' Again, there are several secondary references to the exodus from Egypt which serve to ground a command in Israel's redemptive history (23.15; cf. 23.9). Finally, the parallel use in Ex. 34.18ff. of the laws of the Book of the Covenant (23.10ff.) is another strong indication of an early place of this material within a cultic life of the covenant (cf. Ex. 34).

All these factors indicate a historical setting for this section of the Book of the Covenant in the period prior to the rise of the monarchy. It is evident that some of the material stems from a very early period which may reach back into the wilderness period. Many of the prohibitions are unconnected with a settled agricultural life. Nevertheless, the initial altar law (20.24–26) and the festival calendar clearly point to the period after the conquest. Rather than postulate an alleged Kadesh legislation, it seems more probable to reckon with old material which, however, received its role within the tradition after the land had been settled. The linguistic evidence would also confirm this early dating (cf. Cazelles, *op. cit.*, pp. 103ff.). The parenetic expansions would indicate that the material continued to be treasured in a covenant setting well into the period of the early monarchy.

The problems of the first half of the Book of the Covenant, namely the *mishpatim* of 21.1–22.16, are of a different kind. First of all, we have already noticed its consistent and fully uniform casuistic style. The introduction in 21.1 would also point to its being a unified collection. Moreover, there are no signs of redactional activity within the body of the material. The striking lack of parenetic expansion similar to the latter half of the Book of the Covenant would indicate that its function had been quite different. It also points to the conclusion that the latter half of the book functioned independently of the *mishpatim* and only at a later date were the *mishpatim* incorporated within the Book of the Covenant.

The content of the collection of *mishpatim* would confirm this conclusion. It is universally agreed that the *mishpatim* represented one of the earliest collections of legal material within the Bible. The striking parallels to the other Ancient Near Eastern legal collections has long since removed any doubt regarding its age. But even from internal evidence the early dating is assured. A detailed study of the economic, political, and religious background of the *mishpatim* as undertaken especially by Cazelles points unmistakably to the period immediately after the occupation of the land.

What can one say about the relation of the two parts of the Book of the Covenant? Certainly the lack of reference to a specific Hebrew covenant is noticeable in terms of both form and content. The formula describing the deity's role in the slave law (21.6) contains nothing unique to the covenant. Indeed, the Ancient Near Eastern parallels reveal it to be a common stereotype. These laws have their setting in case law and reflect the daily village life of an unsophisticated, agricultural people. Of course, this is not to suggest that there is nothing specifically Hebrew about these laws. The differences from the parallel Babylonian laws are often considerable (cf. below). The stamp of Hebrew national law is everywhere and affects the stringency and leniency of the different stipulations. The Israelite is to be handled differently from the stranger. Although the institutional setting of the *mishpatim* is distinct from the laws of the latter half of the Book, there are signs of an influence upon the cultic laws from the side of the casuistic. For example, the series of laws regarding cases of capital punishment in 21.12ff. has been modified in vv. 13f. to take account of the institution of asylum by means of a casuistic expansion. However, a direct influence in the reverse direction does not seem to appear. The specific Hebrew characteristics of the *mishpatim* stem more from a tribal consciousness than from a covenantal theology. However, one can argue (as does Greenberg) that the basic stance of the *mishpatim* reflects an attitude toward human life and property commensurate with covenant theology, though the influence is indirect and does not touch on the history of traditions problem.

The question of how the various parts of the Book of the Covenant were joined and at what time has occupied the attention of many commentators. Cazelles (p. 109) has argued that the author used the special 'When you . . .' form as a means of joining together the *mishpatim* of the first half with the religious, cultic laws of the second half. He points to 21.2, 13–14, 23; 22.21 and 23.4–5 as being the critical points of fusion where this form appears. However, this form is not applied with sufficient consistency, in my judgment, to sustain Cazelles' thesis. 23.4–5 interrupts two sections of apodictic laws within the second part of the Book and does not relate to the above issue. Again, the form in 21.13f. seems distinct from the other examples of the 'When you . . .' form.

In my opinion, the fusion of the two halves of the Book occurred at the literary stage. The *mishpatim* were joined to the cultic laws which already had received a place within the Sinai narrative. It is highly likely that the same redactor rearranged his material and gave the altar law its present leading position. However, without sufficient evidence it is idle to speculate on the shape of this material prior to its combination.

5. *Dating*

It is difficult to reach any definite conclusions as to the date at which the Book of the Covenant received its present form. Attempts to assign its composition to Moses have usually failed to take seriously the traditio-historical problems which have just been outlined. A method which simply cites at random Ancient Near Eastern material which is roughly parallel in content to the Book of the Covenant, while older in date, as proof of Mosaic authorship, has not come to grips with the complexity of the problem. Certain terminal points do emerge as an aid in establishing a rough date. The period following the settlement sets the *terminus a quo* for the dating of the second part of the Book of the Covenant. What can one say about a *terminus ad quem* for the addition of the *mishpatim*? Certainly it must be set considerably before the formation of the Deuteronomic laws. The parallel to the slave law in Deut. 15.12ff. indicates that the older *mishpatim* have been fully incorporated into a covenant theology and have long since been used parenetically. Considerable time must be reckoned with for such a development, even allowing for different circles of tradition to have been at work.

6. *Function of the Book*

Again the question must be raised respecting the purpose for which the Book of the Covenant was composed and by which circles within Israel. Our analysis has indicated that the final combining of the two parts of the Book stemmed from circles who sought to bring a collection of early national law more closely under the aegis of Israel's covenant theology. The same forces which we saw at work in shaping the two forms of the Sinai tradition into the one dominant pattern of the covenant renewal seem again to be at work in ordering the Book of the Covenant. As to the purpose toward which the composition of the Book of the Covenant was directed, both Jepsen and Cazelles have argued for seeing it as an effort to resist the inroads of Canaanite culture, particularly in the local sanctuaries. This theory is quite plausible, although admittedly it rests basically on general historical inference. Still the altar law is certainly polemical in tone and would support the theory of opposition toward foreign cults. In a positive sense the formation of the Book sought to bring all of Israel's early laws – many of which were adapted from the surrounding culture – closer in line with the central tenets of the Sinai tradition. For this reason the tradition assigned the authorship of the Book to Moses (20.22; 24.3ff.). It remained for the Deuteronomic period to achieve a complete theological amalgamation which did full justice to the covenant.

7. The order of the laws

Cf. especially CASSUTO, *Exodus*, pp.254ff.; DAUBE, *Studies in Biblical Law*, pp.85ff.; R. HASSE, 'Zur Systematik der zweiten Tafel der hethitischen Gesetze', *RIDA*, 3. série, 7, 1970, pp.51–54; HEINISCH, *Exodus*, pp.278ff.; V. WAGNER, *op. cit.*, *ZAW* 81, 1969, pp.176–182.

Much has been written on the problem of the present order of the laws within the Book of the Covenant. The detailed problems of sequence with the suggested rearrangements of recent commentators are discussed in the exposition. However, several general observations can be made on the larger problem. First, a close logical order is not to be found in the Book of the Covenant. If one were to apply Koschaker's distinction (cited by Jirku, *op. cit.*, p.13) between a *Gesetzeskodex* which represents a unified legal document of a codifier, and a *Rechtsbuch* which is simply a compilation of different laws, the Book of the Covenant certainly falls into the latter classification. Secondly, some of the present order seems to arise from a common Ancient Near Eastern tradition, as Daube, Cassuto and Wagner have demonstrated. However, the possibility that the present order has arisen in part through quite arbitrary reasons must constantly be reckoned with (cf. 21.37ff.). Thirdly, attempts to demonstrate a consistently theological order such as Rothstein's theory of an alleged parallelism to the Decalogue (*op. cit.*) have not succeeded in establishing themselves. Cf. also the theological attempt of H. Frey (see p. 464 below).

The attempts at outlining the laws vary considerably depending on the number and character of the subheadings employed. The repeated effort to introduce a systematic order such as van der Ploeg's three categories of 'religious, moral, and humane' have seldom proved illuminating (*op. cit.*, p. 30). In the end, a somewhat general outline may be the most helpful in providing the larger perspective.

1. 20.22–26. Altar law
2. 21.1–11. Slave law
3. 21.12–17. Capital offences
4. 21.18–36. Laws regulating bodily injuries
5. 21.37–22.16 (EVV 22.1–17). Damage to property
6. 22.17–30 (EVV 22.18–31). Miscellaneous religious and social stipulations
7. 23.1–9. Laws regulating court procedure
8. 23.10–19. Cultic calendar
9. 23.20–33. Parenetic epilogue

8. *Composition of the epilogue*

Ever since Wellhausen's penetrating analysis of this unit, the majority of literary critics (Dillmann, Bäntsch, Holzinger, Driver) have tended to agree that the section consists of an older source (usually assigned to E) into which two blocks of Deuteronomic material have been interpolated. Verses 20–22, 25b–31a make up the older source, 23–25aα, 31b–33 the addition. Signs of lack of unity were found in the repeated sending of a messenger (vv. 20, 23, cf. 27), and between an immediate and gradual conquest (vv. 27f., 29f.). More specifically vv. 23–25a were thought to interrupt the blessing of v. 22 which continues in 25b.

However, more recently less confidence has been attached to this 'solution' of the problems of composition chiefly because this literary analysis leaves some of the major problems unexplained. How is one to interpret the tremendous amount of repetition in the unit which does not corresponding to sources? Note for example: *šlḥ lᵉpānêkā,*

vv. 20, 27, 28; *grš*, vv. 28, 29, 30, 31; *mal'āk*, vv. 20, 23; list of Canaanite nations, vv. 23, 28; *'bd 'elōhêhem*, vv. 24, 25, 33. Again, how is one
to account for a parenetic style which runs through the whole unit?
What is the relation of these verses to Deut. 7? Finally, why is there
no reference to the preceding laws, if this is a homiletical conclusion
to the Book of the Covenant?

First of all, it is clear that the whole unit is parenetic in style. This
fact would speak against seeing just Deuteronomic interpolations
which imply a different style from the original souice. There are some
elements in the unit which are not typically Deuteronomic and would
suggest that an older level of tradition lay at the basis of the passage,
which was then reworked. One thinks especially of the 'messenger'
which is unknown to Deuteronomy. Some of the alleged tensions in
the passage are found paralleled elsewhere (cf. Deut. 7.2ff.), which
would point to a common oral tradition rather than a literary process
of fusion. The theory of a common oral tradition receives further
confirmation in a comparison of the unit with Deut. 7. The striking
similarities have long been noticed. Nevertheless, the differences
both in vocabulary, sequence, and conception would warn against
seeing a literary connection.

One of the most difficult problems arises from the complete
omission in vv. 20–32 of any mention of the preceding laws. This is all
the more surprising because the concluding parenetic section to the
Holiness Code (Lev. 26) and the Deuteronomic Code (Deut. 27)
make explicit reference to the previous legal material, as one would
naturally expect from a conclusion. It has been suggested by some
commentators (Smend, Eissfeldt) that the section is misplaced and
really belongs to the book of Numbers at a time just before the
departure from Sinai. But this solution continues to rest on a predominantly literary approach and has not been illuminating.

In my opinion, the passage was a sermon which once served a
homiletical purpose in Deuteronomistic circles in connection with
the occupation of the promised land. It is much closer to Deut. 7
than Deut. 26. It was placed in its present position as a conclusion to
the Book of the Covenant, but specifically because of the dominant
emphasis on the land which emerged in the last section (23.14ff.).
The section is not really related to the whole Book of the Covenant –
it is not a parenesis on obeying the law – but is a homily on the proper
use of the land.

		C H	Eshnunna	Middle Assyrian	Hittite	Sumerian	Miscellaneous
Ex. 21.2–6	Release of slave	§117, cf. §175–6					Edict of Ammisaduqa, §20–21
5f.		§282					
21.7–11	Stipulation on female slaves	§170–1, §119 cf. 147, 178			cf. §30, 31–33	Lipit-Ishtar §25–6	
21.12	Homicide (murder)		cf. §34	cf. C+G §3	§1–3, 5, 174 cf. 44		
21.13f.	Unintentional homicide	§207					
21.15, 17	Relation to parents	§195, §193					
21.16	Kidnapping	§14			§19–22		
21.18–19	Minor bodily injury	§206	§42–47		§7, 9–11, 13, 15		
21.20–21 26, 27	Injury to slaves	§199			§4, 8, 12, 14, 16		
21.22–23	Miscarriage	§209–214		§A 21, A 50–53	§17, 18	§1–2	
21.24–25	Serious bodily injury	§196, 197, 200	cf. 42			§Ur-Nammu 15–19 cf. §10	
21.28–31 35–37	Goring ox	§250, 251	§53–54				
21.32	Goring ox and slave	§252	§55				
21.33	Accidental death of animal				§75		

					C+G §8, §57–73, F §1 81–85	
21.37; 22.2–3	Theft of animal	§8, 22–23				
22.1	Housebreaking and stealing	§21, 25	§12–13		§93–95	
22.4	Grazing violations	§57, 58			§107	
22.4	Fire damage to field				§104–5	cf. §9
22.6–12	Stipulations for deposits	§120–126, 263, 266–267, 244 cf. §8–9	§36–37			
22.13, 14	Borrowing	cf. §245–6			cf. §74	cf. Lipit-Ishtar 34–7
22.15, 16	Seduction of un-engaged maiden		cf. §31	§A56		
22.17	Witchcraft	§2		§A47	cf. §170	
22.19	Sodomy				§187–8, 199–200	
23.1–3, 6–8	Court procedures	§3–5				Ur. N. §25'–26'

B. The Book of the Covenant and Ancient Near Eastern Parallels

H. BRONGERS, *Oud-Oosters en Bijbels˙recht*, Nijkerk 1960; H. CAZELLES, *Études sur le Code de l'Alliance*, Paris 1946, pp. 156ff.; S. A. COOK, *The Laws of Moses and the Code of Hammurabi*, London 1903; M. DAVID, 'The Codex Hammurabi and its Relation to the Provisions of Law in Exodus', *OTS* 7, 1950, pp. 149–78; Z. A. FALK, *Hebrew Law in Biblical Times*, Jerusalem 1964; J. J. FINKELSTEIN, 'Mishpat' (Hebrew), *Encyclopaedia Biblica* V, Jerusalem 1968, pp. 588ff.; H. FREY, 'Das Ineinander von Kirche und Welt im Licht der Komposition des Bundesbuches', *Wort und Dienst*, 1948, pp. 13ff.; M. GREENBERG, 'Some Postulates of Biblical Criminal Law', *Y. Kaufmann Jubilee Volume*, Jerusalem 1960, pp. 5ff.; J. E. HUESMAN, 'Exodus', *Jerome Bible Commentary*, ed. R. E. Brown, Englewood Cliffs, N.J. 1968, pp. 58ff.; E. JACOB, 'Die altassyrischen Gesetze und ihr Verhältnis zum Pentateuch', *Zeitschrift für vergleichende Rechtswissenschaft* 41, 1925, pp. 319–87; A. JEPSEN, *Untersuchungen zum Bundesbuch*, pp. 58ff.; A. JIRKU, *Altorientalischer Kommentar zum Alten Testament*, Leipzig 1923; *Das weltliche Recht im Alten Testament*, pp. 101ff.; P. KOSCHAKER, *Rechtsvergleichende Studien zum Gesetzgebung Hammurapis*, Leipzig 1917; B. LANDSBERGER, 'Die babylonische Termini für Gesetz und Recht', *Symbolae ad iura orientis pertinentes P. Koschaker*, Leiden 1939, pp. 219–34; D. H. Müller, *Die Gesetze Hammurabis und ihr Verhältnis zur Mosäischen Gesetzgebung sowie zu den XII Tafeln*, Wien 1903; S. PAUL, *Studies in the Book of the Covenant in the Light of Cuneiform and Biblical Law*, Leiden 1970.

The subject of the relation of the Old Testament laws, especially those of the Book of the Covenant, to the laws of the Ancient Near East has been continually investigated ever since the dramatic discovery of the Code of Hammurabi in December 1901 first brought the parallel material to light. Because the subject has been so thoroughly studied, especially in English, there seems little purpose in once again traversing familiar territory. This survey is, therefore, intended to be brief. However, a synopsis indicating the major areas of comparison is offered in order to encourage the reader to study the material for himself. The parallels which are offered vary greatly in character and at times the relation is remote or even antithetical. Obviously no one uniform pattern of relationship is being suggested by such a synopsis. The convenient collection of texts by Pritchard has been cited. However, the critical editions to the cuneiform texts can be found in the introduction of each section of laws. Important literature dealing with the relation of the Old Testament to the Ancient Near Eastern laws is listed above.

3. Old Testament Context

[20.22–26] *Altar Law*

The crucial issue in interpreting the altar law turns on the relation of the ancient law (vv. 24–26) to its present framework. Two major positions have emerged on this issue. On the one hand, the overwhelming number of critical commentaries (Bäntsch, Noth, Te Stroete, etc.) judge vv. 22–23 to be a later redactional framework, and therefore without exegetical significance. Their interest focuses exclusively on the history of religions implications to be found in the original ancient law itself. On the other hand, conservative commentaries (particularly B. Jacob, Cassuto) have attempted to deny all redactional activity, and to tie the altar law specifically to the Sinai account. In my judgment, neither of these two positions has successfully carried out the exegetical task. Certainly the critical commentaries are correct in discerning different levels within the present text; however, equally right is the insistence of the latter that the present position of the law within the Sinai narrative be taken with the utmost seriousness.

Verse 22 gives every sign of being a redactional link, perhaps from the Deuteronomist, which served to join the Book of the Covenant to the Sinai theophany. The parallel with Ex. 19.3 (cf. Deut. 29.1) is striking. The reference to Yahweh's speaking from heaven which is missing from the Exodus account of the theophany represents the subsequent Deuteronomic reflection on the event (4.36). It was not understood as a 'correction', nor was any contradiction between traditions apparently felt by the redactor. Verse 22 has the function of subsuming the whole Book of the Covenant within the framework of the Sinai theophany, and making explicit on the literary level a connection which was deeply rooted in oral tradition (cf. the introduction to the form-critical problems).

Verse 23 is also most probably redactional to the actual law which begins in v. 24. The plural formulation (22.21, 30), as well as the content of the command, would point in this direction. It remains debatable whether the MT offers the original reading (cf. textual notes); however, the fact that the present text reflects an ancient tradition is demonstrated by the versions. The MT is certainly not unintelligible. The first colon, read in the light of its OT parallels, is a prohibition against making gods 'in my company' (cf. Isa. 44.24; 63.3). The second colon makes a similar point in prohibiting the familiar 'gods of gold and silver'. The emphatic 'for you' makes it clear that the entire prohibition is directed against the making and the use of such in the support of worship. Verse 23, coming after the former connecting verses, provides a redactional perspective from which the altar law was now understood. The law which then follows in vv. 24–26 falls specifically under the rubric of the first command: 'You shall have no other gods before me.'

The law itself is extremely old and originally quite independent of its present setting. It stipulates that altars were to be made simply of sod upon which the two major types of offerings, the holocaust, and the 'peace' offering were performed. D. Conrad (*op. cit.*, p. 21ff.) has argued that the 'altars of earth' actually meant sun-dried brick altars. The archaeological evidence that sun-dried brick altars are so widespread in Palestine (e.g. Megiddo, Jericho, Shechem) must be weighed seriously (cf. Galling, *RGG*[3] I, cols. 253ff.). However, this general evidence is not decisive in deciding on the meaning of this passage. The omission of the actual Hebrew word for bricks (*lebēnîm*) remains a major deterrent to this interpretation. E. Robertson (*op. cit.*, pp. 18ff.) has made out a strong case for understanding the earthen altar as one made out of natural building material which would include both earth and field stone. Cf. also J. de Groot, *op. cit.*, p. 63.

These altars were not to be constructed at will, but only in those places where God had 'revealed his name' (cf. textual notes). This is to say, altars were set up only at places of legitimate worship. However, in spite of the efforts of conservative commentators (Jacob) to bring the command into line with later Jerusalem theology, the command presupposes a multiplicity of legitimate places of worship and is not a reference to Jerusalem alone.

When stone altars are built, they are not to be worked upon with tools or constructed of cut stone. No explicit reason for this prohibition is given in the law, but it is highly questionable whether the ready suggestion of a mythological background offers the real solution. Certainly for the later period the redactional framework in which the ancient law has been placed rules such an interpretation out of court. Conrad (*op. cit.*, pp. 43ff.) has argued well the case that the prohibition is not dictated by an aversion to undue luxury, but is specifically directed against the adopting of Canaanite altars which were made of finished stone. M. H. Wiener ('Altars', *op. cit.*, pp. 9ff.) has also pointed out that the finished stone altar was prohibited because of its frequent role in a ceremony of blood manipulation. The original law seems to reflect a semi-nomadic form of life and could even predate the settlement.

The prohibition to mount the altar on steps has also evoked much discussion. Noth (Exodus, *ad loc.*) follows the usual interpretation on the basis of v. 26b and sees the prohibition directed against the introduction of any sexual elements into Yahweh's cult. De Groot (*op. cit.*, p. 64) finds the emphasis of the law does not rest on the steps as such, but rather the law prohibits anyone from standing on the altar. Conrad (pp. 123ff.) offers a new interpretation with extensive backing from archaeological evidence. He argues that the motivation for the prohibition in vv. 26f. must be secondary to the original law, since clothing which covered one's nakedness to this extent, such as breeches, only came into Israel in the eighth century. The original prohibition must have had another concern which has been subsequently forgotten. From his study of the step altar he concludes that this construction was part of a 'high god' cult which was practised throughout the Ancient Near East and against which the prohibition was directed. He makes the further point that steps did enter into the Jerusalem cult through the *debîr* of the temple which he connects with the later worship of Yahweh as a 'high god'. In my judgment, the cultic background of the prohibition is impressive in Conrad's argument. However, his thesis of the secondary nature of v. 26b is not fully convincing.

The redactional history which is still reflected in the text indicates the early concern to bring heterogeneous material more closely into conformity with the dominant covenant theology. Nevertheless, no attempt was made to remove evidence of an earlier historical practice. The redactional pattern is so persistent as to make improbable the suggestion which would attribute the final state of the text to an unwitting inconsistency on the part of the editor.

[21.1–11] *Slave Law*

Verse 1 provides the only superscription in the Book of the Covenant. It appears to indicate that the *mishpatim* once formed a separate collection. The decisive change in style comes at 22.17, which indicates that the original collection extended only this far (cf. the literary analysis above). But by the time of the redaction of Ex. 24.3 the Sinai material had been divided into the 'words of Yahweh' = the Decalogue, and the *mishpatim* = the entire Book of the Covenant. The superscription serves to bestow the full divine authority upon these laws, which were laid upon Israel through the mediation of Moses, in addition to those spoken directly by God.

The laws seek to regulate the treatment of slaves within Israel.

The initial problem has to do with the term 'Hebrew slave'. What is meant? Recent study has made it clear that the term does not designate an ethnic group, but tended to be a perjorative designation of a legal or social status within the Ancient Near Eastern society of the second millennium. The Hebrews were the disadvantaged peoples, which were considered inferior and were employed in menial laboring jobs. In some thirty occurrences of the term in the Pentateuch the term applies to the 'Hebrews' either in contrast to Egyptians (Gen. 39.14; 41.12; 43.32; Ex. 1.15f.; 2.1, 6; 3.18) or in contrast to the Philistines (I Sam. 4.6; 13.3; 14.11, etc.). This would imply that a term which once was used to designate the outsider had been accepted by the Israelites, at least for a time. In the later period the Hebrew slave became identified with the Jewish slave (Jer. 34.9). But already in Ex. 21.2 the term was losing its wider connotation and becoming identified with the Israelite. The contrast lies between being a Hebrew and a 'foreigner' (21.8). In Israel a man could become a slave by being sold by his impoverished parents, or sold for theft (22.2), or by selling himself (Lev. 25.39).

The slave law is presented in classic casuistic style. The initial protasis is introduced by a *kî* clause. This is followed by the apodosis which offers the major stipulation of the law. Then the additional subheadings which fall under the law are introduced by an *'im* (if) clause (v. 4). The law stipulates the release of the Hebrew slave after six years of work. He is to go forth 'free', which is another disputed technical term, and apparently designated a social status free of bondage, but somewhat below that of the full citizen. If he came in single, he leaves single. If he entered married, he leaves married. If the master provided a wife, the woman stays with the master. The sense of cruel inconsistency between this stipulation and the concept of marriage found in Gen. 2.24 – not to speak of Matt. 19.6 – would finally destroy this law within Israel, but only after considerable passage of time. B. Jacob's attempt (*ad loc.*) to avoid the harshness of the law by recalling that the woman had been married without her free choice is far from a satisfactory response to the ethical issue.

However, there is another option offered in the law to the slave. Because of his love for his master and his family, he can renounce his right of ransom and remain a slave permanently. The term 'love' should not be romanticized. Still there is a recognition by the law that a subjective factor can decisively alter the legal situation. The slave shall declare his intention openly. Then he is 'brought to God' – this is a stereotyped term signifying to the nearest sanctuary for a judgment (cf. 22.8, 9) – and marked with a sign of servitude for the rest of his life. Later Jewish law which opposed slavery as degrading the image of God has an interesting theological interpretation of this law. 'The ear which heard at Sinai: "You are my servants" (Lev. 25.42), but nevertheless preferred subjection to men rather than God, deserves to be pierced' (*Tosephta*, Baba Kamma, VII, 5).

The case of the female slave is different in the Book of the Covenant and arises from the fact that she was, as an *'āmāh*, also the concubine of her master. She does not go free after six years (cf. Deut. 15.15), but becomes part of the larger family with stipulated rights which the law assures. Three critical examples are mentioned which might threaten her status: if she does not please her master who designated her (v. 8), if she is designated for his son (v. 9), if the master takes another wife (v. 10). In the first case, she must be ransomed by her own people. In the second case, she must be afforded the privileges of a daughter. In the third case, she must be maintained with her full marital rights.

[21.12–17] *Capital Offences*

The strikingly different form of these sentences from the previous series has long been noticed. Excepting vv. 13f., which provides an excursus on asylum, the stipulations begin with the participle which in Hebrew provides the verb and the subject of the sentence. It seems quite clear that this section once belonged with 22.17ff. These verses form the only major insertion of 'apodictic' law within the *mishpatim* section. The present position is significant and indicates another redactional effort to break down the sharp distinction within Israel between civil and religious law. Since the concept of covenant includes them both as comprising the will of God, the growing amalgamation between traditionally separate categories is an indication of persistent theological reflection on the nature of law and covenant.

The categorical judgment of death pronounced in this series points to a different origin for these laws from the case law which preceded. Usually the suggestion of a cultic background has been defended. Whether one can specify in more detail a specific institutional setting (Schulz) still remains open. The laws parallel in content certain of the Ten Commandments: murder, honoring parents, stealing, and thus mark those areas of life which are categorically prohibited within the covenant community.

The initial prohibition is against manslaughter, and does not take into consideration subjective motivation. This parallels the objective nature of the command against killing in the Decalogue, and is common to Ancient Near Eastern law. However, early within Israel the necessity for distinguishing between murder and accidental death was felt. The need was set over against the tribal background of blood vengeance, an institution which Israel had inherited from her pre-Yahwistic period. Whereas in other states, the growth of a powerful centralized state succeeded in replacing clan vengeance, within Israel the older clan law held on throughout the period of the early monarchy. The law of asylum was the first attempt to check the custom of blood vengeance (cf. Deut. 4.41ff.; 19.11ff.; Num. 35). Verse 13 formulates the exception to the death penalty in a casuistic style which differs slightly from that found in the *mishpatim*. God speaks in the first person and addresses Israel in the second person. The death of Joab (I Kings 2.28ff.) illustrates dramatically how the law was carried out.

Both vv. 15 and 17 describe an abuse directed against one's parents (Lev. 20.9; Deut. 21.18ff.). The Septuagint's rearrangement of the Massoretic sequence arises from a sense of logical order. With the term 'striking', a death blow is obviously not intended since this has already been covered by v. 12. Later Jewish law (cf. *Mekilta*) limited the law to a striking which produced a wound. The term 'curse' has a somewhat wider connotation than to imprecate, and includes other forms of dishonoring parents. The punishment is no less severe than cursing God (Lev. 24.16). There is a syntactical difficulty in v. 16 caused by the uncertainty of determining the antecedent of 'his hand'. It is hardly the hand of the buyer. Still if the seller is intended as antecedent, why would his selling be mentioned (cf. the elaborate discussion in the *Mekilta*)? The RSV offers the best solution by reading the conjunctions as alternatives ('whether . . . or').

[21.18–36] *Laws Regulating Bodily Injuries*

The first instance describes injury arising out of a dispute in which one man assaults another. The injury is such that he recovers in due time. The phrase 'walks around outside', even if with the help of a stick, indicates basic recovery since even a cripple could move around inside his house. The one inflicting the damage is required to compensate for his loss of time and for his care during recovery. The element of motivation does not play a role in a non-fatal injury (contrast with the *CH* §206).

In accordance with general Ancient Near Eastern law the case of bodily injury affecting a slave is dealt with in a separate paragraph. The discrepancy of judgment between the case of a free citizen and of a slave is striking. The very fact that a fatal beating is included in this section of bodily injury would imply that this case did not automatically fall under the stipulations of manslaughter in v. 12. This first impression is confirmed by the formulation of the judgment for a fatal beating: 'he shall surely be punished'. The Samar. text sensed the difficulty and substituted the familiar 'put to death'. Jewish interpreters (*Mekilta*, Rashi, Jacob, Cassuto) continue to defend the view that a death penalty is intended. The Talmud (San. 52b) specifies execution by beheading for such a crime. Cassuto makes much of the Old Testament's 'important innovation' in treating the slave as a human being. But in spite of these good intentions toward the Bible, such an interpretation cannot be maintained. The formula 'he will be punished' is strikingly vague and cannot be identified with the death penalty *per se*. Apparently the determination of the required penalty was left to the discretion of the judge. Any doubt as to whether a different standard from that used for the free citizen was applied to slaves is removed by the final motivation clause. The master is fully exonerated from injuring his slave 'because he is his property'. It is sad to realize that this verse continued to provide a warrant for the 'biblical teaching' on slavery throughout the middle of the nineteenth century in the United States.

Verse 22 begins in typical casuistic style and deals with the case of the injury of a pregnant woman which was inflicted in a brawl. Usually commentators have assumed that the injury was accidental. However, Daube (*op. cit.*, p. 108) has argued for an act of malicious intent (cf. Deut. 25.11f.). If there is no fatal, bodily injury involved, a fine is levied according to the practice common to the Ancient Near Eastern law. The rather imprecise directive 'whatever her husband demands' has troubled commentators, and even called forth emendations. Apparently a common procedure of assessment by an arbitrator was assumed. The order of the law which then followed is not in logical sequence, but arranged by association of the catchword 'harm' (cf. vv. 22, 23). The injuries which are then described are not related specifically to the case of miscarriage, but to bodily injury in general.

There follows then in the case of permanent injury the famous law of retaliation (*lex talionis*): 'life for life, eye for eye, tooth for tooth . . .' (cf. Lev. 24.18ff.; Deut. 19.21). The close parallel in the cuneiform laws (*CH* § 195ff.) as well as the late Punic inscription (cited by Alt, *op. cit.*, *KS* I, pp. 342ff.) demonstrates the common Near Eastern background of this formulation. The principle involved is that a like retribution for injury must be exacted. This stipulation has often been described as a 'primitive' element within the biblical law, and used as evidence for the crassness of Israel's early legislation. However, the recent comparative legal studies of J. J. Finkelstein (*op. cit.*, pp. 91ff.), followed by S. Paul (*op. cit.*, pp. 75ff.), have done much to undercut this position. Finkelstein pointed out that the introduction of the talionic rules in the Code of Hammurabi was an attempt to enlarge the scope of criminal law and embrace a class of delicts which had been previously treated as purely civil torts. The effect was to provide protection to members of inferior social standing and provide equality before the law from acts of physical violence. The wealthy could no longer escape punishment for their crime by simply paying a fine. Thus the principle of *lex talionis* marked an important advance in the history of law and was far from being a vestige from a primitive age.

As is well known, later Jewish midrash reinterpreted the law to mean that the monetary value of a life or an eye must be recompensed (*Mekilta*, B. Talmud, Baba Kamma, 83b–84a). B. Jacob's elaborate attempt (*Das zweite Buch Moses, ad loc.*) to defend this interpretation as the original meaning of the Old Testament text has been rejected by even as traditional a scholar as Cassuto. However, an impressive case has been mounted by Daube (*op. cit.*, pp. 102ff.) for holding that retaliation did include a concept of compensation from the outset. Certainly by the time of Lev. 24.18 the formula 'life for life' had been expanded to cover compensation for both homicide and the destruction of a beast. Daube's attempt to recognize in the law features from the setting of civil law brings an interesting dimension to the subject.

A clear example of the new Hebrew stamp on old material emerges in the law which follows, vv. 26f. If a master injures his slave, whether in a serious way with the loss of an eye, or with the insignificant loss of a tooth, the slave is to be freed. Obviously the law is seeking to prevent any kind of mistreatment toward slaves by lumping all injuries together without distinction. Moreover, the law is a good example of the new direction toward which the Old Testament was moving and casts into a different light the earlier, traditional slave law (vv. 20f.). A slave is not freed because of property damage, but because he is an oppressed human being. For this reason the loss of a tooth represents an act of abuse as well as the loss of an eye.

The law related to the goring ox offers a classic example of common Near Eastern legal tradition. Moreover, the fact that the sequence of the various cases is not arranged according to strict logic – one would expect v. 35 to precede v. 33 – would point to the common practice of placing a supplementary law at the end rather than by combining it with the older material (cf. Daube, *op. cit.*, p. 85). Both the *Code of Hammurabi* §§250ff. and the *Laws of Eshnunna* §§53f. make the distinction between an initial inflicting of damage and the destruction caused by a habitual gorer, known to be vicious. In the first case, the owner is not personally held responsible, although in the case of property loss, he must share the loss (*Eshnunna* §53). In the second case, he is responsible and must pay a fine. Similarly, the biblical law makes a distinction between the first offense and habitual goring. But the decisive difference lies in the severity of the biblical law respecting the latter case. If the owner has been warned and still does not prevent his beast from killing a person, he himself shall be put to death (22.29). As long ago as 1903 D. H. Müller (*op. cit.*, pp. 166ff.) argued that the stipulation of v. 29b was directed against the Ancient Near Eastern pattern of killing a person's son or daughter to compensate for a delict (*CH* §§229f.). In principle the loss of a human life in the Bible cannot be recompensed by a fine. Still the family of the deceased can have the right to temper the law with mercy and reduce the punishment to ransom (v. 30). Greenberg (*op. cit.*, pp. 13ff.) is confident that the stipulation to stone the goring ox (v. 28) is a clear reflection of the uniquely biblical perspective regarding the value of human life. Although this may be true for the later levels of biblical tradition, the initial stipulation seems to reflect a more primitive concept of guilt, as indicated by parallels from other cultures (Frazer, *Pausanias' Description of Greece*, London 1898, II, pp. 370ff., cited by Driver, p. 221).

Verses 33f. presents a slightly different case of injury to animals caused by leaving a pit uncovered. The owner is responsible to make the loss good. In the case of one animal injuring another, the sharing of loss is closely paralleled in the *Code of Hammurabi* §53.

[21.37–22.16] (EVV *22.1–17*) *Damage to Property*

Verse 37 introduces the case of the theft of an ox or a sheep and stipulates a monetary recompense of four or five times depending on the animal. There follow in vv. 2b and 3 two subcategories of theft which are closely related to the initial case and signalled by the particle *'im*. If a man is unable to make restitution, then he is sold in order to provide compensation for the thing stolen. If the stolen animal is found still alive in the possession of the thief, and therefore can be readily restored, the compensation for the theft is reduced to a twofold restitution.

As the MT now stands, another law with a different content is introduced in 22.1, which interrupts the sequence of the law relating to theft. It concerns the case of a thief who is killed in the act of housebreaking and offers a judgment on the legal consequences. This latter is clearly a literary interpolation and separates the subject of the subcategory in v. 3b from its antecedent in v. 37. Most of the modern translations (RSV, NEB) have felt it necessary to rearrange the order of the verses. Nevertheless, the NJPS and Cassuto have retained the sequence of the MT with some good reasons. Certainly, the stipulation in vv. 1–2 is an interpolation into the older law, but it appears to be a very early one and is done most probably with intent. The verses focus attention on the more important problem relating to theft, namely, the loss of life through a resultant act of violence. The law seeks to guard the lives of both parties involved. The householder is exonerated if he kills the intruder at night in the defense of his home. Conversely, the life of the thief is also protected by the law. If he is killed in plain daylight, then the slayer is held responsible for the homicide and is vulnerable to blood vengeance (Num. 35.27; Deut. 19.10). (Cf. Reventlow, *VT* 10, 1960, pp. 311ff.) To my knowledge no other law code seems to have a similar concern for the life of the thief! (For a comparison of Jewish and Roman law on theft, cf. Boaz Cohen, *Jewish and Roman Law* II, New York 1966, pp. 409ff.)

Damage from grazing and from burning are treated in vv. 4–5. The strikingly variant interpretation of these laws which are found in the commentaries arises from the two different meanings of the Hebrew root *b'r* (cf. textual notes). On the one hand, scholars such as

Hoffmann (ZAW 3, 1883, p. 122) and Bäntsch argue for retaining the common meaning of the verb 'to burn' and suggest that the original law had to do with a case of negligent burning of a neighbor's field. They contrast this case with the succeeding law which deals with accidental burning and carries a lighter fine. On the other hand, most other scholars have rejected this view and understand v. 4 to refer to a grazing violation and only v. 5 to fire damage. According to this latter position the confusion arose when the rare meaning of the homonym was misunderstood. The rabbinical commentators saw the philological problem, but introduced a further distinction in v. 4 between damage done by treading and a damage by eating (cf. Rashi). Some additional support for the second position comes from the parallel in the *Hittite Code* §§ 105–107 which, as Cassuto observes, juxtaposes grazing and fire damage. The force in this latter argument is slightly weakened by the fact that the reverse order appears in the Near Eastern code. Nevertheless, the second interpretation has the stronger position.

In the case of damage caused by grazing, if a portion of a neighbor's field is ruined from illegal grazing, the owner of the damaging animals shall still make restitution according to the usual yield of the field which was damaged. In other words, he shall simply make good the neighbor's loss. However, if all the neighbor's field is destroyed and one is therefore unable to determine what the yield of the field would have been, the offending party must compensate from the best of his own field. Rabbinic exegesis subsequently introduced precise distinctions between fields of inferior, average, or best quality (Baba Kamma 6b).

Verse 6–14 treat various cases of damage to deposited goods. Later Jewish interpretation introduced exact distinctions between the paid and unpaid bailee, but in the Old Testament the differentiation is simply on the grounds of the object deposited. Nevertheless, in v. 14 the case of hiring does enter, which is certainly a different category from that of a free deposit.

The first case in vv. 6f. has to do with a deposited article which is stolen. If the thief is caught, the case is simply resolved by requiring a double compensation from the offending party. If the thief is not caught, then the bailee must declare his innocence from the charge of misappropriation before the judge. (The older language 'before God' = at the sanctuary, has been retained.) The owner of the stolen article must then accept the oath in lieu of the object. Verse 8 appears to be an extension of the principle of v. 7 and includes the case of misappropriation by the bailee. Whenever a dispute regarding ownership of an article arises, the case is decided by the judge and the loser must make double restitution. The exact procedure of adjudication is not explained, but rather assumed to be known. The strongly rational tones of the legal procedure speak against the assumption that it was done by means of the old ordeal (Num. 5).

Verses 9–12 treat the case of an injury to an animal which has been deposited for safekeeping. If no one has witnessed the accident, the bailee declares his innocence before a judge, and is exonerated, the reasoning being that it lay outside his area of responsibility. However, if the animal were stolen, he is considered responsible and must make full restitution. He is also not held responsible for damage caused by wild animals, but proof of such is required.

Naturally more responsibility lies with the man who takes the initiative in borrowing an animal from his neighbor. Then in the case of accidental injury, he must make good, the exception being if the owner were present. The latter stipulation implies that the injury was not from neglect and lay beyond the control of the borrower. The last clause of v. 14b is more difficult to explain (cf. textual notes). Some commentators have interpreted the sentence as introducing a completely new subject, namely, the case of an injury to an animal caused by the hired employee. However, it is more natural to interpret the verse as an extension of the previous law. The animal in this case was hired, not borrowed. Since the risk of injury is included in the transaction by its very nature, the ensuing damage must be accepted as a loss by the owner of the rented animal. The difficulty of this interpretation remains, however, the enormous discrepancy between the small profit gained from hiring and the large loss inflicted from injury.

The final case involves the seduction of a maiden who is not yet engaged. Commentators have long since pointed out that such an injury has been included in the Book of the Covenant under the section on property damage. Indeed, this does appear to be a traditional sequence. However, the content of the Hebrew law shows remarkable transformation in respect to the other Ancient Near Eastern codes. First, no distinction is made between the woman's status, whether free or slave. Of course, if the woman had been engaged, this would have been considered adultery, and have required the death penalty (Deut. 22.23ff.). That the seduction of an unengaged maiden was no longer simply viewed as property damage is evident from the stipulation that the seducer must marry the girl. In the Old Testament – in distinction from the New Testament – the laws regulating sexual relationship focus, not so much on condemning pre-marital intercourse as such, but on requiring full responsibility from the male as a consequence of his act. Promiscuity is condemned for its failure to stand by the exploited person which is required in marriage. Only if the father of the girl opposes the marriage – again an ethical note is sounded – is a money settlement substituted to compensate for the wrong done. The bride price (*mōhar*) is infrequently mentioned in the Old Testament and confined to early passages (Gen. 34.12; I Sam. 18.25). A cognate term occurs in Ugaritic. Much which is known about its use stems from inferences from modern Arabic practice which has retained an apparently parallel custom. It is not a dowry but a price paid to the family for the woman who is to become a wife. Because of its minor role in the Old Testament, there is reason to suspect that it dropped out of later practice, but evidence for confirmation of such a thesis is missing.

[22.17–30] *Miscellaneous Religious and Social Statutes*
Verse 17 marks the beginning of the second half of the Book of the Covenant. The casuistic style of the *mishpatim* ends in v. 16 and does not recur in the latter section. The section which follows, often called the *debarim* (words) in contrast to the *mishpatim*, reveals a variety of styles. There is the second person singular imperative (v. 17), second person plural imperative (v. 21), the participle (v. 18), and the 'when you . . .' style (v. 22).

The content of the first paragraph is varied. The modern attempts to separate neatly between the ethical, cultic, and social breaks down completely and indicates that such categories were obviously foreign to Israel. Nevertheless, there is some discernible order in this paragraph, which gives evidence of design. Verses 17–19 deal with three violations which call forth the death sentence: magic, sodomy, and idolatry. Verses 20–26 prohibit different forms of oppression of the poor and the weak. Verses 27–30 appear to be holiness laws with a less unified content.

[17] 'You shall not allow a sorceress to live.' The term 'not allow to live' is a technical term for the ban (Num. 31.15; Deut. 20.16; I Sam. 27.9–11). Nevertheless, it does not seem to be identical with the usual formula of *môṭ yûmāṭ* (surely die). The scope of the former appears wider and includes extermination out of the land. The feminine form 'sorceress' would indicate the frequency with which the practice was identified with women, but the masculine form also occurs. Witchcraft was a form of mantic practice identified with foreign paganism (Deut. 18.12ff.; II Kings 9.22) and a recurrent threat to Israel's worship of Yahweh. It appears from the earliest to the latest period (Jer. 27.9; Ezek. 13.9). Deut. 18.9ff. offers the fullest catalogue of different forms of witchcraft. However, it remains a question how precisely the distinctions between soothsaying, augury, sorcery, etc. were understood in Israel. From the beginning all such practices were outlawed as an 'abomination' which violated the holiness of the people of God. Interestingly enough, in Deuteronomy the office of true prophet is set over against divination and sorcery. The sorcerer laid claim to a power (Isa. 47.9) both of interpreting and controlling the future which opposed the authority of God (Isa. 47.12f.). The sorcerer and mantic were under constant attack and ridicule by the prophets (Isa. 8.18ff.; Micah 5.12). The classic biblical narrative is, of course, the story of Saul and the witch of Endor (I Sam. 28).

[18] Bestiality was always regarded in Israel as a shameful perversion (Lev. 18.23; 20.15f.; Deut. 27.21). Cassuto points out the magical background of the practice, both in Ugarit and Babylon. Hittite law only forbade the practice with certain animals (§§ 187, 188, 199, 200).

[19] (Cf. the textual notes.) The exclusive claim of Yahweh even in this early period is abundantly clear from this law (cf. the discussion of the First Commandment). The once popular phrase 'henotheism' gives a completely inadequate impression of the exclusiveness demanded by the law of Israel. The formulation of II Isaiah is not very different in kind (44.24; 45.21, etc.). The fact that sacrifice to other gods often involved child sacrifice (Deut. 12.31) would further indicate the close connection of this verse in content with the preceding two.

[20–26] These verses treat of various forms of oppression against the poor and weak. The stranger (gēr) was vulnerable to wrong-doing because he lacked the protection of his clan. The widow and the orphan were exposed to violence without the support of husband and father. It is characteristic of the Old Testament to reveal a particularly intense concern for the poor. The style shifts to the first person as God places himself directly in the role of special protector. The vicious nature of money-lending is more than clear from the other references to the practice (cf. Lev. 25.35–37; Deut. 23.20–21; I Sam. 22.2; II Kings 4.1; Ps. 109.11). Rashi points out that the root of 'interest' is *nšk*, meaning 'to bite', and he comments: 'it resembles the bite of a snake . . . inflicting a small wound in a person's foot which he does not feel at first, but all at once it swells, and distends the whole body up to the top of his head. So it is with interest.'

The law permitted a pledge to be taken as security under certain conditions (Deut. 24.17; Amos 2.8; Job 22.6; 24.3; Prov. 20.16), but sought to prevent its abuse. By forcing a creditor to restore a poor man's garment every night, it erected a hindrance to the practice by the fact of sheer inconvenience. However, the actual motivation in the law goes beyond the legal stipulation and appeals to the compassion of the creditor.

The grounds for the prohibition of this paragraph are threefold: (i) Israel knows from her own experience what it is like to be a stranger (v. 20). (ii) It belongs to the nature of God that he is compassionate (v. 26). (iii) The fact of a covenant with God ('my people', v. 24) rules out exploitation with this relationship.

[27–30] These verses treat a variety of topics such as are found together in the Holiness Code (Lev. 17ff.). Verse 27 links together the prohibition to revile God or the ruler (Lev. 24.15f.). Clearly the authority of the ruler in the Old Testament was seen as stemming from God. The theological issue involved in this juxtaposition has traditionally been discussed in reference to the Fifth Commandment (Ex. 20.12). The exact meaning of the term *nāśî'* (ruler) is debated. The word is of quite frequent occurrence, but almost entirely confined to the Priestly source or the book of Ezekiel. Noth (*Das System der zwölf Stämme Israels*, Stuttgart 1930, pp. 151ff.) concluded that the term referred to a representative of the tribe in the amphictyony. Others have argued that the *nāśî'* designated a single over-all ruler, perhaps even the king (cf. van der Ploeg, *RB* 57, 1950, pp. 40ff., and Speiser, *op. cit.*).

The exact meaning of v. 28a remains somewhat obscure by virtue of the philological difficulty (cf. textual notes). In general, the law has to do with the offering of the first fruits, specifically of the vineyard, but with a different vocabulary from that in the more familiar passages (Lev. 23.9ff.; Deut. 26.1ff.). For v. 28b see the discussion in Ex. 13.1f. on the command to offer the first-born of sons as well as animals. The exact means by which the 'giving' was to be done is not explained, but the same verb is used for both men and animals, which lies at the heart of the problem. The firstling is given on the eighth day, before which time it is not acceptable (Lev. 22.27).

Verse 30 has often been eliminated as secondary because of its plural form. However, the content of the law gives an impression of antiquity. A more serious objection to its originality is recorded by Heinisch and Cazelles. Does not Ex. 21.35f. allow an ox killed by another ox to be used? One could reply that 21.35 does not speak of eating. Perhaps only its skin was used. Still one should hesitate to resort to any easy harmonizing which rests on insufficient evidence. How the tension between these verses was resolved is not fully clear. However, this problem seems hardly reason for eliminating v. 30 as secondary. Nor should such tension seem surprising in such a collection of laws. A beast which is torn in the field is prohibited from being eaten because its blood has not been properly drained (Deut. 12.27), but according to Lev. 7.24 a torn animal could be used in every way except eating. The appeal to Israel's holiness is reminiscent of the Holiness Code (Lev. 19.2).

[23.1–9] *Laws Regulating Court Procedure*

Both in terms of form and content vv. 4–5 interrupt a series of laws in vv. 1–3, 6–9 which prohibit various abuses connected with the court. The style of these verses is the 'when you . . .' style in contrast to the prohibitive style of vv. 1–3, 6–9. The use of *kî* and *'ô* only occurs in these verses outside the *mishpatim* section. Verses 4f. deal with conduct toward one's enemy and are not connected with court procedure. Various suggestions have been offered to explain the present form of the text which was brought about by the interpolation. Cassuto's explanation is purely homiletical and without descriptive value. B. Jacob is frank in his inability to offer any reason ('a puzzle'). Noth argues that the term 'enemy' means one with whom one is having a dispute at law and is, therefore, related to the present context. H. Frey, although not attempting a historical explanation as to the origin of the interpolation, sees an order in the present text. He argues that vv. 4–5 do not simply interrupt a closely knit unit. Rather, vv. 1–3 relate primarily to the role of the witness, whereas vv. 6–9 are directed to the judge. Verses 4–5 – whatever the historical reasons for the present position might be – expand the subject of justice in the court for the poor and the stranger to include one's exposed enemy. Indeed, the verses illustrate the extent of the demand by choosing an example lying outside of the court and one which is chiefly under the control of the conscience. The shift from the prohibitive style into a positive formulation points to the parenetic style of the homily.

Verses 1–3 explore with amazing penetration the various temptations which confront a witness in ancient Israel. First, he has the responsibility to guard against dissimulating uncontrolled rumours which destroy a man's reputation and prejudice a case without evidence (Ex. 20.16). Again, the witness is warned against forming 'connections' with the wicked which force him to testify falsely. Clearly the Hebrew law is cognizant of the economic, social, and political pressures which are exercised upon one who has allowed himself to become involved with special interest groups. (On the expression 'set your hand with', cf. II Kings 15.19; Jer. 26.24; Job 30.2).

Verse 2 presents a variety of problems in respect to its original formulation (cf. textual notes). The term *rabbîm* appears in late Hebrew with the meaning of 'the mighty', and designates a high office in Job 35.9, II Chron. 14.10. If one accepts this meaning for v. 2, as does the *NJPS*, an excellent contrast is achieved with the 'humble' of v. 3. Moreover, this was probably the way in which the passage was later understood. However, it is philologically improbable that this was the original sense of the word. Rather, the verse warns against 'following after' the majority to do evil (I Kings 16.21). A similar stipulation is repeated in the second colon with actual reference to giving testimony which distorts the evidence by being swayed by the majority opinion. In the later rabbinical courts the youngest judge was asked to express his opinion first in order not to be influenced by the majority (M. San. 4.2; Rashi). In v. 3 commentators have been tempted to emend the text and read: you shall not show preference to 'a great man' instead of 'a poor man'. The present MT – whether original or not – shows an awareness of the more subtle danger of reverse prejudice in court which is equally a threat to justice. Lev. 19.15 offers the closest parallel: 'You shall not be partial to the poor or defer to the great.'

Deut. 22.1ff. expands at more length on being responsible to one's brother in restoring a lost animal or aiding one in difficulty, even when it relates to action which is unobserved. B. Jacob draws attention quite correctly to the parallel in the Hittite laws (§45), which is a good reminder that such a sense of fairness is not confined to

Israel (cf. the textual notes for an explanation of the last few words).

Verses 6–8 are not really different in kind from vv. 1–3. Nevertheless, Frey has a point in seeing a shift which would be more appropriate in addressing the judge. He is not to bend justice in order to rob a poor man of his right. He is to distance himself from the lie which is the great enemy of the innocent (cf. I Kings 21.13ff.). Again, the bribe, the perennial symbol of personal corruption, is denounced. Finally v. 9 voices the familiar concern over the stranger who is especially vulnerable to acts of violence and injustice by his isolated position. The motivation clause which suddenly shifts to the plural form once again reminds Israel of her Egyptian bondage and points to a parenetic use of this material at some stage of its development.

[23.10–19] *The Cultic Calendar*

The law regarding the sabbath year (cf. Deut. 15.1ff.; Lev. 25.2ff.) and the sabbath day begins this section, which is primarily cultic in content. On the seventh year no crop is to be sown, but the land is allowed to lie fallow and rest. The two verbs in v. 11, *šmṭ* ('let drop', 'remit'), and *nṭš* ('leave', 'abandon'), are almost synonymous. Elsewhere *šᵉmiṭṭāh* becomes a technical term for remission of debt. It is not clear in this law whether the whole land simultaneously celebrated the sabbath year (cf. Lev. 25.2ff.) or whether it varied according to individual properties. It is difficult to image how the former alternative would have worked out in practice.

The original motivation for the sabbatical year has been much discussed. Whether there could have once been a mythical undertone or whether it arose from some agricultural interest, the law in Israel respecting the land was given a theological explanation. At times, particularly in the Priestly writings, the motivation was to preserve the thought of Yahweh's ownership of the land which he simply lent to Israel for use (cf. von Rad, 'The Promised Land and Yahweh's Land', *Problem of the Hexateuch*, pp. 79ff.). In Exodus the social motivation comes to the fore. Whatever grows upon the land is for the poor and the wildlife. The motif of rest and wild animals has led Frey to see the imagery of a 'return of paradise'. However, the thought seems to be far removed from the text at this stage. The concern that the domestic animals rest as well as the slaves and day workers occurs also in the Decalogue. It seems to stem from a genuine humanitarian feeling of sympathy for the underling and creature alike, which in time received a theological support from the covenant. Certainly this emphasis lay at the heart of the Deuteronomic emphasis that 'all Israel' celebrate the sabbath together.

Verse 13, which again returns to the second person plural form and the first person direct address of God, gives the impression of being a homiletical conclusion to the collection. But since it is akin in style to several other homiletical comments within the corpus of laws, such as 22.30; 23.9b, it probably should not be regarded as evidence that the laws originally ended at v. 12. The second part of the verse, which is another variation on a familiar theme, is also more of a parenetic gloss than a formal conclusion.

[14–19] Cf. the classic discussion in Wellhausen, *Prolegomena to the History of Israel*, pp. 83ff., and the more recent discussion of R. de Vaux, *Ancient Israel*, pp. 470ff.; H.-J. Kraus, *Worship in Israel*, pp. 26ff. The relation to Ex. 34 will be discussed in the commentary on that chapter.

Following the references to the sabbath rest, the cultic calendar turns to the three annual pilgrimages, in a section which gives every sign of being originally in independent unit. The discussion of these verses at least for the last hundred years has focused on problems connected with the reconstructing of Israel's cultic history. The reader is referred to the bibliography for an introduction into these larger issues which go beyond the scope of a commentary. It is generally agreed that the calendar in Ex. 23 (with the parallel in Ex. 34) represents the earliest form of the tradition and precedes the later calendars of Deut. 16, Lev. 23, and Num. 28f.

The original calendar in vv. 14–16 is given in the form of the second person singular for the addressee and the first person singular for the addressor. Verse 17 summarizes the law and shifts to a third person. Two additional laws have been attached as an appendix in vv. 18–19. The cultic background to the calendar is immediately apparent. Three times in the year every male was to appear before God at a sanctuary. As is clear from the Gezer calendar (*ANET²*, p. 320), the year was divided into agricultural seasons in early Palestine. (On the whole subject see S. Talmon, *JAOS* 83, 1963, pp. 177ff.) The three festivals in Ex. 23 are likewise attached to annual agricultural periods as occasions for the worship of Yahweh. The 'festival of unleavened bread' (*hammaṣṣōṯ*) for seven days in the month of Abib (Ex. 13.4) marked the beginning of the barley harvest in the spring, either late April or early May. The 'festival of harvest' (*haqqāṣîr*), usually called 'festival of weeks' (*šeḇûʿōṯ* – Deut. 16.9), celebrated the completion of the grain harvest in June. The 'festival of ingathering' (*hā'āsīp̱*) occurred at the completion of the grape and olive season in September at the end of the year.

However, already at this earliest stage in the development of the tradition the agricultural festivals had begun to be attached to historical events within the life of Israel. The feast of unleavened bread commemorated the exodus from Egypt (Ex. 13.3ff.; Deut. 16.3, etc.). One strand of the tradition connects the use of unleavened bread with the haste of the departure from Egypt which gave no time for leavening (Ex. 12.34, 39). Because this motivation appears secondary, scholars have speculated, without reaching a consensus, on the original significance of leaven. Whatever it may have been, it entered the tradition as an inherited item and was given a fresh significance. Of importance is the fact that no explicit mention of the passover is made in Ex. 23 (cf. 34.25). This omission has often been interpreted as indicating a separate development of the traditions of passover and unleavened bread until the period of Deuteronomy (cf. the discussion on ch. 12). Kraus (*op. cit.*, pp. 48ff.) summarizes the process of adaptation of the festival of unleavened bread from the Canaanites under three headings: (i) the whole celebration is directed toward Yahweh, in distinction from any fertility deity; (ii) the festival is centralized; (iii) the festival has been historicized. There would be a broad consensus respecting the first and third points. However, the second point respecting centralization remains highly debatable.

The festival of harvest was set by Deut. 16.9 seven weeks after the sickle was first put to the grain, hence the name 'Pentecost'. The festival reckons with the wheat harvest some seven weeks after the barley harvest. Again some commentators have sought to find an original Canaanite significance in the seven-week period with reference to Ugarit (cf. Kraus, p. 57), but without sufficient evidence. Within the Old Testament itself no historical significance was explicitly attached to this festival, but later Jewish tradition regarded it as commemorating the giving of the law in the third month (cf. Ex. 19.1; II Chron. 15.10ff.).

The festival of ingathering marked the completion of the fruit harvest, and is a festival shared by most agricultural societies (Deut. 16.13). Verse 16 specifies the time of the festival as the 'going out of the year', which has raised several problems. First, the question of the order of the year has been much discussed. It is generally assumed by critical scholars that the early Hebrew year began in the autumn and only at a later period under Babylonian influence was the new year set in the spring (cf. the discussion by de Vaux, *Ancient Israel*, pp. 190ff.). Still other scholars continue to defend two different calendars, a liturgical and a civil, and deny a historical development (Jacob, Cassuto). However interpreted, Ex. 23.16 clearly sets the new year in the fall. Secondly, the question has been raised – especially since Mowinckel – whether there is a connection between the fall festival of ingathering and a New Year's celebration. The festival is also called in the Old Testament a 'feast of tabernacles'. This would seem to point to an agricultural celebration which took place in specially prepared huts and which in the later tradition was then explained in terms of the wilderness tradition (Lev. 23.40ff.). The evidence for a New Year's festival in connection with the autumn festival remains scanty, and at best rests on cumulative rather than direct evidence culled from the total picture of Israel's early cult (cf. Kraus, *op. cit.*, pp. 61ff., for a full bibliography).

Verse 18 prohibits the offering of blood with leaven and the holding over of the fat of the festival until morning. The central issue is whether this verse should be understood in connection with the passover or is to be generally taken for any offering. The traditional view has followed the first option. Already the Targum of Onkelos made the connection explicit: 'Thou shalt not offer with unleavened bread the blood of my passover.' The view is still defended by B. Jacob. However, even Cassuto acknowledges that 'according to the plain meaning of the text' the reference is not specifically to the passover sacrifice. Dillmann, followed by most critical scholars, is probably correct in defending the second option and seeing in v. 18 a general stipulation. Verse 19 also seems to fit into this pattern. Nevertheless, it is hardly by accident that this general stipulation, which had no specific relation to the passover festival, should be joined to the calendar at this point. It is certainly possible that the editor sought to establish a connection between unleavened bread and passover.

The final prohibition in v. 19b (cf. 34.26; Deut. 14.21) has long interested commentators and called forth various explanations (cf. Kalisch, *Exodus, ad loc.*, and Kosmala, *ASTI* 1, 1962, pp. 50ff., for the interesting history of interpretation). New light has been thrown on the text by the Ugaritic parallel in 'The Gods Fair and Beautiful'. The text reads as follows: *ṭb(ḫ g)d bḥlb annḫ bḥmat*, 'cook a kid in milk, a lamb(?) in butter'. Unfortunately, the text is broken in one place and must be restored. Although the reconstruction of Virolleaud is about the only one possible, the argument is not fully free of circular reasoning. Nevertheless, even if the difficulties are admitted, the probability that this is indeed a parallel text is high. Accordingly, the biblical prohibition was directed specifically against a Canaanite ceremony, which was probably connected with its fertility cult.

[23.20–32]   *Epilogue*

This passage which concludes the Book of the Covenant is strikingly different in its style from that which precedes. The unit consists of a series of promises and warnings relating to the possession of the land. In both its form and content this homily is closely parallel to Deut. 7. The passage is characterized by a somewhat loose, repetitive style. Nevertheless, there is a certain discernible structure to its composition. Verses 20–22 move from an unconditional promise to a warning, and then to a conditional promise. Verses 23–26 again go from an unconditional promise to imperatives, and then return to a conditional promise. Finally, vv. 27–32 consist almost entirely of unconditional promises (vv. 27–31) with a concluding imperative.

What has puzzled commentators is the fact that the passage does not take notice of the laws which precede. In contrast to the homiletical conclusion of the Holiness Code and the laws of Deuteronomy, vv. 20ff. do not admonish obedience to these laws. Rather, when obedience is called for it has to do with heeding the instructions of the divine messenger which will be given. The passage returns to the theme of the promised land – note the frequency of the term – which has not been met with since Ex. 13.5 (cf. 3.8, 17; 6.4, 8, etc.). This has led commentators to suggest that the passage is not really a conclusion at all, but a misplaced fragment.

While it can be readily granted that the passage in its present position is redactional and may well have functioned in a different setting originally, it is fundamental to its proper understanding that its present role be not overlooked. It is hardly accidental that this passage concludes the Book of the Covenant and separates the laws from the sealing of the covenant in ch. 24. Actually the homily is related to only one part of the material which precedes, namely to the laws in 23.14ff., which are concerned with the feasts within the land. Following a common biblical principle of association, the editor has added a theological interpretation, not just to the laws, but specifically to the law of the land. In these few verses he deals with the possession of the land, the extent of the land, the blessing of the land, and the purity of the land. The dialectical movement between the unconditional and conditional promises is of great significance and forms a compatible addition to the introduction of the legal material in the initial theophany of ch. 19. Israel is promised unconditionally a special role within God's economy, while at the same time placed under a covenant of obedience. The repeated attempts of recent years to fit the Sinai material into the Hittite treaty pattern has consistently failed to reckon with this essential biblical movement, which is without parallel in the Ancient Near Eastern treaties.

20. 'Behold, I send a messenger before you . . .'. A heavenly messenger or angel is intended, as is clear from the parallel passages (32.34; 33.2; Num. 20.16; cf. Ex. 14.19; Isa. 63.9; Mal. 3.1). Kalisch (*Exodus*, 1855) appears to have made one of the last attempts to identify the messenger with Moses, which certainly lacks a warrant. Perhaps the most eloquent interpretation within this broad tradition is Maimonides (*Guide* II. 34). He draws a parallel between 23.20 and Deut. 18.18 and finds in the warning, 'Beware of him and obey his voice', evidence that both passages speak of a prophet. The tradition of the guiding angel is clearly pre-Deuteronomic and indicates that an older tradition has been employed for the later homily. Moreover, the virtual identification of the angel with God himself – 'My name is in him' – is also a feature common to the earlier sources (Gen. 20.15ff.; Judg. 6.11ff.). (Cf. *TWNT* I, pp. 72f. = *TDNT* I, pp. 74ff., for a bibliography on the subject of the 'messenger of God'.)

The author makes use of the traditional vocabulary of the holy war in describing the possession of the land. In v. 27 God sends his terror before him and throws the enemy into panic. No one is able to stand before them. Verses 29f. then introduce quite a different theme, namely, that the possession of the land will be only a gradual one. Commentators have rightly recognized that a theological explanation is being offered to explain why in fact the conquest did not succeed in eradicating the Canaanite population (cf. Deut. 7.22; Josh. 13.1–7; Judg. 2.1ff.; 3.1ff.; II Kings 17.18f.; Wisd. 12.3–10). The tension caused by this note on the holy war motifs did not arise from a later literary interpolation, but had long since been combined in the oral tradition and hardly recognized as a problem.

The geographical picture (v. 31) is an ideal projection which the tradition attributed to the glorious reign of Solomon (I Kings 4.21).

By the *Yam Sûp* (Reed Sea) the Gulf of Aqaba is undoubtedly meant as in I Kings 9.26 and elsewhere. The Sea of the Philistines is naturally the Mediterranean Sea and 'the river' is the Euphrates.

4. History of Exegesis and Theological Reflection

THOMAS AQUINAS, *Summa Theologica*, Prima Secundae 98–105, 'The Old Law', Blackfriars ed., London and New York, vol. 29, 1969; B. COHEN, *Jewish and Roman Law*, 2 vols., New York 1966, critically reviewed in *JBL* 86, 1967, pp. 238ff.; P. FAIRBAIRN, *The Revelation of Law in Scripture*, Edinburgh 1868; J. J. FINKELSTEIN, 'The Goring Ox. Some Historical Perspectives on Deodands, Forfeitures, Wrongful Death, and the Western Notion of Sovereignty', *Temple Law Quarterly* 46, 1973, pp. 169–290; L. FINKELSTEIN, *The Pharisees*[3], New York 1962; I. HEINEMANN, *Philons griechische und jüdische Bildung*, Breslau 1932; M. HYAMSON, ed., *Mosaicarum et Romanarum Legum Collatio*, London 1913; MAIMONIDES, *Guide for the Perplexed*, trans. M. Friedländer, London 1904, Part III, chs. 34ff.; J. D. MICHAELIS, *Commentaries on the Laws of Moses*, 4 vols., 1770–5, ET London 1814; J. NEUSNER, *The Rabbinic Traditions about the Pharisees before 70* I–III, Leiden 1971; C. PERROT, 'La lecture synagogale d'Ex. XXI, 1–XXII, 23 et son influence sur la littérature néotestamentaire', *A la Rencontre de Dieu. Mémorial A. Gelin*, Le Puy 1961, pp. 223ff.; J. PISCATOR, 'Appendix ad observationes Ex. XXIff.', *Comm. in Exod.*, Herborne 1696, pp. 242ff.; H. WHEELER ROBINSON, *Revelation and Inspiration*, Oxford and New York 1946, pp. 199ff.; J. SPENCER, *De Legibus Hebraeorum Ritualibus*, Cambridge 1685; P. J. VERDAM, *Mosaic Law in Practice and Study throughout the Ages*, Kampen 1959; W. WARBURTON, *The Divine Legation of Moses Demonstrated* I–III, London 1788; A. L. WILLIAMS, *Adversus Judaeos*, Cambridge 1935; H. WITSIUS, *Aegyptica, seu de Aegyptiorum sacrorum cum Hebraïcis collatione*, Amsterdam 1683.

During most of the history of exegesis the Book of the Covenant was not treated as a separate entity distinct from the larger problem of the Old Testament law. Many of the issues which were raised in the prior treatment of the study of the Decalogue overlap with those of the Book of the Covenant (cf. pp. 431ff.). Nevertheless, the use of the laws within the Book of the Covenant did tend to relate to a different set of problems in the history of exegesis and therefore justifies its separate treatment. Whereas the discussion of the Decalogue tended to focus on broad philosophical and theological issues – natural law, law and gospel – reference to the Book of the Covenant turned invariably on the issue whether these specific laws of the Israelite commonwealth still had any binding authority on later generations.

Already in the Hellenistic period a rich variety of hermeneutical approaches to the Old Testament laws had begun to emerge within Judaism. The tradition of strict adherence to the Old Testament law which had developed increasingly in the late post-exilic period was treasured and systematized by the Pharisees. Although the basic collections of rabbinic legal tradition contained in the Mishnah, Tosephta, and halachic midrashim date several centuries after the beginning of the Christian era, many elements of the tradition are clearly pre-Tannaitic and indicate a dominant exegetical direction within Judaism. Although the Jewish sect of Qumran differed significantly in its exegetical tradition from rabbinic exegesis, it did not differ in its attempt to adhere to a strict literal observance of biblical law.

However, another major alternative to the orthopraxis of rabbinic Judaism in respect to the Old Testament laws emerged in the Hellenistic Jewish communities of the Diaspora. Of course the pressure of living in a foreign country turned the problem of the function of the Mosaic law within a Hellenistic state into a burning issue for the Jews. It lies beyond our concern to trace the history of this research (cf. Juster, Mitteis, Schürer, Bickermann, Goodenough, etc.). However, it does seem clear that a variety of solutions were developed to cope with the problem of living both under the law of the state and in accordance with the Mosaic law. Perhaps the most significant development, and certainly the best known, is found in the extensive writings of Philo, particularly in his treatise *On the Special Laws (De Specialibus Legibus)*.

The first thing which strikes even the casual reader is Philo's ability to treat the laws of the Book of the Covenant in a variety of ways. At times he is capable of a very literal exposition which follows the rabbinic tradition, whereas at other times, he exploits the most radical form of allegorical interpretation. However, even in those cases where he offers a literal interpretation he sets them within a broader framework which betrays a totally different approach to these laws from traditional Judaism. For example, in his discussion of the laws of slavery (*Sp.L.* II. 69, 233), although he sets out the stipulations without alteration, he supplies a motivation for compliance which is far closer to Stoic philosophy than to the Old Testament: 'no man is by nature a slave' (cf. Heinemann, *op. cit.*, pp. 329ff.). Again, in his approach to sacrifice he plays down its importance from the outset by sharing the popular Hellenistic piety: 'God does not rejoice in sacrifices . . . but he rejoices in the will to love him . . .' (*Sp.L.* I. 271; Heinemann, pp. 67ff.). Above all, in his allegorical interpretation of the laws of the covenant one sees immediately how far Philo is removed from any literal holding to these laws. Rather, they have value because of an ethical training (*Sp.L* II. 86ff.), rational practicality (II. 110ff.), or a mystical, symbolic function (I. 206ff.). Philo's reflections on Ex. 21.5ff. are a classic example of a philosophical interest for which the literal observance has lost all meaning (*Sp.L.* III. 198ff.).

The new Testament's explicit reference to the laws of the Book of the Covenant are infrequent. Ex. 21.17 is cited in Matt. 15.4, but in a context which shows that it is used simply to elaborate on the parallel command in the Decalogue respecting the honoring of parents. The use of Ex. 21.12 in Matt. 5.21f. has a similar purpose in regard to the prohibition of killing. More important for the New Testament's use of the Exodus laws which are not paralleled in the Decalogue is the reference to the *lex talionis* in Matt. 5.38ff. : 'You have heard it said, "An eye for an eye and a tooth for a tooth," but I say to you . . .' (cf. Luke 7.29f.). It is a basic misunderstanding of these verses to see here evidence that Jesus merely sought to abrogate a particularly cruel law for a more humane, liberal approach. As if he offered a higher spiritualized ethic to replace Israel's primitive morality! It is clear from the other contrasts (cf. v. 39) that the issue at stake in the Sermon on the Mount is on a different level. A far more radical claim is being made. The Gospels are not simply an extension of broad Hellenistic liberalism. The law of Ex. 21.24 is chosen as a good example of human law. Society in general functions on the basis of retaliation. Jesus does not seek to replace it with a better law, but cuts the ground out from under all human law. The evangelist formulates the teaching of Jesus by the conscious use of paradox. The law of God transcends completely the limits set by human society in demanding a complete and limitless response to God. The positive formulation comes in v. 44: 'Love your enemies and pray for those who persecute you.' This is not intended to be a social program (Tolstoy), but an imperative which grows out of a highly theological reflecton on the stark discontinuity between God's call and the rules of human society. In sum, although the Covenant Code is cited, it is used simply illustratively of a highly theological issue and does not touch directly on the question of the Christians' use of Jewish law.

Although there are no specific references to Old Testament laws, the issue of Christian observance of Old Testament laws comes to its sharpest focus in the early controversy reported in Acts 15. In spite of the complexity of the historical-critical problems raised by this chapter (cf. J. Foakes-Jackson and K. Lake, *Beginnings of Christianity* V, New York and London 1933, pp. 195ff., and M. Dibelius, *Studies in the Acts of the Apostles*, London and New York 1956, pp. 93ff.), the decision reported from the Apostolic Council offers a clear picture of how the controversy over the authority of the Jewish law was resolved. The Christian had freedom over against the law and did not need to submit to it. Nevertheless, for the sake of harmony between Jewish and Gentile Christians a compromise was reached. Four stipulations of the Mosaic law set forth a minimum requirement to be observed by non-Jews (vv. 20, 29). However, the implications of this compromise were not at all so clear, as became evident from the ensuing history of Christian interpretation. Was the compromise respecting these laws dictated by a unique historical situation which was never again to be repeated, or did the decision imply that some of the cultic and juridical laws of the Old Testament still held an authority for the Christian? To put the question in another way, did the Pauline antithesis between faith in Christ and works of the law in fact address this problem of the Old Testament law's legitimacy for the Christian? Or was this a different problem, not directly related to the Pauline witness which called forth a different answer? The New Testament did not seem to offer a direct answer to these theological questions, which then began to call forth different solutions from Christian interpreters in the centuries which followed.

In the period of the Apostolic Fathers the most extreme rejection of the Old Testament laws appears in Marcion; however, the position of the Epistle of Barnabas in this respect does not seem too far removed. According to him, Moses had intended the dietary laws to be understood 'in the spirit' (10.2), but an evil angel had persuaded the Jews to understand them literally (9.4). J. B. Lightfoot writes: 'He accuses the Jews of misunderstanding them from beginning to end, and intimates that the ordinances of circumcision, of the sabbath, of the distinctions of meats clean and unclean, were never intended to be literally observed, but had throughout a spiritual and mystical significance' (*Apostolic Fathers*, London 1891, p. 239). In a less extreme form the emphasis on a spiritual understanding of the Old Testament laws became a characteristic feature of the church Fathers, usually in polemics with the Jews, which continued throughout the ages: Justin (*Dialogue with Trypho*, 11.3ff.), Tertullian (*Adversus Judaeos* 3, 5), and Augustine (*On the Spirit and the Letter*, viff.). The attention of the ancient Christian writers focused almost entirely on the Decalogue, which was regarded as containing the moral law intended for all ages.

Within rabbinic Judaism the political disasters which accompanied the destruction of Jerusalem and the scattering of Jews throughout the known world offered a major threat to the continuity of their religious traditions. It was the effort to meet the threat and establish the tradition which resulted in the codification of the law in the Mishnah, the Tosephta, and finally the Babylonian and Jerusalem Talmuds. Although later scholars sought to systematize the tradition further, particularly Maimonides in his monumental code, the Talmud remained the definitive source of all later Jewish reflection on the law in its rich, incredible complexity. Undergirding these sacred books for Judaism was the confession that in addition to the eternally valid written law of Moses God had also provided his people with an oral tradition by which the Torah was to be understood and obeyed.

Although the first Christian writers attributed little importance to the Mosaic laws, a remarkable change did take place. The most striking evidence of the change is the much discussed *Lex Dei*, or the *Collatio Legum Mosaicarum et Romanarum* (ed. by Hyamson; critical bibliography in B. Cohen, *op. cit.* I, p. 3 and Verdam, *op. cit.*, p. 18). This document, written between AD 300–400, consists of sixteen titles which begin with one or more quotations from the Old Testament laws and to which each time a number of quotations from Roman jurists are added. Although the identity of the author and the intention of the document remain contested, it does offer the oldest example of an interest in comparing Mosaic and Roman law for some practical reason, from the side of either a Jew or a Christian.

The period which followed in Western Europe with the decline of the Roman empire is of great significance in respect to the different attitudes which various countries adopted in respect to the Mosaic laws. Verdam (*op. cit.*, pp. 19ff.) points out that instead of concentrating on Roman law as the church's canon law had done, different types of folk law (*Volksrechte*) developed among Christianized people which borrowed much material from the Old Testament and combined it with local tradition. For example, the prohibition on eating flesh with blood continued for a long period of time. The rule of two or three witnesses became the law of civil procedure. The right of asylum was confirmed by church councils. Even the principle of *lex talionis* again acquired significance in legislation of the Middle Ages.

From the side of the theologians, Aquinas' attitude toward the Mosaic law represented a further refinement and continuation of that of the early church Fathers. He attributed authority to the ceremonial law only in so far as it prefigured the 'mystery of Christ' (1a2ae, 103.3). However, respecting the judicial precepts of the Old Testament which regulated a man's relation to his neighbor, he judged them not to be figurative but made void by the coming of Christ. These were national laws which had validity only as long as the regime remained the same (1a2ae, 104).

The Renaissance brought with it a new interest in natural law and humanism, which at the same time evoked fresh attention to the Mosaic law. Verdam (*op. cit.*, pp. 28ff.) interprets this interest in the humanistic school as stemming from an attempt critically to assess Roman law against the sources of the recently discovered antiquity. Indeed a veritable flood of literature appeared on the Mosaic laws in these centuries among which John Selden, *Uxor Hebraica* (1646) and *De Synedriis et Praefecturis Juridicis Veterum Hebraeorum* (1650–5), became standard works. B. Cohen (*op. cit.*, pp. 6f.) lists more than ten Latin books, published during the seventeenth and eighteenth centuries by Christian scholars, which compared Mosaic law with Roman and Canon law.

A different stance toward the Mosaic law began to have its effect on the orthodox theology of the seventeenth century, chiefly among the Calvinists. Luther had made it fully clear that he did not regard the Old Testament legal stipulations as binding on Christians (cf. his essay 'How Christians should regard Moses', Concordia ed., Philadelphia, vol. 35, 1960). Calvin followed him, by and large, in respect to the ceremonial and judicial laws (*Institutes* IV. 20.15). However, among the next generation of Reformed scholars, Piscator (died 1625) felt constrained in his Exodus commentary to enter into an elaborate and often penetrating discussion of whether the juridical laws of the Old Testament still have validity. He concluded that, with proper distinctions, many remain binding on the Christian. Among the English and American Puritans adherence to Old Testament law took its most extreme form. The 'Laws and Liberties of Massachusetts' (1648) mentions fifteen crimes liable to capital punishment, each of which had received a corresponding punishment from the Mosaic laws (cf. Verdam, pp. 37ff.).

Perhaps the beginning of the modern period began with the English deists' attack on the validity of the Old Testament laws.

Lord Bolingbroke in 'A letter occasioned by one of Archbishop Tillotson's Sermons' (*Works* III, Dublin 1793, pp. 292ff.), was typical in writing: 'No law ever operated so weak and uncertain an effect as the Law of Moses did.' He argued that if the law was from 'an infinite wisdom' it must be perfect, which was clearly not the case for the Old Testament laws. Similarly, Spinoza in his *Tractatus Theologico-Politicus* (1670) argued that the laws were not 'conducive to true happiness . . . nay the whole Law of Moses has no other purpose than the supremacy of the Jews' (ET, London 1862, p. 113).

Far more significant in the long run was the brilliant work of John Spencer, *De Legibus Hebraeorum Ritualibus* (1685). Spencer's book was primarily historical and philological in orientation, but he brought a new dimension to bear on the problem by seeking to demonstrate that the Hebrew laws were actually an adaptation of the laws of Egypt. Citing from a wide range of classical writers, he argued that Moses had taken over the basic materal from the Egyptians which he then reworked with the expressed purpose of opposing their idolatry and instilling a religion of monotheism (cf. his classic treatment of the Altar Law, Ex. 20.23ff., in Book II, 4, 5ff.). Spencer is rightly judged the father of modern comparative religion, at least in respect to Old Testament law.

Spencer's work called forth a tremendous storm. His results were accepted and used by J. Clericus, but H. Witsius, an orthodox Calvinist and Hebraist of considerable learning, directed an entire volume against the thesis (*Aegyptica*, 1683). He, in turn, was answered by Warburton's well-known apology, *The Divine Legation of Moses Demonstrated* (1737–1741). Warburton supported Spencer in sharply criticizing Witsius, but he focused much more on a theological defense. 'This is the way of God to accommodate his Institutions to the state, the condition, and contracted habits of his creatures' (Book IV.6). In a remarkable section he sought to find a warrant in Ezekiel's reference to 'statutes that were not good' (20.25) for his view that Mosaic laws had employed the stuff of pagan ceremonies before their being cleansed of superstition (IV. 6). The culmination of this whole development came with the monumental work of Michaelis, *Das Mosäisches Recht* (1770–5). In an exhaustive study for his time, Michaelis brought to bear the full range of philological, archaeological, historical, and comparative religion studies. From the theological point of view it is interesting to note that Michaelis felt confident to summarize in a few short paragraphs why the laws of

Moses could not ever be considered binding on any other nation but Israel. He considered himself free to study them objectively as 'relics of the most ancient legislative policy'.

There is one final feature which is still missing in Michaelis, but which has since become the hallmark of the modern critical approach to the Mosaic law. The reference, of course, is to the discovery of literary sources within the Pentateuch. The discovery of different literary strands opened the possibility of bringing the dimension of historical development into the analysis. Indeed, the failure to sift his material historically is reason enough to designate J. L. Saalschütz, *Das Mosäische Recht* (1846), as the last of the 'pre-critical' treatments. The modern critical development which extends from Ewald, to Wellhausen, to Alt is so well known as to need no extensive review (cf. H.-J. Kraus, *Geschichte der historisch-kritischen Erforschung des Alten Testaments*[2], Neukirchen-Vluyn 1969).

Parallel to the development of the new critical study of Old Testament law went the attempt to interpret the new insights theologically. Space is too limited to trace the history of the various theological approaches in detail. But clearly there emerged in the nineteenth and early twentieth centuries among Christian theologians one dominant position which was then expanded and popularized in different ways. A classic example of this approach is found in the famous Oxford lectures of J. B. Mozley in 1874–5, published under the title *Ruling Ideas in Early Ages*. Mozley was convinced that the Mosaic law was basically a sub-Christian, primitive form of legislation which as such must be rejected as normative for Christian theology. 'The demand . . . of an eye for an eye, and a tooth for a tooth, was the fruit of a very imperfect moral standard, and our Lord passes sentence on it accordingly, as a rule made obsolete by the rise of a higher law' (p. 187). What value then is there in the Old Testament laws? For an answer Mozley fell back on the idea of progressive revelation, which he interpreted as a steady growth of moral insight. 'The morality of a progressive dispensation is not the morality with which it starts, but that with which it concludes' (p. 236). God does not force an immediate moral enlightenment but allows man with his intellectual faculties to move in a 'gradual progressive motion requiring time' until it culminates in the ethics of Jesus. In spite of the fact that the nineteenth-century philosophical foundations of this theory of progressive revelation have been shattered for well over half a century, variations of the theory continue to live in modern biblical textbooks under the guise of Christian theology. At least in the Anglo-Saxon world no other approach to Old Testament law has succeeded in carrying the field to such a degree.

Although the need to provide a far more adequate theological interpretation of biblical law remains primarily the task of the theologian and ethicist, the modern Old Testament scholar can aid in making available pertinent information from his discipline. Specifically in terms of the descriptive discipline of Old Testament law, certain points should be taken into consideration:

1. The historically conditioned nature of the Old Testament law, which includes the Decalogue, has emerged with an even greater clarity on the basis of close study of the Ancient Near Eastern material (cf. the exegesis).

2. The Old Testament laws give evidence of having arisen in different historical periods and often performed different functions; there is, however, no clear pattern of 'ethical progress' which can be established on the basis of Old Testament texts.

3. Most modern New Testament scholars would seriously question whether Jesus ever intended to present 'a higher ethic'. Certainly his relation to the Old Testament was a different one entirely from that represented by the evolutionist.

4. Jewish interpretation of the Mosaic law cannot be dismissed by Christians as 'rigid' or 'legalistic' but it must be understood, first of all, on its own terms before engaging in a theological debate with Christian theology.

Again, several points should be made which affect the constructive task of developing an adequate theology of biblical law:

1. The idealistic categories which admit divine inspiration only to what is regarded as 'eternally valid' or 'perfect' for all contexts must be firmly rejected in handling the Bible.

2. The theological data of Old Testament law cannot be restricted by any *a priori* schema of values, symbols, ontology or the like.

3. A theology of biblical law must relate specifically to the structuring of the concrete historical life of the people of God, who in ancient Israel, in the first-century church, and today continue to participate both in the kingdom of God and in the world.

4. All forms of law, Old and New Testament alike, must be ultimately judged in the light of the living God himself who has revealed himself in Jesus Christ through a life of complete faithfulness under the law.

XIX

THE SEALING OF THE COVENANT
24.1-18

W. Beyerlin, *Origins and History of the Oldest Sinaitic Traditions*, ET Oxford 1965, pp. 14ff., 77ff.; O. Eissfeldt, 'Die älteste Erzählung vom Sinaibund', *ZAW* 73, 1961, pp. 137ff.; M. Haelvoet, 'La Théophanie du Sinai', *ETL* 29, 1953, pp. 386ff.; K. Koch, 'Die Eigenart der priesterschriftlichen Sinaigesetzgebung', *ZTK* 55, 1958, pp. 36ff.; K. Möhlenbrink, 'Josua im Pentateuch', *ZAW* 59, 1942/3, pp. 14–58; L. Perlitt, *Bundestheologie im Alten Testament*, WMANT 36, 1969, pp. 181ff.; H. Schmid, *Mose*, 1968, pp. 64ff.; G. Schmitt, *Der Landtag von Sichem*, Stuttgart 1964; H. Seebass, *Mose und Aaron, Sinai und Gottesberg*, Bonn 1962, pp. 9off.; T.C. Vriezen, 'The Exegesis of Exodus XXIV 9–11', *OTS* 17, 1972, pp. 100–33; C. Westermann, 'Die Herrlichkeit Gottes in der Priesterschrift', *Wort–Gebot–Glaube. Festschrift Eichrodt*, Zürich 1970, pp. 227–49; F. V. Winnett, *The Mosaic Tradition*, 1949, pp. 43ff.

24 ¹Then to Moses he said, 'Come up to the Lord, you and Aaron, Nadab and Abihu, and seventy of the elders of Israel, and worship at a distance. ²Moses alone shall come near to the Lord. They shall not come near, nor shall the people come up with him.'

3 Then Moses came and recounted to the people all the words of the Lord and all the ordinances; and all the people answered with one voice and said, 'All the words which the Lord has spoken we will do.' ⁴So Moses wrote down all the words of the Lord, and rising early next morning he built an altar at the foot of the mountain with twelve pillars for the twelve tribes of Israel. ⁵He then sent young men of the Israelites and they offered burnt offerings and sacrificed peace offerings of oxen to the Lord. ⁶Moses took half of the blood and put it in basins, and the other half of the blood he dashed against the altar. ⁷Then he took the book of the covenant and read it aloud to the people, and they said, 'All that the Lord has spoken we will do and obey.' ⁸Then Moses took the blood and dashed it on the people and said, 'This is the blood of the covenant which the Lord has made with you on the basis of all these words.'

9 Then Moses and Aaron, Nadab and Abihu, and seventy of the

elders of Israel went up, [10]and they saw the God of Israel, and under his feet as it were a pavement of sapphire stone, like the very heaven in purity. [11]Yet he did not lay hand on the leaders of the Israelites, but they beheld God, and they ate and drank.

12 Then the LORD said to Moses, 'Come up to me on the mountain, and wait there, and I will give you the tablets of stone and the teachings and commandments which I have written to instruct them.' [13]So Moses arose with his attendant Joshua, and Moses went up into the mountain of God. [14]To the elders he had said, 'Wait here for us until we come back to you. You have Aaron and Hur with you. Whoever has a dispute, let him take it up with them.'

15 Then Moses went up the mountain and the cloud covered the mountain. [16]The glory of the LORD settled on Mount Sinai, and the cloud covered it six days. On the seventh day he called to Moses from the midst of the cloud. [17]Now the appearance of the glory of the LORD was like a consuming fire on the top of the mountain in the sight of the people of Israel. [18]And Moses entered in the midst of the cloud and went up the mountain, and Moses was on the mountain forty days and forty nights.

1. *Textual and Philological Notes*

24.1. Ordinarily one would have expected a different Hebrew construction for the beginning of a new section, such as *wayyō'mer 'el mōšeh*. Cf. the discussion under the literary problems.

The Samar. adds the names of Eleazar and Ithamar in vv. 1 and 9, completing the list of Aaron's sons (Ex. 28.1).

The LXX's reading of the 3rd person plural προσκυνήσουσι in place of the MT 2nd plural is a later harmonization.

2. Throughout the chapter the LXX tends to read θεός where the MT has Yahweh (vv.2, 5, 16). Its reading of αὐτῶν where the MT has the singular is another harmonization.

3. LXX adds ἀκουσόμεθα following the MT of v.7.

4. Samar. and LXX read the neutral term *'aḇānîm* in place of *maṣṣēḇāh*. This change is understandable in the light of Deut.'s polemic against these pillars (16.22).

5. *na'arê benê*, 'young men'; Targum Onk. *būḵrê* 'first-born', which reflects the midrashic theory that they served as priests before the Levites.

10. *ṭāhôr* in the Priestly source bears the sense of ritual purity (Ex.30.35; 25.11, etc.). The meaning of 'clearness' has been suggested as fitting the context better in this passage. Ugaritic also confirms this interpretation. Cf. C. H. Gordon, *Ugaritic Textbook*, Rome 1965, under *ṭhr*, glossary # 1032. Cassuto remarks that the stem *ṭhr* is commonly used in Ugaritic poetry to signify the brightness of the sapphire. The most interesting parallel is text 51–5: 80–81. The most recent study of the root *ṭhr* is offered by W. Paschen, *Rein und Unrein*, Munich 1970.

11. The etymology of *'aṣîlê* 'leaders' is contested. Gesenius-Buhl and Koehler derive it from a root *'ṣl* 'to be firmly rooted', which is attested in Arabic. Others connect it to a Hebrew verb meaning 'put to the side'. Cf. Num. 11.17, 25. *ḥzh*, 'see'. Cf. Num. 24.4, 16. The verb became a technical word for the prophetic vision (Amos 1.1; Isa. 1.1; etc.)

12. The syntax of vv. 12f. is particularly baffling. The *waw* in the sentence before the word *tôrāh* can be translated in two ways: (i) As a conjunction, 'I will give you the tablets of stone *and* the teaching and the commandment which I have written to instruct them.' (ii) As an explicative (*G–K* §154a): 'I will give you the tablets of stone, namely the teaching and the commandment . . .' But both interpretations present problems in respect to the content. In the first instance, the difficulty lies in the fact that only the tablets of stone were written by God, and not any additional teachings. In the second instance, the difficulty arises from the fact that the Decalogue is not called 'teaching and commandment', nor does it function to 'instruct' according to the usual idiom. Several attempts have been made to avoid the difficulty. Nachmanides suggested that the sentence be so constructed that the verb 'I have written' refers to the stone tablets, and 'to instruct them' refers to the teaching and commandment. The suggestion is logically sound, but grammatically impossible. The text must be actually emended to achieve this effect. Thus Kautzsch, Bäntsch, and Driver suggest transferring the words 'which I have written' to a position after 'tablets of stone'. Although this emendation offers a thoroughly logical solution, it remains doubtful whether the text was ever so constructed. At least the closest parallel in the use of the pair 'instruction and command' (*hattôrāh wᵉhammiṣwāh*), which occurs in II Kings 17.37, appears to reflect the present form of the text of Ex. 24.12. Once again, the attempt to avoid the difficulty by translating 'tables of stone with the teachings . . .' (RSV, NJPS) assumes an implicit emendation which would require an additional preposition (*ʿalêhem*, cf. Dillmann).

In sum, the present form of the text seems to suffer from a later expansion which has confused the syntax. The parallel account of Sinai in Deut. 5.28ff. implies an additional revelation to Moses. Whatever the historical reason, v. 12 has sought to combine the stone tablets which were written in the past with new teachings which were to instruct Israel in the future. Most probably, the *waw* before *hattôrāh* should be construed as a copulative which overlooked the discrepancy caused by the subsequent verb.

13. The LXX reads a plural in the second verb which is an attempt to smooth out the Hebrew text.

14. On the initial construction, cf. Brockelmann, *Hebräische Syntax* §154.

2. *Literary and Traditio-Historical Analysis*

Ch. 24 contains a whole series of compositional problems which have called forth a great divergence of opinion (cf. the latest survey in Perlitt, *op. cit.*). The only point of general consensus is in assigning vv. 15b–18a to the Priestly source. Right at the outset, v. 1 has an unusual opening. Note the syntactical order, the addressee, and addresser. Moreover, it does not appear to attach smoothly to what precedes. Although some have suggested emendation (notably replacing 'to Yahweh' with 'to me', v. 12), the difficulty seems more serious. Noth argues that a whole section must have fallen out.

However, the major literary problem of the chapter has to do with the lack of apparent unity in what follows. Verses 1–2 contain instructions which are carried out first in vv. 9–11, but which form a continuous account. In between, vv. 3–8 appear to constitute an independent account. The striking differences in the portrayal of Moses, the setting of the action, and the action itself would seem to point to two different strands of narrative (cf. Bäntsch for a full characterization). Commentators generally (Bäntsch, Beyerlin, etc.) assign vv. 3–8 to E in spite of the divine name. The parallel with 19.3–8 and the connection with the E strand in 20.18–21 are advanced as evidence. However, opinions vary widely respecting vv. 1f., 9ff. A number of commentators (Dillmann, Bacon, Driver, Hyatt) assign the verses to J. They admit the lack of clear criteria, but assume J to be likely if the other verses are given to E. However, the difficulties of this reasoning are enormous. Nowhere else in J is God pictured being stationed on Mount Sinai in this way, and actually being seen by men. Moreover, it is generally conceded that the J account of the covenant sealing occurs in Ex. 34. Bäntsch and Beyerlin tend to assign it to E, but then to a different stratum from vv. 3–8. The arbitrariness of much of this reasoning does not increase confidence in the suggested source analysis.

There are in addition several other problems which have complicated the picture even more. Verse 2 seems to reverse categorically the instructions given in v. 1 and has therefore been assigned by Beyerlin and others to a separate fragment. Again, vv. 3–8 reflect considerable duplication, especially in vv. 3 and 7. The basis for the covenant ceremony appears at first to be the Decalogue (cf. 19.3ff.), whereas later the Book of the Covenant is expressly made the basis, vv. 7f. As a result of these problems and the increasing complexity of the analysis, the effect has been the complete atomization of the chapter into a myriad of disparate and contradictory fragments.

Perhaps much of the frustration of commentators lies in their effort to trace in great detail the history of the chapter's development, when in fact, the evidence is no longer such as to permit this detailed reconstruction. It may be that the better part of wisdom consists in making clear those areas of general agreement and also simply recognizing those problems which have continued to resist a solution.

Commentators are generally agreed that the difficulties of the chapter lie on both the literary and the pre-literary level. On the literary level, vv. 1, 2, 9–11 attach to vv. 3–8 in a way which suggests the joining of written sources, rather than the fusion of oral tradition. On the oral level, both these sections of the chapter appear to reflect old oral tradition which once functioned independently of their present narrative context.

If we begin with the oral tradition, there is a fairly wide consensus that vv. 3–8 reflect both in form and content a covenant renewal ceremony. The stereotyped pattern of the reading of the law, acknowledgment by the people, sacrifice with blood manipulation, would seem to indicate a ritual pattern with its roots in the institutional life of Ancient Israel (cf. the literature cited in Beyerlin). Again, vv. 1f., 9–11 also appear to reflect an old tradition of a covenant meal following a theophany which was originally unconnected to the Mosaic office of mediator. Because of its highly anthropomorphic description some commentators have even argued for a mythological, pre-Israelite tradition. However that may be, the tradition of a covenant meal of this sort is uncommon in the main streams of Sinai tradition. Nevertheless, there are some lines of continuity with other tradition on the oral level. The presence of the seventy elders, and the meal before Yahweh, finds a historical-traditional link in Num. 11.16ff. and Ex. 18.12 (cf. Seebass, *op. cit.*, pp. 90ff.).

When one comes to assigning sources to the written form of these two bodies of tradition, the grounds for objective judgment begin to disappear. There is a wide consensus in assigning vv. 3–8 to the E source, chiefly because of the consistency in general content with the portrayal of the Sinai events. However, because vv. 1, 2, 9ff. have little in common with either of the older sources, the assignment to a source becomes highly subjective. In the end it does not seem to matter greatly whether one says that it is a separate source within the E strand (E¹), or that it is a separate tradition which J has incorporated. In any case, these verses remain a foreign body which the chapter has difficulty absorbing.

Perhaps the most significant area is the final effort of a redactor to bring these various fragments together into a unified narrative. Indeed, there are many signs of a redactor at work on the chapter. Of course, it is not always possible to know on what level the process of harmonization took place. Although much of it is clearly on the literary level, it is possible that the process had begun earlier.

First of all, whereas v. 1a speaks of the ascent of the elders in a way which seems to disregard Moses' special role as mediator, vv. 1b and 2 have altered the original impact of the verse. Whatever the seventy elders may do, it does not detract from the unique role of Moses who alone can approach God himself.

Secondly, vv. 1–2 and 9–11 have been joined to vv. 3–8 as a literary bracket. The effect was to harmonize the two different accounts of the covenant ceremony. The covenant meal is now seen as a culmination of the rite in 3–8, and not as a rival ceremony.

Thirdly, v. 2 had singled out the special role of Moses. This element is now joined by a literary redactor to vv. 3–8, 12ff. in order to produce the effect of different stages in a series of ascents up the mountain. Verse 2 provides a point from which to make a smooth transition to the command in v. 12.

Lastly, the reversal of the ordinary sequence of Hebrew word order in v. 1 indicates the same stage of literary redaction. Verse 1 is made to connect with 20.22ff. and is addressed to Moses personally, whereas what preceded in ch. 20.22ff. was intended for the people.

There are two additional signs of minor redaction in the chapter but which are due to a different set of forces. The addition of the phrase 'all the ordinances' (v. 3) takes into account the introduction of the Book of the Covenant in its present position within the Sinai narrative. The slight expansion in v. 12 (cf. exegesis) provides a smooth connection to the motif of the broken tablets in ch. 32.

3. *Old Testament Context*

The fact that the text of ch. 24 has received its present form only after a long and complex history of oral and literary transmission should not be used as a reason for failing to see the meaning achieved by this final stage of composition. Indeed, one of the major purposes of tracing the history of a text's development is to be able better to interpret the present form of the text.

It is helpful at the outset to see the key function of ch. 24 in terms of the major lines of movement within the Exodus narrative before examining the meaning of the chapter in more detail. First, ch. 24 brings to completion the sealing of the covenant which had been first announced in 19.3. The repetition by the people of the same response (19.8 and 24.3, 7) marks the beginning and end of the one great covenant event. The theme of Moses' special role as mediator which is adumbrated in ch. 19, and then made explicit in 20.18ff., is climaxed by his role in sealing the covenant in 24.3ff. The careful redaction of the various traditions of the Mosaic office serves in the end to emphasize the unique role which he played.

Secondly, ch. 24 serves as the connecting link with the preceding themes of the book while at the same time pointing forward to the succeeding themes. The chapter forms a bridge to the Priestly account of the ascent of the mountain to receive the instructions for the tabernacle. Similarly, ch. 24 introduces the theme of the golden calf (v. 14), and the need for a renewal of the covenant in Ex. 34.

When we now turn to a detailed examination of the chapter, we immediately become aware of considerable roughness in style and a lack of clear connection between the various parts of the narrative. Of course, seeing the complex history of transmission which lay behind this final stage of the text, it is hardly surprising to find such tensions. In general, two different approaches have been employed to deal with the situation. On the one hand, the ancient versions and translations, particularly the LXX and the Targums, attempted to fill in the missing gaps in the ongoing narrative and to harmonize the difficulties. On the other hand, the recent critical commentaries, abandoning all effort to obtain a coherent account, have tended to highlight the discrepancies and have interested themselves only in historical reconstructions. The weakness of the first approach lies in its failure to deal seriously enough with the given text, substituting one's own opinion of what the text should have said. The weakness of the second lies in its complete atomizing of the narrative in disregard of the final stage of the text, and its failure to realize that the whole is more than its parts. What is needed is a synthetic approach which, while recognizing the historical dimension of the text, will seek to describe as objectively as possible what the final editor actually accomplished with his narrative. In this way the expositor does not himself go beyond the witness of the text. He is also able to offer some value judgments on how successfully the last literary stamping has dealt with the older material of the tradition which was reworked into a new form.

[24.1-2] 'And to Moses he said . . .' There are several immediate difficulties for the reader in these introductory words. To what do these words join in the previous narrative? Who is the speaker, and why is Yahweh addressed in the third person? Certainly it seems far more reasonable to suppose that the reversal of the normal Hebrew syntax has been done by the author with an intent to indicate a shift in emphasis rather than to mark that a prior section has been omitted. The preceding laws in the Book of the Covenant have been presented as direct address from God to Moses which he, in turn, was to transmit to the people (20.22). The introduction of v. 1 in ch. 24 implies that the message which follows is now directed personally to Moses himself. In spite of the roughness of the transition, which is more typical of Hebrew than English, the speaker is clearly Yahweh himself. There are no grounds for following the Jerusalem Targum, which supplies an angel for the speaker to ease the difficulty. Nor is there any evidence for assuming that the author intended a pluperfect use of the verb. Other attempts, such as Rashi's, to transport the whole chapter back to 19.3 cannot be sustained (cf. Nachmanides' decisive criticism).

But is there any reason to suggest why the announcement of the command to the seventy elders in vv. 1 and 2 has been separated from its execution in vv. 9–11? As it now stands, a certain effect seems to have been deliberately achieved by this arrangement. The covenant meal of the elders does not come as a loosely connected anticlimax to ratification of the covenant in vv. 3–8. Rather, the covenant meal is announced to Moses as a continuation of the divine instruction which began at 20.22ff. Moreover, by enclosing the covenant ratification in vv. 3–8 within the announcement and execution of the covenant meal, the latter incident is made to appear not as an afterthought, but as an essential part of the one ceremony. There is a very conscious movement of gradation which separates the elders from the people, and then again Moses from the elders. The covenant meal no longer functions as a parallel ceremony by which to seal the covenant, but rather as a joyous confirmation of the new relationship which had already been accomplished in vv. 3–8.

Commentators (Noth) have emphasized the historical-traditional roots of the seventy elders. Indeed, the number is traditional, and has a connection with other stories which is no longer fully clear (Ex. 18; Num. 11, etc.). In the present narrative the seventy elders function as a select group in between the gradation which separates Moses from the people. However, with this narrative scheme elements of tension remain from the earlier stages of the story. Seven times in the chapter there are references to 'ascending'. Attempts of commentators to iron out the difficulty of repeated ascents by suggesting a variety of nuances cannot be sustained grammatically. Still, if read as a whole and not pressed too hard, a quite coherent picture is achieved of gradual ascent on different levels up to the mount, which climaxes in Moses alone reaching the top.

[24.3–8] These verses describe the ceremony of sealing the covenant with Moses acting as mediator between the people and God. Recent form-critical work has shown a regular pattern for the covenant ratification which includes reading of the law, response from the people, sacrifice, and sealing of the oath (cf. J. Muilenburg, *VT* 9, 1959, pp. 347ff.; K. Baltzer, *Das Bundesformular*, 1960, pp. 37ff.; criticized by L. Perlitt, *Bundestheologie*, pp. 178ff.). But again there is some roughness in the text. In v. 3 Moses recounts all the 'words of Yahweh' and all the 'ordinances' (*mišpāṭîm*). Commentators differ on how to interpret these references. However, in the present context of the narrative the words seem to refer to the Decalogue (cf. 20.1) and the ordinances to the laws which are announced in 21.1. In other words, Moses recapitulates the content of all the law which he had received from Sinai. The fact that the people themselves had heard the Decalogue is irrelevant for the ensuing ceremony. Earlier in the narrative (19.8), actually before the law of God had been announced, the people had affirmed their obedience. The fact that Moses then writes down the laws and once again reads them aloud to the people serves to emphasize the seriousness of knowing exactly the content of that to which they are committing themselves with a solemn oath.

The covenant is sealed in blood. An altar is erected at the foot of the mountain with twelve pillars, symbolizing that all Israel is represented. Young men – the legitimate priesthood had not yet been instituted – perform the sacrifices of burnt offering and peace offering. Then half of the blood is dashed against the altar, and the other half upon the people after they have pledged themselves. Moses then pronounces the performative words: 'Behold the blood of the covenant which Yahweh has made with you' (v. 8). As is frequent in the Old Testament, the precise meaning of the ceremony is not explained in the text, although its effect in sealing the covenant is fully obvious. Consequently, commentators have been forced to offer their own theories as to the exact meaning of each element within the rite. Ever since Clericus' elaborate discussion, the parallels between the Hebrew and ethnic religious rites have been drawn which indicate many elements of striking similarity. Several Old

Testament texts offer additional clues as to the significance. In Gen. 15 a covenant is sealed with God passing between the pieces of animals which had been offered. Jer. 34.18 offers as a threat for disobedience a fate like the calf which had been dissected. Others see in the blood a positive symbol of a community of life established between God and his people, or explain the ritual as a symbol of purification (cf. Lev. 4.22ff.; Heb. 9.18ff.). The dividing of the blood in half would seem to point to a twofold aspect of the covenant. On the one hand, the blood dashed on the altar in place of a sacrifice speaks of God's gracious forgiveness in accepting this as an offering. On the other hand, the blood scattered on the people binds them in a blood oath. However, for the Exodus narrative the importance lies with the effect of the rite and not with the theory behind it. Israel has accepted the divine offer and entered a covenant with her God. Moreover, vv. 7f. makes it explicit that the Book of the Covenant, by which is meant the whole corpus of Sinai laws, formed the basis on which the covenant was made.

[24.9–11] The ascent of the seventy elders which had been commanded in v. 1 is now executed. Nadab and Abihu are now included as sons of Aaron, but whether once another reason dictated the choice can no longer be ascertained. The reference in Num. 26.61 to their death excited the later midrashim to suggest various connections with Ex. 24. The text is remarkable for its bluntness: 'They saw the God of Israel.' Many commentators have followed the LXX in toning down the directness of the statement. Maimonides (*Guide* I. 4) is typical in writing: 'In all these passages the verbs *r'h* and *ḥzh* must be understood as intellectual perception, but in no way as a real perceiving with the eye . . .' However, the passage is not without its parallels. The closest appears in Isaiah's vision (6.1) which also speaks of 'seeing' Yahweh. But in the case of both passages, when the actual description is given, it appears to be far removed from an actual portrayal of God's appearance. In Isaiah the description shifts to the throne, to the accompanying seraphim, and to the skirt of God's garment which fills the temple. In Ex. 24.9ff. even a description of a throne is missing. Rather, what is pictured appears to be the platform under his feet, which is described as if it were a transparency through which one could gaze from below. As in Ezekiel's description (ch. 1), the concrete elements are softened by repeated use of prepositions which emphasize its function as being only an approximate analogy to the reality itself. The sapphire stone, which again appears in Ezek. 1.26 and elsewhere (Ex. 28.18; Job 28.6, 16; Isa. 54.11, etc.) is the familiar opaque blue *lapis lazuli* of Mesopotamia. Its clearness is pictured as that of the heavens itself. The effect of the whole description is one of awe-inspiring majesty leading far beyond the human imagination, but one which recedes from all concrete particulars. The description turns to describe, as if in amazement, the fact that the elders could behold God and still live (cf. 33.20). The shift from the verb *r'h* to *ḥzh*, the latter word being the technical term for prophetic clairvoyance, again appears to be an attempt to characterize this viewing as a special category of perception. The final description 'they ate and drank', places the whole account into the context of a covenant meal (cf. Gen. 31.46, 54; Ex. 18.12) which was celebrated after their safety in God's presence had been assured (v. 11a). The Ugaritic parallel (cf. detailed notes) confirms this interpretation of the terms by reflecting a similar sequence. These verses in their present position in the biblical narrative function as a eucharistic festival in which selected witness celebrate the covenant sealing of vv. 3–8. The God of Israel has not become familiar or less awe-inspiring on account of the covenant, but a new avenue of communion has been opened to his people which is in stark contrast to the burning terror of the theophany in ch. 19.

[24.12–13] Verse 12 again returns to Moses and picks up the theme which was introduced in v. 2. Only Moses is to proceed up the mountain to be in God's immediate presence. The mention of Joshua in v. 13 as Moses' attendant (cf. 17.9) connects with his subsequent role in ch. 32. His unexpected presence at this point in the narrative is hardly recognized as a problem by the Hebrew writer (but cf. the LXX on v. 13). Although the broad movement of the narrative from here on is clear enough – Moses ascends into the mountain leaving Aaron and Hur to care for the people – several of the details in the account are highly perplexing and again indicate a roughness and lack of clear connection in the present form of the text (cf. textual notes on v. 12). Verse 12 seems to imply that Moses obtains not only the tablets of stone, which had been written by God, but also further instruction by which to guide the people. This latter purpose would both clarify the need for a period of forty days on the mountain, and also provide a bridge with which to connect the instructions regarding the tabernacle, which follow in chs. 25ff., with the preceding narrative.

[24.14] This verse presents an additional difficulty in having the message addressed to the elders. As Wellhausen long ago noticed, it is more probable that legal disputes would have arisen among the people in general. Still the problem is more apparent than real within the present contracted style of the narrative. Moses addresses the elders who have approached part way up the mountain with him, but the actual concern is focused on the people. The elliptical style also accounts for the introduction of Hur for the first time into the story. The lack of coherence between the *ad hoc* arrangement by which to adjudicate cases and the institution implied in ch. 18 would be another instance of tension arising from an independent historical development of the two accounts.

[**24.15–18**] The final verses in the chapter furnish the context from which the instructions regarding the tabernacle are given. Although the Priestly account of the theophany which begins in v. 15b appears in terms of source criticism to join with 19.1 within the ongoing narrative of ch. 24, these latter verses connect with little friction to the story and climax the entire chapter. The Priestly imagery of the glory of Yahweh, the descending cloud, and the devouring fire on the top of the mountain, serve to justify the original prohibition in v. 2. Moreover, the chapter is given a symmetry in returning to the theme of the people in v. 18, who now see the burning fire through the cloud. Moses must wait in preparation for six days. Only on the seventh does Yahweh call to Moses. The striking shift in the picture of God in vv. 15ff. when compared to vv. 9–11 has long been noticed as evidence for different sources. However, in the combined form of the present narrative, the shift in imagery also influences the entire reading of the chapter. The terrifying God of Ex. 19 who appeared in his theophany has not changed. He returns at the end of ch. 24 once again in majesty and awe-inspiring terror. What has changed is his relation to Israel. This is dramatically portrayed in the covenant meal of vv. 9–11. But in the light of God's complete otherness, the all-encompassing focus of the chapter falls on God's mercy and gracious condescension. It is this theme which lies at the heart of the witness of the Sinai covenant.

Detailed Exegetical Notes

24.1. On the problem of the seventy elders, cf. H. Schmid, *op. cit.*, pp. 67ff.

7. *sēper habbᵉrît*, 'Book of the Covenant'. Compare with the Deut. phrase, 'Book of the Torah', Deut. 28.61; 29.20; Josh. 1.8.

10. *'ᵉlōhê yiśrā'ēl*, 'the God of Israel'. Cf. on the formula, C. Steuernagel, 'Jahwe, der Gott Israels', *Festschrift Wellhausen*, BZAW 27, 1914, pp. 331ff. The term occurs in some very old passages (Judg. 5.3, 5; Josh. 8.30; I Sam. 1.17), but was later connected with the temple at Jerusalem.

10. On the expression 'a pavement of sapphire stone', cf. Haelvoet's discussion, *op. cit.*, p. 366. The closest content parallel is in Ezek. 1. *Lapis lazuli* is the obvious Ancient Near Eastern counterpart. The terminology of v. 10 has a striking parallel in Ugaritic, in the orders given for the building of Baal's house (51–5: 80–81 = 51–5: 95–97). The parallel extends to the clarity of the stones, the use of pavement (*lbnt*), and the sacrifice accompanied by eating and drinking (51–6: 38–58). (I am indebted to a seminar paper of Bruce Zuckerman for first pointing out the parallels.)

12. 'tablets of stone'. Note the parallel expressions, often assigned to different sources: $š^e n\hat{e}$ $luh\bar{o}t$ $h\bar{a}^{\cdot}\bar{e}dut$, 31.18; 32.15; 34.29; $š^e n\hat{e}$ $luh\hat{o}t$ $^{\cdot a}b\bar{a}n\hat{i}m$, Deut. 4.13; 5.22; 9.9ff.

13. 'mountain of God', Ex. 3.1. Cf. Seebass, *Mose und Aaron*, pp. 83ff. for the traditio-historical problem behind the expression.

16. 'glory of God'. Cf. the literature cited in Ex. 16.10.

4. *New Testament Context*

It is not necessary to review the entire history of exegesis of Ex. 24 because most of the major issues involved in the making of the covenant have already been dealt with in ch. 19. In fact, the inclusion of ch. 24 within ch. 19 – at least that portion which relates to the covenant ratification – had already been suggested by the Jewish midrashim and medieval commentators. Many recent studies have also tended to include ch. 24 within the framework of ch. 19 (e.g. Auzou, *op. cit.*, pp. 268ff.; Plastaras, *op. cit.*, pp. 226ff.). To be sure, Philo has a detailed allegorical exposition of the chapter which is of considerable interest (*Quaest. et Solutiones in Exodum* II, §§27ff.), but little is added to alter his approach to the law discussed above.

There is, however, one particular use of ch. 24 which is of importance enough to warrant notice. The reference is to the use of the Exodus chapter in the New Testament, particularly Heb. 9.18–21. In his discussion of Christ as the mediator of the new covenant, the writer of Hebrews makes use of ch. 24 to prove that even the first covenant was ratified by means of blood. He then reviews Moses' role in reading the commandments, sprinkling the people with blood, and pronouncing the words, 'this is the blood of the covenant which God commanded you' (vv. 19–20). Nevertheless, the fact has long been observed that the description of the first ratification which is given in Hebrews differs noticeably from the one described in Exodus 24. Moffatt (*Hebrews*, ICC, 1924, *ad loc.*) points out at least five distinct points of difference which include the mention of the blood of calves and goats, references to water, scarlet wool and hyssop, the sprinkling of the blood, the tent, and all the vessels.

Various theories have been proposed by commentators on Hebrews to explain the divergence in the New Testament report. E. Riggenbach (KNT 14, 1913) attributes the differences to a citation from memory. Others, such as C. Spicq (Paris 1952–3) and F. F. Bruce (London 1965) weigh the possibility of a special oral tradition lying behind the New Testament account. Indeed, the sprinkling of the tent does appear in Josephus (*Antiq.* III. 206). Additional evidence for an oral tradition has also been sought in Barnabas 8, which may well reflect a type of Christian midrash on Num. 19 (Bruce, *ad loc.*). However, the evidence for the theory is too scanty to be conclusive.

New Testament commentators have also observed that several of the features in Hebrews which are additional to the Exodus account are to be found in Num. 19, the ritual of the red heifer. Indeed, a close study of the relation of the two chapters reveals an unquestionable influence of Num. 19 on Heb. 9 which goes beyond a general similarity in content. Note the parallels in language between σποδὸς δαμάλεως (v. 13) with Num. 19.10; ῥαντίζουσα (v. 13) with 19.4; ἄμωμον (v. 14) with 19.2; λαβὼν τὸ αἷμα (v. 19) with 19.4; κοκκίνου καὶ ὑσσώπου (v. 19) with 19.6; ὕδατος (v. 19) with ὕδατι, 19.7; τὰ σκεύη τῆς λειτουργίας (v. 21) with 19.18; σκηνὴν (v. 21) with 19.4. It is not clear whether the influence of Num. 19 was taken directly from the Old Testament text in a conscious fusion, or whether it entered through a type of traditional midrash, which had made use of the red heifer ritual, or finally through a cycle of lectionary readings (Bruce, *ad loc.*, citing A. E. Guilding, *The Fourth Gospel and Jewish Worship*, Oxford and New York 1960).

Although the motivation behind this reading of the Old Testament remains somewhat obscure, as does the means by which the move was made, the effect of the joining together of Ex. 24 with Num. 19 emerges with clarity. The writer of Hebrews began his theme of the new covenant in 8.1 using Jer. 31.31ff. as his proof-text. In 9.1 he begins to contrast the mediatorship of Christ's new covenant with that of the old, and chooses the picture of the Old Testament tabernacle in order to illustrate the regulation for worship. This leads him to describe the duty of the high priest on the day of atonement in his use of the blood of goats and calves and the ashes of the heifer. When he then turns to describe the ratification of the first covenant under Moses, as reported in Ex. 24, the writer continues using the previous imagery of the high priest's role in the tabernacle, even though the chronology of the Old Testament is thereby fully disregarded. In the Exodus account the blood had functioned as only part of the ceremony of ratification and did not focus on the forgiveness of sins. Whereas in the New Testament account, the writer has transformed the ceremony into a ritual in which the entire emphasis now falls on the forgiveness of sin through the shedding of blood.

On the one hand, one can say that the New Testament is merely reflecting the tendency in the post-exilic period and Tannaitic Judaism to stress the growing consciousness of Israel's sin and need of atonement. On the other hand, the New Testament's reading of the Old Testament is most strongly influenced by the gospel preaching and eucharistic worship (cf. Matt. 26.28; Mark 14.24; I Cor. 11.25) which connected, as if by reflex, the Old Testament symbols of blood, sacrifice, and covenant with the work of Christ who had mediated a new way of life in his life and death.

XX

DIRECTIONS FOR THE TABERNACLE
AND ITS SERVICE

25.1–31.18

K. C. W. Bähr, *Symbolik des Mosaischen Cultus* I–II, Heidelberg 1837–9; 2nd ed. 1874; I. Benzinger, 'Tabernacle', *Encyclopaedia Biblica* IV, London 1903, cols. 4861ff.; W. Brown, *The Tabernacle*, Edinburgh 1871; R. E. Clements, *God and Temple*, Oxford and Philadelphia 1965, pp. 100ff.; F. M. Cross, Jr, 'The Tabernacle', *BA* 10, 1947, pp. 45–68; K. Galling, Beitrag to G. Beer, *Exodus, HAT*[3], 1939; D. W. Gooding, *The Account of the Tabernacle*, Cambridge and New York 1959; P. Grelot, 'La dernière étape de la rédaction sacerdotale', *VT* 6, 1956, pp. 174–89; M. Haran, 'The Complex of Ritual Acts Performed inside the Tabernacle', *Scripta Hier.* 8, 1961, pp. 272–302; 'The Priestly Image of the Tabernacle', *HUCA* 36, 1965, pp. 191–226; 'The Nature of the "'ōhel mô'ēdh" in Pentateuch Sources', *JSS* V, 1960, pp. 50ff.; 'Shiloh and Jerusalem', *JBL* 81, 1962, pp. 14–24; B. Jacob, *Der Pentateuch*, Leipzig 1905, pp. 135—346; C. F. Keil, *Manual of Biblical Archaeology* I, Edinburgh 1887, pp. 98–162; A. R. S. Kennedy, 'Tabernacle', *HDB* IV, pp. 653–68; K. Koch, *Die Priesterschrift von Exodus 25 bis Leviticus 16*, Göttingen 1959; A. Kuenen, *Einleitung im Alten Testament* I[2], 1887, pp. 73–6; A. Kuschke, 'Die Lagervorstellung der priesterschriftlichen Erzählung', *ZAW* 63, 1951, pp. 74–105; B. A. Levine, 'The Descriptive Tabernacle Texts of the Pentateuch', *JAOS* 85, 1965, pp. 307–18; A. Malamat, 'Mishkan YHWH' (Heb.), *Encyclopaedia Biblica* V, Jerusalem 1968, pp. 532–48; J. Morgenstern, 'The Ark, the Ephod, and the Tent', *HUCA* 17, 1942–3, pp. 153–265; 18, 1943–4, pp. 1–52; J. Popper, *Der biblische Bericht über die Stiftshütte*, Leipzig 1862; G. von Rad, *Der Priesterschrift im Hexateuch*, Stuttgart 1934; C. J. Riggenbach, *Die Mosaische Stiftshütte*, Basel 1862; K. H. Walkenhorst, *Der Sinai im liturgischen Verständnis der deuteronomistischen und priesterlichen Tradition*, BBB 33, 1969; J. Wellhausen, *Die Composition des Hexateuchs*[3], 1899, pp. 136ff. (cf. the notes for articles dealing with special problems).

25 [1]The Lord said to Moses, [2]'Tell the Israelites to set aside a contribution for me. You shall accept the contribution for me which everyone shall offer of his own volition. [3]This is the contribution that you shall accept from them: gold, silver, and bronze, [4]blue, purple, and scarlet material, fine linen and goats' hair, [5]tanned rams' skins, dolphin skins, and acacia wood, [6]oil for the lamps, spices for the anointing oil and for the fragrant incense, [7]onyx and other stones for setting, for the ephod and for the breastpiece. [8]Let them make me a sanctuary that I may dwell among them. [9]You must make it exactly as I have shown you, after the design for the tabernacle, and the design of all its furnishings.

10 They shall make an ark of acacia wood, two and a half cubits long, a cubit and a half wide, and a cubit and a half high. [11]You shall overlay it with pure gold – overlay it inside and out – and make a moulding of gold all around it. [12]You shall cast four gold rings for it and put them on its four feet, two rings on one of its side walls and two on the other. [13]You shall make poles of acacia wood, and overlay them with gold, [14]and insert the poles into the rings on the side walls of the ark, to carry the ark by them. [15]The poles are to remain in the rings of the ark, not to be removed from it. [16]You shall put into the ark the testimony which I will give you. [17]You shall make a propitiatory of pure gold, two and a half cubits long and a cubit and a half wide. [18]You shall make two cherubim of gold – make them out of beaten work – at the two ends of the propitiatory. [19]Make one cherub at one end, and the other cherub at the other end; you shall make the cherubim on its two ends of one piece with the propitiatory. [20]The cherubim shall be made with outstretched wings above, screening the propitiatory with their wings. They shall face each other with the faces of the cherubim pointed toward the propitiatory. [21]You shall put the propitiatory above the ark and in the ark you shall place the testimony that I shall give you. [22]There I will meet with you and communicate to you – from above the propitiatory and from between the two cherubim which are on top of the ark of the testimony – all the commands that I have to give you for the Israelites.

23 You shall make a table of acacia wood, two cubits long, one cubit wide, and a cubit and a half high. [24]You shall overlay it with pure gold and make a moulding of gold around it. [25]You shall make a rim of a hand's breadth around it and make a gold moulding for its rim round about. [26]You shall make for it four gold rings, and fasten the rings to the four corners at its four legs. [27]The rings shall be close to the rim as holders for the poles to carry the table. [28]You shall make the poles of acacia wood, and overlay them with gold and the table shall be carried by them. [29]You shall make its plates, bowls, jars, and jugs with which to offer libations, making them of pure gold. [30]You shall set the bread of the Presence on the table, to be before me always.

31 You shall make a lampstand of pure gold. The lampstand, stem and branches, shall be beaten work, its cups, calyxes, and petals, shall be of one piece with it. [32]There shall be six branches extended from its sides, three branches of the lampstand out of one side, and three branches of the lampstand out of the other side of it; [33]three cups shaped like almonds, each with calyx and petals, on one branch, and

three cups shaped like almonds, each with calyx and petals on the other branch – and so for the six branches extending from the lampstand. ³⁴On the lampstand itself there shall be four cups shaped like almonds, with calyx and petals, ³⁵and a calyx of one piece with it under each pair of the six branches extending from the lampstand. ³⁶Their calyxes and their stems shall be of one piece with it, the whole of it a single beaten piece of pure gold. ³⁷You shall make the seven lamps for it and its lamps shall be mounted so as to throw the light forward. ³⁸Its tongs and firepans shall be of pure gold. ³⁹It shall be made out of a talent of pure gold with all its furnishings. ⁴⁰See to it that you follow the design for them which you are being shown on the mountain.

26 ¹The tabernacle itself you shall make of ten curtains of fine twisted linen, of blue and purple and scarlet material, with a design of cherubim worked into them. ²The length of each curtain shall be twenty-eight cubits, and the width of each curtain shall be four cubits, all the curtains to have the same measurements. ³Five of the curtains are to be joined to one another, and the other five curtains joined to one another. ⁴You shall make loops of blue on the edge of the outermost curtain in the first set; and likewise you shall make loops on the edge of the outermost curtain in the second set. ⁵You shall make fifty loops on the one curtain, and fifty loops you shall make on the edge of the curtain that is in the second set, the loops being opposite one another. ⁶You shall make fifty gold clasps, and join the curtains to one another with the clasps, so that the tabernacle will be one whole.

7 You shall make curtains of goats' hair for a tent over the tabernacle, making eleven curtains in all. ⁸The length of each curtain shall be thirty cubits, and the width of each curtain shall be four cubits, the eleven curtains to have the same measurements. ⁹You shall join five of the curtains by themselves, and the other six by themselves, and the sixth curtain you shall double over at the front of the tent. ¹⁰You shall make fifty loops on the edge of the outermost curtain of the one set, and fifty loops on the edge of the curtain of the other set. ¹¹You shall make fifty bronze clasps, and fit the clasps into the loops, and join the tent together so that it becomes one whole. ¹²As for the excess which remains of the curtains of the tent, the extra half-curtain shall overlap the back of the tabernacle. ¹³The extra cubit at each end in the length of the tent curtains shall hang over each side of the tabernacle to cover it. ¹⁴You shall make for the tent a covering of tanned rams' skins, and above that a covering of dolphin skins.

15 You shall make frames for the tabernacle of acacia wood to stand upright. ¹⁶The length of each frame shall be ten cubits and the width of each frame a cubit and a half. ¹⁷There shall be two tenons in each frame joined together. You are to do the same for the frames of the tabernacle. ¹⁸You shall make the frames for the tabernacle as follows: twenty frames

for the south side, [19]and you shall make forty silver bases under the twenty frames, two bases under one frame for its two tenons and two bases under each successive frame for its two tenons, [20]and for the second side of the tabernacle, on the north side, twenty frames, [21]with their forty bases of silver, two bases under one frame, and two bases under each following frame. [22]For the rear of the tabernacle, to the west, you shall make six frames. [23]You shall make two frames for the corners of the tabernacle in the rear. [24]They shall be double at the bottom, but at the top they shall fit into one ring; thus shall it be with both of them, they shall form the two corners. [25]There shall be eight frames with their sixteen bases of silver, two bases under the first frame, and two bases under each of the other frames.

26 You shall make bars of acacia wood, five for the frames of the one side of the tabernacle, [27]five bars for the frames of the other side of the tabernacle and five bars for the frames of the side of the tabernacle at the rear to the west. [28]The middle bar, halfway up the frame, shall run from end to end. [29]You shall overlay the frames with gold and make their rings of gold as holders for the bars, and you shall overlay the bars with gold. [30]Then you shall erect the tabernacle according to the manner which you were shown on the mountain.

31 You shall make a veil of blue, purple, and scarlet material and fine twisted linen. It shall have a design of cherubim worked into it. [32]You shall fasten it with hooks of gold to four posts of acacia wood overlaid with gold upon four bases of silver. [33]You shall hang the veil from the clasps and bring the ark of the testimony there within the veil, and the veil shall separate for you the Holy Place and the Holy of Holies. [34]You shall put the propitiatory upon the ark of the testimony in the Holy of Holies. [35]You shall set the table outside the veil, and the lampstand on the south side of the tabernacle opposite the table. You shall put the table on the north side.

36 You shall make a screen for the door of the tent of blue, purple, and scarlet stuff and fine twisted linen with embroidery. [37]You shall make for the screen five parts of acacia wood and overlay them with gold. Their hooks shall be of gold, and you shall cast five bases of bronze for them.

27 [1]You shall make the altar of acacia wood, five cubits long and five cubits wide – the altar is to be square – and three cubits high. [2]You shall make horns for it on its four corners, its horns are to be of one piece with it, and you shall overlay it with bronze. [3]You shall make pots for removing its ashes, and shovels, basins, forks, and fire pans. All its utensils you shall make of bronze. [4]You shall make for it a grating of bronze network and you shall make upon the net four bronze rings at its four corners. [5]You shall set the mesh under the ledge of the altar, so that it extends half-way up the altar. [6]You shall make poles for the

altar, poles of acacia wood, and overlay them with bronze. 7The poles shall be inserted into the rings so that the poles remain on the two sides of the altar when it is carried. 8You shall make it hollow, of boards. As you were shown on the mountain, so shall they be made.

9 You shall make the court of the tabernacle. On the south side, there are to be hangings for the court of fine twisted linen, a hundred cubits long for one side, 10with their twenty posts and their twenty bases of bronze, the hooks of the posts and their bands being of silver. 11Again for its length on the north side there shall be hangings a hundred cubits long, with their twenty bases of bronze, the hooks of the posts and their bands being of silver. 12For the width of the enclosure, on the west side, there shall be fifty cubits of hangings, with their ten posts and ten bases. 13For the breadth of the court on the front, or east side, there shall be fifty cubits, 14fifteen cubits of hangings on the one flank with their three posts, their three bases. 15On the other flank the hangings shall be fifteen cubits with their three posts and their three bases. 16For the gate of the court there shall be a screen twenty cubits long, of blue, purple, and scarlet material and fine twisted linen, done in embroidery with their four posts and their four bases. 17All the posts around the court shall be banded with silver. Their hooks shall be of silver, and their bases of bronze. 18The length of the court shall be a hundred cubits, the width fifty, and the height five cubits with hangings of fine twisted linen and bases of bronze. 19All the utensils of the tabernacle for all its service, including all its pegs and all the pegs of the court, shall be of bronze.

20 You shall command the Israelites to bring you pure oil of pounded olives for the light, that a lamp may be maintained continually. 21In the tent of meeting, outside the veil which is before the testimony, Aaron and his sons shall tend it from evening until morning before the LORD. It is to be a perpetual statute with the Israelites throughout the generations.

28 1Then you shall bring near your brother Aaron, with his sons, from among the Israelites to serve me as priests: Aaron, Nadab, and Abihu, Eleazar and Ithamar, the sons of Aaron, 2and you shall make sacred vestments for Aaron your brother, for dignity and beauty. 3Next you shall speak with all who are skillful, whom I have endowed with talent to make Aaron's vestments, for consecrating him to serve me as priest. 4These are the vestments which they are to make: a breast-piece, an ephod, a robe, a plaited coat, a turban, and a sash. They shall make these sacred vestments for your brother Aaron and his sons, to serve me as priests. 5Let them receive the gold, blue, purple, and scarlet material and fine linen.

6 They shall make the ephod of gold, of blue, purple, and scarlet material, and of fine twisted linen, worked into designs. 7It shall have two shoulder-pieces attached to it at the two ends and thus joined.

⁸The decorated band that is upon it shall be made like it, of one piece with it: of gold, of blue, purple, and scarlet material, and of fine twisted linen. ⁹Then you shall take two onyx stones, and engrave on them the names of the sons of Israel, ¹⁰six of their names on the one stone, and the names of the remaining six on the other stone in the order of their birth. ¹¹With seal engravings, the work of a jeweler, you shall engrave the two stones with the various names of the Israelites. You shall set them in filigree work of gold. ¹²You shall fasten the two stones upon the shoulder-pieces of the ephod, as memorial stones for the Israelites, and Aaron shall carry their names before the LORD upon his two shoulders for remembrance. ¹³You shall make settings of gold filigree, ¹⁴and two chains of pure gold, and braid these like cords, and you shall attach the corded chains to the settings.

15 You shall make a breastpiece of judgment, worked into a design. Make it in the same style as the ephod. Of gold, blue and purple and scarlet material and fine twisted linen you shall make it. ¹⁶It shall be square and doubled, a span in length and a span in width. ¹⁷You shall set it in four rows of stones. The first row shall be a row of carnelian, topaz, and emerald; ¹⁸the second row: a ruby, a sapphire, and a crystal; ¹⁹the third row: a jacinth, an agate, and an amethyst; ²⁰the fourth row: a beryl, an onyx, and a jasper. They shall be set in gold filigree. ²¹The stones, corresponding to the names of the Israelites, are to be twelve in number. They shall be engraved like seals, each with its name, for the twelve tribes.

22 You shall make for the breastpiece braided chains like cords of pure gold. ²³You shall make two rings of gold for the breastpiece, and put the two rings at the two ends of the breastpiece, ²⁴fastening the two golden cords to the two rings at the ends of the breastpiece. ²⁵The two ends of the two cords you shall fasten to the two settings of filigree, and so fasten it to the shoulder-pieces of the ephod in the front. ²⁶You shall make two rings of gold and attach them to the two ends of the breastpiece on its inside edge which faces the ephod. ²⁷You shall make two rings of gold and attach them in the front of the ephod, to the lower part of the two shoulder-pieces, close to its seam above the decorated band. ²⁸The breastpiece shall be held in place by a cord of blue from its rings to the rings of the ephod, so that it rests on the decorated band of the ephod and that the breastpiece does not come loose from the ephod. ²⁹Aaron shall carry the names of the sons of Israel on the breastpiece of judgment over his heart when he enters the sanctuary for continual remembrance before the LORD. ³⁰In the breastpiece of judgment you shall put the Urim and Thummim, and they shall be upon Aaron's heart when he comes before the LORD. Thus Aaron shall carry the instrument for judgment for the Israelites over his heart before the LORD continually.

31 You shall make the robe of the ephod entirely of blue. ³²There shall be an opening for the head in the middle of it, with a woven binding around the opening, like the opening of a corselet, so that it does not tear. ³³On its hem you shall make pomegranates of blue, purple, and scarlet material, around the hem, with bells of gold between them, ³⁴a golden bell and a pomegranate, a golden bell and a pomegranate, all around the hem of the robe. ³⁵Aaron shall wear it when he ministers so that its sound can be heard when he comes into the sanctuary before the LORD and when he goes out so that he shall not die.

36 You shall make a plate of pure gold and engrave on it the seal inscription: 'Holy to the LORD.' ³⁷You shall attach it to a blue cord and it is to remain on the turban. It shall be on the front of the turban. ³⁸It shall be on Aaron's forehead and Aaron shall bear any sin incurred from the holy things which the Israelites consecrate from any of their sacred donations. It shall always be on his forehead to win acceptance for them before the LORD.

39 You shall weave the plaited coat of fine linen. You shall make a turban of fine linen, and you shall make a sash with embroidered work.

40 For Aaron's sons you shall make coats, and make sashes for them, and make turbans for them, for dignity and beauty. ⁴¹You shall put them on Aaron your brother and upon his sons with him, and shall anoint them, and ordain them, and consecrate them that they serve me as priests. ⁴²You shall make for them linen breeches to cover their nakedness; they shall extend from the loins to the thighs. ⁴³They shall be upon Aaron and his sons when they go into the tent of meeting, or when they approach the altar to minister in the sanctuary, so that they do not incur guilt and die. This shall be a perpetual statute for him and his descendants after him.

29 ¹This is what you shall do to them in consecrating them to serve me as priests. Take a young bull and two rams without blemish, ²and unleavened bread and unleavened cakes mixed with oil, and unleavened wafers spread with oil. You shall make them of choice wheat flour. ³You shall place them in one basket and bring them in the basket, along with the bull and the two rams. ⁴You shall lead Aaron and his sons to the entrance of the tent of meeting and wash them with water. ⁵Then you shall take the vestments, and put on Aaron the tunic and the robe of the ephod, the ephod, and the breastpiece, and gird him with the decorated band of the ephod. ⁶You shall set the turban on his head and place the sacred crown upon the turban. ⁷You shall take the anointing oil, and pour it on his head and anoint him. ⁸Then you shall bring his sons, and put tunics on them ⁹and gird them with sashes, both Aaron and his sons and fix their turbans. They are to have the priesthood for a perpetual statute.

Then you shall ordain Aaron and his sons. ¹⁰You shall bring the bull before the tent of meeting and let Aaron and his sons lay their hands upon the head of the bull. ¹¹You shall slaughter the bull before the LORD at the entrance to the tent of meeting, ¹²and shall take some of the bull's blood and put it upon the horns of the altar with your finger and all the rest of the blood you shall pour out at the base of the altar. ¹³You shall take the fat that covers the entrails, and the long lobe of the liver, and the two kidneys with the fat that is on them, and burn them upon the altar. ¹⁴But the flesh of the bull and its hide and its dung, you shall burn with fire outside the camp. It is a sin offering.

15 Then you shall take one of the rams, and Aaron and his sons shall lay their hands upon the head of the ram. ¹⁶You shall slaughter the ram and take its blood and throw it against the altar round about. ¹⁷You shall cut up the ram into sections, wash its entrails and legs, and put them with its pieces and its head, ¹⁸and burn the whole ram upon the altar. It is a burnt offering to the LORD, a pleasing odor, an offering by fire to the LORD.

19 You shall take the other ram, and Aaron and his sons shall lay their hands upon the head of the ram. ²⁰You shall slaughter the ram, and take some of its blood and put it on the tip of the right ear of Aaron and on the tips of the right ears of his sons, and on the thumbs of their right hands, and on the big toes of their right feet. And throw the rest of the blood against the altar round about. ²¹You shall take some of the blood that is on the altar and some of the anointing oil, and sprinkle it on Aaron and his vestments, and also on his sons and his sons' vestments. And he and his vestments shall be holy, as well as his sons and his sons' vestments.

22 You shall take the fat of the ram, the fat tail, and the fat that covers the entrails, the long lobe of the liver, the two kidneys with the fat on them, and the right thigh – for it is a ram of ordination – ²³and one loaf of bread, and cake made with oil, and one wafer from the basket that is before the LORD. ²⁴You shall put all these in the hands of Aaron and in the hands of his sons, and offer them as a wave offering before the LORD. ²⁵Then you shall take them from their hands and burn them on the altar with the burnt offering as a pleasing odor before the LORD. It is an offering by fire to the LORD. ²⁶Then you shall take the breast of Aaron's ram of ordination and offer it as a wave offering before the LORD. It shall be your portion.

27 You shall consecrate the breast of the wave offering, and the thigh of the priests' portion, which is waved and which is offered from the ram of ordination since it is for Aaron and for his sons. ²⁸It shall be for Aaron and his sons as a perpetual contribution from the Israelites, since it is the priests' portion to be offered by the Israelites from their peace offerings. It is their offering to the LORD.

29 The sacred vestments of Aaron shall pass on to his sons after him,

to be anointed in them, and ordained in them. 30The son who becomes priest in his stead shall wear them seven days, when he enters the tent of meeting to minister within the sanctuary.

31 You shall take the ram of ordination and boil its flesh in a sacred place, 32and Aaron and his sons shall eat the flesh of the ram and the bread that is in the basket at the entrance of the tent of meeting. 33Only they for whose atonement these things were used to ordain and to consecrate them shall eat them, but no unqualified person shall eat of them because they are holy. 34If any of the flesh of the ordination, or any of the bread, is left over until the morning, then you shall burn the remainder with fire; it shall not be eaten because it is holy.

35 Thus you shall do to Aaron and to his sons, just as I have commanded you; throughout seven days you shall ordain them, 36and each day you shall offer a bull as a sin offering for atonement. Offer the sin offering on the altar when you make atonement for it, and consecrate it by anointing. 37Seven days you shall make atonement for the altar and consecrate it and the altars shall become most holy. Whatever touches the altar shall become consecrated.

38 Now this is what you shall offer upon the altar: two lambs a year old, each day, continually. 39The one lamb you shall offer in the morning and the other lamb you shall offer at dusk. 40There shall be a tenth of a measure of choice flour mixed with a quarter of a hin of beaten oil, and a quarter of a hin for a libation. 41You shall offer the other lamb at dusk, and shall offer with it the meal offering of the morning with its libation for a pleasing odor, an offering by fire to the LORD. 42It shall be a continual burnt offering throughout your generations at the entrance of the tent of meeting before the LORD where I will meet with you, to speak with you there. 43There I will meet with the Israelites and it shall be sanctified by my presence. 44I will sanctify the tent of meeting and the altar, and I will sanctify Aaron and his sons to serve me as priests. 45I will dwell among the Israelites and I will be their God. 46They shall know that I am the LORD their God, who brought them out of the land of Egypt that I might dwell among them. I am the LORD their God.

30 1You shall make an altar for burning incense; make it of acacia wood. 2It shall be a cubit long and a cubit wide – it shall be square – and two cubits high. Its horns shall be of one piece with it. 3You shall overlay it with pure gold, its top, its sides round about, and its horns, and you shall make a gold moulding for it round about. 4Make two gold rings for it; under its moulding on two opposite sides of it you shall make them and they shall serve as holders for poles with which to carry it. 5You shall make the poles of acacia wood and overlay them with gold. 6You shall place it before the veil which shields the ark of the testimony before the propitiatory which is over the testimony, where I

will meet with you. ⁷Aaron shall burn fragrant incense on it; every morning when he tends the lamps he shall burn it. ⁸When Aaron sets up the lamps in the evening, he shall burn it at dusk, a perpetual incense before the LORD throughout your generations. ⁹You shall not offer any unholy incense on it, or a burnt offering or a meal offering. You shall not pour a libation upon it. ¹⁰Aaron shall make atonement upon its horns once a year; from the blood of the sin offering of atonement he shall make atonement for it once in the year throughout your generations. It is most holy to the LORD.'

11 The LORD said to Moses, ¹²'When you take the census of the Israelites for the purpose of registration, each person shall pay a ranson for himself to the LORD on being enrolled, that no plague may come upon them through their being enrolled. ¹³This is what every one shall give who is numbered in the census: half a shekel by the sanctuary weight – twenty *gerahs* to the shekel – half a shekel as an offering to the LORD. ¹⁴Everyone who is numbered in the census, from twenty years old and upward, shall give the offering of the LORD. ¹⁵The rich shall not give more, and the poor shall not give less than the half shekel, when giving the LORD's offering as atonement for yourselves. ¹⁶You shall take the atonement money from the Israelites and assign it to the service of the tent of meeting. It shall serve Israel as a memorial before the LORD in order to make atonement for yourselves.'

17 The LORD said to Moses, ¹⁸'You shall make a laver of bronze with a base of bronze for washing; and place it between the tent of meeting and the altar. Put water in it, ¹⁹and let Aaron and his sons wash their hands and their feet from it. ²⁰When they enter the tent of meeting, or when they approach the altar to minister, to burn an offering by fire to the LORD, they shall wash with water, that they may not die. ²¹They shall wash their hands and feet that they may not die. It shall be a statute for them for ever, to him and his descendants throughout the generations.'

22 The LORD said to Moses, ²³'Take the finest spices: five hundred shekels of liquid myrrh, half as much, two hundred and fifty of fragrant cinnamon, two hundred and fifty of aromatic cane, ²⁴five hundred – by the sanctuary weight – of cassia, and a hin of olive oil. ²⁵You shall make of these a sacred anointing oil, a compound expertly blended, to serve as sacred anointing oil. ²⁶You shall anoint with it the tent of meeting, the ark of the testimony, ²⁷and the table with all its utensils, the lampstand with its utensils, and the altar of incense, ²⁸the altar of burnt offerings with all its utensils, and the laver and its base. ²⁹You shall consecrate them that they may be most holy; whatever touches them will become holy. ³⁰You shall anoint Aaron and his sons and consecrate them that they may serve me as priests. ³¹You shall say to the Israelites, "This shall be my holy anointing oil throughout your generations. ³²It shall

not be poured upon the bodies of ordinary men, and you shall not make anything like it in composition; it is sacred and it shall be considered sacred by you. ³³Whoever compounds anything like it, or puts any of it on an unqualified person, shall be cut off from his people.'''

34 The LORD said to Moses, 'Take fragrant spices, stacte, onycha, and galbanum; add pure frankincense to the spices in equal proportions, ³⁵and make an incense expertly blended, refined, pure, sacred. ³⁶You shall beat some of it into powder, and put some before the testimony in the tent of meeting, where I will meet with you; it shall be most holy to you. ³⁷When you make this incense, you shall not make any of it in the same proportions for yourselves; it shall be considered by you sacred to the LORD. Whoever makes any like it to smell of it, shall be cut off from his people.'

31 ¹The LORD said to Moses, ²'See, I have specially chosen Bezalel, son of Uri, son of Hur, of the tribe of Judah. ³I have endowed him with a divine spirit, with skill and intelligence, with ability and knowledge in every kind of craft, ⁴to make designs for work in gold, silver and bronze, ⁵in cutting stones for setting and in carving wood, for work in every skilled craft. ⁶Moreover, I have appointed with him Oholiab, the son of Ahisamach, of the tribe of Dan, and I have granted skill to all who are able, that they may make everything that I have commanded you: ⁷the tent of meeting, the ark of the testimony, and the propitiatory that is upon it, and all the furnishings of the tent, ⁸the table and its utensils, and the pure lampstand and all its fittings, and the altar of incense, ⁹and the altar of burnt offering with all its utensils, and the laver and its base, ¹⁰and the stitched vestments, the sacred vestments of Aaron the priest and the vestments of his sons, for their service as priests, ¹¹and the anointing oil and the fragrant incense for the holy place. Just as I have commanded you, they shall do.'

12 The LORD said to Moses, ¹³'Say to the Israelites, "You shall keep my sabbaths, for this is a sign between me and you throughout your generations, that you may know that I am the LORD who sanctifies you. ¹⁴You shall keep the sabbath, for it is holy for you. Whoever profanes it shall be put to death; whoever does any work on it, that person shall be cut off from his people. ¹⁵Six days shall work be done, but the seventh day is a sabbath of solemn rest, holy to the LORD. Whoever does any work on the sabbath day shall be put to death. ¹⁶The Israelites shall keep the sabbath, observing the sabbath throughout their generations as a perpetual covenant. ¹⁷It is a sign forever between me and the Israelites. For in six days the LORD made heaven and earth and on the seventh day he rested and was refreshed."'

18 When he had finished speaking with him on Mount Sinai, he gave to Moses the two tablets of the testimony, tables of stone, written with the finger of God.

1. *Textual and Philological Analysis with Detailed Notes*

25.2. *t^erûmāh*, 'contribution'. The term designates that which is separated from a larger quantity for a sacred purpose, and can include gifts of produce (Num. 15.19ff.), money (Ex. 30.13ff.), or sacrifice (Ex. 29.27). The specific amount is not designated but left to the decision of the individual.

3. 'bronze', copper with an alloy for hardening.

4. 'blue, purple, scarlet'. For a modern, detailed treatment of these colors, cf. the learned articles by C. L. Wickwire, *IDB*, s.v. Also K. Galling, *BRL*, cols. 150ff., and R. Gradwohl, *Die Farben im Alten Testament*, Berlin 1963. The discussion of Bähr, *Symbolik* I, pp. 303ff., is still of value, especially for its classical references.

šēš. An Egyptian loan word, which most probably designated linen. Cf. Dillmann, *Exodus, ad loc.*, for a review of the older controversy as to whether cotton or woolen material was intended. Cf. J. M. Myers, 'Linen garment', *IDB* III, p. 135.

5. *taḥaš*. The exact meaning of this skin has long puzzled commentators. Already the Talmud found it a problem (Sab. 28b). Its use for women's sandals in Ezek. 16.10 offers little help. The Arabic cognate which means 'dolphin' has tended to be accepted by modern commentators as most probable. Driver 'dugong'; NJPS 'dolphin'; NEB 'porpoise', margin 'sea-cow'; NAB 'tahash skins'. The RSV's 'goat skins' apparently tries to interpret *tḥš* as an archaic form of *tyš* = he-goat. For the latest discussion cf. Haran, *HUCA* 36, 1965, p. 204.

'acacia wood'. Cf. the articles in *IDB* I, p. 23; *BRL*, col. 282, and J. Feliks, 'Akazie', *BHH* I, cols. 54f. The continuing attempt to find a symbolic meaning in the choice of wood, e.g. it was a cedar like the trees of Paradise (B. Jacob), has no basis in the text.

7. 'onyx'. Cf. Ex. 28.17ff.

'ephod'. Cf. Ex. 28.6ff.

'breastpiece'. Cf. 28.15ff.

9. *tabnît*, 'pattern'. Cf. a study of the word by H. Koester, 'Typos', *TWNT* VIII, pp. 187ff. with full bibliography.

10. *'ărôn*, 'ark'. Cf. the latest study of H. J. Zobel, *TWAT* I, pp. 391ff. The LXX's reading of the 2nd singular should be followed instead of the MT's plural, in spite of Jacob's polemic, *Der Pentateuch*, p. 158.

11. *zēr*, 'moulding'. The exact meaning is uncertain, although a moulding or collar of some sort is apparent. Just what its purpose was, other than ornamental, remains conjectural. No details as to its position or size is given. Older commentators speculated on its form and position at some length (cf. Bähr, *Symbolik* I, pp. 377ff.).

12. *pa'ămôt*, 'feet'?. Again the exact meaning is far from clear. The LXX renders it 'corner' (cf. I Kings 7.30). Still the translation of 'feet' seems closest to its basic meaning (cf. Judg. 5.28). Cf. the representation in Galling, 'Kultgerät', *BRL*, col. 342.

16. *'ēdût*, 'testimony'. The P source often speaks of the 'tablets of the testimony' (31.18; 32.15, etc.) which are placed inside the ark. Cf. L. Rost, 'Die Wohnstätte

524   DIRECTIONS FOR THE TABERNACLE: 25.1–31.18

des Zeugnisses', *Festschrift F. Baumgärtel,* 1959, pp. 158ff.; O. Eissfeldt, 'Lade und Gesetzestafeln', *TZ* 16, 1960, pp. 281ff. = *KS* III, Tübingen 1966, pp. 526ff.

17. *kappōret.* LXX renders it ἱλαστήριον, Vulg. *propitiatorium,* Luther *Gnadenstuhl,* from which the English 'mercy seat' (Tyndale). The basic meaning of the root *kpr* is 'to make atonement'. For that reason the usual modern translation 'cover', which reflects a secondary meaning of the verb, is not adequate. It is also clear that the function of the propitiatory is far more than simply to provide a cover, although it serves this purpose as well. Cf. the idiom in Ex. 40.20.

18. 'cherubim'. Cf. the standard dictionaries for the origin and significance of the cherubim. Cf. M. Haran, 'The Ark and the Cherubim', *IEJ* 9, 1959, pp. 30–38; R. de Vaux, 'Les cherubins et l'arche d'alliance', *MUSJ* 37, 1960, pp. 91–124; R. E. Clements, *God and Temple,* pp. 31ff.

23. 'table'. Cf. the detailed note of Kennedy, *HDB* IV, pp. 495ff. The specification of the table has often been compared with that depicted in the Arch of Titus, which shows divergence in its details.

29. Modern archaeological excavations have thrown the question as to the exact shape of the utensils into a new light. Cf. the basic work on ancient pottery by W. F. Albright at *tell beit mirsim* in *AASOR* 12, 1933, and 13, 1934, followed by G. E. Wright, *The Pottery of Palestine,* New Haven 1938. Also the excellent article of K. Galling, 'Keramik', *BRL,* pp. 314ff.; and J. L. Kelso, *The Ceramic Vocabulary of the Old Testament,* New Haven 1948.

30. 'bread of the Presence'. Luther translated it *Schaubrot* from whence Tyndale derived his 'shewbread'. The bread was set out in the presence of Yahweh. The frequent parallels from comparative religion, which are cited to show that originally the bread served as food for the deity, contribute little to understanding the present significance within the priestly writings. Cf. H. F. Beck, 'Bread of the Presence', *IDB*; K. Koch, 'Schaubrot', *BHH* III, col. 1688, and especially M. Haran, *Scripta Hier.* 8, pp. 289ff. The older literature is discussed in detail by Bähr, *Symbolik* I, pp. 425ff.

31. 'lampstand'. A full description by A. R. S. Kennedy, *HDB* IV, pp. 663ff. with a representation. Kennedy discusses the relation to the candlestick which is represented in the Arch of Titus in detail. The fact that many of the specifications of the biblical candlesticks have been omitted makes an exact reproduction impossible. For the more recent discussion of the menorah cf. the following articles: E. Goodenough, 'The Menorah among the Jews of the Roman World', *HUCA* 23, 1950/51, pp. 449–492; W. Eltester, 'Der Siebenarmige Leuchter und der Titusbogen', *Judentum–Urchristentum–Kirche: Festschrift J. Jeremias,* BZNW 26², 1964, pp. 62–76.

26.1. *miškān.* The English 'tabernacle', from the Latin *tabernaculum,* is the dwelling in the form of a tent, supported by a wooden framework, which formed the holy place and the Holy of Holies. Strictly speaking, the curtains, and not the boards, constitute the dwelling of Yahweh. There have been countless attempts to depict precisely the shape of this construction. Kennedy's article (*HDB* IV, pp. 653–668) still represents the most thorough treatment in English and is the culmination of nineteenth-century research on the subject. He also provides a complete bibliography of the older works. Cf. the more recent discussion in *BRL, IDB* and *BHH* which lack the detail of Kennedy's study. The most thorough recent discussion is certainly that of M. Haran, 'The Priestly Image of the Tabernacle', *HUCA* 36, 1965, pp. 191–226. Galling's interesting discussion in *Exodus* (*HAT*), 1939, suffers from his theory of source criticism (von Rad's) which has not been generally accepted.

'skillfully worked'. Haran (*HUCA* 36, 1965, pp. 202ff.) emphasizes the importance of carefully distinguishing the three different techniques of weaving mentioned in these chapters: *ḥōšēb* (26.1), *rōqēm* (26.36), and *'ōrēg* (39.22). Cf. his full discussion on weaving and dyeing of cloth and A. R. S. Kennedy, 'Weaving', *Encyclopaedia Biblica* IV, London 1903, cols. 5289f.

15. *qᵉrāšîm*, 'frames'. Traditionally the boards were thought to be solid wood. The discussion turned on the problem of determining their thickness. In order to secure the correct inner dimension of the required ten cubits on the west end, various theories were advanced (cf. already Josephus, *Antiq.* III, 108ff.). The theory was often defended that the boards were a cubit in thickness (e.g. Rashi to Ex. 26.17). Cf. the review of many traditional explanations in William Brown, *The Tabernacle*, pp. 19ff. Kennedy seems to have been the first to have suggested that the boards were actually wooden frames, not solid boards. His suggestion has much to commend it. It solves the problem of the excessive weight. More important, the theory of open frames allows the decorated curtains to be seen from inside the tabernacle. This difficulty presented a real problem for the older views and called forth different theories on suspending the curtains inside the structure rather than covering it. Although Kennedy's theory cannot be demonstrated conclusively, it remains attractive. However, see the recent strictures of Haran, *HUCA* 36, p. 192. The appeal to the Ugaritic as a confirmation of Kennedy (F. M. Cross, *BA* 10, 1947) is very problematic. Cf. Hyatt, *Exodus*, p. 274.

19. The shape of the sockets is unknown, but a variety of suggestions have been made. Kennedy's theory is highly rational, even if still conjectural.

23–25. The description of the construction of the corners is very obscure. Cf. Ezek. 41.22. Some sort of buttress-type construction is usually accepted. Cf. Kennedy, *op. cit.*, p. 661.

26–29. 'bars'. In a famous article on 'Temple' in Smith's *Dictionary of the Bible*, London 1860–63, a British architect, James Fergusson, proposed an elaborate theory that the central bar was actually a ridge pole. His reconstruction of the tabernacle, although highly improbable, was widely accepted by many English scholars, including the author of Exodus in the *Speaker's Bible*.

27.1. 'the altar'. The LXX and Samar. reading of the altar in v. 1 as an indefinite noun appears to be an attempt to avoid the difficulty caused by the introduction of the incense altar in 30.1. On the form of the altar, cf. the older treatment of Kennedy, *op. cit.*, and the monograph by K. Galling, *Der Altar in den Kulturen des alten Orients*, Berlin 1925.

2. The 'horns' of the altar play an important role in the priestly ritual (Lev. 4.7), and elsewhere (I Kings 2.28). There has been considerable debate as to their appearance, size, and function. Modern archaeological research has shed considerable light on the problem. As early as 1908 H. Gressmann, *Die Ausgrabungen in Palästina und das Alte Testament*, p. 28, connected them with the corners of the *maṣṣēbāh*, rather than being the conventionalized horns of the animal victim. The altars at Megiddo and Gezer show striking resemblances to

the Old Testament's description of the 'horns'. Cf. Galling, *BRL*, col. 19; Smend, *BHH*, col. 63; R. de Langhe, *Biblica* 40, 1959, pp. 476ff.

3. On the utensils for the altar, cf. the articles on 'Kultgerät' in Galling's *BRL*, cols. 340ff. and Fohrer, *BHH*, cols. 1018f.

4. *mikbār*, 'grating'. The bronze grating (pictured by Kennedy, *op. cit.*, p. 658) formed only the bottom half of the altar which rested upon the ground and provided a vertical support for the ledge. Scholars have often conjectured that it was filled with earth when in use, but there is no mention of this.

5. *karkōb*, 'ledge'. It appears to have been the section of the altar on which the priest stood when officiating with the sacrifice and perhaps explains the idiom of 'going up and coming down' connected with sacrificing (Ex. 20.26; Lev. 9.22, etc.).

9. 'court', LXX αὐλη, Vulg. *atrium*. Cf. the standard Bible dictionaries for a diagram of the court. Commentators have long exercised themselves over the mathematical problems involved in the court. How many posts were there? The older commentators tended to reckon 56 (Bähr, Knobel). More recent scholars have often opted for 60. Cf. the exhaustive discussion in B. Jacob, *Der Pentateuch*, pp. 204ff. Bäntsch (*Exodus*, p. 235) is superficial in simply assuming an error in calculation without pursuing the detailed arguments offered by scholars such as Riggenbach (*op. cit.*). For the most recent treatment of the problem cf. Haran, *HUCA* 36, p. 197, who argues for 56.

10. 'bases of bronze'. There is a definite pattern of gradation in the use of the metals. Cf. Haran, *HUCA* 36, pp. 200ff.

14–16. The front is divided into two 'shoulders' or sides, each with fifteen cubits of hangings and three pillars with their bases. In the middle was the door covered by the curtain.

17. 'bands' or 'fillets'. Narrow strips of binding metal used for decoration and not for connecting rods as in I Kings 7.33.

20. 'beaten oil'. The finest quality obtained by beating the olives rather than crushing them in oil presses. Cf. Bible dictionaries for a description of the different methods used in antiquity. Cf. M. Haran, *Scripta Hier.* 8, pp. 277f. for the ritual tending of the lamps.

21. Haran, *Scripta Hieros.* 8, pp. 277f. wants to eliminate the words 'and his sons' as a gloss because of its conflict with Leviticus. Levine's interpretation (*op. cit.*, p. 312) seems more plausible in retaining it and noting the traditional differences between Exodus and Leviticus at several points.

28.1 'priestly vestments'. Eight priestly garments are listed. The four 'inner garments' worn by all priests are the tunic (*ketōnet*), breeches (*miknāsîm*), girdle (*'abnēt*) and hat (*migbā'āh*). Contrast the turban of the high priest. The four 'over garments' worn by Aaron are: robe (*me'îl*), ephod (*'ēpôd*), breastpiece (*hōšen*), and diadem (*ṣîṣ*). In addition to the dictionary articles of J. M. Myers, 'Dress and Ornament', *IDB* III, pp. 869ff.; K. Galling, 'Priesterkleidung', *BRL*, cols. 429ff.; W. Eiss, 'Priesterkleidung', *BHH*, cols. 1491f., cf. the excellent treatment of Haran, *Scripta Hier.* 8, pp. 279ff. The classic seventeenth-century study of J. Braunius, *Vestibus sacerdotum Hebraeorum* (2 vols., 1680), remains unsurpassed in its thoroughness.

4. *hōšen*, 'breastpiece'. It was a type of pouch made of fabric similar to the ephod in which the Urim and Thummim were placed (v. 30), hence the term 'breast-

piece of judgment'. Cf. the fuller treatments of Galling, *BRL*, col.431; Elliger, 'Ephod und Chosen', Festschrift Baumgärtel, pp.9–23; J. Friedrich, *Ephod und Choshen im Lichte des Alten Orients*, Vienna 1968.

'ephod'. It remains a question whether the descripton of the ephod is consistent throughout the entire Old Testament. In the earlier period, especially in the Micah stories (Judg. 17), the ephod is associated with 'house gods' in a manner which is no longer fully clear (cf. also I Sam.2.18; II Sam.6.14, 20). However, in Exodus the ephod is part of the priestly clothing, being a type of apron of different colors on which the breastpiece was attached. Cf. the depiction by Galling, *Exodus*, p.141. The older critical literature is cited by J. Morgenstern, *op. cit.*, pp.114ff., the more recent by R. Smend, *BHH*, col.420 and R. de Vaux, *Ancient Israel*, p.544.

17ff. On the question of the jewelry of the breastpiece, cf. the full discussion by P. L. Garber and R. W. Funk, 'Jewels', *IDB* II, pp.898–905, and W. Frerichs, 'Edelsteine', *BHH*, cols.362ff.

30. 'Urim and Thummim'. The etymology of the words is uncertain in spite of the traditional interpretation of 'lights and perfections'. These objects appear to have been sacred lots which were cast to obtain a judgment (I Sam.14.18). In Exodus they have become the sole possession of the priests for rendering divine oracles. For the older literature, cf. C. F. Keil, *Biblical Archaeology* I, pp.220f.; Driver, *Exodus*, pp.313f. The more recent discussion is covered in R. Press, *BHH*, cols.2066f. and de Vaux, *Ancient Israel*, p.544.

32. *tahrā'*, 'coat of mail' or 'corselet'. A very infrequent word appearing only here and 39.23, whose meaning is not fully clear. The traditional explanation of 'coat of mail', seems still to be the best. It is used here only by way of comparison. On the use of armor in biblical times, cf. B. Reicke, 'Panzer', *BHH*, col.1382.

On the pomegranate design, cf. J. Feliks, 'Granatapfel', *BHH*, col.607, and the two articles by E. Nestle, *ZAW* 25, 1905, pp.205–6; *ZAW* 32, 1912, p.74.

36. The word *ṣiṣ* usually means 'flower', but here it appears to designate a thin burnished plate, which bore the inscription 'Holy to Yahweh'. For the stereotyped character of this formula, cf. Ezek.48.14; Zech.14.20. Cf. A. de Buck, *OTS* 9, 1951, pp.18ff. for Egyptian parallels to the flower symbol.

39. On the high priest's headdress, cf. the detailed notes of H. St J. Thackeray in commenting on Josephus' description in *Jewish Antiquities* III.151ff. (Loeb Class. Lib. Vol. IV, pp.390ff.).

'coat'. Josephus' description of the coat (*Antiq.*III.153) goes far beyond the biblical account. According to him, it reached to the ankles and enveloped the body with long sleeves. The 'open texture' which he mentions could be a reference to the 'chequer work' of v.39. Cf. Driver on the word (*Exodus*, p.310).

40. On the 'turban', cf. G. Fohrer, 'Kopfbedeckung', *BHH*, cols.985f. The turban of the high priest is distinguished in vocabulary from that of the ordinary priest (vv.39 and 40).

'sash'. Josephus describes it at length (*Antiq.*III.154f.).

42. 'breeches'. Cf. Ex.20.26.

29.1. Cf. Leviticus 8 for the ceremony of priestly consecration along with the commentaries of Hoffmann, Noth, and Elliger. The most thorough recent monograph on Ex.29 is that of K. H. Walkenhorst, *op. cit.* The Ancient Near

Eastern parallels are offered by B. A. Levine, *JCS* 17, 1963, pp. 105–12; and *JAOS* 85, 1965, pp. 313ff. Cf. also M. Noth, 'Office and Vocation in the Old Testament', *The Laws in the Pentateuch and Other Studies*, ET Edinburgh 1966, pp. 229ff. E. Lohse, *Die Ordination in Spätjudentum und im Neuen Testament*, Göttingen 1951; R. de Vaux, 'The Installation of Priests', *Ancient Israel*, pp. 346ff.

6. *nēzer*, 'diadem' or 'crown'. The term is not mentioned earlier in Exodus, but is emphasized in Josephus' description. It was the plate of the crown which was fastened around the white turban. Cf. the full treatment of Ancient Near Eastern parallels by Galling, *BRL*, cols. 125ff.

7. 'anointing'. Cf. E. Kutsch, *Salbung als Rechtsakt im Alten Testament*, Berlin 1963; E. Segelberg, 'Salbung', *BHH*, cols. 1646f.

9. 'fill the hands of . . .' is the usual Hebrew idiom for the ordination of priests. The original meaning reflects some part of the ancient ceremony which is no longer fully clear.

10. 'sin offering'. Cf. R. Schmidt, *Das Bundesopfer in Israel*, München 1964; R. Rendtorff, *Studien zur Geschichte des Opfers im AT*, WMANT 24, 1967.

13. Cf. S. R. Driver's learned note on liver divination, *Exodus*, p. 317.

14. 'outside the camp'. Cf. A. Kuschke, *ZAW* 63, 1951, pp. 78ff.

15–18. On the question of burnt offering, cf. L. Rost, 'Erwägungen zum israelitischen Brandopfer', *Von Ugarit nach Qumran. Festschrift Eissfeldt*, Berlin 1958, pp. 177ff.

24. 'wave offering'. *IDB* IV, p. 817; *BHH*, cols. 2142f.

37. Cf. Hag. 2.10ff. for a different approach to holiness.

38–40. 'daily sacrifice'. Cf. R. de Vaux, *Studies in Old Testament Sacrifices*, pp. 37ff.; L. Rost, 'Opfer', *BHH*, cols. 1345ff.

30.1. On the use of incense in the Old Testament, cf. M. Löhr, *Das Rauchopfer*, Halle 1927; R. de Vaux, *Ancient Israel*, pp. 430ff.; M. Haran, 'The Uses of Incense in the Ancient Israelite Ritual', *VT* 10, 1960, pp. 113ff.; G. Sauer, 'Räucherwerk', *BHH*, cols. 1555ff. with full bibliography; N. Glueck, 'Incense Altars', *Translating and Understanding the Old Testament*, ed. H. T. Frank, Nashville 1970, pp. 325–9.

10. On the many problems of the annual Day of Atonement, cf. the commentators on Lev. 16.
kpr, 'make atonement'. S. R. Driver's classic article, 'Propitiation', *HDB* IV, pp. 128ff., sets out clearly the basic issues at stake.

11. E. A. Speiser, 'Census and ritual expiation in Mari and Israel', *BASOR* 149, 1958, pp. 17ff.

13. 'shekel of the sanctuary'. The exact nature of this standard silver weight is unknown. Cf. the learned articles by H. Hamburger, 'Money', *IDB* III, pp. 423ff.; B. Kanael, 'Münzen', *BHH*, cols. 1249ff.; and R. B. Y. Scott, 'Weights, Measures, Money, and Time', *Peake's Commentary on the Bible*, Edinburgh and New York 1962, pp. 37ff.

17–21. 'the bronze laver'. I Kings 7.38f. Cf. also H. Gunkel, *Schöpfung und Chaos*, Göttingen 1898, p. 153; K. Koch, *Der Priesterschrift*, pp. 34f.; P. L. Garber, 'Laver', *IDB* III, pp. 76f.; W. F. Albright, *Archaeology and the Religion of Israel*[3], Baltimore 1953, Oxford 1954, pp. 152–4.

22. 'spice'. J. C. Trever, 'spice', *IDB* IV, pp. 431f.; G. W. van Beek, 'Frankin-

cense and Myrrh in Ancient South Arabia', *JAOS* 78, 1958, pp. 141–52.

31.10. *šerād̠*, 'stitched vestments'? The term is difficult, appearing only in these chapters. LXX understands it as garments of 'service'. Cf. Haran, *HUCA* 36, pp. 214f., for recent theories of its etymology.

12–17. 'sabbath'. Cf. the bibliography cited in Ex. 20.8. On the sabbath as a sign, cf. C. A. Keller, *Das Wort OTH*, Basel 1946, pp. 140ff.

2. Literary and Traditio-Historical Analysis

A. The Source Problem

There has been a wide consensus for well over a hundred years in assigning chs. 25–31 to the Priestly source. Even older commentators such as Driver could summarize the evidence for P quite briefly because it already seemed obvious. The more difficult problem turns on the issue of how to explain the continuing tensions within the P source. The apparent dislocation of chs. 30–31 from their logical position within these chapters was noticed very early. By 1903 Bäntsch had proposed a detailed analysis of the different Priestly redactions (P, Ps, Pss) in an attempt to explain the inner friction. Again, in 1934 von Rad had tried to solve the problem by unravelling two continuous P strands throughout the entire Pentateuch. His thesis was then worked out in considerable detail for Exodus 25ff. by Galling (1939). I think that it is fair to say that this attempt has not been generally regarded as a success. Although at times there have been some genuine insights, by and large, Kuschke's evaluation (*ZAW* 63, 1951, pp. 87f.) is correct when he points out the host of new problems which are raised by von Rad's thesis and the impossibility of continuing very far along this path. The fact that Koch and others have sought a different approach is further testimony of the dissatisfaction with a further analysis of P in terms of literary sources.

Chs. 36–40, which relate the execution of the tabernacle in a style which is often a *verbatim* repetition of the earlier chapters, present a variety of special problems. How is one to explain the basic duplication in these chapters along with the significant variations in sequence and content? Again, what is the reason for the wide variation in the LXX translation? It was the great contribution of J. Popper, *Der biblische Bericht über die Stiftshütte* (1862) not only to have pointed out the full scope of the problems in these chapters for the first time with great precision (cf. his review of earlier research, pp. 18ff.), but to have attempted to explain the literary history of these chapters with a theory which tied literary criticism to the unique textual problems involved.

Popper argued that chs. 36–40 represented a different author from that of 25–31, and one who reflected an approach to the biblical text closely akin to that of the Samaritan Pentateuch. Both schools sought to emphasize the exact correspondence between divine command and Israel's obedience (Ex. 39.1, 5, 7, etc.). Both rearranged the earlier material of 25–31 into a more logical order and showed tendencies toward midrashic expansion (38.8; 39.3). Moreover, Popper argued that the LXX's translation represented an earlier stage in the history of chapters 36ff. which continued to expand in a post-Septuagintal development which is now found in the Massoretic text. Both Kuenen and Wellhausen accepted the broad lines of Popper's theory.

In evaluating Popper's hypothesis it is probably wise to separate, at least at first, the special problem of the Greek translation of chs. 36–40 from the larger literary issues. The text of the Greek version has been discussed at some length without a solid consensus emerging (cf. Swete, *Introduction to the Old Testament in Greek*, Cambridge 1900, pp. 235f.; A. H. McNeile, *Exodus*, p. 226; A. H. Finn, *JTS* 16, 1915, pp. 449–82). Most recently, D. W. Gooding, *The Account of the Tabernacle*, 1959, has devoted an entire monograph to the subject. His conclusions are almost diametrically opposed to those of Popper. He concluded that the same Greek translator was at work in chs. 25–31 as in chs. 36ff. (excepting ch. 38). Also the Hebrew text underlying the Greek was about the same as the MT, and the order of the LXX originally was similar to the Hebrew which was later altered by a Greek editor. While the thoroughness of Gooding's research is impressive and casts doubt on Popper's use of the Greek text to support his thesis, in my judgment the textual problem of these chapters has not been fully settled. (Cf. R. de Vaux's caution in the light of the new Qumran evidence, *RB* 68, 1961, p. 292; however, P. Katz, *ThLZ* 85, 1960, cols. 350–5, seems convinced by Gooding). In regard to the larger thesis of Popper other modifications will be discussed in the section below.

B. *Traditio-Historical Problems*

The historical problems connected with the elaborate Priestly tabernacle have long been recognized. Early nineteenth-century scholars such as de Wette dismissed the whole picture of the tabernacle as mythical, but it was Wellhausen's formulation which won the day, and dominated the field for half a century. According to him (*Prolegomena to the History of Israel*, ET 1885, pp. 38ff.) the representation of the tabernacle rested on a historical fiction and was a projection of the Solomonic temple into the Mosaic age. Wellhausen's reasons for his thesis have continued to be summarized and accepted by many scholars, if in a slightly more palatable form: (*a*) there are inconsistencies within the tabernacle account; (*b*) the transporting of such a construction in the desert is improbable; (*c*) elsewhere in the Old Testament a conflicting picture of an earlier, more primitive Israel emerges; (*d*) there are marks of late post-exilic priestly theology in the tabernacle chapters. (Cf. McNeile, *Exodus*, pp. lxxxff.; Driver, *Exodus*, pp. 426ff.; Hyatt, *Exodus*, p. 260.)

However, within recent years there has been a growing dissatisfaction with Wellhausen's wholesale rejection of the historical basis of the tabernacle. Different modifications have been suggested which seek to recover some elements of older tradition underlying the priestly construction. It is of interest to note the great variety of different approaches which have sought to alter the classic literary-critical method.

J. Morgenstern (*HUCA* 17, 1943, pp. 153ff.) tried to show the continuity between beduin palladia – particularly the pre-Islamic *qubbah* – and the Hebrew tabernacle. Of special interest was the evidence for tent shrines from Sanchuniathon (his dating is uncertain, although Albright and Cross opt for the seventh century BC). The archaeological method was pursued soon thereafter by F. M. Cross (*BA* 10, 1947, pp. 45ff.) who insisted on recovering many archaic elements in the tabernacle. He saw two lines of ancient tradition combined in the tabernacle, namely, a desert tradition of a portable tent shrine and a Syro-Palestinian temple tradition. Again the appeal to Ancient Near Eastern parallels to demonstrate a common sanctuary tradition underlying the tabernacle has been made by Cassuto (*Exodus*, pp. 322ff.), Levine (*JAOS* 85, 1965, pp. 307ff.), and Malamat ('Mishkan', *op. cit.*, pp. 532ff.).

German scholarship has sought to recover evidence of older tradition by means of the form-critical method and to link early tradition with an early institution. Certainly von Rad's early article of 1931, translated as 'The Tent and the Ark' in *The Problem of the Hexateuch and Other Essays*, pp. 103ff., opened up a new front in the discussion. He distinguished sharply between the old tent tradition in which Yahweh 'met' with Moses and the ark tradition which stressed a theology of dwelling. He attempted to trace the history of both traditions until their fusion in the Priestly theology. Of interest was von Rad's conclusion that both traditions which comprised the tabernacle were ancient.

Subsequently Galling (*Exodus, op. cit.*) tried to isolate the older elements of the tent tradition in the description of the tabernacle by reconstructing an early beduin tent structure and relegating the entire frame structure to a later period, but, in my judgment, with unconvincing results. Again Kraus (*Worship in Israel*, pp. 128ff.) sought to reconstruct an early tent festival which was the bearer of the early tent traditions, but without sufficient support to convince.

Far more promising was Haran's attempt to pursue the problem beyond von Rad in several important, independent studies. In his 1960 *JSS* article (*op. cit.*) he agreed with von Rad's description of the early tent tradition as a place of meeting which reflected a different concept and cultic institution from that of the tabernacle. Haran made an important point in insisting that the P account is not a combination of tent and ark, as von Rad had suggested, but rather of tent and tabernacle tradition. 'The tent . . . is amalgamated by P with an entire sanctuary, and not with one of its individual appurtenances' (p. 62). Later, in *JBL* 1962 (*op. cit.*), he attempted to locate the older tabernacle tradition at Shiloh, but with less success.

Perhaps the most ambitious attempt to recover the *Vorlage* of the early Priestly tradition was that of Koch, *Die Priesterschrift*, in 1959. On the basis of stylistic differences in the tabernacle chapters Koch saw evidence to confirm Rendtorff's theory (*Die Gesetze in der Priesterschrift*, 1954) that the Priestly source comprised a collection of ritual material which had been orally transmitted. Koch then attempted to derive this tradition from a cult legend of a non-Jerusalemite sanctuary which possessed its own ark. In my own judgment, Koch's thesis rests on a very fragile basis. It remains a real question whether the alleged stylistic differences really reflect an oral tradition as he describes. Again, the theory suffers from much speculation, as, for example, the alleged etiological function of the tradition and the presence of several different arks. (Cf. a somewhat different criticism of Koch's thesis by J. G. Vink, *OTS* 15, 1969, pp. 101ff.)

To summarize: although there is a growing consensus that ancient material underlies the Priestly tabernacle account, a wide difference of opinion still exists regarding both the nature of the early traditions and the process by which the priestly account took its shape.

C. *The Traditio-Historical Problem Reconsidered*

A starting-point for a reconsideration of the history of traditions problem is provided, in my judgment, by the work of von Rad and Haran in respect to the tent of meeting tradition. The ancient roots of this tradition have become increasingly apparent (cf. the section on the Mosaic offices, pp. 351 ff.). Again, it seems quite clear that the Priestly tradition, in the form found in the tabernacle account of Ex. 25ff., represented a combination of this ancient tent tradition with a completely different tabernacle tradition. This latter tradition in turn reflected both ancient and newer elements. There are now present elements from the old desert tent shrine tradition, as well as common Ancient Near Eastern temple traditions. In the Priestly form of the tabernacle the old temple traditions have also been shaped by elements from the Solomonic temple, which Wellhausen had perceived.

The real problem now lies in determining more precisely how the tradition developed from the early period to the full-blown Priestly account. The brief review of critical research on the problem indicates all too clearly the large areas of uncertainty which still remain. Of course, it may well be that the biblical evidence is too scanty to use to trace the entire history of traditions. However, in my judgment, the tabernacle chapters of Exodus reflect one stage in the development of the tradition which has not been fully exploited up to now.

At the outset, the Priestly framework of chs. 25–31 provides a connecting link between the Sinai tradition and the tabernacle. The cloud covered the mountain for six days, and the glory of God settled on Mount Sinai. Then Moses entered the cloud and remained for forty days and nights (Ex. 24.15–18). At the end of this period Moses descended from the mountain with the tablets (31.18). In the final redaction of the book, the story of the golden calf separates the giving of the tabernacle instructions in chs. 25–31 from their execution in 35–40. This interruption also separates the account of Moses' descent in 34.29–35 from 31.18. Although it is clear that the story of Moses' veil in 34.29–35 reflects early material (cf. exegesis *ad loc.*), it is equally obvious that it has been worked into the Priestly source as part of the framework of the tabernacle chapters. Moses' face shone because he had been speaking with God for forty days. Moreover, the link between Sinai and the tabernacle is furthered established within the chapters by the frequent repetitition of the admonition: 'Make them after the pattern . . . which was shown you on the mountain' (25.9, 40; 26.8, 30; 27.8; Num. 8.4).

Now the interesting thing to observe in these chapters is how the older tent of meeting tradition has been combined with the Priestly tabernacle traditions. First of all, the element of the older tent tradition that God 'meets' Moses there has been retained. Five times in these chapters the verb of meeting is used (Ex. 25.22; 29.42, 43; 30.6, 36). Moreover, in 29.42 the meeting is still pictured at the door of the tent of meeting (cf. 34.34). Closely connected is the theme of Moses' role as speaking with God and mediating his instructions to Israel which was a part of the older tradition of Moses' office (25.22; 29.42; Num. 7.89). Elements of the older office appear most prominently in 34.34–35. Moses retains his ongoing task of mediating between God and the people.

However, elements from the tabernacle tradition have resulted in some major alterations in the older tent tradition. In the majority of cases where there is mention of God's meeting with Moses, the place of meeting is now located 'above the propitiatory . . . between the cherubim' (25.22; 30.6; Lev. 16.2) and not before the tent. Although the terminology of meeting still occurs in these chapters, the emphasis now falls on the new terminology of God's dwelling (*škn*, 25.8; 29.45). The same concentration on the ark appears in putting the two tables of the testimony within the ark (40.20). But perhaps one of the most significant alterations appears in the concept of Moses' office. In 25.22. God promises Moses: 'I will speak with you of all that I will give you in commandment for the people of Israel.' The passage seems to reflect an older concept of the Mosaic office, closely linked with the prophetic, in which Moses continues to mediate the divine instructions to Israel. The parallel with Ex. 33.7ff. is clear in seeing Moses' communication with God as an ongoing activity. Indeed in Ex. 34.34f. the frequentative tense is employed to describe Moses' office. Now it is significant to note that 25.22 is picked up in 34.22: 'He gave them in commandment all that Yahweh had spoken with him on Mount Sinai.' However, rather than the promise of an ongoing office, Moses now discharges once and for all his function at Sinai by giving Israel the divine instructions. In the present context there can be no doubt that the content of the instructions concerns the building of the tabernacle, which follows in chs. 35–40.

The frequent references in chs. 25–31 to Moses' building the tabernacle 'after the pattern which has been shown you on the mountain' has caused some puzzlement among commentators in the past. Von Rad (*Priesterschrift*, p. 181) speculated that this vocabulary once belonged to an older and more detailed tradition of a heavenly image which legitimated the tabernacle. The suggestion is interesting because the idea of a heavenly vision does not belong to the older tent tradition which concentrated fully on the speaking role of Moses. Nor can the later Priestly theology have been the source of the idea since, as we shall shortly observe, chs. 36–40 eliminate the idea completely. It seems, therefore, likely that the idea of a pattern of a heavenly sanctuary belonged to the older tabernacle tradition before it received its stamp from the late Priestly theology. This supposition seems confirmed by the many Ancient Near Eastern parallels to the idea of a heavenly pattern of a divine temple (cf. Cassuto, Cross, etc.). It seems probable that originally the divine legitimation lay in the heavenly vision and in its being received on Mount Sinai. In other words, the Priestly account of the tabernacle in chs. 25–31 reflects a variety of tensions with the older traditions which it incorporated. On the one hand, one can see elements from the older tent tradition which related to Moses' office. On the other hand, there are traces of an ancient tabernacle tradition which legitimated its divine authority through a heavenly vision rather than from instructions on Sinai. The fact that there are such signs of friction serves as a further confirmation of the early age of this material, which the Priestly writer incorporated with some difficulty.

If we now turn to examine Ex. 35–40, there is some evidence to suggest that a still further development of the tradition can be discerned in the redaction of these chapters. Although chs. 35–40 are basically a *verbatim* account of the execution of the building of the tabernacle, there are some redactional changes which seem to point to a later period than that of chs. 25–31. However, since many of the changes are stylistic and logical rather than theological, one must not press the argument from silence too far.

It does seem significant that many of the elements of friction which we pointed out above have been eliminated. The references to the 'pattern which was shown you . . .' have all been removed. In their place appears the repeated clause 'as Yahweh had commanded Moses'. Whereas in chs. 25–31 the reference to following Yahweh's commands is very infrequent indeed (27.20; 31.11), it completely dominates chs. 35–40, occurring ten times in ch. 39 and eight times in ch. 40. The effect of this repetition is to legitimate the form of the tabernacle in its every detail as the explicit command of God to Moses. Certainly Popper (pp. 76ff.) was correct in seeing in this vocabulary a late theological tendency which was shared by the Samaritan Pentateuch. The execution of the commandment must correspond in every way to the divine imperative.

There is also a new understanding of the relation of the Sinai theophany to the tabernacle tradition. Already chs. 25–31 had accommodated older tradition in such a way as to focus the central importance of Sinai on Moses' receiving the instructions for the tabernacle. Now chs. 36–40 extend this cultic emphasis. Ex. 24.16f. had pictured the glory of God (*keḇôḏ YHWH*) settling on Mount Sinai, with the appearance of a devouring fire on the top of the mountain. In 40.34 the same theme is picked up and now transferred from the mountain to the tabernacle.' 'The cloud covered the tent of meeting, the glory of God filled the tabernacle.' The presence of God which had once dwelt on Sinai now accompanies Israel in the tabernacle on her desert journey.

The effect of this transformation is also felt on the description of Moses' office. Moses' role as mediator of the divine word at Sinai has now been confined to the instructions in building the tabernacle. His early prophetic role as ongoing mediator before the tent of meeting which caused some friction in the earlier section has now been fully removed. The change in his position following the erection of the tabernacle is made fully explicit. Once the glory of Yahweh had filled the tabernacle, 'Moses was not able to enter the tent of meeting' (40.35). Moses' prophetic role has been completely absorbed in his new priestly function. Now Moses and Aaron together perform the priest's ritual ceremony before approaching the altar (40.31). Together they bless the people when they leave the tent (Lev. 9.23). But the ongoing institution by which God makes known his will to Israel is through the perpetual priesthood of Aaron (40.15). Moses participates in the ordination of Aaron and his son as he has been commanded (Lev. 8). The tent of meeting is the center of the cultic service (Lev. 8.34); it no longer serves as a place of meeting as in the early tradition. (Interestingly enough, the use of the verb *nôʿāḏ*, which occurs five times in chs. 25–31, is missing completely in chs. 35ff.; however, the reason is probably non-theological.) When God does appear, it is to Aaron before the propitiatory, upon the ark (Lev. 16.2).

To summarize: the study of chs. 25–31 and 35–40 has been able to reveal different stages in the development of the tabernacle tradition. First, we recovered a level of ancient tradition which preceded the Priestly source, but which then was carefully adjusted to the Priestly theology in spite of signs of continuing friction between the levels. Secondly, we detected the signs of a later Priestly redaction in chs. 36–40 which not only sought to eliminate the friction with the older material, but to develop the tabernacle tradition into a more consistent priestly theology which placed the tabernacle at the center of Israel's life and even incorporated Moses fully within the cult.

3. *The Tabernacle in its Old Testament Context*

It does not seem necessary to rehearse the physical structure of the various parts of the tabernacle. Such details are readily available in any Bible dictionary and in most of the older commentaries. The more significant exegetical problem turns on how to understand the meaning of the tabernacle within the book of Exodus. This is, of course, a different question from the usual historical one of determining what the tabernacle originally looked like, or whether Israel really had sufficient precious material for its construction, or how it could have been transported in the desert. These latter questions, although significant in a certain context, are tangential to Israel's own understanding of the tabernacle and contribute little to the exegetical issue at stake.

Already in the Hellenistic period (cf. section on history of exegesis) the attempt had been made to understand the function of the Old Testament tabernacle as basically a symbolic one. It is immediately apparent from the biblical language why this interpretation seemed a natural one. First, the dimension of the tabernacle and all its parts reflect a carefully contrived design and a harmonious whole. The numbers 3, 4, 10 predominate with proportionate cubes and rectangles. The various parts – the separate dwelling place, the tent, and the court – are all in exact numerical relation. The use of metals – gold, silver, and copper – are carefully graded in terms of their proximity to the Holy of Holies. In the same way, the particular colors appear to bear some inner relation to their function, whether the white, blue, or crimson. There is likewise a gradation in the quality of the cloth used. Finally, much stress is placed on the proper position and orientation, with the easterly direction receiving the place of honor.

Several classic symbolic interpretations emerged which sought to deal with these factors. Philo explained the tabernacle as a model of the universe whose four materials represented the elements of nature, and whose precious stones reflected the signs of the Zodiac (*Vita Mos.* II. 88, 126). Again, Maimonides saw the tabernacle and its cultus as a symbolic reflection of a royal palace whose servants sought to do honor to the king with the various rites (*Guide* III. 45–49). Protestant orthodoxy, especially in the tradition of Cocceius, explained the tabernacle as a figurative representation of the kingdom of God in which the vocation of the church was fully realized. But perhaps the most exhaustive defense of a symbolic interpretation was that of Bähr, *Symbolik* (1837), who scrutinized every biblical figure even in the context of extra-biblical parallels to demonstrate a symbolic representation of God's creation and revelation in the tabernacle.

One basic difficulty of the symbolic interpretation which was early recognized even by its defenders was the problem of establishing proper limits. The difficulty did not arise in finding a possible meaning to a symbol, but in choosing between a large group of alternative suggestions and in distinguishing between those elements in the tabernacle which were not to be understood symbolically. Bähr devoted an entire chapter to 'Rules of Interpretation', in which he tried to establish controls. Thus he insisted that the symbolic meaning must agree with the explicit principles of the Mosaic faith. Each symbol must have only one meaning, etc. But the fundamental weakness of the whole method emerged clearly, for example, in Keil's criticism of Bähr. Keil was typical of a whole generation of scholars who wished to retain some degree of symbolic interpretation, but drew back from the extremes to which Bähr's rigorous logic had pushed him. Keil felt that the choice of wood had no symbolic meaning, as Bähr had suggested, nor did the number of pillars at the entrance of the court have a figurative meaning. Nevertheless, the arbitrary selection of what was alleged to be symbolic and what not, often determined by rules of common sense or taste, pointed out the basic weakness of the method. The so-called rules did not overcome an arbitrary, intuitive selection. The real methodological impasse emerged when, in reaction to such attempts, Old Testament scholars such as Clericus responded by rejecting the symbolic method *in toto* and substituting a purely functional interpretation. Accordingly, the reason for incense on the altar was to keep away the flies, and white was chosen for the garments of the priests because they were most easily washed (cited by Bähr, I, p. vi). One wonders whether such a method offers much improvement or is any less dominated by prior assumptions.

The basic methodological problem turns on the fact that nowhere does the Old Testament itself spell out a symbolism by which the role of the tabernacle is to be understood. Therefore, it remains very dubious to seek an interpretation on the basis of symbols constructed from other parts of the Old Testament or from the general history of religions. This is not to deny the fact that much of the description of the tabernacle appears to reflect a symbolic dimension, as we noted above. The issue at stake is how one understands this dimension. It is quite clear from comparative religion and recent archaeological research that the description of the Old Testament tabernacle shares many features with its Ancient Near Eastern background. The construction of the three partitions, indeed the dimensions of the whole tabernacle, appear to be traditional elements. In other words, the Old Testament appropriated a common tradition which was already thoroughly saturated with symbolic meaning.

The exegetical problem turns on how to understand these common elements which included a symbolic dimension. In my opinion, the older Christian orthodoxy and the newer liberal approach were both at fault in failing to distinguish sharply enough between material simply found in the Old Testament and the explicit use which Israel made of this material. It is in Israel's use of common material that one hears the testimony of her faith. Because the use often changed within Israel's history, a full exegesis must also deal seriously with the history of her traditions. The symbolic approach to the tabernacle rested neither on an explicit Old Testament interpretation of a symbol nor on the dimension of the history of traditions. Rather, it sought to penetrate the symbolic language from the perspective of a philosophical system of comparative religions. Therefore, even where it succeeded in disentangling the logic of the symbolism, its results had little or nothing to contribute to the question of how the Old Testament itself understood the role of the tabernacle.

It is this question to which we now turn in an effort to understand the role of the tabernacle in its Old Testament context. First of all, the relationship between the events at Sinai and the role of the tabernacle is clearly expressed in the beginning and ending of the tabernacle chapters. Moses is ordered up on to the mountain to receive the tablets. He enters the cloud and 'the glory of God was like a devouring fire on the top of the mountain' (24.15). There he receives instructions in building the tabernacle. After it has been built, the glory of God which once covered Mount Sinai fills the tabernacle. The cloud representing the presence of God now accompanies Israel above the tabernacle on her journey. The tabernacle serves as a portable sanctuary of the presence of God whose covenant will have been made known at Sinai. What happened at Sinai is continued in the tabernacle.

The purpose of the tabernacle is made explicit in the initial command of God to Moses: 'Let them make me a sanctuary that I may dwell in their midst' (25.8). The tabernacle is, therefore, a sanctuary (*miqdāš*) where God dwells (*šākantî*) in the midst of Israel. The verb is a technical one and sharply distinguished from the usual Hebrew term for inhabiting a place (*yšb*). Indeed, the content of his 'dwelling' is provided in the description of the tabernacle itself. God is continually present in the portable tabernacle. There he 'meets' with his people and walks among them (Lev. 26.12). Yet it is his glory (*kāḇôḏ*) which fills the tabernacle and is represented by the cloud. Lev. 26.13 makes it clear that the tabernacle represents the presence of God in fulfillment of his covenantal pledge, 'I will be your God and you shall be my people', and therefore completes the revelation of God's name: 'I am Yahweh your God, who redeemed you from the land of Egypt' (26.12–13). In the service of the tabernacle the sons of the covenant realize their new life of freedom 'to walk erect'.

The tabernacle was made after the divine pattern shown to Moses (25.9). The later redaction of the instructions emphasized that every detail of the design was made by explicit command of God (35.1, 4, 10, etc.). Bezalel and Oholiab were equipped with the spirit of God and with knowledge in craftsmanship (31.2ff.) to execute the task. For the Old Testament writer the concrete form of the tabernacle is inseparable from its spiritual meaning. Every detail of the structure reflects the one divine will and nothing rests on the *ad hoc* decision of human builders. There is no tension whatever between form and content, or symbol and reality throughout the tabernacle chapters. Moreover, the tabernacle is not conceived of as a temporary measure for a limited time, but one in which the permanent priesthood of Aaron serves throughout all their generation (27.2of.).

The tablets of the Decalogue, the testimony, are placed within the ark of the covenant (25.21; 40.20), which testifies to the continuity between God's past revelation of his will and his ongoing, continual revelation to Israel in the tabernacle. There he meets with the people (29.42f.) and speaks with Moses from above the propitiatory (Num. 7.89). Aaron continues to bear the people of Israel in remembrance before God (28.30). In the ritual of sacrifice he atones continually for the sins of the people (29.14).

The tabernacle testifies in its structure and function to the holiness of God. Aaron bears the engraving on the diadem, 'Holy to Yahweh' (28.36). The priests are warned in the proper administration of their office 'lest they die' (30.21), and the death of Nadab and Abihu (Lev. 10.1) made clear the seriousness of an offense which was deemed unholy to God. Nor can even Aaron appear at will in the holy place, but only at the proper time, clad in the holy garments and having made sin offering for the people (Lev. 16.1ff.). Because its use in the service to God requires a thing to be holy, it must be separated from all profane roles (Ex. 30.32f., 37f.).

The making of the sanctuary was commanded by God; it was not first proposed and then executed by a king (II Sam. 7.2). Moreover, it was carried out by the people as a free-will offering. Indeed, Exodus emphasizes the spontaneous response of the people in supplying the material over and above what was needed (36.5f.). According to the biblical witness, the tabernacle was therefore not an affair of the state or of a priestly clique, but involved the whole nation under divine guidance.

The first account of the tabernacle closes with the sabbath command (31.12ff.); the second account of its building begins with the sabbath command (35.1ff.). The connection between the sabbath and the tabernacle is therefore an important one. The building instructions had outlined in detail the work to be done, but the sabbath command, coming at the conclusion of the instructions, reminds the people of the limits of work. 'Six days shall work be done, but the seventh is a sabbath, holy to Yahweh' (31.15). The tabernacle represents the fulfillment of the covenant promise: 'I will make my dwelling with you ... I will be your God and you shall be my people.' But the actual sign of the covenant is the sabbath. Therefore, the observance of the sabbath and the building of the tabernacle are two sides of the same reality. Just as the sabbath is a surety of Israel's sanctity (31.13), so the meeting of God with his people in the tabernacle serves the selfsame end (29.43). There can be no genuine tension between these two signs. The witness of the tabernacle and that of the sabbath both testify to God's rule over his creation (31.17). To this extent the old Protestant interpretation of the tabernacle as a symbol of God's kingship rests on a solid exegetical basis.

Finally, it is necessary to deal seriously with the present form and position of the tabernacle chapters within the book of Exodus. The fact that their present position represents the final stage of a long redactional process in no way undercuts the importance of hearing their witness. At the outset it is significant to reflect on the effect of the division of the material into its two parts. The instructions are given in chs. 25–31 and then executed with utmost care to detail in chs. 35–40. The point seems obvious that emphasis is being laid by this literary device on the obedience of the people in fulfilling the instructions to the letter.

However, the relation of the tabernacle chapters to the golden calf incident which is recorded in Ex. 32–34 would seem to show that more is involved than at first meets the eye. Both the verses which begin and which end the golden calf incident (31.18 and 34.29ff.) reveal an intentional joining together of the tabernacle chapters with the golden calf story by a Priestly redactor. The present position of chs. 32–34 which now divides the tabernacle account into two parts cannot be seen as accidental. The marks of the Priestly redaction are particularly evident in 34.29 in reworking this old tradition and connecting the commandments given to Moses (v. 32) with the instructions of ch. 35.

In addition, there is a remarkable parallelism in the form of an antitype between the instructions given by God in ch. 25–31 and the incidents connected with the golden calf in ch. 32. The people wish for a representation of God who will accompany them in the wilderness (v. 1). Freely on their own initiative they contribute gold for its construction (v. 3). Aaron uses the gold to make an image to whom the people attribute their redemption from Egypt (v. 4). Then Aaron makes an altar and sacrifices of burnt offering and peace offerings are brought. God says to Moses: 'The people have corrupted themselves' (v. 7). If in the instructions of God to Moses (ch. 25ff.) one can see the true will of God for Israel's worship, in the golden calf one can also see the perversion of worship. If the covenant relation is realized in the service of the tabernacle through which the people are sanctified, the shattering of the relation with its ensuing corruption is also illustrated in her apostasy. The present position of the golden calf story appears to make a double point. First, the alternative to true worship is held up as a terrifying threat which undercuts the very ground of Israel's existence. Secondly, Israel responded to God's forgiveness (ch. 33) and fulfilled her part to the letter in setting up the worship of God which he commanded. The entrance of the presence of God into the tabernacle assured Israel of God's continual presence in spite of her great sin of the past.

Postscript: The full force of this attempt to interpret the tabernacle in the context of its present role within the book of Exodus – that is to say, its Old Testament canonical context – can only be felt when this exegesis is contrasted with the frequent modern method of understanding the passage only in the light of its historical role. (Compare, for example, the careful interpretation of R. E. Clements on 'The Priestly Re-Interpretation of the Cult' in *God and Temple*, pp. 111ff.). The exegetical issue at stake is not whether there were indeed historical forces at work in the formation of the biblical text, which should hardly be denied, but rather the significance that one attributes to the basic integrity of the final or canonical form. In my judgment, the historical dimension has significance for exegesis only to the extent that it can illuminate the final form of the text. To suggest that the 'real' meaning of the text depends on the accuracy of one's historical reconstruction is an assumption which I do not share. Indeed, to read off the meaning of the tabernacle from a reconstructed post-exilic historical context is as subjective a method as the older symbolic interpretation.

4. *The New Testament's Use of the Tabernacle*

The New Testament's reference to the Old Testament tabernacle is infrequent (Acts 7.44; Rev. 13.6; 15.5; 21.3) outside of the Epistle to the Hebrews. Here the reference to the tabernacle goes far beyond the interpreting of single Old Testament verses. Indeed, the Levitical priestly cult which centered in the tabernacle provides the setting from which the author of Hebrews has developed his whole christology. Therefore to deal adequately with the subject would involve a study of the whole of Hebrews, which obviously exceeds the scope of an Exodus commentary. However, at least the attempt will be made here to draw a few of the major lines, lest, because of the enormity of the task, the reader lose all sense of the genuine connection between the testaments.

The theological reflection on the role of the tabernacle along with its offices and ritual provides an important model for understanding the relation of the New Testament to the Old. The author of Hebrews reflects a particular historical stance within early, first-century Christianity, which is often strikingly different from Paul. The writer's practice of hearing the Old Testament through its Greek translation is well-known, as is the evidence of his sharing in the exegetical traditions of his Hellenistic age (9.4!). Moreover, the author of Hebrews is dealing through his epistle with concrete, theological issues which bear directly on the life of his Christian community. He seeks to explain the fact that Christ is no longer with his people who are under growing pressures. He is very much aware of the continuing offense for many that Jesus both suffered and died. Moreover, there remains the ambiguous relation of Christians with their Jewish heritage. On the one hand, awe and reference before their rich religious inheritance; on the other hand, alienation from the old forms in expectation of the new.

What is of great significance is to see how the New Testament writer uses the Old Testament in addressing these problems. First of all, he attempts to understand the Old Testament christologically from the perspective of the life and death of Jesus Christ. Conversely, he shapes the Christian understanding of what Christ actually accomplished by his use of Old Testament categories, often pushed beyond the traditional lines of Christian teaching. Although the writer of Hebrews is not at all a dialectical thinker like Paul, the double movement of thought in structuring the material can be readily seen.

The writer of Hebrews is concerned to show that the Old Testament picture of the tabernacle is a testimony to Jesus Christ, whether in its fulfillment or in its abrogation through a more perfect form. Indeed, the writer is at pains to demonstrate that the old covenant itself speaks of the incomplete nature of old cultic institutions. The Mosaic tabernacle is only a shadow of the true heavenly sanctuary (8.2). Thus there is a perfect tent, not made with hands (9.11) in which Christ ministers. Although the language at times resembles Philo rather than the Old Testament, the christological focus distinguishes it sharply from Hellenistic allegory.

Moreover, the high priestly office of Christ, performed at the right hand of God, reveals its superiority at every point to the older office. The fact that the high priest could only enter into God's presence once a year demonstrated his inability to gain free entrance into his presence (9.8), but in Christ's ministry this restriction is lifted, thus freeing the conscience of the worshipper (9.9) to serve God (9.14). The old ritual required a repeated sacrifice, year after year, but with Christ a sufficient sacrifice has been performed once and for all (9.26). The Levitical priest was forced to atone for his own sins (9.7) and those of the people with the blood of bulls and goats, whereas Christ offered his own blood finally to put away sin by the sacrifice of himself. The old ritual had been of a transitory nature, being only a shadow of the good things to come, obsolete and growing old, but Christ brought an eternal redemption. The old sacrifices could only temporarily cover sins, but not make perfect. Whereas Christ abolished the first sacrifices to sanctify completely through his second offering (10.10).

In addition to arguments regarding the logical superiority of Christ's priesthood, the author employs the more traditional proof-text method. He cites Jer. 31.31ff. as a warrant for the Old Testament promise of a new covenant, but lays the stress in his commentary on the obsolescence of the old (8.8ff.). Again, the writer of Hebrews follows a traditional Christian pattern in citing the prophetic passages which call into question the validity of sacrifice (10.5 citing Ps. 40). His comment makes it clear that it is not sacrifice *per se* which is rejected, but the first order of worship to make room for the second (10.9).

Beside the christological interpretation of the Old Testament, it is equally important to recognize to what extent the Old Testament text in its turn shaped the christology of Hebrews. First of all, the New Testament writer simply takes for granted the Old Testament cultic setting as providing an analogous situation to that in which the redemptive work of Christ was being executed. The author of Hebrews is concerned to work out the exact relationship between Christ and the old Levitical priestly system, but it was his prior commitment to Israel's scripture which caused him to assume that such a relation did in fact exist.

Because of the Old Testament tradition and from early Christian preaching Jesus is presented as the exalted high priest, ministering in a heavenly tabernacle. Indeed, the writer of Hebrews combines two Old Testament offices, that of priest and king, to do justice to Christ's role when seated on the right hand of God (8.1; cf. Ps. 110.1). Like the earthly priest, but in a perfect manifestation, Christ is described in completely sacerdotal terminology: holy, blameless, unstained, separated, and exalted (9.24). His is a permanent priesthood, which does not change from one generation of priests to another, but is eternal (7.23f.). Moreover, his function is to intercede on behalf of his people. This role he performs, not by virtue of his victorious resurrection or his defeat of Satan, but by virtue of the shedding of his own blood (9.12). Only through blood is access to the presence of God available and Christ as the perfect sacrifice offers himself to God (9.14). While the description of Christ's death as a once-and-for-all sacrifice appears in other New Testament books (1 Peter 3.18), its emergence as a major emphasis is derived from its contrast with the repeated sacrifices of the Jewish cult.

Furthermore, it is the writer's concentration with his priestly imagery which causes him to develop only certain aspects of his christology to the exclusion of others. The themes of the incarnation play a role only so far as they relate to Christ's superiority over the earthly priest (4.15; 5.7). The resurrection is passed over to highlight the heavenly ascent of Christ (4.14) to his mediatorial role before the throne of grace. Similarly, the significance of the death of Christ receives a shape dictated by its function in establishing the new covenant through the efficacy of shed blood. Because of his death, 'he opened up a way through the curtain, that is, through his flesh' (10.20).

Likewise when discussing the effect of Christ's death in redeeming his people from sin, the basic lines of the author's theology are formed within priestly imagery. Sin is not the passions of the flesh revived by the law which brings a man into despair before the wrath of God (Rom. 7), but pollution and defilement before the holiness of God (9.13), which, were it not atoned, could infect even the heavenly sanctuary (9.23). Yet the writer of Hebrews is far from being content with an external, mechanical concept of sin. Purification and forgiveness bring a freedom of conscience (9.9, 15) with which to serve the living God. Just as the Old Testament sacrificial system did not atone for 'high-handed' sins, so Christ's sacrifice can be spurned to bring a fearful judgment (10.26).

Finally, it is significant to note the Old Testament's shaping of the writer's use of eschatology. At first one might have thought that the terminology of earthly pattern of a heavenly reality would have little need for a future dimension. Yet it is again evident that the New Testament writer does not move in a timeless world of shadows and forms. The 'true form' is that which is yet to come (10.1). Christ sits down at the right hand of God to await the final victory. The old forms must be replaced by a new age which is different in kind (9.8ff.). Thus the people of the new covenant need endurance to live by hope in the promise of a heavenly home which the Old Testament saints only greeted from afar (11.13).

5. History of Exegesis

B. UGOLINI, *Thesaurus Antiquitatum Sacrarum*, Venice 1744ff., Vols. VIIIff., has reprinted the classic seventeenth-century and early eighteenth-century treatises by S. VAN TIL, *Commentarius Critico-Typicus de Tabernaculo Mosis*; J. BUXTORF, *Historia Arcae Foederis*; H. RELAND, *De Spoliis Templi Hier. in Arcu Titiano Romae Conspicuis* 1716, and many others on the furniture of the tabernacle and its service. Cf. the annotated bibliography of A. CALMET, *Dictionary of the Bible*, London 1732, III, pp. 253ff. for other older works. Cf. also K. C. W. BÄHR, *Symbolik des Mosaischen Cultus* I, Heidelberg 1837, pp. 103ff.; A. DILLMANN, *Der Exodus*[3], 1897, pp. 297ff.; E. W. HENGSTENBERG, *Beiträge zur Einleitung im Alten Testament*, Berlin 1839, pp. 628ff.; B. JACOB, *Der Pentateuch*, Leipzig 1905, pp. 135ff.; M. KALISCH, *Exodus*, 1855, pp. 491ff.

Most modern readers of the book of Exodus have difficulty understanding why the biblical description of the tabernacle has been regarded from the beginning with the greatest possible interest by Jewish and Christian scholars alike. Although a variety of different factors were at work and the interest did shift its focus to different aspects of the issue, the continued interest is reflected in the overwhelming number of treatises on the subject throughout the history of exegesis. Hermann Witsius is typical in summarizing the logic of faith when he writes: 'God created the whole world in six days, but he used forty to instruct Moses about the tabernacle. Little over one chapter was needed to describe the structure of the world, but six were used for the tabernacle' (*Misc. Sacrorum* I, 1712, pp. 394f.).

The earliest interpreters had no doubt that the importance of the tabernacle lay in its hidden symbolism, and the issue at stake was properly to decipher its meaning. Certainly Philo's exegesis (*Vita Mos.* II.88ff.) remains one of the most impressive attempts at a consistent symbolic interpretation, the influence of which for the later history can hardly be overestimated. For Philo the tabernacle was a representation of the universe, the tent signifying the spiritual world, the court the material. Moreover, the four colors signified the four world elements, the lamp with its seven lights the seven planets and the twelve loaves of bread the twelve signs of the Zodiac and the twelve months of the year. Josephus' interpretation (*Antiq.* III, 180ff.) was basically similar and included an explanation of the priestly vestments along the same lines. Among the early church Fathers the influence of the Philonic exegesis was widespread, and is represented particularly in Clement (*Stromata* V), Theodoret (*Quaest. in Exod.* II), Jerome (*Epist.* 64), and others. In fact, much of Philo's symbolism continued to appear right up to the modern period, and seemed to appeal to man's natural reason. Even the last major attempt in Germany to resuscitate a thorough-going symbolic interpretation (Bähr, *op. cit.*) reflected in the end much of Philo's system while explicitly repudiating his natural symbolism.

Nevertheless, another form of symbolic interpretation very soon gained the ascendancy within the Christian church. Origen in his ninth *Homily on Exodus* makes reference to Philo's approach, but then moves in another direction. He saw the tabernacle as pointing to the mysteries of Christ and his church. His moral analogies in terms of the virtues of Christian life – faith compared to gold, the preached word to silver, patience to bronze (9.3) – were picked up and elaborated on at great length throughout the Middle Ages (cf. Bede, *De Tabernaculo*, MPL 91.394ff.; Rabanus Maurus, MPL 108.241ff.; Peter Callensis, *Mosaici Tabernacli Mystica Expositio*, MPL 202.1047ff.).

Perhaps the most learned and detailed treatises in the history of exegesis were called forth in the post-Reformation period in an effort to demonstrate the typology between the kingdom of God in the symbolism of the tabernacle and the church of Christ in its various forms as the invisible and visible, triumphant and militant, congregation of grace. Cocceius had drawn the major lines, but it was left to his successors to work out the thesis in great detail (cf. van Til, *op. cit.*; Witsius, '*De Tabernaculi Levitici Mysteriis*', *Misc. Sacr. I,* 1692, 3rd ed. 1712, pp. 393ff.). The hermeneutical thesis which was assumed throughout these studies was that the New Testament had provided the key to the typological method, but that it was left up to later interpreters to work out the details. Yet in spite of the alleged continuity in method, the enormous gap between the first century and the seventeenth came more and more apparent. Kalisch (*op. cit.*, p. 496) cited J. F. Cramer's curious question: 'In what sense can Christ be square?', as an extreme example of the lengths to which the logic was carried. The inability of classic Christian typology to remain close to the biblical text is finally demonstrated in Bähr's exhaustive study, which in spite of its avowed purpose did not succeed in establishing a closer connection to the actual biblical text than had his predecessors. (Cf. also the classic 'pre-critical' study in English of Patrick Fairbairn, *The Typology of Scripture*, Edinburgh 1876.)

It would be a mistake to leave the impression that interest in the tabernacle only focused on its symbolism. Although this concern was seldom completely absent, there was great interest from an early period in understanding the concrete *realia* of the physical structure. The third-century Baraita on the Tabernacle (ET, J. Barclay, *The Talmud*, London 1878, pp.334ff.) concentrated completely on solving ambiguities in the biblical text which relate to questions such as how the corners of the tabernacle were constructed, or how the bars were arranged, or the shape of the sockets. This same interest in the physical side of the tabernacle continued in the classic Jewish commentators of the Middle Ages, although often combined with traditional symbolic explanations. The historical dimension entered, along with great erudition, in Buxtorf's classic study, *Historia Arcae Foederis* (1654), but was still strongly oriented to the traditional Jewish approach to issues. However, a genuinely modern historical interest which was based on a close empirical study of the evidence appeared in Reland's *De Spoliis Templi* (1716). The growing number of biblical archaeologies from both Protestants and Catholics from the eighteenth century on, testifies to the new historical focus (cf. L. Diestel, *Geschichte des Alten Testaments in der christlichen Kirche*, Jena 1869, pp.579f. for a bibliography).

Still it can hardly be said that the modern historical approach to the tabernacle was a logical extension of the archaeological interest. Indeed often the most learned archaeologies were produced by conservative and orthodox scholars. Rather, several other factors entered in, along with the repudiation of the older typological exegesis. J. Spencer's study of the tabernacle (*De Legibus Hebraeorum Ritualibus*, 1685, III.5), which evoked much heated response because of its thesis of Egyptian influence, was no less theologically oriented than his vigorous opponent, Witsius. Spencer suggested that God had accommodated himself to the older symbols because of the 'crudeness of the age' (*seculi ruditas*), a theme which became increasingly popular. When in 1807 de Wette (*Beiträge zur Einleitung in das AT* II, p.259) characterized the whole wilderness tabernacle as a fable (*Mährchen*), he was not saying anything which had not already been claimed by the English deists. Much more significant for the new critical age were the early literary attempts to date the account of the tabernacle. J. S. Vater (*Commentar über den Pentateuch* III, Halle 1805, p. 556) was convinced of its lateness, but was unable to determine an exact date. P. von Bohlen in *Die Genesis historisch-kritisch erläutert*, Königsberg 1835, had already assumed that the tabernacle was a projection back into the Mosaic age of a late, Priestly document. From this juncture, it was only a matter of time for the full-blown theory of a 'pious fiction' to emerge. It is also evident both in this early stage of literary criticism as well as in its culmination under Kuenen and Wellhausen that a strong antipathy for priestly material accompanied the literary judgments, especially among Protestant commentators. By 1839 Hengstenberg's vigorous defense of the priestly cult as divine revelation (*Beiträge* II, pp. 652ff.) represented for most of the younger German scholars only a voice from the past. Indeed so complete was Wellhausen's victory to become that only well into the twentieth century were once again voices raised which spoke in a positive tone of the Priestly writings (Eichrodt, Welch, von Rad). Certainly there is no inclination for returning to the older, pre-critical approach to the tabernacle. However, one cannot help feeling that contemporary Old Testament scholarship has only begun to find its way back into a whole area of the biblical witness which once was treasured for its incredible richness.

6. *Theological Reflection on the Tabernacle*

The theological task, as we have envisioned it throughout this commentary, is to seek a modern reflection on the biblical witness in the context of both testaments which comprise Christian scripture. Our previous study of the Old Testament revealed that there was no comprehensive symbolic system employed by the writer, but rather a making use of older priestly tradition to testify to God's covenantal promise of dwelling with his people. Again, the New Testament provided a hermeneutical model by its attempt to reinterpret the Old Testament in the light of the priestly office of Jesus Christ, and conversely to understand this new office in the light of the old. Moreover, the history of exegesis served as a reminder that no generation can simply repristinate the past, and it warned of the danger of an exegesis which in fact hangs all too loosely on the text, while claiming the opposite.

First of all, it is striking to note that both testaments testify to the compatibility of the priestly imagery with the biblical message. In neither testaments is there any hint that the priestly language was a temporary accommodation. There is no tension between the priestly institutions and the prophetic word, nor is there any conscious progression from a lower to a higher form. The priestly institution is never regarded as an external shell to be displaced by pure spirit. Rather, the issue at stake is the nature of the priestly office. Both testaments share a common priestly witness respecting the holiness of God, and the indispensible function of the priest, sacrifice and intercession. The point needs stressing particularly in the light of the deep-seated antipathy of most Protestant Christians – one can include a number of modern Catholics as well – to the priestly institutions which are regarded as basically inferior to the prophetic.

Although the Epistle to the Hebrews provides the most thorough-going critique of the old Levitical priestly system within the New Testament, the nature of its criticism has often been misunderstood by failing to recognize the elements of genuine continuity. The presence of God, dwelling concretely among his people, is not spiritualized by the writer of Hebrews, but reinterpreted christologically in a way which reinforces the actual presence of God. The holiness of God is not secularized, as if there was no real tension between God's nature and his sinful world. Hebrews shares fully the Old Testament's awe and trepidation in seeking entrance into his sanctuary. The need for intercession, for sacrifice and reconciliation, cleansing from sin and forgiveness, is fundamental to both testaments and not a vestige of the past to be tolerated. To take the witness of Hebrews seriously is to reject the all too common theological stance which claims the New Testament warrant for understanding sin only in existential categories, the kingship of God exclusively as a political program, and Christ's function as a revealer of unconditioned love.

In spite of these important elements which bind together the testaments, Hebrews offers a major reinterpretation of the role of the Levitical system in the light of the Christian gospel. The old covenant is characterized as incomplete, transitory, and obsolete because of its inability to provide the needed reconciliation between God and his people. Seen from the perspective of the new, the way into the presence of God had not been opened. The old witnessed to the new by means of its failure. Because it foreshadowed the new covenant, the Old Testament prepared the way for the full and final redemption.

Moreover, by interpreting the nature of God and his claims on his people, the Old Testament made clear the role of Christ in his once and for all sacrifice as well as in his present role as heavenly mediator.

Yet the New Testament does not regard the work of Christ in terms of static finality. Christ's intercession continues as he waits for the realization of his priestly kingship. Again, the church is called upon to act in faith and hope in the light of the promised heavenly city. Moreover, the Old Testament continues to provide the needed context for the New Testament parenesis which admonishes endurance. The threat of apostasy symbolized in the Golden Calf which hung over the community of Israel at the very building of the sanctuary remains equally in force for the new. The other alternative to obedient worship is still a live option for the first-century Christian and each successive generation.

It has often been argued that the priestly language of the Bible is no longer meaningful for the modern age and needs radical interpretation. Indeed the hermeneutical issue is real and should not be simply dismissed by biblical scholars. While it is not immediately evident that all lines between modern culture and priestly language have been severed – youth culture seems surprisingly fascinated by the ritual and the cult – still the need for continual reinterpretation is present. The basic theological task is to retain the full dimensions of the biblical witness when seeking its modern proclamation. In regard to the tabernacle chapters in both the New and the Old Testaments, it seems unlikely that the biblical message can be dealt with adequately without considerable instruction in the biblical idiom. However, equally dangerous in an effort to preserve the tradition is an attitude which would tie its message to the language and idiom of the past. Because theology must be both faithful and relevant, there is no theoretical way out of this problem. But theology done in this arena both is serious and exciting.

THE GOLDEN CALF

32.1–35

M. Aberbach, and L. Smolar, 'Aaron, Jeroboam, and the Golden Calves', *JBL* 86, 1967, pp.129–40; L. R. Bailey, 'The Golden Calf', *HUCA* 42, 1971, pp.97–115; W. Beyerlin, *Origins and History of the Oldest Sinaitic Traditions*, ET Oxford 1965, pp.18ff., 126ff.; S. Bochartus, *Hierozoicon*, Leiden 1712, pp.350ff.; G. W. Coats, *Rebellion in the Wilderness*, Nashville 1968, pp.184ff.; R. Edelmann, 'To *ʿannot* Exodus xxxii 18', *VT* 16 (1966), p.355; O. Eissfeldt, *Die Komposition der Sinai-Erzählung Exodus 19–34*, Berlin 1966; 'Lade und Stierbild', *ZAW* 58, 1940/1, pp.190–215 = *KS* II, Tübingen 1963, pp.282ff.; F. C. Fensham, 'The Burning of the Golden Calf and Ugarit', *IEJ* 16, 1966, pp.191–3; A. H. J. Gunneweg, *Leviten und Priester*, Göttingen 1965, pp.29ff.; J. Hofbauer, 'Die literarische Komposition von Ex.19–24 und 32–34', *Zeitschrift für katholische Theologie* 56, 1932, pp.476–529; Y. Kaufmann, *The Religion of Israel*, ET Chicago 1960, London 1961, pp.13f.; S. Lehming, 'Versuch zu Ex.xxxii', *VT* 19, 1960, pp.16–50; J. Lewy, 'The Story of the Golden Calf Reanalysed', *VT* 9, 1959, pp.318–22; S. E. Loewenstamm, 'The Making and Destruction of the Golden Calf', *Biblica* 48, 1967, pp.481–90; M. Noth, 'Zur Anfertigung des Goldenen Kalbes', *VT* 9, 1959, pp.419–22; L. Perlitt, *Bundestheologie im Alten Testament*, WMANT 36, 1969, pp.203ff.; J. J. Petuchowski, 'Nochmals "Zur Anfertigung des Goldenen Kalbes"', *VT* 10, 1960, p.74; H. Schmid, *Mose, Überlieferung und Geschichte*, 1968, pp.81ff.; H. Seebass, *Mose und Aaron, Sinai und Gottesberg*, Bonn 1962, pp.33ff.; R. N. Whybray, *ʿannôt* in Exodus xxxii 18', *VT* 17, 1967, p.122.

32 ¹When the people saw that Moses took so long to come down from the mountain, the people confronted Aaron and said to him, 'Come on, make us gods to go before us. As for that fellow Moses who brought us up out of the land of Egypt, we do not know what has become of him.' ²Aaron said to them, 'Tear off the gold rings which are in the ears of your wives, your sons and your daughters, and bring them to me.' ³So all the people took off the gold rings which were in their ears and brought them to Aaron. ⁴He took it from them, and shaped it with an engraving tool, and made it into a molten calf. Whereupon

they exclaimed: 'These are your gods, O Israel, who brought you up out of the land of Egypt!' ⁵When Aaron saw this, he built an altar in front of it, and Aaron issued this proclamation: 'Tomorrow shall be a feast to the LORD.' ⁶They rose early in the morning and offered up burnt offerings and brought peace offerings. Then the people sat down to eat and drink and rose up to play.

7 Then the LORD said to Moses, 'Go down at once, for your people, whom you brought up out of the land of Egypt, have corrupted themselves. ⁸They have been quick to turn aside from the way which I commanded them. They have made themselves a molten calf and have worshiped it and sacrificed to it and said, "These are your gods, O Israel, who brought you out of the land of Egypt." '⁹And the LORD said to Moses, 'I have watched this people and indeed they are a stiff-necked people. ¹⁰Now then let me alone so that I can let my anger loose upon them to annihilate them, but I will make of you a great nation.'

11 But Moses sought to placate the LORD his God, and he said, 'O LORD, why should you vent your anger on your people, whom you have brought out of the land of Egypt with great power and with a mighty hand? ¹²Why let the Egyptians say, "With an evil intention he brought them out, to slay them in the mountains, and to annihilate them from the face of the earth"? Turn from your anger and change your mind about doing evil against your people. ¹³Remember your servants, Abraham, Isaac, and Jacob, to whom you swore by yourself and said to them: "I will increase your descendants as the stars of heaven, and I will give to your descendants all this land which I promised and they shall possess it for ever." ' ¹⁴So the LORD changed his mind about the evil that he considered doing to his people.

15 Then Moses turned and went down from the mountain with the two tablets of the testimony in his hand, tablets inscribed on both surfaces; on one side and on the other side they were inscribed. ¹⁶The tablets were the work of God, and the writing was God's, engraved on the tablets. ¹⁷When Joshua heard the uproar which the people were making, he said to Moses: 'There is the sound of war in the camp.' ¹⁸But he answered, 'It is not the sound of the cry of victory, nor the sound of the cry of defeat; it is the sound of singing that I hear!' ¹⁹As soon as he came near the camp and saw the calf and the dancing, he became enraged, and he flung the tablets from his hands, and shattered them at the foot of the mountain. ²⁰Then he took the calf which they had made and burnt it with fire, and ground it to powder, and scattered it on water and forced the Israelites to drink it.

21 Then Moses said to Aaron, 'What did this people ever do to you that you have brought such great sin upon them?' ²²Aaron replied, 'Do not let my lord be angry. You know that this people are intent on evil. ²³They said to me, "Make us gods to go before us. As for that

fellow Moses who brought us out of the land of Egypt, we do not know what has become of him." 24And I said to them, "Whoever has any gold, let him tear it off", and when they gave it to me, I threw it into the fire, and out came this calf!'

✗ 25 When Moses saw that the people were out of control – Aaron had let them get out of control to be a derision among their enemies – 26then he took his stand at the gate of the camp, and said, 'Whoever is on the LORD's side come to me', and all the Levites rallied to him. 27He said to them, 'Thus says the LORD, the God of Israel, "Arm yourselves each with his sword, and go back and forth throughout the camp from gate to gate, and let each man slay his brother, his friend, and his neighbor."' 28The Levites followed Moses' instruction, and some three thousand of the people fell that day. 29'Then Moses said, 'Today you have installed yourselves as priests to the LORD, indeed each at the cost of his son, and his brother, that he may bestow a blessing upon you today.'

30 The next day Moses said to the people, 'You have committed a great sin. But now I will go up to the LORD, perhaps I can make atonement for your sin.' 31So Moses returned to the LORD and said, 'Alas, this people have committed a great sin and have made for themselves gods of gold. 32But now if you will forgive their sin – if not, then blot me out of the book which you have written!' 33But the LORD said to Moses, 'Whoever has sinned against me, him I will blot out of my book. 34But now go, lead the people where I told you. See, my angel will lead you. But on the day that I do punish, I will punish them for their sins.'

35 Then the LORD sent a plague upon the people because they had made the calf (which Aaron made).

1. *Textual and Philological Notes*

Cf. the fragment of a Qumran text of Ex. 32 (provisionally 4Q Ex²) published by P. Skehan, *JBL* 74, 1955, pp. 182ff., which reflects the Samaritan recension.

32.1. zeh mōšeh, 'that Moses'. Brockelmann, *Hebräische Syntax* §23a, translates it 'Mose da' and speaks of the original 'deictic force' of the demonstrative.

2. LXX omits 'your sons' in the series.

4a. This verse raises a series of extremely difficult syntactical and exegetical problems which have called forth an enormous secondary literature. Cf. especially in the bibliography the survey of opinions in Rosenmüller, *Scholia, ad loc.*; Noth, *VT* 9, 1959, pp. 419ff.; Loewenstamm, *Biblica* 48, 1967, pp. 480ff. The first problem turns on determining the antecedent of 'ōṭô (it) in v. 4. Does it relate to zāhāb (gold) in v. 3, or to 'ēgel (calf) in v. 4? The second problem is closely connected. What is the meaning of the noun ḥereṭ (engraving tool?)? Traditionally (cf. LXX) it has been interpreted in the light of Isa. 8.1 as a tool for engraving metal. But how can one form a molten calf with such an instrument? The third problem concerns the verb wayyāṣar which in form can be either a qal of *ṣwr* or a hiphil of *ṣrr*. What does it mean in this verse? Usually the verb *yṣr*, not *ṣwr*, means 'to fashion'. However, a warrant for such a meaning for *ṣwr* is found in I Kings 7.15, which may denote 'to cast out of metal'.

On the basis of these difficulties two other major interpretations have been put forward. The one follows the Targ. Onk. and Peshitta (cf. NJPS) in translating 'to cast in a mold'. But the major problem, already pointed out by Bochartus, is that there is no good evidence that the noun *ḥereṭ* ever carried this meaning. To suggest a logical bridge from bag to mold is an illegitimate semantic transfer. The other interpretation, suggested by Bochartus and strongly defended by Noth, emends the noun to *ḥārîṭ* with the meaning 'bag', and takes the verb from *ṣûr*. This interpretation has its strongest warrant in II Kings 5.23. Accordingly, Aaron accepted the gold from the people, secured it all in a bag, and subsequently made it into a golden calf. Two objections can be levied against this interpretation. First, it does require an emendation. Secondly, from a literary perspective it does not add anything significant in the story which is surprising in the light of the otherwise brilliant narrative style. Cf. the elaborate refutation in J. Clericus, *ad. loc.*

I am inclined to accept the traditional interpretation of 'engraving tool' in the light of the clear warrant in Isa. 8.1. The problem of sequence is not too serious in the light of the frequent use in the Old Testament of *hysteron proteron* (Gen. 23.20; 49.27; Ex. 16.20; Isa. 14.17, etc.). For the use of *ṣûr* with a meaning of fashion, cf. *BDB*, p. 849. Stylistic considerations of the chapter as a whole also favor this interpretation (cf. exegesis).

4b. The subject 'god(s)' can be translated either singular or plural. The issue is exegetical rather than grammatical. Cf. the parallels in I Kings 12.28 (pl.) and Neh. 9.18 (sg.).

The LXX reads the verb *wayyō'm^erû* in the singular, thus attributing the statement to Aaron! However, the reading is secondary in the context of vv. 5 and 6. On *'ēlleh* (these) as an interjection, cf. A. S. Van der Woude, *Jaarbericht ex Oriente Lux* 18, 1964, pp. 309f.

5. The NEB ill-advisedly follows the Syriac in repointing the first verb to mean 'to fear'.

6. LXX reads the sg. in the first three verbs.

l^eṣaḥēq, = 'to play'. The verb can have a neutral sense (Gen. 19.14) or a decidedly sexual connotation (Gen. 26.8; 39.14). The LXX retains a neutral sense, but most modern translations prefer the latter (NEB, NAB). This move had, of course, been long since made by the Targums (*Pseudo-Jonathan*, *Neofiti*) and midrashim. Cf. the exegesis below.

7. The slightly divergent LXX reading in v. 7a appears to be influenced by Deut. 9.12.

10. Targ. Onk. offers the interpretative paraphrase: 'Refrain from thy prayer.'

13. *z^ekōr l^e* has the technical denotation of 'remember to one's credit'. Cf. H. J. Boecker, *Redeformen des Rechtslebens im AT*, WMANT 14, 1964, pp. 106ff.

18. There are several much debated problems in v. 18. (Cf. F. I. Andersen, *VT* 16, 1966, pp. 108ff.; R. Edelmann, *VT* 16, 1966, p. 355; R. N. Whybray, *VT* 17, 1967, p. 122.) A poetic metre has generally been recognized, although the length of the final colon has been debated. Several scholars contest that the

last two words ('I hear') should be included within the poem itself. Warrant for textual corruption, particularly haplography, has been sought in the LXX's reading of 'those beginning with wine' (φωνὴν ἐξαρχόντων οἴνου). However, the LXX is much more likely a secondary interpretation. Other emendations have been suggested, such as the reading 'the sound of ʿAnat', the Canaanite goddess (Edelmann).

According to the MT the poem contains a play on words between the qal form in the first two cola and the piel of the last, and therefore affords a contrast in meaning between noise and special noise or singing. Some have sought to find a homonym for the root ʿnh. Andersen's suggestion of cultic music is quite attractive, whether one derives it from the common Hebrew root ʿnh (sing) or a homonym.

25. The exact meaning of *pāruaʿ* remains uncertain. The Arabic cognate and the parallel in Prov. 29.18 suggest 'let loose' or 'lack restraint'. The LXX's rendering is of little help. The Vulgate has *nudatus*.
   šimṣāh (shame, derision) is also uncertain. The root *šmṣ* is 'to whisper', and the LXX suggests the meaning 'secret joy' or 'derision'.

28. The Vulgate and the NT (I Cor. 10.8) read 23,000 instead of the MT's 3000 men.

29. *biḇnô*. Gunneweg (*op. cit.*) suggests taking this as a *beth pretii*= in exchange for. Cf. R. J. Williams, *Hebrew Syntax*, Toronto 1967, § 246.

35. The verse is difficult because of its contradictory content: 'because they made the calf which Aaron made'. The problem is not one of textual corruption. *BH³* suggests emending to ʿāḇeḏû on the basis of Targum Onkelos. But this is misleading since Onkelos has the same Aramaic root in both places and simply avoids the difficulty by pointing the first form as a *ištap'el*. A more serious attempt to avoid the difficulty is the NJPS's translation: 'for what they did with the calf that Aaron made'. The problem of this translation does not lie in understanding the *'eṭ* as a preposition, but in the conjunction ʿal *'ašer*. The conjunction in Hebrew consistently functions to introduce a purpose clause ('because') followed by a verb (cf. Num. 20.24; Deut. 29.24; Jer. 16.11; Esth. 8.7, etc.). Even the phrase ʿal-dᵉḇar *'ašer* which would be closer to the suggested translation, functions also as a conjunction and not as a noun clause. Therefore, the translation does not seem to be defensible on syntactical grounds. It can also be challenged from the context of the chapter. In sum, the last three words appear to be a clumsy, secondary addition.

2. Literary and Traditio-Historical Analysis

A. The Redaction of chapters 32–34

There are many signs which indicate that chs. 32–34 were structured into a compositional unit in one of the final stages of the development of the book of Exodus. First of all, the chapters have been placed within an obvious theological framework of sin and forgiveness. Chapter 32 recounts the breaking of the covenant; ch. 34 relates its restoration. Moreover, these chapters are held together by a series of motifs which are skillfully woven into a unifying pattern. The tablets are received, smashed in ch. 32, recut, and restored in ch. 34. Moses' intercession for Israel begins in ch. 32, continues in ch. 33, and comes to a climax in ch. 34. The theme of the presence of God which is the central theme of ch. 33 joins, on the one hand, to the prior theme of disobedience in ch. 32, and on the other hand, to the assurance of forgiveness in ch. 34.

The achieving of this compositional unity appears to stem from the hand of a literary redactor, who composed his story. Of course, he made much use of older sources, but it is important to recognize that his task was far wider in scope than simply piecing together parallel accounts from the J and E sources. Indeed, it is the decisive role of the redactor in the formation of chs. 32–34 which distinguishes the character of this section from that of Ex. 19–24. (Cf. the discussion of his work in ch. 34.)

B. *Chapter 32*

Commentators have been quick to point out the inconsistencies within the chapter. For example, vv. 7–14 anticipate the discovery by Moses of the golden calf which occurs in 15ff. In the first passage he learns by direct communication from God, whereas in the second he discerns it from the uproar in the camp. Again, the forgiveness for which Moses interceded in vv. 11ff. and which he received in v. 14 does not tally well with the punishment in vv. 25ff., nor the refusal of forgiveness in vv. 33ff. Finally, others see a duplicate punishment in the water (v. 20) and the plague (v. 35). For these reasons there is considerable agreement among commentators in characterizing vv. 7–14 as a Deuteronomic addition and seeing vv. 25–29 as an independent tradition from a much later period. The majority of commentators, therefore, see only one original source in ch. 32 – often designated vv. 1–6, 15–20, 35 – to which later accretions have been joined. The question of whether the one source belongs to J or E remains contested and usually has been decided on cumulative evidence culled from material outside the one chapter (so Noth=J; Beyerlin=E).

In my opinion, this usual analysis is only partially true and has suffered from a failure to observe correctly some of the important literary features of the text. By a concentration on the analysis, the synthetic achievement of the whole chapter has frequently been overlooked. If we turn again to the chapter, vv. 1–6 introduce the story and are clearly of one piece (*contra* Noth). But the story evidently needs vv. 7–8 to connect with Moses' return in v. 15. The alleged contradiction between God's informing Moses (vv. 7–8) and his own discovery (vv. 17ff.) arises from failure to recognize the literary nature of the story. A topical scheme of contrasting scenes often dislocates the chronological sequence of the narrative. The author had an old piece of poetic tradition in v. 18 which he had to work into his story. He introduced it by having Joshua raise the question which called forth the poetic response. The fact that a certain tension exists between the prose and the poetic section is to be expected and is common in the Old Testament (cf. Gen. 9.20–27; Ex. 17.15; Josh. 10.12ff.). Similarly the delayed outburst of anger on seeing the calf is a typical literary device with many parallels (cf. Num. 12.2, 9), and offers no evidence for the lack of literary unity.

It is also most probable that Moses' intercession in vv. 30ff. belongs to the original story. The objection of Lehming (*op. cit.*), for example, that the punishment of 'poison water' in v. 20 excludes forgiveness, has over-interpreted the symbolism. The Ugaritic parallel (cf. below) indicates that the calf is completely exterminated and the people humiliated, but there is no indication that an ordeal with all the implications of Num. 5 is intended. Moreover, the fact that there is the lack of forgiveness (v. 33) stands in tension with the larger framework of the chapters and offers further evidence for its being in the original story.

To summarize up to this point: Exodus 32 reflects one basic source – probably J – to which there have been two expansions. Verses 7–14 are saturated with Deuteronomic language (cf. Deut. 9.25ff.), but the expansion appears to have attached to an element within the original story. This would account for the different sequence of events between vv. 7–14 and Deut. 9.25ff. The second expansion in vv. 25–29 reflects an independent tradition and introduces another issue into the story which goes beyond the original intention of the narrative (cf. below).

We turn next to the traditio-historical problem of the chapter. There has been a wide consensus among critical scholars since the turn of the century that Ex. 32 is related in some way to the events recounted in I Kings 12.25ff., in which Jeroboam I set up two golden calves. In both chapters the expression occurs: 'These are your gods, O Israel, who brought you out of the land of Egypt.' The plural form of 'gods' fits in I Kings 12, but is singularly out of place in Ex. 32. For this reason, the majority of scholars treat ch. 32 as a late interpolation into the pentateuchal narrative which has been composed by the Deuteronomic writer as a polemic against Jeroboam's policy and projected back etiologically into the Mosaic period.

Although the evidence for seeing a connection between the two chapters is strong, and in my opinion convincing, the crucial issue turns on whether the Deuteronomic editor of I Kings 12 actually created the Exodus story *de novo* in the light of the situation created by Jeroboam, or whether he was dependent on an existing story which he adjusted to suit his later polemic against Jeroboam. In my judgment, the evidence supports this second alternative. First of all, Ex. 32 has been built into a well-constructed pattern of sin and forgiveness along with chs. 33 and 34. Since these chapters show every sign of a pre-Deuteronomic redaction (cf. below), it seems highly probable for ch. 32 as well. Again, Ex. 32 shows several points of friction with the larger framework in which it now functions, which also indicates an earlier stage of the tradition. For example, Moses' intercession according to the later Deuteronomic expansion (vv. 7-14) was successful, whereas it was refused in the original story (vv. 33f.). Then again, Ex. 32 reflects several important differences from Deut. 9, which again points to a pre-Deuteronomic redaction. Finally, Beer has made the significant observation that the Deuteronomist would hardly have created as a polemic against Jeroboam a story which indicted the entire nation of idolatry had there not been an earlier tradition to that effect which he could make use of.

What then can be said about the *Sitz im Leben* of this tradition and the circle in which the story functioned? The story does not appear to have its roots in the more familiar traditions. It differs from the murmuring tradition in not sharing the motif of murmuring against Moses or seeking to return to Egypt. Then again, it does not appear to stem from traditions which arose through reflection on the office of Moses as mediator, particularly since Moses' intercession is specifically denied in this case. Nevertheless, it is of interest to note that Ex. 32 does share some elements from both these circles of traditions. In respect to the murmuring tradition, the people are pictured 'gathering against' Aaron, which is often the technical term of rebellion (cf. Num. 16.3), and are derogatory in their speaking about Moses. Moreover, in both Deut. 9 and Ps. 105 the golden calf story has been explicitly drawn into the orbit of the murmuring tradition. In respect to the traditions of Moses' office, it is significant that the problem begins with the absence of Moses in his function as mediator. Moreover, the motif of his intercession does become dominant in the later development of Ex. 32 and Deut. 9.

We conclude, therefore, that there was an independent oral tradition lying behind the story which, even in the oral stage, was attracted into the orbit of other traditions. It passed into a literary form, probably in the J source, before it was incorporated by a pre-Deuteronomic redactor into his larger narrative of chs. 32–34. Although I disagree with those scholars who have sought to recover an early tradition with a favorable attitude toward the fashioning of the calf (Gressmann; M. Newman, *The People of the Covenant*, Nashville 1962, p. 182), the original story, even in its J form, might well have lacked some of the details regarding the calf which reflect specifically Jeroboam's later practice. However, the possibility of Israel's having such an image in the pre-settlement period has been strongly defended by Eissfeldt on archaeological grounds (*op. cit.*). This undercuts Te Stroete's denial that such an image would have been possible for this period (*Exodus*, p. 218).

Finally, the passages which refer to Aaron warrant a special treatment. The problem is especially perplexing because of the lack of sufficient historical information to know exactly what is involved. The tradition seeks to legitimate the special office of the Levites within the priesthood. The heart of the tradition is found in v. 29, called by Gunneweg 'Levitenregel', which explains the special position at the cost of son and brother. The fact that this tradition is now set within a larger anti-Aaronite framework ties the chapter to the whole complicated history of the relation of the Levites to Aaron (cf. Gunneweg). A specific concern of Ex. 32 is whether this tradition arose as a reaction to the policy of Jeroboam who, as we know from I Kings 12.32, replaced the legitimate Levite priests with his own priests (so Lehming, pp. 44ff.). Another alternative, defended by Gunneweg, is to regard vv. 25–29 as an independent tradition which was only subsequently worked into an anti-Aaronite polemic, perhaps at the time of Jeroboam. This latter alternative appears to me to be far more likely and accords with the relation of the rest of the chapter to a later Deuteronomistic appropriation.

I am inclined to agree with Rudolph in regarding the confrontation between Aaron and Moses (vv. 21–24) as belonging to the original story and not part of the subsequent tendentious polemic. The description of Aaron's reaction is of one piece with his role in vv. 1–6 and, far from being a later defence of him, presents him in an awkward and ludicrous light. The omission of Moses' response is again part of the narrative style and offers no evidence of being an unexpected rupture within the story.

3. *Old Testament Context*

Exodus 32 forms an integral part of the larger literary complex which includes chs. 33 and 34. This can be easily observed in the series of major themes which run through the three chapters and tie them closely together. For example, the motif of Moses' speaking with God ends in ch. 31.11, but is picked up in 33.11, 23 and 34.29. Similarly, the major theme of Moses' intercession on behalf of Israel occurs in 32.11ff., 30ff.; 33.12ff; 34.8ff. The theme of the tablets of the law ends in 31.14 as the conclusion of the giving of the law at Sinai, but is then picked up, in their being broken in 32.15ff. and then finally restored in 34.1ff., 28f. The theme of God's presence which accompanies Israel dominates ch. 33 (1ff., 12ff.), but it had already been introduced in 32.34 and continues in 34.9. Again, the theme of God who both judges and forgives continues as a red cord throughout the three chapters (32.10ff., 14, 34; 33.3, 19; 34.6, 14).

Nevertheless, the fact that ch. 32 begins a larger literary unit does not distract from the integrity of the chapter itself, which forms an impressive example of Hebrew narrative style. Unfortunately in recent years the complexity of the critical questions has tended to obscure the literary achievement of the final stage of composition. Several of these features should be kept in mind as one attempts to understand this chapter within its present Old Testament context.

First of all, the chapter is characterized by the juxtaposition of the sharpest contrasts possible. Representative of this is the simultaneous action going on between God and Moses on the top of the mountain and between Aaron and the people at the foot of the mountain. Chapter 31 ends the period of forty days of divine instruction with Moses receiving the tablets. But down below the long period is described from the people's perspective as a long 'delay'. On the summit an architectonic calm reigns, below in the valley a restlessness which erupts into frenzied activity and boisterous noise.

The movement of the chapter progresses by a series of confrontations between two persons, in which again the sharp contrasts are juxtaposed in a very effective manner. It begins with the confrontation of Aaron and the people, shifts to the conversation between God and Moses. Then there is an encounter in turn between Moses and the people, Moses and Aaron, Moses and the Levites, before Moses returns to the mountain to intercede with God. The role of Moses as mediator ties the various parts closely together. Although it was the absence of Moses which prompted the initial confrontation between Aaron and the people, in the remaining encounters Moses is always present. Indeed, he is the one figure who has experienced both worlds, the top of the mountain with God and the valley below with the people. Moreover, the contrasting style of narrative appears also in the variety of roles which Moses fulfils. He is initially characterized as the leader who brought Israel up from Egypt, but shortly emerges as intercessor in the style of Deuteronomy, judge as in Num. 5, classic prophet who speaks the word of God in v. 27, and spiritual father of the Levite priests in contrast to Aaron.

Because the style of the chapter focuses on the series of polarities which reflects a topical interest in the content of the story, the logical sequence of the narrative is often distorted. The failure to evaluate properly this literary shaping has often led literary critics to fragment the chapter into multiple layers and sources which lack all cohesion. For example, Moses is first informed of the golden calf by God (vv. 7ff.), and only later discovers it himself (vv. 15ff.). However, the disclosure of God cannot therefore be eliminated as a disturbing interpolation. Rather, it is essential for the contrast of perspectives which the biblical author portrays between the same scene when viewed from below and from above. Again, Moses secures God's forgiveness in v. 14, but there follows a series of judgments (25ff., 35). The contrast here is between Moses' intercession for the people when he is with God and his judgment of the people when he faces them in the valley. Finally, it has often been considered illogical that Moses would have questioned Aaron only after his judgment of the people, but the scene fits into a topical sequence which progresses from people, false leadership, to faithful remnant (cf. the different sequence in Deut. 9.13ff.).

There are many other stylistic features in the chapter which reveal a remarkable narrative skill. Thus, the threat to Israel's election brought about by the golden calf is reflected in the slight change of pronouns. God speaks to Moses of 'your people' (v. 7), while Moses reminds God that they are 'your people' (v. 11). The uncertainty of the outcome is then continued in the use of the neutral term 'this people' (v. 31). Again, the contrast between Moses' identification with the people in their sin (vv. 11, 31) and Aaron's low estimate (v. 22) is striking. Finally, the retelling of the incident by Aaron is of interest and reflects a high level of subtlety.

[32.1–6] The story of the golden calf begins with the theme of Moses' absence and shows that it is closely connected with the preceding chapter which relates Moses' role during the period after the theophany (ch. 19) and the ratification of the covenant (ch. 24). There is a looser connection with 24.14 in which Aaron is appointed as Moses' substitute. Later Jewish midrash is troubled by the omission of Hur in ch. 32 and seeks to find a place for him also (cf. *Exodus Rabbah*).

There is a certain note of threat in the choice of the verb to describe the people's initial approach to Aaron: 'they gathered against' (cf. Num. 16.3). The abusive reference to Moses with flippant unconcern sets the tone for the coming activity, and reflects the absolute disapproval of the author who, in contrast to Aaron, sees the disaster from the outset. The people's request is for a substitute to take Moses' place in leading them. Clearly Aaron's response is to this demand. He has no idea of rejecting Yahweh (cf. v. 5). However, the request is now formulated by the writer from the perspective of the later outcome. Indeed, one can say that the whole subsequent history of Israel's unfaithfulness (note especially Jeroboam I) has been reflected in the request. Accordingly, the people demand a substitute for Yahweh himself: 'Make us gods who will go before us.' The people are portrayed by the narrator as apostate and polytheistic from the outset. They want 'gods' which can be fabricated. In the words of Ps. 106.20, 'They exchanged the glory of God for the image of an ox that eats grass' (cf. Neh. 9.18).

Of course, this formulation raises a whole battery of possible questions, both in respect to literary and history of religions problems. How could this have happened if the people had heard the Decalogue? Again, did they really believe that gods themselves could be 'made', or was the issue that of a symbol for God? Although obviously such questions have a validity in themselves, they do not aid greatly in understanding the present form of the narrative, but reflect problems which are somewhat oblique to it. From the writer's perspective the request was clearly idolatrous. However, when he allows Aaron to speak, there does emerge a certain ambiguity in the incident which was undoubtedly closer to the historical reality. In other words, the writer is reporting and interpreting at the same time. He is reporting the events of the great apostasy, but in a manner which makes it representative of all subsequent idolatry. The theological aims of the author, far from being a disturbing secondary element, form the warp and woof of the entire narrative.

Aaron responds to the request by ordering them to strip the gold earrings from their wives and children and bring the gold to him. No motivation is given to Aaron except that of acquiring gold, nor can any other intention be attributed to him without reading it into the story (cf. the typical midrashic move continued by Rashi). The people respond immediately and bring the gold to him. What happens then in v. 4 has continued to puzzle commentators (cf. the textual notes). Did he fashion the calf with an engraving tool, or cast the figure in a mould, or simply secure it in a bag? In spite of the exegetical difficulty of v. 4a, the essential emphasis of the verse focuses on the outcome, namely, Aaron *made* the gold into a molten calf. The fact that this straightforward summary conflicts with Aaron's own account of the calf is clearly intentional, and offers no grounds whatever for an attempted harmonization. In fact, the traditional interpretation of v. 4a – 'he formed it with an engraving tool' – fits best the movement of the story. By altering the logical sequence of its actual construction – the place for an engraving tool is surely after the form has been cast – the active participation of Aaron is purposely highlighted.

Why Aaron chose to make expressly a calf is not explained in the text, but has evoked a variety of theories from commentators. B. Jacob's explanation (*loc. cit.*) that Aaron wanted to make something completely nonsensical to expose their folly misses the mark badly. Older commentators derived the calf from the influence of Egypt during the long period of slavery there. There is obviously a *religionsgeschichtliche* background to the choice. Among the Egyptians the bull represented Apis in the pantheon while among the Canaanites he symbolized Baal. It was not by accident that Jeroboam chose the calf. However, for the story itself the consideration in selection of a calf plays no role, but a common Near Eastern reflex has exerted a force even when it was unconscious to the biblical writer.

The people on seeing the calf immediately respond by assigning the image a function: 'These are your gods, O Israel, who brought you out of Egypt.' Commentators have long been struck by the obvious disparity between the plural form and the reference to the one calf and have rightly pointed out the parallel to Jeroboam's calves (I Kings 12.28). From the perspective of the Exodus writer the people now confirm their idolatrous intent. However, Aaron's response begins to reveal the ambiguity of the original situation for the first time. When he saw their reaction, he proclaimed: 'Tomorrow will be a feast to Yahweh.' Obviously Aaron had a different intention from the people when he made the calf. The fact that he could incorporate the calf in a Yahweh festival indicates that he did not understand it as blatant apostasy from Yahweh. Nor does v.5 imply that Aaron had identified the calf with Yahweh as some older commentators suggest (Lapide). The portrayal of Aaron in this verse surely does not belong to some allegedly late attempt to mitigate his responsibility. Rather, the author allows Aaron to remain in an awkward and compromising position which is not resolved, but only intensified by his own apology in vv. 21ff.

The first scene closes with a burst of frenzied activity the effect of which is achieved by a skillful piling up of verbs. The people themselves assume control. They rise early, offer the sacrifices, eat and drink, and 'rise to play'. The final verb in Hebrew carries both a positive and negative connotation. But from what has been said regarding the writer's perspective, it seems clear enough that he means it in a negative sense. A religious orgy has begun. Certainly v. 25 confirms this impression.

For Y. Kaufmann (*op. cit.*), vv. 1–6 provide a classic example for his theory that Israel became so committed to monotheism after Sinai as to no longer even comprehend polytheism. He argues that the issue of the calf is not syncretism, namely representing Yahweh in the figure of an ox, but the replacement of him by a fetish. The point is well taken in respect to the standpoint of the author who composed the story in its present form. Israel sought to replace the living God by a statue which they saw being constructed from the gold of their earrings! However, Kaufmann has failed to reckon with the prehistory of the story. There are many signs, especially in the portrayal of Aaron, that suggest the original issue was syncretistic in character.

Yahweh was not being replaced, but represented. Clearly this was Jeroboam's intention in I Kings 12, even though the action is condemned by the Hebrew writer as perverting the true worship of Yahweh.

[32.7–14] It is essential to the narrative that God's informing Moses of the golden calf should not be removed as an interpolation (cf. literary problems). Rather the contrast between what is occurring in the valley and what is transpiring on the top of the mountain forms the very heart of the story. The disturbance in logical sequence is obvious from a comparison with Deut. 9, in which the same prayer is offered by Moses after the descent into the valley (cf. the discussion by Ibn Ezra).

The scene shifts abruptly from Israel's merry-making before the calf to Yahweh's reaction. The urgency of his command, 'Go, descend', is not reflected in 31.18 where God has finished speaking. In v. 7 there is a harsh dissidence, as if he had suddenly broken off. There is no purpose in continuing with covenant laws when the covenant has been shattered. His description of the people as '*your people*' is the divine reaction to the people's cry, 'These are *your* gods'. There is no ambiguity in Yahweh's judgment: Israel has corrupted herself. The evidence is marshalled in words from her own mouth. The Deuteronomic expansions add a further commentary in emphasizing Israel's inclination toward sin (v. 9). Nor can one soften this judgment by suggesting that apostasy is not the issue, but rather a false mode of worship (so B. Jacob). Israel's election is surely at stake because God is now prepared to annihilate her completely (cf. Num. 14.11f. and Ezek. 20.13ff.).

Nevertheless, the classic Jewish interpreters have correctly sensed a profound paradox in Yahweh's response which runs through the Bible (cf. *Exodus Rabbah* or Rashi). God vows the severest punishment imaginable, but then suddenly he conditions it, as it were, on Moses' agreement. 'Let me alone that I may consume them.' The effect is that God himself leaves the door open for intercession. He allows himself to be persuaded. That is what a mediator is for! As B. Jacob correctly observes, God could have shut the door – indeed slammed it – as he did in Deut. 3.26 when Moses requested permission to enter the promised land. Moreover, the personal promise to Moses to make him into a great nation picked up the identical words of the prior promise to Abraham (Gen. 12.2), giving Moses his strongest argument by which to counter the threat.

However, the appeal to a paradox is misunderstood if it takes the edge off the seriousness of the threat, or the intensity of Moses' intercession. Deut. 9.25 speaks of his lying prostrate for another forty days and nights. Moses uses three arguments which appear in slightly different order in Deut. 9. He appeals to God's miraculous delivery of Israel from Egypt, which includes the gentle reminder of 'thy people'. He calls to mind how the Egyptians would interpret Israel's destruction, bringing shame on God himself (cf. Deut. 9.28; Ezek. 20.14). Finally, he appeals to the promise of God to the Fathers: 'Remember Abraham, Isaac, and Israel, thy servants . . . .' To summarize this appeal under the traditional rabbinic rubric of 'the merits of the Fathers', as Cassuto does, runs the danger of badly blurring the central issue. Moses' appeal is not to some accumulated deposit of merit which can be tapped, but to the *promise* of God himself. Moses does not attempt to excuse or mitigate Israel's sin, but he seeks to overcome it by falling back ultimately on what God can do in making a future possible.

The writer brings this scene to a close by an explicit reference to its effect on God. Yahweh changes his mind regarding his intention to destroy Israel. If this sentence is read by itself, it makes the God of Israel as arbitrary as Zeus. If it is read in its full context, it epitomizes the essential paradox of the Hebrew faith: God is 'merciful and gracious . . . but will not clear the guilty' (34.7).

[32.15–20] The description of Moses' return is a marvellous account of the slow build-up of suspense and its sudden explosion into action. However one regards the verse which relates God's conversation about the calf, the description of the actual descent is described in a way completely unrelated to this prior knowledge. Moses starts down the mountain carrying the two tablets of the testimony. He descends as if the covenant were still in order. Indeed, the writer has time, as it were, to describe in some detail the tablets – they were written on both sides with the very writing of God himself – before Moses meets Joshua half-way down the mountain. The suspense mounts by a sensitive use of sound. The camp is too far away to see, but it can be heard. Joshua, the younger man, misunderstands the sound, but Moses has the sharper ear and the experience of years. With a clever play on words, he identifies the sound as singing. Still only a hint has been given of what is to follow.

Finally, Moses reaches the foot of the mountain – Joshua has already fallen out of the narrative once his role is over – and draws near to the camp. Then he sees . . . in an instant, the calf and the dancing. The writer pauses for one brief glimpse at Moses' reaction: he became enraged. Then he plunges into describing an unbroken series of violent actions. He threw down the tablets and shattered them, not because he was tired, but to dramatize the end of the covenant. Then he took the calf, burnt it with fire, ground it to powder, scattered it on the water and forced the people to drink the mixture.

The old crux as to how the golden calf would be both burnt and ground to powder has been partially resolved by a Ugaritic parallel (cf. the detailed notes). The text describes how 'Anat cleaves Mot with a sword, burns him with fire, grinds his body with millstones, and strews his flesh upon the field. In this parallel at least three of the important verbs are similar to the Exodus narrative, even in the order of burn, grind, and scatter. The significance is that the text depicts Mot's total annihilation by a series of actions regardless of whether the different images employed were logically compatible (cf. Loewenstamm, *op. cit.*). This appears to be the intention behind the biblical description. Likewise the feature of forcing the people to drink the water is a further sign of the total destruction of the cursed image in which Israel participates to her shame. An allusion to the ordeal in Num. 5 may also be in the background, but again should not be pressed. The issue at stake is not to determine the guilt, but to eradicate it.

[32.21–24] The passage which preceded culminated in a violent display of anger and judgment on the part of Moses. It was described in an unbroken series of verbs. But up to now Moses has not spoken any words. In the two scenes which follow, Moses first addresses Aaron before calling for a faithful remnant to mete out judgment. A contrast between the old priesthood represented by Aaron and the new faithful priesthood represented by the Levites has often been suggested, but in fact, the relation between the two units is far less precise.

Moses accosts Aaron with a typical idiom of the disputation (cf. Gen. 20.9), and demands an explanation. After a suitably humble introduction, Aaron briefly recapitulates the events and concludes with the astonishing statement: 'I threw the gold into the fire and out came this calf'! It is remarkable to see how widely the commentators vary in their evaluation of this defense by Aaron. On the one hand, commentators such as Bäntsch and Gressmann characterize the answer as evidencing 'childish naïvety'. Others speak of an attempt at humor (Fensham), or reject it as a classic example of face-saving (Heinisch). On the other hand, Jewish commentators tend to defend Aaron and accept his defense at face value (Jacob, Cassuto). Loewenstamm (*op. cit.*) appeals to the various midrashic passages as leaving no doubt that they accepted Aaron's claim for the calf to have been self-produced, and seeks support in Ugaritic literature for holding this to be an ancient and widespread motif.

Perhaps the best clue to the author's intention is afforded by his technique in summarizing the event. When Aaron relates the role of the people, he repeats *verbatim* the entire dialogue as recorded in v. 1 along with its demand for other gods and the abusive reference to Moses. When he comes then to his own role in gathering the gold, the account is considerably abbreviated and minimizes Aaron's own role. The people bring the gold of their own accord, as if it had not been requested by him. When he reaches the crucial point on the actual construction of the calf, Aaron's story diverges completely from the original account. He pictures himself uninvolved. The calf came out all by itself. Moreover, the fact that Aaron commences his defence with a broad condemnation of the people as evil by nature and ends up disavowing any responsibility for himself, hardly speaks well for Aaron. Perhaps the failure of the biblical writer to press the issue further or offer any comment on this defense would indicate that his concern did not lie with Aaron himself. Rather Aaron's whole behavior, both in his original weakness and subsequent defense, serves merely to highlight by contrast the role of the true mediator. Aaron saw the people 'bent on evil'; Moses defended them before God's hot anger (v. 11). Aaron exonerated himself from all active involvement; Moses put his own life on the line for Israel's sake. Aaron was too weak to restrain the people; Moses was strong enough to restrain even God.

[32.25–30] There is a real sense in which the judgment wrought by the Levites serves as a commentary on the role of Aaron in the story even though the commentary probably reflects a later period. Whatever its actual historical roots, there is a strongly anti-Aaron polemic reflected in its formulation. Moses observes that the people 'were out of control' to the 'delight of their enemies'. Unfortunately the exact meaning of both Hebrew words is unclear, but significantly the author places the blame for the sorry situation solidly on Aaron: 'He had let them break loose.' For this author one can be guilty for failing to act.

Then Moses stood in the gate of the camp and sounded the appeal. 'Those who are with Yahweh, come to me.' Up to this point in the story no distinctions had been made among the people. 'All the people' had responded to Aaron's call for gold (v. 3) and had celebrated the worship of the calf. Consequently 'this people' as a collective entity received the divine condemnation (v. 9). Suddenly a distinction within Israel is called for. Certainly it is to misunderstand fully the point of this story to argue that here is evidence to indicate how small the group was which was apostate. Of the six-hundred-thousand people (*sic!*) only three thousand were involved, and probably foreigners at that! (Cf. *Exodus Rabbah*). Clearly the point of the story is the reverse. Moses called for supporters of Yahweh and only the Levites came forward. Aaron had sought to combine worship of the calf with worship of Yahweh (v. 5). Now the sharpest possible distinction is made, which forced upon all the choice of a decision for or against Yahweh and cut away all the middle ground.

Moses now assumes the role of prophet and in one of the rare usages of the idiom in the Pentateuch, proclaims the divine word: 'Thus says Yahweh'. The word is of judgment directed to the Levites as its agent who immediately proceed to execute the awesome punishment. Verse 29 contains the heart of the narrative. 'Today' marks the decisive moment in the life of the tribe, and as in Ps. 2.7, it designates the act of special ordination. At the cost of son and brother the Levites have won their position as the blessed of the Lord. Implicitly the story condemns Aaron as representative of the old priesthood for his failure to separate rigorously between the faith of Yahweh and its rivals. The Levites were faithful at an enormous cost. It is likely that the particular formulation of this story reflects a later history of struggle for the priesthood in which Aaron had become a prototype of an unfaithful priest. Particularly in the light of Aaron's later prestige, it is all the more remarkable that this story was retained in the tradition.

[32.30–35] In the last section Moses once again returns to his role as mediator. Nor should it be regarded as too disturbing that he had already secured God's forgiveness in v. 14. Anticipation and repetition are the hallmarks of the whole narrative. The intercession displays the same features of intense struggle. To the people Moses can only hold out the hope that 'perhaps' God would forgive. But with God Moses is prepared to exchange his life for their forgiveness. The inner movement of this intercession and response is strikingly different from the earlier one in vv. 9ff. There God let himself be persuaded, but here there is no room for negotiation. God rejects Moses' plea for a full forgiveness. Indeed the people will not be destroyed *en masse* and the promise of the possession of the land is reiterated. But an ominous warning of coming judgment against the evil-doers is held out. 'In that day' they will be judged. Some commentators find in the future threat an explicit reference to Jeroboam's policy. Within the present context the threat which is introduced at the end of ch. 32 forms a bridge to ch. 33 and ultimately to the restored covenant of ch. 34. The final verse rounds off the theme of judgment in the chapter without having a close relation to the verses which precede.

Detailed Notes

32.1. *yiqqāhēl 'al* = 'assemble against'. Cf. G. Coats, *Rebellion in the Wilderness*, p. 188, on the use of the verb in the wilderness traditions.

4. The literature dealing with the technical problem of fashioning the image of a calf in gold, in addition to the history of religions problems, is extensive. Cf. the bibliography to ch. 32. Above all the discussion in Bochartus, Eissfeldt, Noth, and Loewenstamm.

10. On the role of Moses as intercessor, cf. F. Hesse, *Die Fürbitte im Alten Testament*, Erlangen 1949; G. von Rad, *Old Testament Theology* I, pp. 294f.; J. Muilenburg, 'The Intercession of the Covenant Mediator', *Words and Meanings. Essays . . . to D. Winton Thomas*, ed. P. R. Ackroyd, Cambridge 1968, pp. 159ff.

13. Cf. S. Schechter's classic essay on 'The Zachuth of the Fathers', *Some Aspects of Rabbinic Theology*, New York 1923, pp. 170ff.

15. On the terminology of the tablets in the Old Testament, cf. the more recent discussions in S. Lehming, *op. cit.*, pp. 32ff., and Perlitt, *op. cit.*, p. 211. The older literary critics felt that the divergent vocabulary divided nicely into the traditional sources: E says 'tables of stone' (24.12); P uses 'the two tables of the testimony' (31.18a; 32.15a, etc.); J and D speak of 'the two tables of stone' (34.1, 4; Deut. 4.13). Deuteronomy uses also 'the tables of the covenant' (9.9). However, it is a question whether this theory can be fully sustained because the argument was often circular.

16. On the formula 'the work of God', cf. G. von Rad, 'Das Werk Jahwes', *Studia Biblica et Semitica . . . Th. C. Vriezen Dedicata*, Wageningen 1966, pp. 290ff.

18. The problem of poetic meter in v. 18 is discussed by F. I. Andersen, *VT* 16, 1966, pp. 108ff.

20. The Ugaritic passage often cited as a parallel is 49:11:31–36 in C. H. Gordon, *Ugaritic Textbook*, Rome 1965, and translated by H. L. Ginsberg in *ANET²*, p. 140:

> 'With sword she doth cleave him.
> With fan she doth winnow him –
> With fire she doth burn him.
> With hand-mill she grinds him –
> In the field she doth sow him.
> Birds eat his *remnants* . . .'

24. On the tradition of the self-producing idol, cf. Loewenstamm, *op. cit.*, pp.488ff.
25. The problem of Aaron is treated in most detail by Gunneweg, *op. cit.*, pp.88, but cf. also Lehming, pp.40ff.
34. On the accompanying angel cf. Ex.23.23.

4. *New Testament Context*

The golden calf episode is referred to explicitly in two different passages within the New Testament (I Cor. 10.7f.; Acts 7.38ff.). In the first passage Paul makes a homiletical use of a series of Old Testament stories taken from the wilderness wandering period – the crossing, the manna and quail, the golden calf, the fiery serpents – in order to draw a warning for the church from Israel's failure. In spite of the fact that the Israelites shared in the selfsame sacraments – they were baptized and partook of the same spiritual food and drink – they became idolaters. Paul applies the golden calf story to the Christian community as a direct lesson which was 'written down for our instruction', even though the church has experienced the 'end of the ages'.

The second reference, in Acts, is a more complex interpretation and played a far greater role in the subsequent history of the Old Testament passage within the Christian church. Nevertheless, it is significant that some of the basic notes of the New Testament's understanding of the passage shortly ceased to be heard in the church. In the first place, one is struck by the strong sense of identification which the author of Acts makes between Israel and the Christian community. It was to 'our fathers' that Moses received 'living oracles to give to us'. Indeed, through the LXX translation the 'assembly' in the wilderness becomes the *ekklesia* in the wilderness which further supports the continuity between Israel and the church. Again, although the whole point of the story is judgmental and a parallel is drawn between the rejection of Moses and of Jesus, the condemnation of Israel's sin is proclaimed from the perspective of one standing within the community. The judgment on Israel had already been passed by the prophets and is simply renewed and intensified by the disciples. Clearly the writer of Acts sees Stephen as a prophetic figure who employs the Old Testament idiom in condemning them as 'stiff-necked . . . uncircumcised in heart and ears . . . Which of the prophets did not your fathers persecute?' Moreover, in the portrayal of Stephen's death, the writer of Acts appears to be painting him as one who stands in the line of Moses and Jesus and who died interceding for his people.

The actual interpretation of the golden calf story shows a number of features which are consistent with the writer's use of the Old Testament throughout the speeches. The making of the calf is preceded by a description of the act as open rebellion: 'they refused to obey him, but thrust him aside'. Commentators have suggested that the influence of Ezekiel's interpretation (20.8) is present, but the parallel expression in 7.27 would rather seem to indicate a characteristic heightening of the element of conscious disobedience. Likewise, the New Testament writer supplies an inner motivation for the demand for the calf: 'in their hearts they turned to Egypt', which is the similar technique used in the interpretation of 7.25. The folly of the deed is brought out by emphasizing that the calf was an idol and the 'works of their own hands'.

A major point of the speech lies in the accusation that if Israel had been obedient to living oracles given to Moses, they would not have fallen into idolatry, but would have recognized Christ. Later Christian interpretation saw in the expression (v. 42), 'God gave them over to worship the host of heaven' (cf. Rom. 1.24) a complete severing of the covenant with the Jews and an abandonment of them by God. However, the framework of the speech, particularly its concluding note, would indicate that this judgment did not at first carry such an absolute tone of finality.

5. History of Exegesis

K. BARTH, *Kirchliche Dogmatik*, IV/1, pp.470ff., ET *Church Dogmatics* IV/1, pp.427ff.; W. W. BAUDISSIN, 'Kalb, goldenes', *RE* IX, pp.708–10; PHILLIPS BROOKS, 'The Fire and the Calf', *Sermons Preached in English Churches*, New York 1883; WILHELM VISCHER, *Das Christuszeugnis des Alten Testaments* I, Zürich 1946, pp.251ff.; H. HELLBARDT, *Das Bild Gottes*, Munich 1939; S. E. LOEWENSTAMM, 'The Making and Destruction of the Golden Calf', *Biblica* 48, 1967, pp.481ff.; E. MIHALY, 'A Rabbinic Defense of the Election of Israel', *HUCA* 35, 1964, pp.103ff.; F. MONCAEUS, *Aaron purgatus* (Atrebati 1606), reprinted in *Critici Sacri*, I/2; R. DE PURY, *Der Exodus*, Neukirchen 1961, pp.62ff.; L. SMOLAR and M. ABERBACH, 'The Golden Calf Episode in Postbiblical Literature', *HUCA* 39, 1968, pp.91ff.; M. WALZER, 'Exodus 32 and the Theory of Holy War: The History of a Citation', *HTR* 61, 1968, pp.1–14.

The early church made frequent reference to Ex.32, most often in a polemic against the synagogue. Some of the major points of the attack had already been adumbrated in Acts 7. Israel had refused to obey the 'living oracles' (v. 38) received by Moses, but turned to idols and sacrificed to a calf. Therefore, God gave them over to their folly and in their blindness they failed to recognize the Christ. Although the language of Acts was influential in shaping the use of the early church, the perspective from which the attack was launched very soon diverged from that of the New Testament. Consistently the church was contrasted with the disobedience of the synagogue. Perhaps the most extreme form of the polemic appears in the *Epistle of Barnabas* (14.4; 4.7ff.), which argued that the covenant had been withdrawn from Israel because of her idolatry, symbolized by the breaking of the tablets, and given to the church. Indeed, it was argued that the burden of observing the ceremonial law was a punishment derived from her sin with the golden calf (Justin, *Dialogue* 20.3; 21.1; 22.1; *Apostolic Constitutions* VI. 20.6; cf. Smolar, *op. cit.* p. 96). It remained a common theme among the Fathers to castigate the Jews for their idolatrous, foolish abandoning of the covenant of God (Origen, *Contra Celsum* II. 74; Irenaeus, *Adv. Haer.* IV.3; Tertullian, *Adv. Jud.* 1). Augustine saw in the calf worship a sign of everlasting damnation because Israel had given herself over to the body of the Devil (*Quaest. in Hept.* II. 142).

For the synagogue the story of the golden calf had been a source of embarrassment from the outset. Josephus omitted the story from his history, and Philo (*V. Mos.* II. 161ff.) did his best to exonerate most of Israel and Aaron from the blame (cf. his use of Num. 17). However, the dilemma increased with the church's polemical use of the story. Smolar and Aberbach (*op. cit.*) have made out a good case that the rabbinic defense varied in relation to the audience. On the one hand, the Jews frankly admitted the seriousness of the offense in accordance with the clear testimony of scripture. Indeed, in homilies addressed to the Jews themselves the rabbis agreed that the evil consequences stemming from the event had never been exhausted: 'No punishment ever comes upon Israel in which there is not a part payment for the sin of the golden calf' (*B. Sanh.* 102a and elsewhere). R. Simeon ben Yoḥai went so far as to say that Israel had been without any sickness when she stood on Mount Sinai, but these afflictions appeared after the sin of the golden calf (*Lev. Rabbah*, XVIII. 4, cited Smolar, p. 14).

On the other hand, there grew up among the Jews an extensive apologetic literature which sought to blunt the attack which had arisen from the church's use of the story. The form of the defense varied considerably in the midrashic literature, but certain classic arguments became popular. First, Israel as a nation was not chiefly to blame, but the trouble began with the 'mixed multitude' who came from Egypt (Saadia, Rashi). Israel had miscalculated the period of forty days announced by Moses and therefore was tricked by Satan into supposing that Moses was dead (*Pseudo-Jonathan*; *Exodus Rabbah* 41.7; Rashi). A variant of this theme was that Satan tricked Israel in shaping the golden calf (*Neofiti* I). Secondly, Aaron had sought to restrain the people by various tactics. By demanding the earrings of the wives and daughters he anticipated that they would refuse (*PRE* 45; Rashi). He postponed the festival a day hoping that Moses would return. Saadia argued that he had the calf made to discover the idolaters within Israel (cited and criticized by Ibn Ezra). Finally, Aaron acquiesced because he feared that he would be killed along with Hur, and he sought to spare Israel this additional sin. Moses' failure to judge Aaron is cited as additional evidence of his innocence (Nachmanides). But above all, the apology sought to dispel the charges which had been levelled against the eternal covenant between God and the Jewish people. Because of the 'merits of the Fathers' and the intercession of Moses, Israel had been forgiven.

In the period which followed, particularly after the political hegemony of the Christian church, a variety of other issues were reflected in the interpretation of the golden calf story. Interestingly enough, the rabbinic tradition of interpreting the story continued to play an increasingly important role in Christian exegesis up to the Post-Reformation period. Particularly through Nicholas of Lyra the major rabbinic interpretations were popularized, and transmitted without serious criticism (cf. the *Postilla ad loc.*, and especially the notes of Paul of Burgos). First of all, Christian theologians began to sense that the attack on the apostasy of the Jews could easily backfire. Lapide is typical of the Roman Catholic position in denying that 'all the people', now understood as the *tota ecclesia*, could have been apostate. They erred in their profession of faith, not in the faith itself (*ad loc.*). Similarly Calvin, with his emphasis on God's eternal covenant, denied that the covenant was altogether annulled; it was only temporarily ruptured: 'He at least had some hidden roots from whence the church sprang up anew' (*ad loc.*). Paul of Burgos argued that the breaking of the tablets did not signify the end of the law, since the moral law continued unimpared.

Again, Moses is greatly praised for his passionate intercession and frequently seen as a type of Christ (I Clem. 53; Cyril of Alexandria, *Glaphyrorum in Ex. Liber* III, MPG 69.530; Bede; Piscator). He stood in the breach and was willing to die for Israel. Then again, the story lent itself very early in Christian preaching to a moralistic application as it had previously been used by Philo. Tertullian (*De Cultu Feminarum* II.13) warns against the continuing danger of gold. Ambrose (*De Elia et Jejunio* VI. 16, MPL 14.705) makes much of the drunkenness and immorality which always accompanies idolatry and contrasts this behavior with the *abstentia* in which the law was first given (cf. Gregory, *Moralia* I. VIII. 10, MPL 75.532). Bede spiritualizes the event to see the calf as a sign of the body of the devil which must be burnt by fire in order to mortify the flesh (*Comm. in Exod.* 32, MPL 91.330).

It is also significant that quite early in the Christian era, Christian interpreters began to follow the Jewish tradition in defending Aaron's reputation. Augustine is quite sure that Aaron would not have lied to Moses because he knew that God had shown Moses what had really happened (*Quaest. in Hept.* II. 145). Likewise, Theodoret (*ad loc.*) defends Aaron's faithful intention of serving God with arguments similar to those of the rabbis. Clarius (*Critici Sacri, ad loc.*) goes so far as to accept the legend that the Magi created the calf after Aaron had sought to destroy it. But perhaps the most elaborate defense of Aaron is found in F. Moncaeus' classic essay *Aaron Purgatus* of 1606 (reprinted *Critici Sacri*, I/2). Moncaeus argues that Aaron not only did not commit an evil act, but also intended the calf to serve as the cherubim. It was the people who corrupted the symbol into something evil. Of course, there continued to be commentators who objected to these apologetic moves and who judged Aaron to be without excuse (cf. Fagius, *Critici Sacri, ad loc.*).

Further, it is remarkable to observe how particular verses in the story have assumed a new importance because of an association with Christian doctrine. Verse 10, in which God says to Moses 'Let me alone', is discussed at great length both by the church Fathers, Scholastics, and Reformers. Usually Christians agreed with the rabbis that God was speaking 'in a human fashion' (*kilšōn bᵉnē 'āḏām*, Ibn Ezra). Lyra spoke of *more humano* since God is not in fact subject to human pressure. Theodoret sees God as exciting Moses to intercede for Israel. Gregory follows a similar approach that God wants to be restrained. Calvin senses a testing of Moses' faith as God sets before him an apparent contradiction in his word. He declares his intention to destroy his people while at the same time quickening his mind to intercede.

Again, Moses' request, 'Blot me out of thy book' (v. 32), caused considerable difficulty for Christian interpreters. On the one hand, it seemed highly irresponsible for Moses to wager his 'eternal salvation' in this way. On the other hand, Moses sought the impossible because God had already determined the righteous in his immutable will. Augustine considered the statement 'careless', and due to his passionate concern (*Quaest in Hept.* II. 147). Hugo Victorinus commented that it stemmed from the 'impetuosity of his human affection' (cited by C. a Lapide *ad loc.*). Others spoke of his being carried away by vehemence (Calvin) or honest zeal (Joseph Hall). In sum, no one was prepared to accept that Moses' salvation was in jeopardy. Only occasionally did anyone question whether the 'book of life' in the New Testament sense was intended.

The transition to the historical-critical approach of the modern period was prepared in a variety of ways. Whereas classic orthodox Christian exegesis had continued to emphasize the folly and stupidity of Israel's idolatry, Moncaeus' essay (*op. cit.*) derived the element of stupidity from a mistaken reading of the story. He judged it incredible to make the high priest of Israel responsible for idolatry. He sought, therefore, to find another avenue into the story. Again, Clericus and others sought a depth dimension when insisting that the calf was only a symbol of the deity and cited classical sources to show that no religion has ever identified their god with the image itself (cf. Clericus on Gen. 31.30). Bochartus, Rosenmüller and others had already recognized the parallel of Ex. 32 with I Kings 12, but deduced from this that Jeroboam had also derived the idea of a calf from Egypt.

The historical-critical position emerged from a new appraisal of the literary problem. Ewald had suggested that a later writer – he used the term 'Fourth Narrator' – had transferred an event which happened some centuries after Moses to the wilderness period, namely, that Israel worshipped Yahweh in the form of a bull (*History of Israel* II[2], ET London 1869, pp. 182ff.). But it was the work of Kuenen and Wellhausen which drew the full literary consequences. Accordingly, Ex. 32 was a projection back into the Mosaic period of a polemic intended against the northern kingdom in the period subsequent to Jeroboam I. The classic literary-critical approach usually derived the narrative from the period of Hezekiah (cf.

Kennedy, *HDB* I), but some like Pfeiffer (*Introduction to the OT*, New York 1948, London 1952, p. 377) pushed the date up to 600. In more recent years reaction against the excesses of the literary-critical method has set in. A connection between Ex. 32 and Jeroboam's policy has been maintained, but often an older tradition has been sought behind the Exodus story (cf. Beyerlin).

Finally, it is of interest to note the extensive theological usage which the story of the golden calf has had in the modern period largely unaffected by the historical-critical development. Moreover, the contemporary appraisal is strikingly different from classic Victorian sermons, such as that of Phillips Brooks. H. Hellbardt's essay, *Das Bild Gottes* (1939), was written against the background of the church's conflict with the threat of Nazism. Hellbardt used the story as a vehicle for vigorously condemning the church's seeking a visible substitute for God himself (p. 24) which was only a projection of a people's dreams (p. 33), and which concealed naked paganism. He contrasted the image of Christ with all forms of cultural deities which belong to the demonic. Also Karl Barth (*op. cit.*) found in the story a good example of how man's religion could confuse the *vox populi* with the *vox Dei*. The institution can at any moment produce the calf on its own. Indeed, de Pury (*op. cit.*) finds in Aaron the father of Liberal Protestantism and the natural theology of Catholicism! He sought to be relevant to the people's 'religious need' and ended up losing the faith itself.

6. *Theological Reflection in the Context of the Canon*

The Old Testament's witness attributes an unusual importance to the story of the golden calf. Not only does it form the heart of a lengthy unit of three chapters, but it assigns its massive bulk to a place right in the middle of the divine instructions at Sinai. It produces a rupture of enormous proportions and stands as a threat to the covenant from the beginning. In spite of the miraculous delivery from Egypt, of the majesty and awe of Sinai, the Old Testament testifies that Moses had not even descended from the mountain before Israel was apostate. Indeed, embedded at the heart of the sacred tradition lies Israel's disobedience and rebellion. The Old Testament understood this episode of flagrant disobedience, not as an accidental straying, but as representative in its character. The story of the divine redemption includes the history of human resistance and rebellion. The New Testament understands this story as equally relevant to the life of the church. The threat of apostasy does not lie in the distant past or attach solely to the people of Israel. One does not ever reach a state of immunity from this basic temptation. Not even the sure signs of divine grace, as in the sacraments (I Cor. 10.1ff.), form a secure resting place of this basic threat.

What gives the story such a cutting edge is its penetrating insight that religion itself can be the means to disobedience. Aaron, who is the representative of the cult, is left to squirm as a dubious ally. He has no word from God and yet he tries to adjust to the situation by throwing the mantle of religion over their program for change. What was proposed as a device to salvage the faith shortly produced a compromise which struck a blow at the heart of the divine-human relation.

Both testaments testify to the sheer folly of the episode. The Psalmist marvels that Israel could have actually 'exchanged the glory of God for an image of an ox that eats grass'. Isaiah's satire on the stupidity of idolaters (ch. 44) finds echoes in the New Testament's description: 'they rejoiced in the works of their hands' (Acts 7.41). However, the note of folly is sounded from the context of the worshipping community. When one can catch a glimpse of God's true majesty and praise him for his mighty works (Ps. 106.1ff.), from that perspective the irrational madness of the human response emerges with great clarity. The story of the calf testifies to the extent of man's vision when he has cut himself off from the sight of the God of Sinai, and growing restless and bored, sets out to construct his own gods. By adding the phrase: 'they turned in their hearts to Egypt', the New Testament has begun to probe the roots of human alienation from God by projecting it deep into the heart long before its manifestation in the actual deed of renunciation.

Then again, the story of the golden calf has found a place in scripture as a testimony to God's forgiveness. Israel and the church have their existence because God picked up the pieces. There was no golden period of unblemished saintliness. Rather, the people of God are from the outset the forgiven and restored community. There is a covenant – and a new covenant – because it was maintained from God's side. If there ever was a danger of understanding Sinai as a pact between partners, the rupture of the golden calf made crystal clear that the foundation of the covenant was, above all, divine mercy and forgiveness.

Finally, in between Israel and God was the mediator, who wrestled with God and stood in the breach. Alongside the figure of Moses as the great law giver, stands Moses the intercessor, who knowing the full wrath of God, shielded Israel from its full force and secured for his people the renewal of the promise.

GOD'S PRESENCE ENDANGERED

33.1–23

R. E. CLEMENTS, *God and Temple*, Oxford and Philadelphia 1965, pp. 26ff.; F. DUMERMUTH, 'Joshua in Ex. 33.7–11', *TZ* 19, 1963, pp. 161ff.; M. HARAN, 'The Nature of the *"'ōhel mô'ēdh"* in the Pentateuchal Sources', *JSS* 5, 1960, pp. 50–65; A. R. JOHNSON, 'Aspects of the use of the term *pānîm* in the Old Testament', *Festschrift O. Eissfeldt*, Halle 1947, pp. 155–60; J. MAIER, *Das altisraelitische Ladeheiligtum*, Berlin 1965, pp. 12ff.; J. MUILENBURG, 'The Intercession of the Covenant Mediator, Exodus 33:1a, 12–17', *Words and Meanings: Essays ... to D. Winton Thomas*, ed. P. R. Ackroyd and B. Lindars, Cambridge 1968, pp. 159ff.; F. NÖTSCHER, *'Das Angesicht Gottes Schauen' nach biblischer und babylonischer Auffassung*, Würzburg 1924; G. VON RAD, 'The Tent and the Ark', *The Problem of the Hexateuch*, ET 1966, pp. 103ff.; J. REINDL, *Das Angesicht Gottes im Sprachgebrauch des Alten Testaments*, Leipzig 1970; F. STIER, *Gott und sein Engel im Alten Testament*, Münster 1934; G. WESTPHAL, *Jahwes Wohnstätten nach den Anschauungen der alten Hebräer*, BZAW 15, 1908, pp. 114ff.

33 ¹Then the LORD said to Moses, 'Go up, depart from here, you and the people that you have brought from the land of Egypt to the land of which I swore to Abraham, Isaac, and Jacob, saying: "To your descendants I will give it." – ²and I will send an angel before you, and I will drive out the Canaanites, the Amorites, the Hittites, the Perizzites, the Hivites, and the Jebusites – ³to a land flowing with milk and honey, but I will not go up in your midst, lest I consume you on the way, for you are a stiff-necked people.'

4 When the people heard this harsh word, they went about like mourners, and no one put on his ornaments. ⁵The LORD said to Moses, 'Say to the Israelites, "You are a stiff-necked people. If for one moment I were to go in your midst, I would consume you. Now take off your ornaments that I may decide what to do with you."' ⁶Therefore the Israelites remained stripped of their ornaments from Mount Horeb onward.

7 Now Moses used to take the tent and pitch it outside the camp, at a distance from the camp. It was called the tent of meeting. Whoever sought the LORD would go out to the tent of meeting which was outside the camp. ⁸Whenever Moses would go out to the tent, all the people would rise and stand, each at the entrance of his tent, and follow Moses with their eyes until he had entered the tent. ⁹When Moses entered the tent, the pillar of cloud would descend and stand at the entrance to the tent while he spoke with Moses. ¹⁰When all the people saw the pillar of cloud standing at the door of the tent, all the people would rise and bow low, each at the entrance of his tent. ¹¹The LORD would speak to Moses face to face, as one man speaks to another. When he would then return to the camp, his young attendant, Joshua, the son of Nun, would not stir out of the tent.

12 Moses said to the LORD, 'Look, you say to me, "Bring up this people," but you have not let me know whom you plan to send with me. Moreover you have said, "I know you by name, and indeed you have gained my favor." ¹³Now then if I have gained your favor, show me your ways that I may know you and continue in your favor. Consider, too, that this nation is your people.' ¹⁴He said, 'My presence will go and I will set your mind at rest.' ¹⁵And he said to him, 'If your presence will not take the lead, do not let us leave this place. ¹⁶For how can it ever be known that I have gained your favor, I and your people, except you go up with us, and we be distinguished, I and your people, from all other people on the face of the earth?' ¹⁷Then the LORD said to Moses, 'This very thing that you have asked, I will do because you have gained my favor and I know you by name.'

18 Then he said, 'Let me see your glory.' ¹⁹He answered, 'I will make all my goodness pass before you and I will proclaim the name LORD before you. I will be gracious to whom I will be gracious and I will show mercy on whom I will show mercy. ²⁰'But', he said, 'you cannot see my face, for no mortal man can see me and live.' ²¹And the LORD said, 'Look, there is a place beside me. Station yourself on the rock, ²²and, as my glory passes by, I will put you in a crevice of the rock and shield you with my hand until I have passed by. ²³Then I will remove my hand and you will see my back, but my face shall not be seen.'

1. Textual and Philological Notes

33.2. LXX reads 'my angel . . . he will drive out'.

3. LXX has an initial verb εἰσάξω which eases the difficulty of the MT. In the MT v. 3 must be seen as a continuation of v. 1 with v. 2 functioning as a parenthesis. The LXX's reading is hardly original. Of course, other literary-critical solutions are possible. Cf. Kuenen's suggestion of seeing vv. 1b and 2 as an interpolation (cited by Dillmann-Ryssel, p. 381).

6. Rudolph claims that the last two words are senseless and emends to *mahēr wᵉnāḏōḇ* ('with haste and willingly'). The suggestion is ingenious, but unnecessary.

7. The verbs in vv. 7–11 have a frequentative sense (*G–K* §112e).

hā'ōhel. In terms of Hebrew grammar, the definite article could be generic (*G–K* §126r, s), but this is unlikely from the context (cf. Driver, *Exodus, ad loc.*). The problem of the antecedent for *lô* has been much discussed. The syntactical problem has frequently been combined with the larger literary-critical question. Knobel (1857) first suggested that a report of the construction of the ark had once stood between vv. 6 and 7. However, the *lô* should not be taken as a direct object since this use of the preposition is common only in late Hebrew (cf. Gen. 12.8; 26.25, etc.). Dillmann and Bäntsch suggest a dative usage, which has a parallel in II Sam. 6.17. Cf. the full bibliography on the question cited by Haran, *JSS* 5, 1960, p. 53.

13. LXX has γνωστῶς ἴδω σε which appears to reflect a different Hebrew text. Cf. the suggested reconstruction of BH³. LXX has γνῶ = *wᵉ'ēḏaʿ* instead of the MT *ûrᵉ'ēh*, which makes good sense and is defended by Rudolph as original.

14. Because of the difficulty in the sequence of the sentence, it has been suggested that v. 14 be read as a question (Tremellius, Ewald). Although there is a grammatical warrant for such a move (*G-K* §150a), it is more of an escape than a solution in this instance.

There is no textual evidence to warrant taking the root of the second verb from *nḥh* as Ehrlich (*Randglossen* I, p. 405) and the AmTr propose, but as a conjecture it merits consideration.

23. *'aḥōrāy*. The hinder part of a man or animal (I Kings 7.25).

2. *Literary and Traditio-Historical Analysis*

The literary analysis of this chapter is extremely difficult and no consensus has emerged. There is some agreement that separate stories have been rather loosely collected, but the issue remains highly contested whether one can speak of literary sources or not. The older commentators generally tried to sort out the discrepancies within the chapter by assigning the verses to J, E, and a JE redactor (JEᴿ, so Bäntsch, Driver). The alternative solution is represented by Noth who feels that source analysis is impossible here because the chapter consists of a conglomerate of secondary accretions formed around one central theme. Most modern commentators (e.g. Beyerlin) adopt a compromise position and speak of sources and separate stories. It should be acknowledged, however, that the usual criteria for source divisions are lacking and one is dependent on other considerations when assigning sources.

It is generally recognized that vv. 7–11 is a unit which joins closely neither with what precedes nor with what follows. The theory, apparently first proposed by Knobel and subsequently defended by Wellhausen, Dillmann and Eissfeldt, sought to explain the abrupt beginning of the passage – note the *lô* in v. 7 – by suggesting that the construction of the ark from the ornaments in v. 6 had been suppressed in order to make room for the priestly account (cf. 25.10–32). However, in spite of its continual supporters (von Rad, Beyerlin, etc.), the theory has its difficulties (cf. Maier, *op. cit.*, pp. 12ff., and Clements, *op. cit.*, pp. 36ff.). At best it remains an argument from silence. The available evidence does not seem to be such as to resolve the question decisively. Scholars remain sharply divided on assigning these verses to a source. More important is the fact that an old piece of independent tradition regarding the tent has been incorporated within the narrative framework of the chapter. The reasons will be discussed below.

There is considerable agreement in seeing two separate units in the verses which follow, 12–17 and 18–21, although both seem to have suffered from occasional expansions. Moreover, the view is held by many that the beginning of the first unit (vv. 12–17) is to be sought in the first verses of the chapter (1f.). Muilenburg's thesis (*op. cit.*) of an ancient liturgy underlying these verses is suggestive, but unlikely. His analysis remains highly subjective. The most perplexing task is to analyze vv. 1–6. Here the various opinions diverge widely because of the usual criteria by which to be guided.

Briefly, the literary problems are as follows: vv. 1–3 appear to understand the command to go up to the land accompanied by the angel in a good sense which would parallel the earlier promise (23.23). However, v. 3b sharply reverses this judgment and sees this as a judgment. Then both sections in vv. 12ff. and 4ff. are reactions to this announcement of judgment. Moreover, in vv. 4ff. there appears to be a doublet in the manner in which the jewels are removed, once spontaneously, once by command. I am inclined not to split up vv. 1–3 into sources (*contra* Rudolph, Muilenburg), but to see different layers upon one basic source.

Probably the most definite thing which one can say is that all these stories revolve about the one theme of God's presence. Although they appear to have arisen in different historical settings, they have been brought together by a redactor to illuminate the one issue. Moreover, there is a clear line connecting ch. 33 with ch. 32 in the speech of judgment in 32.34. An angel – not Yahweh – will accompany

Israel. In the same way a line connects ch. 33 with what follows in ch. 34, both in terms of the theophany (34.6ff.) and the promise of accompaniment (v. 9). This evidence would confirm the conclusion which has already emerged in ch. 32 that the decisive stage in the formation of the chapter stems from a redactor's hand, rather than from existing sources.

3. Old Testament Context

Chapter 33 contains a number of difficult exegetical problems in respect to which a commentator must come to some decision:

1. What is the chronological relation of ch. 33 to chs. 32 and 34, particularly in terms of the forty-day periods on the mount, which are mentioned (cf. Ex. 24.18; 34.28; Deut. 9.18, 25; 10.10)?

2. How does one understand the 'messenger' or 'angel' which is a substitute for Yahweh's personal accompaniment (33. 2f.), and the messenger who appears to embody the divine presence (Ex. 23.23; 32.34; Mal. 3.1, etc.)?

3. What is the significance of the 'ornaments' which are removed in vv. 4ff.?

4. What is the nature of the 'tent' (vv. 7ff.) and why is it introduced at this point in the narrative?

5. How does the final request of Moses to see God's glory (18ff.) function within the chapter?

Two strikingly opposed methods of exegesis among commentators have sought to offer solutions to these questions. On the one hand, there is the classic midrashic method of the medieval Jewish commentators, followed in part by 'pre-critical' Christian scholars (e.g. Calvin), and modern Jews (e.g. Cassuto). The strength of the method is its attempt to explain the present form of the text with utter seriousness. Its weakness lies in its frequent recourse to going beyond the text in order to solve a difficulty, either in the form of a rationalistic harmonization, or a homiletical glossing over the tension. On the other hand, there is the historical-critical method – whether in its literary critical or traditio-historical form is immaterial – which seeks to explain the text in terms of a reconstructed history of development. Its strength lies in the often genuine insights which it brings to the text by means of the historical dimension. Its weakness lies in its failure to take seriously the final stage of the canonical text, and its unwarranted speculation regarding the early stages of the text on which it seeks to build a theology.

My own attempt will be to take the present shape of the text with great seriousness, and yet to use the historical dimension which has been opened up by critical exegesis as a check against going beyond the witness of the text in the form of rationalistic harmonizations.

[33.1–3] The passage is in the form of a discourse of God with Moses, but without explicit information regarding either the time or place of the communication. Because of both its form and content, commentators have long suggested that the order of these verses was topical and needed to be rearranged if one sought to establish a genuine chronology. Thus Calvin proposed that these verses preceded in time the prayer of Moses in 32.31. However, the attempt to achieve this interpretation by translating the introductory verb in the pluperfect ('God had said to Moses . . .') is ruled out in terms of Hebrew grammar (cf. Driver, *Hebrew Tenses*[3], pp. 84ff.). Cassuto offers a more elaborate theory of an epic style to justify seeing vv. 1–3 as a continuation of the divine discourse in vv. 33ff. The speech is paralleled in order to include the additional reservation that God will nevertheless not accompany his people.

In my judgment, there is no justification for seeking a closer connection to ch. 32 than has been actually provided in 33.1ff. The divine speech is explicitly set off from ch. 32 by a new introduction. Moreover, this break is not simply caused by the historical notice in v. 35, but by a strikingly different emphasis. In 32.33ff. the mention of the accompanying divine messenger is part of the renewed promise of the land which is set over against the continuing threat of ultimate judgment on the wicked. But in 33.2f. the mention of the angel is a sign of judgment and indicates that God himself will no longer guide Israel on its way. The theory that v. 2 is a later interpolation does not affect this basic contrast of motifs in the two chapters. In other words, the exact chronological relation of ch. 33 to what precedes and follows is left unspecified and should not be pressed.

This approach to the problem presents no difficulties except for those who would insist on fitting ch. 33 into the chronology of the forty days on the mountain. According to Exodus Moses went up initially for forty days to get the tablets (24.18). Following his descent to destroy the calf in which he broke the first tablets, he returned on the next day (32.30) to intercede. Then he came up again on Mount Sinai with new tablets and remained forty days (34.28). However, in

Deut. 9 we read that he interceded before God for forty days in a prayer similar to that in Exodus (9.18, 25; 10.10). These accounts appear to represent different traditions of the sequence at Sinai, and do not show any signs of having been harmonized, especially in relation to Ex. 33. (The theory that Moses stayed a period of forty days on three occasions was held both by Jewish and Christian harmonists. Cf. J. Lightfoot, *A Handful of Gleanings out of the Book of Exodus, Works* II, London 1822, p. 389.)

Of course, vv. 1–3 make it absolutely clear that the sin of the golden calf has been assumed as the background of the passage. The intercession of Moses has succeeded in sparing the people from immediate annihilation. Indeed the promise of possession of the land is reiterated in 32.34; 34.1f. However, the problem of the chapter turns on the reservation, which, as an aftermath of Israel's great sin, remains even after God's forgiveness. He himself will not go up in Israel's midst. The reason is given in terms of the catchword 'stiff-necked people' from 32.9. Because they are inclined to evil, God fears that his presence would now be a threat to their existence: '. . . lest I consume them on the way'. Therefore, he proposes to send his messenger instead.

The general sense of the immediate context of these verses is clear enough. God plans to withdraw his presence as a sign of judgment. The difficulty arises when one attempts to understand how this role of the angel as a poor substitute relates to the other messenger who rather embodies the divine presence (Ex. 23.23). The midrashic method is quick to offer a harmonization. E. W. Hengstenberg, for example (*Christology of the Old Testament* I², Edinburgh 1858, pp. 119f.), distinguished two different kinds of angels, only one of which is a form of the divine presence (cf. Ibn Ezra). But once again, this proposed solution goes beyond the biblical text, which is silent on such a combination. Nor does Ex. 33 indicate that the refusal of God to accompany Israel has any effect on the cloud and pillar of fire which had guided the people earlier. Rather, the issue of the chapter turns on the ensuing events which had the effect of changing God's announced purpose.

[33.4–6] The first reaction to the intention of God not to accompany Israel came from the people. 'When they heard the evil news, they mourned and no man put on his ornaments.' Commentators have long speculated on what ornaments were meant (cf. Targ. Onk.). Cassuto tries to combine them with the 'washed clothes' of

19.10, 14 but must admit that this connection has not been made by the text itself. Again, literary critics have long argued that the ornaments were removed in order to construct the ark from them, but again this theory lacks support from the text and can only remain hypothetical. In the end, whatever garments or ornaments were meant, the only clear point of the text is that their removal indicates a sign of mourning on the part of the people. Further than this one cannot go with any degree of certainty.

A more difficult problem has to do with the repetition within these same verses. Verse 4 relates that the people on hearing the bad news refrained from putting on their ornaments. However, v. 5 then reports a command of Yahweh to the people which ordered them to put off the ornaments. Again several different solutions to the difficulty have been proposed. The Septuagint has tried to ease the problem by shortening the text. The classic midrashic solution is to suggest that the people only removed them for a short time and intended putting them back on (Saadia), or that the command included far more than did the original action of the people (Nachmanides).

Over against such attempts at a solution which assume the unity of the text, the literary-critical approach offers the easy historical alternative of seeing two variants of the same story. Indeed, the language of vv. 5f. would seem to point to a later source or redaction. (Note the plural form of the second person, v. 5, in contrast to v. 4; the form of address common to P: 'Yahweh said, say to the people', v. 5; Horeb instead of Sinai, v. 6.) Although the theory of a doublet is probably correct, nevertheless, the need remains to determine the effect of the combination of traditions on the present form of the text. Two elements occur in the second form of the command which are additions to the first account and which provide the key to the passage's function in the chapter. First, God is still undetermined what he will do with his people (v. 5), which would seem to open the way for the renewed intercession of Moses which follows. Secondly, the people's sign of mourning was not a temporary display, but a continuous one: 'from the time of Mount Horeb onward'. This change in attitude evidenced by their continual mourning would offer reason for Moses to seek complete forgiveness. Although the terminology of repentence is not used, the tradition of the stripping of ornaments – whatever it may have once meant – now serves in the narrative to demonstrate Israel's change of heart.

[33.7–11] This section which is basically unified has no obvious connection with either what precedes or follows. In terms of its content, it appears to interrupt the theme of God's denying Israel his accompanying presence, which is picked up again in v. 12. Again, the style of vv. 7ff. is markedly different. The form of the Hebrew verbs is frequentative and marks a continuous activity, rather than a single historical occurrence.

Pre-critical expositors have always been hard pressed to explain the tent which is described as the meeting place with God 'outside the camp'. The difficulty arises because 'the tent' – note the definite article – is explicitly identified with the 'tent of meeting' ('ōhel mō'ēḏ), which at that time had not yet been erected according to the chronological sequence of the book of Exodus (40.16ff.). Moreover, the description of this 'tent of meeting' is very different from the tent in Ex. 33 and has a different function (cf. Num. 3.1ff.). The usual way of avoiding the problem was by constructing a theory that this tent was Moses' own private tent (LXX, Ibn Ezra, Grotius, Jacob, etc.; cf. Calvin's objections to the theory), or the tent was some provisional structure (Cassuto), or an old sanctuary which the Israelites had previously possessed (Michaelis, Rosenmüller). However, all these theories not only remain unsupported from any evidence within the biblical text itself, but fail to explain what evidence there is.

It is clear from several other passages in the Pentateuch that there existed another tradition within Israel in respect to the 'tent of meeting' (cf. Num. 11.16, 24, 26f.; 12.4, 10; Deut. 31.15). The tent is much simpler than the one pictured in the Priestly description of Ex. 25–31. Rather than being in the center of the camp (Num. 2.17), this tent was outside the camp (Num. 11.26f.). Instead of the group of Levites which attended it (Num. 3.5ff.), it appears to have been served by one attendant, Joshua. Again, this earlier tradition of the tent of meeting conceives of the function of the tent as a place which God visits periodically to make known his will to Moses. The cloud descends upon the entrance of the tent, and does not remain as ever-present in the Holy of Holies. Finally, there is no mention of its being a housing for the ark.

In the light of this evidence historical critics, particularly since Kuenen and Wellhausen, have come up with an interpretation of vv. 7–11 which differed completely from all the pre-critical theories, which were mentioned above. The passage is viewed as a fragment of an old tradition, usually assigned to the E source, which has nothing to do with the present context of the chapter, but which has preserved an earlier concept of Israel's tabernacle. In the later history of the development, this earlier view was replaced by the more elaborate Priestly theory and was virtually lost from view in the Old Testament. Wellhausen and his school argued that the dominant Priestly account of the tabernacle, which then replaced the earlier account, was a projection back into the Mosaic period of a post-exilic institution (cf. the introduction to ch. 25 for a full discussion). Although in recent years Wellhausen's historical theory of the tabernacle has eroded considerably, nevertheless, the basic approach of the critical school to 33.7–11 in regarding it as a fragment of a different and older tradition has been maintained by modern scholars (e.g. Beyerlin, Haran, Te Stroete, etc.). Accordingly the interest in the passage has focused, by and large, on historical information which it has been thought to provide on the early history of Israel's religious institutions.

I fully agree with the literary-critical assessment of the passage as reflecting an old tradition of the tent of meeting which parallels the later Priestly account. Because of the need for historical perspective, the classic midrashic interpretations are inadequate. However, I disagree basically with the usual approach of the critical commentary in failing to reckon with the role of the passage in its present literary context. Regardless of what the pre-history of the text was, the task of determining its present role in ch. 33 remains the primary one for the study of the Old Testament as scripture.

What can one say about the function of vv. 7–11 within the present chapter? First of all, there are no evident literary connections which the redactor supplied to his older material in order to bring it more in line with his new composition. He does not offer a redactional framework in terms of a fresh introduction or conclusion. Nor does he seem to have made serious inroads within the body of the unit. He has retained the style of the older tradition even with its unusual verbal forms. Therefore, if the redactor of the chapter has made a purposeful use of these verses in his composition, its new role must emerge in terms of its function in the larger narrative pattern. Of course, the possibility that these verses found a place within the chapter by sheer accident must remain an open alternative, especially in the light of their earlier history.

There is a certain progress of thought in the chapter which strikes the reader immediately. The initial discourse of Yahweh to Moses reports the bad news of God's decision not to accompany this people (vv. 1–3). There follows then the people's reaction of mourning which is explicitly connected to the bad news (vv. 4–6). Moses' reaction to the news is picked up in vv. 12–17 in which he addresses God specifically on the issue of his accompanying presence and intercedes on behalf of the people. In other words, vv. 4–6 treat the people's reaction, whereas vv. 12–17 deal with Moses' reaction to the same issue. In between these two reactions of the people and of Moses comes the verses of the older tradition. These verses, in contrast to what precedes and what follows, do not address themselves directly to this same issue. However, the passage does speak of Moses' office as intercessor before God, and the people's reaction to this intercession. Furthermore, the activity of both Moses and the people extends over a period of time. In terms of topical sequence vv. 7–11 serve as a connection between what precedes and what follows by combining Moses, God, and the people within one activity. The people do not simply mourn (v. 4), but respond with reverent behaviour – they rise and worship (v. 10) – before the presence of God with Moses. In its present position, without being specifically altered, the section witnesses to the obedient and worshipful behavior over an extended period of time, thereby providing Moses with a warrant to intercede in vv. 12ff.

Moreover, if one begins to look in more detail at the passage, other signs of its new function within the composition become evident. In the older tradition, the position of the tent 'outside the camp' appeared to carry no negative overtones (Num. 11.24, etc.). However, in the later tradition the overwhelming number of passages which use the formula 'outside the camp' carry an overtone of impurity (Ex. 29.14; Lev. 4.12; 13.46; Num. 15.35; Deut. 23.12, etc.). It seems therefore most probable that this negative understanding of the expression provided the redactor with a suitable transition by which to introduce the passage into his composition. Moses took the tent 'outside the camp' because the people had just proved themselves unfit for God to dwell in their midst. In recognizing this connection, the older midrashic interpretation, which was followed by Calvin and others, was certainly on the right track.

Other elements within the text lend themselves admirably to the new context. The major part of ch. 33 focuses on the intercession of Moses. The connection with Moses' office in vv. 7ff. is therefore a natural one. Moreover, the same people who began their folly with the calf by showing utter disrespect for Moses (32.1), now rise and stand in his presence (v. 8) as well as before the theophany itself

(v. 10). In addition, the tent tradition now provides a setting for the display of individual piety. Even though the presence of God now was to be found outside the camp, individuals 'who sought the LORD' could go out to the place of meeting. What better sign of a transformed people!

Furthermore, the passage addresses the issue of God's accompanying his people at least in an indirect way. The visible sign of God's guidance out of the land of Egypt and through the dangers of the wilderness had always been the pillar of cloud by day and the fire at night. Now the people see that the pillar of cloud has not departed fully. It still descends to the door of the tent.

Finally, there is a certain parallelism between vv. 7–11 and the basic features of the divine revelation on Mount Sinai (cf. Haran, *JSS, op. cit.*, p. 57). The theophany at Sinai took place outside the camp. Moses prepared the people to meet God at some distance. God descended in a pillar of cloud and Moses was seen speaking with God. When he went up to the mountain, he was followed by his attendant, Joshua. The inclusion of vv. 7–11 as a pale shadow of Ex. 19 provides another link to the renewal of the broken covenant which is consummated in ch. 34.

In sum: although vv. 7–11 had once an independent role in early tradition, they have now assumed a new and most appropriate role within the writer's story of Moses' intercession for sinful Israel.

[33.12–17] The broad lines of the dialogue which follows between God and Moses are basically clear, but many details of the passage remain difficult and perplexing. First of all, the question of the length of the unit is debated, and several scholars suggest that verses from the beginning of the chapter originally introduced the section (Muilenburg includes v. 1a, Beyerlin vv. 1a, 3). However, there is no compelling reason to hold that the beginning is missing. The passage simply presupposes the bad news of vv. 1–4, and begins a new episode within the larger narrative with the direct intercession of Moses. A more important issue is the problem of determining the conclusion of the passage. Traditionally v. 17 has been regarded as belonging to the passage which follows. However, in terms of both form and content v. 17 provides the natural conclusion to the dialogue without which the whole passage is left hanging (so also the NAB).

The initial plea of Moses to Yahweh begins on a high note of intensity marked by the exclamation: 'Look'. The first plea contains two parts, both of which are introduced by Moses' first quoting a word of Yahweh himself. 'You say, "Bring up this people," but you have not told me whom you will send with me.' Again, 'You have said, "I know you by name . . .," then show me your ways.' The plea is then concluded by a short affirmation, again introduced by the same exclamation: 'Look, this nation is your people.' The final sentence serves to ground the plea in the covenant between God and Israel which Moses continues to regard as still operative throughout his intercession. The first part of the plea, 'You have not told me whom you will send with me,' does not match too well with the mention of the angel in v. 2. In fact, the angel plays no role whatever in the rest of the chapter. The intercession focuses only on the issue of whether or not God himself will accompany his people. The two parts of the plea are basically parallel in content, and seek not simply information about Yahweh's plans with Israel, but a further commitment on her behalf.

The divine response to the intercession follows in v. 14: 'My face (or presence) will go with you and I will give you rest.' Some commentators have argued that the response does not seem to fit the plea and perhaps has been misplaced. When Moses again takes up his intercession, he continues to pray for what has already been granted. Others have tried to avoid the difficulty in the divine response by suggesting that God's answer is actually a question. However, this latter suggestion hardly recommends itself either in terms of the style or content of the dialogue.

Perhaps the logical consistency of the dialogue should not be overworked. There is an emotional tone of the highest intensity throughout the conversation as Moses seeks unswervingly to wrest from God a further concession. From the larger context it is clear that Moses is not satisfied with the first response, but certainly he has gained a partial concession. God's face or presence will accompany them. More difficult to understand is the second half of the response: 'I will give you rest.' To give rest in the Old Testament is often connected with the possession of the promised land (Deut. 3.20; 12.10, etc.). If this is the sense intended, then God is reiterating his promise of the land. Still the explicit use of the singular pronoun – give *thee* rest – may point in another direction. God's promise remains focused on Moses personally. He is offered the comfort of God.

At least some confirmation of this interpretation is found in the second plea of Moses which again consists of two parts, vv. 15–16. Moses' initial response seems to pass roughshod over the concession.

God has said: 'My presence will go with you.' Moses replies: 'If thy presence will not go, then do not make us leave this place.' The effect is to minimize the partial concession in order to press for the full request. Indeed, what Moses is really after comes out clearly in his repetition of the phrase 'I and thy people'. God's response had continued to attach itself to Moses himself. Moses shakes it off and demands that the response include the people. The issue is whether God will again accompany his people in such a way as to make them again distinct from all other peoples. This was the essence of the original covenant promise. The concluding response comes in v.17. God will do all that Moses requested. Moses has wrested from God a full restoration. The way is now prepared for a formal renewal of the covenant within the narrative.

[33.18–23] There are several fundamental exegetical problems involved in this passage. The most difficult one is to determine the role of this passage in its larger context. In what way is it related to what has preceded, and to what then follows in 34.6ff.? Up to now Moses had been interceding for the people who had grievously sinned over the golden calf. Is this passage suddenly an individual matter of a metaphysical or mystical nature? Again, is the passage a unity or does it reflect inner disorder?

There is considerable evidence to suggest that lying behind the present form of the story was an earlier tradition about Moses which the author of the chapter has reworked into his larger composition of the breaking and restoring of the covenant (chs. 32–34). The fact that God speaks three times in reply to Moses' request, each time with a separate introduction, would certainly point to an expansion of an original story. (Cassuto's attempt at a literary evasion is not convincing.) Moreover, there are some further tensions within the present form of the account which can be best explained on the basis of the earlier tradition. Moses requests to see God's *glory* (*kābôd*), to which God replies, 'You cannot see my *face*.' When his glory does pass by, Moses, who is hidden in a fissure of a rock, is only allowed to see God's back, and not his face. It would appear that in the earlier account, the request turns on Moses' attempt to have some concrete, visible experience of God's person. This request is paralleled to Moses' earlier desire to know God's name (3.14; cf. Gen. 32.29). His request to have God reveal himself in an unmediated form is then denied. There are limits placed even on God's chosen mediator. No man can so experience God and live. But a partial concession is made and for this reason the story was undoubtedly treasured in a cycle which was related to Moses' special office. Moses is allowed to catch a fleeting glimpse of the 'back' of God. Of course, a tremendous anthropomorphism is involved, but the extreme caution with which it is used is an eloquent testimony to the Hebrew understanding of God. Even to be allowed to catch a glimpse of his passing from the rear is so awesome to the man Moses that God himself – note the strange paradox – must shield him with his own hand.

However, the present form of the story has shifted the emphasis and made the story play a somewhat different role within the context of Ex. 33. First of all, the special divine revelation which Moses requested and God provided is no longer seen primarily in terms of a visible appearance. Rather, God let all his 'goodness' (*ṭûḇî*) pass by, which in v. 22 is identified with his 'glory' (*keḇōḏî*). The revelation of God is in terms of his attributes rather than his appearance. Usually in the Old Testament the goodness of God signifies his benefits which are experienced by Israel (Hos. 3.5; Jer. 31.12, 14; Ps. 27.13, etc.). Of course, the usage in v. 19 is unique and without an exact parallel, but the concern is clearly to define God's revelation in terms of his activity toward Israel. Thus along with the display of goodness is the proclamation of the name. The name of God, which like his glory and his face are vehicles of his essential nature, is defined in terms of his compassionate acts of mercy. The circular *idem per idem* formula of the name – I will be gracious to whom I will be gracious – is closely akin to the name in Ex. 3.14 – I am who I am – and testifies by its tautology to the freedom of God in making known his self-contained being (cf. the discussion on 34.6ff.).

The second shift in the focus of the story is in the author's relating this tradition in an integral way to the context of the present chapter. In the earlier account the issue seemed to turn on a request of Moses for a special, individual revelation. It has bothered commentators that Moses' request appeared to have little to do with Israel's plight. Did Moses have time at this crucial juncture for a flight into metaphysics (cf. Jacob's comments)? The revelation to Moses is promised in ch. 33, but its fulfillment is now pictured as occurring in 34.6ff. within the context of the restoration of the broken covenant. Moses' response to the theophany, far from being an exclamation of mystical delight, returns rather to the major theme of ch. 33: 'go in the midst of us . . . a stiff-necked people . . . pardon our iniquity and our sin . . .'

Finally, the theophany to Moses has been worked into the account of the reiteration of the law in ch. 34 so as to provide a parallel to the theophany-law sequence of the original covenant. In the same way as once all Israel experienced the thunder and lightening on the mountain before the giving of the Decalogue, so now Moses as the mediator of the restored covenant once again encounters the majesty of God before hearing his will and receiving it on the tablets of the law.

In sum: the final section of ch. 33 now serves to climax the intercession of Moses for Israel on account of her sin, and forms the bridge to the restoration of the covenant in the succeeding chapter.

Detailed Notes

33.2. 'angel'. Cf. the literature cited in Ex. 23.23.

7. 'tent of meeting'. Cf. the fundamental study of G. von Rad, *op. cit.*, pp. 103ff., and the more recent discussion of M. Haran, *op. cit.*, with full bibliography.

11. 'his servant Joshua'. F. Dumermuth (*op. cit.*) has argued the case that Joshua had the role of medium in the sacred tent on the basis of numerous parallels from the history of religion. In my opinion, the evidence for the thesis is not compelling.

12ff. On the varied terminology of the presence of God – his name, face, glory, etc. – cf. Eichrodt, *Theology of the OT* II, pp. 23ff. Two monographs, which represent quite different positions, deal with the broader issues at stake: W. J. Phythian-Adams, *The People and the Presence*, London and New York 1942, and R. E. Clements, *God and Temple*, 1965.

18. 'glory of God' is a technical expression, derived from the root *kbd* = to be heavy, and denotes that side of the divine nature which can be perceived by man through revelation. On the subject cf. the article by von Rad, 'Doxa', *TWNT* II, pp. 235ff. = *TDNT* II, 232ff., and the more recent studies listed by G. H. Davies, *IDB* II, pp. 401–3.

19. On the name formula, cf. Ex. 34.6ff. and the literature cited there.

4. History of Exegesis

The story of Moses' request to see God's glory and the subsequent theophany (vv. 18–23) has continued to evoke considerable interest from interpreters from the earliest times. There does not seem to have emerged any characteristic exegetical tendency which fundamentally separated Jew and Christian, as has been seen so frequently in the book of Exodus. Rather, the variety of forces which were at work in influencing and shaping the questions and answers arising from this particular passage left a similar impact on both confessions.

The refusal of God to comply in full with Moses' request for a revelation of himself called forth a similar reaction from both Jew and

Christian. The classic Jewish and Christian commentators of the medieval period were fully agreed that no mortal man can see the essence of God and live (e.g. Maimonides, Augustine). Obviously the Old Testament is unambiguous at this point. Moreover, Onkelos had employed the concept of the 'Shekinah' to denote the accompanying divine presence in distinction from God himself. There was more disagreement on what God actually allowed Moses to see. Saadia suggested that he saw an appearance of light which God had created in his moment of passing by. Judah Halevi reported two opinions: the glory of God was a fine substance which assumed any form God desired to reveal, or else it meant the whole of the spiritual world (*Kuzari*, IV.3). Christian writers often simply paraphrased the Hebrew terminology and spoke of glory, majesty, and power (Lyra, Drusius, Tremellius, etc.).

The distinction between the essence of God and his attributes came early into both Jewish and Christian theology. Maimonides is typical in remarking: 'The knowledge of the works of God is the knowledge of his attributes, by which he can be known' (*Guide* I.54). Thomas Aquinas made a similar distinction (*Summa* 1a, 12.1ff.). In spite of a basic similarity, the Exodus passage took on a particular meaning in Jewish interpretation because it was understood as recording the moment when God taught Moses the formula for prayer, demonstrating its use, and proclaimed his thirteen attributes (Rosh ha-Shanah 17b; Rashi).

A more philosophic direction in Christian theology had been provided early by the Vulgate translation *omne bonum*. Thus Paul of Burgos made the point that God did not say, 'I will show you my goodness (*bonum meum*)', but 'all goodness (*omne bonum*)' (Additio IV, *Biblia Sacra*). He then proceeded to reflect on the nature of universal goodness and its various manifestations in the world (cf. the parallels in Abarbanel). In general, Jewish interpreters resisted making Moses' experience mystical or exclusively metaphysical (Kalisch, *Exodus*, is an exception). Moses did acquire an understanding of God's nature which was beyond that of any other man, but it was in his office as prophet. However, a similar concern to relate the theophany to Moses' office as intercessor was shared by Grotius, who interpreted the theophany as the goodness which God will do to the people of Israel.

The classic christological interpretation is given by Augustine (*Quaest. in Hept.* II.154) who seeks to understand the phrase 'I will pass before you' (*transibo ante te*) in the light of John 13, and sees it as a future prophecy of Christ's resurrection. An interesting formal parallel to this use occurs in the *Abot de Rabbi Nathan* where 'face' is referred to 'this world', and 'back' to the 'world to come' (ch. 25).

Finally, the introduction of the historical-critical method in the late nineteenth century tended to bring with it the philosophical categories of liberal Protestant theology. Both Dillmann and Bäntsch characterize the theophany as a revelation of God's 'ethical' nature. McNeile summarizes the divine appearance in a way which is hardly less philosophical than the schoolmen: 'It is a spectacle of outward beauty as a visible sign of His moral perfection.'

5. *Theological Reflection*

This chapter offers a variety of themes, but they all circle about the role of the faithful mediator, Moses, who wrestles with God for the sake of Israel. The portrayal of God's servant actively striving with him for the forgiveness of his people is a recurrent one in the Old Testament. One thinks of Abraham's role before the destruction of Sodom (Gen. 18.22ff.), and the prophet's place as intercessor (Amos 7; Jer. 14, etc.). But above all, the biblical theme is developed in terms of Moses' role who repeatedly put his own life at risk for the sake of sinful Israel (Ex. 32.11; Deut. 9.25ff.). These Old Testament passages provide the background for the christological development of the New Testament in picturing Jesus as the true mediator between God and man.

Ex. 33 provides an excellent illustration of the biblical approach to sin and forgiveness. Israel's disobedience has shattered the covenant relation. God declines to accompany this people any longer because his holiness now threatens the very existence of the transgressor. But God has provided a mediator between himself and his people, not to discount the seriousness of Israel's sin, but to plead God's own mercy on the basis of his former promise. This tension between God who both judges and forgives which is present in Ex. 33 will later reach a point of genuine paradox (Job 19.25ff.; Rom. 8.1ff.). The Old Testament rather runs the risk of humanizing God through its extreme anthropomorphism – God changes his mind, v. 5 – than undercut the absolute seriousness with which God takes the intercession of his servant. Moses, on his part, refuses anything less than the full restoration of Israel as God's special people.

The struggle between sin and forgiveness which Moses wages with God also involves the people. Whereas the intercession of Moses in ch. 32 focuses on Moses' single role before God, ch. 33 addresses the issue of the people's participation through repentance without reducing Moses' role. The people strip themselves in mourning and rise expectantly as Moses intercedes for them.

Verses 17–23 prepare the way for the renewal of the covenant by means of a theophany, which recapitulates the action of the initial giving of the law in ch. 19. The giving of the law is above all a revelation of God as 'a God merciful and gracious, slow to anger, and abounding in steadfast love and faithfulness . . . forgiving iniquity, transgression, and sin . . .' This essential message of the gospel did not have to await the New Testament's proclamation, but was fundamental to the old covenant from the outset.

THE RENEWAL OF THE COVENANT

34.1–35

W. F. Albright, 'The Hebrew Expression for "Making a Covenant" in Pre-Israelite Documents', *BASOR* 121, 1951, pp.21ff.; 'The Natural Face of Moses in the light of Ugaritic', *BASOR* 94, 1944, pp.32–5; K. Baltzer, *Das Bundesformular*, WMANT 4, 1960, pp.48ff.; W. Beyerlin, *Origins and History of the Oldest Sinaitic Traditions*, ET Oxford 1965, pp.24ff., 77ff.; J. B. Carpzov, 'Disp. de Nummis Effigien Moysis Cornatum Exhibentibus', 1659, reprinted in B. Ugolini, *Thesaurus Antiquitatum Sacrarum*, Venice 1769, vol. XXVIII, cols.1416ff.; H. Cazelles, 'Ex.34, 21 traite-t-il du Sabbat?', *CBQ* 23, 1961, pp.223–6; R. C. Dentan, 'The literary affinities of Exodus 34, 6f.', *VT* 13, 1963, pp.34–51; F. Dumermuth, 'Moses strahlendes Gesicht', *TZ* 17, 1961, pp.241–8; A. Eberharter, 'Besitzen wir in Ex 23 und 34 zwei Rezensionen eines zweiten Dekalogs?', *BZ* 20, 1932, pp.157–62; B. D. Eerdmans, *Das Buch Exodus*, 1910, pp.77ff.; O. Eissfeldt, 'Die älteste Erzählung von Sinaibund', *ZAW* 73, 1961, pp.137ff.; J. de Fraine, 'Moses "cornuta facies" (Ex.34, 29–35)', *Bijdragen, Tijdschrift voor filosophie en theologie* 20, 1959, pp.28–38; H. Horn, 'Traditionsschichten in Ex 23, 10–33 und Ex 34, 10–36', *BZ*, NF 15, 1971, pp.203–22; A. Jirku, 'Die Gesichtsmaske des Mose', *ZDPV* 67, 1944/5, pp.43ff.; H. Kosmala, 'The So-called Ritual Decalogue', *ASTI* 1, 1962, pp.31–61; F. Langlamet, 'Israël et "l'habitant du pays"', *RB* 76, 1969, pp.321–50, 481–507; A. Lommel, *Masks, Their Meaning and Function*, ET New York 1972; J. Morgenstern, 'The Oldest Document of the Hexateuch', *HUCA* 4, 1927, pp.1–148; 'Moses with the Shining Face', *HUCA*, 1925, pp.1–27; R. H. Pfeiffer, 'The Oldest Decalogue', *JBL* 43, 1924, pp.294–310; G. von Rad, *Die Priesterschrift im Hexateuch*, Stuttgart 1934, pp.78ff.; H. H. Rowley, 'Moses and the Decalogue', *Men of God*, London and New York 1963, pp.1–36; J. Scharbert, 'Formgeschichte und Exegese von Ex.34, 6f. und seine Parallelen', *Biblica* 38, 1957, pp.130–50; N. Walker, 'Concerning Ex.34, 6', *JBL* 79, 1960, p.277; F. E. Wilms, 'Das jahwistische Bundesbuch in Ex 34', *BZ*, NF 16, 1972, pp.24–53.

34 ¹The Lord said to Moses, 'Cut two tablets of stone like the first and I will write upon the tablets the words which were on the first tablets which you broke. ²Be ready by morning and in the morning come up Mount Sinai and present yourself there to me on the top of the mountain. ³No one else shall come up with you, and no one else shall

be seen anywhere on the mountain, neither shall flocks or herds graze in front of that mountain.

4 So Moses cut two tablets of stone like the first, and rising early in the morning, went up Mount Sinai, as the LORD had commanded him, taking the two tablets of stone in his hands. 5Then the LORD descended in the cloud, and stood with him there, and proclaimed the name LORD (YHWH). 6The LORD passed before him and proclaimed: 'The LORD, the LORD, a God compassionate and gracious, long-suffering, rich in steadfast love and faithfulness, 7extending steadfast love to thousands, forgiving iniquity, rebellion, and sin. Yet he does not remit all punishment, but avenges the iniquity of the fathers upon the sons and grandsons to the third and fourth generation.' 8And Moses hastened to bow to the ground and he prostrated himself. 9He said, 'If I have gained your favor, O Lord, then may the LORD go in our midst, although it is a stiff-necked people, and pardon our iniquity and our sin, and take us as your own possession.'

10 He said, 'I hereby make a covenant. Before all your people I will do such wonders as have not been performed in all the earth or in any nation. All the people among whom you are living shall see how awesome is the LORD's work which I will do for you. 11Pay attention to what I command you this day. I will drive out before you the Amorites, the Canaanites, the Hittites, the Perizzites, the Hivites, and the Jebusites. 12Be careful not to make a covenant with the inhabitants of the land which you are about to enter, lest they become a snare in your midst. 13But you shall tear down their altars, smash their pillars, and cut down their sacred posts. 14You shall not worship any other God for his name is the LORD, the Jealous One, and a jealous God he is. 15You must not make a covenant with the inhabitants of the land, lest, when they lust after their gods and sacrifice to their gods, and someone invites you, you will eat of his sacrifice. 16And if you were to marry their daughters to your sons, their daughters will lust after their gods, and cause your sons to lust after their gods.

17 'You shall not make for yourselves molten gods.

18 'You shall observe the feast of unleavened bread. Seven days you shall eat unleavened bread, as I commanded you, at the appointed time in the month of Abib, for in the month of Abib you came out from Egypt. 19Every firstling of the womb belongs to me: all the males of your herds, both cattle and sheep. 20But the firstling of an ass you shall redeem with a lamb, or if you do not redeem it, you must break its neck. Every firstling among your sons you shall redeem. None shall appear before me empty-handed.

21 'Six days you shall work, but on the seventh day you shall cease work. Even at plowing time and harvest you shall cease work.

22 'You shall observe the feast of weeks, the first fruits of the wheat

harvest, and the feast of ingathering at the turn of the year. ²³Three times a year shall all your males appear before the Lord God, the God of Israel. ²⁴For I will drive out the nations before you and enlarge your territory, nor shall any one covet your land when you go up to appear before the LORD your God three times a year.

25 'You shall not offer the blood of my sacrifice with anything leavened, and the sacrifice of the feast of passover shall not be left over until the morning.

26 'The choice of the first fruits of your ground you shall bring to the house of the LORD your God.

'You shall not boil a kid in its mother's milk.'

27 The LORD said to Moses, 'Write down these words for in accordance with these words I have made a covenant with you and with Israel.' ²⁸He was there with the LORD forty days and forty nights, neither did he eat any bread or drink any water. And he wrote upon the tablets the words of the covenant, the Ten Commandments.

29 When Moses descended from Mount Sinai – the two tablets of the testimony were in Moses' hands as he descended – Moses himself was not aware that the skin of his face shone because he had been talking with God. ³⁰When Aaron and all the Israelites saw how the skin of Moses' face shone, they were afraid to come near him. ³¹But Moses called out to them and Aaron and all the leaders of the congregation returned to him, and Moses spoke to them. ³²Afterward all the Israelites came near and he instructed them concerning all that the LORD had spoken with him on Mount Sinai. ³³When Moses had finished speaking with them, he put a veil over his face, ³⁴but whenever Moses went in before the LORD to speak with him, he would take off the veil, until he came out. When he came out, he would tell the Israelites what he had been commanded. ³⁵Then the Israelites would see how the skin of Moses' face shone. So he would put the veil back on over his face until he went in to speak with him.

1. Textual and Philological Notes

34.5. In terms of Hebrew syntax the subject of the two verbs *yityaṣṣēb* and *yiqrā'* can either be Yahweh or Moses. The issue can only be decided in terms of the context. Accordingly, commentators have been divided in their interpretation. Yahweh as subject is defended by AV, RSV, NJPS, NEB, NAB; Moses as subject by AV margin, Dillmann, Bäntsch, Driver, Hyatt. The first view finds its support in the wording of 33.21 and 34.2, while the second finds its warrant in 33.19. Most probably the problem arose because of the subsequent expansion in vv.6–9 which clearly understood Yahweh to be the subject of the proclamation. Originally v.5 may well have intended Moses as subject. In the present context of the whole chapter in which v.5 is read in the light of v.6, Yahweh is most naturally the subject of the proclamation.

6. Most probably the translation of the name as a repeated exclamation: 'Yahweh, Yahweh', is correct, and is so understood by the Hebrew accents. However, it is possible to take the first 'Yahweh' as the subject of the verb *wayyiqrā*'. This interpretation finds its support in the parallel, Num.14.17–18 (cf. margin NJPS). LXX lacks one of the names.

7. On the translation of '*ªlāpîm*, cf. the note on 20.6.

10. The problem of translating the term *bªrîṯ* (covenant, pact) is closely related to the larger exegetical issues. Cf. the notes on ch.19 and ch.24 and the literature cited there of Jepsen, Kutsch, Fohrer, and Perlitt.

13. The text of the end of the verses is somewhat fluid. The LXX has an extra colon which appears to have entered from Deut.7.5. The reading '*ªšêrêhem* instead of the MT has support from one Hebrew manuscript, the Greek, the Syriac, and the Samar.

19. The *waw* before *wªḵol* is explicative. It is not necessary to assume (as do Dillmann, Bäntsch) that a verb has fallen out or been combined in a textual corruption.

The MT *tizzāḵār* is clearly an error for *hazzāḵār*, which has support from the versions.

23. On the Massoretic pointing of *yērā*'*eh*, cf. the note on 23.15.

28. LXX has a different order of the words in the second colon, but there is no reason to suggest that this is more original.

'he wrote upon the tablets'. The subject of the verb is ambiguous. On the basis of v.27 one would expect Moses to do the writing. However, in the light of Ex.34.1 (cf. Deut.10.4) Yahweh should be the subject.

29. The verb *qrn* is a denominative of the noun *qeren* (horn) which, however, appears in the sense of ray as a symbol of divinity in the Ancient Near East (cf. Hab.3.4). The Vulgate translation took it literally: *Quod cornuta esset* and led to the artistic representation of Moses with horns on his head. Jirku (*ZDPV* 67, 1944/5, pp.43ff.) still argued for the literal rendering of 'horn' on the basis of Ps.69.32. Cf. Albright, 'The Natural Face', *op. cit.*

34. The verbs shift to the frequentative in the last two verses.

35. It is syntactically possible to translate the sentence as follows: 'When the Israelites would see that Moses' face shone, he would put back the mask . . .' However, in the light of the clear sense of v.33 that Moses spoke officially to them without a mask, this option is not advisable. Cf. Rashi's paraphrase to avoid the difficulty.

2. Literary and Traditio-Historical Analysis

A. A Review of Proposed Solutions

Ch.34 is one of the most difficult chapters in Exodus to analyze and opinions diverge widely. The chapter is integrally related to one's understanding of chs.19–24, and indeed to the entire Sinai tradition. The burning problem which had already been recognized by Goethe in 1773 (*Zwo wichtige bisher unerörterte Fragen*) and even anticipated by a fifth-century Greek writer (cf. E. Nestle, *ZAW* 24,

1904, pp. 134f.), turns on the issue of the relation of the Decalogue in Ex. 20 with the laws of ch. 34. If ch. 34 was simply a rewriting of the original laws upon fresh tablets, one would expect to find an exact repetition, which does not seem to be the case. However, if ch. 34 does not contain the laws of Ex. 20, but other laws relating to worship which are preserved in the Book of the Covenant, then these laws were not those written on the first tablets which Moses broke. Driver sums up the critical problem: 'The great difficulty is that one thing is commanded, and another done' (*Introduction to the Literature of the Old Testament*[9], Edinburgh 1913, pp. 39f.).

The starting-point for the modern critical debate began with Wellhausen's analysis, which isolated ch. 34 as a parallel account to ch. 20 of the Sinai covenant (*Composition des Hexateuchs*, 1879, pp. 85ff.). After Kuenen's criticism had cleared the way for assigning ch. 34 to J (1881), Wellhausen's theory received its classic form (*Composition*[3], 1899, pp. 329ff). Ex. 34 had been altered by a redactor to give it the form of a covenant renewal, but actually it was a parallel account. Whereas E's chapter 20 contained an 'ethical decalogue', J's ch. 34 had a 'ritual decalogue'. Wellhausen then characterized J's decalogue as more primitive in character and more ancient in age than the ethically oriented 'ethical decalogue' of E.

Wellhausen's analysis of ch. 34 as J's parallel account, which contained a ritual decalogue, received wide acceptance, although the debate continued on the exact details of the literary analysis. Kuenen sought to find in 34.1, 4, 28 a continuation of E's account of a covenant renewal. His views were then further refined by Bäntsch who increased the role of the Deuteronomist. By and large, there appeared to be a consensus regarding the two decalogues in spite of the disagreement on the details of the literary development.

However, it is fair to say that this classic literary solution suffered a gradual erosion from several sides in the decades which followed. First of all, it became increasingly difficult to defend the view of an actual decalogue in ch. 34. Wellhausen himself made two quite different divisions. Attempts to produce ten commandments remained highly subjective and unconvincing (cf. the criticisms of Eerdmans, *Das Buch Exodus*, pp. 88ff.; R. Kittel, *Geschichte des Volkes Israel* I[2], Gotha 1912, pp. 468ff.). Secondly, the overall picture of the history of Israel's religion, which had contributed to the theory of the two decalogues as levels of ethical awareness, became increasingly untenable. Finally, added to these factors, the new emphasis on form and traditio-historical criticism appeared to open up other solutions to the old crux of ch. 34. Especially influential was Alt's essay in 1934 on the 'Origins of Israelite Law', which denied that Ex. 34 was a ritual decalogue, and rather characterized it as a secondary, conflated form which had been derived from common Israelite traditions.

Within more recent times two major types of solutions to the problem of ch. 34 have emerged. The first group remained basically literary-critical in its orientation, but sought to make considerable refinements on the classic position of Wellhausen. Characteristic of this group were scholars such as Eissfeldt, Pfeiffer, and Rudolph. Without reviewing all the details of their various proposals, in general the effect has been to picture a much more complicated process of literary redaction than that described by Wellhausen. As a result, little consensus has emerged.

The second group has sought to take more seriously the oral stage in the development of tradition and combine this with a literary analysis. Noth is representative of this approach. He holds that the laws in Ex. 34 and those of 23.14–19 were two different series of apodictic law which rested on common oral tradition. But then Noth is very vague in attempting to trace the temporal relationship between the two passages and he seems to leave many of the problems of redaction unresolved.

For this reason, Beyerlin has attempted to pursue the issue further and particularly to solve the problem of how it came about that laws similar to the Book of the Covenant have now taken the place of J's decalogue. Beyerlin's own solution is a combination of literary and traditio-historical factors. He argues that originally ch. 34 had a decalogue closely akin to ch. 20, but subsequently this decalogue was dislocated and replaced at a later date by an abbreviated form of the Book of the Covenant in an effort to check Canaanite infiltration (p. 87). But the effect of Beyerlin's solution is that a 'displacement theory' is defended which is almost as complicated as Rudolph's, and the arguments by which to explain the motivation for this alteration remain highly illusive, in my judgment.

Finally, Kosmala (*op. cit.*) also combines literary and traditio-historical methods in a detailed article in which he argued that vv. 18–24 were in reality an ancient feast-calendar with an appendix (vv. 25–26) of four additional laws relating to the passover. Although Kosmala has undoubtedly made some keen observations, it is highly questionable that his overall construction can be sustained. His initial literary critical observations seem exceedingly arbitrary, particularly his identifying the Book of the Covenant with the covenant agreements found in the homiletical sections of Ex. 23.20–23 and 34.10–16.

In sum: although the classic Wellhausen analysis has been generally abandoned as inadequate, no recent attempt has been able to muster widespread support. Only in terms of methodology is there a theoretical agreement that a solution will have to take account of a development on both the literary and traditio-historical levels.

B. *The Problem Reconsidered*

In the light of the many unresolved problems, it seems in order to attempt a fresh synthesis. First of all, the initial insight of Wellhausen that ch. 34 is J's parallel account of the Sinai covenant seems to be sound. A close look at the contents of the chapter confirms the thesis that an original covenant is being discussed. The theme of covenant renewal, which is confined to vv. 1, 4, 28b, is redactional.

In the J source the covenant is made on the basis of 'these words' (34.27). These laws reflect a tradition of Israelite law containing elements in common with both the Decalogue (Ex. 20) and the Book of the Covenant (21–23). However, in Ex. 34 there is no distinction made between the two. Laws shared in common with both these other collections are simply designated the 'words of the covenant'. In my judgment, it is a mistake to suggest any 'displacement theory'. Verses 10–27 contain J's covenant laws; however, in the original J account there is no indication of their being only ten words.

The covenant pattern which emerges in Ex. 34 is distinct from that found in chs. 19–24 and appears to reflect a different form of the Mosaic office (cf. discussion in ch. 19). Thus, Moses alone ascends the mountain and God reveals himself in his name with a theophany (34.5ff.). Then Yahweh announces that he will make a covenant (v. 10) on the basis of his words (chs. 19–23), which he does. Moses writes down the words of the covenant (vv. 27b–28a). Whereas in chs. 19–24 Moses acts as covenant mediator who seals the covenant between God and the people in a ritual of radification, in ch. 34 God makes his covenant alone with Moses without any covenant ceremony. Moreover, it is indicative that the chapter concludes with the tradition of Moses' ongoing function of communicating to the people God's will (34.29–34; cf. 33.7ff.).

In the original E account, Moses' office as mediator arose from the people's fear of the theophany (20.18–20). Moses then received the covenant law and, on the basis of these laws, ratified the covenant with Israel (24.3ff.). Both 19.3ff. and 24.3 indicate that the legal basis of the covenant, according to E, was the Decalogue alone. The E account of Sinai reflects the old tradition of the covenant renewal ceremony of the tribal league.

The present shape of the Sinai tradition in Exodus bears the decisive shaping of a redactor who combined J and E. Moreover, the evidence is strong that this redaction was pre-Deuteronomic. In respect to chs. 19–24 this JE redactor introduced the legal traditions contained in the Book of the Covenant into the Sinai narrative. He did this by moving 20.18–20 from its original position before the Decalogue to its present position after the Decalogue. Thereby he provided a bridge to the Book of the Covenant. According to his new pattern the covenant was sealed on the basis of both the Decalogue and the Book of the Covenant. Therefore, the JE redactor made this change explicit in both Ex. 24.3 and 12. The latter verse also provided the link with ch. 32. Moses climbed the mountain to get the tablets upon which were written the 'law and the commandments'.

The redaction of Ex. 34 by the same hand was also far-reaching and decisive. The redactor built ch. 34 into the pattern of sin and forgiveness by joining it to chs. 32 and 33. He did this by introducing the tablet motif of a covenant restoration into J's account and transforming it into a renewal of the broken covenant (34.1, 4). He also added the words of v. 28b to match his introduction: 'he (God) wrote upon the tablets the words of the covenant'. The fact that the J account did not contain the Decalogue of Ex. 20 presented no problems to the redactor because he already understood the original covenant to have been sealed on the basis of both the Decalogue and the Book of the Covenant. The laws in ch. 34 represented a convenient abbreviation of both these collections of laws on which the covenant was to be renewed.

The basic confusion of the chapter arose subsequently from the Deuteronomic understanding that the covenant was sealed solely on the basis of the Decalogue (Deut. 5.22; 9.8ff.). On the basis of this understanding, the Deuteronomic editor added the phrase 'the ten commandments' to Ex. 34.28. This gloss introduced a distinction into the chapter which was hitherto unknown. As a result, the laws of Ex. 34 no longer matched their new framework. Other less disruptive expansions can also most likely be attributed to his hand (34.11–13, 15–16).

It remains an interesting question to consider where Deuteronomy got the idea that the covenant was sealed only on the basis of the Decalogue? Does it reflect an ancient tradition which is independent of the rest of the Pentateuch, or is it to be explained in terms of a literary process? In my opinion, the evidence points to the latter alternative. Deuteronomy's portrayal of the establishing of Moses' office as covenant mediator after the receiving of the Decalogue (Deut. 5.22) appears to reflect the pentateuchal narrative after the alterations made by the JE redactor. In fact, Deut. 5.4 appears to be the Deuteronomist's own correction of the older E tradition found in 5.5. In the same way, both the motif of the broken and restored tablets and the golden calf story follow the Exodus narrative after it had received its shaping by the JE redactor.

C. 34.29–35

The final unit in the chapter calls for a special treatment because of its unusual problems. This passage has been almost always assigned to the Priestly source during the period of classic literary criticism (Wellhausen, Dillmann, Bäntsch, Driver). This judgment was made on the basis of several characteristic P phrases in the passage such as 'two tablets of the testimony' (v. 28), 'congregation' (v. 31), etc. Also the passage seemed to serve as the Priestly source's account of the descent from the mountain. The fact that there seemed to be a literary break after v. 33 which described an ongoing practice led some commentators to distinguish between two different layers in the P source (Bäntsch, von Rad).

In more recent times much more doubt has been expressed as to whether the passage has been correctly assigned to P (Gressmann, Eerdmans, Noth). Most of the characteristic P phrases could easily have entered at a later period of transmission. Particularly the content shows little affinity with the Priestly source (cf. Noth).

The more difficult problem lies in assessing the form and function of this tradition in its original form. Gressmann appears to have been the first modern scholar who suggested that the story was an etiological saga and was connected with the use of a ritual mask by the priest. In recent times the theory has been defended by Jirku (*op. cit.*), who argued that Moses is pictured as wearing a mask with horns which he covered with a veil in order not to frighten the people. Still, it seems quite clear from Near Eastern parallels that the original reference to *qeren* was to a divine glow, and not to horns. It is difficult to avoid the conclusion that a much more primitive tradition, not at home in Israel, lay at the root of the old form of the story. However, the striking fact is that in the present form of the biblical story, the 'veil' functions in exactly the opposite way from the priestly mask in primitive religion (cf. Rudolph's criticism of Gressmann). Ex. 34.33 states explicitly that the veil was worn when Moses functioned as a private citizen, whereas he removed it when speaking to God in his office as mediator. Thus whatever the original source of this ancient tradition, already in the oral stage it had been transformed and incorporated into the tradition respecting Moses' special office as a divine mediator before the tent of meeting.

D. *The Redaction of Chs. 32–34*

A brief summary of our understanding of the formation of chs. 32–34 is now in order. The decisive stage in the formation of 32–34 can be attributed to the hand of the JE redactor, whose work was so far-reaching as to approach that of an author rather than a redactor. In this regard, the development of chs. 32–34 is clearly different from that of chs. 19–24. Naturally the JE redactor made wide use of the older literary sources. Generally speaking, only one literary source underlies each of the stories, and the criterion for determining which source is not very clear. Particularly ch. 33 shows an accumulation of independent stories around a central theme. It is also likely that a particular oral tradition relating to the Mosaic office influenced the choice of stories in this section. In the period following the JE redactor, the hand of the Deuteronomic editor can also be detected. In ch. 32 the present form of the story reflects his polemic against Jeroboam I. In ch. 34 brief expansions bring the earlier story more into line with the Deuteronomic theology.

In the end, the redactional structuring of chs. 32–34 produced a superb, new literary composition which went far beyond the individual elements of the earlier sources. Moreover, this new composition, both by its scope and depth, offered a profoundly theological interpretation of the meaning of the Sinai covenant which left a decisive stamp on the entire Old Testament.

3. *Old Testament Context*

Ex. 34 forms the climax of the narrative which began in 32 with the story of the golden calf. Chapter 32 related the breaking of the

covenant, while ch. 34 recounts its restoration. Chapter 33 bridges
the two parts of the narrative with an account of Moses' intercession
which finally achieved the healing of the breach. Because the present
narrative has been composed from earlier material, and gives
evidence of a complex literary and traditional development (cf.
section above), there is some tension in the details of the story.
Nevertheless, it remains an important task of the interpreter to seek
to understand the final stage of the story in its present form.

[34.1–10] Moses is commanded to cut two tablets of stone which
were like the first ones which he had broken. The explicit mention of
the first tablets ties ch. 34 closely to the golden calf incident. But,
whereas the first time God himself provided the tablets, this time
Moses is ordered to bring with him the tablets on which God is to
write. In the past some scholars have made much of this change in
the origin of the tablets, as if the heavenly tablets would have been a
similar temptation toward idolatry as had been the calf. Actually
there is no sign that this difference carried any significance for the
narrator. What is, however, emphasized is that God himself would
write on the tablets, and he would write the same words of the former
tablets. This promise was the concrete sign that Israel had been
forgiven and the relationship had been restored from God's side.

The description of the preparation and execution of the instructions
followed by the theophany is reminiscent of elements in ch. 19 both in
its specific vocabulary and general description. In the morning
Moses alone was to climb Mount Sinai and to present himself before
God. In ch. 19 there was a certain tension between Moses' role with
the people and his role as the sole mediator. However, in ch. 34 only
the latter tradition plays a role. The people enter into the narrative
only upon Moses' return from the mountain (vv. 29ff.). Once again
the prohibition of 19.12 is repeated: neither man nor beast is to enter
the sacred precinct (34.3). The actual theophany is in terms of
Yahweh's 'descent in the cloud' (v. 5) which combines elements from
both the theophanic traditions of ch. 19: 'Yahweh descended in fire'
(v. 18) and 'the cloud rested on the mountain' (v. 16). It is not fully
clear in the subsequent description of the theophany (v. 5b) whether
it was God or Moses who stood and proclaimed the divine name.
Some commentators have suggested that at an earlier level of the
narrative Moses' response was found in a type of liturgical use of the
divine name. However that may be, v. 5 now receives its clearest
interpretation from what follows in v. 6. Clearly God is the one who

pronounces the divine name. Before this revelation of the name Moses can only silently bow and worship (v. 9).

In the present context the actual theophany is portrayed as a fulfillment of Moses' request in the previous chapter to see God's glory (33.17ff.). The repetition of the key words 'pass by' and 'proclaim the name' establishes the author's intention. The effect of placing the theophany within the context of the restoration of the covenant shifts the focus of the special revelation from the realm of an individual experience of Moses to a ratification of God's covenant relation with Israel through his mediator. The God who now makes himself known through his name as the God of mercy and judgment makes good his claim by forgiving his sinful people. The intention of an explicit reference to the sin of the golden calf comes out forcefully in v. 9, which picks up all the various themes of the last two chapters: 'finding favor with God', 'going in our midst', 'stiff-necked people . . . iniquity and sin', and 'your possession'.

The frequent use through the rest of the Old Testament of the formula in v. 6 by which the nature of God is portrayed (Num. 14.18; Neh. 9.17; Ps. 86.15, etc.) is an eloquent testimony to the centrality of this understanding of God's person. The whole formula does not occur in the original account of the covenant in ch. 19, but it is retained for its restoration, which would seem to indicate that the biblical tradition itself understood the formulation as a reflection of a considerable history of Israel's relation with her God. The community which treasured these traditions was not the generation who could confidently say: 'all that Yahweh has spoken we will do' (24:7), but the people who stood beyond the great divide caused by the sin of the golden calf. The faith which Israel learned to prize was not a proud tradition that once in the past God had singled out a people, but rather that God had continued to sustain his original purpose with a sinful nation both in mercy and judgment.

The function of v. 10 in the present narrative is not immediately clear. In an earlier stage of the tradition it seems to have followed directly the descent of God in v. 5 and introduced the stipulations of the covenant in vv. 11ff. However, there are difficulties to this interpretation, particularly the fact that v. 10, if it is now a response, does not address the question raised in v. 9. Actually the verse picks up a theme which occurs in the former chapter, in 33.16. There Moses argues that Israel is made distinct from all other peoples by God's presence in her midst. Verse 10 makes no mention of God's accompanying presence, but rather picks up the other motif. God will make a covenant such that all people will testify to the wonder of God's work. Indeed the intervention of God on Israel's behalf requires the use of creation language: he will perform marvels never before created! Both the thought and the language are not far removed from Second Isaiah.

[34.11–16] Literary critics have long observed that vv. 11–16 appear to reflect a later literary expansion which has been strongly influenced by Deuteronomy. In the context of the present narrative, placed after the final announcement of the covenant and before the actual stipulations, the section serves as a homilectical introduction which both interprets the covenant and commends its obedience. The whole emphasis of the admonition falls on Israel's complete separation from the inhabitants of the land. The warning is grounded in the nature of God who is a jealous god and will not tolerate the worship of another (v. 14), and in the subtle temptation to idolatry which contact with the Canaanites inevitably brings. This homily also serves to remind of the golden calf episode by its similar language: not worship, nor sacrifice, nor eat, nor play the harlot (cf. 32.6ff.).

[34.17–26] The actual laws of the covenant now follow. The literary critical problems associated with them are difficult and complex (cf. the section above). Whatever the explanation for this selection of laws, the fact with which one has to reckon is the close parallelism, often *verbatim*, between these laws and those in Ex. 13.13, 14 and 23.15–19. (Cf. Driver, *Exodus*, or Pfeiffer, *op. cit.*, for a synopsis in parallel columns.)

Several generalizations respecting these laws can be made:

1. The laws in Ex. 34.18–26 are unquestionably related to those in Ex. 13 and 23, but the nature of the relationship remains debatable. The facts to be explained should be carefully noted. There are some laws which are identical in every detail (34.26 // 23.19), some which show minor variation (34.20 // 13.13), and some which diverge significantly (34.19 // 13.12). When there is variation, it sometimes extends throughout the law; at other times it consists of a significant addition (34.25 // 23.18). In the light of this complexity it is not clear whether one set of laws is dependent on another in a literary relationship (so Pfeiffer), or whether there are two recensions of a common written set of laws (Driver), or whether common oral tradition underlies them both (Beyerlin). It is certainly possible that both literary

recensions and oral tradition were involved. The parallelism in sequence between Ex. 34.21–26 and 23.12ff. could reflect a common oral tradition, but the dividing of 23.15a and 15b in 34.18 and 34.21, with verses parallel to ch. 13 placed in between, points more to a literary development.

2. The attempt to determine the relationship between the parallels by means of a scheme of religious development has not resulted in any assured conclusions (*contra* Pfeiffer), and must be made with considerable caution. In general, the laws seem to be of the same age as the Book of the Covenant (chs. 21–23) and reflect Israel's life after the settlement in the land. Historical decisions on specific problems, such as the reference to passover in 34.25 // 23.18, will have to be made on the basis of cumulative evidence from the entire Old Testament rather than on a literary theory affecting only ch. 34.

3. There appears to be no one discernible pattern in the present arrangement of the laws, neither literary, historical, nor theological. It is not clear why the sequence of the three festivals, such as one has in Ex. 23, has been broken in ch. 34, or whether one can regard the position of the final laws as anything but an historical appendix. Attempts such as that of Benno Jacob to find a theological reason for the position of each law runs the danger of simply producing a modern midrash. For example, there is little evidence to suggest that the position of the law forbidding work on the seventh day in v. 21 has been determined by a concern to dispel any uncertainty regarding the position of the sabbath during the period between the feast of unleavened bread and the feast of weeks (Jacob *ad loc.*). In sum, the intention of the author in making use of these laws is best reflected in the framework into which they have now been set (vv. 11–16, 27–28), rather than in his reshaping the form or content of the laws themselves.

4. The laws in Ex. 34 contain elements which parallel both the Decalogue and the Book of the Covenant from the tradition of the original covenant at Sinai. Parallels to the Decalogue relate to the prohibition of other gods (20.3 // 34.14), the making of images (20.4 // 34.17), and the sabbath (20.8 // 34.21). The parallels to the Book of the Covenant have been discussed above. The reason for this particular selection seems to be a historical one. The author of the present text made use of a set of laws from an earlier source (J). However, various theological implications were drawn from the formal parallelism, as the concluding framework shows (vv. 27f.).

The laws which regulated the renewal of the covenant were not different in kind from those of the first covenant.

[34.27–28] The giving of the laws concludes with a divine command to Moses to write down 'these words', a description of Moses' sojourn on the mountain, and a final sentence describing the writing down of the Ten Commandments upon tablets. But the apparently simple prose conclusion contains some extremely difficult problems of interpretation which call for a historical dimension.

As the text now stands, Moses is first commanded to write down 'these words', which, as the following sentence specifies, form the basis of the covenant. The antecedent must refer to the instructions which have just been transmitted to Moses orally by God and include both the admonitions (vv. 11ff.) and the laws (vv. 17–26). These words which Moses wrote, however, are distinguished from the words of the Ten Commandments which Yahweh wrote upon the stone tablets. Although the agent who inscribed the tablets is ambiguous in the Hebrew of v. 28b (cf. critical note), the clear reference in 34.1 makes evident the author's intention. Accordingly, the present narrative distinguishes between admonitions and laws which Moses wrote down, and the Decalogue which God himself inscribed (24.12). Nevertheless, there remains some unclarity how both sets of words specifically relate to each other. What Moses wrote down is designated as the words 'according to which the covenant has been cut', whereas the Ten Commandments which God inscribed are also called the 'words of the covenant'. Allowing for this unclarity, the impression left by the chapter is that Moses first received admonitions and laws which were specifically focused on the threat of idolatry and called to mind Israel's recent unfaithfulness. Thereafter, God restored the tablets with the original words of the Decalogue.

However, there are other difficulties in the text which would indicate that the interpretation offered by the final redactor of the chapter differed somewhat from an earlier stage. For example, the distinction between instructions which Moses wrote and the Decalogue which God wrote is not evident even in ch. 34 outside the concluding framework. Again, the terminology of the divine law as the 'ten words' does not occur elsewhere in Exodus and appears to be a Deuteronomic phrase (Deut. 4.13; 10.4). The fact that some of the parallel laws to the Decalogue are included within the instructions written down by Moses in v. 27, would be additional evidence to suggest the lack of an originally sharp distinction between the

Decalogue and the Book of the Covenant. Furthermore, the covenant terminology in Ex. 24 would indicate that the distinction was redactional and that the Decalogue had not yet been designated with a separate title. In addition the introduction of the motif of the tablets, which is missing on the earlier levels of the tradition, aided in separating the Decalogue as an entity distinct from the other covenant laws.

Although it does remain a theoretical projection, there is considerable evidence to suggest that three different stages of literary development can be traced in ch. 34. There is a level which contained the early covenant laws of the J source. These laws paralleled in general those in ch. 19–23, and contained elements of both the Decalogue and the Book of the Covenant. Secondly, this source was reworked by the redactor of chs. 32–34 and placed within the context of the golden calf story and the renewal of the covenant. On this level, the motif of the tablets of stone was introduced. Thirdly, a Deuteronomic editor designated the contents of the tablets of stone as the Decalogue in v. 28, and thereby forced into ch. 34 a distinction between the laws written by Moses and the Ten Commandments inscribed by God.

In spite of the evidence of a development within the text with some accompanying signs of inner tension, it would be a serious mistake to regard this redactional process as a 'growth in confusion', as critical commentators often imply. The later stages have certainly introduced new distinctions which were not originally present, and which reflected, for example, the growing importance of the Decalogue as a separate entity, or the centrality of the passover (34.25). However, there are several lines of continuity which should not be overlooked. All levels of the development are agreed in recognizing as an integral part of the Sinai tradition both the material of the Decalogue and that of the Book of the Covenant. The relation between the various collections of laws changed throughout the years and a historical reconstruction of an alleged original level seems quite impossible. Furthermore, there is no evidence of a growth from cultic to ethical law. Indeed, the so-called 'ethical decalogue' of Ex. 20 increased in importance, but never in such a way as to call into question the divine origin of other legal traditions. Finally, there is a strong continuity running through all the history of development in seeing the centrality of Moses' office, not only as the immediate vehicle for the reception of God's commandments for Israel, but as a continuous channel of the divine will, which interpreted for each generation the the living will of God (Ex. 20.18ff.; 33.7ff.; 34.29ff.; Deut. 5.28ff.; 18.15ff.).

[34.29–35] In the earlier section on literary problems the case was argued for seeing the story of Moses' shining face as a tradition from a special cycle of stories which treated the office of Moses. The question was left open as to what extent the Mosaic office was related to Ancient Near Eastern practices, especially in the light of parallels to the 'divine glow' and the mask. The present task is to determine the role of the story within the Exodus narrative. Thus, why is the story related in this manner? Again, if the story is akin to 33.7ff. in terms of its genre, why has it been reserved for the end?

The story is related in two distinct styles of Hebrew prose, which is made possible by a different use of the verb. Verse 29–33 recount in the historical past the episode of Moses' return from the mountain with a glowing face, the people's reaction, and Moses' use of a veil. However, vv. 34–35 employ a frequentative tense to describe an ongoing practice of Moses in his office as divine mediator. The first verses give a specific historical setting, and relate specifically to Moses' final descent from Mount Sinai. The initial reaction to the shining face, both by Moses and the people, is related. The last two verses in the paragraph, however, are given no specific historical setting, either in time or space, although the cumulative evidence from other passages would tend to tie the practice to the tent of meeting.

The reference to the descent from the mount with the tablets forms a smooth transition from v. 28; however, the passage is not closely related to the preceding incident of the Golden Calf. In terms of content, the story could have just as easily been attached to 31.18, as many literary critics have suggested. In fact, the story has a decidedly different emphasis from the main body of Exodus tradition. Whereas in Ex. 19ff. (cf. Deut. 5.22) the focus of the Sinai tradition fell on the once-and-for-all proclamation of the divine laws of the covenant, which were then inscribed upon stone tablets, the main point of this story has to do with Moses' ongoing practice of speaking with God and communicating his words to the people. The seven occurrences of the word 'to speak' in this brief passage give ample indication of the author's intention. However, there is a certain parallelism to the earlier account of Moses' function as covenant mediator in 20.18ff. In this story the people are terrified before the thunder and lightning of the theophany; in 34.29 they are fearful before the mere reflection from Moses' face of the theophany. In both stories the people retreat and are afraid to draw near. In both stories Moses hears the word of God in their stead and communicates his will to them.

The distinctive content of the story concerns Moses' use of a veil or mask. This motif ties the two parts of the story so closely together that the shift in style is often overlooked. The author relates the first use of the mask in a typical Hebrew narrative style (cf. Gen. 6.11ff.; 18.1ff.; 19.24ff.; Ex. 3.2ff. etc.). First he describes what has happened from the perspective of the author who views it from a position removed from the historical sequence. Moses had acquired a divine glow because of his long speaking with God. Then, the author describes how the discovery of the glow was experienced by those within the story. Moses himself was unaware that his skin shone, but the people . . . 'looked, and behold the skin of his face shone . . .'. They were afraid to come near to Moses, so that he had to call them. Then he established the pattern which would be repeated. He gave them in commandment all that God had spoken to him, and only when he had finished speaking did he put on his veil.

At this point in the story, the author shifts his style to describe the continuation of the practice. The clause, 'whenever Moses went in before Yahweh to speak with him', has introduced a new setting without feeling the need to explain. What is presupposed is that Moses continues to speak with God, no longer on the top of the mountain, but in the tent of meeting (Ex. 33.11). Moreover, the same immediacy between God and Moses is present which results in the same afterglow of the divine majesty. The veil or mask is removed when Moses speaks with God. It is put on only after he has finished speaking God's words to the people. Both vv. 33 and 35 make it clear that the people continue to see the glow on Moses' face. In other words, the veil covers his face only in the period in which he is not performing his office of receiving or communicating God's word.

There is a certain tension between the two parts of the story in respect to this mask which has long been observed (cf. Gressmann). What was the purpose of the mask if it was not to cover Moses' shining face which continued to cause the people's anxiety? The initial introduction of the mask in response to this fear begins to make this obvious connection. As the text now stands, one could understand the use of the mask only after his initial communication

(v. 33) as having been dictated by the unusual situation, namely, he did not know his face shone. Then later on as a concession to the people's fear he covered his face before them except in those periods in which he was speaking to God. Accordingly, the use of the mask would have been quite straightforward. But the present form of the story does not understand the use of the mask in this way. Verse 35 makes it unequivocal that Moses came out from speaking with God and addressed the people, both times, without a mask. What function the mask has is then not fully clear. Commentators have deduced that he wore it at those times in which he did not function in his particular office as mediator. But this is not really stated in the text, and makes very little sense.

It is possible that the tradition was explicitly resisting having Moses speaking to the people with a mask because of some Ancient Near Eastern practice of the shaman. Indeed, the biblical story is concerned that the divine glow on Moses' face should not be understood as a type of metamorphosis. Moses did not himself become a deity. He was unaware of any transformation. The whole point of the story emphasizes that his was only a reflection of God's glory. By placing the story in this form in its present position the author has given an interpretation of how he wants the entire Sinai tradition to be understood. God and the revelation of his will stand at the center. But Sinai is also the story of Moses, the mediator between God and Israel, who continued to function as a mortal man and yet who in his office bridged the enormous gap between the awesome, holy, and zealous God of Sinai and the fearful, sinful, and repentant people of the covenant.

Detailed Notes

34.1. On the terminology of the tablets cf. footnote on Ex. 32.15.

6. The name formula occurs elsewhere in the following places: Num. 14.18; Neh. 9.17; Pss. 86.15; 103.8; 111.4; 112.4; 116.5; 145.8; Joel 2.13; Jonah 4.2; Nahum 1.3; II Chron. 30.9. There are echoes of it in still other verses. Cf. the two detailed studies of Scharbert, *op. cit.*, and Dentan, *op. cit.*, along with the interesting observations of E. Bickerman, *Four Strange Books of the Bible*, New York 1964, p. 41, in regard to its use in Jonah. Near Eastern parallels to the 'love of God' are offered by W. Moran, *CBQ* 25, 1963, pp. 81ff.

7. On the formula 'to visit the iniquity of the fathers upon the children', cf. the striking parallel of Muršiliš II: 'And so it is: the sins of the father come upon the son; and so my father's sins have come upon me' (V. Korošec, *Hethitische Staatsverträge*, Leipzig 1931, p. 103). (I am indebted to Thomas Mann for this parallel.)

17. Cf. the exegesis of Ex. 20.4ff.
18. Cf. Ex. 23.15ff.
19. On the subject of the first-born, cf. 13.1ff.
21. On the sabbath, cf. 20.8ff. Cf. Kosmala's interpretation of the 'plowing time and harvest', *op. cit.*, pp. 38ff.
22. On the feast of weeks and feast of ingathering, cf. 23.16f.
25. Cf. Ex. 23.18 and the literature on the passover cited in ch. 12.
26. Cf. 23.19.
33. 'veil'. Cf. the article by F. Dumermuth, *op. cit.*, and the discussion of 'teraphim' by G. Fohrer, *BHH* III, col. 1951.

4. *New Testament Context*

D. GEORGI, *Die Gegner des Paulus in 2 Korintherbrief*, WMANT 11, 1964, pp. 246ff.; J. GOETTSBERGER, 'Die Hülle des Mose nach Ex 34 und II Cor 3', *BZ* 16, 1924, pp. 1–17; A. OEPKE, '*κάλυμμα*', *TWNT* III, pp. 561f. = *TDNT* III, pp. 556ff.; S. SCHULZ, 'Die Decke des Moses', *ZNW* 49, 1958, pp. 1–30; H. ULONSKA, 'Die Doxa des Mose', *EvTh* 26, 1966, pp. 378–88; W. C. VAN UNNIK, '"With unveiled Face", an Exegesis of 2 Cor. 3, 12–18', *Novum Testamentum* 6, 1963, pp. 153–69.

Most of the major issues in the history of interpretation of this chapter have already appeared in the study of earlier passages of the Sinai tradition. Therefore it does not seem necessary to review this material. However, the New Testament's use of the last portion of the chapter is so unusual that some notice of the problem seems called for.

The difficulties of understanding II Cor. 3 are so many that one hesitates to enter the arena. For example, how does the section which begins in vv. 7ff. relate to the larger issue of Paul's controversy with his opponents with which the chapter begins and which continues in ch. 4? Is there a logical sequence of thought which ties together the various allusions to Moses and the old covenant in the chapter? To what extent is Paul making use of an exegetical tradition on Ex. 34 in shaping his argument? Unfortunately, there has emerged nothing which even begins to resemble a consensus of opinion among New Testament scholars in spite of considerable attention to these problems within recent years. It is not my intention to unravel all the problems which continue to baffle the experts in the field. This would be arrogance indeed. Rather, my concern is to approach the New Testament text from the insights gained in the exegesis of the Old Testament, and to focus my attention on the theological problems at stake in its New Testament application. Obviously I do not share the view that the text is so *ad hominem* in nature as to prevent one from drawing any conclusions respecting Paul's own use of the Old Testament (*contra* Ulonska).

In v. 7 Paul begins his use of Ex. 34. He describes the divine splendor on Moses' face which attended the giving of the old covenant as having such a brightness that the Israelites were not able to look at it. Although Paul does not make use of the specific vocabulary of either the Massoretic text or the Septuagint, he has reflected adequately enough the sense of Ex. 34.30. But what causes the initial exegetical problem is that Paul then adds a phrase which appears to have no basis at all in the Old Testament, namely, that the divine splendor 'was soon to fade' (v. 7). Indeed, on the basis of this characterization of the nature of the Old Testament splendor, Paul builds his argument using the familiar rabbinic device of *a minore ad maius*. If the splendor of the old dispensation was too great for the Israelites to view, fading as it was, how much greater would be the splendor of the new which is permanent.

Now it is important to notice that the weight of the argument falls on establishing the contrast between the old and the new manifestations of splendor. But what Paul simply assumes from his readers is their agreement with his description of the first splendor as 'about to fade away'. Paul does not establish this point even though it has no obvious basis in the Old Testament text. He takes it for granted even though, if it were to be denied, the force of his argument would have been lost. This would suggest that the interpretation of the splendor as fading was not a creation of Paul, but was already well known by his readers. He simply made use of a generally accepted interpretation on which to build his own argument.

What can one say about the nature of this interpretation? Because of the lack of contemporary parallels, there can be no certain judgment. However, the fact that later rabbis did comment on the duration of the splendor on Moses' face (cf. Rashi), one could assume that the question was raised in the earlier period as well. At least two factors from the Old Testament would probably have entered into their interpretation. First, outside of Ex. 34 there is never again mention made of Moses' shining face. Secondly, Ex. 40.35 states that Moses was not able to enter the tent of meeting because of God's glory. Consequently, it is possible for a midrashic exegesis to have deduced from this combination of texts that the splendor of Moses' face did in fact not endure. Nor is there any reason for supposing that this interpretation would indicate a Christian origin which sought to minimize the Old Testament's account of the splendor. The specific Christian interpretation rather appears in the contrast which Paul established on the basis of this accepted reading of the Old Testament text, and which was implied in the initial rubric of a 'dispensation of death' (v. 7).

The problem of understanding Paul's argument intensifies in the verses which follow (12–18), and it is not easy to be sure of the movement of thought. Paul contrasts the boldness of the Christian with Moses who covered his face with a veil lest the Israelites see the fading glory. He then designated them as hardened. At that point there is a marked shift in the thought and the theme of the veil is related directly to the present situation: 'to this very day' the same veil is there 'when they read the old covenant'. Paul has moved from the Old Testament Israelites to the synagogue of his day, and from an episode in the history of the old covenant to the record of that episode which is read as scripture. Verse 15 clarifies the ambiguity in v. 14 by making explicit that the veil lies over the minds of the Jews whenever the Old Testament scriptures are read.

The basic exegetical difficulty is to understand the relation between these various parts. What is the starting-point from which to trace the sequence of thought? Van Unnik (*op. cit.*) has argued that the connection between the 'boldness' ($\pi\alpha\rho\rho\eta\sigma\iota\alpha$, v. 12) and the veil is a philological one. He believes that Paul is thinking in Aramaic and makes an unconscious connection between the Aramaic equivalent of the Greek 'boldness' which is 'to uncover the face' and the story of Moses' covering his face with a veil. He finds a further confirmation to his theory in v. 8 where the expression 'with unveiled face' occurs. It is possible, although far from certain, that this factor did play a role. However, it seems to me that von Unnik has not dealt seriously enough with the midrashic background in Paul's exegesis, and consequently has not succeeded in fully illuminating the various connections within the chapter.

In v. 12 Paul introduces the theme of boldness. It is a concept attested elsewhere in his writings (II Cor. 7.4; Phil. 1.20), and joins to his argument in vv. 7–11 quite smoothly. It now functions as a contrast to Moses' behavior who covered his face. We have already argued that Paul made use of an accepted midrashic interpretation of Ex. 34 on which to mount his case in vv. 7–11. In v. 13 he repeats the same interpretation, again without feeling the need to establish it. What is new in v. 13 is the reference to the veil and the assumption that Moses' motivation in covering his face was timidity, thus providing a contrast to the call for Christian boldness. The introduction of the veil, however, is a natural one if Paul was following a midrash because only at this point in the Exodus story is it first mentioned.

How then can one explain the motivation of timidity within the midrash? First of all, the problem of understanding the motivation for Moses' use of the veil has long been seen by rabbinic commentators (cf. Ibn Ezra). The usual critical explanation that this is a mythological motif in which Moses put on the veil to protect the people from the radiant splendor rests on a reconstruction of the text. According to the biblical text Moses always spoke to God and the people without the mask (cf. exegesis of 34.33, 35). The fact that the text itself does not offer a motivation for the wearing of the veil would naturally evoke a midrashic interpretation. We have already argued that the theory of the 'fading glory' arose to explain why there is no further mention in the Old Testament of this phenomenon. But what about the motivation of Moses' timidity in concealing its passing? The account in Num. 12 of the challenge of Mirian and Aaron to Moses is closely akin to Ex. 34. The issue at stake is whether Moses has sole claim of being God's mediator. The action takes place also before the tent of meeting. God affirms that only to Moses does he speak 'mouth to mouth, clearly, and not in dark speech'. Moses even sees the form of Yahweh (Num. 12.8). Rabbinic commentators naturally connected this passage with the theophany to Moses in Ex. 33 and 34. But there is another element in Num. 12. Moses, who alone sees the form of God, is 'very meek, more than all men on the face of the earth' (v. 3). Is it possible that Moses' meekness was connected through this passage with his covering of his face to hide the fading glory?

In v. 14 there is a decided shift in style, which is well rendered by the NEB: 'but in any case . . .'. Paul turns from his comparison of Moses to characterize the present generation of Jews as 'hardened'. They have the same veil over their minds whenever they read the Old Testament. Clearly Paul has suddenly transformed the term 'veil' into a metaphor by which to make quite a different point. The difference of the next verses both in form and content indicate that Paul is no longer following a well-received tradition, but making an *ad hoc* application within his argument. Only in v. 16 does he again return to the Old Testament text, and specifically to the conclusion of the Exodus passage. However, Paul is no longer following a traditional interpretation. In striking contrast to the earlier style of argument he is forced now to justify his interpretation from scripture. First he cites the passage regarding Moses: 'whenever he turns to the Lord the veil is removed'. Then he interprets: the 'Lord' of this passage is the Spirit, namely of Christ. He concludes: 'and where the Spirit is, there is liberty.' Finally, he draws the application by tying together all the various elements of his exegesis: 'Because we are free, we have no veil, we are bold to reflect the splendor of Christ and are thus transfigured by his Spirit.'

There are several implications which one can draw from Paul's use of the Old Testament. The apostle comes to the Old Testament text from the perspective of the Christian gospel. The old covenant is fading; its splendor is passing in comparison to the permanent glory of the new. But Paul is not simply concerned to establish the superiority of the new, as one might expect in Hebrews. Rather, he argues that already the Old Testament witnesses to the coming of the new. Indeed, Moses is the dispensation of death on whom a veil rests when read without the Spirit, but 'when he turned to the Lord' his veil was removed (v. 16). Moses is therefore an agent of both the old and the new. Again, Paul makes use of traditional Jewish exegesis, some of which is certainly midrashic in character. Moses reflected a divine *doxa*, which he covered with a veil in order to hide its fading splendor. The fact that Paul builds his own argument upon it points to the conclusion that he works with an inherited interpretation of many Old Testament passages, which he shares with his readers.

But basically Paul gives evidence of a serious wrestling with the biblical text in an effort to penetrate to the content of the witness. Indeed he brings to the text a framework of Christian theology and a midrashic inheritance of his age. But he finds in the text an understanding of Christian boldness as liberty, of the Spirit at work in removing the veil, and a reflection of God's glory in the gradual transformation of the Christian into his likeness.

In sum, Paul's interpretation of II Corinthians 3 is a classic example of genuine theological dialectic. He brings to the text the perspective of faith which had learned to hope in Christ (v. 12), but he brings from the text a witness which conversely forms his understanding of God and shapes the Christian life through his Spirit.

XXIV

TABERNACLE INSTRUCTIONS EXECUTED

35.1–40.38

35 ¹Then Moses called together the whole Israelite community and said to them, 'These are the things that the LORD has commanded you to do. ²On six days work may be done, but on the seventh day you shall have a sabbath of complete rest holy to the LORD; whoever does any work on it shall be put to death. ³You shall not light any fires in any of your dwellings on the sabbath day.'

4 Moses said to the whole community of Israelites, 'This is the thing that the LORD has commanded. ⁵Take from among you a contribution to the LORD. Let whoever is willing bring a contribution for the LORD: gold, silver, and bronze; ⁶blue, purple, and scarlet material and fine linen and goats' hair, ⁷tanned ram skins, dolphin skins, and acacia wood, ⁸oil for the lamps, spices for the anointing oil and for the fragrant incense, ⁹onyx and other stones for setting, for the ephod and for the breastpiece.

10 'Let all who are skilled among you come, and make all that the LORD has commanded; the tabernacle, ¹¹its tent and its covering, its hooks and its frames, its bars, its posts, and its bases; ¹²the ark with its poles, the propitiatory and the veil of the screen; ¹³the table with its poles and all its utensils, and the bread of the Presence; ¹⁴the lampstand for lighting, with its furnishings and its lamps, and the oil for lighting; ¹⁵the altar of incense with its poles, the anointing oil and the fragrant incense, and the screen for the door at the entrance of the tabernacle; ¹⁶the altar of burnt offering with its bronze grating, its poles, and all its utensils, the laver and its base, ¹⁷the hangings of the court, its posts and its bases, and the screen for the gate of the court; ¹⁸the pegs for the tabernacle, and the pegs for the court and their cords, ¹⁹the stitched vestments for ministering in the holy place, the sacred vestments of Aaron the priest, and the vestments of his sons for serving as priests.'

20 Then the whole Israelite community left Moses' presence. ²¹And

they came, everyone who was willing and whose spirit moved him, and brought the contribution to the LORD to be used for the tent of meeting, and for all its service, and for the sacred vestments. ²²So they came, both men and women, all who were of a willing heart brought brooches, earrings, rings and pendants, gold ornaments of all kinds, everyone dedicating an offering of gold to the LORD. ²³Everyone who possessed blue, purple, and scarlet material, fine linen, goats' hair, tanned ram skins, and dolphin skin, brought them; ²⁴everyone who could contribute silver or bronze brought it as a contribution to the LORD, and everyone who possessed acacia wood for any use in the work, brought it. ²⁵All the skilled women spun with their hands, and brought what they had spun in blue, purple, and scarlet material, and in fine linen. ²⁶All the women who excelled in that skill spun the goats' hair. ²⁷The leaders brought onyx stone and other stones for setting, for the ephod and for the breastpiece, ²⁸and spices and oil for lighting, and for the anointing oil, and for the fragrant incense. ²⁹All the Israelite men and women who were willing to bring anything for the work which the LORD had commanded through Moses to be done, brought it as a freewill contribution to the LORD.

30 Moses said to the Israelites, 'See, the LORD has specially chosen Bezalel, son of Uri, son of Hur, of the tribe of Judah. ³¹He has endowed him with a divine spirit; with spirit and intelligence, with ability and knowledge in every kind of craft, ³²to make designs for work in gold, silver, and bronze, ³³in cutting stone for setting and in carving wood, for work in every skilled craft. ³⁴He has granted him ability to teach, both him and Oholiab son of Ahisamach, of the tribe of Dan. ³⁵He has endowed them with ability to do every sort of skill done by a carver, designer, embroiderer in blue, purple, and scarlet material, and in fine linen, and by a weaver – as workers in all crafts and as makers of designs.

36 ¹Then Bezalel and Oholiab and all the skilled persons whom the LORD has endowed with skill and ability to perform well all the tasks in the service of the sanctuary, shall carry out all that the LORD has commanded.'

2 Moses then called Bezalel and Oholiab and every skilled man whom the LORD had endowed with skill, everyone who was willing to come to do the work; ³and they received from Moses all the freewill offering which the Israelites had brought for doing the work on the sanctuary. But when they continued to bring freewill contributions morning after morning, ⁴all the craftsmen who were engaging in the various tasks on the sanctuary came, each from the task which he was engaged, ⁵and they said to Moses, 'The people are bringing far more than is needed for the work which the LORD has commanded us to do.' ⁶Whereupon Moses had the proclamation made throughout the camp, 'Let neither man or woman make anything more for the contribution to the sanctuary.' So

the people were restrained from bringing. [7]Their efforts had been more than enough for all the tasks to be done.

[8]Then all the skilled men among the workmen made the tabernacle with ten curtains. They were made of fine twisted linen and of blue and purple and scarlet material with a design of cherubim worked into them. [9]The length of each curtain was twenty-eight cubits, and the width of each curtain four cubits; all the curtains had the same measurements. [10]He joined five of the curtains to one another, and the other five curtains he joined to one another. [11]He made loops of blue on the edge of the outermost curtain of the first set; likewise he made them on the edge of the outermost curtain of the second set. [12]He made fifty loops on the one curtain, and he made fifty loops on the edge of the curtain that was in the second set; the loops were opposite each other. [13]He made fifty gold clasps, and joined the curtains with the clasps, so that the tabernacle was one whole.

14 He also made curtains of goats' hair for a tent over the tabernacle; he made eleven curtains in all. [15]The length of each curtain was thirty cubits, and the width of each curtain was four cubits; the eleven curtains had the same measurements. [16]He joined five curtains by themselves and the other six by themselves. [17]He made fifty loops on the edge of the outermost curtain of the one set, and fifty loops on the edge of the curtain of the other set. [18]He made fifty bronze clasps to join the tent together that it become one whole. [19]He made for the tent a covering of tanned rams' skins and above that dolphin skins.

20 Then he made the frames for the tabernacle of acacia wood. [21]The length of each frame was ten cubits, and the width of each frame a cubit and a half. [22]There were two tenons in each frame, joined together; he did the same for all the frames of the tabernacle. [23]He made the frames for the tabernacle as follows: twenty frames for the south side, [24]and forty silver bases under the twenty frames, two bases under one frame for its two tenons and two bases under each following frame for its two tenons. [25]For the second side of the tabernacle, on the north side, he made twenty frames, [26]with their forty bases of silver, two bases under one frame, and two bases under each following frame. [27]For the rear of the tabernacle, to the west, he made six frames. [28]He made two frames for the corners of the tabernacle in the rear. [29]They were double at the bottom, but at the top they fitted into one ring. He made two of them so, for the two corners. [30]There were eight frames with their sixteen bases of silver: sixteen bases, under every frame two bases.

31 He made bars of acacia wood, five for the frames of the one side of the tabernacle, [32]and five bars for the frames of the other side of the tabernacle and five bars for the frames of the tabernacle at the rear to the west. [33]He made the middle bar, halfway up the frame, to run from end to end. [34]He overlaid the frames with gold and made their

rings of gold for holders for the bars, and overlaid the bars with gold.

35 He made the veil of blue, purple, and scarlet material and fine twisted linen. It had a design of cherubim worked into it. [36]He made four posts of acacia wood and overlaid them with gold. Their hooks were of gold, and he cast for them four bases of silver. [37]He also made the screen for the door of the tent, of blue, purple, and scarlet material and fine twisted linen with embroidery, [38]and its five posts with their hooks. He overlaid their tops and their bands with gold, but their five bases were of bronze.

37 [1]Bezalel made the ark of acacia wood, two and a half cubits long, a cubit and a half wide, and a cubit and a half high. [2]He overlaid it with pure gold – inside and out – and made a molding of gold all around it. [3]He cast four gold rings for its four feet, two rings on one of its side walls and two on the other. [4]He made poles of acacia wood and overlaid them with gold, [5]and inserted the poles into the rings on the side walls of the ark, to carry the ark. [6]He made a propitiatory of pure gold, two and a half cubits long and a cubit and a half wide. [7]He made two cherubim of beaten gold at the two ends of the propitiatory, [8]one cherub at one end and the other cherub at the other end; he made the cherubim on its two ends of one piece with the propitiatory. [9]The cherubim spread out their wings above, screening the propitiatory with their wings. They faced each other with the faces of the cherub pointed toward the propitiatory.

10 He also made the table of acacia wood, two cubits long, one cubit wide, and a cubit and a half high. [11]He overlaid it with pure gold, and made a molding of gold around it. [12]He made a rim of a hand's breadth around it and made a gold molding for its rim round about. [13]He cast for it four gold rings, and fastened the rings to the four corners at its four legs. [14]The rings were close to the rim as holders for the poles to carry the table. [15]He made the poles of acacia wood to carry the table, and overlaid them with gold. [16]He made the utensils of pure gold that were to be upon the table, and its plates, bowls, jugs, and jars with which to offer libations.

17 He also made the lampstand of pure gold. The lampstand, stem and branches, were made of beaten work, its cups, calyxes, and petals, were of one piece with it. [18]There were six branches, extending from its sides, three branches of the lampstand out of the one side of it, and three branches of the lampstand out of the other side of it, [19]three cups shaped like almonds, each with calyx and petal, on the one branch, and three cups shaped like almonds, each with calyx and petal, on the other branch – and so for the six branches extending from the lampstand. [20]In the lampstand itself there were four cups shaped like almonds with calyx and petal, [21]and a calyx of one piece with it under each pair of the six branches extending from it. [22]Their calyxes and their stems were

of one piece with it, the whole of it was a beaten piece of pure gold. [23]He made the seven lamps, its tongs, and its firepans of pure gold. [24]He made it all and its furnishings out of a talent of pure gold.

25 He made the altar of incense of acacia wood. It was a cubit long and a cubit wide – it was square – and two cubits high. Its horns were of one piece with it. [26]He overlaid it with pure gold, its top, its sides round about, and its horns, and he made a molding of gold round about it, [27]and he made two rings of gold for it under its molding on two opposite sides of it, as holders for the poles with which to carry it. [28]He made the poles of acacia wood and overlaid them with gold. [29]He made the sacred anointing oil also, and the pure fragrant incense expertly compounded.

38 [1]He made the alter of burnt offering of acacia wood, five cubits long and five cubits wide – the altar was square – and three cubits high. [2]He made horns for it on its four corners, its horns were of one piece with it, and he overlaid it with bronze. [3]He made all the utensils for the altar, the pots, shovels, basins, forks, and fire plans. All its utensils he made of bronze. [4]He made the altar a grating of bronze network under its ledge extending halfway up. [5]He cast four rings on the four corners of the bronze grating as holders for the poles. [6]He made the poles of acacia wood and overlaid them with bronze. [7]He inserted the poles into the rings on the sides of the altar to carry it with them. He made it hollow with boards.

8 He made the bronze laver and its bronze basin from the mirrors of the serving women who served at the door of the tent of meeting. [9]He made the court. On the south side there were hangings for the court of fine twisted linen, a hundred cubits long; [10]their posts were twenty and there were twenty bases of bronze, but the hooks of the posts and their bands were of silver. [11]On the north side a hundred cubits, their posts were twenty, their bases twenty, of bronze, but the hooks of the posts and their bands were of silver. [12]On the west side the hangings were of fifty cubits, their posts ten, and their bases ten; the hooks of the posts and their bands were silver. [13]For the front, to the east, fifty cubits. [14]The hangings for one flank were fifteen cubits with three posts and three bases. [15]And so for the second flank, on each side of the gate of the court were hangings of fifteen cubits with their three posts and three bases. [16]All the hangings around the court were of fine twisted linen. [17]The bases for the posts were of bronze, but the hooks of the pillars and their bands were of silver. The overlay of their tops was of silver and all the posts of the court were banded with silver. [18]The screen for the gate of the court was embroidered in blue, purple, and scarlet material and fine twisted linen. It was twenty cubits long and five cubits high in its width, corresponding to the hangings of the court. [19]There were four posts; their four bases were of bronze, their hooks of

silver and the overlay of their tops and their bands of silver. ²⁰All the pegs of the tabernacle and of the court round about were of bronze.

21 These are the reckonings for the tabernacle, the tabernacle of the testimony, which were drawn up by command of Moses for the work of the Levites under the direction of Ithamar, the son of Aaron, the priest. ²²Bezalel, the son of Uri, son of Hur, of the tribe of Judah, had made all that the LORD had commanded Moses. ²³With him was Oholiab, the son of Ahisamach, of the tribe of Dan, an engraver, a craftsman and embroiderer in blue, purple, and scarlet material and fine twisted linen.

24 The total amount of gold that was used for the work in the complete building of the sanctuary, the gold from the contributors, was twenty-nine talents and seven hundred and thirty shekels by the sanctuary weight. ²⁵The silver from those of the community who were recorded came to one hundred talents and a thousand seven hundred and seventy-five shekels by the sanctuary weight: ²⁶a *beka* a head, half a shekel by the sanctuary weight, for everyone who was entered on the records, from the age of twenty years up, were six hundred and three thousand, five hundred and fifty men. ²⁷The hundred talents of silver were for casting the bases of the sanctuary and the bases for the veil, a hundred bases for the hundred talents, a talent for a base. ²⁸Of the thousand seven hundred and seventy-five shekels he made hooks for the bases and overlaid their tops and made bands for them. ²⁹The bronze that was contributed was seventy talents, and two thousand and four hundred shekels. ³⁰With it he made the bases for the door of the tent of meeting, the bronze altar and the bronze grating for it and all the utensils of the altar, ³¹the bases round about the court, and the bases of the gate of the court, all the pegs of the tabernacle, and all the pegs round about the court.

39 ¹Of the blue, purple, and scarlet material they made the woven vestments for ministering in the sanctuary; they made the sacred vestments for Aaron, as the LORD had commanded them.

2 He made the ephod of gold, blue, purple and scarlet material, and of fine twisted linen worked into designs. ³Gold leaf was hammered out and cut into thin strips to work into designs wih the blue, purple, and scarlet material and with the fine twisted linen. ⁴They made for it shoulder-pieces, attached at its two ends. ⁵The decorated band that was upon it was made like it, of one piece with it; of gold, blue, purple, and scarlet material, and fine twisted linen, as the LORD had commanded Moses.

6 They prepared the onyx stones set in filigree work of gold and engraved with seal engravings of the names of the Israelites. ⁷They were fastened on the shoulder-pieces of the ephod, to be stones of remembrance for the Israelites, as the LORD had commanded Moses.

8 He made the breastpiece, worked into a design, in the same style

as the ephod, of gold, blue, purple, and scarlet material, and fine twisted linen. ⁹It was square; the breastpiece was doubled, a span in length and a span in width when doubled. ¹⁰They set it in four rows of stones. A row of carnelian, topaz, and emerald was the first row; ¹¹and the second row, a ruby, a sapphire and a crystal; ¹²and the third row, a jacinth, an agate, and an amethyst; ¹³and the fourth row, a beryl, an onyx, and a jasper. They were set in gold filigree. ¹⁴There were twelve stones with their names corresponding to the names of the Israelites. They were engraved like seals, each with its name, for the twelve tribes.

15 They made on the breastpiece braided chain like cords of pure gold. ¹⁶They made two settings of gold filigree and two gold rings and put the two rings at the two ends of the breastpiece; ¹⁷and they fastened the two gold cords to the two rings at the ends of the breastpiece. ¹⁸Then they fastened the two ends of the cords to the two settings of filigree. Thus they attached them at the front to the shoulder-pieces of the ephod. ¹⁹Then they made two rings of gold and attached them to the two ends of the breastpiece, at its inside edge which faced the ephod. ²⁰They made two other rings of gold and attached them on the front of the ephod, to the lower part of the two shoulder-pieces, close to its seam above the decorated band of the ephod. ²¹The breastpiece was held in place by a cord of blue from its rings to the rings of the ephod, so that it rested on the decorated band and did not come loose from the ephod, as the Lord had commanded Moses.

22 He also made the robe of the ephod woven all of blue. ²³The opening of the robe in its middle was like the opening in a corselet with a binding around the opening so that it would not tear. ²⁴On the hem of the robe they made pomegranates of blue, purple, and scarlet material and fine twisted linen. ²⁵They also made bells of pure gold, and put the bells between the pomegranates upon the hem of the robe round about between the pomegranates; ²⁶a bell and a pomegranate, a bell and a pomegranate all around the hem of the robe for ministering, as the Lord had commanded Moses.

27 They also made the coats, woven of fine linen, for Aaron and his sons, ²⁸and the turban of fine linen, and the decorated turbans of fine linen, and the linen breeches of fine twisted linen; ²⁹and sashes of fine twisted linen, blue, purple, and scarlet material, embroidered, as the Lord had commanded Moses.

30 They also made the plate of the sacred crown of pure gold and engraved upon it the seal inscription: 'Holy to the Lord.' ³¹They attached to it a cord of blue to fasten it on the turban above, as the Lord had commanded Moses.

32 Thus all the work of the tabernacle of the tent of meeting was completed. The Israelites had done according to all that the Lord had commanded Moses. So they had done. ³³They brought the tabernacle

to Moses, the tent with all its furnishings, its hooks, its frames, its bars, its posts, and its bases, ³⁴the covering of tanned ram skins, the covering of dolphin skins, and the veil of the screen; ³⁵the ark of the testimony with its poles and the propitiatory; ³⁶the table with all its utensils, and the bread of the Presence; ³⁷the lampstand of pure gold and its lamps – all fitted out – and all its utensils, and the oil for the light; ³⁸the altar of gold, the anointing oil, and the fragrant incense, and the screen for the door of the tent; ³⁹the bronze altar with its bronze grating, its poles, and all its utensils, the laver and its base, ⁴⁰the hangings of the court, its pillars, and its bases, and the screen for the gate of the court, its cords and its pegs, and all the utensils for the service of the tabernacle, for the tent of meeting; ⁴¹the woven vestments for ministering in the sacred place, the sacred vestments for Aaron the priest, and his sons' vestments, when serving as priests. ⁴²The Israelites carried out all the work, just as the LORD had commanded Moses. ⁴³When Moses saw that they had carried out all the work and that they had done exactly as the LORD had commanded, Moses blessed them.

40 ¹The LORD said to Moses, ²'On the first day of the first month you shall set up the tabernacle of the tent of meeting. ³You shall put the ark of the testimony in it, and you shall screen the ark with the veil. ⁴You shall bring in the table and put it in order, and you shall bring in the lampstand and set up its lamps. ⁵You shall place the gold altar of incense before the ark of the testimony and set up the screen for the door of the tabernacle. ⁶You shall place the altar of burnt offering before the door of the tabernacle of the tent of meeting, ⁷and place the laver between the tent of meeting and the altar, and put water in it. ⁸You shall set up the court round about, and hang up the screen for the gate of the court. ⁹Then you shall take the anointing oil and anoint the tabernacle and all that is in it, and consecrate it and all its furnishings, so that it becomes holy. ¹⁰Then you shall anoint the altar of burnt offering and all its utensils to consecrate the altar, so that the altar shall be most holy. ¹¹You shall also anoint the laver and its base, and consecrate it. ¹²Then you shall bring Aaron and his sons to the door of the tent of meeting and shall wash them with the water, ¹³and put upon Aaron the sacred vestments, and you shall anoint him and consecrate him that he may serve me as priest. ¹⁴You shall also bring his sons and put coats on them, ¹⁵and anoint them, as you have anointed their father, that they may serve me as priests. Their anointing shall qualify them to a perpetual priesthood from one generation to another.'

16 This Moses did; he did just as the LORD had commanded him. ¹⁷In the first month of the second year, on the first of the month, the tabernacle was set up. ¹⁸Moses set up the tabernacle: he laid its bases, erected its frames, and inserted its poles, and set up its posts. ¹⁹He spread the tent over the tabernacle, and put the covering of the tent on

top of it, as the LORD had commanded Moses. [20]He took the testimony and put it into the ark and placed the poles on the ark, and put the propitiatory on top of the ark. [21]Then he brought the ark into the tabernacle, and set up the veil of the screen and screened off the ark of the testimony, as the LORD had commanded Moses. [22]He put the table in the tent of meeting, on the north side of the tabernacle, outside the veil, [23]and arranged the bread in order on it before the LORD, as the LORD had commanded Moses. [24]He put the lampstand in the tent of meeting, opposite the table on the south side of the tabernacle, [25]and set up the lamps before the LORD, as the LORD had commanded Moses. [26]He placed the altar of gold in the tent of meeting before the veil, [27]and he burnt fragrant incense upon it, as the LORD had commanded Moses. [28]He put the screen in place before the door of the tabernacle. [29]He set the altar of burnt offering at the door of the tabernacle of the tent of meeting, and offered upon it the burnt offerings and the meal offerings, as the LORD had commanded Moses. [30]He placed the laver between the tent of meeting and the altar, and put water in it for washing. [31]From it Moses and Aaron and his sons washed their hands and their feet. [32]When they entered the tent of meeting, and when they approached the altar, they washed, as the LORD had commanded Moses. [33]He set up the court round the tabernacle and the altar and put up the screen for the gate of the court. So Moses finished the work.

34 Then the cloud covered the tent of meeting and the glory of the LORD filled the tabernacle. [35]Moses was not able to enter the tent of meeting because the cloud had settled upon it and the glory of the LORD filled the tabernacle. [36]Whenever the cloud was lifted from the tabernacle, the Israelites used to set out on their journey, [37]but if the cloud was not lifted, they would not set out until the day that it was lifted. [38]The cloud of the LORD was over the tabernacle by day, and there was fire in it by night, in the sight of all the house of Israel through all their journeys.

1. *Literary Analysis*

The textual and traditio-historical problems of these chapters are treated in the introduction to chs. 25–31.

Chapters 35–39 report how the divine instructions which were given to Moses for building the tabernacle were executed. The account is basically a *verbatim* repetition of the earlier chapters, but with some significant alterations and omissions. Several different principles appear to be involved in the changes. The most important factor, which was clearly observed by Noth (*Exodus*, p. 277), is that instructions which relate to the positioning and use of the elements connected with the tabernacle are omitted. The motivation seems to be a logical one. The author first describes the making of the tabernacle and only when completed does he turn to its assembly. Thus the placing of the bread of the Presence (25.30), the lamps (25.37), and the hanging of the veil (26.33) are omitted in the initial description and reserved for 40.16ff.

Still there seem to be other factors involved which cannot be explained in the same manner. It is hardly possible that the omission of the details of hanging the excess curtain in 26.12f. arose from this same desire for a systematic order of presentation. Rather, the somewhat unclear directions may have led to its being omitted. Theological factors seem to be involved in the omission of all reference to the 'pattern on the mountain' (25.21f.; cf. Introduction to chs. 25–31). Finally, there are abbreviations and omissions which have no obvious explanation (e.g. 37.29).

The order of these chapters is far more systematically arranged than in chs. 25–31, which factor has often been used as evidence for a later date. Thus, the incense altar which appeared out of place in ch. 30 assumes its logical place with the other furniture in 37.25–38. There are only occasional additions over and above the previous instructions, notably 38.8 (cf. LXX 38.22). The tendency for summary and enumeration is very strong throughout these chapters (38.24ff.).

2. Old Testament Context

[35.1–3] // 31.12–17 The Sabbath Command

The sabbath command had ended the section which reported the divine instructions for the tabernacle. In ch. 35 it assumes a position of new importance and introduces the execution of the instructions. The earlier passage has been adjusted in its form as a speech of Moses. Moreover, it has been sharply abbreviated. Only v. 2 is basically the same. The covenantal elements in 31.13f. and 16f. have not been repeated. The prohibition of fire is new and without a direct parallel elsewhere (cf. 16.23). The background of this formulation of the law is unknown, and it is unclear whether this is a new stipulation to meet a new condition (Hyatt) or an older law which has been simply appended.

[35.4–9] || *25.1–9 The Voluntary Offering*
The older form has been adjusted to the new pattern of command-execution which characterizes chs. 35–39. There is no parallel to 25.8–9, which speaks of the heavenly pattern.

[35.10–19] *The Invitation to Skilled Workmen*
There is no correspondence in the early account of this invitation. The section interrupts the narrative of the freewill offering which then continues in v. 20. The strong tendency to enumeration is evident in this section which may well point to old priestly inventories.

[35.20–29] *The Presentation of Offerings*
Again there is no correspondence to the account of the people's response to the call for material. The precise listing of the material, such as the four different sorts of gold ornament (nose rings, earrings, signet rings, armlets) as well as attention to the different classes of people among the contributors, probably reflects official records of some kind.

[35.30–36.1] || *31.1–6 The Commissioning of Bezalel and Oholiab*
The commissioning of the overseers assumes its logical position at the beginning of the work in distinction from the earlier account. The enumeration in 31.7–11 is not repeated.

[36.2–7] *The Response of the People*
The freewill offering of material for the tabernacle calls forth such a generous response from all the people of Israel that further contributions are restrained. A strong theological interest of the narrative is evident which takes note of the people's zealous response to the cult whenever possible.

[36.8–19] || *26.1–14: The Making of the Curtains*
The account is basically a duplication of the earlier account. The omission of 26.9b, 12, 13 has puzzled commentators, and the reason is not immediately obvious. The frequent suggestion that the writer was himself confused over these instructions is conjectural and impossible to prove. Later midrashic exegesis tended to simplify and explain the difficulties rather than to omit them.

[36.35–38] || *26.31–37: The Making of the Veil and Screen*
The omission of 26.33–35 in the account is explained by the consistent omission of instructions regarding position and use. A summary of these instructions appears in 40.20f.

[37.1–9] // *25.10–22*: *The Making of the Ark and Propitiatory*
The placing of the tablets within the ark occurs in 40.20. 25.15f.
and 21f. are missing in the second account.

[37.10–16] // *25.23–30*: *The Making of the Table*
The second account is virtually the same as the earlier one. The
omission of 25.30 is best explained by its logical postponement until
40.23.

[37.17–24] // *25.31–40*: *The Making of the Golden Lampstand*
Again basically a repetition with an abbreviation of 25.37b, 40.

[37.25–28] // *30.1–10*: *The Making of the Incense Altar*
The strikingly different order of the altar in the second account
has often been noticed, and often used as evidence of a later date
(cf. Noth). The reference to the ritual of the day of atonement in
30.6–10 has been omitted. The major reason seems to be a logical one
since the ritual is reserved for Lev. 16.

[37.29] // *30.22–28*: *Oil and Incense*
The longer account in 30.22ff. is sharply abbreviated to a bare
enumeration of the two elements.

[38.1–7] // *27.1–8*: *The Construction of the Bronze Altar*
The accounts are basically the same with an abbreviation of
27.8b. The LXX (38.22) adds a reference in midrashic style to
Num. 17.1ff (EVV 16.36ff.): 'He made the bronze altar out of the
bronze censors which belonged to the men who rebelled with the
company of Korah.'

[38.8] *The Bronze Laver*
This verse, which has no earlier correspondent, has evoked much
discussion as to its meaning. Who were the 'ministering women'?
Why is their work described by the verb *ṣb'* which denotes an organized service like the professional Levites? Some commentators have
suggested a cleaning and repairing service, others singing and dancing. The only parallel is I Sam. 2.22 which is of little real help.
Driver suggests that the verse implies that the service of the tabernacle
had already been under way. There is insufficient evidence to decide
whether older historical material is involved or later midrashic
exegesis. The literary form would favor the first alternative.

[38.9–20] // *27.9–19*: *The Making of the Court*
The substance of the two accounts are the same, but with con-

siderable variation in formulation, especially toward the conclusion of the description. The second account both abbreviates and expands in different places, the reasons for which are not evident.

[38.21–31] *Summary of the Materials Used*
This summary which has no earlier parallel and interrupts the sequence of the construction, provides a variety of details regarding the amount of material employed in the work. The reference to the census in v.25 (cf. Num. 1), as well as the reference to Ithamar for service in the tabernacle (cf. Num.3–4), has suggested to many commentators a later period (cf. Driver's note).

The most recent study of Hebrew weights by R. B. Y. Scott (*Peake's Commentary on the Bible*, London and New York 1962, sect. 35) reckons the talent at about 64lbs. (29kg.) and the sanctuary shekel ⅓oz. or 9·7gr. According to this calculation there would be some 1,900lbs. of gold, 6,437lbs. of silver, and 4,522lbs. of bronze.

[39.1–31] *// 28.6–43:* The Priestly Vestments
The description of the ephod is considerably shorter, but new material is introduced in 39.3. Similarly, the description of the onyx stones shows abbreviation. Somewhat more significant is the variation in the nomenclature of the breastpiece, which is no longer called 'breastpiece of judgment'. Commentators have also speculated on why the Urim and Thummim are not mentioned. The abbreviations in 28.35b and 41.42b, 43 seem to fall under the general principle followed by the author of omitting elements which refer specially to their use or position within the tabernacle.

[39.32–43] *Final Enumeration*
Once more the author summarizes the work of the tabernacle to confirm that all had been done according to command. The explicit reference to Moses' blessing seems to reflect a traditional element.

[40.1–33] *The Erection of the Tabernacle*
The structure of this chapter reflects the same command-execution pattern which was found in the two blocks of the tabernacle chapter. In vv. 1–15 Yahweh instructs Moses regarding the erection of the tabernacle and the consecration of Aaron and his sons. The later seems a surprising anticipation of Lev. 8, but the writer disregards the strictly chronological sequence for the sake of his narrative conclusion. The work must be finished and the glory of God enter. Then vv. 16–33 report on Moses' exact execution of the order. The repetition of the

phrase 'as Yahweh had commanded Moses', which occurs eight times in this section, epitomizes the dominant redactional intention throughout chs. 35–40.

[40.34–38] *The Glory and the Tabernacle*

The climax of all the building comes with the covering of the tent by the cloud and the entrance of God's glory into the tabernacle. The parallel with the description of the cloud and glory on Mount Sinai (24.17f.) clearly reveals the author's theological intention. The presence of God which once abode on Mount Sinai, now dwells in the sanctuary and accompanies Israel on her way. The notice of Moses' inability to enter the tent of meeting would appear to point to the new state of affairs which now operates in the cult. Moses' older role before the tent of meeting (Ex. 33.7) has been replaced by a new priestly role which he shares with Aaron (Lev. 9.23).

INDEX OF SUBJECTS

INDEX OF AUTHORS

INDEX OF BIBLICAL REFERENCES